THE ROUTLEDGE HANDBOOK OF ADOPTION

Adoption is practiced globally yielding a multidimensional area of study that cannot be characterized by a single movement or discipline. This handbook provides a central source of contemporary scholarship from a variety of disciplines with an international perspective and uses a multifaceted and interdisciplinary approach to ground adoption practices and activities in scientific research. Perspectives of birth/first parents, adoptive parents, and adopted persons are brought forth through a range of disciplinary and theoretical lenses.

Beginning with background and context of adoption, including sociocultural and political contexts, the handbook then addresses the diversity of adoptive families in terms of family forms, attitudes about adoption, and characteristics of adopted children. Next, research examining the lived experience of adoption for birth parents, adoptive parents, and adopted individuals is presented. A variety of outcomes for internationally and domestically adopted children and adoptive families is then discussed and the handbook concludes by addressing the development, training, and implementation of adoption competent clinical practice.

With cutting-edge research from top international scholars in a diversity of fields, *The Routledge Handbook of Adoption* should be considered essential reading for students, researchers, and practitioners across the fields of social work, sociology, psychology, medicine, family science, education, and demography.

Gretchen Miller Wrobel, Ph.D., is a Professor of Psychology at Bethel University, USA and co-investigator on the Minnesota-Texas Adoption Research Project. Dr. Wrobel's research interests include information seeking related to curiosity about one's adoption and adoptive family communication. She is past editor of *Adoption Quarterly*.

Emily Helder, Ph.D., is an Associate Professor of Psychology at Calvin University, USA. Dr. Helder is a clinical neuropsychologist whose research and training have focused on the impact of early experience on later development, language, and the experience of abuse, neglect, and early deprivation.

Elisha Marr, Ph.D., is an Associate Professor of Sociology and Director of Gender Studies at Calvin University, USA. Dr. Marr's research on transracial adoption includes identifying trends in adoption rates, experiences of transracial adoptees and their adoptive parents, and racial preferences of adoptive parents. More recently, Marr has expanded to exploring motivations to adopt.

ROUTLEDGE INTERNATIONAL HANDBOOKS

Routledge International Handbook of Human Trafficking
A Multi-Disciplinary and Applied Approach
Edited by Rochelle L. Dalla and Donna Sabella

The Routledge Handbook of Comparative Rural Policy
Edited by Matteo Vittuari, John Devlin, Marco Pagani, and Thomas Johnson

Routledge International Handbook of Masculinity Studies
Edited by Lucas Gottzén, Ulf Mellström, and Tamara Shefer

Routledge Handbook of European Welfare Systems, 2e
Edited by Sonja Blum, Johanna Kuhlmann, and Klaus Schubert

Routledge International Handbook of Heterosexualities Studies
Edited by James Joseph Dean and Nancy L. Fischer

Routledge Handbook of Contemporary European Social Movements
Protest in Turbulent Times
Edited by Cristina Flesher Fominaya and Ramón A. Feenstra

The Routledge International Handbook of Military Psychology and Mental Health
Edited by Updesh Kumar

Routledge International Handbook of Green Criminology
Edited by Avi Brisman and Nigel South

Routledge International Handbook of Contemporary Racisms
Edited by John Solomos

For more information about this series, please visit: www.routledge.com/Routledge-International-Handbooks/book-series/RIHAND

THE ROUTLEDGE HANDBOOK OF ADOPTION

Edited by Gretchen Miller Wrobel, Emily Helder, and Elisha Marr

Routledge
Taylor & Francis Group
LONDON AND NEW YORK

First published 2020 by Routledge

2 Park Square, Milton Park, Abingdon, Oxon OX14 4RN
605 Third Avenue, New York, NY 10017

Routledge is an imprint of the Taylor & Francis Group, an informa business

First issued in paperback 2021

British Library Cataloguing-in-Publication Data
A catalogue record for this book is available from the British Library
Library of Congress Cataloging-in-Publication Data
Names: Wrobel, Gretchen Miller, editor. | Helder, Emily, editor. | Marr, Elisha, editor.
Title: The Routledge handbook of adoption / edited by Gretchen Miller Wrobel, Emily Helder, and Elisha Marr.
Description: Abingdon, Oxon ; New York, NY : Routledge, 2020. | Includes bibliographical references and index.
Identifiers: LCCN 2019043547 (print) | LCCN 2019043548 (ebook) | ISBN 9781138362505 (hardback) | ISBN 9780429432040 (ebook)
Subjects: LCSH: Adoption.
Classification: LCC HV875 .R665 2020 (print) | LCC HV875 (ebook) | DDC 362.734–dc23
LC record available at https://lccn.loc.gov/2019043547
LC ebook record available at https://lccn.loc.gov/2019043548

ISBN: 978-1-138-36250-5 (hbk)
ISBN: 978-1-03-217377-1 (pbk)
DOI: 10.4324/9780429432040

Typeset in Bembo
by Swales & Willis, Exeter, Devon, UK

CONTENTS

CONTRIBUTORS

Donna M. Aguiniga, Ph.D., MSW, is an Associate Professor with the University of Alaska Anchorage School of Social Work, USA and interim director of the UAA Center for Community Engagement & Learning. Dr. Aguiniga's research interests include adoption, permanency outcomes for foster care youth, poverty and family functioning, and civic engagement. Her practice background is in child welfare and community mental health.

Anne J. Atkinson, Ph.D., is president and founder of PolicyWorks, Ltd., an independent program evaluation and policy research firm established in 1995 and based in Virginia, USA. Her research in child welfare, education, juvenile justice, school safety, and prevention is informed by decades of practice and administration in these fields and a strong commitment to creating usable best practice tools and training for professionals on the front lines. She especially enjoys assisting state-level policy leaders to improve public policy and strengthen services systems and creating the tools and training that frontline professionals need to engage in effective, evidence-based practice.

Mary Beek, Ph.D., is a Research Fellow in the Centre for Research into Children and Families at the University of East Anglia, UK. She has a background in social work practice and management in foster care and adoption. Over the last 20 years she has been involved in a range of related research, including studies of long-term foster care, contact after adoption, and supporting children's transitions to adoption.

Johanna Bick, Ph.D., is an Assistant Professor in the Psychology Department of the University of Houston, USA. She examines how early life stress, including psychosocial deprivation, shapes neurodevelopmental and behavioral trajectories of children and how parenting interventions can mitigate many consequences of early adverse experiences.

Sebilu Bodja, MPA, is the Director of Africa Programs for Bethany Christian Services Global. His role involves program development for orphaned and vulnerable children and their families in different countries of Africa.

Megan Bresnahan, OTR/L, received her degree in occupational therapy from the University of Wisconsin-La Crosse, USA and has been working as an occupational therapist since 2001. She has worked closely with the Adoption Medicine Clinic at the University of Minnesota Masonic Children's Hospital for 13 years, including working with patients who have been adopted and their families. Megan works with children who have been adopted internationally and domestically, and children in foster care, along with their families, to provide support and help them progress with many areas of development.

Krystal K. Cashen, M.S., is currently a Doctoral Candidate in Developmental Science in the Department of Psychological and Brain Sciences at the University of Massachusetts Amherst, USA. Broadly, her work focuses on how experiences unique to adoption and LGBTQ-parented families shape the development of identity and close relationship functioning into emerging adulthood.

Rachael Clemens, Ph.D., is Adjunct Faculty in the School of Information & Library Science at the University of North Carolina at Chapel Hill, USA. Her research examines human information behavior in contexts of personal crisis, particularly situations in which shame and social stigma may impede effective information seeking and thus compromise informed decision-making behavior. She enjoys teaching research methods, information behavior, and information literacy courses.

Monica Dalen, Ph.D., is a Professor at the University of Oslo, Norway in the Department of Special Needs Education. Her research focus is mainly on international adoption, academic achievement, learning difficulties, and special needs education.

Andrew Dismukes, Ph.D., is a Postdoctoral Scholar in the gene-environment interplay lab at Pennsylvania State University, USA. He is most interested in genetic and environmental influences that shape the stress response system, with a particular focus on neuroendocrine functioning, and how this influences health and behavior across the lifespan.

Judith Eckerle, M.D., is the Medical Director of the Adoption Medicine Clinic at the University of Minnesota, USA. Dr. Eckerle assists families pre- and post-adoption with consultation, referral, and clinical services. Her academic interests include FASD research, adoption and foster care issues, and global advocacy for children.

Marko Elovainio, Ph.D., is a Professor of Psychology at the University of Helsinki, Finland. His research interests include psychosocial factors and health, occupational health psychology, and social epidemiology.

Rachel H. Farr, Ph.D., received her Ph.D. from the University of Virginia, USA and completed a postdoc at the University of Massachusetts Amherst, USA. Dr. Farr is an Assistant Professor of Psychology at the University of Kentucky, USA. She has conducted a large longitudinal study about how parental sexual orientation relates to child, parent, and family outcomes among diverse adoptive families, and the results have been cited in the media as well as amicus briefs for the Supreme Court. With William T. Grant Foundation funding, Dr. Farr is currently studying racially and socioeconomically diverse adolescents with LGBTQ parents.

Francine Fishman, LCSW, has spent the past 15 years working at Nassau Board of Cooperative Educational Services (BOCES) and Eastern Suffolk BOCES, USA, as a school social worker. She is committed to empowering and advocating for students with special needs. During her tenure as a social worker she has done extensive work in the field of adoption both in direct practice and research. She has earned an advanced certification in School Building and District Leadership from the College of St. Rose, USA, an MBA in business management from Adelphi University, USA, and an MSW from Stony Brook University, USA.

Jody M. Ganiban, Ph.D., is a Professor of Psychology at George Washington University, USA. Her research interests include genetic and environmental contributions to children's socioemotional development and physical health.

Karin Garber, Ph.D., is an Assistant Professor at Pacific University (Hillsboro, OR, USA), and the Associate Director of Pacific Psychology and Comprehensive Health Clinics. Her research interests include identity in marginalized populations, social justice for diverse individuals and families, and mentorship in the context of adoption.

Kristi Gleason, LMSW, serves as Vice President of Global Programs at Bethany Christian Services. In this role, she manages Bethany's portfolio of programs, including family preservation, domestic and intercountry adoption, family-based care, and refugee services. She has worked in the arena of child welfare and child rights for the past 19 years in Albania, China, Tibet, Haiti, and the United States. She has experience in community development, foster care, and working with vulnerable children. As a Fulbright Fellow, she researched domestic violence and its effect on family systems in Eastern Europe. Gleason's areas of expertise include program development in international settings, child protection, project management, and grant writing.

Sharon L. Glennen, Ph.D., is a Professor in the Speech Language Pathology & Audiology Department at Towson University, USA. She began researching language development in internationally adopted children after the adoption of her two children from Russia. This work led to the creation of developmental guidelines regarding typical language outcomes in internationally adopted children. This research has been published widely and presented at many national and international conferences.

Danielle Godon-Decoteau, Ph.D., is a Visiting Lecturer at Mount Holyoke College, USA in the Psychology and Education Department. Her research focuses on race, ethnicity, and culture; internalized racism; transracial adoption; and Asian American mental health. Godon-Decoteau serves as treasurer for the Asian American Psychological Association's new Division of Asian Americans with Multiple Heritages.

Harold D. Grotevant, Ph.D., holds the Rudd Family Foundation Chair in Psychology at the University of Massachusetts Amherst, USA, where he is the Founding Director of the Rudd Adoption Research Program, which connects adoption research with policy and practice through conferences, workshops, graduate and postdoctoral training, and stimulation of research activities. His research focuses on relationships in adoptive families (especially open adoption) and on identity development in adolescents and young adults, and has resulted in over 150 articles and chapters as well as several books, including *Openness in adoption: Exploring family connections* (with Ruth McRoy, 1998). He is a Fellow of the American Psychological Association, the Association for Psychological Science, and the National Council on

Family Relations; and a recipient of awards for research, teaching, mentoring, outreach, educational leadership, and adoption scholarship.

Sally Guyer is a Data Analyst for the Early Growth and Development Study (EGDS) at the Prevention Science Institute at the University of Oregon, USA. She has been working in the field of research in various positions for 19 years and with EGDS for 12 years.

Mary Eschelbach Hansen, Ph.D., is a Professor of Economics at American University, USA. Hansen's research about child welfare primarily measures the extent to which federal and state statutes and policies impact the goals of safety, stability, and permanence for children. Her research on adoption has been funded by the NIH/NICHD and the Annie E. Casey Foundation.

Emily Helder, Ph.D., is an Associate Professor of Psychology at Calvin University, USA. Dr. Helder is a clinical neuropsychologist whose research and training have focused on the impact of early experience on later development, language, and the experience of abuse, neglect, and early deprivation. Most recently, she has initiated an intervention study with international adoptees to improve peer social relationships.

Eveliina Holmgren, Ph.D., is a Clinical Psychologist and Psychology Lecturer at Metropolia University of Applied Sciences, and Researcher in the Finnish Adoption Study (FinAdo). Her research interests include adopted children's experiences of bullying, risk, and protective factors within and outside the adoptive family, and the many ways of supporting resilience among adopted children and their families.

Dana E. Johnson, M.D., Ph.D., is a Professor of Pediatrics and member of the Divisions of Neonatology and Global Pediatrics at the University of Minnesota, USA, where he co-founded the International Adoption Program in 1986. His research interests include the effects of early institutionalization on growth and development and the outcomes of children who experience early adversity. He has authored numerous scholarly works, including co-editing *Adoption Medicine* published by the American Academy of Pediatrics.

Megan M. Julian, Ph.D., is a Clinical and Developmental Psychologist, and Clinical Lecturer in the Department of Psychiatry at the University of Michigan, USA. In both her research and clinical work, she specializes in early childhood, and studies how early relational care (or relational deprivation, in the case of orphanage rearing) affects the course of development, and how caregiver–child relationships can be enhanced in order to support children's development.

Adam Y. Kim, B.S., is a Doctoral Candidate at University of Minnesota, USA specializing in cultural and personality psychology. Current projects include exploring the role of politicization in inter-minority solidarity, and advancing our understanding of the experience of displacement, separation, and migration for transnationally adopted individuals. He approaches these projects through a critical race and ethnic studies perspective, acknowledging the role of systems of power and privilege in human development and centering the experiences of the oppressed.

JaeRan Kim, Ph.D., LISW, is an Assistant Professor at the University of Washington, Tacoma, USA, in the Social Work and Criminal Justice Program. Her research is focused on adoption, addressing disabilities, race, and transnational experiences on post-adoption stability and the preparation of social work professionals working in the adoption field. Kim has over 15 years of experience working with fostered and adopted children and families and has developed numerous training curricula for child welfare professionals.

Bibiana Koh, Ph.D., LICSW, is an Associate Professor, MSW Field Director, and Batalden Scholar in Applied Ethics at Augsburg University in Minneapolis, Minnesota, USA. Dr. Koh's research focuses on adoption, social work pedagogy, and ethics in social work practice.

Rose M. Kreider, Ph.D., is the Chief of the Fertility and Family Statistics Branch in the Social, Economic, and Housing Statistics Division at the US Census Bureau. Her research includes work on interracial marriage, children's living arrangements, cohabitation, one-person households, and marital patterns in the US, in addition to international and transracial adoption.

Maria Kroupina, Ph.D., is an Associate Professor in the Department of Pediatrics at the University of Minnesota, USA. The overarching goal of Dr. Kroupina's combined research-clinical program is to design a research-based clinic for young children with a history of early adversity and toxic stress, including those with histories of institutional care, multiple foster placements, and early emotional trauma. The Birth to Three Clinic and Early Childhood Mental Health Program focus on early identification of high-risk children in order to prevent long-term negative mental health and neurodevelopmental outcomes by providing early intervention.

Helena Lapinleimu, M.D., Ph.D., has acted as Specialist of Pediatrics and Neonatology in the Department of Pediatrics and Adolescence of the University Hospital of Turku, Finland and as Adjunct Professor in the Department of Pediatrics of the University of Turku, Finland. She has worked as the principal investigator of the Finnish Adoption Study (FinAdo) that was launched in 2007. She has also been working as a consulting pediatrician for the all Finnish Adoption Organizations since 2007.

Richard M. Lee, Ph.D., is a Distinguished McKnight University Professor in the Department of Psychology at the University of Minnesota, Twin Cities, USA. He has been conducting research on the psychology of international adoption for 20 years with a focus on the transracial and transnational experiences of adopted Korean youth and their families.

Leslie D. Leve, Ph.D., is the Alumni Faculty Professor in the College of Education at the University of Oregon, USA. She also serves as past president of the Society for Prevention Research. Her research interests focus on understanding risk and protective factors for youth who are adopted, in foster care, or in the juvenile justice system.

Rebecca Lipschutz, M.S., is a third-year Graduate Student in the Child Clinical Psychology Ph.D. program at the University of Houston, USA. She previously earned her Master's in Neuroscience at Tulane University, USA. Her research interests include studying how early life adversity shapes the development of biological systems and pathways for risk and resiliency in children.

Yanhong Liu, Ph.D., is an Assistant Professor with the Department of Counseling and Human Services at Syracuse University, USA. Her scholarly work focuses on marginalized youth and their supporting systems. She has published in areas of adoption, attachment, and bullying and school-based intervention.

Albert Y.H. Lo, M.S., is a Doctoral Student in Clinical Psychology at the University of Massachusetts Amherst, USA. He currently works with Dr. Harold Grotevant as part of the Rudd Adoption Research Program. His research interests are in the areas of parenting and identity development.

Rachel D. Ludeke, MSW, is a Doctoral Student at the Silver School of Social Work at New York University, USA. She holds a Master's in Social Work and B.A. in English and History/Political Science from Rutgers University. She has worked in the child welfare field as an administrator for transitioning foster youth programs in New Jersey and has also served as a program coordinator for various projects related to homelessness, disaster relief, and nonprofit management and governance.

Elissa E. Madden, Ph.D., is an Associate Professor in the Diana R. Garland School of Social Work at Baylor University, USA. Her primary research interest is in the area of child welfare. She has co-authored publications on the experiences of birth mothers who have placed a child for adoption, barriers to adoption from the public child welfare system, the post-secondary experiences and needs of foster alumni, and child welfare workforce issues. Dr. Madden currently serves as the associate editor of *Adoption Quarterly*, a peer-reviewed, international, multidisciplinary journal that addresses continuity in adoption issues.

Elisha Marr, Ph.D., is an Associate Professor of Sociology and Director of Gender Studies at Calvin University, USA. Dr. Marr's research on transracial adoption includes identifying trends in adoption rates, experiences of transracial adoptees and their adoptive parents, and racial preferences of adoptive parents. More recently, Marr has expanded to exploring motivations to adopt.

Jessica A.K. Matthews, Ph.D., is a postdoctoral research scholar in the Rudd Adoption Research Program in the Department of Psychological & Brain Sciences at the University of Massachusetts Amherst, USA. She completed her Ph.D. in Child Study and Human Development at Tufts University, USA, with Professor Ellen Pinderhughes. Her research interests include maltreatment in adoptive homes; cultural, ethnic, and racial socialization of adoptees; and the experience of children in foster care.

Ruth McRoy, Ph.D., is the Donahue and DiFelice Professor Emerita at the Boston College School of Social Work, USA, and is Research Professor and the Ruby Lee Piester Centennial Professor Emerita at the University of Texas at Austin School of Social Work, USA. McRoy has been involved in adoption practice, teaching, and research for many years, and has focused on such topics as openness in adoption, transracial adoptions, kinship care, special needs adoptions, African American adoptions, and adoptive family dynamics. Since 2007, she has led a team evaluating AdoptUSKids, the national photolisting service. She was selected as the recipient of the 2010 St. John's Outstanding Scholar in Adoption Award and the 2013 Adoption Excellence Award from the US Children's Bureau.

Darcey H. Merritt, MSW, Ph.D., is an Associate Professor at NYU Silver School of Social Work, USA and a Faculty Fellow at the school's McSilver Institute for Poverty

Policy and Research. She is also an associate editor for *Children and Youth Services Review* and a member of the board of directors of the Society for Social Work and Research. Dr. Merritt has extensive experience as a practitioner in the private and public child welfare systems, and as a researcher with interests including child maltreatment prevention, maltreatment type definitional issues, neighborhood structural impact on maltreatment, and experiences of those served by public child welfare systems. More specifically, her research focuses on parenting in socioeconomic contexts, considering the impact of working memory on parental decision-making. Overall, her scholarship is dedicated to providing empirical and meaningful knowledge useful to bolstering the well-being of children and families, specifically through contributing their voices in the discussion of prevention methods.

Isabel Narciso, Ph.D., is an Associate Professor on the Faculty of Psychology of the University of Lisbon, Portugal and serves as a family therapist. Dr. Narciso has been participating in undergraduate, postgraduate, master's, and doctoral courses, and developing research in several areas of family psychology, particularly parenting in non-normative and adverse contexts, with a main interest in adaptative parenting, parent–child relationships, and family and child adaptation. She is currently a member of the CICPSI (Research Center for Psychological Science; R&D unit).

Jenae M. Neiderhiser, Ph.D., is a Distinguished Professor of Psychology and Human Development and Family Studies at Pennsylvania State University, USA. She is interested in how genes and environments work together to shape development across the lifespan, with a particular focus on family relationships and prenatal environment.

Elsbeth Neil, Ph.D., is a Professor of Social Work at the University of East Anglia, Norwich, England. Her research interests are in how adoption is experienced by adoptees, birth relatives, and adoptive parents, and particularly how birth and adoptive families keep in contact; she is also interested in understanding the support needs of all affected by adoption and the role of social workers on helping families.

Jesús Palacios, Ph.D., is Professor of Developmental and Educational Psychology at the University of Seville, Spain. His teaching, research, and practice-related activities have focused on foster care and adoption, playing an active role in connecting adoption researchers around the world. Besides publications and training activities, Prof. Palacios consults regularly with governmental agencies about how to improve systems of foster care and adoption on behalf of children.

Hanna Raaska, M.D., Ph.D., is a specialist in child psychiatry and currently works as Chief Physician in the Pediatric Neuropsychiatric Unit at Helsinki University Hospital, Finland. She is a member of the Finnish Adoption Study group, in which her interests are mainly in developmental problems and their association with emotional and behavioral problems in adopted children.

Elizabeth Raleigh, Ph.D., is Associate Professor of Sociology at Carleton College, USA. She is the author of *Selling transracial adoption: Families, markets, and the color line* (2017). Currently, Dr. Raleigh is working on a project examining "Dear Birthmother" letters written by prospective adoptive parents to expectant women considering adoption.

Patricia Ramsey, Ph.D., is Professor Emerita in the Department of Psychology and Education at Mount Holyoke College in South Hadley, MA, USA. She has studied early social and attitude development and has written several books, chapters, and articles on multicultural education for young children and the development of friendships in preschools. More recently, Dr. Ramsey has been working in the field of adoption studies and has done work on identity development of transracial adoptees, their decisions to search for their birth families, and the perceptions and experiences of adoptive parents.

Marta Reinoso Bernuz, Ph.D., holds a Ph.D. from the University of Barcelona, Spain. She is currently a Lecturer on the Faculty of Psychology and Education Sciences at the Open University of Catalonia and member of the research group PSiNET. Her research, teaching, and clinical interests focus on early childhood, families, adoption, stress, and resilience. She is especially concerned about adopted children's viewpoints on the experience of adoption.

Debbie Riley, LCMFT, CEO, The Center for Adoption Support and Education, is a national leader in mental health services for the foster care and adoption community. Ms. Riley is a nationally recognized adoption expert, author, and dynamic public speaker, and has more than 35 years of professional experience, including extensive health care management and administrative expertise and hands-on experience at designing and developing nationally acclaimed adoption competent programs for professionals. Her direct (and current) delivery of specialized adoption competent mental health services to adopted children, teens, adults, and their families affords her the broad knowledge and nationally respected expertise needed to promote health education, child advocacy, and public policy development. She is also an adoptive parent.

Scott Ryan, Ph.D., MSW, is the Jenkins Garrett Professor and Dean of the University of Texas at Arlington's School of Social Work, USA. He is also the editor of the journal *Adoption Quarterly*. He has worked extensively with at-risk families for almost two decades as a clinician, educator, trainer, and researcher. Dr. Ryan has published numerous scholarly articles and book chapters on adoption and has presented his research nationally and internationally. For his work in the area of adoption, Dr. Ryan has received the Friend of Children Award from the North American Council on Adoptable Children, an Angel in Adoption Award from the Congressional Coalition on Adoption Institute, and an Adoption Excellence Award from the US Children's Bureau.

Marta Santos-Nunes, Ph.D., works in Clinical Psychology at the University of Lisbon, Portugal and University of Coimbra, Portugal. She is currently a member of the Research Center for Psychological Science at the University of Lisbon. Dr. Santos-Nunes specializes in family issues and adoption and has been working with adoptive families over the last ten years in the assessment process of candidates seeking adoption as well as in clinical interventions with adoptive parents and children. She is the author of international articles and book chapters in the field of adoption.

Kristina M. Scharp, Ph.D., is an Assistant Professor of Communication at the University of Washington and a Director of the Family Communication and Relationships Lab. She researches difficult family transitions such as parent–child estrangement and the processes by which family members cope with their distress. Her research has won top paper awards at both the International and National Communication Associations and has garnered attention from outlets such as *The New York Times*, PBS, NPR, and *The Washington Post.*

Peter Selman, Ph.D., is Visiting Fellow in the School of Geography, Politics & Sociology at Newcastle University, UK, where he was Head of Department of Social Policy until his retirement in 2002. He is editor of *Intercountry Adoption; Development, trends and perspectives* (2000) and has written many articles and chapters on adoption policy. His main research focus in recent years has been on the demography of child adoption with a special emphasis on intercountry adoption. He has made regular presentations on this topic at international conferences and has acted as research consultant to international organizations such as the UN Population Division, the Hague Conference on Private International Law, and the Innocenti Research Centre in Florence.

Ellen Singer, LCSW-C, is Senior Therapist/Training Coordinator at the Center for Adoption Support and Education (CASE), USA. She provides clinical services to the foster and adoption community with special interest in adult adoptees. Ellen is a lead trainer for parent and professional groups, key author of CASE publications, and contributor to other adoption-related publications. She is an adoptive mother.

Cherry Smith is a Doctoral Student in Educational Psychology at the University of South Florida, USA. Her research interests include educational resilience, conflict resolution in schools, social-emotional well-being of children, and children's mental health.

Kathryn A. Sweeney, Ph.D., is an Associate Professor of Sociology at Purdue University Northwest, USA. Her research examines how structural racial and gender disparities shape everyday life, with recent work focusing on adoptive parent choices, children's adoption-themed books, media portrayal of the Baby Veronica case, and use of DNA ancestry testing.

Tony Xing Tan, Ph.D., is a Professor of Educational Psychology at the University of South Florida, USA and an Affiliated Professor at Xi'an Jiaotong University, China. His research interests include adopted children's development and how drastic social change affects Chinese children's cultural socialization, social-emotional well-being, and academic outcomes.

Steinar Theie, Ph.D., is an Associate Professor at the University of Oslo, Norway in the Department of Special Needs Education. Dr. Theie's main research interests are children's social and emotional development with a specific focus on internationally adopted children. Other topics of interest are children with social and emotional problems, inclusion of children at risk in pre-school and school settings, and school choice and school movement among immigrants.

Lindsey J. Thomas, Ph.D., is an Assistant Professor of Communication Studies at Illinois State University, USA. Her program of research focuses on intersections of (postmodern) families, health, and culture. Her current research examines the ways in which formerly fostered young adults make sense of their experiences and how experiences and sense-making processes might connect with well-being outcomes.

Cassandra P. Vázquez is a first-year Developmental Psychology Doctoral Student at the University of Kentucky, USA, under the supervision of Dr. Rachel Farr. Her research interests broadly include adoptive families, youth in foster care, LGBTQ issues, sexuality development, and parent–child socialization.

Salomé Vieira-Santos, Ph.D., is an Assistant Professor on the Faculty of Psychology at the University of Lisbon, Portugal. She has taught in undergraduate, postgraduate, master's, and doctoral courses, and has developed research in the areas of clinical psychology, pediatric psychology, and child protection, with a main interest in the parent–child relationship and family and child adaptation. She is currently a member of the CICPSI (Research Center for Psychological Science; R&D unit).

Dorothy White, M.A., is a Doctoral Student in Clinical Psychology at George Washington University, USA. Her research to date centers on early childhood social and personality development, specifically callous-unemotional behaviors.

Amy L. Whitesel, Ph.D., LCSW-C, is an Assistant Research Professor of Psychology at George Washington University, USA. Dr. Whitesel has been working in the adoption field for more than 20 years, in both direct practice and research. Dr. Whitesel's research focus has been the study of the birth parent experience, with special emphasis on birth fathers.

Gretchen Miller Wrobel, Ph.D., is a Professor of Psychology at Bethel University, USA and co-investigator on the Minnesota-Texas Adoption Research Project. Dr. Wrobel's research interests include information seeking related to curiosity about one's adoption and adoptive family communication. She is past editor of *Adoption Quarterly*.

TABLES

FIGURES

INTRODUCTION

There is a vast amount of literature on the topic of adoption, yet it is difficult to find a central source of the most contemporary scholarship from a variety of disciplines. The primary purpose of this handbook is to make scientific research easily accessible, comprehensible, and useful for the various stakeholders involved in adoption. This includes members of the adoptive kinship network of birth and adoptive family members, the professionals who work with them, and those involved in adoption research and education. In order to increase the utility of the handbook for adoption professionals, each chapter includes a section in which the authors explicitly connect their academic findings to implications for policy and practice.

In an effort to cultivate a diversity of topics and perspectives, the editors were strategic and intentional about soliciting and incorporating chapters from global scholars, resulting in both US and international content from experts in a variety of fields including psychology, social work, sociology, medicine, family science, demography, political science, law, economics, information science, education, communication, occupational therapy, and speech pathology. Many viewpoints are included and represented since a number of contributing authors' academic work is informed by their own personal experience with adoption and child welfare, either as a birth parent, adoptee, or adoptive parent. In addition to these personal experiences described by some, contributing authors discussed a variety of factors leading to their initial and continued interest in investigating topics related to adoption. Common themes included enjoying the complexity of adoption as a topic that is intersectional and interdisciplinary at its core, that studying it allows researchers to examine fundamental questions about family and key aspects of human experience, the desire to contribute to a better understanding of adversity or trauma in early life, and the ability of adoption research designs to answer questions about the role of experience in development and its interaction with genetic predispositions.

When asked about hopes for the future of adoption many authors discussed their strong wish for a reduction in stigma and increased awareness about adoption in the general public, including for birth parents making an adoption plan, for adoptees themselves, and for adoptive families. Additionally, authors outlined their hope that research in various fields could lead to improvements in child welfare policy and practices and in mental health services provided to adoptees, birth parents, and adoptive parents. Authors highlighted the increasing emphasis on centering the voices of adoptees in research, policy, and practice as a positive development that they hoped would continue to be realized. Last, several authors discussed their hope that definitions of family could continue to be broadened beyond simply those with whom we have biological ties.

Even as authors highlighted the positive possibilities of adoption in creating family ties, they advocated for a more nuanced understanding of adoption, that acknowledges inherent losses, ethical complexities, and historical and current inequities.

Section descriptions

The handbook is a multifaceted and interdisciplinary book grounding adoption practices and activities in scientific research, and is divided into five parts. Part I, 'Adoption in context', provides an understanding of the background and context of adoption, including the sociocultural and political contexts in which adoption occurs. The editors (Chapter 1) begin with a historical overview of adoption in the US, highlighting significant issues and controversies. Kreider (Chapter 2) provides a contemporary portrait of the demographics of adopted children in the US, including basic estimates of the number of internationally adopted children and transracially adopted children. Hansen (Chapter 3) continues the discussion, arguing that the economic way of thinking provides useful tools for developing adoption policy that allocates limited resources wisely, while at the same time taking into account the ethical problems in adoption. From an international perspective, Bodja and Gleason (Chapter 4) describe an initiative by Bethany Global to partner with the Ethiopian government to provide care options for children to be raised in families instead of orphanages. Discussed are program development contexts where legal and policy supports are in place, yet there may be a gap in the infrastructure to provide practical implementation. Facilitating the transition to adoptive families in the United Kingdom is the focus of Neil and Beek (Chapter 6). Using data from research conducted at the University of East Anglia, the chapter explores the value of children's relationships with birth parents, previous foster parents and other caregivers, and describes some key principles for helping children to make successful transitions to their adoptive families. From the perspective of those who place children for adoption, Clemens (Chapter 5) presents a qualitative and interpretive inquiry into information seeking and information use of birth mothers surrounding the process of decision-making, coping, and living with the act of child relinquishment. Last in this part, Whitesel and colleagues (Chapter 7) from the Early Growth and Development Study, discuss the benefits of the adoption research design to address heritable and environmental contributions to behavior and also adoption-specific outcomes.

The diversity found in contemporary adoptive families, such as family form, attitudes about adoption, and characteristics of adopted children, is explored in Part II of the handbook, 'Diversity in adoption'. Farr and Vázquez (Chapter 12) offer an insightful review of the interdisciplinary research exploring the outcomes and experiences of adoptive families headed by LGBTQ parents using multiple theoretical perspectives. Outcomes for Black children adopted in the US, including multiracial identification, are described by Raleigh and Kreider (Chapter 10) using analyses at the population level. Comparisons of the demographics of families with Black children headed by White parents, Black parents, and White interracially or interethnically married parents are provided. Turning to attitudes of potential adopters, Sweeney (Chapter 11) summarizes relevant research on potential adoptive parent preferences for child gender and race within the restrictions of policies, practice, availability, and social norms. Identifying the increase in the number of children placed who have recognized or potential medical problems, Johnson, Eckerle, Bresnahan, and Kroupina (Chapter 14) trace the history of adopting children with disabilities, and discuss how new knowledge on the effects of adversity in early childhood has expanded our understanding of which children are at risk for short- and long-term medical, developmental, emotional, and behavioral problems.

International adoption is approached through several lenses. Reinoso Bernuz (Chapter 8) presents the challenges inherent in international adoption while presenting adoption as an effective intervention, offering children the possibility of recovery and healthy development within an adoptive family. Exploring attitudes regarding transracial adoption, Kim and Lee (Chapter 9) employ an integrated critical adoption studies framework, with an Asian Americanist perspective, to focus on discrimination, ethnic-racial identity, cultural socialization, and the way in which adopted persons pursue cultural engagement. Julian (Chapter 13) discusses the developmental impact of children who were adopted from institutional care at a relatively older age, from a globally depriving institution or from a socially-emotionally depriving institution. The part ends with a focus on the use of international adoption in the face of natural disasters such as earthquakes, floods, and famines. Selman (Chapter 15) provides reflection on policy that expedites adoption and movement of children from their birth country at a time of trauma.

In Part III, 'Lived experience', the intricacies of day-to-day life for members of the adoption kinship network (including birth parents, adoptive parents, and the adopted individual) and how they are shaped by larger cultural and external forces are considered. Madden, Aguiniga, and Ryan (Chapter 16) give insight into the experiences of women who placed a child for adoption. An overview of the thoughts, considerations, and experiences of birth mothers who relinquished a child during the era of open adoptions is provided. Search and reunion with birth parents is discussed by Godon-Decoteau and Ramsey (Chapter 17) who explore how the sociocultural context surrounding being a transracial adoptee impacts the complex search process. Thomas and Scharp (Chapter 18) provide an overview of several family communication and sense-making theories that are salient to the study of the methods, content, and importance of communication in and around adoptive families. Grotevant (Chapter 19) addresses the implications of adoptive openness in the context of domestic adoption of infants, adoptions from the child welfare system, and international adoptions. Turning to the perspectives of adoptive parents, Lo and Cashen (Chapter 20) bring insight to research and theory on cognitive parenting processes experienced by adoptive parents as well as their relation to adoptee and family outcomes. Additionally, Helder and Marr (Chapter 21) examine the relationship between religiosity and the activities of potential and current adoptive parents. Religious motivations to adopt are discussed in the context of ethnicity, choices parents make in the adoption process, and outcomes for adopted children. Last, difficult experiences of adopted persons are considered. Garber (Chapter 22) focuses on the budding area of microaggressions, an overt or covert discriminatory message, as it relates to the experiences of adopted individuals and families living in a bionormative society. Matthews (Chapter 23) brings light to the small, but growing literature regarding maltreatment of adopted children in their adoptive homes. Based on a discussion of maltreatment etiology, ideas for targeted prevention are discussed.

A variety of outcomes for internationally and domestically adopted children and adoptive families comprise Part IV ('Outcomes') of this handbook. Glennen (Chapter 24) discusses the unique situation of internationally adopted children learning a new language after adoption. Neurobiological information about second language learning, developmental milestones, and language outcomes are discussed in depth. Lipschutz and Bick (Chapter 26) further the discussion of neurobiological impact through a review of evidence indicating that early deprivation exposures, secondary to institutional rearing, shape key underlying neurobiological systems that subserve higher level domains of cognitive and emotional development. Adjustment of adopted persons is addressed by three chapters. Holmgren, Raaska, Elovainio, and Lapinleimu (Chapter 25) analyze issues surrounding behavioral and emotional adjustment of adopted persons, leading to the conclusion that there are many open questions among confirmed answers with regard to behavioral and emotional adjustment. Social development of internationally adopted children is discussed by Tan, Liu, and Smith (Chapter 27) with an emphasis on child–parent attachment, relationship quality, peer relations, ethnic identity development, self-esteem, and social and academic competence. Dalen and Theie (Chapter 28) focus on the academic performance and school adjustment among internationally adopted children in Norway and other northern countries, paying particular attention to early intervention. Adoptive parenting stress across the family life cycle is discussed by Santos-Nunes, Narciso, and Vieira-Santos (Chapter 29). The relationship between parenting stress and child characteristics and parental characteristics is reviewed. Palacios (Chapter 30) provides important insight into adoption breakdown, when an adoption fails to result in full and lasting permanence, through a discussion of levels of instability as related to differing types of breakdown.

The handbook concludes with Part V, 'Adoption competency', addressing the development, training, and implementation of adoption competent clinical practice. Such practice is essential for providing quality services and supports to members of the adoption kinship network. Atkinson (Chapter 31) describes the growing consensus around clinical competencies that distinguish adoption competent practice as a specialized area of mental health practice and the application of those competencies in major areas of clinical intervention in work with adoptive families. The discussion continues as Riley and Singer (Chapter 32) describe the Training for Adoption Competency program, an in-person training, and the National Adoption Competency Mental Health Training Initiative web-based training for child welfare and mental health professionals. Evaluation data on the programs are reviewed. Next, curricular issues are addressed. Fishman (Chapter 33) discusses how schools are often underprepared and lack knowledge to adjust curricula to be sensitive to the history and needs of adopted children. She provides a theoretical framework for educators to begin to understand the challenges manifest in schools. Koh, Kim, and McRoy (Chapter 35) examine adoption-specific curricula in higher education – particularly among baccalaureate and graduate degree programs. They discuss the potential challenges in filling this gap in adoption-related curricula. Merritt and Ludeke (Chapter 34) move us to the topic of services available to families after the adoption has been completed. Through their overview, specific attention is given to post-adoption service needs, availability, and access for children adopted from the child welfare system into non-relative or kinship placements, as well as domestic and international/intercountry adoptive placements.

Our goal was to provide readers with a comprehensive volume on adoption that included an international perspective. While the handbook is not exhaustive in its coverage of adoption, it does integrate a wide variety of established and emerging adoption research and experts from around the world. Perspectives of birth/first parents, adoptive parents, and the adopted person are brought forth through a range of disciplinary and theoretical lenses. It is our expectation that the volume will spark discussion surrounding common issues in adoption, resulting in thoughtful, robust research initiatives and evidence-based policy and practice.

We would like to extend our gratitude and appreciation to our editorial assistant, Gwyneth Findlay, and our student assistant, Elena van Stee, for the efforts they contributed to the project. We would also like to thank Samuel Perry for thoughtful and constructive input and insight. Additionally, we would like to acknowledge the Council for Christian Colleges and Universities and our home Universities, Calvin University and Bethel University, that provided us with the time and financial resources to make this handbook a reality.

PART I

Adoption in context

1

HISTORICAL AND CONTEMPORARY CONTEXTS OF US ADOPTION

An overview

Elisha Marr, Emily Helder, and Gretchen Miller Wrobel

Complex family forms, such as those created through adoption, are becoming increasingly commonplace in the US. Our contemporary familiarity with adoptive families, whether through personal connections or through media portrayals, makes it difficult to believe that adoption is a relatively new practice in the US. In fact, prior to the 1900s, few families formally adopted unrelated children (Davis, 2011; Perry, 2017). The current US adoption system was created and shaped by a variety of factors including immigration, race, war, poverty, affluence, disease, and medical developments as well as changing cultural perspectives about the value of children and norms for women and families. To provide some foundational context for this handbook, we first provide a brief history of adoption in the US and then describe some of the major adoption-related topics and controversies.

Prior to the 1900s

Some of the earliest instances of adoption involved White settlers adopting Native American children. Though ostensibly based – at least initially – on an agreement between White missionaries and Indigenous groups, Native Americans often interpreted the practice as an ongoing, reciprocal establishment of kinship and peaceable relations between the two groups; whereas the White settlers treated it as formal severance of relationships between the child and their tribe. Once the Native Americans learned that the agreement was nonreciprocal and irrevocable, they stopped willingly participating in the practice (Leacock, 1980). Yet the willingness of Native Americans became irrelevant since this period was followed by massacres of Indigenous people allowing Whites to take possession of their now-orphaned children (Ward Gailey, 2010). This practice continued through the early 20th century, during which White Americans not only "adopted" Native American orphans, but also forcibly removed children from their parents in order to "civilize," "Christianize," and "Americanize" them in boarding schools (Briggs, 2012; Davis, 2011; Perry, 2017).

The 19th-century influx of European immigrants to eastern coastal cities resulted in the practice of White immigrant children being adopted by rural White families. Travel to the US, poverty, and disease resulted in growing numbers of orphans living on the streets. These were not only children whose families had died, but also those whose parents were too poor to provide them with basic necessities. Although some improperly supervised or homeless children became vagrants engaging in criminal activities to survive, others were taken in by families where they would work for room and board (Carp, 2005; Davis, 2011; DellaCava, Kolko Phillips, and Engel, 2004; Perry, 2017). Around the mid-19th century, there were about 30,000 parentless Irish children in New York City alone (Perry, 2017). Urban and church-related organizations, such as the Children's Aid Society of New York, would put many of these children on "orphan trains" to the western US to become formally adopted into families or to work as farm hands (Perry, 2017; Solinger, 2004). It has been estimated that from about 1850 to 1930 around 200,000–250,000 of these children were placed into homes; however, only 90,000 were formally adopted (Davis, 2011; Perry, 2017).

1900–1960s

The formal private adoption of infants began around the turn of the 20th century and took shape throughout the Depression Era. The formality arose from efforts to standardize and professionalize child placements. The US Children's Bureau, which was established in 1912, and the Child Welfare League of America, which was established in 1921, began to create and institute adoption standards for both public and private agencies. By the 1930s, all 48 states instituted statutes governing adoption; the federal government followed suit (Carp, 2005; DellaCava, Kolko Phillips, and Engel, 2004). The infant adoptions resulted from the maternity home movement, which offered unwed pregnant women a place to live until their child was born. The main message conveyed to birth mothers was that their infant would be promptly adopted by married couples, providing good homes, who would raise the child to be a good citizen (Davis, 2011). Until this point in time, safe, effective infant formulas and bottles were not easily accessible or affordable, making it almost logistically impossible for an infant to be adopted by another couple without a wet nurse. Once infants could be fed by someone other than a lactating mother it created the opportunity for childless couples to adopt, and conversely the opportunity for unwed mothers to place their child for adoption (Hanan, 1997).

These systems, policies, and practices continued into the post-World War II (WWII) era baby boom. Married women who were able to biologically reproduce were able to create the idealized nuclear family, yet infertile married women conspicuously lacked the children needed to make their couple into what they considered a real family (Carp, 2005; Sandelowski, 1990). Conversely, pregnant unmarried women often did not have access to jobs paying a living wage and feared the social stigma of raising an illegitimate child (Solinger, 2004). Thus, they were pressured by society to marry, or to quietly and surreptitiously surrender their child for adoption. The aforementioned maternity homes made it possible for infertile White middle class couples to gain access to healthy, White infants available for adoption, while protecting the birth mother and her family from shame and stigma (Davis, 2011; Patton, 2000; Solinger, 2004). Although private adoption seemed like a good solution to the issues of both White married women who were infertile and White unmarried women who were pregnant, some birth mothers reported a sense of choicelessness and being coerced into surrendering their infants (Fisher, 2003; Solinger, 2001).

Adoption was not an option for all women in the US. Throughout US history and into this post-WWII era, African American women were effectively excluded from these early forms of formal adoption. They did not have access to many of the postwar programs, supports, and resources White women were using to create idyllic American families, and most worked in formal or informal wage labor (Davis, 2011; Solinger, 2004). Similar to White couples, unmarried African American couples who learned of their pregnancy were expected to marry to avoid the stigma of raising an illegitimate child (Gutman, 1976). Yet, African American women who did not marry did not also have the choice of a private, confidential, and formal means for placing their child with a vetted middle or upper class unrelated couple of their same race. Consequently, their unwed pregnancies were handled informally by their familial and kinship communities, a practice that had always been utilized by African American families (Gutman, 1976; Higdon, 2008; Solinger, 2004). During slavery, Black women had very little control over the residence and raising of their child, yet could count on the related and unrelated people in their network to support and provide for both of them to the extent it was possible (Abdullah, 1996; Davis, 2011; Gutman, 1976; Higdon, 2008). These informal adoptions could simply involve the network assisting the woman in raising her child, or another woman or couple might raise it as they would one of their own biological children. Regardless of the arrangement, it was more likely to be verbal, informal, and without any organizational oversight or approval (Abdullah, 1996; Higdon, 2008). Asian, Hispanic, and Latino families in the US similarly relied on informal arrangements among extended family for the care of single-parent and orphaned children (Higdon, 2008). Yet their mid-20th-century immigration to the US (History.com, 2018) coincided with the establishment of a more structured adoption system with legal oversight and enforcement, resulting in the informal aspect of adoption being a much smaller portion of their US history than it was for African Americans (Higdon, 2008). In summary, although the 1930s through the 1960s are commonly viewed as the beginning of adoption in the US, it should be recognized that the adoption of unrelated children has been a practice, for better or worse, since the arrival of Europeans (Davis, 2011; Higdon, 2008).

During the post-WWII period, White couples in the US were also able to adopt children from other countries. Part of the de-Nazification program involved placing orphans from Germany and other European countries with both US military and civilian families (Ward Gailey, 2010). Unlike the adoptions of the previous century where the primary goal of adoptive families was to provide a home for the child, often in exchange for work, White couples seeking to adopt internationally desired a child that they would intimately raise as they would their own biological child. Adoption agencies sought to match children with parents with similar eye and hair color in an attempt to minimize differences in appearance (Davis, 2011; Ward Gailey, 2010). This was the beginning of international adoption; however, many would describe these as same-race adoptions due to the matching of adoptive parents' and adoptees' phenotypes.

The conclusion of the Korean War in 1953 began the first international adoptions to the US where adoption agencies did not practice racial matching. Very few adoptions of children of one race by parents of a different race had occurred prior to this time (DellaCava, Kolko Phillips, and Engel, 2004; Perry, 2017). Yet the pressure of White families in the US to cross racial-ethnic lines to adopt from Korea was spurred by the notable number of war orphans. Many of these children had been fathered by US soldiers, but excluded from the mother's Korean family (Perry, 2017). Additionally, civilian evangelical Christians, Harry and Bertha Holt, were moved to adopt these mixed-race children after watching a documentary about an orphanage in Korea. Despite having six biological children, the Holts adopted eight Korean orphans and eventually established Holt International Services to facilitate adoptions from Korea to the US. The Holts are credited with beginning what we now know as the practice of private international adoption (DellaCava, Kolko Phillips, and Engel, 2004; Perry, 2017).

Public foster care also coalesced during this period of the 1930s through the 1960s. As children began to be valued for sentimental and emotional reasons, as opposed to their economic value as workers, adoption practices began to prioritize the best interests of the child (Davis, 2011). Additionally, as the federal government instituted more social welfare and oversight programs, a link between child welfare and adoption was made. Systems were established to investigate child abuse and neglect, as well as to rehome children who were victims of these practices (Davis, 2011; Solinger, 2004). Children involuntarily removed from their parents' homes were to be temporarily placed with family members or with unrelated families that had met certain standards. The overarching goal of public foster care was to help the parents meet the child welfare standards and reunify the family; however, lack of resources and ethnic bias in the system had a particularly devastating impact on Black families. Social workers were trained in a culture within which White family forms were considered the norm. In comparison, Black families were perceived as dysfunctional and broken by slavery, evidenced by the prevalence of irresponsible and promiscuous Black single mothers (Briggs, 2012; Patton, 2000). Thus, even though some White birth parents also struggled with access to the housing, education, and medical care necessary to provide for their children, the ethnic bias against Black familial cultural practices resulted in disproportionately large numbers of Black children being involuntarily removed from their birth families (Briggs, 2012; Patton, 2000; Solinger, 2004; Ward Gailey, 2010). A smaller proportion of Black children were reintegrated into their birth families in comparison to White foster children. These ethnic differences also characterized Black parents seeking to adopt; consequently, they struggled to be approved as foster and/or adoptive parents (Briggs, 2012; Carp, 2005; Davis, 2011; Solinger, 2004). Some identify this as the beginning of the crisis in the foster care system in which there are more children of color, specifically Black children, than there are of same-race adoptive parents (Solinger, 2004). Because adoptions across racial lines were rare during this time period, these children of color, relative to their White counterparts, experienced longer wait times for placement or languished in institutions (Briggs, 2012; DellaCava, Kolko Phillips, and Engel, 2004; Simon and Altstein, 1977).

The essential structure of the current US adoption system grew out of these practices, policies, government organizations, and private agencies established during this period of the 1930s to the 1960s. Public adoption commonly refers to state governments being primarily responsible for the administration of the adoption and foster care of children who have been involuntarily removed from the homes of birth parents by child welfare agencies. These children are often older, may have physical, mental, or behavioral challenges, and are commonly labeled as hard-to-place or special-needs (CWIG, 2011; Davis, 2011; Vandivere, Malm, and Radel, 2009). Private adoptions are those facilitated by non-government adoption agencies or attorneys (Biafora and Esposito, 2007; Child Welfare Information Gateway (CWIG), 2011; Vandivere, Malm, and Radel, 2009; Ward Gailey, 2010). Birth parents seeking to voluntarily surrender an infant for adoption work with these private agencies or attorneys to facilitate permanent adoption by adoptive parents. Private domestic adoption describes when birth parents and adoptive parents reside in the US. Private international adoption describes when adoptive parents reside in the US, the birth parents reside in a country other than the US, and adoption agencies or organizations in both countries facilitate the adoption (Biafora and Esposito,

2007; Child Welfare Information Gateway (CWIG), 2011; Vandivere, Malm, and Radel, 2009; Ward Gailey, 2010). Private international adoption can also involve birth parents in the US and adoptive parents from a country other than the US, yet this is rare (Buckwalter-Poza, 2014). Since international, federal, and state laws may differ, there are some variations to these practices (e.g., state government contracting with private agency to facilitate foster care; Hansen, 2009); yet these categories and descriptions reflect the primary differences between public and private, domestic and international adoption (Child Welfare Information Gateway (CWIG), 2011; Vandivere, Malm, and Radel, 2009; Ward Gailey, 2010).

1960s-2000

Formal domestic and international adoption in the US continued into the 1960s and 1970s, yet there were marked changes among birth parents and adoptees. Increased access to contraception and abortion, as well as increased acceptance of single parenthood, led to a decrease in the number of healthy White infants being surrendered for adoption (Fisher, 2003; Patton, 2000; Simon and Altstein, 2000; Ward Gailey, 2010). At this time of more integrative attitudes toward race, White potential adoptive parents began to consider, and became more willing to adopt children of color (Patton, 2000; Simon and Altstein, 2000; Ward Gailey, 2010). Government and private adoption agencies considered these transracial adoptions to be second best to same-race adoptions, yet they began to permit the practice (Simon and Altstein, 2000). The vast majority of adoptions in the US continued to be same-race; however, this was the beginning of agencies making transracial placements (predominately White parents adopting children of color) when they desired (Patton, 2000; Simon and Altstein, 2000; Ward Gailey, 2010).

Adoption during the 1980s and 1990s was characterized by three major shifts: (1) the increase in transracial adoptions, (2) the increase in international adoptions (Biafora and Esposito, 2007; Simon and Altstein, 2000; Ward Gailey, 2010), and (3) the move from extremely limited contact between adoptees and birth parents (commonly known as closed adoptions) to encouraging some level of contact between adoptees and birth parents (commonly known as open adoptions; Grotevant and McRoy, 1998). Domestically, growing societal and political support for transracial adoption resulted in federal legislation eliminating barriers for transracial placements. The 1993 Multiethnic Placement Act (MEPA) and the 1997 Adoption and Safe Families Act (ASFA) were established to prioritize adoptive homes for children rather than having them wait for same-race adoptive parents. Agencies were prohibited from using race to delay or deny the adoption of a child (Patton, 2000; Simon and Altstein, 2000). Since private adoption agencies do not report information about their adoptions to an umbrella organization, it is not possible to determine if MEPA/ASFA increased the number of transracial adoptions domestically. However, beginning in the early 1990s, government agencies were required to report data on public adoptions to the Adoption and Foster Care Analysis and Reporting System (AFCARS). It has been estimated that during the period in which MEPA/ASFA were implemented, transracial placements increased from making up 10.8% of public adoptions in 1995 to 15% in 2001 (Hansen and Simon, 2004).

Internationally, the previously discussed adoptions from South Korea to the US continued. In fact, through 1990 most of the children adopted internationally were Korean (Beck, 1992). However, world events, practices, and policies soon changed the composition of children internationally adopted. Following the fall of the Soviet Union, Romanian women surrendered thousands of their children to orphanages. Many White adoptive parents from the US now had the opportunity to internationally adopt White-skinned children. Yet after a year of permitting international adoptions, Romania enacted strict policies on international adoption to avoid being perceived as needing US assistance in taking care of Romanian children (Beck, 1992; Simon and Altstein, 2000).

In the early 1990s, 15 years after the US withdrawal, South Vietnam began to allow international adoption of its children to the US (Simon and Altstein, 2000). Around this time, China also began allowing their children to be internationally adopted due to increasing numbers of girls being surrendered to orphanages. In this patriarchal culture, when faced with China's policy limiting families to one child, many were choosing to surrender their infant girls. The number of Chinese children adopted to the US increased markedly throughout the 1990s (Simon and Altstein, 2000; Ward Gailey, 2010).

Conversely, prior to the 1990s, South American children made up more than one in five of all international adoptees; most were from Columbia. Yet by 1998, less than one in 20 international adoptions were from South America. This decrease is attributed to fewer South American countries making adoptees available and China providing a new source of internationally adoptable children (Simon and Altstein, 2000). International adoption from Mexico, the Caribbean, and Central America fluctuated slightly throughout the 1980s and 1990s, yet they accounted for approximately one in ten international adoptees each year, with Guatemala being the largest source (Simon and Altstein, 2000).

The other major change in adoption practice in the 1980s was movement toward more openness in adoption. Traditionally, confidentiality in adoption was viewed as protecting the birth mother, adopted child, and adoptive family from one another so that all could move on from the adoption and continue with their lives (Chapman, Dorner, Silber, and Winterberg, 1986). Birth mothers would be better able to grieve the loss of their child (Kraft, Palambo, Mitchell, Woods, and Schmidt, 1985a), adoptive parents would be able to bond with their child and feel more secure in their role as parent without the presence of the birth mother (Kraft, Palambo, Mitchell, Woods, and Schmidt, 1985b), and adopted children would not become confused as to who their parents were by internalizing only one set of parents (Kraft, Palambo, Mitchell, Woods, and Schmidt, 1985c). In the 1980s, dissatisfied with traditional practice, proponents of openness advocated that contact would benefit all members of the adoptive kinship network (Pannor and Baran, 1984). Birth mothers would know the wellbeing of the child they placed (Chapman, Dorner, Silber, and Winterberg, 1986), adoptive parents would feel equipped to answer their child's adoption-related questions (Berry, Dylla, Barth, and Needell, 1998), and children's access to information about their adoption would positively influence their satisfaction with adoption (Mendenhall, Berge, Wrobel, Grotevant, and McRoy, 2004). Agencies began to practice openness in adoption by facilitating agreements between birth and adoptive parents about the type and frequency of future contact. From simply providing detailed information about the birth parents to the adoptee and their adoptive parents, to in-person visits, the amount of contact among those in the adoption triad has increased, a significant change from previous adoption arrangements (Grotevant, 2012; Siegel and Smith, 2012). Contact between birth and adoptive families has become common and is seen as in the best interests of the child (Siegel and Smith, 2012).

2000s–the present

The major development in adoption in the 2000s involved changes to laws, policies, and practices regarding lesbian, gay, bisexual, trans, and queer (LGBTQ) individuals and/or same-sex couples' adoption of a child. Although the first known adoption to a gay man occurred in

1968, and the first gay couple to jointly adopt a child occurred in 1979 (Mombian, 2017), adoption agencies formally or informally did not regularly place children with LGBTQ identifying individuals or couples for much of the 20th century (Appell, 2011). In 1993, Vermont and Massachusetts became the first states to permit same-sex couples to adopt jointly, yet the final state to overturn its ban on adoption by LGBTQ people was Florida in 2010 (Appell, 2011; Mombian, 2017). Adoption agencies were then able to prevent same-sex couples from jointly adopting by banning unmarried couples; however, the 2015 Supreme Court ruling of *Obergefell* v. *Hodges* legalized same-sex marriage in all states (Kazyak, 2018; Moreau, 2019). Most same-sex couples who had previously been denied the ability to adopt due to being unmarried could now legally pursue the adoption of children; however, barriers still exist. At the writing of this chapter, ten states do not require state-licensed adoption agencies to place children with LGBTQ individuals or same-sex couples if the practice conflicts with the agency's religious beliefs. It is expected that this decision will be challenged and ultimately decided at the federal level (Kazyak, Woodell, Scherrer, and Finken, 2018; Moreau, 2019). In 2013, it was estimated that almost 27,000 same-sex couples were raising 58,000 adopted and foster kids in the US (Gates, 2015).

The National Council for Adoption's (NCFA) longitudinal research on adoption trends shows that although a notable number of unrelated adoptions continue to occur each year, there has been a decrease since the early 2000s, particularly among international adoptions. In 2014 approximately 75,000 children were adopted by unrelated parents in the US, with almost 6,000 of them having been adopted from countries other than the US (domestic 92%, international 8%; Jones and Placek, 2017). This differs greatly from the 96,000 unrelated adoptions in 2007, of which 19,500 were international (domestic 80%, international 20%; Rosman, Johnson, and Callahan, 2011) and 2002 with 97,000 unrelated adoptions of which 21,000 were international (domestic 79%, international 21%; Atwood, Allen, Ravenel, and Callahan, 2007). These early 2000s figures also differ from 1996, during which the total of all unrelated adoptions was about 66,000 with approximately 11,300 adopted internationally (domestic 83%, international 17%; Atwood, Allen, Ravenel, and Callahan, 2007). A review of NCFA's periodical reports shows that the number of unrelated adoptions in the 1980s and 1990s fluctuated between 60,000–66,000 with international adoptions comprising minimally 10% of these figures (Atwood, Allen, Ravenel, and Callahan, 2007; Jones and Placek, 2017; Rosman, Johnson, and Callahan, 2011). In short, the number of children adopted by unrelated parents domestically and internationally increased toward the end of the 20th century and peaked in the early 2000s. Yet in the past decade these numbers have been declining, particularly among international adoptions.

Reports from the US Census Bureau have provided some of the most recent and comprehensive information on the characteristics of adoptees in the US (see Chapter 2 for statistics on adoption). In 2010 there were approximately 1,557,000 adoptive children (under the age of 18) in the US, of which almost 17% were born outside of the US, 24% were transracial, and 10% differed in Hispanic ethnicity (i.e., child was Hispanic yet the head of household was not and vice-versa) (Kreider and Lofquist, 2014). In 2000, of the 1,586,000 adopted children (under the age of 18), about 12.5% were born in a country other than the US, 17% were transracial, and 6.5% differed from their head of household in Hispanic ethnicity (Kreider, 2003). These categories overlap (e.g., many of the children adopted internationally also differed in race from their adoptive parents), yet illustrate that a notable portion of adoptions cross national, racial, and ethnic lines; very different from the adoption patterns of the early 20th century. The variations between the composition of adoptive families in 2000 and 2010 also reflect the increases in domestic transracial placements and international adoptions in the 1980s and 1990s; however, same-race adoptions continue to make up the vast majority of adoptions (Kreider and Lofquist, 2014) (information relevant to this topic can be found in Chapter 10).

Issues and areas of controversy in adoption

Openness

Adoption is a process that is shaped by personal, social, and political attitudes in the context of history and culture. Openness in adoption is one aspect that is shaped by these contexts and can be thought of as a continuum from confidential or no contact, to mediated contact with exchange of information through an intermediary (often the adoption agency), to fully disclosed with direct contact (Grotevant and McRoy, 1998). More recently the concept of openness has shifted to a description of the type and frequency of contact (Grotevant et al., 2007). Contact can take many forms: letters and photos placed at the adoption agency, in-person visits, and communication through social media (Fursland, 2013; Grotevant, 2012).

Openness or contact between adoptive and birth family members has seen much change in the last 40 to 50 years. Moving from a culture where adoption was practiced in a context of secrecy, to the adoption process including consideration of how much contact to have between birth and adoptive families, has been a major shift influencing all aspects of adoption (Siegel and Smith, 2012). The decision about contact impacts all members of the adoption kinship network (AKN; Grotevant and McRoy, 1998) of birth and adoptive family members who might have differing desires related to amount and type of contact (Grotevant, Wrobel, Fiorenzo, Lo, and McRoy, 2019) (see Chapters 6, 7, and 19 for information on relationships and contact among the AKN).

Contact in adoption can change over time, including increasing the amount of contact or stopping contact between birth and adoptive family members. Contact can be stopped for a variety of reasons, including a loss of interest or contact did not work out (Grotevant, Wrobel, Fiorenzo, Lo, and McRoy, 2019). One impetus for an increase in contact is curiosity about one's adoption (Wrobel, Grotevant, Samek, and Von Korff, 2013). This curiosity, which can be satisfied through many approaches, exists in adoptions with all types of contact, not just for those in confidential adoptions. Yet, it is important to remember that some adopted individuals are satisfied with the information they have and feel no need to seek out more (Wrobel and Dillon, 2009). One concern that can bring tension to the information-gathering process is at what age is it best for an adopted person to seek out the information. If the adopted person is not of legal age to access information independently, the adopted parents must make decisions about helping their child find information. Responses can vary from assisting their child to asking that the child wait until they reach the age of majority (Wrobel, Kohler, Grotevant, and McRoy, 2003).

Searching for birth parents with the goal of reunion is one way adopted persons seek to increase contact (see Chapter 17 for information on search and reunification among transracial adoptees). This process is characterized by the unknown: Will I be able to find my birth parent? Will my birth parent want to have contact with me? Will the relationship work out? What is the best way to find my birth parent? Howe and Feast (2001) found that most adopted persons who engaged in a search for a birth mother, regardless of outcome with regard to an ongoing relationship, found the process satisfying and worthwhile. Sixty-three percent of their sample remained in contact with their birth mother eight years post-reunion. For those who do have contact with birth parents, establishing contact with additional members of the AKN can also provide avenues to additional adoption-related information. Wrobel, Carlson, Phillips, Ruff, and Grotevant (2016, November) found for persons adopted domestically as infants, that as the adopted persons became emerging adults the number of birth family members with whom contact was established increased. Obtaining information does not always need to be accomplished through expanding the AKN. AKN members can provide information to each other as the need arises.

One force that cannot be ignored is the use of the internet and social media sites to seek out adoption-related information and maintain relationships in the AKN. Whitesel and Howard (2013) conducted a survey of over 2,000 AKN members regarding their adoption-related internet use. Their findings paint a picture of widespread use of the internet and social media to search for birth family members, maintain ongoing contact in the AKN that can feel less intrusive than visits, and follow AKN members without their knowledge. It is clear that confidentiality is harder to maintain in the era of new technologies, yet Whitesel and Howard report that few of their respondents reported that internet or social media use led to unwelcome intrusions.

Newest to the discussion of information seeking by adopted individuals is genetic testing. Determining a genetic-relative family health history or the use of direct-to-consumer genetic ancestry testing can lead to finding members of the AKN. The bioethics surrounding the use of genetic testing and subsequent search and reunions is in its infancy (Lee, Kim, and Lee, 2016).

Transracial adoption

Although currently, and throughout US history, adoption agencies primarily match children with adoptive parents of the same race, the number and proportion of children adopted by parents of a different race (predominately children of color adopted by White parents) has grown since the 1960s (Kreider and Lofquist, 2014; Simon and Altstein, 2000). When adoption agencies began to permit transracial placements, it was strongly opposed, particularly by African American and Native American groups. The National Association of Black Social Workers published a paper in 1972 detailing their concerns, including that White parents could not teach Black children Black culture, effectively decreasing the transmission of Black culture to future generations. Additionally, White parents would not be able to equip Black children with the survival skills necessary to living in a racist society (Butler-Sweet, 2011; Patton, 2000; Simon and Altstein, 2000). Transracial adoption was not viewed as the altruistic action to provide Black children with familial homes, but a strategy to fulfill White childless couples' need for a child due to the dwindling number of White children available for adoption (Patton, 2000; Simon and Altstein, 1977). Native American groups echoed these sentiments, asserting that the adoption of Native American children by White parents decimates Indian tribes and results in a cultural genocide (Simon and Altstein, 2000).

> [T]he leaders of black American and Native-American organizations argued that nonwhite children who are adopted by white parents are lost to the communities into which they were born. The experience of growing up in a white world makes it impossible for black and Indian children to ever take their rightful place in the communities of their birth.
>
> *(Simon and Altstein, 2000, p. 45)*

The 1978 Indian Child Welfare Act was established to protect Native American families and intergenerational transmission of their culture; however, the mid-1990s MEPA/AFSA legislation removed barriers from the transracial adoption of all other children (Butler-Sweet, 2011; Simon and Altstein, 2000). Thus, the central issue has moved from considering whether transracial adoptions should occur, to how much importance should be placed on race in adoption decisions. Some argue that adoption agencies should not use race as a factor in choosing adoptive parents; finding familial homes, regardless of race, is in the best interests of the child (Bartholet, 1991). Others assert that because adoptive parents have racial preferences for children who are Asian, Hispanic, or Latino over children who are Black, the failure of adoption agencies to consider race in placements will result in Black children being less likely to be adopted (Banks, 1998; Maldonado, 2006) (see Chapter 11 for information on adoptive parents' race and gender preferences). However, despite the increase in transracial adoptions, and multiracial families in general in the US, research continues to identify areas of concern, including transracial adoptees' issues with identity and adjustment surfacing as young adults (Butler-Sweet, 2011; Patton, 2000) and adoption agencies' struggle to prepare White parents for parenting children of color without discouraging them from adopting (Raleigh, 2018).

International adoption

International adoption is a practice that also contains inherent tensions, with advocates and challengers emphasizing different values and research findings (Rotabi, 2012). Those that support the practice of international adoption, emphasize the inherent right of children to be raised within a family, the large numbers of children currently residing in institutions in nations without robust child welfare infrastructure, the risks that come with aging out of institutional care when domestic placements are not available, and the research findings indicating that adoption from institutional settings into families results in improvements in cognitive, behavioral, and emotional outcomes (Bartholet and Smolin, 2012) (see Chapters 24, 25, 26, 27, and 28 for information on outcomes of international adoptees).

In contrast, those that strongly critique the practice of international adoption place a high value on the reciprocal ties and rights to contact between the birth family (including extended family and community) and the child (Bartholet and Smolin, 2012), as well as the child's right to maintain their birth language, culture, and heritage in order to ground the identity development process (Hollingsworth, 2003). Given that most sending countries involved in international adoption are often lower-resource nations, concerns have also been raised about the vulnerability of birth families to coercion or misunderstanding regarding relinquishment decisions, child kidnapping, and trafficking (Selman, 2009). For example, the practice of placing a child in an institution temporarily due to poverty and/or lack of access to education may lead some children to be incorrectly identified as abandoned. Critics raise the concern that the high fees paid by adoptive parents to agencies can also lead to a commodification of children (Bartholet and Smolin, 2012; Solinger, 2001). Additionally, emphasizing the use of international adoption as a humanitarian response to poverty, conflict, or other disasters in lower-resource nations can de-emphasize the structural and systemic causes and solutions to these problems and might perpetuate, rather than address, the factors that would reduce relinquishment and increase reunification efforts (Brookfield, 2008) (see Chapter 15 on adoptions following natural disasters). The shadow of colonialism and imperialism looms over the practice, for critics, given that the majority of receiving countries are Western nations. Some worry that it perpetuates the narrative of rescue by the "Western savior," prioritizing the rights of relatively affluent adoptive families above those of poorer birth families (Briggs, 2012; Solinger, 2001).

In response, supporters of international adoption argue that the poor conditions of institutions and the lack of in-country familial options for children, especially those that are older and/or have disabilities, should override these concerns (see Chapter 13 about the impact of institutionalization on adoptees and Chapter 14 about parenting adoptees with disabilities). Also, they tend to view abuses in the system (trafficking, bribes) as rare occurrences that can be addressed through enforcement and strengthening of laws, rather than as a sign of widespread corruption (Bartholet and Smolin, 2012). No matter the position taken, it is important to recognize the complexity of the issue and that it is not merely an intellectual argument, but involves individuals with deep emotional ties to both their adoptive families and their birth family and culture, even when contact with biological relatives has not been established (see Chapters 8 and 9 for information on international adoptions).

In order to address several of the concerns above, in addition to broader issues of child rights and welfare, several international agreements have been established. First, the United Nations Convention on the Rights of the Child (UNCRC; United Nations, 1989) delineates a variety of protections and rights, including protections based on gender and a call for countries to address poverty and lack of access to nutrition, clothing, and housing, in the context of international cooperation. Specific to international adoption, the UNCRC states that children are best raised in a family context and that contact between the child and birth family should be maintained, even in the context of adoption or foster care, as long as it is in the best interests of the child. The UNCRC also highlights the importance of cultural continuity in upbringing, specifically with regard to ethnic, religious, cultural, and linguistic background. The UNCRC does, however, allow for international adoption when in-country options are not suitable for a particular child and outlines several goals for preventing abuse within the international adoption system. These include separation of the child from their family only in cases where judicial review determines it is in the best interest of the child, and that governments would implement measures to prevent the trafficking of children and improper gain by adoption service providers and their intermediaries. To date, 194 countries have signed the UNCRC, with only the United States and Somalia not yet ratifying it.

In order to establish coordination and cooperation among countries involved in international adoption, the Hague Convention on the Protection of Children and Co-operation in Respect of Intercountry Adoption was drafted in 1993 (Hague Conference on Private International Law (Conférence de La Haye de droit international privé; HCCH), n.d.), with 101 countries currently considered contracting parties to the Convention. The Convention established standards for inter-country adoption that were intended to protect the rights and interests of children, birth parents, and adoptive parents, all while preventing abuses such as child trafficking. This included requiring each country to delineate a central authority to oversee international adoption (in the United States it is the Department of State) and accrediting adoption service providers as a way to ensure transparency and appropriate levels of regulation. Similar to the UNCRC, the Convention also prioritizes in-country options for children, encouraging the development of kinship care and domestic alternative care models when possible and in the best interests of the child (see Chapter 4 for information on domestic adoption in Ethiopia). A number of critiques have emerged over time regarding the Convention (for review, see Rotabi and Gibbons, 2012), with one of the most prominent being that countries that have not signed or ratified the Convention may continue to operate international adoption programs without these safeguards and regulations in place.

LGBTQ adoption

Even as public opinion supporting same-sex marriage has been increasing steadily in the US and Europe, public approval of adoption by same-sex couples may vary from LGBTQ marriage support (Schwartz, 2010; Takács, Szalma, and Bartus, 2016). In the US, polling by Gallup

(McCarthy, 2019) indicated that 75% of those surveyed believed that same-sex couples should be legally allowed to adopt, which represents a steady increase over the last 40 years. Additionally, research examining the level of public support for adoption by LGBTQ couples has found that both micro (i.e., degree of religious involvement) and macro (i.e., country surveyed) level variables (Takács, Szalma, and Bartus, 2016) significantly influence the level of support. Within the US, conservative political ideology and more frequent religious attendance were the strongest predictors of lower support for same-sex adoption (Schwartz, 2010).

The relationship between opposition to same-sex adoption and political and religious beliefs are results of cultural wars and strategic campaigns to prevent LGBTQ people from parenting children. Save our Children, the Moral Majority, Concerned Women for America, and Focus on the Family were established in the 1970s and 1980s to advance evangelical (formerly referred to as fundamentalist) Christian values in US culture, with preserving traditional nuclear families as one of the major principles. Gay people were often characterized as dangerous pedophiles who were a danger to all children, which justified not only preventing them from adopting, but also keeping custody of their own biological children when relevant. These groups worked to change public opinion through books, television, and films, as well as public policy by lobbying, introducing and promoting legislation, influencing elections, and litigation when necessary. Consequently, a relationship was established between conservative political ideology and religious evangelical Christianity, commonly referred to as the "Christian Right." The impetus and continued priority of the Christian Right is opposition to same-sex relationships and family formation, including the ability for LGBTQ people to adopt children (Briggs, 2012; Herman, 1997).

Thus, currently the most significant tension surrounding LGBTQ adoption is the policy of adoption agencies in several states to decline placement to LGBTQ couples due to religious beliefs about same-sex marriage (Kazyak, Woodell, Scherrer, and Finken, 2018). This tension between the right of LGBTQ individuals to be free from discrimination when seeking adoption services, especially from state-contracted agencies, with the religious freedom of faith-based agencies is currently on display across several states in the US. In Michigan, *Dumont* v. *Gordon*, a lawsuit filed by two gay couples who were rejected by state-contracted agencies that had religious objections to same-sex marriage, reached a settlement and resulted in new policy that state-contracted agencies were required to accept qualified LGBTQ couples. One of the agencies named in the case chose to adjust their policy correspondingly, while the second agency has filed a new lawsuit (*Buck* v. *Gordon*) (LeBlanc, 2019). The legal landscape in Europe is quite varied, with the Netherlands being the first country to allow same-sex couples to jointly adopt beginning in 2001, and close to 20 countries having some form of adoption process available to LGBTQ couples (Takács, Szalma, and Bartus, 2016). Of note, joint adoption by LGBTQ parents seeking to adopt internationally is not allowed by many sending countries and several countries do not allow single LGBTQ adoption (Kazyak, 2018).

In this context, researchers have attempted to evaluate a wide range of process variables and outcomes for families headed by LGBTQ couples and individuals (see Chapter 12 for information) and have found generally equivalent outcomes compared with families headed by opposite sex couples.

Inequality in adoption as a reproductive option

When most think of adoption they consider it to be one of the options that couples have to become parents once biological reproduction and fertility treatments have failed (Fisher, 2003; Hanan, 1997; Park and Wonch Hill, 2014). However, the aspect of adoption that is less visible is that birth parents must surrender their rights to parent the child they bore (Fisher, 2003; Perry, 1998; Solinger, 1992). Research shows that many birth mothers relinquish their child after considering the few poor choices available to them (Fisher, 2003; Jones, 2000; Madden, Ryan, Aguiniga, and Crawford, 2016; Solinger, 2001) (see Chapters 5, 7, and 16 for information about birth parent experiences and decisions). Thus, although adoption is often perceived as an additional option for reproduction and parenting, this option is dependent on the relative choicelessness experienced by birth parents. Employing an intersectional lens, scholars in this area have learned how larger systems of gender, sexuality, marital status, socioeconomic status, race and ethnicity, and nationality shape one's reproductive options regarding adoption. An examination of macro-level adoption trends reveals a flow of children from those in disadvantaged groups to those in more privileged groups: from unwed women to heterosexually married couples, from poor women to middle and upper classes, from women of color to people who are White, and from nations with fewer resources or experiencing a crisis to the US (Briggs, 2012; Perry, 1998; Solinger, 2001).

Historically women's reproductive options were minimal or non-existent. As one of the many assets to men, they were obliged to reproduce based on the desires of their husband as well as societal expectations (Baca Zinn and Eitzen, 2002; Roberts, 1997; Sandelowski, 1990; Thorton Dill, 1999; Weitz, 2016). The growing autonomy of women in US society, as well as the development of safe, effective birth control methods, has afforded them a number of reproductive options (Baca Zinn and Eitzen, 2002; Sandelowski, 1990; Solinger, 2001). However, their ability to exercise their choice of these options continues to be highly influenced by familial, cultural norms (Petchesky, 1998; Ross and Solinger, 2017; Sandelowski, 1990). Despite increasing acceptance of diverse family forms in the US, the traditional nuclear family continues to be the ideal for many. There is social, political, and economic support and pressure for women to marry heterosexually and to have a few (although not many) children (Baca Zinn and Eitzen, 2002; Sandelowski, 1990). This impacts adoption as a reproductive option in two primary ways: (1) adoption is perceived as an option for heterosexually married couples who do not have children or have only one child (Hanan, 1997; Park and Wonch Hill, 2014; Schwartz, 2010) and (2) people with the power to make adoption decisions consider heterosexual married couples to be the best familial homes for adoptive children (Briggs, 2012; Davis, 2011; Hanan, 1997; Raleigh, 2012).

The influence of familial cultural ideals on adoption has resulted in unwed pregnant women who are pressured to place their child for adoption (Madden, Ryan, Aguiniga, and Crawford, 2016; Solinger, 1992), whereas heterosexually married women who experience fertility challenges are pressured to adopt (Hanan, 1997; Park and Wonch Hill, 2014). Those who are LGBTQ, cohabitating, never married, divorced, or widowed are discouraged from adopting a child (Briggs, 2012; Davis, 2011; Hanan, 1997; Raleigh, 2012). There is both explicit and implicit discrimination against sexual minorities and the unmarried in the adoption approval process (Appell, 2011; Briggs, 2012; Hanan, 1997; Raleigh, 2012). There is also less societal acceptance and support for their creation of a family through adoption (Briggs, 2012; Davis, 2011; Schwartz, 2010). Although increasing numbers of LGBTQ and unmarried people are approved as adoptive parents, some research shows that they may be matched with the children who have not been selected by heterosexual married couples and are deemed the least desirable (Goldberg, Downing, and Sauck, 2007; Raleigh, 2012). Thus, adoption by sexual minorities and the unmarried may be a reproductive option, yet their choices continue to be limited in comparison to heterosexual married couples.

Having the resources to raise a child is another aspect fundamental to having adoption as a reproductive option. Lack of material resources and access to quality service resources are cited by birth mothers as one of the greatest factors considered when surrendering their child (Jones, 2000; Madden, Ryan, Aguiniga, and Crawford, 2016). Faced with the limited choices of not being able to provide for their child and the potential for their child to be parented by someone with more resources, poor women sometimes choose to place their child for adoption. Conversely, those who seek to adopt a child in the US must have notable financial resources and demonstrate access to quality services in order to be approved (Davis, 2011; Hanan, 1997). The ability of those in the middle and upper classes to choose to parent through adoption, is highly dependent on poor and working class birth parents' disadvantages.

Similarly, racial-ethnic categorization impacts reproductive options. Since the arrival of Europeans to what is now known as the US, social, political, and economic forces encouraged fertility, reproduction, and parenting among White married women, while simultaneously attempting to stymie the births among racial-ethnic minority women unless their children could be controlled by Whites and/or used for instrumental purposes (Roberts, 1997; Thorton Dill, 1999; Weitz, 2016). Although the eugenics movement, which promoted the reproduction of White people (Anglo-Saxon or Nordic heritage), did not take root in the US until the early 1900s, it simply elucidated, structured, and strategized the prominent reproductive and parenting practices (Sandelowski, 1990; Weitz, 2016).

The more recent manifestation of reproductive racial inequality is less explicit and takes the form of cultural and political encouragement or discouragement of reproduction (Davis, 2011; Roberts, 1997; Weitz, 2016). It also involves less of a focus on population control and more of a focus on socialization and parenting (Patton, 2000; Solinger, 2001). Since people of color in the US are disproportionately represented in the poorer and working classes, the inequality in reproductive choices previously identified regarding social class are consistent with reproductive choices for racial-ethnic groups (Patton, 2000; Ward Gailey, 2010). However, independent of social class, racial-ethnic minority groups who have material resources and access to quality services can be discouraged from reproduction and parenting based on stereotypes and perceptions about their race and cultural practices (Patton, 2000; Sandelowski, 1990). The standards used to determine child abuse or neglect have been deemed to be culturally biased against people of color, resulting in disproportionately larger numbers of children of color being involuntarily removed from their birth parents and available for foster care or adoption (Briggs, 2012; Cooper, 2013; Patton, 2000; Roberts, 2002). Similarly, people of color seeking to adopt children encounter the same cultural bias in the approval process (Briggs, 2012; Hanan, 1997; Roberts, 2002). This cultural bias results in inequality, as people of color are less likely than people who are White to be able to exercise their reproductive choice to adopt a child. It also limits the ability of parents of color to parent the children they bore.

Race and ethnicity shaping the pool of approved adoptive parents and the children available for adoption is also relevant to transracial adoption (previously discussed in an earlier section). During the period of racial matching in the US, White adoptive parents were forced to compete over the White children available for adoption (Simon and Altstein, 2000; Solinger, 1992). As fewer White infants were surrendered for adoption, racial matching limited adoption as a reproductive option for potential White adoptive parents. The increasing social and political support for transracial placements beginning in the 1970s not only increased the chance that children of color would be matched with an adoptive family, it also provided White parents with an additional reproductive option (Patton, 2000; Simon and Altstein, 2000). This has resulted in Whites being the vast majority of foster care and adoptive parents, children of color being disproportionately overrepresented in foster care and as adoptees, and most transracial adoptions being comprised of White parents and children of color (Marr, 2017; Vandivere, Malm, and Radel, 2009).

Regarding nationality, countries that allow their children to be adopted internationally are more likely to be struggling with after effects of war (e.g., Korea), natural disasters (e.g., Haiti), political unrest (e.g., Romania), as well as those that have fewer resources (e.g., Guatemala), and/or are predominately non-White (e.g., China, Ethiopia) (Briggs, 2012; Perry, 1998; Selman, 2009; Simon and Altstein, 2000). In these areas of relative disadvantage or circumstantial crises, birth parents who struggle to provide for their child might deem surrendering their child for adoption to be the best of the few choices available to them (Bloch Jones, 1993; Briggs, 2012; Fisher, 2003; Manley, 2006). This makes it possible for potential adoptive parents in the US, who have relatively greater resources and political power, to add international adoption as an option for reproduction.

Reproductive justice is a framework put forth by Ross and Solinger (2017) to address inequality in reproductive options. They argue that individuals should have: (1) the right *not* to have a child, (2) the right to *have* a child, and (3) the right to parent a child in a safe and healthy environment. These rights can only be realized when individuals have access to community-based resources (high quality health care, education, and housing), a living wage, and a safety net for situations when these resources fail (Ross and Solinger, 2017). Logically, increasing resources and rights to disadvantaged groups will positively impact their reproductive options; however, it is more complex when applied to the reproductive option of adoption. Since one person's ability to have adoption as a reproductive option is dependent on another person's choicelessness (Solinger, 2001), the equality achieved through reproductive justice will effectively remove adoption as one of the reproductive options currently available to advantaged groups.

Emerging areas of exploration and practice

Although during the 20th century organized, formal adoption was shrouded in secrecy, the practice, the kinship network, and the related social services have grown in visibility and openness throughout the 21st century. Recognizing that adoption is not only familial, but involves politics, economics, health, communication, and education for individuals and society on a global scale, it has increasingly become an important area of research in the academy. Much of the initial scholarship focused on the adjustment of adoptees, yet the diversity of adoption-related research illustrates how and why adoption should be studied by a variety of disciplines. Reviewing historical and contemporary fundamental information about adoption provides the context necessary for in-depth exploration of the subject. It is this richness of context that promotes a broad understanding of adoption that undergirds research that promotes knowledge of specific adoption-related topics.

References

Abdullah, S. B. (1996). Transracial adoption is not the solution to America's problems of child welfare. *Journal of Black Psychology*, *22*(2), 254–261. doi:10.1177%2F00957984960222011

Appell, A. R. (2011). Legal issues in lesbian and gay adoption. In D. M. Brodzinsky & A. Pertman (Eds.), *Adoptions by lesbians and gay men: A new dimension in family diversity* (pp. 36–61). Oxford: Oxford University Press.

Atwood, T. C., Allen, L. A., Ravenel, V. C., & Callahan, N. M. (Eds). (2007). *Adoption factbook IV: The most comprehensive source for adoption statistics nationwide.* Alexandria, VA: National Council for Adoption.

Baca Zinn, M., & Eitzen, D. S. (2002). *Diversity in Families* (6th ed.). Boston, MA: Allyn and Bacon.

Banks, R. R. (1998). The color of desire: Fulfilling adoptive parents' racial preferences through discriminatory state action. *Yale Law Journal, 107*, 875-964. https://digitalcommons.law.yale.edu/ylj/vol107/iss4/1

Bartholet, E. (1991). Where do Black children belong? The politics of race matching in adoption. *University of Pennsylvania Law Review, 139*, 1163–1256. https://scholarship.law.upenn.edu/penn_law_review/vol139/iss5/1

Bartholet, E., & Smolin, D. (2012). The debate. In J. L. Gibbons & K. Smith Rotabi (Eds.), *Intercountry adoption: Policies, practices, and outcomes* (pp. 233–251). Farnham, UK: Ashgate Publishing.

Beck, S. (1992). Persona non grata: Ethnicity and Romanian nationalism. In C. Ward Gailey (Ed.), *The politics of culture and creativity* (pp. 119–145). Gainesville: University Press of Florida.

Berry, M., Dylla, D. J. C., Barth, R. P., & Needell, B. (1998). The role of open adoption in the adjustment of adopted children and their families. *Children and Youth Services Review, 20*, 151–171. doi:10.1016/S0190-7409(97)00071-6

Biafora, F., & Esposito, D. (2007). Adoption data and statistical trends. In R. A. Javier, A. L. Baden, & A. Camacho-Gingerich (Eds.), *Handbook of adoption* (pp. 32–42). Thousand Oaks, CA: SAGE Publications, Inc.

Bloch Jones, M. (1993). *Birthmothers: Women who reliquish babies for adoption tell their stories.* Chicago, IL: Chicago Review Press.

Briggs, L. (2012). Somebody's children: The politics of transracial and transnational adoption. Durham, NC: Duke University Press.

Brookfield, T. (2008). Maverick mothers and mercy flights: Canada's controversial introduction to international adoption. *Journal of the Canadian Historical Association, 19*(1), 307–330. doi:10.7202/037436ar

Buckwalter-Poza, R. (2014). America's unseen export: Children, most of them Black. Retrieved 21 July 2019 from https://psmag.com/news/outgoing-adoption-americas-unseen-export-children-black-84084

Butler-Sweet, C. (2011). "A healthy Black identity": Transracial adoption, middle-class families, and racial socialization. *Journal of Comparative Family Studies, 42*(2), 193–212. doi:10.3138/jcfs.42.2.193

Carp, E. W. (2005). A historical overview of American adoption. In E. W. Carp (Ed.), *Adoption in America: Historical perspectives* (pp. 1–27). Ann Arbor: The University of Michigan Press.

Chapman, C., Dorner, P., Silber, K., & Winterberg, T. S. (1986). Meeting the needs of the adoption triangle through open adoption: The birthmother. *Child and Adolescent Social Work, 3*, 203–213. doi:10.1007/BF00758252

Child Welfare Information Gateway (CWIG) (2011). *How many children were adopted in 2007 and 2008?* Washington, DC: Department of Health and Human Services, Children's Bureau.

Cooper, T. A. (2013). Racial bias in American foster care: The national debate. *Marquette Law Review, 97*(2), 215–277. Retrieved from https://scholarship.law.marquette.edu/mulr/vol97/iss2/3

Davis, M. A. (2011). *Children for families or families for children* (Vol. 29). Dorderecht: Springer Science + Business Media.

DellaCava, F. A., Kolko Phillips, N., & Engel, M. H. (2004). Adoption in the US: The emergence of a social movement. *Journal of Sociology and Social Welfare, 31*(4), 141–160. Retrieved from https://scholarworks.wmich.edu/jssw/vol31/iss4/8

Fisher, A. P. (2003). Still "Not quite as good as having your own"? Toward a sociology of adoption. *Annual Review of Sociology, 29*, 335–361. www.jstor.org/stable/30036971

Fursland, E. (2013). *Facing up to Facebook: A survival guide for adoptive families.* London: BAAF.

Gates, G. J. (2015). *Demographics of married and unmarried same-sex couples: Analysis of the 2013 American Community Survey.* Los Angeles, CA: Williams Institute, UCLA School of Law. Retrieved from https://williamsinstitute.law.ucla.edu/wp-content/uploads/Demographics-Same-Sex-Couples-ACS2013-March-2015.pdf

Goldberg, A. E., Downing, J. B., & Sauck, C. C. (2007). Choices, challenges, and tensions. *Adoption Quarterly, 10*(2), 33–64. doi:10.1300/J145v10n02_02

Grotevant, H. D. (2012). What works in open adoption. In P. A. Curtis & G. Alexander (Eds.), *What works in child welfare* (pp. 309–327). (2nd ed.). Washington, DC: Child Welfare League of America.

Grotevant, H. D., & McRoy, R. G. (1998). Openness in adoption: Exploring family connections. Thousand Oaks, CA: SAGE Publications, Inc.

Grotevant, H. D., Wrobel, G.M., Fiorenzo, L., Lo, A.Y.H., & McRoy, R. (2019). Trajectories of birth family contact in domestic adoptions. *Journal of Family Psychology, 33*, 54–63. doi:10.1037/fam0000449

Grotevant, H.D., Wrobel, G.M., Von Korff, L., Skinner, B., Newell, J., Friese, S., & McRoy, R. (2007). Many faces of openness in adoption: Perspectives of adopted adolescents and their parents. *Adoption Quarterly, 10*(3–4), 79–101. doi:10.1080/10926750802163204

Gutman, H. (1976). *The Black family in slavery and freedom, 1750–1925*. New York: Pantheon.

Hague Conference on Private International Law (Conférence de La Haye de droit international privé; HCCH). (n.d.). Adoption section. Retrieved from www.hcch.net/en/instruments/conventions/specialised-sections/intercountry-adoption

Hanan, J. I. (1997). The best interests of the child: Eliminating discrimination in the screening of adoptive parents. *Golden Gate University Law Review, 27*(2), 167–222. Retrieved from https://digitalcommons.law.ggu.edu/ggulrev/vol27/iss2/3

Hansen, M. E. (2009). Using private contracts to create adoptions from foster care. In S. J. Quintero (Ed.), *Child welfare issues and perspectives* (pp. 113–126). New York: Nova Science Publishers.

Hansen, M. E., & Simon, R. J. (2004). Transracial placement in adoptions with public agency involvement: What can we learn from the AFCARS data?. *Adoption Quarterly, 8*(2), 45–56. doi:10.1300/J145v08n02_03

Herman, D. (1997). T*he antigay agenda: Orthodox vision and the Christian Right*. Chicago: University of Chicago Press.

Higdon, M. J. (2008). When informal adoption meets intestate succession: The cultural myopia of the equitable adoption doctrine. *Wake Forest Law Review, 43*, 223–281. doi:10.2139/ssrn.1009981

History.com. (2018). US Immigration Timeline. Retrieved 21 July 2019 from www.history.com/topics/immigration/immigration-united-states-timeline

Hollingsworth, L. D. (2003). International adoption among families in the United States: Considerations of social justice. *Social Work, 48*(2), 209–217. www.jstor.org/stable/23720845

Howe, D., & Feast, J. (2001). The long-term outcome of reunions between adult adopted people and their birth mothers. *British Journal of Social Work, 31*(3), 351–368. doi:10.1093/bjsw/31.3.351

Jones, J., & Placek, P. (2017). Adoption by the numbers: *A comprehensive report of US adoption statistics*. Alexandria, VA: National Council for Adoption. Retrived from https://indd.adobe.com/view/4ae7a823-4140-4f27-961a-cd9f16a5f362

Jones, M. B. (2000). *Birthmothers: Women who have reliquished babies for adoption tell their stories* (2nd ed.). Chicago: Chicago Review Press.

Kazyak, E., Woodell, B., Scherrer, K., & Finken, E. (2018). Law and family formation among LGBQ-parent families. *Family Court Review, 56*(3), 364–373. doi:doi.org/10.1111/fcre.12353

Kraft, A. D., Palambo, J., Mitchell, D. L., Woods, P. K., & Schmidt, A. W. (1985a). Some theoretical considerations on confidential adoptions, Part I: The birthmother. *Child and Adolescent Social Work Journal, 2*, 13–21. doi:10.1007/bf00757531

Kraft, A. D., Palambo, J., Mitchell, D. L., Woods, P. K., & Schmidt, A. W. (1985b). Some theoretical considerations on confidential adoptions, Part II: The adoptive parents. *Child and Adolescent Social Work Journal, 2*, 69–82. doi:10.1007/bf00757473

Kraft, A. D., Palambo, J., Mitchell, D. L., Woods, P. K., & Schmidt, A. W. (1985c). Some theoretical considerations on confidential adoptions, Part III: The adopted child. *Child and Adolescent Social Work Journal, 2*, 139–153. doi:10.1007/BF00758065

Kreider, R. M. (2003). Adopted children and stepchildren: 2000. Census 2000 Special Reports: US Census Bureau. Retrieved from www.census.gov/prod/2003pubs/censr-6.pdf

Kreider, R. M., & Lofquist, D. A. (2014). Adopted children and stepchildren: 2010. Population characteristics: US Census Bureau. Retrieved from www.census.gov/prod/2014pubs/p20-572.pdf

Leacock, E. B. (1980). Montagniais women and the Jesuit program for colonization. In M. Etienne & E. Leacock (Eds.), *Women and colonization* (pp. 25–42). New York: Praeger.

LeBlanc, B. (2019, April 15). Adoption agency sues state over new gay adoption rules. *Detroit News*. Retrieved from www.detroitnews.com/story/news/local/michigan/2019/04/15/agency-sues-michigan-new-gay-adoption-rules/3471204002/

Lee, R., Kim, O. M., & Lee, H. (2016). Unpacking reasons for genetic testing of adoptees. *The American Journal of Bioethics, 16*(12), 39–40. doi:10.1080/15265161.2016.1239793

Madden, E., Ryan, S., Aguiniga, D., & Crawford, M. (2016). Understanding options counseling experiences in adoption: A quantitative analysis of birth parents and professionals. New York, NY: The Donaldson Adoption Institute. Retrived from www.adoptioninstitute.org/wp-content/uploads/2017/03/Understanding-Options-Counseling-Experiences-in-Adoption-Qualitative-Study.pdf

Maldonado, S. (2006). Discouraging racial preferences in adoptions. *UC Davis Law Review*, *39*, 1415–1480.

Manley, K. L. (2006). Birth parents: The forgotten members of the international adoption triad. *Capital University Law Review*, *35*(Winter), 627–653.

Marr, E. (2017). US transracial adoption trends in the 21st century. *Adoption Quarterly*, *20*(3), 222–251. doi:10.1080/10926755.2017.1291458

McCarthy, J. (2019). Gallup first polled on gay issues in '77. What has changed? *Gallup*. Retrieved from https://news.gallup.com/poll/258065/gallup-first-polled-gay-issues-changed.aspx

Mendenhall, T. J., Berge, J. M., Wrobel, G. M., Grotevant, H. D., & McRoy, R. G. (2004). Adolescents' satisfaction with contact in adoption. *Child and Adolescent Social Work Journal*, *21*, 175–190. doi:10.1023/b:casw.0000022730.89093.b7

Mombian. (2017). A very brief history of LGBTQ parenting. Retrieved 21 July 2019 from www.mombian.com/2017/10/10/brief-history-lgbtq-parenting/?_ga=2.264909391.1553046052.1563776676-1991323456.1563776676

Moreau, J. (2019). LGBTQ parents face "state-sanctioned discrimination," American Bar Association says. *Out Politics and Policy*. Retrieved 21 July 2019 from www.nbcnews.com/feature/nbc-out/lgbtq-parents-face-state-sanctioned-discrimination-american-bar-association-says-n968456

Pannor, R., & Baran, A. (1984). Open adoption as standard practice. *Child Welfare: Journal of Policy, Practice, and Program*, *63*(3), 245–250.

Park, N. K., & Wonch Hill, P. (2014). Is adoption an option? The role of importance of motherhood and fertility help-seeking in considering adoption. *Journal of Family Issues*, *35*(5), 601. doi:10.1177/0192513X13493277

Patton, S. (2000). *Birthmarks: Transracial adoption in contemporary America*. New York and London: New York University Press.

Perry, S. L. (2017). *Growing God's family: The global orphan care movement and the limits of evangelical activism*. New York: New York University Press.

Perry, T. L. (1998). Transracial and international adoption: Mothers, hierarchy, race, and feminist legal theory. *Yale Journal of Law and Feminism*, *10*, 101–164.

Petchesky, R. P. (1998). Negotiating reproductive rights: Women's perspectives across countries and cultures. *Reproductive Health Matters*, *6*(11), 186–189. doi:10.1016/S0968-8080(98)90188-4

Raleigh, E. (2012). Are same-sex and single adoptive parents more likely to adopt transracially? A national analysis of race, family structure, and the adoption marketplace. *Sociological Perspectives*, *55*(3), 449–471. doi:10.1525%2Fsop.2012.55.3.449

Raleigh, E. (2018). *Selling transracial adoption: Families, markets, and the color line*. Philadelphia, PA: Temple University Press.

Roberts, D. (1997). *Killing the Black body: Race, reproduction and the meaning of liberty*. New York: Panthenon.

Roberts, D. (2002). *Shattered bonds: The color of child welfare*. New York: Basic Civitas Books.

Rosman, E. A., Johnson, C. E., & Callahan, N. M. (Eds.). (2011). *Adoption factbook V: The most comprehensive source for adoption statistics nationwide*. Alexandria, VA: National Council for Adoption.

Ross, L., & Solinger, R. (2017). *Reproductive justice: An introduction* (1st ed.). Oakland, CA: University of California Press.

Rotabi, K. S., & Gibbons, J. L. (2012). Does the Hague convention on intercountry adoption adequately protect orphaned and vulnerable children and their families?. *Journal of Child and Family Studies*, *21*, 106–119. doi:10.1007/s10826-011-9508-6

Sandelowski, M. J. (1990). Failures of volition: Female agency and infertility in historical perspective. *Signs*, *15*(3), 475–499. Retrieved from www.jstor.org/stable/3174424

Schwartz, J. (2010). Investigating differences in public support for gay rights issues. *Journal of Homosexuality*, *57*, 748–759. doi:10.1080/00918369.2010.485875

Selman, P. (2009). The movement of children for international adoption: Developments and trends in receiving states and states of origin, 1998–2004. In D. Marre & L. Briggs (Eds.), *International adoption: Global inequalities and the circulation of children* (pp. 32–51). New York: New York University Press.

Siegel, D. H., & Smith, S. L. (2012). Openness in adoption: From secrecy and stigma to knowledge and connections. New York: Evan B. Donaldson Adoption Institute.

Simon, R. J., & Altstein, H. (1977). *Transracial adoption*. New York: John Wiley & Sons.

Simon, R. J., & Altstein, H. (2000). *Adoption across borders: Serving the children in transracial and intercountry adoptions*. Lanham, Maryland: Rowman and Littlefield Publishers, Inc.

Solinger, R. (1992). *Wake up little Susie: Single pregnancy and race before Roe v. Wade*. New York: Routledge.

Solinger, R. (2001). *Beggars and choosers: How the politics of choice shapes adoption, abortion, and welfare in the United States*. New York: Hill and Wang.

Solinger, R. (2004). Adoption. In G. Mink & A. O'Connor (Eds.), *Poverty in the United States: An encyclopedia of history, politics, and policy* (Vol. 1 A-K, pp. 51–53). Santa Barbara, CA: ABC-CLIO.

Takács, J., Szalma, I., & Bartus, T. (2016). Social attitudes toward adoption by same-sex couples in Europe. *Archives of Sexual Behavior, 45*, 1787–1798. doi:10.1007/s10508-016-0691-9

Thorton Dill, B. (1999). Fictive kin, paper sons, and *Compadrazgo*: Women of color and the struggle for family survival. In S. Coontz, M. Parson, & G. Raley (Eds.), *American families: A multicultural reader* (pp. 2–19). New York and London: Routedge.

United Nations. (1989). Convention on the right of the child. Retrieved from www.ohchr.org/en/professionalinterest/pages/crc.aspx

Vandivere, S., Malm, K., & Radel, L. (2009). *Adoption USA: A chartbook based on the 2007 national survey of adoptive parents*. Washington, DC: The US Department of Health and Human Services, Office to the Assistant Secretary of Planning and Evaluation. Retrieved from https://aspe.hhs.gov/report/adoption-usa-chartbook-based-2007-national-survey-adoptive-parents

Ward Gailey, C. (2010). *Blue-ribbon babies and labors of love: Race, class, and gender in US adoption practice*. Austin, TX: University of Texas Press.

Weitz, R. (2016). A history of women's bodies. In B. K. Scott, S. E. Cayleff, A. Donadey, & I. Lara (Eds.), *Women in culture: An intersectional anthology for gender and women's studies* (pp. 248–255). Hoboken, NJ: Wiley-Blackwell.

Whitesel, A., & Howard, J. A. (2013). *Untangling the web II: A research-based roadmap for reform*. New York: Donaldson Adoption Institute. Retrieved from www.adoptioninstitute.org/wpcontent/uploads/2013/12/2013_12_UntanglingtheWeb2.pdf

Wrobel, G., Carlson, V., Phillips, A., Ruff, M., & Grotevant, H. (2016, November). Profiles of contact between adoptive and birth family members across time. In B. Hepp (Discussant), *Emerging trends in adoption openness and birth family contact*. Symposium conducted at the annual meeting of the National Council on Family Relations, Minneapolis, MN.

Wrobel, G. M., & Dillon, K. (2009). Adopted adolescents: Who and what are they curious about? In G. M. Wrobel & E. Neil (Eds.), *International advances in adoption research for practice* (pp. 217–244). London, UK: Wiley.

Wrobel, G. M., Grotevant, H. G., Samek, D. R., & Von Korff, L. (2013). Adoptees' curiosity and information-seeking about birth parents in emerging adulthood: Context, motivation, and behavior. *International Journal of Behavioral Development, 37*(5), 441–450. doi:10.1177/0165025413486420

Wrobel, G. M., Kohler, K., Grotevant, H. D., & McRoy, R. (2003). The family adoption communication model (FAC): Identifying alternative pathways of adoption related communication. *Adoption Quarterly*, 7(2), 53–84. doi:10.1300/j145v07n02_04

2

US ADOPTION BY THE NUMBERS

Rose M. Kreider

This chapter provides a portrait of adopted children under 18 in the United States, focusing on internationally adopted children and transracially adopted children. There is no administrative data source that tracks all types of adoption (e.g. non-relative children, stepchildren) in the US, and few data sources are large enough to permit detailed analysis of the type of relationship (i.e. biological, step, or adoptive) between children and the parents with whom they live. This chapter analyzes the largest nationally representative data sets available for the US that includes details on how children are related to the parents in their home: Census 2000 data and the 2013–2017 American Community Survey 5-year data.

Methods

Census 2000 was the first decennial census to include "adopted son/daughter" as a specific type of relationship between the householder (who owns or rents the home) and their child(ren). It was also the last decennial census to include a short form and a long form. All US residents were counted via the short form, while the long form was sent to a sample of about 16 percent of the US population. The long form included questions about characteristics of the people in the home, and of the housing unit itself. The short form included about ten questions, asking about the age, sex, race, origin, and relationship to householder for all household members, as well as a few key housing characteristics.

The American Community Survey (ACS), which replaced the long form decennial census, was fully implemented in 2005. The ACS is in the field every month and produces annualized estimates for the calendar year. The ACS is a very large nationally representative sample, with over 2 million households responding annually. Multiyear estimates are also published using five years' worth of sample data. The 5-year ACS data provide the largest sample of the population in the US. Compared with the annualized estimate provided in the 1-year files, the 5-year file provides estimates for smaller geographic areas and for smaller population groups. This chapter uses the 2013–2017 ACS 5-year data because of its larger sample size. The internal US Census Bureau files were used for both analyses, since they are larger than the public use files, and allow for more accurate estimates of relatively small groups, such as transracially adopted children and internationally adopted children (US Census Bureau, 2018). Reports have been previously published on adopted and stepchildren from Census 2000 (Kreider, 2003) and the ACS and 2010 Census data (Kreider and Lofquist, 2014). This chapter compares estimates of adopted children from 2000 to the most recent ACS 5-year data from 2013–2017.

In Census 2000 and the ACS, it is the household address that is sampled. The respondent is asked to list everyone living in the home and the specific relationship of each person (e.g., husband or wife, brother or sister) to the householder (the person who owns or rents the home). When children of the householder are present, they can be reported as a "biological son/daughter," "stepson/stepdaughter," or "adopted son/daughter." These data reflect the relationships among people living in the household at the time of the interview, and so do not provide a measure of the number of adoptions occurring in a given period of time.

There are a few limitations to working with the census and ACS data. First, the information is based on the people within a household, thus, it does not capture familial relationships among people who do not live in the same household. If the child lived with two parents, decennial census and ACS data do not identify whether the second parent was the child's biological, step, or adoptive parent. For reference, the 2017 Current Population Survey, which asks about the type of relationship between the child and each coresident parent, was examined for comparison and it was determined that 91.2 percent of children under 18 who lived with at least one adoptive parent were the adopted child of the householder (comparisons were tested at the 90 percent confidence level). Only children of the householder are discussed in this report, usually those under 18, except as noted in Figure 2.1.

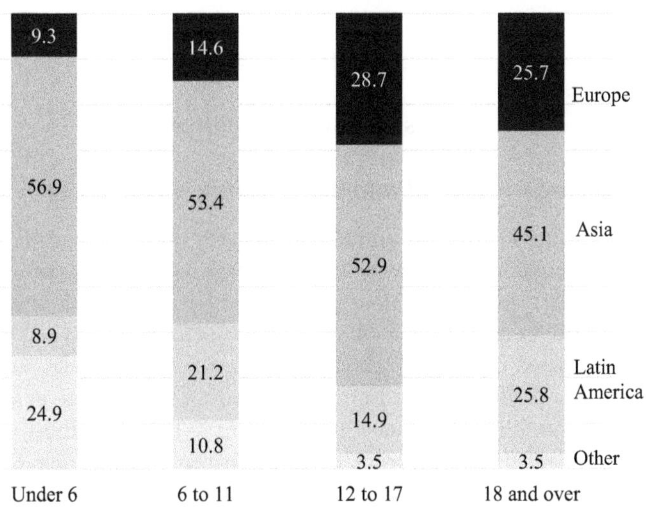

Figure 2.1 Percent distribution of internationally adopted children of the householder by age of child and place of birth: 2013–2017

Note: Other includes Africa, Northern America, and Oceania. Mexico is included in Latin America.

Totals may sum to more than 100, due to rounding.

Source: US Census Bureau, 2013–2017 ACS. (For information on confidentiality protection, sampling error, nonsampling error, and definitions, see www.census.gov/acs/www)

Additionally, because the type of relationship between parents and children is reported by respondents, it includes all variations of individuals they may view as their adopted child, such as: adoption of biologically related and unrelated children, adoption of stepchildren, adoption through private and public agencies, domestic and international adoptions, and independent and informal adoptions. Households where the adults have divorced, remarried, and/or cohabitated may report the biological child of their unmarried partner as their adopted child if they are involved in raising them, even though no legal adoption has taken place. Research has found that in comparison to White families, informal adoptions are more common among non-White racial-ethnic families, particularly those which are Black and Hispanic (Suarez Hamm, 1999), reflecting the diversity of ways in which family relationships and the process of adoption can be defined. A qualitative study prepared for the US Census Bureau found that informal adoption of biological grandchildren was common in Inupiaq communities in Alaska (Craver, 2001). Even international adoptions are not uniformly legally recognized as such. An analysis comparing Census 2000 data and State Department reports of visas concluded that a substantial proportion of foreign-born Latin American children reported as adopted had not come into the US on visas that indicated that they had been legally adopted (Kreider, 2007). Conversely, other studies have determined that some parents who have legally adopted children related to them may not report the child as adopted (Radel, Bramlett, and Waters, 2010). We cannot distinguish among children who were adopted by their stepparents, children adopted by their biological grandparents or other relatives, and children adopted by people to whom they were not biologically related. An estimate for 1992, derived from court records, found that about 42 percent of all adoptions were by stepparents or by a relative (Flango and Flango, 1995). Despite the fact that the data reflect various types of relationships between adoptive parents and their children, data from Census 2000 and ACS are nationally representative, large-scale data sources that provide an excellent opportunity to create a profile of adopted children under 18 in the US.

Shifts in adoption patterns

Decreasing number of adopted children under 18 since 2000

In 2013–2017, of the 64.6 million children under 18, 94.1 percent were the biological children of the householder, 3.7 percent were stepchildren, and 2.2 percent were adopted children (see Table 2.1). In 2000, 2.5 percent of the householder's children under 18 were adopted. The estimated total of 1.4 million adopted children in 2013–2017 is lower than the 1.6 million estimated in Census 2000 long form data. This change was evident in the younger age groups. While 1.5 percent of children under age six in 2013–2017 were adopted, the corresponding percentage was 1.9 in 2000. For those ages six to 11, 2.4 percent were adopted in the recent data, compared with 2.6 percent in 2000. The percentage of children who were adopted did not differ statistically for the older two age groups shown (ages 12 to 14 and ages 15 to 17).

This decrease in the percentage and number of adopted children between 2000 and 2013–2017 is due to the lower number of international adoptions by US parents. China and South Korea altered their laws, resulting in fewer international placements. Adoptions from Guatemala were shut down based on the country's failure to meet the Hague Convention rules. Russia banned new adoptions to the US in 2013, and Ethiopia ended international adoptions in 2017 (Breuning, 2013; Budiman and Hugo Lopez, 2017; Efrat,

Table 2.1 Children of the householder, by type of relationship and age

Relationship	*Under 18 years*				
	Total	*Under 6*	*6 to 11*	*12 to 14*	*15 to 17*
2000					
Total children of householder	64,650,000	20,120,000	22,800,000	11,200,000	10,530,000
Adopted children	1,586,000	389,200	598,300	316,600	281,700
Stepchildren	3,292,000	328,400	1,271,000	847,100	845,700
Biological children	59,770,000	19,400,000	20,930,000	10,040,000	9,400,000
Percent of age group	100.0	100.0	100.0	100.0	100.0
Adopted children	2.5	1.9	2.6	2.8	2.7
Stepchildren	5.1	1.6	5.6	7.6	8.0
Biological children	92.5	96.4	91.8	89.6	89.3
2013–2017					
Total children of householder	64,630,000	20,330,000	21,980,000	11,190,000	11,130,000
Adopted children	1,441,000	296,000	535,300	307,500	302,400
Stepchildren	2,380,000	243,800	857,200	612,300	667,100
Biological children	60,810,000	19,790,000	20,590,000	10,270,000	10,160,000
Percent of age group	100.0	100.0	100.0	100.0	100.0
Adopted children	2.2	1.5	2.4	2.8	2.7
Stepchildren	3.7	1.2	3.9	5.5	6.0
Biological children	94.1	97.3	93.7	91.8	91.3

Source: US Census Bureau, Census 2000, 2013–2017 American Community Survey
(For information on confidentiality protection, sampling error, nonsampling error, and definitions, for Census 2000 data see www.census.gov/prod/cen2000/doc/sf3.pdf, for ACS see https://www.census.gov/programs-surveys/acs/technical-documentation/code-lists.html)

Leblang, Liao, and Pandya, 2015; Selman, 2012a). The decrease in adopted children in the US, specifically international adoptees, is not only evident in this analysis but Efrat, Leblang, Liao, and Pandya (2015) also find a decrease of 38 percent between 2004 and 2010 in international adoptees, while Montgomery and Powell (2018) find a decrease of 72 percent since 2005. Statistics available on the US State Department website also reflect the dramatic decline. They document a high of about 23,000 international adoptions in 2004, declining to about 4,700 in 2017 (US State Department, 2018). Changes in several of the main sending countries had a large effect on the number of children available for adoption by parents in the US.

Which states have higher percentages of children under 18 who are adopted?

In the nation, 2.2 percent of the householder's children under 18 were adopted (see Table 2.2). The right column on Table 2.2 indicates whether the percentage differed statistically between 2000 and 2013–2017 at the 90 percent level. The percentage of householder's children under 18 who were adopted declined in each region (for a list of the states included in each region see US Census Bureau Geographic Reference Manual, 1994), but states and the District of Columbia varied; some saw no significant change, while others saw an increase or decrease in the percentage of children under 18 who were adopted. Nineteen states experienced a significant change,

Table 2.2 Number and percentage of householder's adopted children for the United States, regions, and states

Area	Children under 18 years 2000: Total under 18 years	Children under 18 years 2000: Adopted children Number	Children under 18 years 2000: Adopted children Percent	Children under 18 years 2013–2017: Total under 18 years	Children under 18 years 2013–2017: Adopted children Number	Children under 18 years 2013–2017: Adopted children Percent	Significant difference[1]
United States	64,650,000	1,586,000	2.5	64,630,000	1,441,000	2.2	Yes
Region							
Northeast	11,790,000	284,200	2.4	10,580,000	210,800	2.0	Yes
Midwest	15,230,000	389,100	2.6	14,060,000	337,700	2.4	Yes
South	22,580,000	548,300	2.4	24,470,000	551,800	2.3	Yes
West	15,050,000	364,400	2.4	15,520,000	341,000	2.2	Yes
State							
Alabama	995,300	24,940	2.5	943,300	22,650	2.4	No
Alaska	175,300	6,910	3.9	163,600	7,402	4.5	No
Arizona	1,198,000	28,970	2.4	1,390,000	37,980	2.7	Yes
Arkansas	604,500	15,970	2.6	608,200	15,900	2.6	No
California	8,028,000	167,200	2.1	7,814,000	132,800	1.7	Yes
Colorado	1,007,000	29,440	2.9	1,130,000	31,000	2.7	No
Connecticut	775,200	19,240	2.5	692,800	15,250	2.2	No
Delaware	172,400	3,452	2.0	175,200	3,755	2.1	No
District of Columbia	87,890	2,649	3.0	98,120	2,474	2.5	No
Florida	3,204,000	82,180	2.6	3,565,000	73,440	2.1	Yes
Georgia	1,903,000	49,190	2.6	2,169,000	46,030	2.1	Yes
Hawaii	238,300	6,941	2.9	234,500	5,975	2.6	No
Idaho	344,500	9,562	2.8	398,100	10,560	2.7	No
Illinois	2,886,000	73,640	2.6	2,634,000	50,220	1.9	Yes
Indiana	1,441,000	37,000	2.6	1,403,000	37,780	2.7	No
Iowa	688,600	18,570	2.7	671,000	18,590	2.8	No
Kansas	662,200	19,730	3.0	653,600	19,180	2.9	No
Kentucky	906,900	20,660	2.3	869,200	25,270	2.9	Yes
Louisiana	1,052,000	22,830	2.2	951,100	18,000	1.9	Yes
Maine	343,600	7,137	2.5	230,300	7,323	3.2	Yes
Maryland	1,576,000	32,270	2.7	1,176,000	23,800	2.0	Yes
Massachusetts	1,850,000	35,650	2.6	1,250,000	27,230	2.2	Yes
Michigan	3,046,000	61,230	2.6	1,971,000	51,300	2.6	No
Minnesota	1,479,000	31,380	2.6	1,191,000	28,840	2.4	No
Mississippi	886,300	16,300	2.5	599,900	12,980	2.2	No
Missouri	1,635,000	33,160	2.5	1,227,000	32,780	2.7	No
Montana	255,300	6,803	3.2	202,200	6,996	3.5	No
Nebraska	507,200	11,810	2.8	430,400	11,440	2.7	No
Nevada	561,600	10,590	2.3	586,800	12,090	2.1	No
New Hampshire	358,300	6,864	2.4	238,600	6,436	2.7	No
New Jersey	2,601,000	42,610	2.3	1,801,000	29,550	1.6	Yes

(Continued)

Table 2.2 (Cont.)

	Children under 18 years 2000			Children under 18 years 2013–2017			
	Total under 18 years	Adopted children		Total under 18 years	Adopted children		Significant difference[1]
Area		Number	Percent		Number	Percent	
New Mexico	5,690,000	11,760	2.6	423,300	9,234	2.2	Yes
New York	5,768,000	100,700	2.4	3,673,000	62,580	1.7	Yes
North Carolina	2,230,000	42,910	2.4	2,020,000	49,440	2.5	No
North Dakota	182,600	3,647	2.4	156,100	4,258	2.7	No
Ohio	3,385,000	62,650	2.4	2,341,000	51,150	2.2	Yes
Oklahoma	989,900	23,520	2.9	832,600	26,540	3.2	No
Oregon	940,400	23,900	3.1	770,400	20,590	2.7	Yes
Pennsylvania	3,556,000	62,330	2.3	2,393,000	53,590	2.2	No
Rhode Island	304,600	5,496	2.4	189,700	4,825	2.5	No
South Carolina	1,159,000	22,030	2.5	932,300	23,880	2.6	No
South Dakota	222,900	5,691	3.0	187,900	5,187	2.8	No
Tennessee	1,619,000	30,980	2.5	1,295,000	36,840	2.9	Yes
Texas	6,591,000	110,300	2.1	6,263,000	126,900	2.0	No
Utah	831,000	19,430	2.9	829,200	23,510	2.8	No
Vermont	168,400	4,181	3.0	108,200	4,182	3.9	Yes
Virginia	2,000,000	38,290	2.4	1,655,000	34,830	2.1	Yes
Washington	1,698,000	38,880	2.8	1,456,000	39,570	2.7	No
West Virginia	493,200	9,849	2.7	320,500	9,032	2.8	No
Wisconsin	1,583,000	30,580	2.4	1,189,000	26,950	2.3	No
Wyoming	141,300	3,997	3.4	125,500	3,253	2.6	Yes

Note:
1 Indicates whether change in the percentage from 2000 to 2013–2017 was significant at the 90 percent level.
Source: US Census Bureau, Census 2000, 2013–2017 American Community Survey
(For information on confidentiality protection, sampling error, nonsampling error, and definitions, for Census 2000 data see www.census.gov/prod/cen2000/doc/sf3.pdf, for ACS see https://www.census.gov/programs-surveys/acs/technical-documentation/code-lists.html)

including an increase from 3.0 to 3.9 percent in Vermont, and a decrease in Wyoming from 3.4 percent to 2.6 percent in the percentage of householder's children under 18 who were adopted. In Alaska, the shift from 3.9 percent to 4.5 percent was not statistically significant.

In terms of geographic variation in the 2013–2017 ACS in the percentage of children who were adopted, the Northeast had the lowest percentage of adopted children (2.0 percent) while the Midwest had the highest (2.4 percent). Among states, Alaska had the highest percentage, at 4.5, although it did not differ statistically from Vermont (3.9 percent). Substantively, these are small variations, yet the most important observation about geographic patterns in the percentage of children who are adopted is that adoption is a family-building process that is evident across all states in roughly the same proportions. Census data include various types of adoption, each of which may have its own geographic pattern, which might also contribute to the lack of distinct geographic patterns when considering all types of adoptions.

Characteristics of transracially adopted children

Transracial adoption results in perhaps the most visible group of adoptive families. Based on the 2007 National Survey of Adoptive Parents (NSAP), 40 percent of adopted children (not including those adopted by their stepparents) were involved in a transracial, trans-ethnic, or transcultural adoption (Vandivere, Malm, and Radel, 2009).

In the past, transracial adoption faced opposition and restrictions. For example, the 1978 Indian Child Welfare Act created federal standards for removing American Indian children from their birth families, and, when removal was necessary, required that the adoptive and foster care homes reflect the unique values of the Indian culture (McRoy and Griffin, 2012). Yet as transracial adoption gained acceptance, policies were created to remove barriers to crossing racial and cultural lines by prohibiting race from being the only factor for placement, or denial of placement, the basis for the 1994 Multiethnic Placement Act (MEPA; McRoy and Griffin, 2012). Debate continues over whether or how much race or culture should be a factor when children are matched with adoptive parents. An assessment after the passing of the 1994 MEPA found that transracial adoptions through the public foster care system increased from 11 percent of adoptions in 1995 to 15 percent in 2004 (Eschelbach and Simon, 2004). Yet, this increase has not eliminated the overrepresentation of African American children in foster care (Argys and Duncan, 2013; Jacobson, Nielsen, and Hardeman, 2012; McRoy and Griffin, 2012), and more recent data do not show a sizable effect of MEPA on numbers of transracial adoptions of young children (Marr, 2017).

In this chapter, children of the householder are considered to be transracially adopted if the householder parent and their adopted child are of different race or origin groups, where the groups are:

1. White alone non-Hispanic
2. Black alone non-Hispanic
3. Asian or Pacific Islander alone non-Hispanic
4. American Indian or Alaska Native alone non-Hispanic
5. Some other race alone non-Hispanic
6. White/Black
7. White/Asian
8. White/Native Hawaiian and Pacific Islander
9. White/American Indian and Alaska Native
10. White/Some Other Race
11. Hispanic

Or either parent or child is some other multiracial combination.

In 2013–2017, there were approximately 469,600 transracially adopted children under the age of 18, about one in three (32.6 percent) of all adopted children under 18 (See Table 2.3). Only the difference between the race/origin of the householder and the child is considered. As Marr (2017) points out, it would be possible to look at the race/origin of the spouse of the householder as well. In 2013–2017 ACS data, 32.7 percent of the adopted children of the householder (for those whose householder has a spouse present) would be considered transracially adopted using this same definition, but comparing only the race/origin of the child and the spouse of the householder; thus

Table 2.3 Characteristics of transracially adopted children under 18: 2013–2017

Characteristic of child	*Transracially adopted children* Number	*Margin of error*[1]	*Percent*	*Margin of error*[1]	*Other adopted children* Number	*Margin of error*[1]	*Percent*	*Margin of error*[1]
Total children	469,600	10,660	100.0	(X)	971,700	8,797	100.0	(X)
Age of child								
0–2 years	32,220	1,737	6.9*	0.32	78,260	2,315	8.1	0.23
3–5 years	59,310	2,313	12.6	0.35	126,200	3,172	13.0	0.29
6–8 years	80,820	2,699	17.2*	0.41	159,300	2,854	16.4	0.25
9–11 years	105,800	2,861	22.5*	0.43	189,400	3,234	19.5	0.28
12–14 years	101,900	3,027	21.7	0.47	205,600	3,706	21.2	0.30
15–17 years	89,510	2,746	19.1*	0.37	212,900	2,861	21.9	0.29
Race and Hispanic origin of child								
White alone	30,040	1,440	6.4*	0.28	646,700	6,876	66.6	0.45
Black or African American alone	87,300	3,043	18.6*	0.47	132,400	3,782	13.6	0.38
American Indian and Alaska Native alone	11,430	903	2.4*	0.20	8,957	706	0.9	0.07
Asian or Pacific Islander alone	114,800	3,150	24.5*	0.49	29,230	1,489	3.0	0.15
Some Other Race alone	4,642	533	1.0*	0.12	1,410	335	0.1	0.03
Two or more races								
White-Black	50,850	2,106	10.8*	0.33	1,544	419	0.2	0.04
White-American Indian and Alaska Native	6,349	594	1.4*	0.12	2,221	338	0.2	0.03
White-Asian	10,300	746	2.2*	0.15	822	258	0.1	0.03
White-Native Hawaiian or Pacific Islander	1,074	257	0.2*	0.05	358	280	0.0	0.03
White-some other race	604	226	0.1*	0.05	64	51	0.0	0.01
Other multiple races	10,420	915	2.2*	0.18	2,085	419	0.2	0.04
Hispanic or Latino (of any race)	141,700	4,256	30.2*	0.51	145,800	4,007	15.0	0.38
Child Hispanic, householder non-Hispanic, or child non-Hispanic, householder Hispanic	169,400	4,794	36.1	0.54	(X)		(X)	(X)
Foreign born	145,100	4,366	30.9*	0.62	74,890	2,440	7.7	0.23
Disability status								
Age 5 and over	399,200	8,878	100.0		810,500	7,947	100.0	(X)
At least one disability	49,890	2,115	12.5	0.43	95,230	2,216	11.7	0.26

(*Continued*)

Table 2.3 (Cont.)

Characteristic of child	*Transracially adopted children*				*Other adopted children*			
	Number	*Margin of error*[1]	*Percent*	*Margin of error*[1]	*Number*	*Margin of error*[1]	*Percent*	*Margin of error*[1]
Hearing disability	5,430	470	1.4*	0.11	7,426	598	0.9	0.07
Vision disability	4,924	507	1.2	0.12	11,530	741	1.4	0.09
Cognitive disability[2]	41,950	1,967	10.5	0.42	81,750	1,995	10.1	0.24
Ambulatory disability	4,893	476	1.2	0.11	8,647	724	1.1	0.09
Self-care disability	9,009	681	2.3*	0.16	14,100	768	1.7	0.10
Independent living	5,475	524	1.4	0.55	11,850	719	1.5	0.33
Multiple disabilities[3]	14,210	960	3.6	0.22	26,700	1,107	3.3	0.14

Notes:
1 These questions were asked only of people aged 5 and over.
2 The question asks if the person has difficulty learning, remembering, or concentrating.
3 This includes children age 5 to 17 with any combination of two or more of any of the disabilities.
* Indicates that the difference between the percentage for interracially adopted and same-race adopted children is statistically significant at the p<.10 level.
Note that the race/origin categories are mutually exclusive – the race categories show non-Hispanics.

Source: US Census Bureau, 2013–2017 American Community Survey
(For information on confidentiality protection, sampling error, nonsampling error, and definitions, for Census 2000 data see www.census.gov/prod/cen2000/doc/sf3.pdf, for ACS see https://www.census.gov/programs-surveys/acs/technical-documentation/code-lists.html)

not a statistical difference from the 32.6 percent when comparing householder's race/origin to their adopted child. About 29.1 percent of the adopted children who have married parents would be considered transracially adopted in relation to both parents.

An additional but expected limitation of using self-reporting data is that the racial identification of the child is likely reported by the parent and might not be categorized in a way that fits how the Census Bureau defines the various groups. In addition, whether the child is viewed by others as having been transracially adopted might be independent of the race reported for them and their parent. The proportion of adopted children who fit the particular definition of transracial adoption used here is also affected by the fact that census and ACS data include all types of adoption, as well as parents who report the child as their adopted child when no legal measures have been taken. For example, there is no way to distinguish parents who might report the biological child of their partner as their adopted child, or those who report their nephew or niece as their adopted child, simply because the child is living in their household and they have assumed responsibility for their education, for example. These sorts of informal situations can affect the overall estimate of the proportion of children under 18 who are transracially adopted.

Table 2.3 profiles selected demographic characteristics of transracially adopted children under 18 compared with their other adopted counterparts. A lower proportion of transracially adopted children were under age 3 or ages 15 to 17 than other adopted children. While 6.9 percent of transracially adopted children were under 3 years old, this was true of 8.1 percent of other adopted children. At the other end of the age spectrum, 19.1 percent of transracially adopted children were age 15 to 17, while 21.9 percent of other adopted children belonged to this age group. Instead, higher percentages of transracially adopted children were age 6 to 8, or 9 to 11.

These differences may reflect shifts in the numbers of internationally adopted children over time, and the age of internationally adopted children, since a significant proportion of transracially adopted children are also foreign born (30.9 percent).

The race distributions of the two groups are markedly different. Two-thirds (66.6 percent) of same-race adopted children are White non-Hispanic, compared with just 6.4 percent of transracially adopted children. For the transracially adopted children, one-fourth (24.5 percent) were Asian or Pacific Islander, 18.6 percent were Black, 10.8 percent were White/Black, and 1 percent were Some Other Race.

Census and ACS collect race as a separate question from whether or not the respondent is of Hispanic origin. Thus, this chapter shows a mutually exclusive set of race/origin categories, with everyone identified as Hispanic shown in that category. For transracially adopted children, 30.2 percent were reported as Hispanic, while 15.0 percent of other adopted children were reported as Hispanic. Thirty-six percent of transracially adopted children differed from their parent in terms of whether or not they were Hispanic.

The report on adopted children and stepchildren in 2010 (Kreider and Lofquist, 2014) used ACS 2009–2011 data (US Census Bureau, 2018) to provide estimates of transracially adopted children using the parameter used in this chapter of the child differing from their householder parent by race/origin. A comparison with the 2013–2017 data reveals that a higher percentage of transracially adopted children were Black or White-Black at the later time point, while a lower percentage were Asian or Pacific Islander. In 2009–2011, 15.3 percent of transracially adopted children were Black and 9.5 percent were White-Black. In 2013–2017 the corresponding percentages were 18.6 and 10.8, respectively. In contrast, 28.3 percent of transracially adopted children were Asian in 2009–2011, compared with 24.5 percent in 2013–2017. These shifts were likely affected by the decline in adoptions from China and the rise in adoptions from Ethiopia (Efrat, Leblang, Liao, and Pandya, 2015; Marr, 2017).

Overall, 30.9 percent of the transracially adopted children were foreign born, compared with 7.7 percent of their other adopted counterparts. This reflects the race difference between White US parents and the racial makeup of the birth countries of most of the internationally adopted children. The percentage of transracially adopted children who were foreign born in the 2013–2017 data is lower than it was in the ACS 2009–2011 data, when it was 36.5 percent (Kreider and Lofquist, 2014). As Marr (2017) notes, transracial adoption in the US is heavily affected by international adoption, which is often transracial.

About 12.5 percent of transracially and 11.7 percent of other adopted children age 5 and over had at least one disability, which did not differ statistically across the two groups. For transracially and other adopted children, the only category of disability that differed statistically between the two groups of adopted children was self-care disability. However, it could be argued that the difference between the 1.7 percent of other adopted children with a self-care disability and the 2.3 percent of transracially adopted children with the same disability is not substantively important. A higher percentage of both transracially adopted and other adopted children had at least one disability in the 2013–2017 data, compared with 2009–2011 (Kreider and Lofquist, 2014). While 12.5 percent of transracially adopted children and 11.7 percent of other adopted children had at least one disability in 2013–2017, 9.7 percent of transracially adopted children and 9.9 percent of other adopted children had at least one disability in 2009–2011. Part of this increase was due to an increase in the percentage of children with a cognitive disability, which increased from 7.7 percent to 10.5 percent for transracially adopted children and from 8.3 percent to 10.1 percent for other adopted children. The percentage of children with multiple disabilities also increased, from 2.6 percent to 3.6 percent for transracially adopted children, and from 2.5 percent to 3.3 percent for other adopted children.

Place of birth of internationally adopted children

A variety of factors combine to make internationally adopted children a subgroup of adopted children who share particular characteristics and challenges. Internationally adopted children receive special attention as a group, in part because these adoptions are often transracial, and so more visible to the public eye. Another reason for the high profile of international adoptions is the intercountry dynamics involved. Sending countries often establish restrictions on who can adopt, and many create a standardized process by which the adoptions take place.

Internationally adopted children are defined here as foreign-born adopted children of the householder when the householder and their spouse (if present) are US citizens by birth. This excludes foreign-born children who come to the US with their biological parent who marries a US native who then adopts the child. Based on estimates from the NSAP, about one in every four adopted children were adopted internationally. However, the sample of adoptive parents for the NSAP did not include those who adopt a stepchild (Vandivere, Malm, and Radel, 2009), so the percentage of adopted children who were adopted internationally is lower in census surveys due in part to this difference in the denominator of adoptive parents, which, in census surveys includes all those who report an adopted child.

There is likely a substantial increase in the numbers of children adopted internationally to the US since the mid-20th century; however, this assertion is based on estimates from general knowledge of adoption trends, since the data are not available. The first trend is the decreasing number of US-born children available for adoption since the mid-20th century. Although there are multiple factors involved, increasing acceptability of single parenting and declining teen births after the peak in 1970 are both related to the decrease in native-born children available for adoption (Martin, Hamilton, Osterman, Driscoll, and Drake, 2018; Martin et al., 2009). Conversely, the number of children adopted internationally increased from the mid-20th century through the early 2000s (Jones, 2009; US State Department, 2018). Globally, the US adopts the largest number of children from abroad, although when considering the number of adopted children in proportion to the country's population, some other countries adopt at a higher rate, such as Norway, Spain, and Sweden in 2004 (Selman, 2012a). This long-term increase corresponds with the decrease in native-born children in the US who were available for adoption, perhaps encouraging parents to seek other opportunities to adopt.

The high point for international adoptions occurred in 2004, with an estimated global total of 45,000 international adoptions, nearly 23,000 of which were completed by parents in the US. Annual totals decreased after that, and by 2009, fewer international adoptions occurred than in 1998 – nearly 30,000 globally in 2009, compared with about 32,000 in 1998 (Selman, 2012b). By the late 2000s, further changes in the policies of particular countries and the implementation of the Hague Convention and Intercountry Adoption Act (IAA), which established operating standards to protect children from abusive practices, had the overall effect of reducing international adoptions to the US (Daugherty Bailey, 2009). The IAA took effect in 2008 and required that adoption agencies be accredited. As the largest sending country since 1995, China's restrictions in the eligibility criteria for international adoptive parents in the mid-2000s had a significant impact on the decline in all international adoptions. These restrictions corresponded with changes that had already been made to encourage domestic adoption within China, which decreased the number of children made available for adoption (Dowling and Brown, 2009). Additionally, in January of 2008, the US halted adoptions from Guatemala, another of the main sending countries, while issues with the Guatemalan adoption system were addressed (Selman, 2012b). More recently, a diplomatic rift with the US resulted in Russia stopping adoptions to the US, and Ethiopia increased domestic laws for adoption leading to a suspension of all international adoptions in 2017 (Budiman and Hugo Lopez, 2017). The overall decrease in international adoption is reflected in the number of immigrant visas issued to children coming to the US for adoption, which decreased from about 15,700 in 1999 to about 4,700 in 2017 (US State Department, 2018).

Shifts in the birth countries of internationally adopted children are evident in Table 2.4, which provides a detailed examination of the place of birth. Figure 2.1 graphs the percent

Table 2.4 Internationally adopted children under 18 by place of birth and age: 2013–2017

	Under 18 years				
Nativity and place of birth	*Total*	*Under 6*	*6 to 11*	*12 to 14*	*15 to 17*
Number					
Total[1]	174,600	15,870	71,650	46,760	40,330
Europe[1]	36,860	1,471	10,430	11,170	13,790
Russia	26,590	1,070	8,072	8,341	9,102
Asia[1]	93,350	9,025	38,290	25,750	20,280
China	58,950	5,734	24,920	16,500	11,790
Korea	17,620	2,004	6,792	4,712	4,111
Africa	14,100	3,832	7,579	1,704	990
Latin America[1]	29,590	1,416	15,160	7,918	5,096
Central America[1]	23,080	499	13,360	5,950	3,268
Guatemala	21,390	254	12,960	5,524	2,647
South America[1]	3,773	306	921	1,167	1,379
Oceania	596	99	153	201	143
Percent					
Total[1]	100.0	100.0	100.0	100.0	100.0
Europe[1]	21.1	9.3	14.6	23.9	34.2
Russia	15.2	6.7	11.3	17.8	22.6
Asia[1]	53.5	56.9	53.4	55.1	50.3
China	33.8	36.1	34.8	35.3	29.2
Korea	10.1	12.6	9.5	10.1	10.2
Africa	8.1	24.2	10.6	3.6	2.5
Latin America[1]	16.9	8.9	21.2	16.9	12.6
Central America[1]	13.2	3.1	18.7	12.7	8.1
Guatemala	12.2	1.6	18.1	11.8	6.6
South America[1]	2.2	1.9	1.3	2.5	3.4
Oceania	0.3	0.6	0.2	0.4	0.4

Notes:
1 Includes areas not shown separately.
Note that Mexico is included with Central America.
Source: US Census Bureau, 2013–2017 American Community Survey
(For information on confidentiality protection, sampling error, nonsampling error, and definitions, for Census 2000 data see www.census.gov/prod/cen2000/doc/sf3.pdf, for ACS see https://www.census.gov/programs-surveys/acs/technical-documentation/code-lists.html)

distribution by world regions and the current age of the child in 2013–2017. Changes in the distribution by age of the child may reflect change over time in the most common birth countries for those under 18. Since most adults 18 and over do not live with their parents, shifts in the distribution for that age group are less closely connected to the total distribution by birth country for these adoptees.

In 2013–2017, 12.1 percent of adopted children under 18 were internationally adopted. About half (53.5 percent) of the internationally adopted children were born in Asia, about one-sixth (16.9 percent) in Latin America, and about one-fifth (21.1 percent) in Europe (see Figure 2.1). Sixty-three percent (63.1 percent) of the children from Asia were born in China, and an additional 18.9 percent were born in Korea. Korea was one of the largest birth countries for adopted children prior to the 1990s (Selman, 2012b). In 2013–2017, the majority (72.1 percent) of internationally adopted children under 18 from Europe were adopted from Russia. The majority (72.3 percent) of children under 18 adopted from Latin America were born in Guatemala. China was the largest single-country source of internationally adopted children, comprising about 58,950 children or about one-third (33.8 percent) of all internationally adopted children under 18.

Conclusion

This chapter reviewed nationally representative estimates of adopted children under 18 in the US in 2000 as well as 2013–2017, with a particular focus on transracially adopted children and internationally adopted children. Census 2000 long form data and the 5-year ACS data are two of the largest nationally representative samples available, which make them good sources for estimates of these relatively small subpopulations of children. Policy makers can use this information to make empirical estimates of the characteristics of adopted children in the US. For example, the increase shown in this chapter in the percent of adopted children who have a disability, compared with earlier estimates, may be informative to policy makers as they plan how to best make resources available to support adoptive families. Policy makers and researchers can make use of these data to investigate more detailed questions about the changing characteristics of adopted children in the US.

Author note

Disclaimer: Any views expressed on statistical, methodological, or technical issues are those of the author and not necessarily those of the US Census Bureau.

References

Argys, L., & Duncan, B. (2013). Economic incentives and foster care adoption. *Demography, 50*(3), 933–954. doi:10.1007/s13524-012-0166-0

Breuning, M. (2013). Samaritans, family builders, and the politics of intercountry adoption. *International Studies Perspectives, 14*(4), 417–435. doi:10.1111/insp.12016

Budiman, A., & Hugo Lopez, M. (2017). Amid decline in international adoptions to U.S., boys outnumber girls for the first time. Retrieved from www.pewresearch.org/fact-tank/2017/10/17/amid-decline-in-international-adoptions-to-u-s-boys-outnumber-girls-for-the-first-time/

Craver, A. (2001). *Complex Inupiaq Eskimo households and relationships in two northwest Alaska rural communities.* Anchorage, AK: Alaska Native Science Commission. University of Alaska.

Daugherty Bailey, J. (2009). Expectations of the consequences of new international adoption policy in the US. *Journal of Sociology and Social Welfare, XXXVI*(2), 169–184.

Dowling, M., & Brown, G. (2009). Globalization and international adoption from China. *Child and Family Social Work, 14*, 352–361. doi:10.1111/j.1365-2206.2008.00607.x

Efrat, A., Leblang, D., Liao, S., & Pandya, S. (2015). Babies across borders: The political economy of international child adoption. *International Studies Quarterly, 59*, 615–628. doi:10.1111/isqu.12206

Eschelbach Hansen, M., & Simon, R. J. (2004). Transracial placement in adoptions with public agency involvement: What can we learn from the AFCARS data? *Adoption Quarterly, 8*(2), 45–55. doi:10.1300/J145v08n02_03

Flango, V., & Flango, C. (1995). How many children were adopted in 1992? *Child Welfare, LXXIV*(5), 1018–1024.

Jacobson, C. K., Nielsen, L., & Hardeman, A. (2012). Family trends and transracial adoption in the US. *Adoption Quarterly, 15*, 73–87. doi:10.1080/10926755.2012.681591

Jones, J. (2009). Who adopts? Characteristics of women and men who have adopted children. *NCHS Data Brief No. 12*, Hyattsville, MD: National Center for Health Statistics.

Kreider, R. M. (2003). Adopted children and stepchildren: 2000. *Census 2000 Special Reports, CENSR-6RV*, Washington, DC: US Census Bureau.

Kreider, R. M. (2007). Foreign-born adopted children in the US, 2000. In T. Atwood, L. Allen, and V. Ravenel (Eds.), *Adoption factbook IV* (pp. 133–153). Washington, DC: National Council for Adoption.

Kreider, R. M., & Lofquist, D. (2014). Adopted children and stepchildren: 2010. *Current Population Reports*, P20-572. Washington, DC: US Census Bureau.

Marr, E. (2017). US transracial adoption trends in the 21st century. *Adoption Quarterly, 20*(3), 222–251.

Martin, J. A., Hamilton, B. E., Osterman, M. J. K., Driscoll, A. K., & Drake, P. (2018). Births: Final data for 2017. *National Vital Statistics Reports, 67*(8), 1–50. Hyattsville, MD: National Center for Health Statistics.

Martin J. A., Hamilton, B. E., Sutton, P. D., Ventura, S. J., Menacker, F., Kirmeyer, S., & Matthews, T. J. (2009). Births: Final data for 2006. *National Vital Statistics Reports, 57* (7). Hyattsville, MD: National Center for Health Statistics.

McRoy, R., & Griffin, A. (2012). Transracial adoption policies and practices. *Adoption and Fostering, 36* (3–4), 38–49. doi:10.1177/030857591203600305

Montgomery, M., & Powell, I. (2018). International adoptions have dropped 72 percent since 2005 – here's why. Retrieved from http://theconversation.com/international-adoptions-have-dropped-72-percent-since-2005-heres-why-91809

Radel, L. F., Bramlett, M. D., & Waters, A. (2010). Legal and informal adoption by relatives in the US: Comparative characteristics and well-being from a nationally representative sample. *Adoption Quarterly, 13*, 268–291. doi:10.1080/10926755.2010.537957

Selman, P. (2012a). Global trends in intercountry adoption: 2001–2010. *Adoption Advocate, 44*, 1–17.

Selman, P. (2012b). The rise and fall of intercountry adoption in the 21st century: Global trends from 2001 to 2010. In J. L. Gibbons and K. Smith Rotabi (Eds.), *Intercountry adoption: Policies, practices, and outcomes* (pp. 7–27). Surrey, UK: Ashgate.

Suarez Hamm, M. (1999). Latino adoption issues. In W. L. Pierce (Ed.), *Adoption factbook III* (pp. 257–260). Alexandria, VA: National Council for Adoption.

US Census Bureau. (1994). *Geographic areas reference manual*. Washington, DC. Retrieved from www.census.gov/programs-surveys/geography/guidance/geographic-areas-reference-manual.html

US Census Bureau. (2018). Retrieved from www.census.gov/programs-surveys/acs/guidance/estimates.html

US State Department, Bureau of Consular Affairs. (2018). Retrieved from https://travel.state.gov/content/travel/en/Intercountry-Adoption/adopt_ref/adoption-statistics.html

Vandivere, S., Malm, K., & Radel, L. (2009). *Adoption USA: A chartbook based on the 2007 National Survey of Adoptive Parents*. Washington, DC: US Department of Health and Human Services.

3

AN ECONOMIC PERSPECTIVE ON ETHICS IN ADOPTION POLICY

Mary Eschelbach Hansen

US adoption policies changed considerably between 1980 and 2015. Congress encouraged adoption of all types through changes to the tax code. Congress specifically encouraged adoption from foster care by subsidizing it. In international adoption, the US, like most countries, signed a United Nations agreement that discourages child trafficking. These changes to policy increased the number of adoptions from foster care, but about 100,000 children still wait in foster care for an adoptive family. In contrast, the changes to international policy have *decreased* adoptions of children from abroad by families in the US, while two million or more children worldwide remain waiting.

The mixed success of adoption policies reflects a lack of coordination in their development. A coordinated theory of adoption policy has the potential to produce better results. A theory of adoption policy should take into account two key facts about adoption: first, adoption presents ethical problems, and second, resources that society is willing and able to spend on adoption and adoption policy are limited. This chapter argues that the economic way of thinking provides useful tools for developing adoption policy that allocates limited resources wisely while, at the same time, promoting ethical practice in adoption.

The economics of adoption policy are straightforward. Policymakers aim to achieve the greatest cumulative benefits that are possible for all members of the adoption triad and for society as a whole. Using this utilitarian principle, policymakers balance costs with benefits to allocate efficiently the limited pool of resources that is available for adoption and adoption policy.

The ethical issues in adoption are many and complex. Society seeks to eliminate baby stealing and baby selling in private domestic and international adoption. Society also aims to protect the right of children to safety from abuse and neglect in their birth families, while birth parents in families who are at risk of becoming involved in the child welfare system seek to limit the unwarranted intrusion of the government. For children who are orphaned or whose parents' rights are terminated by a court, society seeks to advance their right to be raised in a loving and permanent family. Meanwhile, adoptive parents seek parental rights and rights to privacy that are on par with the rights of birth parents.

Typically, each of the ethical issues in adoption is considered separately by policymakers, but economics provides a way to think cohesively about the ethical issues in adoption.

Economics sees the ethical issues as "market failures" that stem from imperfect information and from positive externalities. There is imperfect information in adoption because, for example, it is hard for prospective adoptive parents to verify if adoption service providers illegally traffic children or if they truthfully reveal a child's special needs. There are positive externalities in adoption because even members of society who are not part of an adoption triad benefit from adoption.

The first section below shows how economic logic helps to identify the kinds of regulation that are needed in order for policy to lead to the optimal number of adoptions. It emphasizes how using the economic way of thinking helps policymakers to design policy that takes into account the key ethical challenges of imperfect information and positive externalities in adoption. The second section briefly reviews the available data on the number of adoptions and the number of waiting children, to show that existing policy has created too few adoptions. The third section reviews the history of adoption policy in the US. This history illustrates how subsidies have been successful in addressing the positive externality problem in adoption. In contrast, efforts to address the problem of imperfect information in international adoption have caused the number of international adoptions to fall rather than to rise. The final section outlines how policymakers might use economics to further refine adoption policy.

The right number of adoptions

To formulate adoption policy that achieves the greatest benefits at the lowest possible cost, it is necessary for policymakers to undertake a systematic analysis of the trade-offs between the benefits and costs of each option. Such an economic analysis helps to define the characteristics of a coordinated adoption policy that creates the "right number" of adoptions.

It is important to understand that an economic analysis does *not* require that adoption be treated as though it is a market for a child or a market for parental rights (See Freundlich, 2000; responding to Landes & Posner, 1978). Instead, an economic analysis considers the market for the professional services required to facilitate the various types of adoption (Hansen & Hansen, 2006; Hansen & Pollack, 2010). In this way, and as noted in the introduction, an economic analysis takes into account the ethical principles and problems in adoption policy.

In economic analysis, the fundamental rule to obtain the benefit-maximizing outcome is to allocate resources so that the last dollar spent on each option society values yields the same net benefits as the first dollar spent. More specifically, in a benefit-maximizing outcome in the market for professional adoption services, resources are allocated to each type of adoptive placement until enough children are placed in each type so that the net benefits to society from the last placement of each type is equal. Adoptive parents in the US choose between three main sources of adoption: foster care, international adoption, and private domestic adoption.

To understand the logic, consider Figure 3.1, which shows the benefit-maximizing division of resources between two types of adoption. On the horizontal axis is the total number of waiting children at any one point in time. To keep the analysis simple, ignore the differences between children typically placed through the different types of adoption. Also ignore the boundaries between types of adoption that were created by historical adoption policy. That is, assume that prospective adoptive parents can easily switch between Type A and Type B adoption (if the analysis is performed separately for waiting children with different characteristics, or for different types of adoption, the basic logic is unchanged;

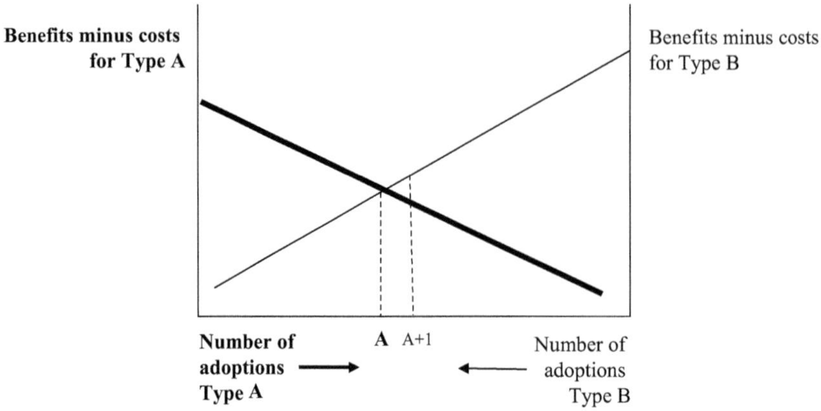

Figure 3.1 Benefit-maximizing division of resources between two types of adoption

however, with separate analyses it is more difficult to use the figure to illustrate the case "too few" adoptions, as discussed below). On the left-hand vertical axis is the net benefits – i.e., benefits minus costs – of adoptions facilitated through Adoption Type A, while on the right-hand vertical axis is the net benefits of Adoption Type B.

Description: Net benefits (benefits minus costs) of each type of adoption decline as the number of adoptions of that type increases. To maximize the total benefits to society of adoptions, resources for the different types of adoption should be allocated so that **A** children are placed in Type A adoptions. All remaining waiting children are placed in Type B adoptions.

For both types of adoption, the net benefits decline as the number of adoptions increases. The main driver of the decline is cost. The cost of facilitating an additional placement, regardless of the type of adoption, always increases. For example, in the case of adoption from foster care, recruiting the first few adoptive parents may be relatively low-cost because a few prospective adoptive parents are already fostering children, or because a few proactively apply to adopt. However, the cost of recruiting additional adoptive parents goes up quickly because finding and training them takes time and money and because many drop out along the way (Kamarck, Hansen, Wilson, & Katz, 2012). In the case of private adoption, the increasing cost of matching birth parents with adoptive parents is likely to be the force behind declining net benefits.

To reach the benefit-maximizing outcome, each child should be placed so that the net benefit from their adoption could not be greater if they were placed through a different option. Following this rule, **A** children should be placed in Adoption Type A, as shown in Figure 3.1. The logic is easiest to see by supposing that, instead of placing **A** children through Type A, we place one more than that, A+1. As Figure 3.1 shows, if child A+1 had been correctly placed in a Type B adoption, the net benefit would have been greater than it is in their actual placement.

Figure 3.1 shows a scenario in which the costs for the two types of adoptions increase relatively slowly. If costs increase slowly, then the benefits of adoption exceed the cost of adoption for each waiting child. Thus, it is possible to match all waiting children with an adoptive family. If costs were to increase quickly, the lines representing net benefits would be steep and would cross the horizontal axis before crossing each other. This means that even at the benefit-maximizing outcome, some children would remain waiting and the benefit-maximizing solution has net benefits equal to zero for the last adoption of each type.

There is an important qualification to using the economics underlying Figure 3.1 to develop adoption policy. The economics relies on the assumption there are no ethical absolutes. For example, the argument for the position that favors restricting of transracial and trans-cultural adoptions that rely on "cultural genocide" is based on an ethical absolute (for an excellent summary of the debate over transracial adoption, see Bartholet, 1990). Ethical absolutes imply unlimited benefits or costs and therefore imply that no resources ought to be spent on one or more of the available options. In contrast, the argument here assumes that all types of adoption have value to society.

Without some adoption policies, the market for adoption services is unlikely to reach the benefit-maximizing outcome shown in Figure 3.1. There will be too few adoptions, resulting in not all waiting children achieving permanency. There are two reasons for the smaller number of adoptions, each reason an example of "market failure," in the lexicon of economists. First, the information available to members of the adoption triad is imperfect. Second, the benefits of adoption to society as a whole are greater than the benefits that go directly to the members of the adoption triad.

Imperfect information aspect

It is not uncommon for a producer or seller to know more than the buyer about the quality of the product or service. If it is difficult to assess every important aspect of a product or service, it might not be feasible for the consumers to find out everything they might need to know. In adoption, it is difficult for prospective adoptive parents to know whether an adoption service provider has high ethical standards. Specifically, prospective adoptive parents might be unable to observe whether an adoption service provider only places children who are truly legally available for adoption, is non-profit, does not condone illegal fees, and aims to create the best match between family and child.

Imperfect information reduces the expected value of adoption services in the eyes of prospective adoptive parents; they must discount its value by the probability that their service provider engages in unethical behaviors. Because imperfect information has no impact on the actual costs of facilitating adoptions, the existence of this kind of market failure decreases the net benefits of placements of all types, as illustrated by the dashed lines in Figure 3.2. Because of imperfect information, the number of prospective adoptive parents might be too small to find appropriate families for all waiting children. At most, A′ children (where A′ is less than A) are placed in Type A adoptions, while a maximum of B children are placed in Type B adoptions. Many children – i.e., a total of A′ minus B children – remain waiting.

Description: When there is a market failure such as imperfect information or a positive externality, the perceived net benefits are below true net benefits of adoption. As a result, the total benefits to society of adoptions are not maximized and A′ – B children remain waiting. Policy to address the market failures has the potential to move the outcome toward the benefit-maximizing outcome shown, in which all waiting children are adopted and resources are divided so that **A** children are placed in Type A adoption.

Regulation can move markets with imperfect information, including the market for adoption services, toward the benefit-maximizing outcome. Policymakers can set minimum standards, such as standards of ethics in social work practice. Second, policymakers can

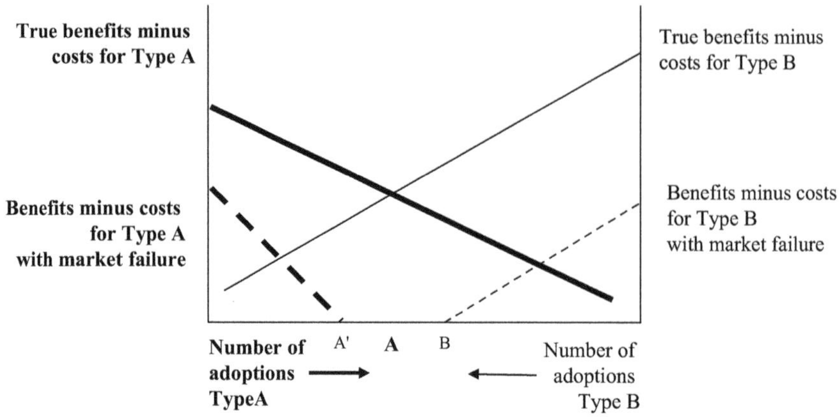

Figure 3.2 Market failure impact on two types of adoption

require that adoption service providers demonstrate that they follow the standards by requiring audits. Audits can check the documentation of the legal status of adopted children, require proof of sources of revenue and destinations of disbursements, and verify the types of information and criteria used for matching children with prospective adoptive parents. Effective regulations that resolve the problems of imperfect information reduce uncertainty on the part of prospective parents. In Figure 3.2 the curves indicating net benefits shift up to their original positions (the solid lines), which has the potential to ensure that there are enough families to place all waiting children.

Positive externality aspect

If the production and consumption of the good or service being exchanged has no effect on people outside the market, then an unregulated market generates the benefit-maximizing amount of the good or service. This is not the case in adoption. When a child is adopted, there are two ways in which people outside the adoption triad benefit. First, when a professional adoption service facilitates the adoption of a child whose birth parents cannot care for them, society benefits. For example, a permanent adoption of a child from foster care reduces the probability that the child will have poor outcomes and require social services as an adult (Hansen, 2007a). Second, in order for professionals to facilitate an adoption legally and ethically, the government must provide protection of the rights of children and families involved in adoption. For example, the government must protect adopted children from trafficking, and it must protect the parental rights of both birth parents and adoptive parents from unnecessary intrusion into the family and unnecessary separation from their children. Such protection is provided through enactment of laws, the enforcement of laws by the relevant authorities, and resolution of disputes in court. The protection of the rights of children and families has benefits to society that are greater than the benefits to any single individual. Further, even those who are never part of an adoption triad benefit from the protections of the members of the triad. These are examples of how adoption has "positive externalities," another type of market failure.

Figure 3.2 can also be used to illustrate how the positive externality aspect of adoption results in the failure to place some waiting children. The dashed lines now represent the net benefits that accrue only to the members of the adoption triad, while the solid curves representing net benefits illustrate the full value of adoption to society. Once again, market failure results in too few adoptions. The policy remedy is to incentivize adoptions. For example, lawmakers can offer ongoing subsidies to families who adopt children from foster care, and they can allow tax benefits for all kinds of adoption. If the subsidy/tax benefit is as large as the difference between private and total net benefits for each type of adoption, well-designed policy can support a benefit-maximizing division of placements across types of adoption and help to ensure all waiting children achieve permanency.

Existing policy creates too few adoptions

Although the historical statistics are not very complete, the number of adoptions finalized in the US probably peaked in the late 1960s at about 175,000 annually (Herman, 2012). These were mostly private domestic adoptions. The decrease since the 1960s in private domestic adoptions is attributed to birth control becoming more readily available and single motherhood becoming more socially acceptable. Yet through the 1990s, most adoptions were of this type. Again, though historical statistics on the demand for adoption are not available, it seems likely that the number of parents seeking private domestic adoption in the US was always larger than the number of children placed for adoption by their birth parents (Landes & Posner, 1978). In contrast, although adoptions from foster care in the US tripled from the mid-1990s to the mid-2000s, peaking at just under 60,000 annually, at no time did the number of children waiting in foster care fall below 100,000 (US Department of Health and Human Services, 2018). Also, in the 1990s to the mid-2000s, international adoptions approximately doubled, peaking at just over 20,000 annually (US Department of State, 2017), while at least 2 million children resided in orphanages worldwide (UNICEF, 2009). Since the mid-2000s the number of adoptions has fallen. In 2007, about 134,000 adoptions – in total, of all types – were finalized; in 2017 there were only about 110,000 (Jones & Placek, 2017). Clearly, current adoption policy fails to result in the placement of all waiting children, and it is unlikely that it results in the benefit-maximizing number of adoptions.

The failure of policy to reach the benefit-maximizing number of adoptions has been most thoroughly studied for adoption from foster care. My article on the value of adoption (Hansen, 2007a) reviews the literature on the costs and benefits of a child's adoption from foster care as compared to the child's remaining in foster care until the age of emancipation. I calculate the present discounted value of net benefits to show that the return to investment in adoption is many times the return to investment in most public goods. There are several reasons that the returns on investment in adoption from foster care are so high. First, for children in foster care whose birth parents' rights have been terminated, the cost of adoption to the child welfare system is about half the cost of the child remaining in long-term foster care (see also Barth, Lee, Wildfire, & Guo, 2006). Second, children adopted from foster care are less likely to use special education services than children who remain in foster care, thus, adoption lowers the costs of public schools. Children adopted from foster care also are less likely to commit crimes as teens and young adults than children who remain in foster care, so adoption reduces criminal justice costs. Finally, children adopted from foster care are more likely to finish high school and obtain post-secondary education or training than children who remain in foster care. Adoption increases earnings and decreases the cost of welfare programs. In short, a dollar spent on the adoption of a child from foster care yields about three dollars in benefits (Hansen, 2007a), indicating that society would benefit from spending additional resources on adoption.

Creating more adoptions

As mentioned above, to address the positive externalities aspect of adoption, policymakers can offer subsidies. The first section discusses the evidence that subsidies to families contributed to the surge in adoptions from foster care in the 1990s and early 2000s. To address the imperfect information aspects, policymakers can regulate adoption service providers. However, if regulation significantly increases the cost of placements, or if it directly restricts placements, it can reduce adoptions instead of increase them. The second section summarizes the research showing that regulation in international adoption was likely the force behind the decline in international adoptions during the 2000s.

Increasing adoptions using subsidies

A primary driver of the increase in adoptions from foster care was federal support for subsidies to adoptive parents (Hansen, 2007b; Hansen & Hansen, 2006). The Adoption Assistance and Child Welfare Act of 1980 (CWA) established the largest of the subsidies (for a summary of federal law on child welfare, see Child Welfare Information Gateway, 2016). The CWA had three goals. The first was to require states to make "reasonable efforts" to reunify children with their families of origin. The second was to care for foster children in families rather than institutions. The third was to encourage adoption if the foster child could not return to their family of origin. The CWA supported these goals by authorizing federal reimbursement of a state's expenditures on monthly payments to certain foster families and to families that adopt eligible foster children. Under the CWA, each state decides the amount of a monthly subsidy to offer, although subsidies to adoptive families cannot exceed subsidies to foster families for the same child. A 1986 law subsidized the up-front costs of adoption from foster care (Child Welfare Information Gateway, 2016); typically, families who adopt from foster care pay nothing and the federal government reimburses states' expenses.

Offering subsidies to families who adopt increased the number of adoptions from foster care, particularly the ongoing monthly subsidies (Avery & Mont, 1992; Hansen & Hansen, 2006). In the federal fiscal year 1997, states that offered the highest monthly subsidies finalized adoptions for about 20 foster children per 100,000 people in the state, while states that offered the lowest monthly subsidies finalized about eight adoptions from foster care for each 100,000 people in the state. In a simple cross-sectional regression analysis, an increase of one percent in the monthly subsidy was associated with a 1.5 percent increase in the adoption rate (Hansen & Hansen, 2006). This one percent increase in subsidy amounted to paying an extra 36 dollars per month to all adoptive families to achieve ten additional adoptions. A more sophisticated panel analysis showed that states that increased their monthly subsidies increased the number of families that chose to grow by adoption from foster care relative to the number of families that chose to grow by childbirth. On average, states that increased subsidies had three times more adoptions from foster care than states that did not increase their incentives to families (Hansen, 2007b).

Yet, by the late 1990s, it was clear that policymakers had more work to do (Provencher, Kahn, & Hansen, 2017; US Department of Health and Human Services, 2018). The number of children entering foster care was rising while, despite an increasing number of adoptions, the total number of children exiting foster care was falling. At this time stays in foster care exceeded two years on average. Long periods in foster care harm child well-being by increasing the risk of behavior problems (Early & Mooney, 2002), delinquency, and adult dependency (see, among many, Doyle, 2007). To address the situation, Congress passed the Adoption and Safe Families Act of 1997 (ASFA). Through ASFA, Congress signaled that it recognized the value to society of adoption in several ways. ASFA clarified the limits of "reasonable efforts" to reunite foster children, and it freed states from reunifying a child in the presence of specific "aggravated circumstances," such as when the parent had caused the death of a sibling. The law required that states move to terminate parental rights once a child had been in foster care for 15 out of 22 months. ASFA required permanency hearings for all foster children, and it promoted "concurrent planning," in which local child welfare authorities worked toward locating an adoptive family for a child even as efforts to reunify the child with their birth parents continued. It also forbade states from delaying or denying adoptions based upon the geographic location of prospective adoptive parents. Finally, as part of ASFA, Congress allocated new money to adoption. It funded adoption promotion and support services, and it created incentive payments for states to improve performance in adoptive placements.

After ASFA, states took steps to increase adoptions, including increasing the number of social workers devoted to adoption (Congressional Research Service, 2004), increasing contracts with private agencies (Blackstone, Buck, & Hakim, 2004), and increasing average subsidies paid to families (Hansen, 2007b). At the same time as it changed policy on adoption from foster care, Congress recognized the high value of all types of adoption to society, by greatly increasing the tax benefits of adoption. In 1981, Congress had created an itemized tax deduction for expenses related to any type of adoption. In 1996, it converted the deduction to a credit (tax credits are much more valuable; credits reduce tax liability dollar-for-dollar, while deductions only decrease tax liability by the applicable marginal tax rate). Because the up-front costs of adoption from foster care were already subsidized, these tax benefits went mostly to families who adopted privately and internationally (US Department of the Treasury, 2000). However, the 2001 Tax Relief Act offered a $10,000 unqualified tax credit to families who finalize the adoption of a child with special needs. Even though they had no adoption expenses, families who adopted children from foster care were able to take advantage of the 2001 unqualified tax credit (for a detailed history of the adoption tax credit, see Donovan, 2013). Together with the monthly subsidies to adoptive families, ASFA and the 2001 Tax Relief Act increased the number of adoptions from fewer than 28,000 per year in 1995 to more than 50,500 in 2005.

Improving information without reducing adoptions is difficult

Concerns about the imperfect information aspect of adoption have long led countries in the Americas and in Northern and Western Europe to execute regional agreements on ethical practices for providers of international adoption services. Regional agreements, however, did not prevent all instances of unethical practices such as trafficking in children worldwide. The international press uncovered cases of child-stealing for adoption and cases of child-selling by parents and by orphanages (Parra-Aranguren, 1994). To reduce these unethical practices, and as an outgrowth of the discussion regarding children's rights in general, in the 1980s the United Nations led an effort to establish a single international agreement for the regulation of international adoption (Bartholet, 1995; Kapstein, 2003), leading to the creation of the 1993 Hague Convention on Intercountry Adoption.

The Hague Convention encourages all providers of international adoption services to focus on meeting the needs of waiting children rather than fulfilling the desires of prospective adoptive parents. A focus on the child ought to ensure that all members of the adoption triad can be confident that providers of international adoption services meet high ethical standards. Specifically, the Hague Convention delegates to the country of the child's origin the responsibility for ensuring that proper consent to adoption has been given. To the receiving country, the Convention delegates responsibility for ensuring the legal status of the adopted child, including keeping documentation requirements for immigration reasonable. The Hague Convention also prohibits financial gain from adoption. Fees and "donations" paid by adoptive parents must be spent on the actual costs, which can include social services, travel, and child support during the period before the adoption takes place. To ensure full financial disclosure, receiving countries must accredit all providers of international adoption services. (For a summary of the Hague Convention and related federal law, see Hansen & Pollack (2006). For a summary of aspects of the Hague Convention that are not directly relevant to the information problem, including the requirement that countries consider national solutions for waiting children before allowing them to be adopted internationally, see Hansen & Pollack (2008).)

It took the US Congress almost a decade to implement the Hague Convention by passing the Intercountry Adoption Act (ICA) of 2000. The biggest challenge was deciding which federal agency would regulate international adoption. Like most of family law, regulation of all aspects of adoption was the responsibility of states. The fiscal carrots and sticks in the CWA and the ASFA gave some regulator-like authority over adoption from foster care to the federal Department of Health and Human Services (DHHS), but Congress decided to assign the role of regulator of international adoption to the Department of State. Congress decided that the State Department's responsibility for issuing visas and its networks in sending countries, which had gathered evidence used to prosecute cases of unethical and illegal practices in adoption, was more important than the DHHS' knowledge of adoption more generally.

It took several years for the Department of State to finalize regulations under the ICA. They went into effect in 2006. Under the regulations, providers of international adoption services are required to meet most, but not all, of the standards for ethical performance. That is, only substantial compliance, not strict compliance is required. Nonetheless, many agencies in the US have been sanctioned under the ICA (US Department of State Bureau of Consular Affairs, 2018). Although ethical concerns about so-called independent adoptions remain (Hayes, 2011), in a survey conducted several years after ICA regulations went into effect, most participants in international adoption in countries that signed the Hague Convention perceived adoption practice as being more consistently ethical than it was previously (Pinderhughes, Matthews, Deoudes, & Pertman, 2013). Professionals in countries that typically send children in international adoption were more confident that the Hague Convention had improved ethical practice than professionals in receiving countries were. On the other hand, professionals in sending countries that were not signatories to the Hague Convention were unlikely to agree that ethical standards had improved since the 1990s.

Unfortunately, apparent improvements in information under the Hague Convention and the ICA have not increased international adoptions to the US, as Figure 3.2 suggests they should. International adoptions peaked in 2005 and began to decline as regulations under the ICA went into effect.

Although it was hoped that the improvements made by the Hague Convention would reduce the "delays, complications and [the] considerable costs" of international adoption (Duncan, 2000, p. 47), the decline in the number of adoptions suggests that the costs have more than offset any perceived increase in the net benefits of international adoption.

In the US, becoming an accredited agency is expensive. In addition to being licensed by states to provide adoption services, professionals who wish to provide their services in international adoption must also undergo an entirely separate accreditation process under the ICA. As part of this separate process, adoption service providers must purchase $1 million in liability insurance.

A second type of cost is borne by the US taxpayer. Although, as noted above, the Hague Convention places the responsibility for verifying the availability of children for adoption on the sending country, the ICA requires the US Attorney General to affirm independently the availability of each child for adoption. The redundancies almost certainly contribute to improvements in conforming to ethical standards; however, they also increase wait times. Said one adoption professional, "There is a burden of bureaucracy that many times delays children from going to their families" (Pinderhughes, Matthews, Deoudes, & Pertman, 2013, p. 79). If the attorney general is unable to verify the availability of a child who has previously been cleared for adoption by their country of origin, that child could ultimately become unadoptable and might remain in an orphanage until adulthood.

Of course, bureaucracy can also delay domestic adoptions. Interstate adoptions of waiting children may be restricted by states' desires to reserve a pool of in-state prospective adoptive parents for in-state foster children and by the complexity of interstate placement (Kamarck, Hansen, Wilson, & Katz, 2012). Formal or informal restrictions on transracial adoption or adoption by non-traditional families, including same-sex headed families, can delay or entirely prevent the adoption of waiting children (for a recent example of state restrictions on LGBT adoption, see Fortin, 2018). Reducing bureaucratic inefficiencies and eliminating restrictions are policies that move society toward the benefit-maximizing "right" number of adoptions.

Creating better adoptions

Thus far, the information in this chapter is based on the assumption that all adoptions result in permanency. However, a small number of adoptive placements disrupt (meaning the adoptions are not completed) or dissolve (meaning that adoptive parents relinquish their rights to the child or that their parental rights are terminated) (for a review, see Palacios, Rolock, Selwyn, & Barbosa-Ducharne, 2018). The existence of disruptions and dissolutions suggests that some adoptive families are not well-matched with children (see Chapter 30 in this volume for a discussion of adoption disruption). Poor matching is part of the imperfect information problem previously discussed. For example, adoption service providers might fail to gather information about a child's early exposures to toxins or traumatic experiences, or providers might fail to transmit all information to prospective adoptive parents. As a result, about 10 percent of adoptive parents report that they receive insufficient information on the educational, physical, mental, and behavioral health needs of the children that they adopt (Vandivere, Malm, & Radel, 2009). Without good and complete information, adoptive parents may be under-prepared when their children later experience problems tied to their early experiences.

In the past, the matching-information problem has not been a significant part of adoption policy. To see how policy could improve the matching-information problem, consider the way matching occurs in adoption from foster care. Some prospective adoptive parents might take steps toward adoption after viewing a segment on a local news program about a particular waiting child (Metropolitan Washington Council of Governments, 2018). Alternatively, they might view state and national websites that list descriptions of waiting children in foster care (Adoption Exchange Association, 2018). However, during the process of applying to adopt, prospective parents who might have viewed a particular child's profile are typically encouraged to consider other waiting children.

The process of deciding which children to match with which adoptive families requires significant resources and adequate information about potential adoptive families and waiting children. Although family–child matches have changed considerably since the 1960s

(Melosh, 2002), the information used in matching has hardly changed. The central document is the home study, which is prepared by an adoption service provider. The narrative of the home study includes a statement by the family regarding the preferred characteristics of children they are willing and able to adopt, plus the opinion of the adoption service provider regarding the capacity of the family to parent children with different characteristics.

Home studies vary greatly in the quality, amount, and type of information they contain. Despite efforts to promulgate the use of a common home study (Crea, Barth, Chintapalli, & Buchanan, 2009), the content and format of the home study is not always uniform across jurisdictions within a state, much less across states. In order to make a match, adoption service providers have to compare families and children along numerous dimensions: family size; attitude toward siblings; age of parents and child; physical, emotional, and mental disabilities; and other concerns. The information conveyed in a home study completed by one provider might not be the information desired by another provider. In contrast to the way states recognize drivers licensed in other states, some jurisdictions do not accept home studies prepared in other jurisdictions (Kamarck, Hansen, Wilson, & Katz, 2012).

Policymakers can create both better adoptions and more adoptions – and move toward maximizing net benefits – by encouraging development of a comprehensive system for adoptive matching. Such a system might build on the one that identifies the "best possible match" between medical doctors seeking residencies and hospitals seeking residents (Roth, 1986) and between students and charter schools (Abdulkadiroğlu, Pathak, & Roth, 2005). The key is to leverage what is known about successful adoptions to design a home study and a child evaluation for universal use that accurately assesses each family's capabilities and each child's needs. A standardized format would mitigate the information problem. Further, a standardized format would facilitate automated matching. With automated matching, the pools of prospective adoptive parents and waiting children worldwide could effectively be combined. Resources needed to identify good matches for all waiting children could be greatly reduced.

Conclusion

This essay has shown that regulation of adoption is necessary if society desires to maximize the benefits of adoption to all. Regulation is needed because the market for adoption services suffers from two "market failures": imperfect information and positive externalities. Each of the market failures has an ethical element. The imperfect information problem refers to the difficulty that prospective adoptive parents face in knowing whether adoption service providers behave ethically. The positive externality problem stems from the fact that even members of society who are not part of an adoption triad benefit from adoption; thus society has an ethical obligation to encourage adoption.

A review of the history of adoption policy in the US shows that the positive externality in adoption can be effectively addressed using subsidies. Past success in using subsidies to increase adoptions from foster care suggests that higher subsidies are warranted. In contrast, the history of implementation of the Hague Convention in the US shows that policymakers have not yet effectively addressed the problem of imperfect information. Past approaches to ensure ethical adoption practice have been so expensive that international adoptions have fallen instead of risen. A new approach is needed. One potentially promising approach is to standardize the collection of high-quality information about prospective adoptive families and waiting children.

References

Abdulkadiroğlu, A., Pathak, P. A., & Roth, A. E. (2005). The New York City high school match. *American Economic Review, 95*(2), 364–367. doi:10.1257/000282805774670167

Adoption Exchange Association. (2018). AdoptUSKids. Retrieved December 18, 2018, from www.adoptuskids.org

Avery, R. J., & Mont, D. (1992). Financial support of children involved in special needs adoption: A policy evaluation. *Journal of Policy Analysis and Management, 11*(3), 419–441. doi:10.2307/3325070

Barth, R. P., Lee, C. K., Wildfire, J., & Guo, S. (2006). A comparison of the governmental costs of long-term foster care and adoption. *Social Service Review, 80*(1), 127–158. doi:10.1086/499339

Bartholet, E. (1990). Where do Black children belong? The politics of race matching in adoption. *University of Pennsylvania Law Review, 139*, 1163–1256.

Bartholet, E. (1995). International adoption: propriety, prospects and pragmatics. *Journal of the American Academy of Matrimonial Lawyers, 13*, 181–210.

Blackstone, E. A., Buck, A. J., & Hakim, S. (2004). Privatizing adoption and foster care: Applying auction and market solutions. *Children and Youth Services Review, 26*(11), 1033–1049. doi:10.1016/j.childyouth.2004.08.004

Child Welfare Information Gateway. (2016). Major federal legislation concerned with child protection, child welfare, and adoption. Retrieved December 15, 2018, from www.childwelfare.gov/pubs/other pubs/majorfedlegis/

Crea, T. M., Barth, R. P., Chintapalli, L., & Buchanan, R. L. (2009). Structured home study evaluations: Perceived benefits of SAFE versus conventional home studies. *Adoption Quarterly, 12*(2), 78–99. doi:10.1080/10926750902978824

Donovan, C. A. (2013). The adoption tax credit: progress and prospects for expansion. Retrieved December 15, 2018, from https://lozierinstitute.org/adoptiontaxcredit/

Doyle, J. J. (2007). Child protection and child outcomes: Measuring the effects of foster care. *The American Economic Review, 97*(5), 1583–1610. doi:10.1257/aer.97.5.1583

Duncan, W. (2000). The Hague Convention on protection of children and cooperation in respect of intercountry adoption. In P. Selman (Ed.), *Intercountry Adoption: Developments, Trends, and Perspectives* (pp. 40–52). London: British Agencies for Adoption and Fostering.

Early, T. J., & Mooney, D. D. (2002). *Mental health service use for children in foster care in Illinois.* Champaign, IL: Children and Family Research Center, School of Social Work, University of Illinois at Urbana-Champaign.

Fortin, J. (2018, May 13). Oklahoma passes adoption law that LGBT groups call discriminatory. *The New York Times.* Retrieved from www.nytimes.com/2018/05/12/us/oklahoma-gay-adoption-bill.html

Freundlich, M. (2000). *The market forces in adoption: Adoption and ethics* (Vol. 2). Washington, DC: Child Welfare League of America.

Hansen, M. E. (2007a). The value of adoption. *Adoption Quarterly, 10*(2), 65–87. doi:10.1300/J145v10n02_03

Hansen, M. E. (2007b). Using subsidies to promote the adoption of children from foster care. *Journal of Family and Economic Issues, 28*(3), 377–393. doi:10.1007/s10834-007-9067-6

Hansen, M. E., & Hansen, B. A. (2006). The economics of adoption of children from foster care. *Child Welfare, 85*, 559–583.

Hansen, M. E., & Pollack, D. (2006). The regulation of intercountry adoption. *Brandeis Law Journal, 45*, 105–128.

Hansen, M. E., & Pollack, D. (2008). Trade-offs in formulating a consistent national policy on adoption. *Family Court Review, 46*(2), 366–374. doi:10.1111/j.1744-1617.2008.00206.x

Hansen, M. E., & Pollack, D. (2010). Transracial adoption of black children: An economic analysis. In M. B. Goodwin (Ed.), *Baby Markets: Money and the New Politics of Creating Families* (pp. 133–145). New York: Cambridge University Press.

Hayes, P. (2011). The legality and ethics of independent intercountry adoption under the Hague Convention. *International Journal of Law, Policy and the Family, 25*(3), 288–317. doi:10.1093/lawfam/ebr016

Herman, E. (2012). Adoption history: Adoption statistics. Retrieved December 15, 2018, from https://pages.uoregon.edu/adoption/topics/adoptionstatistics.htm

Jones, J., & Placek, P. (2017, February 15). Adoption: by the numbers. Retrieved December 11, 2018, from www.adoptioncouncil.org/publications/2017/02/adoption-by-the-numbers

Kamarck, E. C., Hansen, M. E., Wilson, J. B., & Katz, J. (2012). Eliminating barriers to the adoption of children from foster care. *Harvard Kennedy School Faculty Research Working Paper, RWP12-040.* Retrieved from www.hks.harvard.edu/publications/eliminating-barriers-adoption-children-foster-care

Kapstein, E. B. (2003). The baby trade. *Foreign Affairs, 82*(6), 115–125. doi:10.2307/20033761

Landes, E. M., & Posner, R. A. (1978). The economics of the baby shortage. *Journal of Legal Studies*, 7, 323–348. doi:10.1086/467597

Melosh, B. (2002). Adoption stories: Autobiographical narrative and the politics of identity. In E. W. Carp (Ed.), *Adoption in American: Historical Perspectives* (pp. 218–246). Ann Arbor: University of Michigan Press.

Metropolitan Washington Council of Governments. (2018). Wednesday's child. Retrieved December 18, 2018, from www.mwcog.org/community/planning-areas/child-welfare/wednesdays-child/

Palacios, J., Rolock, N., Selwyn, J., & Barbosa-Ducharne, M. (2018). Adoption breakdown: concept, research, and implications. *Research on Social Work Practice, 29*(2), 130–142. doi:10.1177/1049731518783852

Parra-Aranguren, G. (1994). Explanatory report on the 1993 Hague Intercountry Adoption Convention. Retrieved December 17, 2018, from www.hcch.net/en/publications-and-studies/details4/?pid=2279

Pinderhughes, E., Matthews, J., Deoudes, G., & Pertman, A. (2013). *A changing world: Shaping best practices through understanding of the new realities of intercountry adoption.* New York: The Donaldson Adoption Institute. Retrieved from www.adoptioninstitute.org/old/publications/2013_10_AChangingWorld.pdf

Provencher, A. J., Kahn, N. E., & Hansen, M. E. (2017). Adoption policy and the well-being of adopted children in the United States. *Child Welfare, 95*, 27–55.

Roth, A. E. (1986). On the allocation of residents to rural hospitals: A general property of two-sided matching markets. *Econometrica, 54*(2), 425–427. doi:10.2307/1913160

Congressional Research Service. (2004). Child welfare: implementation of the Adoption and Safe Families Act (P. L. 105-89). Retrieved December 15, 2018, from www.everycrsreport.com/reports/RL30759.html

UNICEF. (2009). Progress for children: A report card on child protection (No. 8). Retrieved December 11, 2018, from www.unicef.org/publications/index_50921.html

US Department of Health and Human Services. (2018). Adoption & foster care statistics. Retrieved December 11, 2018, from www.acf.hhs.gov/cb/research-data-technology/statistics-research/afcars

US Department of State. (2017). Adoption statistics. Retrieved December 11, 2018, from https://travel.state.gov/content/travel/en/Intercountry-Adoption/adopt_ref/adoption-statistics.html

US Department of State Bureau of Consular Affairs. (2018). Agencies denied or subject to adverse action. Retrieved December 17, 2018, from https://travel.state.gov/content/travel/en/Intercountry-Adoption/about-adoption-service-providers/agencies-denied-or-subject-to-adverse-action.html

US Department of the Treasury. (2000). Report to the Congress on tax benefits for adoption. Retrieved December 15, 2018, from www.treasury.gov/resource-center/tax-policy/Documents/Report-Adoption-2000.pdf

Vandivere, S., Malm, K., & Radel, L. (2009, November 1). Adoption USA: A chartbook based on the 2007 National Survey of Adoptive Parents. Retrieved December 19, 2018, from https://aspe.hhs.gov/report/adoption-usa-chartbook-based-2007-national-survey-adoptive-parents

4
DOMESTIC ADOPTION IN ETHIOPIA

Sebilu Bodja and Kristi Gleason

Background

Domestic adoption, as an organized and legal care option, does not have a long history in Ethiopia. Adoption was not included in the Ethiopia Civil Code of 1961, the first comprehensive enactment of law in Ethiopia. The Ethiopian Constitution (which came into force in 1995) and the Revised Family Code (enacted in 2000) provided principal legal guidance on the facilitation of adoption services, both local and international. Additionally, guidelines were created to streamline child welfare services, especially the Alternative Child Care Guideline of 2009 (Ministry of Women Affairs (MOWA), 2009), which detailed operational procedures to be followed during implementation or service provision (MOWA, 2009).

This chapter begins by providing a description of the historical and cultural understanding of adoption among several people groups in Ethiopia, which form the basis for the legal and policy frameworks that regulate adoption in Ethiopia currently. Following this, the history of international adoption of children from Ethiopia is discussed, as well as the forces that led to a movement toward prioritizing domestic options for orphaned and vulnerable children. Bethany Global, the international development arm of the Michigan-based organization Bethany Christian Services, began intercountry adoption (ICA) from Ethiopia in 2008. Shortly thereafter, in an effort to place more children into families, they also began a foster care adoption program for children not served through ICA. Bethany Global's foster-to-adopt program is described as an example of an innovative program that established a domestic adoption infrastructure within two regions in Ethiopia. The chapter outlines the steps in program implementation and key features that were central to establishing this program where there was, initially, a lack of a strong child welfare and domestic adoption infrastructure.

Gudifecha has very strong social and cultural roots in Ethiopia and refers to the adoption of a child into a family through customary arrangements that enable the child to become a full member of the new family and enjoy equal rights to biological children (Duressa, 2002). *Gudifecha* is an Afaan Oromo (the largest language group in Ethiopia, comprising one-third of the country according to the 2007 Census (FDRE, 2007)) word, adopted by other local languages, that represents all the major aspects of the conventional understanding of adoption as defined in international conventions. *Gudifecha* is said to have become part of the cultural practice of the Oromo people during their migration to various parts of present-day Ethiopia. They practiced *gudifecha* in adopting a people group that they subjugated or children of an opposing group that had been taken captive. The practice involved adopting communities or individuals to integrate them into the Oromo society. The Oromo people also practiced *gudifecha* to take in a child left without parental care. There are variations of *gudifecha* where willing families within a clan participated by giving a family that could not bear a child the chance to raise a child for the family lineage to continue. In such cases, the other family that gave their child to a childless family would have many biological children of their own, from whom they chose one to give (Duressa, 2002). It was done with the assumption that the new family would provide the best care for the child out of their earnest desire to have a child of their own. One could, however, ask whether this was in the best interest of the child involved, from the standpoint of best practices and mechanisms that should be in place to protect the long-term welfare of the child.

Gudifecha is a very public ceremonial event where community leaders and members gather to colorfully celebrate the adoption of a child. At the ceremony, elders in the community issue a decree to community members acknowledging the inclusion of the child into the new family. The decree also denounces any potential derogatory inferences to the child emanating from previous loss of biological parents. The purpose of the decree is to officiate that the child is a legitimate part of the new family with all the rights of a biological child (Duressa, 2002).

Children that came under parental care through *gudifecha* would enjoy all the same rights as biological children. They were entitled to inheritance and were fully embraced as part of the Oromo lineage through *mogassa*, another cultural practice used to graft the adopted child into the new family by giving them a new name (Duressa, 2002).

While *gudifecha* is largely used as an Afaan Oromo and Amharic[1] substitute for adoption, there are few studies that examine whether it is uniformly applied across cultures, including cultural sub-groups within a single people group. Hence, the cultural and customary use of *gudifecha* as an indigenous adoption institution requires further study in terms of compliance with legal procedures and requirements. Further studies are also required to examine whether *gudifecha*, as a cultural practice, meets standards of best practice in sustainably protecting the welfare of children.

Legal and policy frameworks for domestic adoption

UNCRC and ACRWC

Ethiopia is a signatory to the United Nations Convention on the Rights of the Child (UNCRC), which was ratified in Ethiopia in 1991, and the African Charter on the Rights and Welfare of the Child (ACRWC), which was ratified in 2002. Related to the care of orphaned and vulnerable children, the UNCRC states that a

> child temporarily or permanently deprived of his or her family environment, or in whose own best interests cannot be allowed to remain in that environment, shall be entitled to special protection and assistance provided by the State. State Parties shall in accordance with their national laws ensure alternative care for such a child.
>
> *(United Nations, 1990, p. 7)*

Relatedly, the ACRWC outlines that children who are separated from their parents should get special protection and should be provided with alternative family care, and states should also take all possible steps to trace and re-unite children with parents (African Commission on Human and Peoples' Rights, 1999). Both the UNCRC and ACRWC have equal application in the legal system of Ethiopia as any other national laws of the land. Hence, the provisions on adoption in both conventions equally set principles and implementation modalities for administration of the services. Article 20 of the UNCRC and Article 25 of the ACRWC are cited in the Alternative Child Care Guideline of the government of Ethiopia, described in more detail below, as the overarching principles that form the basis for formulating care options (MOWA, 2009).

The Ethiopian constitution

Article 36 of the Constitution of the Federal Democratic Republic of Ethiopia, which came into force in 1995, provides for the right of the child to have a family (FDRE, 1995). The provisions in the article outline measures that should be taken to safeguard the welfare of children, including orphaned and vulnerable children without parental care. One of the measures that the constitution encourages is the creation of institutions that facilitate the adoption of children. As the supreme law of the land, the constitution offers clear guidance on measures that would be required for the institutionalization of adoption (FDRE, 1995).

The Revised Family Code proclamation of 2000

The Revised Family Code of Ethiopia also enshrines clear provisions for adoption procedures and assigns various responsibilities to actors that are involved in facilitating it (FDRE, 2000). The government of Ethiopia has, over the years, developed policies and guidelines to regulate and govern delivery of services. Chapter 10 of the Code is entirely devoted to adoption, covering a broad range of provisions for administration and implementation of adoption, both domestic and intercountry. The provisions enlist safeguard mechanisms and rights an adopted child is entitled to as the adoption is completed through the legal system. Article 192 stipulates provisions for orphanages to keep legal custody of the children under their care and ways they can make decisions about the child's adoption, considering the best interest of the child. According to the Revised Family Code, adoption is strictly tied to children under the custody of orphanages, referred to in Ethiopia as child care institutions (FDRE, 2000).

Alternative child care guidelines

Government agencies such as the Ministry of Labor and Social Affairs and Ministry of Women and Children Affairs have been mandated to regulate services for orphaned and vulnerable children. With the reorganization of the ministerial mandate and an increased focus on these children, a separate department was created within the Ministry of Women and Children Affairs that deals with alternative care (MOWA, 2009). The ministry has been mandated to provide policy guidance, streamline systems, and implementation across regions of the Federal government. Hence, local care options received increased attention after the Alternative Child Care Guidelines were published in 2009 (MOWA, 2009). Services in the Alternative Child Care Guidelines lists Community-based Childcare (a term referring to kinship care), reunification and reintegration, domestic adoption, foster care, intercountry adoption, and institutional care as the care options in order of preference. The main objectives of the Guidelines are:

a) To facilitate the provision of quality and effective care and support to orphaned and vulnerable children, based on the principles that they ensure the best interests of the child;
b) To set minimum conditions on the delivery of alternative childcare services in the country, so that organizations can adopt and apply them in the context of the objective reality of their regions;
c) To develop sound child-oriented operational frameworks in accordance with the rights-based approach both at institutional and community levels, so that all children will be ensured of the necessary protection;
d) To promote a participatory approach of dealing with the care and support of orphans and vulnerable children.

(MOWA, 2009, p. 6)

The Guidelines also set broad operational modalities and criteria for actors and individuals that were involved in providing services on any or all care options. Various sections of the Guidelines consistently refer to the best interest of the child as the principal driver of decision-making by any stakeholder affecting the welfare of the child.

While it is clear that Ethiopia has well-defined policies and procedures that outline the best way for alternative care to be implemented for children outside of parental care, it has only been in the past 10–15 years that alternatives such as foster care and adoption have been real options for children. Due to the HIV epidemic in the late 1990s, large numbers of children were orphaned and needed immediate care. Institutional care was the only option available for these children, and the practice of institutionalizing children as a primary care option has remained in effect for Ethiopia, even up to the present day. The only other viable option for children needing families in Ethiopia at that time was through intercountry adoption (ICA).

Intercountry adoption

The history and evolution of ICA in Ethiopia is not well documented. The legal basis for formal ICA was created after the first Civil Code of Ethiopia was ratified in 1961; chapter 11 of the entire civil code is devoted to adoption. Formal adoption is said to have been started locally by missionaries that were given permission to take in orphaned children that had come under their care during their mission activities (Alemu Osman, 2006).

Historically, ICA was rarely an option for children from the mid-1970s to early 1990s when Ethiopia was under Communist rule. The late 1990s saw ICA grow significantly because of a nation-wide orphan crisis following the HIV/AIDS pandemic. The crisis prompted the formation of several NGO-run orphanages that took in children who lost their parents to HIV/AIDS and related illnesses. Orphanages struggled with the huge inflow of children and did not have the option of placing children into local families due to a lack of child welfare infrastructure, as well as a lack of expertise in recruiting and supporting foster families. As a result, ICA became a preferred option since there was great interest from the international community to respond, in some form, to the orphan crisis (Alemu Osman, 2006). The government of Ethiopia required these NGOs to also run programs helping orphaned and vulnerable children in Ethiopia if they wanted to also facilitate ICA. The revenue generated through ICA fees funded new orphanages, which then were filled with children who many times had one or two living parents. While the intentions were good, it also ensured that ICA and the institutionalization of Ethiopian children would remain the first option for children, rather than the last resort as outlined in both Ethiopian and International law.

As a result, Ethiopia became the largest sending country in Africa and became a destination for many internationally adopting families from the USA, Italy, Spain, France, and the Netherlands (ACPF, 2012). The African Child Policy Forum (ACPF) report shows that the total number of ICAs for the whole of Africa for the period between 2002–2010 was 33,434, and Ethiopia was the top sending country with 21,368 adoptions for the same period (ACPF, 2012). The US State Department reported there were 2,511 adoptions out of Ethiopia to the United States for the year 2010 alone. The number steadily reduced after 2010, until a total ban was declared in 2017 (US Department of State, 2019). Growing concerns over unethical practices by orphanages and Adoption Service Providers, weak government oversight, the desire to keep children in their country of origin, and alleged non-compliance by Adoption Service Providers on post-adoption reports are stated as the reasons that led to the ban.

Both the growth and decline of ICA triggered an important discussion in the country as to how best to care for orphaned and vulnerable children domestically. Due to negative media coverage over the last decade, of children who had been internationally adopted from Ethiopia and then experienced abuse and/or neglect at the hands of their adoptive parents, an important question was raised as to what could be done to keep children in their home country. These discussions were rooted in a desire to consider what was in the best interests of Ethiopian children, but also signified an alignment with the UNCRC's article 7 which states that a child has a right to "know and be cared for by his or her parents." In addition, the decline and eventual ban raised a practical question that other countries around the world were asking, as to how a society should respond to the needs of children who no longer have ICA as a care option.

Domestic adoption

Culturally speaking, Ethiopian society has included the practice of adoption informally, as mentioned above. However, legal domestic adoption, as an organized and regulated alternative, became a viable option only over the last decade, with a push for more local options for children requiring alternate forms of care.

As a signatory to the UNCRC and ACRWC, which apply as key legal instruments to guide child welfare practices, the government of Ethiopia accepted the practice of domestic adoption as a viable option. The Family Law of Ethiopia and the Alternative Care Guideline of the Ministry of Women and Children Affairs (previously MOWA) created clear provisions and operational procedures to guide activities of the sector.

Kinship care is the most widely used customary care option for orphaned and vulnerable children in Ethiopia. The Alternative Child Care Guideline lists it as the preferred alternative under community-based care options. A national assessment conducted by FHI360, an international NGO focused on human development, and MOWA on the status of family and community-based care in Ethiopia in 2013 showed that the customary use of kinship care has positive aspects and requires serious considerations in terms of bringing formality into the institution for accountability and ensuring the well-being of children under care. Out of the estimated 4.2 million orphaned and vulnerable children in the country, the majority continue to be supported via kinship arrangements outside of the formal child welfare system. This form of care principally uses local community-based organizations to place children with close or distant relatives. Reunification and Reintegration are also used for children separated from their families for different reasons (Tadele, Ayode, and Kifle, 2013).

In the past, family-based care options, such as foster care and domestic adoption, have been rarely available as alternative care options. Since the adoption of the Alternative Care Guideline in 2009, however, the country has seen meaningful growth of these options. The rise and growth of domestic adoption can be attributed to several factors, including increasing awareness of the importance of family-based care, governmental interventions, and a ban on ICA.

Increased awareness on benefits of family-based care to children

There had been a focus on promoting local care options in response to the proliferation of orphanages and the increasing number of children leaving Ethiopia through ICA. The bigger question was whether this was the only option for children, hence ICA should be considered a measure of last resort as is outlined in the Alternative Child Care Guidelines of the government of Ethiopia (MOWA, 2009). However, there were huge gaps both in identifying and developing local family-based care options, due to lack of awareness. With a global shift to family-based options, as opposed to institutional care, there were concerted efforts to raise awareness in the community and the work force regarding the child welfare system. As a result, most efforts were cascaded to a local level, creating conducive conditions for the development of family-based local options (Tadele, Ayode, and Kifle, 2013).

Government-induced interventions

One of the criteria set forth by the government of Ethiopia during the licensing process of international adoption agencies was to require them to be involved in some form of development or social services activity. As a result, several agencies initiated or supported reunification, reintegration, foster care, and domestic adoption programs in addition to community-based interventions that assisted children in kinship settings. Some agencies did this out of necessity, while other agencies leveraged their expertise in international social services and introduced innovative family-based services that considered the socio-cultural context of the country.

Ban on intercountry adoption

Before the government of Ethiopia temporarily banned ICA in 2016, the number of children leaving the country had been sharply declining from a peak in 2011. The official ban came in April 2017 when the Parliament approved an amendment to the Family Law that prohibited foreign nationals from adopting Ethiopian children. The sharp decrease of ICA over the years, coupled with the ban, created unprecedented demand to create local alternatives for children in orphanages. Children that would otherwise be adopted by foreign nationals were left in the care of orphanages, both those run by the state and private agencies. As a result, the demand for services increased, and so did the interest and investment from several stakeholders.

Foster-to-adopt: the case of Bethany Global

Bethany Global started the first formalized foster care program in Ethiopia in 2009 with the main purpose of de-institutionalizing the care of children by creating new care options. The aim was to place children into Ethiopian families through long-term foster care arrangements. The program commenced in the city of Adama. Following a series of awareness-raising and sensitization workshops, the program was officially started through a partnership between Bethany Global, Adama town Women and Children Affairs Office, and an orphanage caring for orphaned and vulnerable children. Children served through this program came from the local NGO-operated orphanage, while adoptive and foster parents were recruited using faith-based and community-based organizations.

Bethany Global, along with its partners, was the first to introduce and implement formal foster care in Ethiopia. Although foster care was one of the options in the Alternative Child Care Guidelines of the government of Ethiopia (MOWA, 2009), the Guidelines lacked clarity as to how foster care could be operationalized, including much needed legal provisions to facilitate placement. While foster care usually implies temporary placement of children in families, Bethany's strategy was to use foster placement as an intermediary intervention before permanency was ensured through legal domestic adoption (see Figure 4.1).

In the initial stages of program development, Bethany discovered that most of the families that took in children were only interested in either long-term or permanent placement. Families had strong cultural and/or religious convictions for wanting to care for foster and adoptive children permanently. This resulted in the change of both the design and name of the program; hence the foster-to-adopt program was established. The program has now expanded to several cities beyond Adama, including Ethiopia's capital, Addis Ababa. The broader geographic coverage has enabled Bethany Global to not only serve more children but to examine the practicality of the program design in different socio-cultural and religious contexts.

Steps in program implementation

Figure 4.2 outlines the program implementation steps utilized by Bethany Global and each is described in more detail below.

Awareness raising

Kinship care was widely practiced in the community, while foster care was little known or practiced. The concept of taking in biologically unrelated children is even more uncommon. Bethany's approach of awareness raising was centered on the need for children to be raised in families and without the negative effects of institutional care. It also advocated for the need for children, irrespective of their social background, to belong in

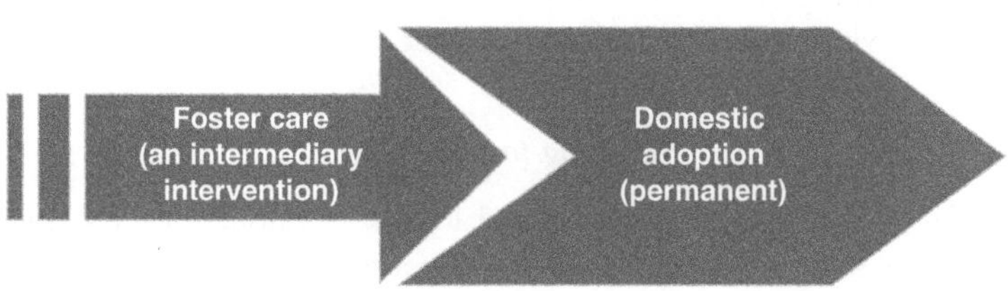

Figure 4.1 Bethany Global's strategy in establishing formal foster care in Ethiopia

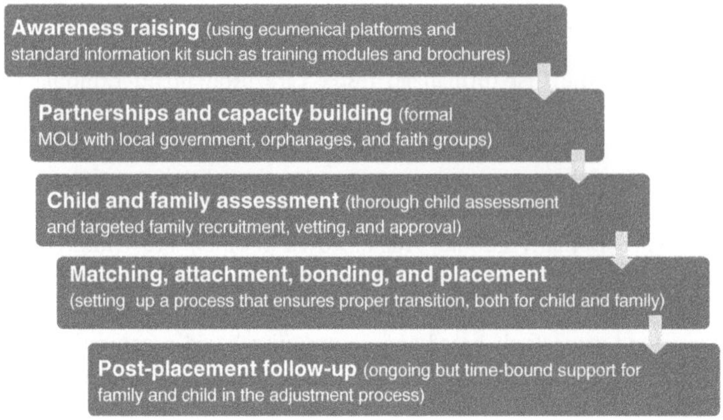

Figure 4.2 Program implementation steps

loving families. This advocacy was both supportive of the government's Alternative Child Care Guidelines (MOWA, 2009), as well as in line with national laws that stated that children have the right to a family (FDRE, 1995). The effort, in this regard, built cultural and religious contexts to raise strong convictions in the community's understanding of foster care and domestic adoption as a new care option.

Partnerships and capacity building

Formal partnership was preceded by thorough awareness raising and training programs for local government, leaders of faith groups, and orphanages. The aim was to bring consensus around program objectives and design. Due to the lack of availability of foster care as a care option, Bethany Global needed to build the capacity of local staff and the social work workforce in various government offices around best practices in child welfare and clinical skills in case management.

Child and family assessment

Introducing a new care option to Ethiopia required learning from countries with strong programs. A process for child and family assessment that met the requirements of, and was informed by, standards of best practice, was one of the key aspects during program development. This included creating child and family assessment processes and tools informed by what was available in countries such as the US, UK, and South Africa. It also meant standardizing assessment processes to make best interest determinations for orphaned and vulnerable children, which was previously non-existent in the child welfare system.

Matching-to-placement

The child welfare system seriously lacked a social work workforce that was equipped with the necessary clinical social work skills to meet the needs of families and children. While the training of case workers and managers focused on clinical skills, the task of taking a child through the process of matching to eventual placement into the new family required establishing a standard process, as well as ensuring the process safeguarded the best interest of the child. Transitioning a child from the institutional care setting to the new family life required the concerted effort of orphanage staff, case workers, the new adoptive parents, and staff of regulatory government agencies. The effort included agreeing on a process that met basic standards and helped the child and the new family make a smooth transition.

Post-placement services

The demand for post-placement service was necessitated by the practical needs of foster/adoptive families and their children and was highly instrumental for the success of the program. Beyond ensuring the permanency of the transition, post-placement services helped create the support system for foster/adoptive families using resources available in the community and beyond. The families remained in the Bethany caseload until legal adoption was finalized in the local courts.

Key aspects of Bethany's role in innovating alternative care

Initiating all care options according to the Alternative Child Care Guidelines has paramount importance in ensuring that Ethiopia is meeting all its commitments related to the UNCRC and ACRWC conventions and domestic laws, which prioritize family-based care for children. Such efforts require innovative intervention, and the following section describes key features of that effort.

Deinstitutionalization of care

Due to the lack of availability of other care options for the reasons discussed above, institutional care was the preferred option in Ethiopia for many years. This can be attributed to several factors. First, the Revised Family Code (FDRE, 2000) and the Alternative Child Care Guidelines (MOWA, 2009) stipulated that only children under the care of child care institutions, meaning orphanages, were eligible for ICA placement (an exception would be relative adoption). Hence, ICA, to some extent, induced the rapid growth of private orphanages, particularly during the peak years from 2008 to 2012. Second, there were misconceptions around the benefits of institutional care, especially for low-income families who thought children received better education, medical care, and clothing in child care institutions.

Hence, moving toward a strategy that prioritized in-country family-based services required deconstructing misconceptions and demonstrating that domestic family-based care options were viable. Before Bethany introduced the foster-to-adopt approach, family-based care options were very limited for children in child care institutions. The creation of new options for the deinstitutionalization of care meant that child care institutions had alternative avenues of serving children with domestic services that uphold the best interest of the children (Tadele, Ayode, and Kifle, 2013).

The sharp increase in the number of placements of children through foster care and domestic adoption through Bethany's program in 2018 (n=129) from the previous year (n=37), after the ban on ICA in April 2017, is evidence of the role these domestic services are playing to meet the needs of younger children whose most likely option in the past was ICA (see Table 4.1). The creation of a broader range of care options not only expands the range of service lines, but also reduces the length of time children stay in child care

Table 4.1 Number of placements by year through Bethany Global Ethiopia office

Year	*2010*	*2011*	*2012*	*2013*	*2014*	*2015*	*2016*	*2017*	*2018*	*Jan–April 2019*
Placements	1	23	8	15	35	35	31	37	129	57

institutions. It is important to note, however, that children with special needs and older children, the principal beneficiaries of ICA prior to the ban, remain underserved after the ban, with few viable domestic services available for them.

Building infrastructure for a new care option

The alternative child welfare landscape was characterized by two different processes. On the one hand, there was and is a huge focus on community-based care options in Ethiopia, which includes preventive kinship-based community responses. On the other hand, there was a disproportionate placement of children through ICA until it was banned in 2017. Reunification services were highly skewed to serving children on the streets and in child care institutions. Nevertheless, both foster care and domestic adoption were barely available as care options and were the missing middle.

Building new services from the ground up required significant investments in creating systems, processes, tools, and building a social work workforce equipped with clinical skills to be able to support children and families in the program. This is especially true when the regulatory government body does not have the legal, administrative, and programmatic means to operationalize services. In such cases, the burden of laying the infrastructure for program implementations rests on the practitioner organization. While legal and policy directives as well as systems are principal responsibilities of the government, creating tools and processes for program implementation and forging close public–private partnership for systems strengthening are best carried out by practitioner organizations with the required capacity. Current tools for child and family assessment, training, home studies, and other clinical services to children and families were created during program development and are widely utilized with the endorsement of the government of Ethiopia.

Partnership with the faith community

The faith community, particularly churches, have been instrumental in the recruitment of local families for the foster-to-adopt program. While there is a need for further study to identify reasons for program failure or success in the Ethiopian context, Bethany's foster-to-adopt program would not have been a success without the involvement of the local church. The role of churches was indispensable for two reasons. First, churches provided the platform to have access to the community; the message on the need for the community to step up its efforts to care for the orphans in its midst was better accepted coming from church/community leaders. Second, families that were recruited through churches had ongoing support systems within the churches and beyond during and after fostering or adoption was completed.

However, the implementation did not come without challenges. Frequent turnover of government officials, lack of streamlined referral pathways for children in need, and lack of awareness on the benefits of family-based care at the grassroots level were significant barriers. It is also a huge burden on one single organization to build specialized service skills from the ground up, and sustaining that effort is an even greater challenge. Most foster and adoptive families have preferences for younger children and the inability to place older children and children with special needs is among the most significant programmatic challenges. These challenges slowed down program implementation and affected the number of placements, in addition to constraining Bethany's ability to meet the needs of children in institutional care

Current state of domestic adoption in Ethiopia

There is a lack of consolidated national statistics on the placements of children through domestic adoption in Ethiopia. Although Bethany Global's domestic adoption program could be considered as the largest both in placement figures and geographic distribution, there are also other actors with smaller operations in different parts of the country. Kidmia Foundation, Positive Action for Development, Bethel Children's Home, and My Father's House are local NGOs involved in domestic adoption. Some government offices such as Bureaus of Women, Children and Youth in Regional States also report facilitating local adoptions without the use of the services of a placement agency. Faith-based organizations and NGOs promoting in-country, family-based programs have organized regular annual events, where Bethany Global is a key player, to promote domestic adoption and continue to build on existing momentum. However, it is hard to be empirically certain about statistics, trends, and the future of domestic adoption except the fact that it has grown significantly in the last few years with more actors involved in implementation.

Conclusions

Orphaned and vulnerable children in Ethiopia have different needs that require diversified interventions. According to what is stipulated in international conventions that Ethiopia has ratified, and the overarching principles stated in the child welfare policies, domestic family-based care is highly prioritized over other forms of care. Children in alternative care settings will have a better chance of enjoying the promises of the conventions with diversified care options.

However, studies have shown that the efforts to lay the infrastructure, coordinate the system, and invest in the development of domestic programs has been slow if not non-existent (Tadele, Ayode, and Kifle, 2013). The government of Ethiopia has created legal and policy frameworks that guide implementation. However, there are limitations in operationalizing services in the Alternative Child Care Guidelines. There is a need for detailed guidelines and, in some cases, revision of current laws to align the delivery of services with the intent to protect the best interest of the child. For instance, there is a need to create provisions for foster care in the Family Code of Ethiopia, which were not included at the last revision in 2000.

The development of alternative care programs requires the concerted effort of various actors. In the case of Bethany Global, it required close partnership between the government, non-profit sector, and the faith community to develop sustainable and impactful programs with strong community ownership. Governments in developing countries are intent on addressing the problems of orphaned and vulnerable children but are constrained by resources, both financial and technical, to develop quality services that are diverse and accessible. NGOs, such as Bethany Global, bring expertise, specialized skills, and resources for development of such programs which could be complemented with close partnership with the government to lay the infrastructure for smooth implementation. Government agencies better serve program development by focusing their efforts on streamlining laws and policies, creating a smooth referral pathway for children in need, and building the capacity of the social work workforce within its structure to be appropriately responsive to the needs of at-risk children. The Bethany Global foster-to-adopt program is a clear demonstration of what can be achieved to serve the needs of children and families when government, civil society, and the faith community work together for the same goal.

The foster-to-adopt program of Bethany Global has been instrumental in bridging the gap and, at times, the disconnect between policy and practice. The following can be said of key learning outcomes.

1. During program implementation, stakeholders have been able to identify vital features of program implementation that are required to create alignment between policy and practice.
2. The program brought to the surface the need for effective and sustained awareness raising at the grassroots level to mobilize families and communities to come around a societal need that can be addressed using local resources.
3. Building the capacity of social work workforce by providing essential skills and tools of implementation is a necessary preparatory step in developing services for children.
4. Putting in place systems, processes, and tools requires close partnership of various actors with clear ownership of the regulatory bodies of the government. This is also a necessary step toward standardizing service quality and delivery across actors and regions.

In conclusion, the current state of the program, as evidenced by the increasing number of placements and wide geographical coverage, speaks to the viability of the program not only to scale but its ability to cater to the needs of children in institutions, thereby serving as a key driver of deinstitutionalization of care in Ethiopia. Considering the key learning outcomes of the program development process, there is a body of knowledge, skills, and expertise transferrable to similar contexts. Bethany Global has been able to leverage the experience from Ethiopia to support and inform service development in countries such as Ghana, Zambia, Haiti, and South Africa. Such could also be the case for many other sub-Saharan countries where the context is closely similar.

Note

1 Amharic is widely spoken across Ethiopia and is the working language of the Federal Government of Ethiopia (FDRE, 1995).

References

African Child Policy Forum. (2012). Africa the frontier for intercountry adoption. ACPF, Addis Ababa, Ethiopia. Retrieved from www.childwatch.uio.no/news/2012/africa—the-new-frontier-for-inter country-adoption-en.pdf

African Commission on Human and People's Rights. (1999). *African charter on the rights and welfare of the child*. Retrieved from www.achpr.org/instruments/child/

Alemu Osman, T. (2006). *The operation of adoption agencies in the context of the best interest of orphan and vulnerable children to alternative care in Ethiopia*. (Unpublished Master's thesis). Addis Ababa University, Addis Ababa, Ethiopia. Retrieved from www.academia.edu/7691763/Inter_Country_Adoption_Ethiopia_By_Tesfaye_Almu

Duressa, A. (2002). *Guddifachaa: Adoption practice in Oromo society with particular reference to the Borana Oromo*. (Unpublished Master's thesis). Addis Ababa University, Addis Ababa, Ethiopia. Retrieved from http://etd.aau.edu.et/bitstream/handle/123456789/3059/Ayalew%20Duressa.pdf?sequence=1&isAllowed=y

Federal Democratic Republic of Ethiopia (FDRE). (1995). *The constitution of the Federal Democratic Republic of Ethiopia*. Retrieved from www.wipo.int/edocs/lexdocs/laws/en/et/et007en.pdf

Federal Democratic Republic of Ethiopia (FDRE). (2000). *The revised family code*. Retrieved from www.refworld.org/pdfid/4c0ccc052.pdf

Federal Democratic Republic of Ethiopia Population Census Commission. (2007). *Summary and statistical report of the 2007 population and housing census*. Retrieved from www.ethiopianreview.com/pdf/001/Cen2007_firstdraft(1).pdf

Ministry of Women's Affairs (MOWA). (2009). *Alternative childcare guidelines on community-based childcare, reunification and reintegration program, foster care, adoption and institutional care service*. Retrieved from https://resourcecentre.savethechildren.net/node/5359/pdf/5359.pdf

Tadele, G., Ayode, D., & Kifle, W. (2013). Assessment of community and family-based alternative child-care services in Ethiopia. FHI360, Durham, NC. Retrieved from www.fhi360.org/sites/default/files/media/documents/Assessment%20of%20Community%20and%20Family-Based%20Alternative%20ChildCare%20Services%20in%20Ethiopia.pdf

United Nations. (1990). *Convention on the rights of the child*. Retrieved from www.ohchr.org/en/professionalinterest/pages/crc.aspx

United States Department of State. (2019). *Adoption statistics*. Retrieved from https://travel.state.gov/content/travel/en/Intercountry-Adoption/adopt_ref/adoption-statistics.html.

5

INTERSECTION OF INFORMATION SCIENCE AND CRISIS PREGNANCY DECISION-MAKING

Rachael Clemens

This chapter explores the information behavior of women surrounding the decision-making and coping processes in relinquishing a child to adoption, and how the nature of this context influences access to and fruitful engagement with information that supports decision-making. Situated in a context of personal crisis, grounding frameworks of human information behavior, coping, and decision-making are presented briefly. Next, the findings from a qualitative and interpretive inquiry into the experience of birthmothers are reviewed (Clemens, 2017). The chapter concludes with suggestions for ways these findings can inform policy and practice in the field of adoption.

Information plays a ubiquitous role in shaping the decisions we make in our everyday lives. The ways we look for information, perceive potential sources of information, engage with information, dismiss information, create information, and share information influence and/or stem from our understanding of the world and our place in it. Throughout my survey of the literature on birthmothers as well as my own research, I have come to conclude that information plays a central role to expectant mothers as they consider and explore options, construct and evaluate versions of future possible selves, and frame their situation in order to move forward. But this relationship with information is complex, fluid, and extremely personal within a context of crisis pregnancy and child relinquishment decision-making and coping. The voices of birthmothers in this study describe their experience with child relinquishment as steeped in secrecy and shame; they also characterize information sources as similarly tinged and filtered through the same stigma. Information is scarce and involves significant levels of trust on the part of expectant and birthmothers. Navigating unfamiliar information pathways to support such an emotional and deeply personal decision impacts a woman's means to explore and critically assess options surrounding decisions about an unintended pregnancy. Lack of role models, relevant information, and support systems contribute to feelings of uncertainty, vulnerability, and powerlessness for women who make and live with a decision to relinquish their child for adoption. The power dynamic surrounding information access and trustworthiness as expressed in the voices of birthmothers in this study is neither new nor unique; researchers at the Evan B. Donaldson Adoption Institute reported a similar finding that helped to prompt this research:

> Principally because adoption is not well understood by the public generally, most women struggling to make decisions about unplanned pregnancies do not have accurate information with which to make an informed choice about whether this is a reasonable option for them.
>
> *(Smith, 2007, p. 5)*

Frameworks

Human information behavior has emerged as an umbrella framework (Savolainen, 2007) in the world of information and library science, encompassing research surrounding "the totality of human behavior in relation to sources and channels of information, including both active and passive information seeking and information use" (Wilson, 2000, p. 49). Through life experience we become familiar with the processes involved in making everyday decisions, and generally develop a confidence in gathering information with which to make satisfying choices. Yet, occasionally, we might find ourselves confronted with a situation that shatters or confounds our established means of finding and using information to make a decision. Additionally, although gathering new information can often clarify a situation, uncover reasonable options, or offer hope for a positive resolution of a crisis, it could also add to the uncertainty and stress of the response process due to its unavailability, complexity, or overwhelming nature.

Research in the area of coping examines human responses to threatening situations at both the cognitive and behavioral levels. Folkman & Lazarus (1988) identify a two-stage process in mediating or navigating a stressful incident. First, a cognitive appraisal raises one's awareness of the existence, nature, and scale of a "threat." Second, a process of coping, managing the threat, is set in motion. The way a person chooses (albeit not necessarily overtly) to address and deal with such a stressful and threatening environment may be influenced by several factors, including the perception of control. If the person senses the possibility of control or change in the situation, they might be more likely to employ problem-focused coping reactions and strategies. Yet if they feel the impending threat is completely outside their ability to influence or control, their coping response may be focused on controlling emotions and tempering the unpleasant feelings of stress (Folkman & Lazarus, 1985). Individuals facing a personal crisis may experience cognitive difficulties (Sniezek, Wilkins, Wadlington, & Baumann, 2002) or find themselves vulnerable to some form of information poverty by exhibiting behavior fueled by secrecy, deception, and risk-taking (Chatman, 1996).

These complex and overwhelming issues regarding information behaviors, crisis, and coping are clearly evident in the nature of child relinquishment to adoption; birthmothers routinely identify the experience of surrendering a child to adoption as the single most stressful event in their lives (Mantecon, 1994; Stiffler, 1991; Winkler & van Keppel, 1984). Deciding to place a child for adoption has immense and life-long consequences for both mother and child (Jones, 2004; Lauderdale & Boyle, 1994; Pugh, 2010). Uncertainty regarding options, outcomes, trustworthiness of information, and even one's confidence in making such a decision are compounded by the pressure of having a nine-month (or less) time deadline. Information pathways relating to adoption plans, alternatives, resources, and support are usually unfamiliar and abstract to the general population (Madden, Ryan, Aguiniga, & Crawford, 2016); thus, it is not surprising that the greatest barrier to adoption-related services for birthmothers is reported to be lack of knowledge (Conlon, 2005). Defensive responses to stress surrounding a birthmother's situation, through denial, fantasy, and repression, are also commonly reported (Rynearson, 1982).

Another factor in this crisis context that may stretch it beyond the boundaries of everyday life relates to social norms, stigma, and shame due to the lingering legacy of mystery and prejudice that continues to characterize relinquishing a child to adoption (March, 2014). The parental loss that a birthmother experiences is often socially unacknowledged, and the devastating grief has life-long repercussions (Stiffler, 1991). Intentional concealment (secrecy) and outright deception surrounding child relinquishment can significantly impact the opportunities for information-gathering and evaluation as a woman contemplates such a decision. The "conspiracy of silence" (Lifton, 1994), as reflected in adoption legislation and practice in the 20th century, has been decreasing, yet still shields information pathways from transparency and access (Winkler, Brown, van Keppel, & Blanchard, 1988).

Methods

The participants or key informants in this study (Clemens, 2017) were women who voluntarily relinquished a child for adoption between 2000 and 2015, and who were willing and able to share their experience in light of their decision-making, coping, and information behavior. Using an Interpretative Phenomenological Analysis (IPA) study design, a purposeful sample of eight birthmothers from across the US participated in face-to-face, semi-structured interviews about their own lived experiences. Generally speaking, the phenomenological approach to inquiry aims to reveal the common threads of meaning attributed to a phenomenon as ascribed by those who have lived through the experience. A fairly recent incarnation of the interpretive or hermeneutic branch of phenomenology, IPA offers guidance in designing studies into how people make sense of major and transformative life experiences, matters that are of *existential import* to the participant (Eatough & Smith, 2008; Smith, 2011). This aim aligns well with the context and sensitive nature of the phenomenon in this study, the birthmother experience.

Interview questions and prompts were developed to elicit responses to the overarching research topic: the birthmothers' experience of decision-making and coping to be analyzed through the lens of information behavior. The interview schedule was developed around the loose chronological process of the decision-making journey: (1) *decision-making pre-adoption*; (2) *adoption placement event*; (3) *post-adoption phase*. However, in keeping with the inductive epistemology of IPA, the interview guide was treated as a flexible tool to help facilitate each participant's ability to tell her own story in her own words. Participants were also invited to give the researcher a *guided tour* of any material relating to the adoption experience that she keeps and what it means to her (e.g. legal documents, photographs, diaries, or other artifacts relating to the adoption).

Analysis of all collected data followed IPA protocol as outlined in Smith, Flowers, and Larkin (2009). Initially each interview transcript was addressed separately through a process of deep engagement in order to yield a within-case thematic structure that represented the unique experiential account articulated by the birthmother, in keeping with the idiographic nature of IPA. Next, the researcher looked for patterns across cases to identify cross-case emergent themes. The specific steps in analyzing each interview were: (1) reading and re-reading the transcript multiple times; (2) initial noting of descriptive comments, linguistic comments, and conceptual comments; (3) developing emergent codes; and (4) searching for connections across emergent codes to develop overarching themes.

Table 5.1 provides a brief overview of the eight birthmothers, from six different states, who participated in the study. Coincidentally, all participants are engaged in some form of open adoption, meaning they participated in selecting adoptive parents and have varying levels of ongoing contact with the adoptive family and the child(ren) they relinquished.

Table 5.1 Overview of participants

Pseudonym	*Age at interview (2015–2016)*	*Year of child's birth*	*Age of child at interview*	*Adoption description and contact*
Laurel	27	2009	6 years, daughter	* Open and identified, child lives in same state; frequent contact via social media, phone; regular meetings
Liz	25	2012	3 years, daughter	Open and identified, child lives in another state; frequent contact via social media, phone, Skype; occasional meetings
May	27	2008	7 years, son	Open and identified, child lives in another state; regular contact via phone, Skype; occasional meetings
Robin	34	2011	4 years, (twins) sons	Open and identified, children live in same state; regular contact through email, phone, pictures; regular meetings
Stella	20	2001	4 years, daughter	Open and identified, child lives in another state; frequent contact via social media, phone; occasional meetings
Jenny	32	2014	18 mos, (twins) sons	Open and identified, children live nearby, in same state; regular contact via phone; frequent meetings
Becky	31	2006	9 years, daughter	Open and identified, child lives in different state; regular contact via phone, email; regular meetings
Bronwyn	29	2003	12 years, daughter	Semi-open, unidentified initially but now identified, child lives in same state; regular contact via email and social media; no ongoing meetings

*Identified means full identifying information is shared between birthmother and adoptive family; this includes full name, address, phone, email, and social media.

Findings

Several themes arose across all the participating birthmothers' reflections on their experiences with adoption. These include: (1) envisioning future possible selves, pre-adoption; (2) envisioning future possible selves, post-adoption; (3) trading of trust and power; (4) developing trust in information providers; and (5) negotiating trust with the adoptive parents. Information behavior is evident through each of these processes. These themes help us better understand the birthmothers' relationships with information during their decision-making and coping journeys, but they are also iterative and non-linear as evidenced by the meaning birthmothers continue to make of the experience.

Envisioning future possible selves, pre-adoption

Acts of self-reflection and envisioning alternative futures were evident in all participants' experiences, both in their immediate response to the unintended pregnancy and during subsequent years post-adoption.

> I was mad at the situation, thinking different things, thinking abortion, thinking adoption, thinking maybe I can do this on my own, but all at once. I wanted someone else's opinion, so I talked to family and also friends about opinion-based *[sic]*. What do you think I should do, and how do you think I should even start thinking about this stuff? My dad would just say, "Think about not only your heart choices but think about the practical choices of every day. How are you going to provide for them? Have you literally sat down and written down what your life would be like on this amount of money that you'd make, this amount of support, living probably in the system indefinitely?" I mean things like that. He helped me really see the practical side, and I'm grateful for that.
>
> *(Robin)*

> I started to ask … what's my five-year plan – what do I see myself, like, where do I see myself? What do I think I'll miss out on if I have this child or what will I gain if I give it up for adoption, those kind of things, but really thinking about in the future. It's hard to think in the future in that situation, but if you can at all, it's helpful.
>
> *(May)*

The theory of *possible selves* (Markus & Nurius, 1986) describes this phenomenon as conceptions of ourselves in future states, imagined visions of one's self in the future. An individual contemplates representations of who she might become in the future; these may be positive (hoped-for selves) or negative (feared selves). These possible selves provide a context for evaluating the current self and situation and may provide direction for motivation, decision-making, and behavior. Information utilized in generating possible selves is internal (attitudes, beliefs, biases, and self-concept) as well as external (cultural and social contexts). We understand experiences and interactions as being shared with other people (Bruner, 1986); thus, possible selves derive their meaning from social context and inter-subjectivity (Erikson, 2007).

Across the board, participants were initially overcome with emotion and disbelief upon learning of the pregnancy. Robin recalls full-fledged denial at the news, demanding additional tests for confirmation. May felt embarrassment and shame, "wanting everything to just go away." Bronwyn avoided confronting the possibility of pregnancy until more than halfway through the term; when it was confirmed, she admits feeling as though her life was over. Yet, after a period of processing and living with the news, each woman began to assess the situation in light of her circumstance.

Participants recalled difficulty in pulling themselves out of denial and into a frame of mind where they could consider the future. This difficulty corresponds to the assessment of the severity of the negative event stage described in crisis decision theory (Sweeny, 2008); participants in this study perceived the unintended pregnancy news as overwhelming, a negative life event of significant magnitude. Various prompts in their lives motivated participants to shift into conscious consideration of possible outcomes or *possible selves*. Time was the most obvious prompt; the nature of pregnancy is bounded by a specific time frame with an equally imminent decision-making time frame. Participants were also prompted to think about their future by those in whom they confided, often by friends and family, and sometimes by the information resources they consulted, such as an adoption professional or information found through Internet searches.

Taking stock and assessing where she was in life, each participant identified a veritable list of qualifiers by which to judge whether or not she could see herself successfully parenting the child(ren). Each participant envisioned a future as a mother to her unborn child(ren) and judged the probability of a positive outcome based on her current self. "Possible selves furnish criteria against which outcomes are evaluated" (Markus & Nurius, 1986, p. 956). The list of qualifiers was virtually the same for all cases: financial status and prospects for near-future stability; social support including biological father, immediate family, and friends; emotional and mental stability; comparison between her own childhood and prospective upbringing of this child; and co-crisis and extenuating circumstances that complicated the situation.

As each participant began to try on different responses and outcomes relating to the pregnancy, she engaged in some form of information-seeking behavior. May visited a Planned Parenthood facility to collect information on abortion options and then a crisis pregnancy agency to explore parenting and adoption possibilities. Jenny sought out a pregnancy counselor for information on options to support both a parenting decision and an adoption decision. She credits the nonjudgmental support of the social worker as she explored these two very different possible selves. She found the extensive and detailed information to be helpful as she crafted mental depictions of her choices; the resulting vivid portrayals of the possible future selves helped her make an informed decision.

In addition to information provided directly by the adoption professionals (usually social workers), participants consulted with other birthmothers (women who had previously relinquished a child to adoption) in the search for information with which to construct a birthmother version of a future self. Direct and unmediated access to women who had already placed a child for adoption was noted in all cases as beneficial and important in learning about what the future *could* look like (for better or worse).

Other birthmothers were a vital source of information for participants as they considered an adoption decision. They were able to provide authentic answers to the question, *What is the experience going to be like*? While each situation is different and surrounded with unique complexities, the voices of women who have already begun a journey through adoption can be a rich source of inspiration (both positive and cautionary) for decision-makers as they construct and consider their own possible selves.

Generating possible selves to aid in decision-making and coping with the pregnancy crisis is a theme apparent across all cases. Information behavior (search, evaluation, use, etc.) directly supports this iterative activity and involves both internal resources (self-reflection and imagining different futures) and external information sources. As participants solidified an adoption decision and began to refine the birthmother version of their future selves, information-gathering efforts focused exclusively on the adoption pathway. Participants purposefully restricted or stopped other information search activities and moved into a space of intentional avoidance and insulation. Restricting information engagement to sources focused solely on adoption planning allowed women to shelter their decision from conflicting information and opinions.

Efforts to narrow information searching and engagement to sources supporting an adoption decision may be interpreted as a coping strategy. Purposeful pruning of information sources to those that nurture the adoption choice follows the earlier flurry of information-gathering about any and all options. Limiting information and intentionally avoiding conflicting information serve a self-protective function and as a way of reducing post-decisional conflict (Fischer, Fischer, Weiswelier, & Frey, 2010). Participants welcomed a safe haven from the emotional storm of information engagement and decision-making; once the decision to move forward with relinquishment is reached, participants focus on information to aid in clarifying the adoption plan. Women sought information to nurture a future self as birthmother and shifted attention to resources that would help them reach that outcome. At this point, participants began to focus on the details of the adoption process, such as the level of openness they desired, selecting an adoptive family, contact agreements, birth planning, and timing.

Envisioning future possible selves, post-adoption

> I was trying to find information about what it was like to be a birthmom. And there was, like, nothing. There are so many blogs and stories of what adoptive couples experience, but really not much about what birthmoms experience. There's no real kind of playbook out there for how to go about any of it. So that's what makes it really kind of challenging.
>
> *(Laurel)*

In the years since Laurel placed her son in an open adoption, she continues to re-envision and redesign her future self in the role of "birthmother in an open adoption"; she actively seeks information to help construct and figure out what that can/should look like. In the quotation above, she describes her disappointment with the scarcity of information, role models, and research that might help her further develop the open and ongoing relationship she has with the adoptive family and her son.

While the decision-making process toward relinquishment is steeped in intense emotions, the post-adoption years are also laden with uncertainty and emotional decisions. All birthmothers in this study participate in some kind of open adoption that includes varying degrees of communication and information exchange with the child(ren) and adoptive families. Open adoption involves more choices and decisions for a birthmother in subsequent years as she navigates the relationship with the child, the adoptive family, and her own identity as a birthmother. Thus, the crafting and refining of the self as a birthmother remains a work in progress; as time passes and the open adoption relationship progresses, women continue to envision future possible selves and seek information for support. Engagement with information in this context is prompted by different life situations that arise, a desire for guidance or insight, and often a need for community with other people involved in adoption.

Boundaries within the open adoption dynamic become a frequent cause of concern for birthmothers in terms of what their role/identity should look like, and what is appropriate and comfortable for everyone. The lack of information and exemplars on this front leaves women to figure things out without benefit of significant and evidence-based resources. This desire for information and best practices for maintaining and building a strong and positive open adoption relationship is heard clearly across the sample. Birthmothers are left to imagine and cautiously reconstruct models of their possible future selves in a vacuum, relying on the trust they place in the adoptive family's information and intentions.

May notes disappointment that her vision for the open adoption, the possible self she crafted during the decision-making process and even in the early days of the adoption, is not coming to fruition. Now, seven years later, she must recreate that image from a position of powerlessness and with almost no guidance to inform her hopes for the future.

> I just think that it's not going to be what I envisioned as an open adoption because of the couple that I chose. That came to light afterwards. I just wish that I had been able to build a relationship or gone about the process sooner, that I could have picked someone that I felt more comfortable with or that was just more like me. Maybe if we had similar interests that we could connect with. Because now I have this couple that I really have nothing in common with, and I'm trying to build a relationship with, other than the fact that they are raising the child that I gave up for adoption.
>
> *(May)*

Trading of trust and power

> In a lot of ways, I was scared to ask for different things or come off as demanding. It's kind of like this whole *trading of trust*. You're going into it, they're just really trusting and hoping that you're going to give them a child, but then afterwards you are really just trusting and hoping that they don't cut off ties. So it was always just trying to get that balance of asking for things that you wanted but at the same time not making them feel like you are being demanding or you're asking too much.
>
> *(Laurel)*

The dynamics of power and trust are prevalent across all cases in this study. Laurel's quotation above exemplifies the fragility and uncertainty of trust surrounding the information and intentions conveyed by others involved in the adoption. In this example, Laurel characterizes the precarious balance of power between herself as a birthmother and the adoptive couple; she recognizes the trust that the prospective parents are investing in her before the adoption event, while in the same breath she expresses her fear about the level of trust she must commit related to ongoing contact post-adoption. (Laurel's home state offers no legal protection to birthparents in terms of an enforceable contact agreement.) This theme of *trading of trust* manifests in many forms across cases in this study and at varying points both pre- and post-adoption. There are both positive and negative experiences surrounding trust as participants engage with information and information providers such as adoption agencies, social workers, and prospective adoptive couples before and following the adoption event. Trust becomes an even more pronounced theme in the context of open adoption, specifically the ongoing relationship between birthmother and adoptive family. Examples from the data offered in this section highlight the vulnerability participants experience when making a determination to trust information and other people; also presented are examples of reassurance and empowerment that participants recall when an information source lives up to the outlay of trust.

Developing trust in information providers

In making decisions about adoption, Robin relied on the information provided by the adoption agency she selected; she placed her trust in the authenticity and accuracy of this information.

> In choosing this adoption agency, what made a difference was the fact that they offered post-adoption counseling, and they told me in writing, in the brochure, they told me verbally about birthparent counseling. But that never happened. And I'm very – to this day, I'm very mad about that. The director said that she was sorry but they had some staffing changes. No birthmother should ever go through this without counseling, ever.
>
> *(Robin)*

In the end, Robin's trust in the information supplied by the adoption agency and social worker was misplaced, and the breakdown in services promised by the agency had a significant (and negative) impact on Robin's experience. Although she does not regret the adoption decision, she recalls her vulnerability and distress at learning the information was ultimately untrustworthy. Because of her financial situation and emotional fragility, Robin felt she had no recourse in securing professional help to cope with the grief she was experiencing. She urges other women contemplating an adoption plan to carefully scrutinize and hold agencies accountable for the services they advertise: "Nail down deadlines, write emails, have a paper trail." May describes similar feelings of abandonment following the adoption event: "I felt obsolete after my pregnancy." The attentiveness and promises of emotional support from adoption professionals and adoptive parents that expectant mothers experience often disappear with the legal relinquishment of the child; the shift in power is complete.

Bronwyn points to the trust a woman relinquishes to an adoption agency in its role as initial gatekeeper of information about prospective adoptive families. "With an agency, there are screenings and home studies and you would hope that everybody they choose, that they let through to adopt, that they're great people." Expectant mothers rely on adoption professionals to vet prospective adoptive families and the information they provide about themselves and their desires surrounding an adoption plan. But ultimately, in the midst of overwhelming emotions and uncertainty, women must use their own judgment in determining the trustworthiness of the information and intentions of prospective adoptive families. This information is particularly vital when women pursue an open adoption and make decisions based upon shared visions for the future. Depending upon state law, birthparents might or might not have any legal recourse when open adoption agreements and expectations fall through.

Amid examples of misplaced trust, participants also expressed occasions and layers of trust that have fulfilled and empowered their experience with adoption. Jenny recalls the breadth and depth of information she received through the adoption agency.

> The pregnancy counselor, she went over everything with me, explained every little detail about how it works and how it doesn't work. Even when it came time to go to court to sign papers, she went over everything with me beforehand, even showed me samples of the papers I was going to have to sign. It was everything, down to the last detail, to make sure I completely 100 percent understood what I was doing.

Jenny speaks with confidence about the preparation and information the social worker provided as she began considering adoption for her twin boys. In her case, the adoption professional made extensive efforts to educate Jenny about the process, options, and legal aspects of adoption, far beyond merely providing information. This knowledge empowered Jenny in her decision-making; the trust she placed in the information and the expertise of the social worker has been fulfilled.

Negotiating trust with the adoptive parents

As a theme, trading of trust and power is most pronounced as participants navigate their ongoing relationship with the adoptive family, in these cases most directly with the adoptive mother. Jenny characterizes the emotions and dynamics she experiences surrounding her frequent and regular visits with her twin boys.

> That's the hard thing I guess, saying goodbye over and over and over again because you never know if it's the last time. I never know. I could say goodbye, and she could call me 10 minutes later and say, "Well, you know, you said this at the visit, and I didn't like it … so you're not seeing them again." It's really hard to have that hanging over your head, that anytime I go see them, anytime I talk to them or any picture I get could be the last … you just don't know. That's rough, that's really rough. There's nothing that compares to that feeling. … I feel like if I do one thing wrong, she's going to close the adoption because she can. It's hard, it's kind of like you're walking around on eggshells all the time.

The open and ongoing relationship with her twin boys and the adoptive parents is extremely important to Jenny; open adoption was a significant factor in her decision to choose adoption. She describes the close ties and support she continues to experience with the adoptive couple; however, the undercurrent of uncertainty is a constant reminder of her position of vulnerability. Jenny experiences her situation as one of perpetual dependence on trust; as her state does not recognize post-adoption contact agreements, power in terms of the open adoption relationship resides completely with the adoptive parents. Becky uses the same analogy to describe the precarious nature of ongoing contact with her daughter's adoptive family: "Since the adoptive parents control everything now, I feel like I'm walking on eggshells." Even though Becky's post-adoption contact agreement is legally binding in her state, she still experiences a sense of vulnerability and powerlessness in the relationship.

Evaluating information and determining trustworthiness are fundamental tenets of the decision-making process in any circumstance. In the emotional and high stakes context of an adoption decision, women often feel themselves in a position of vulnerability, with few guarantees about the trustworthiness of information and other people. Participants in this study experience a perpetual dependence on trust – certainly during the information-gathering and decision-making phase, but especially in terms of the open adoption arrangements. Becky suggests that this overall sense of powerlessness is propagated by a culture of shame and stigma.

> The shame of getting pregnant foreshadows this whole thing, and women feel like they don't have any rights to make decisions for themselves. The shame of getting pregnant, the shame of not having the support, of having bad circumstances, you have this horrible self-esteem. That's the hardest thing, I think, not feeling like you're worth enough to demand what you need to make it work and to put yourself back together afterwards. You don't feel worthy of this child.

Across the experiences of participants in this study, we see the immense levels of trust that women place in the providers of information. Trust extends from the legitimacy and fullness of information a woman encounters relating to her options (including information encountered online or through other sources) to the reliability of the adoption professionals with whom birthmothers engage. The theme of trust and trading of trust is clear regarding the authenticity of the information prospective adoptive parents provide; with an open adoption plan, birthmothers must continue to trust the adoptive family to adhere to the agreed-upon arrangements for ongoing contact.

Implications for adoption research and practice

Among all cases in this study, adoption professionals played an enormous role in providing and explaining a wide variety of types of information as women faced an unintended pregnancy. In each interview the adoption professional appears as a direct provider and information conduit for a variety of information needs. From counseling options, to presenting prospective adoptive families to birthmothers, to explaining legal rights, the adoption professional was the central hub for much of the information women used throughout the relinquishment process. The significance of this role is also well documented in the literature (Johnson & Faasse, 2012; Smith, 2007).

Overwhelmingly, participants wanted informed guides and role models for the future as they made an adoption plan. Laurel clarifies this information need: "There's no real kind of playbook out there for how to go about any of it. So that's what makes it really kind of challenging." Participants were disappointed at the scarcity of information resources relevant to their situation – both in online and print formats. Content was particularly sparse with regard to open adoption relationships (e.g., best practices for preparing and developing post-adoption contact agreements; launching and maintaining a positive open adoption relationship). Support groups played an important role for birthmothers as they attempted to mitigate the lack of available information and meet some of their information needs through adoption communities (both online and in-person). Likewise, women who had already placed a child for adoption were key informants for participants in the decision-making processes. Finally, a lack of substantive, consistent, ongoing, and free professional counseling was detrimental to the emotional well-being of several participants, especially post-adoption. Table 5.2 recounts the unresolved information and support needs expressed by participants.

A recent report from the Donaldson Adoption Institute (Madden, Ryan, Aguiniga, & Crawford, 2016) also identifies the lack of uniformity across agencies, adoption professionals, and states regarding the information presented to women who are considering relinquishing a child to adoption. Several recommendations to improve adoption practice are offered in the report that relate directly to the findings from this research study. These include recommendations for adoption professionals to: (1) develop and adopt best-practice guidelines for the provision of options counseling; (2) develop and disseminate evidence-based written materials about options; (3) increase expectant parents' access to support groups and other parents; and (4) develop best-practice guidelines for therapeutic work with expectant parents.

These recommendations for adoption professionals are clearly echoed in the information needs expressed by participants in this study. While many women participating in this study spoke highly of the information and support they received from adoption professionals, participants identified specific gaps and unresolved information needs that mirror the recommendations from the Donaldson Adoption Institute report (Madden, Ryan, Aguiniga, & Crawford, 2016).

An additional consideration is that the desire for opportunities to engage with other people who "get it" is fierce; adoption support groups, whether in-person or online, are often the only

Table 5.2 Unresolved information and support needs

Emotional support • Non-existent or insufficient grief counseling • Bare-boned and outdated online support forums • Lack of community in terms of support for birthmothers
Easy and direct contact with other birthmothers to learn from their experiences (the good, the bad, and the ugly)
What is the birthmother experience going to be like over a lifetime?
What is a good family? How to determine if a prospective adoptive family will be the right fit for the type of adoption I want?
Examples and/or role models for open adoption relationships
Guidance and continuing support to launch and develop a successful open relationship with the child and adoptive family

resource birthmothers perceive as available, free, and relevant following the adoption event. These communities serve a vital role in providing women a safe space to seek and share information. Adoption professionals can enhance their role as information providers and conduits by promoting such opportunities for women to connect with other birthmothers during both the decision-making phase and in the years and decades following the relinquishment and adoption events. As more birthfathers engage in pre- and post-adoption decisions and relationships, adoption professionals could increase support for these often-unheard voices by facilitating similar and more inclusive opportunities for dialog.

Conclusion

The voices of birthmothers in the study described here clearly articulate specific information needs during the decision-making process leading up to the adoption event as well as ongoing and yet unresolved information needs post-adoption. These needs include (1) options counseling surrounding an unintended pregnancy; (2) extensive and ongoing emotional support; (3) legal information and counsel; and (4) preparation and ongoing support for maintaining an open adoption. Participants characterized the information landscape through which they tried (and continue to try) to identify supporting information as sparse, difficult to navigate, and often irrelevant to their situation-specific needs. The information needs identified in this study correlate very closely with the findings from a recent, large-scale, mixed-methods study into the options counseling experiences of expectant mothers and adoption professionals (Madden, Ryan, Aguiniga, & Crawford, 2016).

The themes of this study highlight the important role of sustained and ongoing information and communication support for the broader adoption kinship network as well, including the biological extended family of the child (birthfather, birthfather's extended family, maternal grandparents, and siblings), as well as members of the extended adoptive family. Cultivating safe spaces for members of the adoption kinship network to share and explore information could offer tremendous and authentic opportunities for information exchange and first-hand insight into what is working or not working for other people similarly affected by adoption.

References

Bruner, J. S. (1986). *Actual minds, possible worlds.* Cambridge, MA: Harvard University Press.

Chatman, E. A. (1996). The impoverished life-world of outsiders. *Journals of the American Society for Information Science, 47*(3), 193–206.

Clemens, R. A. (2017). *Human information behavior, coping, and decision-making in the context of a personal crisis: An interpretative phenomenological analysis of the voices of birthmothers on relinquishing a child for adoption* (Doctoral dissertation). Retrieved from Proquest Dissertations & Theses Global (Order No. 10285384).

Conlon, C. (2005). *Mixed methods research of crisis pregnancy counseling and support services.* Dublin: Crisis Pregnancy Agency. Retrieved from www.lenus.ie/handle/10147/305318

Eatough, V., & Smith, J. (2008). Interpretative phenomenological analysis. In C. Willig & W. Stainton-Rogers (Eds.), *The SAGE handbook of qualitative research in psychology* (pp. 179–195). London, England: SAGE Publications Ltd. doi:libproxy.lib.unc.edu/10.4135/9781848607927.n11

Erikson, M. G. (2007). The meaning of the future: Toward a more specific definition of possible selves. *Review of General Psychology, 11*(4), 348–358. doi:10.1037/1089-2680.11.4.348

Fischer, P., Fischer, J., Weiswelier, S., & Frey, D. (2010). Selective exposure to information: How different modes of decision making affect subsequent confirmatory information processing. *British Journal of Social Psychology, 49*, 871–881. doi:10.1348/014466610X499668

Folkman, S., & Lazarus, R. S. (1985). If it changes it must be a process: A study of emotion and coping during three stages of a college examination. *Journal of Personality and Social Psychology, 48*, 150–170.

Folkman, S., & Lazarus, R. S. (1988). Ways of coping questionnaire, research edition. Retrieved from Mental Measurements Yearbook database.

Johnson, C., & Faasse, K. (2012). Birthparent counseling in policy and practice. *Adoption Advocate, 45*, 1–10. Retrieved from www.adoptioncouncil.org/publications/2012/03/adoption-advocate-no-45

Jones, K. L. (2004). *Birthmothers' experiences of open and closed adoption* (Master's thesis). Retrieved from ProQuest Dissertations and Theses. (Order No. MQ98972).

Lauderdale, J. L., & Boyle, J. S. (1994). Infant relinquishment through adoption. *IMAGE: Journal of Nursing Scholarship, 26*(3), 213–217.

Lifton, B. J. (1994). *Journey of the adopted self: A quest for wholeness.* New York, NY: Basic Books.

Madden, E., Ryan, S., Aguiniga, D., & Crawford, M. (2016). *Understanding options counseling experiences in adoption: A quantitative analysis of first/birth parents and professionals.* Retrieved from www.adoptioninstitute.org/wp-content/uploads/2016/11/Understanding-Options-Counseling-Experiences-in-Adoption-Phase-One-Report.pdf

Mantecon, V. H. (1994). *Re-membering broken bonds: An in-depth exploration of the phenomenology of the experience of child-surrender* (Doctoral dissertation). Available from ProQuest Dissertations and Theses database. (UMI No. LD03198).

March, K. (2014). Birth mother grief and the challenge of adoption reunion contact. *American Journal of Orthopsychiatry, 84*(4), 409–419. doi:10.1037/ort0000013

Markus, H., & Nurius, P. (1986). Possible selves. *American Psychologist, 41*(9), 954–969.

Pugh, A. (2010). *Adoption is an option: A personal narrative* (Master's thesis). Retrieved from ProQuest Dissertations and Theses database. (Order No. 1486381).

Rynearson, E. K. (1982). Relinquishment and its maternal complications: A preliminary study. *American Journal of Psychiatry, 139*(3), 338–340.

Savolainen, R. (2007). Information behavior and information practice: Reviewing the "umbrella concepts" of information-seeking studies. *Library Quarterly, 77*(2), 109–132.

Smith, J. A. (2011). Evaluating the contribution of interpretative phenomenological analysis. *Health Psychology Review, 5*(1), 9–27. doi:10.1080/17437199.2010.510659

Smith, J. A., Flowers, P., & Larkin, M. (2009). *Interpretative phenomenological analysis: Theory, method and research.* London: SAGE Publications Ltd.

Smith, S. (2007). *Safeguarding the rights and well-being of birthparents in the adoption process.* (White paper). New York, NY: Evan B. Donaldson Adoption Institute.

Sniezek, J. A., Wilkins, D. C., Wadlington, P. L., & Baumann, M. R. (2002). Training for crisis decision-making: Psychological issues and computer-based solutions. *Journal of Management Information Systems, 18*(4), 147–168.

Stiffler, L. H. (1991). Adoption's impact on birthmothers: "Can a mother forget her child?". *Journal of Psychology and Christianity*, *10*(3), 249–259.

Sweeny, K. (2008). Crisis decision theory: Decisions in the face of negative events. *Psychological Bulletin*, *134*(1), 61–76. doi:10.1037/0033-2909.134.1.61

Wilson, T. D. (2000). Human information behavior. *Informing Science*, *3*(2), 49–55.

Winkler, R. C., Brown, D. W., van Keppel, M., & Blanchard, A. (1988). *Clinical practice in adoption*. New York, NY: Pergamon Press.

Winkler, R. C., & van Keppel, M. (1984). *Relinquishing mothers in adoption: Their long-term adjustment*. Melbourne: Institute of Family Studies.

6

RESPECTING CHILDREN'S RELATIONSHIPS AND IDENTITIES IN ADOPTION

Elsbeth Neil and Mary Beek

For the large majority of children, adoption confers lifelong relationships and a sense of belonging in the adoptive family. But adoption also involves the legal severance of the child from the birth family and often the loss of key relationships with birth family members and others who have had important roles in the child's life. With this comes the loss of the child's identity as a member of their birth family community. Each of these losses can have lifelong impact. This chapter will further explore these losses and ways in which they might be eased. It is written from the perspective of the English child care system, but it is suggested that issues of relationships and identity in adoption are universal, affecting adopted children and adults across all contexts and cultures.

The purpose and context of adoption varies across legal jurisdictions, and within states and countries its practice has varied over time. The current situation in England is that adoption is mostly used for children in foster care who cannot return to their families. This practice of adoption for children in care without parents' consent is firmly established and has been encouraged by successive governments, though not without attracting controversy (Featherstone, Gupta, and Mills, 2018; Kirton, 2013). Most children are adopted under the age of five and are placed in families previously unknown to them (Department for Education, 2018). Permanency is the underpinning framework for child care social work, the goal being "to ensure that children have a secure, stable and loving family to support them through childhood and beyond and to give them a sense of security, continuity, commitment, identity and belonging" (Department for Education, 2015, pp. 22–23).

Adoption policy in England shares many similarities to the US, where the Adoption and Safe Families Act (1997) also focuses on promoting adoption within timescales for children who are unable to return to their biological families. There are differences, however; notably that most children in the US are adopted by foster carers or biological kin (Hegar and Scannapieco, 2017).

Adoption addresses concerns about children "drifting" in the care system, having no chance of returning home but not establishing any sense of permanence or family belonging, or even a stable base in just one foster home (Fanshel and Shinn, 1978; Rowe and Lambert, 1973). For most children, adoption does provide stability, family belonging, and opportunities for developmental recovery, though many children need ongoing support services (Biehal, Ellison, Baker, and Sinclair, 2010; Hodges, Steele, Hillman, Henderson, and Kaniuk, 2005; Neil, Beek, and Ward, 2015; Neil, Young, and Hartley, 2018). However, adoption also involves multiple losses. Separation from significant others is ambiguous, since birth relatives may be physically absent but still present in the child's mind (Boss, 1999). Losses are often unrecognized, and adoptees' grief disenfranchised (Brodzinsky, 2011; Leon, 2002). Children may feel an immediate and keen sense of loss when separated from people who have been closely involved in their daily lives. They can also have a sense of loss about relationships they have not had the chance to experience (Brodzinsky, 2011).

In adoptions from the care system, children will often lose their previous foster family relationships. In England, adopted children will have typically spent an average of 15 months in foster care (Department for Education, 2018) where, hopefully, they will have developed a sense of security and trust in their foster carers. Placement for adoption involves separation from these primary caregivers, as well as their network of friends and family, home, pets, and community.

Each of these losses has an impact on the child's sense of identity, creating complexity and often uncertainty around key questions such as "Who am I?", "Where do I come from?", and "Where do I belong?" (Grotevant and Von Korff, 2011). It is important, therefore, to consider adopted children's loss of identity and relationships through both an ethical and a psychological lens. When the focus is on the best interests of the child, both of these perspectives lead us to think about how the negative impact of loss can be mitigated or minimized. The key to addressing this loss is to work so that children experience some degree of *continuity* of identity and relationships with birth family members and previous caregivers. Continuity in this context refers to a variety of activities, including open communication within the adoptive family about the child's past relationships and identity (Brodzinsky, 2005), respect for items connected with the child's past, and consideration given to the full range of indirect and face-to-face contact with significant others (Fahlberg, 2012).

In terms of openness in adoption in England, the right of adoptees to access birth records (and hence to be able to trace birth family members) has been enshrined in law since 1975. Whether or not a child should have any ongoing contact with birth family members must be considered in adoption proceedings, but the law stops short of saying that such contact should be promoted (Adoption and Children Act 2002, Sec 46/6). Most adoptions include plans for children to remain in contact with birth parents through letters exchanged by the adults via the adoption agency, although in practice more than half of these arrangements are not sustained (Neil, 2018). Few children have visits with birth family members (referred to in this chapter as face-to-face contact); when they do, visits are mostly with a biological sibling who has been adopted or fostered or with grandparents rather than birth parents (Neil, Young, and Hartley, 2018). This has been a static picture over the past 20 years in the UK (Neil, 2018). Practices in other countries vary widely. For example, research from the US suggests that rates of face-to-face contact in care adoptions are growing, though not planned for all (Brodzinsky and Goldberg, 2016). In New South Wales, Australia, adopted children are expected to have ongoing contact with birth parents (Collings, Neil, and Wright, 2018).

Questions about whether or how adopted children should maintain relationships with birth family members do not have easy answers. Research has demonstrated that while contact is often beneficial for children, adoptive parents, and birth relatives, outcomes of the contact and experiences are mixed, and careful decision making is needed to take account of individual factors (Boyle, 2017; Neil, 2018). Contact works best when adoptive parents and birth family members can work together for the sake of the child, and this requires empathy, commitment, relationship skills, and flexibility (Grotevant, 2009).

Regarding the child's ongoing contact with foster carers, in the English context this is usually discussed before the child is placed with their adoptive family, yet contact may be discouraged or delayed (Swain, 2016). There is some professional uncertainty regarding the nature and value of sustaining relationships with foster carers, with differing views as to whether too much closeness and intensity might negatively affect the child in their adoptive family. Similarly, there is varying advice to adopters on the benefits of keeping the foster family identity "alive" in the child's mind by talking about foster family members or displaying their photographs.

Despite some changes in adoption practice, therefore, the issue of respecting children's relationships and identities in adoption remains an area of uncertainty and ambivalence for adoption professionals, adopters, foster carers, and birth family members.

Three important studies at the University of East Anglia, UK, have explored these issues in depth. The "Contact after Adoption" study is a longitudinal study of children adopted under the age of four (most of whom were adopted from care), their adoptive parents, and birth relatives. Families took part when the children were pre-school age, in middle childhood, and in late adolescence (Neil, Beek, and Ward, 2015). This study explored families' experiences of indirect (letterbox) contact and direct (face-to-face) contact with birth family members. The "Supporting Direct Contact" study interviewed adoptive parents and birth relatives who had face-to-face contact, to explore their experiences of contact and contact support services (Neil, Cossar, Jones, Lorgelly, and Young, 2011). The third project, called "Moving to Adoption," involved the development and piloting of a practice program to help professionals support the moves of children from their foster to adoptive families in a child-focused way (Neil, Beek, and Schofield, 2018). This chapter will draw on findings from these studies to consider ways in which adoption can be respectful and supportive of children's pre-adoption relationships and identity, while also providing children with love, security, and a family for life.

Birth family relationships and identity

Relationships

The loss of secure attachment relationships is universally difficult for children to manage (Bowlby, 1973), but when children are adopted from care, relationships with parents have often been marred by abuse, neglect, or instability. In such circumstances, children's attachments to parents are likely to be insecure, even disorganized (Howe, 1998). Separation from caregivers is difficult, whether attachment relationships have been secure or insecure (Schofield and Beek, 2018). Where previous relationships have been positive, benefits of staying in touch are likely to outweigh challenges (Neil, 2018). Where relationships have been difficult and attachments are insecure, the challenges can be significant; these must be balanced against the challenges of ending relationships and the loss and identity issues that may follow (Neil, Cossar, Jones, Lorgelly, and Young, 2011).

When children have had difficult relationships with birth parents, it is tempting to defer to the idea of a "clean break" or "fresh start." This might be the right decision in some cases, and it is important to listen to children who express strong feelings about people with whom they do not want to stay in touch (Thomas, Beckford, Lowe, and Murch, 1999). For children who have been abused or neglected, their behavior before, during, or after contact with parents might suggest significant fear, and adults may need to make a decision to end contact (Howe and Steele, 2004). For many children adopted from care, feelings toward their parent will be mixed and can fluctuate over time. This was clearly demonstrated in our longitudinal study (Neil, Beek, and Ward, 2015), where adopted young people who had lived with a parent before adoption sometimes missed or even idealized this parent, but at other times felt angry, anxious, or rejected by them.

For example, Reece, adopted at age four, had only indirect contact with his mother, and she did not respond to letters. He accepted this when in middle childhood, even saying about his birth parents, "They are out of my life now." However, in early adolescence he started thinking "constantly" about his birth mum and wanted to get back in touch. He found it hard to make sense of his relationship with her, veering between blaming himself ("Was it something I done ... why me out of everyone?") and being angry with her ("What's her problem ... why won't she contact me?"). At the age of 16 he tracked her down using social media. He felt an instant connection but could not develop a closer relationship because his birth mother's views of why he was adopted did not fit with his own understanding. He ultimately distanced himself: "I have little contact with her now ... she's not mother material."

Where children are able to stay in touch with birth parents, meetings can elicit a range of positive and negative feelings, allowing adoptive parents and (sometimes) birth parents the chance to understand and manage their child's adoption-related emotion (Neil, Beek, and Ward, 2015). Adoptive parents have reported the ways they felt maintaining a relationship had been helpful to their child (Neil, Cossar, Jones, Lorgelly, and Young, 2011). Some parents felt their child would not have been able to commit to adoption without this: "[it] would be ripping her away from the family she loved ... and she would never allow herself to love us if that was the case." Others felt that contact helped children feel less worried about family members: "She needed the reassurance that her mum was okay," or that maintaining relationships gave their child important lessons for adult life: "[it's] better for his relationships when he grows up. If he sees it is not losing all the time, then it is good for him" (Neil, Cossar, Jones, Lorgelly, and Young, 2011, p. 160).

Contact can prompt communication between adoptive parents and children (Von Korff and Grotevant, 2011), giving adoptive parents opportunities to help children think about and make sense of their relationships with birth family members. For example, Luke, who was adopted at age four, had face-to-face contact with his birth mother. His adoptive mum felt this brought up feelings of sadness and loss, but also guilt: "he feels guilty that he wants to go [to see his mum], he feels guilty that he thinks he is letting me down. He feels guilty because he is not there looking after her." She tried to give him permission to hold and share these emotions by acknowledging his positive feelings for his birth mother:

> [S]ome of the toys that she has given him in the past, when it has come to turfing out things that he has grown out of, I say "well you really loved that rabbit when [birth mum] gave it to you, I wouldn't throw it out yet, keep it because it reminds you of her."

We explored the extent to which adoptive parents were "communicatively open" – the extent to which they were open to thinking and talking about adoption with their child (Brodzinsky, 2005). We found that having face-to-face contact was associated with higher levels of adoption communication openness in adoptive parents. This may have been because parents who were more communicatively open chose to have more contact, but it was also clear that having contact helped adoptive parents to talk with their child about adoption and it built their empathy for birth relatives (Neil, 2007). We also found that adoptive parents who were more communicatively open helped make contact meetings comfortable for adopted children and birth relatives, for example, by reassuring the child that it was OK for them to have a range of feelings about seeing their birth family, or by making the birth parent feel included and welcomed (Neil, Cossar, Jones, Lorgelly, and Young, 2011).

Where adopted children have had positive relationships with parents, grandparents, or siblings before adoption, feelings of sadness, loss, and anxiety can be strong when relationships are cut off. Children generally find staying in touch with siblings or grandparents less emotionally complex than contact with parents, and contact with these birth family members is often lasting and rewarding (Neil, Beek, and Ward, 2015; Neil, Cossar, Jones, Lorgelly, and Young, 2011).

For example, Keira, adopted at age two and interviewed at age 17, had face-to-face contact with her grandmother who had been supportively involved in her life from birth. She felt comfortable spending time with her grandmother, saying the meetings "felt like we were a real family." Grandparents often have fewer problems and more resources than birth parents, and they can be more accepting of the child's adoption (Neil, 2006). Children can benefit from knowing their grandparents care about them. Grandparents can be an important conduit of information between the adoptive family and the birth parents; in some cases, grandparents can provide practical and emotional support to children and adoptive parents (Neil, Beek, and Ward, 2015).

Being adopted poses great risks in terms of the loss of sibling relationships (Monk and Macvarish, 2018). At a minimum, children need to know who and where their siblings are, and why they have been unable to grow up together (Cossar and Neil, 2013). Staying in touch with siblings can mitigate children's sense of loss and provide reassurance and information. An adoptive mother described how her son (11) had been able to settle down more in the adoptive family after getting back in touch with his younger brother and sister (Neil, Cossar, Jones, Lorgelly, and Young, 2011):

> He was just delighted, he almost matured in front of us and he seemed to grow up … he seemed grounded and settled, almost relieved and more content in himself … he was able to relax knowing that they were fine.

However, maintaining sibling relationships is not always straightforward. Siblings sometimes have very different experiences and perceptions of birth parents, and the different adoptive and foster families involved might not always get along (Cossar and Neil, 2013). Some children and young people might need help to make sense of and repair sibling relationships, and some sibling contact arrangements will need professional support.

Many children are adopted when they are very young and will not have formed relationships with their birth family before adoption. The need for relationships to be promoted after adoption can be too easily dismissed in this scenario, the argument being that children do not remember their family and therefore will be confused by face-to-face contact. However, the child's lack of emotional connection to birth family members can make some aspects of staying in touch easier. For example, in our longitudinal study, adoptive parents of children adopted in infancy told us that their children's responses to birth family contact meetings were low-key, much like going to see a distant relative or friend of the family (Neil, 2004b). In middle childhood, children were starting to develop some understanding of adoption and their birth family (Neil, 2012), and their interest in meetings increased. In late adolescence, almost all young people who had maintained direct contact with the birth parent were positive about this even though few felt they had a close relationship with their parent. They felt they had benefited from knowing their birth parent cared about them and from learning more about their identity and why they needed to be adopted.

Identity

For adoptees, learning about where they have come from and why they needed to be adopted are key to understanding their adoptive identity (Grotevant and Von Korff, 2011). Curiosity about birth parents is normative among adoptees, the predominant question being, "Why was I adopted?" (Wrobel and Dillon, 2009). Identity formation can be thought about in terms of narratives – the evolving stories we tell about ourselves – where we have come from, who we are now, and where we see ourselves heading (McAdams, 2001). Our life stories feature significant people with whom we have shared time and space in our lives. Our autobiographical memories are essentially co-constructed with significant others who help us tell and retell our personal stories (Pasupathi, 2001). Thus, when adopted children lose contact with important people, they also lose memories, storytelling opportunities, access to information, and ultimately, identity.

Where face-to-face birth family contact has been maintained, adoptive parents have emphasized the identity benefits for the child, arguing this can help children fill in gaps, learn about their roots, or put their past together (Neil, Cossar, Jones, Lorgelly, and Young, 2011). Adoptees' own accounts also demonstrate the benefits of staying in touch with birth family for identity development. Qualitative analysis of adopted young people's interviews identified four patterns of adoptive identity development: cohesive, unexplored, fragmented, and developing (Neil, Beek, and Ward, 2015). In the "cohesive" group, young people who had thought a lot about their adoption over the years, they told consistent stories including details and examples. They reflected on their own thoughts and feelings, as well as those of their adoptive parents and birth relatives. They seemed at ease with their adoption story in the present, though some recognized they might wish to explore the story in more detail in the future. Young people with an "unexplored" pattern showed a low level of interest in their adoption and were satisfied with very simple explanations. "Fragmented" identity described young people who felt that their adoption story did not make sense to them, and they had negative feelings around adoption. Young people with a "developing" sense of adoptive identity were curious and questioning but felt unsatisfied, and they wanted more answers. Compared to the young people in the other identity groups, those with "cohesive" adoptive identities had the highest levels of face-to-face contact with birth relatives and were more likely to still be in touch with someone from their birth family.

Adopted children and young people can also find out about their life stories through exchanges of written information, though there are more barriers here to achieving a good mutual understanding (Neil, 2004a). Mediated letterbox contact is a difficult and unfamiliar way for families to communicate. Both adopters and birth family members can find letters hard to write and each can feel that the information they receive is bland or uninformative (Neil, Beek, and Ward, 2015). In our longitudinal study, 16 years after adoption, 60 percent of letterbox contact arrangements had stopped completely, many of these having failed at an early stage. This left some young people with information gaps and unresolved feelings about their birth family, making it hard for them to piece together their life story (Neil, Beek, and Ward, 2015). Letterbox contact had worked well in just a few cases and had provided a good platform for people to meet up later to explore whether a relationship could be developed.

Relationships with foster carers and other previous caregivers

In optimum circumstances, the child's relationships with the foster carers who have cared for them prior to adoption will be close and loving. The foster carers will have provided a secure base (Schofield and Beek, 2014) for the child over a significant number of months and sometimes years.

These secure base attachment relationships are crucial for children to begin their recovery from early harm. When infants and children come into foster care from difficult family backgrounds, their trust in relationships and their development are likely to have been affected. They need positive experiences of available, sensitive caregivers who not only meet their physical needs, but also their emotional needs. This reduces their anxiety so that they can feel safe and secure enough to play, learn, and enjoy their world. These positive experiences and expectations of the self and other people will continue to have significance for the child when children are placed for adoption. The secure attachment relationships with foster carers cannot be "transferred" to the adopters, as the child will first need to learn to trust the adoptive parents. Instead, positive relationships with foster carers will provide a sound foundation from which the child will gradually "take the risk" of trusting in their new adoptive parent(s) and building a new attachment relationship that will provide a secure base for the future (Schofield and Beek, 2008).

However, it is important not to underestimate the impact on the child when separated from their foster carers. Separation from trusted caregivers and building trust in new caregivers is especially difficult for vulnerable children who may experience fear, an acute sense of abandonment, and negative memories of past separations (Bowlby, 1973; Hindle and Shulman, 2008; Lanyado, 2003). Rushed or stressful moves can be very distressing for children; they have been linked with poorer outcomes at older ages (Neil, Young, and Hartley, 2018) and to unsettled or disrupted adoptions (Selwyn, Meakings, and Wijedasa, 2015). It is vital, therefore, to consider both the way in which the move is managed and the extent to which there can be positive continuity of relationships between the child and the foster carers after the move has occurred. Key helping factors are how the loss is planned for, how it is managed, and how gradual the separation is (Breier et al., 1988; Winnicott, 2018). Browning (2015) proposes that the impact of the move can be "softened" for the child by a progressive transition process with gradually decreasing contact with foster carers, overseen by a well-functioning professional team.

In our recent study (Neil, Beek, and Schofield, 2018), a practice program providing a theory and research-based framework for a more gradual transition process was piloted on 40 children's moves to adoption (the children were aged from 5 months to 6 years old). The practice program is not prescriptive about timescales but rather suggests six key principles to be considered when moving a child, as follows:

- Opportunities for the foster carers and adopters to build a positive relationship should be promoted at an early stage in the moving process.
- The child and the adopters should be given opportunities to become familiar with each other through play and observation prior to adopters undertaking any caregiving tasks.
- All arrangements and timescales should focus on the needs of the child.
- The child's feelings about the move should be held in mind and responded to sensitively.
- Some continuity of foster family relationships and environment will support the child in managing the loss of the foster family and building trust in the adoptive family.
- Planning should be in consultation with the child, the families, and the social workers, and be flexible to allow for emerging circumstances and needs.

The pilot data were used to develop a model for supporting children's moves (the University of East Anglia [UEA] model). This describes three key stages of the moving process.

Stage 1: Getting to know each other, is a period of familiarization in which the foster carers and the adopters, as well as the adopters and the child, get to know each other informally and begin to build trust.

Stage 2: Making the move, is an intensive period of about 14 days for these very young children. Adopters and the child have almost daily contact, initially in the foster home, and then the child and foster carer spend time in the adoptive home. The foster carers remain physically and psychologically available during this stage, but incrementally take more of a back seat as the adopters gain confidence in their caregiving tasks and children gain confidence that the new parents can meet their needs.

Stage 3: Supporting relationships after the move, covers the first four weeks of the adoption placement where the main focus is on the adopters and child building their relationship, wherever possible with support from the child's foster carer.

At all stages, it is important to ensure that plans are flexible and individualized, adjusted according to age, the nature of the child's attachment with the foster carer, the child's personality, and the child's previous history of change and loss. The longer timescales and gradual relationship building between the adults promote some continuity of environment.

Although the period immediately following the move is significant, it is also important to think about the ongoing continuity of relationships with the foster carers and other adults who have been significant to the child in the longer term (Brodzinsky, 2011).

In UK adoptions, longer term contact between the foster family and the adoptive family has been variable, with many children having no further contact after the move, although some adopters choose to remain in touch (Boswell and Cudmore, 2017). When relationships have endured, they are reported to be extremely valuable to the child, providing welcomed support and links with the past (Thomas, Beckford, Lowe, and Murch, 1999; Neil, Young, and Hartley, 2018). Longer timescales and increased opportunities for the adults to build trust in each other frequently resulted in plans for a range of indirect contact and face-to-face visiting arrangements in the future (Neil, Beek, and Schofield, 2018).

Although our study focused on moving younger children from foster care to adoption, the key principles underpinning the UEA model could be applied to a range of other situations. Even in inter-country adoption, where timescales may be more limited, the creative use of Skype, video, and photo sharing can provide some continuity of relationships for the child. This can also happen through the careful transfer of information about the child and the birth family, important objects, or photographs. Relevant preparation and training are key to helping all parties understand the purpose and value of these practices.

Building a secure base in the adoptive family

We have seen that secure base relationships with previous caregivers are important in shaping children's expectations of themselves and others and enabling them to take the risk of building trust in the new family. The key task for adoptive parents is to support the child in building this trust and to enable the child to feel a sense of belonging, being loved, and being loveable in the adoptive family.

The Secure Base Model (Schofield and Beek, 2014) provides a framework for thinking about the sort of parenting that can contribute to this task. It identifies five dimensions of

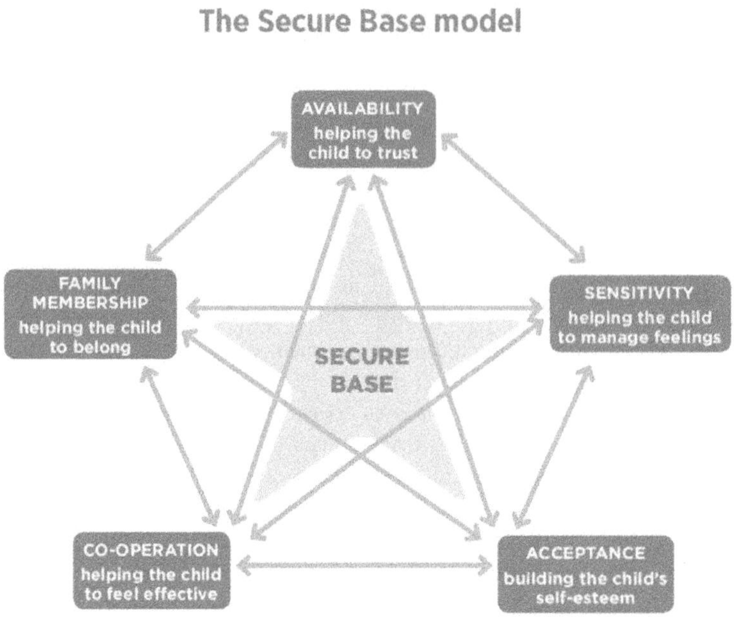

Figure 6.1 The Secure Base Model

caregiving which overlap and interact with each other to form a secure base for the child. Each caregiving dimension has a corresponding developmental benefit to the child, and these are illustrated in Figure 6.1.

Sensitive adopters will reflect these dimensions of parenting through the innumerable interactions of family life – ranging from the moment-to-moment interactions over breakfast through to evening and bedtime routines. Gradually, children will feel more secure, form trusting relationships, and feel a sense of belonging in the adoptive family.

Parenting within these dimensions will also prompt sensitive adopters to think about how children's previous relationships and identities can be helpfully supported. For example, in demonstrating their own physical and emotional *availability*, adopters will be mindful of the ways in which previous caregivers have breached or built the child's trust and the ways in which this might have shaped the child's expectations of adults. They will show *sensitivity* to the child's thinking and feeling about their previous relationships and identity, and they will help the child to acknowledge, name, and manage these feelings. Showing non-judgmental *acceptance* of both the strengths and difficulties of the birth family and previous caregivers is essential to helping the child to build a positive sense of self and identity. It is important for adopters to demonstrate *co-operation* by working together with the child to establish comfortable levels of openness, allowing the child some safe and appropriate choice and agency, and understanding that the child's needs and understandings will change through different developmental stages. Finally, as well as building a positive adoptive family identity, adopters need to help the child to establish a comfortable sense of their birth family identity, mediated on an individualized basis, through the full range of contact arrangements from no contact through to regular face-to-face meetings. Again, children's needs and feelings about their birth family identity are likely to change over time, and adopters will need to be alert and responsive to this. The ideas generated by the Secure Base Model connect closely to those of adoption communication openness (Brodzinsky, 2005).

Planning and supporting adoptions that respect children's relationships and identities: Connections to policy and practice

Over the last 20 years, a wide range of research studies from different parts of the world, including our own at UEA, have shown that adoption involves a lifelong process of resolving loss and building a coherent sense of identity. In 2013, a group of UK charities reported on how best to achieve stability and a positive sense of identity and belonging for children in care. They identified children's past relationships as "the golden thread" that runs through their lives, querying why children who cannot be brought up in their birth families should frequently lose so many important relationships from the past (The Care Inquiry, 2013). We suggest that adoption practice should also regard every important pre-adoption relationship and identity as having the potential to be an ongoing "golden thread" in the child's life.

In terms of adoption policy, it is important that the legal frameworks around adoption do not create and enforce barriers that prevent children from maintaining connections to important people, through restricting or preventing birth family contact or sealing adoption records. However, it is also important that legal frameworks allow an individualized consideration of the quality of such contact and the impact of this on the child, including any risks. Courts making adoption orders need to "set the tone" for a more inclusive model of adoption by requiring the child's existing relationships to be taken into account and strongly encouraging the maintenance of contact unless it is clearly not in the child's best interests (Neil, 2018).

In terms of implications for practice, the first-level step in minimizing the loss of relationships and identities for children is the careful gathering and preservation of as much information as possible about the child's background history, the communities and cultures that this includes, and the people who have been significant to them. Consideration should be given to the child's relationship and identity needs not just in the near future, but later in their life: what and who will the child want or need to know?

The personal circumstances, wishes, and resources of birth family (and foster family) members need to be explored. Attention should be paid to considering who in the child's existing network has something to offer in terms of providing background information or ongoing news of how significant people are doing. Who can reassure the child that they are cared about and remembered? Which individuals are most able to support the child as a member of their adoptive family? What help might birth parents need to manage adoption-related loss, anger, and shame so they can focus on their child's needs (Neil, 2006)?

The feelings and resources of adoptive parents should also be explored (Neil, 2007). What is their understanding of the child's losses, and how do they think they can work with birth and foster families to meet the child's needs? What are their thoughts and feelings about the child's birth family, the reason they needed to be adopted, and how do they plan to talk with the child about this? What worries them about contact, and what support or information would help them feel comfortable in connecting with birth family members?

In collaboration with adoptive parents, birth relatives, and children (when old enough), professionals then need to consider the full range of contact arrangements with birth relatives, from "no contact" (in a small minority of cases, this may be the best or only option) through to face-to-face contact on a regular basis. Our research suggests that "formulaic" contact plans are not helpful, but that, instead, planning should be underpinned by the following key principles. That is, contact should be *purposeful* (of some benefit to the child); *individualized* (according to the particular needs of the child and the particular relevant qualities of the child, the adopters, and the birth relative); and should be viewed as a *relationship-based process* that is *dynamic* over time. The foundation of successful contact is trust between birth and adoptive families (Neil, 2010), and trusting and mutually comfortable relationships take both time and effort to grow (Grotevant, 2009). From the start it is important to think about how best to promote trust and empathy between birth and adoptive families and to provide early opportunities for people to meet up and start these discussions.

Whether or not families might need help from professionals to maintain contact after the adoption order should be considered and the nature of this support negotiated with those involved, with the goal of contact that is comfortable and family-like, with risks managed (Neil, 2010). Both the contact itself and any professional support services need to be reviewed from time to time, particularly when circumstances change or children reach new stages in their lives. Figure 6.2 summarizes these ideas in a model for planning and supporting contact (Neil, Beek, and Ward, 2015, p. 284).

Children's connections with previous caregivers also need to be respected when they move to adoption. Gradual transitions that are sensitive to the child's feelings and allow the child to build trust in the new parents, *while at the same time* using the previous caregivers as a secure base, can help the child to grieve their losses as well as enjoy their new family life. Some continuity of relationships with previous caregivers should be considered in all cases and, wherever appropriate, ongoing contact (ranging from an annual card to regular face-to-face contact) will help the child to fill the gaps in their identity and to know that they are still held in mind by their previous caregivers.

The aim of every adoption is to provide a secure base for the child through to adulthood and beyond. Research has shown us that this is rarely achieved by the total severance of the past, but rather through an acknowledgment of the role of birth relatives, previous caregivers, and adoptive parents in helping the child to achieve a coherent sense of the past in ways that are comfortable and individually tailored to changing needs across the lifespan.

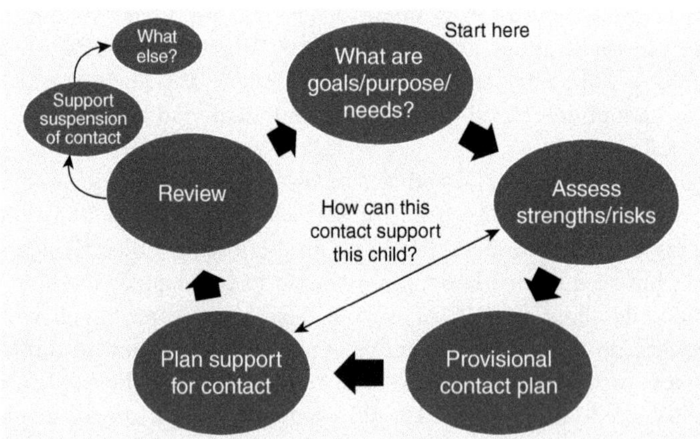

Figure 6.2 Planning and Supporting Contact Model

References

Biehal, N., Ellison, S., Baker, C., & Sinclair, I. (2010). *Belonging and permanence: Outcomes in long-term foster care and adoption.* London: British Association of Adoption and Fostering (BAAF).

Boss, P. (1999). *Ambiguous loss: Learning to live with unresolved grief.* Cambridge: Harvard University.

Boswell, S., & Cudmore, L. (2017). Understanding the "blind spot" when children move from foster care into adoption. *Journal of Child Psychotherapy, 43*(2), 243–257. doi:10.1080/0075417X.2017.1323946

Bowlby, J. (1973). *Attachment and loss, vol. II: Separation* (Vol. 2). New York: Basic Books.

Boyle, C. (2017). "What is the impact of birth family contact on children in adoption and long-term foster care?" A systematic review. *Child & Family Social Work, 22*, 22–33. doi:10.1111/cfs.12236

Breier, A., Kelsoe, J. R., Kirwin, P. D., Beller, S. A., Wolkowitz, O. M., & Pickar, D. (1988). Early parental loss and development of adult psychopathology. *Archives of General Psychiatry, 45*(11), 987–993. doi:10.1001/archpsyc.1988.01800350021003

Brodzinsky, D. M. (2005). Reconceptualizing openness in adoption: Implications for theory, research, and practice. In D. Brodzinsky & J. Palacios (Eds.), *Psychological issues in adoption: Research and practice* (pp. 145–166). Westport, CT: Praeger.

Brodzinsky, D. M. (2011). Children's understanding of adoption: Developmental and clinical implications. *Professional Psychology: Research and Practice, 42*(2), 200–207. doi:10.1037/a0022415

Brodzinsky, D. M., & Goldberg, A. E. (2016). Contact with birth family in adoptive families headed by lesbian, gay male, and heterosexual parents. *Children and Youth Services Review, 62*, 9–17. doi:10.1016/j.childyouth.2016.01.014

Browning, A. (2015). Undertaking planned transitions for children in out of home care. *Adoption and Fostering, 39*(1), 51–61. doi:doi/10.1177/0308575914565072

The Care Inquiry. (2013). Making not breaking: Building relationships for our most vulnerable children. Retrieved from www.nuffieldfoundation.org/sites/default/files/files/Care%20Inquiry%20-%20Full%20Report%20April%202013.pdf

Collings, S., Neil, E., & Wright, A. C. (2018). Practices to improve communication between birth parents and permanent families. *Advances in Social Work and Welfare Education, 20*(2), 144–150.

Cossar, J., & Neil, E. (2013). Making sense of siblings: Connections and severances in post-adoption contact. *Child & Family Social Work, 18*(1), 67–76. doi:10.1111/cfs.12039

Department for Education. (2015). The Children Act 1989 guidance and regulations (June 2015). Retrieved from https://assets.publishing.service.gov.uk/government/uploads/system/uploads/attachment_data/file/441643/Children_Act_Guidance_2015.pdf

Department for Education. (2018). *Adoption leadership board headline measures and business intelligence: Quarter 4 2016 to 2017 update.* Retrieved from https://assets.publishing.service.gov.uk/government/uploads/system/uploads/attachment_data/file/704518/ALB_Business_Intelligence_Quarter_4_2016_to_2017.pdf

Fahlberg, V. (2012). *A child's journey through placement.* London: Jessica Kingsley Publishers.

Fanshel, D., & Shinn, E. B. (1978). *Children in foster care: A longitudinal investigation.* New York: Columbia University Press.

Featherstone, B., Gupta, A., & Mills, S. (2018). *The role of the social worker in adoption – Ethics and human rights: An enquiry.* London: British Association of Social Workers.

Grotevant, H. D. (2009). Emotional distance regulation over the life course in adoptive kinship networks. In G. Wrobel & E. Neil (Eds.), *International advances in adoption research for practice* (pp. 295–316). Chichester: Wiley-Blackwell.

Grotevant, H. D., & Von Korff, L. (2011). Adoptive identity. In S. J. Schwartz, K. Luyckx, & V. L. Vignoles (Eds.), *Handbook of identity theory and research* (pp. 585–601). New York, NY: Springer.

Hegar, R. L., & Scannapieco, M. (2017). Foster care to kinship adoption: The road less traveled. *Adoption Quarterly, 20*(1), 83–97. doi:10.1080/10926755.2016.1149535

Hindle, D., & Shulman, G. (2008). *The emotional experience of adoption: A psychoanalytic perspective.* London: Routledge.

Hodges, J., Steele, M., Hillman, S., Henderson, K., & Kaniuk, J. (2005). Change and continuity in mental representations of attachment after adoption. *Psychological Issues in Adoption: Research and Practice*, 93–116.

Howe, D. (1998). *Patterns of adoption.* Oxford: Blackwell Science.

Howe, D., & Steele, M. (2004). Contact in cases in which children have been traumatically abused or neglect by their birth parents. In E. Neil, and D. Howe (Eds.), *Contact in adoption and permanent foster care* (pp. 203–223)). London: BAAF.

Kirton, D. (2013). "Kinship by design" in England: Reconfiguring adoption from Blair to the coalition. *Child & Family Social Work, 18*(1), 97–106.

Lanyado, M. (2003). The emotional tasks of moving from fostering to adoption: Transitions, attachment, separation and loss. *Clinical Child Psychology and Psychiatry, 8*(3), 337–349. doi:10.1177/1359104503008003005

Leon, I. G. (2002). Adoption losses: Naturally occurring or socially constructed? *Child Development, 73*(2), 652–663. doi:10.1111/1467-8624.00429

McAdams, D. P. (2001). The psychology of life stories. *Review of General Psychology, 5*(2), 100. doi:10.1037//I089-2680.5.2.100

Monk, D., & Macvarish, J. (2018) Siblings, contact and the law: An overlooked relationship? Retrieved from www.nuffieldfoundation.org/sites/default/files/files/Final%20Siblings%20Summary.pdf

Neil, E. (2004a). The "Contact after Adoption" study: Indirect contact and adoptive parents' communication about adoption. In E. Neil, and D. Howe (Eds.), *Contact in adoption and permanent foster care* (pp. 46–64). London: BAAF.

Neil, E. (2004b). The "Contact after Adoption" study: Face-to-face contact. In E. Neil and D. Howe (Eds.), *Contact in adoption and permanent foster care* (pp. 65–84). London: BAAF.

Neil, E. (2006). Coming to terms with the loss of a child: The feelings of birth parents and grandparents about adoption and post-adoption contact. *Adoption Quarterly, 10*(1), 1–23. doi:10.1300/J145v10n01_01

Neil, E. (2007). Post-adoption contact and openness in adoptive parents' minds: Consequences for children's development. *British Journal of Social Work, 39*(1), 5–23. doi:10.1111/j.1469-7610.2010.02330.x

Neil, E. (2010). The benefits and challenges of direct post-adoption contact: Perspectives from adoptive parents and birth relatives. *Aloma: Revista de Psicologia, Ciències de l'Educació i de l'Esport, 27*, 89–115. Retrieved from http://revistaaloma.net/index.php/aloma/article/view/23/12

Neil, E. (2012). Making sense of adoption: Integration and differentiation from the perspective of adopted children in middle childhood. *Children and Youth Services Review, 34*(2), 409–416. doi:10.1016/j.childyouth.2011.11.011

Neil, E. (2018). Rethinking adoption and birth family contact: Is there a role for the law? *Family Law, 48* (2018, September), 1178–1182.

Neil, E., Beek, M., & Schofield, G. (2018). *Moving to adoption: A practice development project, project report.* Norwich: Centre for Research on Children and Families. Retrieved from https://ueaeprints.uea.ac.uk/69318/1/Moving_to_Adoption_research_briefing.pdf

Neil, E., Beek, M., & Ward, E. (2015). *Contact after adoption: A longitudinal study of post adoption contact arrangements*. London: Coram BAAF.

Neil, E., Cossar, J., Jones, C., Lorgelly, P., & Young, J. (2011). *Supporting direct contact after adoption.* London: BAAF.

Neil, E., Young, J., & Hartley, L. (2018). *The joys and challenges of adoptive family life: A survey of adoptive parents in the Yorkshire and Humberside region.* Norwich: Centre for Research on Children and Families.

Pasupathi, M. (2001). The social construction of the personal past and its implications for adult development. *Psychological Bulletin, 127*(5), 651–672. doi:10.1037//0033-2909.127.5.651

Rowe, J., & Lambert, L. (1973). *Children who wait: A study of children needing substitute families.* London: Association of British Adoption Agencies.

Schofield, G., & Beek, M. (2008). *Achieving permanence in foster care: A good practice guide.* London: BAAF.

Schofield, G., & Beek, M. (2014). *The Secure Base model: Promoting attachment and resilience in foster care and adoption.* London: CoramBAAF.

Schofield, G., & Beek, M. (2018). *Attachment handbook for foster care and adoption* (2nd ed.). London: CoramBAAF.

Selwyn, J., Meakings, S., & Wijedasa, D. (2015). *Beyond the adoption order: Challenges, interventions and adoption disruption.* London: BAAF.

Swain, V. (2016) *Keeping connected: Maintaining relationships whilst moving on.* (July, 2016). Retrieved from www.thefosteringnetwork.org.uk/sites/www.fostering.net/files/uploads/pdf/keep_connected_4_feb_v2.pdf

Thomas, C., Beckford, V., Lowe, N. V., & Murch, M. (1999). *Adopted children speaking.* London: BAAF.

Von Korff, L., & Grotevant, H. D. (2011). Contact in adoption and adoptive identity formation: The mediating role of family conversation. *Journal of Family Psychology, 25*(3), 393–401. doi:10.1037/a0023388

Winnicott, C. (2018). Face to face with children (1963). In J. Kantor (Ed.) *Face to face with children: the life and work of Clare Winnicott* (pp. 163–183). London: Routledge.

Wrobel, G. M., & Dillon, K. (2009). Adopted adolescents: Who and what are they curious about? In G. Wrobel & E. Neil (Eds.), *International advances in adoption research for practice* (pp. 217–244). Chichester: Wiley-Blackwell.

7

THE EARLY GROWTH AND DEVELOPMENT STUDY

Using an adoption design to understand family influences and child development

Amy L. Whitesel, Andrew Dismukes, Dorothy White, Sally Guyer, Jody M. Ganiban, Leslie D. Leve, and Jenae M. Neiderhiser

Introduction

This chapter describes the Early Growth and Development Study (EGDS). The EGDS is a prospective, longitudinal adoption study that was designed to explore the development of adoptive and birth families over time, and to understand the contributions of heritable and environmental processes to child development. The EGDS comprises an adoption kinship network consisting of birth parents, children adopted at birth, and their adoptive parents.

In the first part of this chapter, we present data from the EGDS related to birth parents, as they are a historically understudied population in adoption research. We describe their experiences with the adoption process, including information about events, characteristics, and relationships prior to and following the adoption placement, to provide a comprehensive picture of the short- and long-term impacts of adoption for birth families in the adoption kinship network. Next, we focus on adoptive families and examine how adoption research designs can be a powerful tool for disentangling the effects of the rearing environment on child development above and beyond heritable characteristics and prenatal factors. We additionally summarize key research findings that have emerged from the EGDS over the course of the study and consider implications and future directions for adoption research.

The relationships among heritable and environmental influences on child health and behavior have been studied in many ways, including through adoption designs such as the EGDS and the Colorado Adoption Project (Rhea, Bricker, Wadsworth, & Corley, 2013), through twin designs, and in molecular genetic research. An adoption design featuring birth parents, adoptive parents, and the adopted child is an especially powerful tool for identifying the effects of the rearing environment distinct from the effects of potentially heritable characteristics shared between biological parents and their children. In this chapter, we focus on the EGDS in order to provide an accessible, informative introduction to the benefits of a longitudinal adoption design that includes biological and adoptive parents and the adopted child.

Within a parent–offspring adoption research design, birth parents' characteristics are used as indicators of heritable tendencies, while birth mothers' pregnancy experiences and prenatal care are used to characterize their offspring's prenatal environments. Adoptive parents' behaviors and features of the adoptive home (e.g., parenting style, marital conflict, sibling relationships, neighborhood characteristics) are used as indicators of the postnatal rearing environment. In this design, the birth and adoptive families are not genetically related. Consequently, similarities between adoptive parent characteristics and the adopted child's characteristics reflect environmental processes, and similarities between birth parents' characteristics and the adopted child reflect putative heritable influences and/or prenatal exposures.

A central goal of the EGDS is to understand how family processes influence the expression of children's heritable predispositions and prenatal exposures over time (Leve, Neiderhiser, Scaramella, and Reiss, 2010). Research in the EGDS reflects four general aims: (1) to examine postnatal environmental influences on child development, (2) to examine evocative gene–environment correlations, (3) to examine gene × environment (G×E) and prenatal × postnatal environment interactions, and (4) to examine longitudinal pathways of continuity and change across development in relation to genetic, prenatal, and environmental influences (Leve et al., 2013). An evocative gene–environment correlation occurs when inherited factors influence children's rearing environments. For instance, a young child might show an interest in music, and parents might respond by arranging piano lessons for the child or by frequently exposing the child to music. Gene–environment interactions in adoption studies occur when the characteristics of the postnatal environment alter the expression of heritable tendencies (Dick, 2011), or vice versa. For example, genetic factors contribute to children's risk for becoming overweight or obese. However, a home environment that encourages healthy diets and physical activity could mitigate the expression of this risk. Alternatively, children's heritable risks for obesity in conjunction with home environments that provide access to unhealthy foods and foster sedentary habits could increase the child's risk for becoming obese. Because the EGDS has followed children over time, it is also possible to examine the impacts of evocative gene–environment correlations and gene–environment interactions on the emergence of new abilities and behaviors in children.

In addition to these study aims, the EGDS also focuses on the adoption kinship network, and has assessed a variety of elements related to adoption, such as characteristics of birth parents and their experience with making an adoption plan. The EGDS has also explored reasons that adoptive parents choose adoption and patterns of openness, and the level of contact between birth and adoptive families.

The EGDS recruited two cohorts, with recruitment beginning in 2003 and ending in 2009. Participating families were recruited with the help of private, licensed adoption agencies or service providers who conduct voluntary domestic adoptions across the country (See Figure 7.1).

The EGDS has systematically recruited one of the largest known samples of birth mothers and birth fathers involved in domestic adoption to date, and is one of the largest studies to have recruited "yokes," a designation stipulating that adoptive families and corresponding birth parents consist of a linked unit connected via the adopted child. The first cohort includes 361 families and the second includes an additional 200 families, for a total of 561 linked units, or yokes.

Following the study's eligibility guidelines, adoption agencies contacted adoptive families through the mail, and birth parents by phone, to describe the study. Interested individuals were subsequently contacted by EGDS staff for recruitment. Separate staff members contacted the adoptive parents and birth parents in order to maintain a strict firewall, so that information about participation or any other information related to the adoption is never

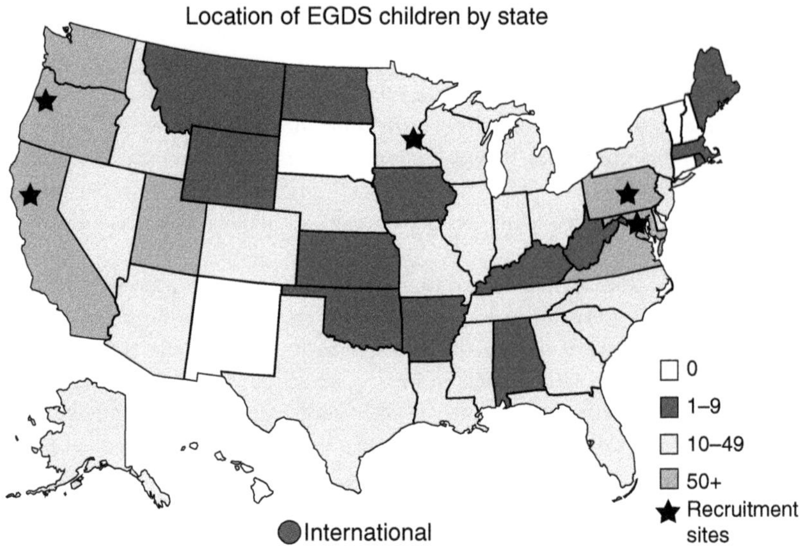

Figure 7.1 EGDS recruitment sites and volume by state

shared across yoked families by study staff. Leve et al. (2013) provide detailed information about the EGDS recruitment procedures.

Once recruited, birth parents were interviewed in person for the first time three to six months following the birth of the child, and adoptive families were interviewed for the first time by phone when the adopted child was approximately six months old. The adopted children, along with their birth and adoptive families, have been assessed in regular intervals via phone, mail, web, and in-person interviews. The participant retention rates for the sample has exceeded 80 percent over the past 10–15 years. While historically considered a difficult population to track, birth mothers and fathers have remained involved in the EGDS, providing a rich window into the lives of birth parents.

Birth parents

In this section, we provide an overview of the previous, but limited, research with birth parents and provide a detailed description of birth parents in the EGDS. This includes demographic characteristics, reasons for placing, adoption planning, and an examination of their adjustment following placement.

Birth parents and their experiences with adoption are historically understudied (Whitesel, 2008; Zamostny, Wiley, O'Brien, Lee, and Baden, 2003). There is interest in the adoption community to better understand the experiences of both birth mothers and birth fathers, given the lifelong and systemic impact of adoption (Claridge, 2014). This interest has been partially driven by the increased attention to adoption in general, a decrease in the secrecy around adoption for birth mothers as out-of-wedlock births have become less stigmatized, and greater communication within the adoption kinship network as open adoption has become more common (Brodzinsky, 1990; Farr, Ravvina, and Grotevant, 2018).

For decades, adoption was a secretive event and many women felt coerced into adoption (De Simone, 1996). Early literature on birth mothers was characterized by anecdotal evidence describing babies born out of wedlock. Women who placed their infants for adoption were expected to "move on" following the birth. However, the experience of unresolved grief is a common thread throughout birth mother research across the decades (Brodzinsky and Smith, 2014). These include reports of a poor sense of self, guilt, shame, anxiety, and depression post-placement (Brodzinsky and Smith, 2014; De Simone, 1996; Wiley and Baden, 2005). Birth mothers also feel a lack of social and emotional support when those around them avoid any discussion of the pregnancy or their feelings after the adoption (Madden, Ryan, Aguiniga, Killian, and Romanchik, 2018), and strain on intimate relationships, including with the birth father or other partner, is common (Madden et al., 2018). Last, the process of making an adoption plan leads some birth mothers to question future parenting and the quality of the relationship with their other children (Claridge, 2014).

Fewer studies have focused on birth fathers, in part because it is often assumed that birth fathers are less involved than birth mothers in the adoption plan (Wiley and Baden, 2005). Within existing studies, birth fathers have reported similar consequences following the adoption as birth mothers, including feelings of guilt, shame, anger, and loss (Clapton, 2007). Birth fathers specifically also report greater substance use, risky sexual behaviors, violence, or acting out following adoption (Clapton, 2007). Making an adoption plan has been found to cause substantial stress in the birth father's relationship with the birth mother, specifically, and in his relationships within his family (Clapton, 2007; Whitesel, 2008). Findings differ between birth mothers and fathers in regard to the benefits of the birth parents staying together post-adoption. A study of birth mothers reported that birth parents have greater difficulty in overcoming grief when they remained in a relationship (Christian, McRoy, Grotevant, and Bryant, 1997). In contrast, Whitesel (2008) found that greater feelings of connectedness with the birth mother were associated with fewer feelings of depression and anxiety in birth fathers post-adoption. Interventions designed to prepare birth mothers and fathers for placement and to assist them in the healing process post-adoption, with a focus on the birth parent relationship as a risk or protective factor in post-adoptive grief resolution, are critical going forward.

The existing research on birth parents is still generally retrospective, focuses almost exclusively on birth mothers, and does not traditionally characterize birth parents' pre- and postnatal experiences. Methodologically, many of the samples of birth parents have also been clinical samples or were self-selected (Smith, 2006), limiting the generalizability of the findings. The reliance on retrospective data can yield an incomplete picture of the birth parents' experiences and cannot easily be compared, given continual changes in adoption practices over time. The EGDS addressed these concerns by utilizing a systematic recruitment strategy and prospective data collection.

The birth parent sample in the EGDS is summarized in Table 7.1. On average, the birth mothers were 24 years old and birth fathers were 26 years old at the time of the adoption, which challenges a common stereotype that most birth mothers are teens (Brodzinsky and Smith, 2014). The majority of birth parents were White, and the median education level of birth mothers and fathers at the start of the study was a high school diploma. At this point, four percent of birth mothers and three percent of birth fathers had completed their bachelor's degree. At the last interview they participated in, 10 to 15 years after their start in the study, almost nine percent of birth mothers and eight percent of birth fathers had completed their bachelor's degree. Birth families most often reported $25,000 or less in median household income at the start of the study. In comparison, 29 percent of adults age 25–29 had a bachelor's degree (US Census Bureau, 2004), and the median household income in the United States was $42,409 (US Census Bureau, 2003). Based on these

Table 7.1 Birth parent demographics at placement

	Birth mothers	*Birth fathers*
N	556	209
Age	24.4 ± 6	26.1 ± 7.8
Range	13–43	15–58
Race		
White	70.1%	69.9%
African American	13.3%	11.5%
Hispanic/Latino	6.7%	9.6%
Multi-ethnic	4.9%	4.8%
Other	5%	4.2%
Income	< $15K	$15–25K
Education	High School	High School

findings, birth families participating in the EGDS, on average, had fewer socioeconomic resources and lower educational attainment than US averages at the initiation of the EGDS. At the most recent interview, slightly more than half of birth mothers and only 37 percent of birth fathers reported that their income had increased since the start of the study. These data indicate that birth parents tend to struggle more financially than same-age peers and may lack resources and social support. These data are also informative for the adoption community to understand the context and resources available to individuals facing an unintended pregnancy.

Collecting information about the birth parents' medical and physical histories, along with their social environments prior to and during the pregnancy, is standard practice in adoption planning. The medical history may include the birth parents' general physical health and presence of chronic illnesses, as well as the amount of prenatal care a woman received and any complications she experienced during her pregnancy. The social history includes information about use of substances during pregnancy, where the birth parents lived, and their social support. This information informs adoptive parents about their children's potential heritable and prenatal risk and protective factors, and may help explain unanticipated medical problems or conditions later in their child's life.

The EGDS collected the birth mothers' obstetric and delivery records and asked birth parents to complete several questionnaires that focused on pregnancy experiences as well as their social support systems during and following the pregnancy. The EGDS found that the majority of participating birth mothers (84 percent) reported receiving prenatal care at some point during their pregnancy. Birth mothers participating in EGDS have experienced higher levels of perinatal risk than national averages (Marceau et al., 2015). In regard to substance use during pregnancy, 28.5 percent of birth mothers in the EGDS used one substance, with cigarette smoking, alcohol use, and marijuana use being the most common (Marceau et al., 2015). The rates of use in the EGDS for most substances were higher than in the general population, except in the case of alcohol use, for which the rates were comparable (Marceau et al., 2015). These data suggest that despite higher rates of substance use, many birth mothers remained mindful of their health during their pregnancy by accessing prenatal care.

Birth parent mental health was examined by measuring depression and anxiety symptoms; two symptoms commonly reported across previous studies with birth parents. Using the Beck Anxiety and Depression Inventories (Beck, Epstein, Brown, and Steer, 1988), symptoms were assessed at approximately five months post-partum and again one year later. For anxiety symptoms, birth mothers reported mild anxiety while birth fathers reported minimal anxiety symptoms five months post-partum. Anxiety symptoms decreased for both birth mothers and fathers a year later. These reported symptoms are lower than a similarly aged group of young adults (Blalock and Joiner, 2000). Birth mothers reported greater depressive symptoms at their initial interview, approximately five months post-partum, than birth fathers. When compared to a study of young adults, both females and males reported lower levels of depressive symptoms than did our birth parent sample, both at five months post-partum and one year later (Bernert, Merrill, Braithwaite, Van Orden, and Joiner Jr., 2007). Depressive symptoms for birth mothers also decreased a year later, while birth fathers reported a slight increase. These findings suggest that depression is more prominent than anxiety among birth parents who have placed a child for adoption, compared to the general population of young adults.

In regard to the social environment during pregnancy and adoption planning, birth parents were asked about their levels of social support. Prior research has shown that the birth parents' own parents have a great deal of influence on adoption planning and can lead some birth parents to feel coerced into making an adoption plan (Clapton, 2007; De Simone, 1996), and that birth mothers who report higher levels of feeling coerced also tend to have more unresolved grief (De Simone, 1996). In the EGDS, birth parents were asked to describe how their parents, the other birth parent, and a close confidant reacted to the news about the pregnancy. Birth mothers reported that their parents were more often angry and worried than they were supportive; their close confidant was mostly supportive and worried; and the birth father was anxious. Birth fathers reported similar reactions from their own parents and close confidant: they personally felt more anxious and worried than other emotions. Whitesel (2008) found that birth fathers reported a more positive adjustment post-adoption when they openly discussed the adoption plans with their parents versus not disclosing the pregnancy to them at all. These findings highlight the importance of support systems for birth parents.

The EGDS also examined relational dynamics within birth families, with a focus on the relationship between birth parents and their romantic partners, whether or not it was the other birth parent. Birth parents reported on their relationship status throughout their participation in the study, allowing us to understand how their interpersonal relationships changed over time. At the time birth parents enrolled in the study, about half reported they were in a relationship. In 8.5 percent of the cases, birth mothers reported the pregnancy resulted from rape and therefore we did not ask additional questions about her relationship with the birth father.

While most birth parents are not together currently, a small percentage (about 6 percent) have remained together throughout the 15 years of the study. Few birth parents were married at the start of the study, but 15 years later, more than half of birth parents reported being married or living in a committed, marriage-like relationship. About a third of the birth parent sample was not parenting at the start of EGDS and have not parented children at any time during their participation, while 45 percent were parenting at the time of enrollment, when the adoptee was born. Following the adoption placement, half of the birth parents added children to their family, regardless of whether they were already parenting or not. This suggests that birth parents' life circumstances may change, and their readiness to parent may also change as they become older.

Few studies have explored how placing a child for adoption influences birth parents' lives. Within EGDS, birth parents were asked how different areas of their lives were affected by making an adoption plan five months after placement and one year later. Some of these areas include their relationships with others, finances, physical and emotional health, happiness and self-worth, and the ability to plan for the future. Birth mothers and fathers reported negative influences on their adjustment at five months post-placement, but this effect attenuated over time. The area that was impacted the most was mental and emotional health at both five and 18 months post-placement. One year after placement, birth mothers reported their ability to plan for the future was the most improved area; for birth fathers, it was general life satisfaction. These findings indicate evidence of positive adjustment for birth parents a year after the adoption placement in regard to planning for the future. However, the healing process continues over time, and birth parents need time and continued support to move forward positively in their journey. The next section will focus on what leads birth parents toward making an adoption plan and highlight the thoughtfulness and caring often put into adoption planning.

Factors that lead to choosing adoption

Both adoption professionals and adopting parents benefit from knowing why birth parents choose to make an adoption plan. Adoptive parents, in particular, need to be able to convey information to their child about decisions birth parents make. The EGDS explored reasons birth parents placed their infants for adoption. They most often chose adoption due to circumstances related to their home environment, such as not residing in a stable living situation (Early Growth & Development Study, 2012). Birth parents reported not having the financial resources to parent a child or an additional child, not being able to parent on their own, or not being ready for parenting. The idea of adoption as the best option was also noted by birth parents, especially as an alternative to abortion.

The EGDS further explored what birth families considered when selecting an adoptive family. Birth parents were asked about the types of adoptive family characteristics that were important to them when selecting a family. As summarized in Figure 7.2, the most important factor for birth mothers and fathers was that the adoptive parents could provide educational opportunities for their child. Other "very important" factors included the adopting parents having a close marital relationship, being financially secure, and offering the type of family the birth parent would have liked to have had when they were growing up. More than half of birth parents reported that it did not matter to them if there were already other children in the adoptive home.

A unique attribute of the EGDS is the in-depth examination of birth fathers' characteristics and their role in adoption planning. In the EGDS, most of the birth fathers were involved in the decision for adoption (70.8 percent) and had some interaction with adoption professionals. The adoption decision-making activities that birth fathers engaged in included helping select an adoptive family, providing a medical and social history, and/or receiving counseling and support. For the small number who reported never working with the adoption agency, most of them still reported either signing a consent to the adoption and/or providing social and medical background about themselves and their families. Only 15 birth fathers did not report any involvement with an adoption agency. Birth fathers who did not work directly with the agency indicated most often that they refrained because they were following the birth mother's wishes or that they did not want to be a direct part of the process. In sum, the EGDS demonstrates a pattern of high involvement with the creation of the adoption plan by birth fathers. This finding challenges stereotypes of birth fathers as being absent throughout the adoption process (Clapton, 2007).

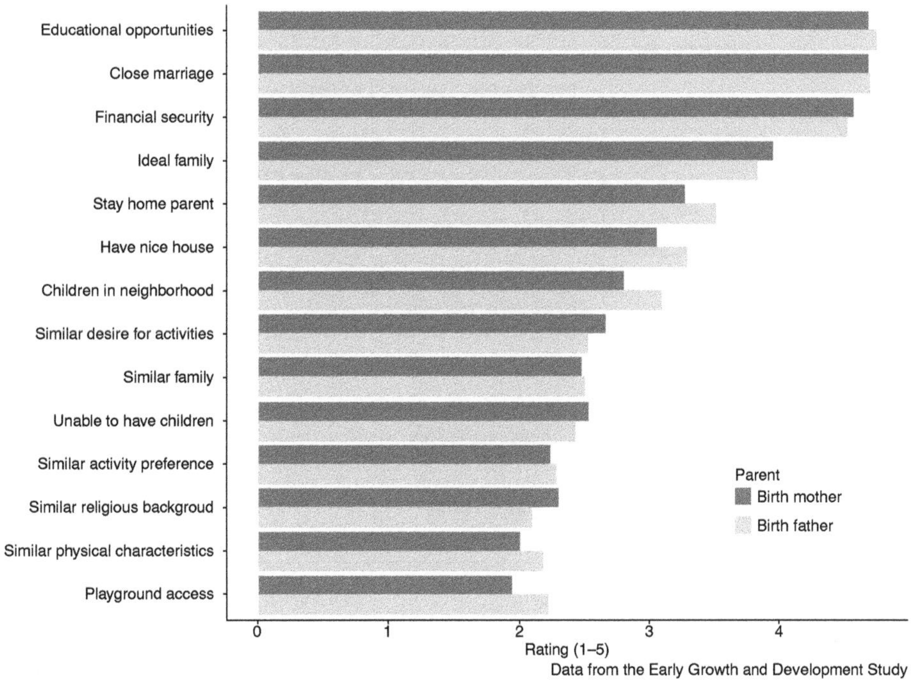

Figure 7.2 Factors important to birth parents when selecting an adoptive family

Having as much information as possible about the birth parents and their story may help facilitate the child's own narrative and understanding of themselves and assist adoptive parents in their comfort with communicating adoption to their child (Brodzinsky, 2011). These data also highlight that most birth parents are thoughtful and concerned about the homes in which their children will be placed. This finding challenges the stereotype that birth parents "give up" their children and do not care about them. These data can help to inform individuals and couples seeking to adopt by providing a better understanding of the needs and desires of birth parents who are considering an adoption plan.

Birth parents are not the only members of the adoption kinship network subject to stereotypes; adoptive parents are subject to assumptions and negative social stigma due to the perception that adoptive parenting is somehow lesser than parenting biological children (Wegar, 2000). Assumptions also exist around why individuals and couples choose to adopt, with the most common perception being infertility (Goldberg, Kinkler, and Hines, 2011). There are a number of other driving forces that lead individuals and couples to adoption, especially in light of the growing diversity in family type (e.g., single, gay, lesbian). The EGDS created a measure aimed at exploring the reasons adoptive parents chose to adopt; results are shown in Figure 7.3. The measure included a list of eight statements that reflect different motivations for adoption, and the adoptive parents rated how much each statement applied to them. The primary reason endorsed was an overarching desire to be a parent. While many men and women cited their inability to have a biological child, they also decided to adopt for other reasons, such as wanting to provide a home to a child or because adoption was already a part of their family. These data suggest that infertility is not always

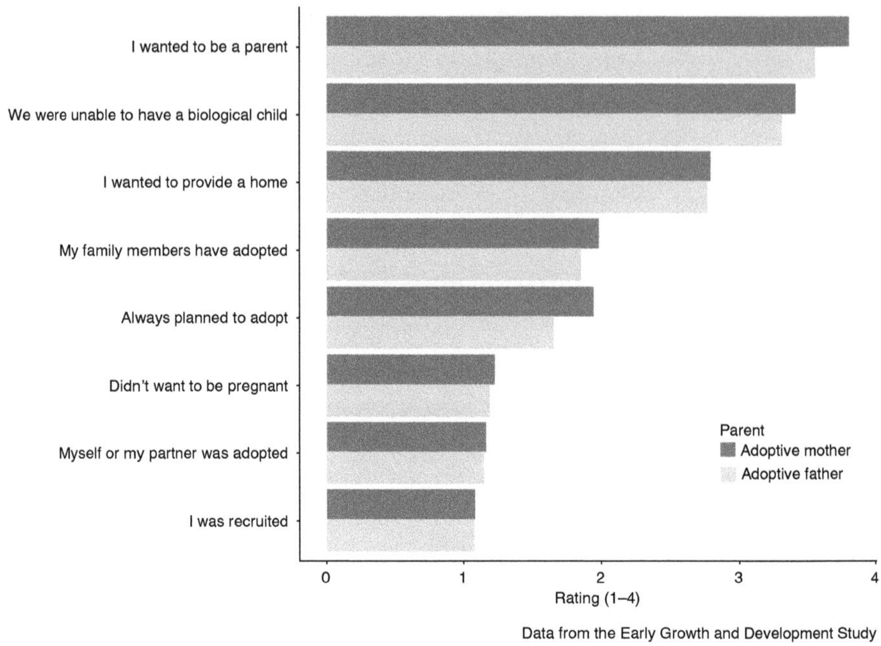

Figure 7.3 Factors important to adoptive parents when choosing to make an adoption plan

the deciding factor for individuals who want to become parents. Instead, adoption becomes an option to experience the journey of parenthood and provide a nurturing and loving environment for a child.

Adoptive families

In this section, we describe some general trends in research on adoptive families, followed by a careful examination of adoptive families within the EGDS from a holistic and family-focused perspective. Finally, we highlight a number of important genetic, environmental, and gene–environment interaction findings that have emerged as families in the EGDS have matured over the course of the study.

There is a great deal of heterogeneity in adoption in the United States (Brodzinsky, 2005), with three primary pathways to adoption: private domestic organizations and intermediaries, child welfare/foster care systems, and international organizations (Grotevant and McDermott, 2014). Adoption represents the addition of a new family member into an existing network (Rosnati, 2015), and the formation of an adoptive family is better thought of as a transition or journey rather than as a singular event (Brodzinsky and Huffman, 1988).

Much of the existing literature on adoption has focused on the development of the adopted child. Common research designs include comparing the developmental progress of adopted children to that of non-adopted children, or investigating the ability of adopted children to "recover" from adverse early life experiences. Adoption studies, however, can also be used to disentangle the influences of genetic factors and prenatal environment from postnatal experiences on children's emotional, behavioral, and physical development (Palacios and Brodzinsky, 2010). The EGDS utilizes this strategy.

Adoptive families within the EGDS reflect the diversity observed in adoption more generally. Demographics at placement can be seen in Table 7.2. Twenty percent of EGDS families represent transracial adoptions (i.e. the child does not match the race of either adoptive parent) and roughly half of the adopted children match the race of both adoptive parents (54.5 percent), while 5.3 percent match the race of only one parent. For the remaining 20 percent, adopted children were listed as multi-racial; therefore it is unknown if they match the race of an adopted parent. Seventy-nine of the adoptive parents were divorced after 15 years (14 percent) and seven parents had had more than one divorce in that time span; six adoptive parents were widowed. The EGDS sample has expanded over time. The original 561 adoptive and birth families have grown over time through the addition of siblings into the study. When the study began, 64 percent of adopted children were the only child in the home; now more than half of adopted children have siblings.

Research within the EGDS can be considered under the four general aims mentioned earlier in this chapter. The adoptive family unit is essential for discerning environmental influences on the child (Aim 1), and parenting behavior has emerged as a particularly salient domain of influence. Overreactive parenting (such as parents exhibiting harsh, irritable, or overly angry behavior) is particularly important and has been found to contribute directly to child externalizing behaviors (e.g. acting out, impulsivity) independent of inherited risk in early childhood (Marceau et al., 2015). In addition, parenting interacts with children's temperament characteristics. Overreactive parenting coupled with negative emotionality (such as fussiness, difficulty to soothe, and irritability) during infancy predicted externalizing behaviors in toddlerhood above and beyond prenatal risk (Lipscomb et al., 2011). Findings from the EGDS also highlight the important role of positive parenting (e.g., warmth, responsiveness). Adoptive mothers' warm parenting at age 6 predicted lower levels of child externalizing behaviors at age 7 compared to children whose adoptive mothers displayed less warm parenting (Reuben et al., 2016). Higher levels of positive reinforcement during a clean-up task were related to lower levels of child behavior problems during early childhood (Waller et al., 2017). The EGDS provides a unique lens through which positive parenting can be explored, and has highlighted that, independent from a child's inherited characteristics, positive parenting is critical for child development.

Table 7.2 Adoptive family demographics at placement

	Adoptive mothers	*Adoptive fathers*	*Child*
N	568	559	561
Age (range)	37.6 ± 5.7 (24–55)	38.1 ± 5.7 (25–60)	<12 weeks
Race			
White	91.3%	89.5%	55.6%
African American	3.5%	5.1%	13%
Hispanic/Latin	2.1%	2%	10.9%
Multi-ethnic	0.9%	1.1%	19.3%
Other	2.2%	2.3%	1.3%
Income	$100–125K	$125–150K	NA
Education	College degree	College degree	NA

Aims 2 and 3 reflect circumstances under which genetic and/or prenatal influences work together with the adoptive family environment to influence child development. For example, for children with high prenatal risk (e.g., toxin exposure, pregnancy complications, or substance use during pregnancy), adoptive mothers' overreactive parenting was associated with a less variable cortisol rhythm, while adoptive fathers' overreactive parenting was associated with a more variable cortisol rhythm. These findings suggest that parenting affects the impact of prenatal risks on children's stress responses, and that mothers and fathers influence this association differently (Marceau et al., 2013). Thus, the adoptive family unit shapes the expression of an underlying characteristic present before birth.

Adoption designs are essential to understanding child development because they are able to tease apart what influences can be attributed to the child's environment in their adoptive home, and what influences can be attributed to the child's inherited and prenatal background provided by their birth family. While this design does allow for identification of inherited contributions to development, it also facilitates our understanding about which environmental factors, such as differences in parenting practices, may influence child development.

Implications for practice and policy

The broad goals of this chapter thus far have been to describe the experiences of birth and adoptive families in an adoption design using the EGDS as an example, to emphasize the role of birth parents as critical participants in research utilizing an adoption design, and to highlight select research from the EGDS. The focus on birth parents in this chapter and in the adoption design more broadly parallels an increased involvement of birth parents in the lives of adopted children. Adoptive families and birth parents are linked through the unique relationships established through the adoption process, alternatively referred to as a "shared fate" (Kirk, 1964) or as "weak ties" (Granovetter, 1977). Adoption openness (operationalized as perceived openness, knowledge, and contact between adoptive and birth parents) has been measured in the EGDS families since first enrollment. The EGDS has also focused on satisfaction with openness, separate from actual contact, as a means to understand how this relationship may be associated with individual and family life. Ge and colleagues (2008) first characterized this relationship in the EGDS. The authors were interested in the relationship between satisfaction with the adoption process and birth mother adjustment after adoption, and found that openness in adoption was significantly and positively associated with satisfaction as well as better post-placement adjustment of birth mothers. This fits with a general theory of adoption openness, which suggests that more openness is generally associated with a decreased sense of loss and grief for birth parents (Henney, Ayers-Lopez, McRoy, and Grotevant, 2007) as well as improved adjustment to life as an adoptive parent in adoptive families (Grotevant, McRoy, Elde, and Fravel, 1994). Research from the EGDS indicates that openness is a key factor in birth mother and father satisfaction with the adoption process and with post-adoption adjustment (Ge et al., 2008). In a different sample of adopted children, greater levels of satisfaction with contact in the adoptive family were associated with less externalizing behaviors during adolescence (Grotevant, Rueter, Korff, and Gonzalez, 2011). Levels of openness can change over time between adoptive and birth families, and the "right amount" of openness can change across the life course (Henney, Ayers-Lopez, McRoy, and Grotevant, 2007). This can be seen in the EGDS, where average levels of openness decrease across time, but satisfaction with adoption openness is stable. Figure 7.4 provides openness data from the first EGDS cohort, which includes children born before 2006. These findings support the idea that openness in adoption can be positive for all members of the adoption kinship network,

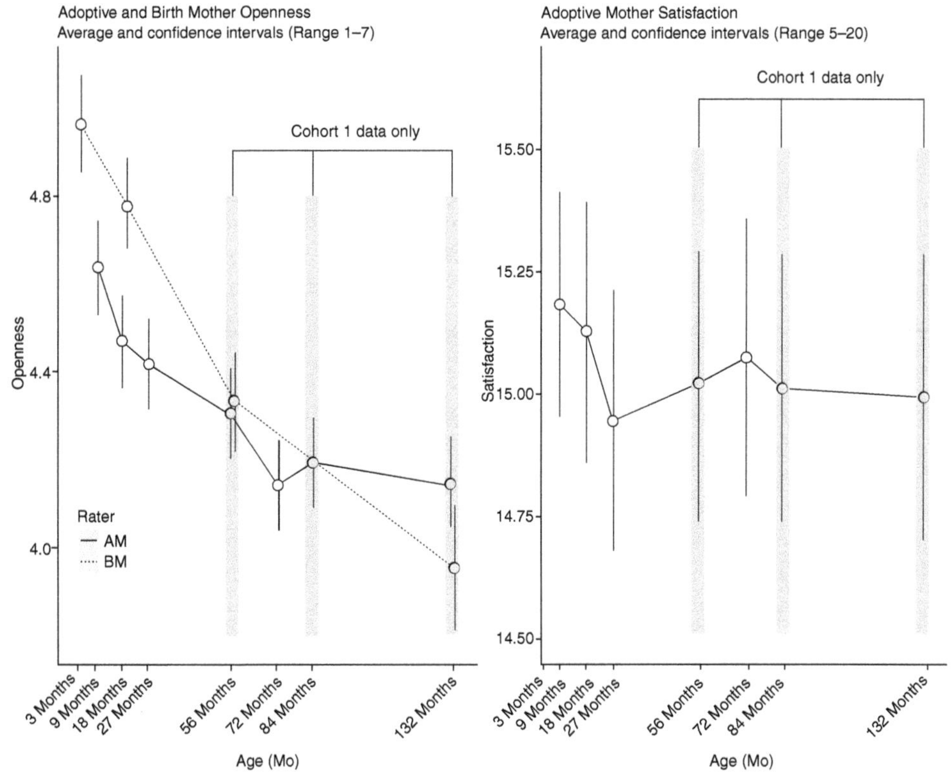

Figure 7.4 Trajectories of openness and satisfaction in the EGDS

despite varied definitions of openness across families. Adoption practitioners must be well versed in educating birth parents and adoptive families about openness, its benefits, and how to navigate an ongoing relationship that might change over time.

Beyond providing insight into the impact of openness and the adoption process itself, birth parents provide critical information about inherited and prenatal environmental influences on the developing child. Much of the early literature specifically about birth mothers viewed their actions as neurotic (Pannor, Baran, and Sorosky, 1978) and was extremely judgmental by modern standards. This viewpoint no longer holds credence, and the literature on birth parents has become much more empathetic. The adoption can be considered a life stressor for birth families (Brodzinsky and Smith, 2014), and can result in unmet needs for these individuals (Coleman and Garratt, 2016; Memarnia, Nolte, Norris, and Harborne, 2015). However, despite improved understanding of the experiences of birth parents and the adopted child which refutes those early conceptualizations, some stigma remains for birth parents. In the future it will be critical for investigators to acknowledge that adoption is not a single event, but a journey that plays out across the lives of both birth and adoptive families over time. The continued involvement of birth families in EGDS (and other adoption designs) allows for these families to continue to relate how the experience of adoption has shaped their lives. One of the most apparent lessons from the EGDS is that birth parents can play a central role in design and execution of research whose goal is to capture a holistic and complete understanding of adoption within and between families. This research can also inform adoption practitioners in their work with birth parents, not only around the time of placement but also help them better understand the struggle birth parents may continue to experience years later and target services aimed at promoting more positive long-term outcomes.

The EGDS now includes birth and adoptive siblings in the sample, providing a greater opportunity to examine inherited and environmental effects both across multiple levels of genetic relatedness within birth and adoptive families. For example, comparisons can be made across biologically related siblings being parented in different environments, and the study will explore if changes in the birth family composition are related to changes in other aspects of their adjustment over time.

The study of birth parents, coupled with analysis of the adoptive family environment, furthers our understanding of the ways in which heritable and environmental influences shape each individual child. Parenting behavior within the adoptive family has been especially informative of child health and behavior across the study, and influences the expression of heritable risk factors. Adoption practitioners can emphasize to adopting parents the important influence of positive parenting while also providing them with a better understanding of the complexity of potential risk factors. Practitioners can empower parents by reinforcing the critical role the adoptive family environment plays in child development.

Studies such as the EGDS demonstrate not only the many benefits of the adoption design and its role in understanding parenting and child development, but also illuminate elements of adoption that are of interest to adoption researchers and practitioners, with a goal of providing data-informed services to all members of the adoption kinship network.

References

Beck, A.T., Epstein, N., Brown, G., & Steer, R.A. (1988). An inventory for measuring clinical anxiety: Psychometric properties. *Journal of Consulting and Clinical Psychology, 56*(6), 893–897. doi: 10.1037/0022-006X.56.6.893

Bernert, R.A., Merrill, K.A., Braithwaite, S.R., Van Orden, K.A., & Joiner, T.E. (2007). Family life stress and insomnia symptoms in a prospective evaluation of young adults. *Journal of Family Psychology, 21*, 58–66. doi: 10.1037/0893-3200.21.1.58

Blalock, J.A., & Joiner, T.E. (2000). Interaction of cognitive avoidance coping and stress in predicting depression/anxiety. *Cognitive Therapy and Research, 24*(1), 47–65. doi: 10.1023/A:1005450908245

Brodzinsky, A.B. (1990). Surrendering an infant for adoption: The birthmother experience. In D.M. Brodzinky & M.D. Schechter (Eds), *The psychology of adoption* (pp. 295–315). New York, NY, US: Oxford University Press.

Brodzinsky, D., & Huffman, L. (1988). Transition to adoptive parenthood. *Marriage & Family Review, 12*(3–4), 267–286. doi: 10.1300/J002v12n03_13.

Brodzinsky, D., & Smith, S.L. (2014). Post-placement adjustment and the needs of birthmothers who place an infant for adoption. *Adoption Quarterly, 17*(3), 165–184. doi: 10.1080/10926755.2014.891551

Brodzinsky, D.M. (2005). *Psychological issues in adoption: Research and practice*. Westport, CT, US: Praeger Publishers/Greenwood Publishing Group.

Brodzinsky, D.M. (2011). Children's understanding of adoption: Developmental and clinical implications. *Professional Psychology: Research and Practice, 42*(2), 200–207. doi: 10.1037/a0022415

Christian, C.L., McRoy, R.G., Grotevant, H.D., & Bryant, C.M. (1997). Grief resolution of birthmothers in confidential, time-limited mediated, ongoing mediated, and fully disclosed adoptions. *Adoption Quarterly, 1*(2), 35–58. doi: 10.1300/J145v01n02_03

Clapton, G. (2007). The experiences and needs of birth fathers in adoption: What we know now and some practice implications. *Practice, 19*(1), 61–71. doi: 10.1080/09503150701220515

Claridge, A.M. (2014). Supporting birth parents in adoption: A couple treatment approach. *Adoption Quarterly*, *17*(2), 112–133. doi: 10.1080/10926755.2014.891545

Coleman, P.K., & Garratt, D. (2016). From birth mothers to first mothers: Toward a compassionate understanding of the life-long act of adoption placement. *Issues in Law & Medicine*, *31*(2), 139–163.

De Simone, M. (1996). Birth mother loss: Contributing factors to unresolved grief. *Clinical Social Work Journal*, *24*(1), 65–76. doi: 10.1007/BF02189942

Dick, D.M. (2011). Gene-environment interaction in psychological traits and disorders. *Annual Review Of Clinical Psychology*, 7, 383–409. doi: 10.1146/annurev-clinpsy-032210-104518

Early Growth & Development Study (2012). *Agency report: national summary statistics*. Unpublished manuscript.

Farr, R.H., Ravvina, Y., & Grotevant, H.D. (2018). Birth family contact experiences among lesbian, gay, and heterosexual adoptive parents with school-age children: Birth family contact among LG and heterosexual adoptive parents. *Family Relations*, *67*(1), 132–146. doi: 10.1111/fare.12295

Ge, X., Natsuaki, M.N., Martin, D.M., Leve, L.D., Neiderhiser, J.M., Shaw, D.S., & Reiss, D. (2008). Bridging the divide: Openness in adoption and postadoption psychosocial adjustment among birth and adoptive parents. *Journal of Family Psychology*, *22*(4), 529–540. doi: 10.1037/a0012817

Goldberg, A. E., Kinkler, L. A., & Hines, D. A. (2011). Perception and internalization of adoption stigma among lesbian, gay, and heterosexual adoptive parents. *Journal of GLBT Family Studies*, 7, 132–154. doi: http://dx.doi.org/10.1080/1550428x.2011.537554.

Granovetter, M.S. (1977). The strength of weak. In S. Leinhardt (Ed.), *Social Networks* (pp. 347–367). doi: 10.1016/B978-0-12-442450-0.50025-0

Grotevant, H.D., & McDermott, J.M. (2014). Adoption: Biological and social processes linked to adaptation. *Annual Review of Psychology*, *65*, 235–265. doi: 10.1146/annurev-psych-010213-115020

Grotevant, H.D., McRoy, R.G., Elde, C.L., & Fravel, D.L. (1994). Adoptive family system dynamics: Variations by level of openness in the adoption. *Family Process*, *33*(2), 125–146. doi: 10.1111/j.1545-5300.1994.00125.x

Grotevant, H.D., Rueter, M., Korff, L.V., & Gonzalez, C. (2011). Post-adoption contact, adoption communicative openness, and satisfaction with contact as predictors of externalizing behavior in adolescence and emerging adulthood. *Journal of Child Psychology and Psychiatry*, *52*(5), 529–536. doi: 10.1111/j.1469-7610.2010.02330.x

Henney, S.M., Ayers-Lopez, S., McRoy, R.G., & Grotevant, H.D. (2007). Evolution and resolution: Birthmothers' experience of grief and loss at different levels of adoption openness. *Journal of Social and Personal Relationships*, *24*(6), 875–889. doi: 10.1177/0265407507084188

Kirk, H.D. (1964). *Shared fate: A theory of adoption and mental health*. New York: Free Press.

Leve, L.D., Neiderhiser, J.M., Scaramella, L.V., & Reiss, D. (2010). The early growth and development study: Using the prospective adoption design to examine genotype–environment interplay. *Behavior Genetics*, *40*(3), 306–314. doi: 10.1007/s10519-010-9353-1

Leve, L.D., Neiderhiser, J.M., Shaw, D.S., Ganiban, J., Natsuaki, M.N., & Reiss, D. (2013). The early growth and development study: A prospective adoption study from birth through middle childhood. *Twin Research and Human Genetics*, *16*(1), 412–423. doi: 10.1017/thg.2012.126

Lipscomb, S.T., Leve, L.D., Harold, G.T., Neiderhiser, J.M., Shaw, D.S., Ge, X., & Reiss, D. (2011). Trajectories of parenting and child negative emotionality during infancy and toddlerhood: A longitudinal analysis. *Child Development*, *82*(5), 1661–1675. doi: 10.1111/j.1467-8624.2011.01639.x

Madden, E.E., Ryan, S., Aguiniga, D.M., Killian, M., & Romanchik, B. (2018). The relationship between time and birth mother satisfaction with relinquishment. *Families in Society*, *99*(2), 170–183. doi: 10.1177/1044389418768489

Marceau, K., Laurent, H.K., Neiderhiser, J.M., Reiss, D., Shaw, D.S., Natsuaki, M.N., & Leve, L.D. (2015). Combined influences of genes, prenatal environment, cortisol, and parenting on the development of children's internalizing versus externalizing problems. *Behavior Genetics*, *45*(3), 268–282. doi: 10.1007/s10519-014-9689-z

Marceau, K., Ram, N., Neiderhiser, J.M., Laurent, H.K., Shaw, D.S., Fisher, P., & Leve, L.D. (2013). Disentangling the effects of genetic, prenatal and parenting influences on children's cortisol variability. *Stress*, *16*(6), 607–615. doi: 10.3109/10253890.2013.825766

Memarnia, N., Nolte, L., Norris, C., & Harborne, A. (2015). "It felt like it was night all the time": Listening to the experiences of birth mothers whose children have been taken into care or adopted. *Adoption & Fostering*, *39*(4), 303–317. doi: 10.1177/0308575915611516

Palacios, J., & Brodzinsky, D. (2010). Adoption research: Trends, topics, outcomes. *International Journal of Behavioral Development*, *34*(3), 270–284. doi: 10.1177/0165025410362837

Pannor, R., Baran, A., & Sorosky, A.D. (1978). Birth parents who relinquished babies for adoption revisited. *Family Process*, *17*(3), 329–337. doi: 10.1111/j.1545-5300.1978.00329.x

Reuben, J.D., Shaw, D.S., Neiderhiser, J.M., Natsuaki, M.N., Reiss, D., & Leve, L.D. (2016). Warm parenting and effortful control in toddlerhood: Independent and interactive predictors of school-age externalizing behavior. *Journal of Abnormal Child Psychology*, *44*(6), 1083–1096. doi: 10.1007/s10802-015-0096-6

Rhea, S.A., Bricker, J.B., Wadsworth, S.J., & Corley, R.P. (2013). The Colorado adoption project. *Twin Research and Human Genetics*, *16*(1), 358–365. doi: 10.1017/thg.2012.109

Rosnati, R. (2015). Family resources in the transition to adoption: Introduction to the Special Section. *Family Science*, *6*(1), 38–42. doi: 10.1080/19424620.2015.1080962

Smith, S.L. (2006). *Safeguarding the rights and well-being of birthparents in the adoption process*. Retrieved from www.adoptioninstitute.org/publications/2006_11_Birthparent_Study_All.pdf

US Census Bureau. (2003). *Income in the United States: 2003*. Retrieved from www.census.gov/prod/2003pubs/p60-221.pdf.

US Census Bureau. (2004). *Education attainment in the United States: 2003*. Retrieved from www.census.gov/prod/2004pubs/p20-550.pdf.

Waller, R., Shaw, D.S., Neiderhiser, J.M., Ganiban, J.M., Natsuaki, M.N., Reiss, D., & Hyde, L.W. (2017). Toward an understanding of the role of the environment in the development of early callous behavior: Early CU behavior and the environment. *Journal of Personality*, *85*(1), 90–103. doi: 10.1111/jopy.12221

Wegar, K. (2000). Adoption, family ideology, and social stigma: Bias in community attitudes, adoption research, and practice. *Family Relations*, *49*(4), 363–370. doi: 10.1111/j.1741-3729.2000.00363.x

Whitesel, A.L. (2008). *Post adoption adjustment of birth fathers: The effects of relationships with birth mothers and family*. Retrieved February 20, 2019, from https://search.proquest.com/openview/ce96dfac8384f396b360dff7510b8b77/1?pq-origsite=gscholar&cbl=18750&diss=y

Wiley, M.O., & Baden, A.L. (2005). Birth parents in adoption: Research, practice, and counseling psychology. Practice-Science Integration Section of the Scientific Forum. *Counseling Psychologist*, *33*(1), 13–50. doi: 10.1177/0011000004265961

Zamostny, K.P., Wiley, M.O., O'Brien, K.M., Lee, R.M., & Baden, A.L. (2003). Breaking the silence: Advancing knowledge about adoption for counseling psychologists. *The Counseling Psychologist*, *31*(6), 647–650. doi: 10.1177/0011000003258082

PART II

Diversity in adoption

8

UNIQUE CHALLENGES AND STRENGTHS FOR FAMILIES FORMED THROUGH INTERNATIONAL ADOPTION

Marta Reinoso Bernuz

International adoption has become an important phenomenon in contemporary society. At its peak in 2004, approximately 45,000 children were adopted from other countries, 5,541 of those into Spain, which registered the second highest figure for international adoptions in the world after the United States. Although the figures have dropped dramatically worldwide (an analysis of the subject can be found in Selman, 2012), the total number of children adopted from other countries by Spanish families, according to official sources, has reached 54,792 since its legal regulation (1997–2017). In 2004, children mainly came from China (2,389), Russia (1,618), Ukraine (349), Colombia (256), and Ethiopia (220). However, this trend has changed and, currently, Vietnam (98), China (85), India (57), Russia (54), and Ethiopia (52) represent the principal countries of origin (Ministry of Health, Consumer Affairs, and Social Welfare, 2019).

Awareness of the fluctuating numbers of international adoptees is essential to those who work in the area and must prepare for the supports and services unique to these adoptees' challenges and risks. Issues international adoptees have to deal with throughout their development (see Gunnar & Kertes, 2005; Miller, 2005) include early experiences such as abandonment, abuse, neglect, malnutrition, social or emotional poverty, and institutionalization, which create situations of cumulative risk and often lay the foundation for less successful development paths. A second set of stressors include their personal experiences during the separation that adoption entails, including residential moves, moving to another country, changes in personal relationships, and interethnic experiences. The last set of challenges include the experiences and behavioral challenges typical of their age. Adoptees work through these matters with varying success according to risk factors from early childhood experiences and developed adaptive skills. Difficulties can thus become entrenched from the outset, or development can be progressively transformed through experiences and appropriate progress (Brodzinsky, Schechter, & Henig, 1992; Brodzinsky, Smith, & Brodzinsky, 1998).

The adoption process can also entail extremely painful and exhausting experiences for the adoptive parents, perhaps including infertility diagnosis, unsuccessful assisted reproduction procedures, infertility grief, procurement of a suitability certificate, and/or financial investment. Despite the fact that adoptive parenting has many aspects in common with biological parenting, important differences stem from the way parenthood is established. Moreover, international adoption is distinct from domestic adoption and presents a number of specific features worthy of consideration. These are primarily related to prior experiences in the country of origin, and to the potential for ethnic, cultural, and language differences.

Consequently, the challenges and specific processes faced by internationally adoptive families primarily include the establishing and redirecting of the emotional bond, managing communication about adoption, monitoring psychosocial development and adjustment, managing ethnic and cultural differences, and searching for origins (see, among others, Brodzinsky et al., 1992). According to Brodzinsky (1990), the way in which the adoptive family copes with and adjusts to these shifting challenges has a significant influence on the development and well-being of the adoptee and the system as a whole. This means that all of these processes can be a significant source of stress for adoptive families while also providing opportunities to grow stronger.

The most significant contributions and implications of the international literature in these different areas are reviewed below. The available evidence in Spain will be accorded special consideration, in view of the significance of the Spanish case in the global context.

The process of bonding and family integration

The experience of a secure attachment is a sensation of comfort and well-being stemming from a figure of affection and protection and is the basis of emotional regulation and future relationships (Bowlby, 1982; Fonagy, Target, Gergely, & Jurist, 2002). But problems can arise when bonding's natural development is interrupted by numerous disruptions in early relationships. For example, meta-analytic research conducted by Van Den Dries, Juffer, Van IJzendoorn, and Bakermans-Kranenburg (2009) reveals a lower incidence of secure attachment and a higher incidence of disorganized attachment in adopted children as compared to non-adopted children. The risk of developing attachment disorders is reduced in cases of adoption at an early age – during the child's first year – and is higher for children adopted from highly depriving circumstances, such as orphanages in Eastern Europe.

Bond co-building with the adoptive family and changes in attachment patterns are processes that follow varying cycles, and it is therefore considered appropriate to speak of a transition to adoptive parenthood. During this process of change and unification, family dynamics – understood in terms of roles, responsibilities, and expectations assigned to or assumed by the different members – play an important part in regulating the child's adaptation and the family system as a whole (a deeper analysis of this specific area can be found in Arranz, Oliva, Olabarrieta, & Antolín, 2010; Berástegui, 2007; Bertrán, 2013; McKay, Ross, & Goldberg, 2010). A unique feature of the international adoption process is that emotional ties are constructed independently of genetic inheritance and the cultural or ethnic origin of the child. Adopted children must therefore establish their differentness from others and build relationships of individuality as well as of similarity or belonging, especially with the adoptive family. The appropriate organization of these elements promotes acceptance of the self and identity formation (Brodzinsky et al., 1992; see also San Román, 2013, for an analysis within the Spanish context).

It is also important to consider the experiences of different family members. The results of some comparative studies (e.g. Hawkins et al., 2007; Reinoso, Juffer, & Tieman, 2013; Stryker, 2011) indicate that the majority of children are satisfied with their adoptive family and that mothers and fathers, in general, have a fairly accurate idea of their children's perceptions of adoption. Despite this, important discrepancies exist in the conceptualization of the term "family." Transracial international adoptees have a broader and more heterogeneous vision of family than their adoptive parents, including their birth parents and other significant relationships from their country of origin in that vision, and in their assessments of communication about adoption, cultural identity, and discrimination. We will return to these aspects in greater detail later.

With regard to adoptive parents, protective factors identified by research include acceptance of the child's history prior to adoption, realistic and accurate expectations of the potential conflicts that can ensue, and realistic and accurate expectations of the adoption project itself (Berástegui, 2007; Corbella & Gómez, 2010). Previous research has recognized the high degree of involvement of the adopters in their work as parents and in the education of their children (Gibson, 2009; Hamilton, Cheng, & Powell, 2007), which is consistent with the fact that these families have been selected based on their ability to provide a suitable family environment. Recently, some critics (e.g. Pylypa, 2016) have warned of the dangers of societal promotion of intensive parenting practices in families of internationally adopted children, arguing that such practices are highly demanding and that their implementation is not backed by sufficient scientific evidence. Other authors have shown that large numbers of adoptive parents express important doubts and insecurities about their role (Bertrán, 2013) and that fear of failure as adoptive parents leads to a great deal of anxiety and stress (Verbovaya, 2016). In this context, the adoptive family's ability to recognize the particular challenges it faces, as well as its own resources and limitations, is a key factor for the success of the adoptive project (Berástegui, 2007; Kirk, 1964).

Adoptive parents' own histories of attachment also contribute to their parenting skills and the development of healthy attachments, and it is especially important that they resolve their own feelings of deprivation and grief prior to the arrival of the child (McKay et al., 2010). Similarly, for couples, the dynamic of their relationship exerts an effect on the attachment pattern they offer their child, and therefore on family adjustment (Corbella & Gómez, 2010). Baden, Gibbons, Wilson, & McGinnis (2013), in a critical review of the literature, recognize the lack of research on the difficulties and needs of adoptive parents, especially in the pre-adoption stage. This information is essential to create strategies for effective bonding and integration.

Less common family models – single-parent families, same-sex parents, blended families, etc. – can add complexity to the process of attachment between parents and children. Each of these models has its own specific, potentially stigmatizing, issues that must be addressed at the same time as those directly related to the adoption itself (Arranz et al., 2010).

An extreme expression of tension for adoptive families is the disruption of the adoption, estimated to occur in less than 5 percent of cases according to European research, and in 5 to 10 percent of cases according to studies conducted in the US. The chief causes of adoption disruption have been established as a sustained accumulation of risk factors, chronic or escalating difficulties, and either a lack of specialized support, or support arriving too late (see Berástegui, 2017; Festinger, 2014; Palacios, Rolock, Selwyn, & Barbosa-Ducharne, 2019; Verbovaya, 2016, for an in-depth analysis). Various studies therefore point to the importance of an early holistic and integrated therapeutic approach (e.g. Baden et al., 2013; Hegar & Watson, 2013; Weir et al., 2013).

Communication about adoption

There is currently agreement on the importance of an open, flexible, and empathetic communicative attitude within the adoptive family in promoting acceptance of the adoptive status and psychological well-being (see Chapter 18 in this volume). Spanish research draws similar conclusions to other international research on international adoption, finding that children consider their adoptive parents to be the most important figures with whom to talk about their adoption (Reinoso et al., 2013) and that, regardless of the information available on the child's origins, it is the adoptive parents who control what subject matter is addressed or avoided (Freeark, Rosenblum, Hus, & Root, 2008; Passmore, Feeney, & Foulstone, 2007). It is also known that the issues that are addressed later and less frequently are physical/racial differences and the reasons for the child's separation from their birth family (Berástegui & Jódar, 2013; Palacios, Sánchez-Sandoval, & León, 2005).

Communication about origins implies accepting and addressing the differences involved in the adoptive relationship; the events discussed often involve intense emotions and the challenges posed are numerous (e.g. Frekko, Leinaweaver, & Marre, 2015). Recent studies conducted in Spain, such as Aramburu et al. (2018), show that the majority of adolescents adopted from other countries rate their family's communication about their adoption positively; and that a greater degree of openness is associated with less likelihood of behavioral disorders among children. The same study showed that adolescents who had experienced abuse or neglect prior to their adoption reported less open communication surrounding their adoption.

In the case of children adopted from other countries, it is also necessary to consider the difficulties involved in finding and maintaining contact with the birth family. In spite of the existing controversy, uncertainty, and complexity of the open adoption process – that is, adoptions in which the birth family maintains some kind and degree of contact with the child and their adoptive family (Grotevant, 2012) – research shows it to have a positive impact on the individuals involved (Ge et al., 2008; Siegel, 2012; Wolfgram, 2008). Although this measure has a long tradition in many EU countries, Australia, New Zealand, Canada, and the United States, its legal recognition and implementation in Spain is very recent, in 2015, and still raises important questions (see Rosser & Berástegui, 2017). In this respect, it is fortunate that a great variety of materials and resources exist that facilitate expression, dialog, and reflection on identity and origins, including stories, books, and films (suggested sources and conversation techniques can be found in Wolfs (2008, 2010) and Reinoso, Requena, and Miró (2018), for example).

Psychosocial development and adjustment

Given the discontinuity between the pre- and post-adoption periods, the development, adaptation, and psychological adjustment of children adopted abroad is one of the questions having aroused the most interest and debate. The majority of studies have been aimed at determining whether adopted children present more problems than non-adopted children, and the results have not always been consistent. Early research (see Wierzbicki's meta-analysis, 1993) concluded that adopted children received psychological treatment to a greater degree than comparable non-adopted children, and presented a greater risk for psychosocial maladjustment, particularly externalizing behavioral problems and academic difficulties. However, various authors (e.g. Haaguard, 1998; Sharma, McGue, & Benson, 1996; Warren, 1992) have pointed out that the differences found were small and were a reflection of a greater predisposition on the part of the adoptive parents to seek psychological help. They also underscored the need to take into account the comparison group employed (see Palacios (2017) and Wilson (2004) for additional critical review).

New research investigating the effects of early deprivation on children's development by Juffer, Van IJzendoorn, and their team at Leiden University are of particular interest. A total of five meta-analytical studies were conducted with reference to aspects such as physical growth, cognitive development, school performance, attachment formation, behavioral problems, and self-esteem. The overall results present very positive data on the evolution and adjustment of children after adoption (see Juffer, Van IJzendoorn, and Palacios (2011) and Van IJzendoorn and Juffer (2006) for a detailed overview). Adopted children obtained better results in all the analyzed developmental areas compared with currently institutionalized children and showed significant recovery from the developmental delays present at the time of their adoption. At the same time, comparison with their current non-adoptive peers did reveal the existence of delays and difficulties, though these tended to be relatively small in some areas (behavioral problems) and somewhat more significant in others (head circumference, attachment problems, school performance, language). No significant differences between adopted children and non-adopted peers were found in other areas (weight, height, intelligence, self-esteem). Studies conducted in Spain obtained similar results and indicated adoptees' satisfactory socio-emotional adjustment (Aramburu et al., 2018; Barcons-Castel, Fornieles-Deu, & Costas-Moragas, 2011; Loizaga, Louzao, de Aranzabal, & Labayru, 2009; Palacios et al., 2005; Reinoso & Forns, 2012). The inconsistency found between cognitive abilities and academic results merits special mention, given the important influence of schooling and relationships formed in school on the life and well-being of adoptees. The authors suggest that the negative interference of socio-emotional demands encountered by adoptees over the years is a causal factor of poorer school performance relative to intellectual functioning.

The meta-analyses also demonstrate the strongly negative impact of early adversity on child development, while showing that the age at the time of adoption and the child's area of origin might not always be stable predictors of adjustment difficulties. The developmental stage of the child is revealed as another important factor for consideration: developing cognitive capacity in middle childhood improves the child's understanding of adoption and leads to increased risk of behavioral disorders. Generally speaking, the authors interpret these findings as a demonstration of the protective, albeit limited, effect of adoption as compared to the previously suffered adversity, and conclude that adoption is indeed an effective intervention that offers children the possibility of recovery and healthy development within an adoptive family.

Christoffersen (2012) conducted a systematic review of the literature to compare the progress of internationally adopted children with that of their peers or non-adopted siblings who remained with their birth families, in foster families, or in institutions in the country of origin. The comparison produced significant results in favor of the former in terms of cognitive function and academic performance, leading the author to conclude that adoption has a positive impact on these development areas. Results in relation to behavioral problems, mental health, and self-esteem were similar, though with heterogeneous results. The tentative conclusion is that the quality of the developmental context impacts results in such a way that adopted children who are in surroundings that are hostile or disrespectful of the adoption present lower levels of self-esteem and more mental health problems.

Similarly, a recent meta-analysis carried out by Behle and Pinquart (2016) showed that, in the event of a psychiatric diagnosis, adopted children and their families are as inclined as others to seek professional help; and that adopted children are twice as likely as non-adopted children to receive psychiatric treatment or a diagnosis of mental illness. This last figure is higher than that found in previous studies and meta-analyses which explored the symptomatology with continuous measurement (e.g. Barcons-Castel et al., 2011; Juffer et al., 2011; Loizaga et al., 2009; Reinoso & Forns, 2012), and supports the idea that differences in the level of psychological functioning of adopted children are found in its most serious expression (Haaguard, 1998). In addition, the meta-analysis indicates greater vulnerability to diverse disorders (ADHD, anxiety, behavioral problems, depression, substance abuse, and psychosis), which seems to suggest that the multiple risk factors associated with adoption are non-specific. (Chapters 24 through 28 in this volume provide more detailed information on emotional, behavioral, social, language, and academic outcomes for adoptees.)

Finally, it is important to note that, while much emphasis has been placed on the problems of adoptive families, few studies have focused on their capabilities. Some experts point to the important difference in favor of adopted children with respect to prosocial behavior (Sharma et al., 1996) and their popularity within their peer group (Stams, Juffer, Rispens, & Hoksbergen, 2000). These are elements of strength and play a key role in an individual's adjustment, buffering the impact of stressful situations and promoting resilience and successful results (Rutter, 2005).

Ethnic and cultural differences

In an important percentage of international adoptions, there are obvious racial differences between the children, their parents, and the community in which they live. Differences in physical characteristics can generate tension and unease (Juffer, 2006; Juffer & Tieman, 2009), and feelings of loss in relation to ethnic, racial, and genealogical ties (Brodzinsky et al., 1992). The ethnic and cultural origin of adopted children, the development of ethnic identity, and the influence these factors have on the child's adjustment and integration into their context is an important area of ongoing study (reviews of this issue can be found in Boivin & Hassan, 2015; Chen, 2016; Hollingsworth, 1997; Lee, 2003; Simon & Alstein, 1996). Empirical research conducted in Spain (Reinoso et al., 2013) shows that, compared with intraracial adoptive families, children of transracial adoptive families expressed a greater sense of belonging to and interest in their birth culture, while the parents reported a lesser degree of satisfaction and family identity on the part of their children. On the same subject, different authors (e.g. Grotevant, Dunbar, Kohler, & Esau, 2000; Hollingsworth, 1997; Lee, 2003) argue that transracial adoptees may have greater difficulty developing positive racial or ethnic identity.

Moreover, there is a need for negotiation of the expectations of the adoptive parents and the choices of the adoptee in relation to belonging and transnational identities. They must decide, for example, how they wish to incorporate the child's cultural origins – customs, festivals, language, etc. – into the life of the adoptive family (Friedlander, 1999; Scherman, 2010; Thomas & Tessler, 2007; Vonk & Massatti, 2008). Travel to the child's birth country is another way of maintaining this connection, as we shall see below. As transracial adopted children grow up, they acquire an increasingly complex and integrated view of their ethnic and cultural experiences, and can develop a biracial identity naturally, provided they are exposed to both adoptive and birth cultures, and if the adoptive parents cultivate open dialog around this question (see Friedlander et al., 2000). Moreover, different studies show that parents and children of adoptive families, in spite of their dissimilarities, tend to feel emotionally close and identify with each other (Juffer, 2006; Juffer & Tieman, 2009; McGuinness & Pallansch, 2000; Reinoso et al., 2013). This feeling of family cohesion and commitment is another strength of this family model that merits special mention.

As the years go by, however, transracial adoptees also become more aware of potential negative reactions from their surroundings (Powell & Affi, 2005). Physical or racial differences within the family make the adoption obvious to all and compromise the family's privacy, very often triggering thoughtless curiosity, questions, and comments (see Chapter 22 in this volume), which present a risk for the socialization and consolidation of a healthy ethno-cultural adoptive identity (Grotevant, 1997; Hollingsworth, 1997). In the context of Spain, the work of Reinoso, Pereda, Van Den Dries, and Forero (2016) shows that adoption-specific stressors most frequently expressed by internationally adopted children are interpersonal problems of victimization; also, in general, these stressors are appraised as less controllable than other generic stressors and tend not to be disclosed spontaneously. Longitudinal research extending into adulthood is essential for a better understanding of the experiences, issues, and responses of transracial adoptees.

Searching and reconciliation with origins

Understanding of and experiences relating to origins evolve according to developmental stage and the tasks encountered during that stage (see Brodzinsky et al. (1992) for a detailed description of these). Adoptive parents face the same challenges, their ultimate goal being to help their children assimilate and come to terms with their adoption. Reconciling the dichotomy of abandonment-adoption, which the adopted child begins to be aware of in middle childhood, is especially important in this ongoing adjustment process. For many adoptees, this not only involves experiencing a sense of loss concerning their birth parents, but it also affects other areas: ethnic and racial connections, genealogical ties, robustness of the adoptive bond, social status, and identity. This type of loss differs from others, such as the death or divorce of a parent, because it is more omnipresent, more profound, and less socially acknowledged. It is also usually linked to a lack of information surrounding the circumstances of the adoption and the possibility of re-establishing a relationship with the missing individuals. For all of these reasons, the grieving process can at times be especially complex and difficult (see, among others, Brodzinsky, 1990; Bowlby, 1982; Leon, 2002; Newton, 1993; Pivnick, 2010; Powell & Affi, 2005).

Questions about their biological parents, their birth country, and the circumstances of their adoption are natural in adoptees, responding to their need to find out more about themselves and give meaning, continuity, and coherence to their personal history (e.g. Grotevant, 1997; Howe & Feast, 2003; Maguire-Pavao, 2005). The search for origins, no longer viewed as an indication of psychopathological disorders or of the failure of the adoption, enjoys greater social and legal recognition. In Spain, for example, the law states that adopted children must know they are adopted before they reach 12 years of age. Nonetheless, the potential for stress should be acknowledged. Experts in the area (Berástegui & Gómez, 2007; Wilson & Summerhill-Coleman, 2013) therefore point to the importance of the process being conducted gradually, and always in accordance with adoptees' characteristics and needs, to ensure they have sufficient resources to work through and assimilate the information. They also stress the need for the adoptee to be supported and accompanied, ideally by the adoptive parents, and to request mediation and the help of a post-adoptive service where necessary. See Chapter 17 for more information on motivations to search and the search and reunification process for transracial adoptees.

In the context of international adoption, travel to their birth country can change adoptees' perception and comprehension of their own experience (Wilson & Summerhill-Coleman, 2013). It supplies continuity and context to their life history, encourages the adoptee to explore and work through lingering grief, reinforces the connection with the adoptee's ethnic group and culture of origin, validates the dual family (birth and adoptive), and encourages communication and the building of shared meaning within the adoptive family, among other aspects. However, the experience is not always positive, nor is it free from important challenges. Difficulties often arise, along with feelings of disappointment, discouragement, and failure when expectations are not met, or when the information obtained is incomplete and/or contradictory. Feelings of insecurity, shame, confusion, and rejection are also common (Wilson & Summerhill-Coleman, 2013). When a meeting with the birth family takes place, this encounter is often a very intense and significant experience. A lack of connection or resemblance to the birth parents, disagreement about the kind of future contact the parties wish to maintain, and cultural differences are some of the difficulties that can arise (Docan-Morgan, 2016). In addition, managing the dual family connection post-reunion may be difficult, particularly negotiating two mother–daughter relationships. Findings from Richardson and Davey's (2013) study suggest that when adoptive mothers feel secure and maintain open communication about the adoption, adoptees report fewer loyalty conflicts. In contrast, when adoptive mothers have closed communication styles about the adoption, adoptees could feel they have to hide any contact with their biological mothers from adoptive mothers to preserve relationships with their adoptive mothers.

Today the search for origins has been revolutionized by the internet and social media, increasing the possibility of contact between adoptees and their birth families. In view of the debate and controversy surrounding the right to know and the right to privacy, and the potential for these to be reconciled in the area of international adoption, the opportunities and dangers posed by new technologies merit additional consideration (Black, Moyer, & Goldberg, 2016; Fursland, 2013; Howard, 2012).

Practical implications and future lines of research

The review of the literature presented here has important practical implications and draws attention to current challenges and perspectives for research on international adoption. These are rooted in the context of Spain but can, to a large extent, be extrapolated to other contexts.

First, the research conducted conveys a positive and normalizing message: the majority of international adoptees develop satisfactorily with adequate personal and social adjustment. This fact is of summary importance and underscores the reparative effect of adoption and its contribution to the healthy and successful development of the child. Notwithstanding, it is evident that adopted children face important challenges on their development path, and this can generate problems. It is therefore necessary to continuously and closely monitor adoptees' progress, considering the person as a whole and paying special attention to the early detection of difficulties of any kind.

Second, it is fundamental that adopted children feel supported. This involves talking openly about origins and creating an appropriate space for listening to children's experiences, with respect and understanding, particularly during adolescence. The fact that families decline to take part in research and talk about questions related to the adoption is an indication of the delicate nature of the subject and may lead to skewed results in existing research.

Third, and despite the interest in knowing the experiences of internationally adopted children, there is insufficient research that incorporates the testimony of the children themselves. It is known that adopted children, from a relatively young age, are capable and willing to reflect on their personal history as well as identify circumstances and problems that affect them. Listening to the opinions of adoptees is important because it lets us know their real needs. It would also be useful for future studies to incorporate the perspective of other members of the adoptive family, particularly that of siblings and grandparents. The results of different studies show that the nuclear and extended family acquires a prominent role for the adopted individual in coping with adoption-specific issues, and points to the existence of differing opinions on some matters.

Adoptive families must also be aware of the need to prepare children to deal with situations of overt discrimination as well as more subtle forms of slights and insults that can negatively impact self-esteem and integration into groups in society. Accordingly, there is a need to work explicitly on the issue of stigma and discrimination from an early age, particularly with children adopted transracially, or who belong to "new" family models (i.e., headed by LGBTQ parents). At the same time, it is fundamental to raise awareness and sensitize the general population to the issue of international and transracial adoption within the framework of a diverse and pluralistic society.

Future studies should be concerned with new issues which are increasingly becoming vitally important, such as the results of travel to the country of origin and meeting the birth family; perceptions and needs of the birth family; implications of open adoption; factors that promote school adjustment and learning; effectiveness of interventions directed at the adoptive population; and the social perception of adoption and associated stigma. Research along these lines will contribute to greater knowledge and understanding of the reality of adoption.

Finally, it is essential that professionals working with adopted children and their families are equipped with up-to-date knowledge and resources to enable them to successfully perform their responsibilities (see Chapters 31 and 32 in this volume). The adoptive population presents a number of specific health care, educational, and social characteristics and needs that must be recognized and adequately addressed, though to date this has not always been the case. Correspondingly, more prospective longitudinal studies are needed to determine their outcomes in the long term and the factors that contribute to their development and adjustment paths. This would be of tremendous use in improving the effectiveness of adoption support services.

Conclusions

Data presented worldwide demonstrate the nuances and peculiarities of international and transracial adoption processes and the specific challenges that can lead to risks and stress for families. Some of the results – e.g. added complexities in identity formation, increased risk of psychiatric diagnosis – may be considered in terms of differential exposure to stressors prior to and throughout the adoption process. At the same time, the many positive outcomes after adoption proves the capacity for resilience of these children and their families.

References

Aramburu, I., Pérez-Testor, C., Mercadal, J., Salamero, M., Davins, M., Mirabent, V., Martínez, B., & Brodzinsky, D. (2018). Influence of communicative openness on the psychological adjustment of internationally adopted adolescents. *Journal of Research on Adolescence*. doi:10.1111/jora.12464

Arranz, E., Oliva, A., Olabarrieta, F., & Antolín, L. (2010). Análisis comparativo de las nuevas estructuras familiares como contextos potenciadores del desarrollo psicológico infantil. *Infancia y Aprendizaje*, *33*(4), 503–513.

Baden, A.L., Gibbons, J.L., Wilson, S.L., & McGinnis, H. (2013). International adoption: Counseling and the adoption triad. *Adoption Quarterly*, *16*(3–4), 218–237. doi:10.1080/10926755.2013.794440

Barcons-Castel, N., Fornieles-Deu, A., & Costas-Moragas, C. (2011). International adoption: Assessment of adaptive and maladaptive behavior of adopted minors in Spain. *The Spanish Journal of Psychology, 14*(1), 123–132. doi:10.5209/rev_SJOP.2011.v14.n1.10

Behle, A.E., & Pinquart, M. (2016). Psychiatric disorders and treatment in adoptees: A meta-analytic comparison with non-adoptees. *Adoption Quarterly, 19*(4), 284–306. doi:10.1080/10926755.2016.1201708

Berástegui, A. (2007). La adaptación familiar en adopción internacional: Un proceso de estrés y afrontamiento. *Anuario de Psicología, 38*(2), 209–224.

Berástegui, A. (2017). El papel de los profesionales en la prevención de rupturas en adopción. *Revista Clínica Contemporánea, 8*, 1–10. doi:https://doi.org/10.5093/cc2017a7

Berástegui, A., & Gómez, B. (2007). *Esta es tu historia: identidad y comunicación sobre los orígenes en adopción.* Madrid: Universidad Pontificia de Comillas.

Berástegui, A., & Jódar, R. (2013). Comunicación sobre adopción: Logros y lagunas en la adopción internacional en España. *Familia: Revista de ciencias y orientación familiar, 46*, 43–55.

Bertrán, M. (2013). Being a mother and father in international adoption in Spain: Towards the child's wellbeing. *Childhood, 20*(4), 507–520. doi:10.1177/0907568212471403

Black, K.A., Moyer, A.M., & Goldberg, A.E. (2016). From face-to-face to Facebook: The role of technology and social media in adoptive family relationships with birth family members. *Adoption Quarterly, 19*(4), 307–332. doi:10.1080/10926755.2016.1217575

Boivin, M., & Hassan, G. (2015). Ethnic identity and psychological adjustment in transracial adoptees: A review of the literature. *Ethnic and Racial Studies, 38*(7), 1084–1103. doi:/10.1080/01419870.2014.992922

Bowlby, J. (1982). *Attachment and Loss (Vol. 1). Attachment* (2nd ed.). New York: Basic Books.

Brodzinsky, D.M. (1990). A stress and coping model of adoption adjustment. In D.M. Brodzinsky & M.D. Schechter (Eds.), *The Psychology of Adoption* (pp. 3–24). New York: Oxford University Press.

Brodzinsky, D.M., Schechter, M.D., & Henig, R.M. (1992). *Being Adopted: The Lifelong Search for Self.* New York: Doubleday.

Brodzinsky, D.M., Smith, D.W., & Brodzinsky, A.B. (1998). *Children's adjustment to adoption: Developmental and clinical issues.* Thousand Oaks: Sage Publications.

Chen, Z.J. (2016). Exploring the relationship between adoptive parents and international adoptees: From the perspectives of cross-cultural communication and adaptation. *Adoption Quarterly, 19*(2), 119–144. doi:10.1080/10926755.2015.1113218

Christoffersen, M.N. (2012). A study of adopted children, their environment, and development: A systematic review. *Adoption Quarterly, 15*(3), 220–237. doi:10.1080/10926755.2012.700002

Corbella, S., & Gómez, A.M. (2010). Características de las familias adoptivas que facilitan la adaptación y consideraciones sobre los aspectos facilitadores de la integración. *Aloma: Revista de Psicologia, Ciencies de l'Educacio i de l'Esport, 27*, 51–66.

Docan-Morgan, S. (2016). Cultural differences and perceived belonging during Korean adoptees' reunions with birth families. *Adoption Quarterly, 19*(2), 99–118. doi:10.1080/10926755.2015.1088109

Festinger T. (2014). Adoption disruption. In G.P. Mallon & P.M. Hess (Eds.), *Child welfare for the 21st century: A handbook of practices, policies, and program* (2nd ed., pp. 437–454). New York: Columbia University Press.

Fonagy, P., Target, M., Gergely, G., & Jurist, E. (2002). *Affect regulation, mentalization, and the development of the self.* New York: Other Press.

Freeark, K., Rosenblum, K.L., Hus, V.H., & Root, B.L. (2008). Fathers, mothers and marriages: What shapes adoption conversations in families with young adopted children?. *Adoption Quarterly, 11*, 1–23. doi:10.1080/10926750802291393

Frekko, S., Leinaweaver, J., & Marre, D. (2015). How (not) to talk about adoption: On communicative vigilance in Spain. *American Ethnologist, 4*(42), 703–719. doi:10.1111/amet.12165

Friedlander, M.L. (1999). Ethnic identity development of internationally adopted children and adolescents: Implications for family therapists. *Journal of Marital and Family Therapy, 25*(1), 43–60. doi:10.1111/j.1752-0606.1999.tb01109.x

Friedlander, M.L., Larney, L.C., Skau, M., Hotaling, M., Cutting, M.L., & Schwam, M. (2000). Bicultural identification: Experiences of internationally adopted children and their parents. *Journal of Counseling Psychology, 47*, 187–198. doi:http://dx.doi.org/10.1037/0022-0167.47.2.187

Fursland, E. (2013). *Facing up to Facebook: A survival guide for adoptive families.* London: British Association for Adoption and Fostering.

Ge, X., Natsuaki, M., Martin, D., Leve, L., Neiderhiser, J., Shaw, D.S., … Reiss, D. (2008). Bridging the divide: Openness in adoption and postadoption psychological adjustment among birth and adoptive parents. *Journal of Family Psychology, 22*(3), 529–540. doi:10.1037/a0012817

Gibson, K. (2009). Differential parental investment in families with both adopted and genetic children. *Evolution and Human Behavior, 30*, 184–189. doi:10.1016/j.evolhumbehav.2009.01.001

Grotevant, H.D. (1997). Coming to terms with adoption: The construction of identity from adolescence into adulthood. *Adoption Quarterly, 1*(1), 3–27. doi:10.1300/J145v01n01_02

Grotevant, H.D. (2012). What works in open adoption. In P.A. Curtis & G. Alexander (Eds.), *What works in child welfare* (2nd ed., pp. 309–327). Washington: Child Welfare League of America.

Grotevant, H.D., Dunbar, N., Kohler, J.K., & Esau, A.M.L. (2000). Adoptive identity: How contexts within and beyond the family shape developmental pathways. *Family Relations, 49*(4), 379–387. doi:10.1111/j.1741-3729.2000.00379.x

Gunnar, M., & Kertes, D. (2005). Prenatal and postnatal risks to neurobiological development in internationally adopted children. In D. Brodzinsky, & J. Palacios (Eds.), *Psychological issues in adoption: Research and practice* (pp. 47–65). Westport: Praeger.

Haaguard, J.J. (1998). Is adoption a risk factor for the development of adjustment problems?. *Clinical Psychology Review, 18*, 47–69.

Hamilton, L., Cheng, S., & Powell, B. (2007). Adoptive parents, adaptive parents: Evaluating the importance of biological ties for parental investment. *American Sociological Review, 72*, 95–116. doi:10.1177/000312240707200105

Hawkins, A., Beckett, C., Rutter, M., Castle, J., Groothues, C., Kreppner, J., … Sonuga-Barke, E. (2007). Communicative openness about adoption and interest in contact in a sample of domestic and intercountry adolescent adoptees. *Adoption Quarterly, 10*(3–4), 131–156. doi:10.1080/10926750802163220

Hegar, R.L., & Watson, L.D. (2013). Managing special needs and treatment approaches of intercountry adoptees and families. *Adoption Quarterly, 16*(3–4), 238–261. doi:10.1080/10926755.2013.790863

Hollingsworth, L.D. (1997). Effect of transracial/transethnic adoption on children's racial and ethnic identity and self-esteem: A meta-analytic review. *Marriage and Family Review, 25*(1–2), 99–130. doi:10.1300/J002v25n01_07

Howard, J. (2012). *Untangling the Web: The internet's transformational impact on adoption*. New York: Donaldson Adoption Institute.

Howe, D., & Feast, J. (2003). *Adoption, search and reunion: The long-term experience of adopted adults*. London: British Association for Adoption and Fostering.

Juffer, F. (2006). Children's awareness of adoption and their problem behavior in families with 7-year-old internationally adopted children. *Adoption Quarterly, 9*(2), 1–22. doi:10.1300/J145v09n02_01

Juffer, F., & Tieman, W. (2009). Being adopted: Internationally adopted children's interest and feelings. *International Social Work, 52*(5), 635–647. doi:10.1177/0020872809337682

Juffer, F., Van IJzendoorn, M.H., & Palacios, J. (2011). Recuperación de niños y niñas tras su adopción (Children's recovery after adoption). *Infancia y Aprendizaje, 34*(1), 3–18. doi:10.1174/021037011794390102

Kirk, H.D. (1964). *Shared fate*. New York: Free Press.

Lee, R.M. (2003). The transracial adoption paradox: History, research, and counseling implications of cultural socialization. *The Counseling Psychologist, 31*, 711–774. doi:10.1177/0011000003258087

Leon, I.G. (2002). Adoption losses: Naturally occurring or socially constructed?. *Child Development, 73*(2), 652–663. doi:10.1111/1467-8624.00429

Loizaga, F., Louzao, I.I., de Aranzabal, M., & Labayru, M. (2009). *Adopción internacional: Cómo evolucionan los niños, las niñas y sus familias?*. Bilbao: Mensajero.

Maguire-Pavao, J. (2005). *The family of adoption*. Beacon, NY: Boston.

McGuinness, T., & Pallansch, L. (2000). Competence of children adopted from the former Soviet Union. *Family Relations, 49*(4), 457–464. doi:10.1111/j.1741-3729.2000.00457.x

McKay, K., Ross, L.E., & Goldberg, A.E. (2010). Adaptation to parenthood during the post-adoption period: A review of the literature. *Adoption Quarterly, 13*(2), 125–144. doi:10.1080/10926755.2010.481040

Miller, L.C. (2005). *The handbook of international adoption medicine: A guide for physicians, parents, and providers*. New York: Oxford University Press.

Ministry of Health, Consumer Affairs, and Social Welfare. (2019). Estadísticas sobre adopción. Retrieved from www.mscbs.gob.es/ssi/familiasInfancia/Infancia/adopciones/estadisticas.htm

Newton, N. (1993). *The primal wound: Understanding the adopted child*. Baltimore: Gateway Press.

Palacios, J. (2017). Adopción no es patología. *Clínica Contemporánea, 8*(2), 1–10. doi:10.5093/cc2017a9

Palacios, J., Rolock, N., Selwyn, J., & Barbosa-Ducharne, M.A. (2019). Adoption breakdown: Concept, research and implications. *Research on Social Work practice, 29*(2), 130–142. doi:10.1177/1049731518783852

Palacios, J., Sánchez-Sandoval, Y., & León, E. (2005). Adopción y problemas de conducta. *Revista Iberoamericana de Diagnóstico y Evaluación Psicológica, 19*(1), 171–196.

Passmore, N., Feeney, J.A., & Foulstone, A.R. (2007). Secrecy within adoptive families and its impact on adult adoptees. *Family Relationships Quarterly, 5*, 3–5.

Pivnick, B.A. (2010). Left without a word: Learning rhythms, rhymes, and reasons in adoption. *Psychoanalytic Inquiry, 30*(1), 3–24. doi:10.1080/07351690903200101

Powell, K.A., & Affi, T.D. (2005). Uncertainty management and adoptees' ambiguous loss of their birth parents. *Journal of Social and Personal Relationships, 22*, 129–151. doi:10.1177/0265407505049325

Pylypa, J. (2016). The social construction of attachment, attachment disorders and attachment parenting in international adoption discourse and parent education. *Children & Society, 30*, 434–444. doi:10.1111/chso.12159

Reinoso, M., & Forns, M. (2012). Adaptación psicosocial en niños adoptados internacionalmente: Percepción personal y parental. *Anales de Pediatría, 76*(5), 268–278. doi:10.1016/j.anpedi.2011.08.001

Reinoso, M., Juffer, F., & Tieman, W. (2013). Children's and parents' thoughts and feelings about adoption, birth culture identity and discrimination in families with internationally adopted children. *Child & Family Social Work, 18*(3), 264–274. doi:10.1111/j.1365-2206.2012.00841.x

Reinoso, M., Pereda, N., Van Den Dries, L., & Forero, C.G. (2016). Internationally adopted children's general and adoption-specific stressors, coping strategies and psychological adjustment. *Child & Family Social Work, 21*(1), 1–13. doi:10.1111/cfs.12099

Reinoso, M., Requena, E., & Miró, T. (2018). *Per fi junts! Parlem d'adopció*. Barcelona: Abadia de Montserrat.

Richardson, A., & Davey, M.P. (2013). Female adoptees' experiences balancing relationships with biological and adoptive mothers post-reunification. *Journal of Marital and Family Therapy, 39*(3), 358–372. doi:10.1111/j.1752-0606.2012.00321.x

Rosser, A., & Berástegui, A. (2017). Retos y dificultades para la implantación de la adopción abierta en España. El papel de la mediación. *Mediaciones Sociales, 16*, 175–191. doi:10.5209/MESO.58115

Rutter, M. (2005). Adverse preadoption experiences and psychological outcomes. In D. Brodzinsky & J. Palacios (Eds.), *Psychological Issues in Adoption: Research and Practice* (pp. 67–92). Westport: Praeger.

San Román, B. (2013). "I am White … even if I am racially Black" "I am Afro-Spanish": confronting belonging paradoxes in transracial adoptions. *Journal of Intercultural Studies, 34*(3), 229–245. doi:10.1080/07256868.2013.787400

Scherman, R.M. (2010). A theoretical look at biculturalism in intercountry adoption. *Journal of Ethnic & Cultural Diversity in Social Work, 19*, 127–142. doi:10.1080/15313201003771742

Selman, P. (2012). The global decline of intercountry adoption: What lies ahead?. *Social Policy and Society, 11*(3), 381–397. doi:10.1017/S1474746412000085

Sharma, A.R., McGue, M.K., & Benson, P.L. (1996). The emotional and behavioral adjustment of United States adopted adolescents: Part I. an overview. *Children andYouth Services Review, 18*, 83–100. doi:10.1016/0190-7409(95)00056-9

Siegel, D.H. (2012). Growing up in open adoption: Young adults' perspectives. *Families in Society, 93*, 133–140. doi:10.1606/1044-3894.4198

Simon, R.J., & Alstein, H. (1996). The case for transracial adoption. *Children and Youth Services Review, 18*, 5–22. doi:10.1016/0190-7409(95)00051-8

Stams, G.J.J.M., Juffer, F., Rispens, J., & Hoksbergen, R.A.C. (2000). The development and adjustment of 7-year-old children adopted in infancy. *Journal of Child Psychology and Psychiatry, 41*, 1025–1037. doi:10.1111/1469-7610.00690

Stryker, R. (2011). The war at home: Affective economics and transnationally adoptive families in the United States. *International Migration, 49*(6), 25–49. doi:10.1111/j.1468-2435.2010.00607.x

Thomas, K.A., & Tessler, R.C. (2007). Bicultural socialization among adoptive families: where there is a will, there is a way. *Journal of Family Issues, 28*(9), 1189–1219. doi:10.1177/0192513X07301115

Van Den Dries, L., Juffer, F., Van IJzendoorn, M.H., & Bakermans-Kranenburg, M.J. (2009). Fostering security? A meta-analysis of attachment in adopted children. *Children and Youth Services Review, 31*, 410–421. doi:10.1016/j.childyouth.2008.09.008

Van IJzendoorn, M.H., & Juffer, F. (2006). The Emanuel Miller memorial lecture 2006. Adoption as intervention. Meta-analytic evidence for massive catch-up and plasticity in physical, socio-emotional, and cognitive development. *Journal of Child Psychology and Psychiatry*, *47*, 1228–1245. doi:10.1111/j.1469-7610.2006.01675.x

Verbovaya, O. (2016). Theoretical explanatory model of international adoption failure: Attachment and ecological systems perspectives. *Adoption Quarterly*, *19*(3), 188–209.

Vonk, M.E., & Massatti, R.R. (2008). Factors related to transracial adoptive parents' levels of cultural competence. *Adoption Quarterly*, *11*(3), 204–226. doi:10.1080/10926750802421966

Warren, S.B. (1992). Lower threshold for referral for psychiatric treatment for adopted adolescents. *Journal of the American Academy of Child and Adolescent Psychiatry*, *31*, 512–517.

Weir, K.N., Lee, S., Canosa, P., Rodrigues, N., McWilliams, M., & Parker, L. (2013). Whole family theraplay: Integrating family systems theory and theraplay to treat adoptive families. *Adoption Quarterly*, *16*(3–4), 175–200. doi:10.1080/10926755.2013.844216

Wierzbicki, M. (1993). Psychological adjustment of adoptees: A meta-analysis. *Journal of Clinical Child Psychology*, *22*, 447–454. doi:10.1207/s15374424jccp2204_5

Wilson, S.L. (2004). A current review of adoption research: Exploring individual differences in adjustment. *Children and Youth Services Review*, *26*, 687–696. doi:10.1016/j.childyouth.2004.02.013

Wilson, S.L., & Summerhill-Coleman, L. (2013). Exploring birth countries: The mental health implications of heritage travel for children/adolescents adopted internationally. *Adoption Quarterly*, *16*, 262–278. doi:10.1080/10926755.2013.790865

Wolfgram, S. (2008). Openness in adoption: What we know so far – a critical review of the literature. *Social Work*, *53*(2), 133–142.

Wolfs, R. (2008). *Adoption conversations. What, when and how to tell.* London: British Association of Adoption and Fostering.

Wolfs, R. (2010). *More adoption conversations. What, when and how to tell.* London: British Association of Adoption and Fostering.

9

A CRITICAL ADOPTION STUDIES AND ASIAN AMERICANIST INTEGRATIVE PERSPECTIVE ON THE PSYCHOLOGY OF KOREAN ADOPTION

Adam Y. Kim and Richard M. Lee

There is a growing interest in research that centers the experiences of adopted individuals, including the role of culture, ethnicity, and race in the lives of transnationally, transracially adopted individuals. Within psychology and related fields, this research has largely focused on the content, prevalence, and impact of perceived discrimination, cultural socialization, and ethnic-racial identity. Given the prevalence of transnational adoption from Korea, research on transnationally, transracially adopted individuals has largely focused on adopted Koreans. We review this research to highlight some of the ways in which adopted Koreans, and their adoptive parents, navigate these cultural, ethnic, and racial experiences during childhood, adolescence, and into adulthood. We integrate a critical adoption studies framework (Homans et al., 2018) with an Asian Americanist perspective (Lee, Kim, & Zhou, 2016b) to guide our review and to suggest policy implications and future directions for research.

Adoption as natural experiment and intervention

Adoption research typically approaches adoption as a natural experiment or a natural intervention. Adoption as a natural experiment uses the lack of genetic similarity found in families formed through adoption to disentangle the roles of nature and nurture (Haugaard & Hazan, 2003). This use of adoption as a study design has been applied to study genetic and environmental influences on a wide range of psychological phenomena (e.g., Buchanan, McGue, Keyes, & Iacono, 2009). Adoption as a natural intervention characterizes adoption as an event that alters the developmental trajectory of the adopted child. Seminal studies by Rutter (1998) have highlighted how adoption can promote developmental catch-up among Romanian children who had experienced severe institutional neglect and abuse growing up in orphanages. Similarly, Juffer and colleagues concluded that adopted individuals are generally well-adjusted (e.g., Juffer & van IJzendoorn, 2005) and that "adoption is an impressive intervention leading to astonishing catch-up" (van IJzendoorn & Juffer, 2006, p. 1240). While these two types of adoption studies contribute to our understanding of human development, adoption is utilized as a research methodology. The adoptive experiences of individuals and families are not central to the research.

Adoption (and race) as a risk factor

Haugaard (1998) argues that adoption can function as a risk factor for adjustment problems due to an over-representation of adopted individuals in the tail ends of distributions despite similar mean scores. National registry studies of transnationally adopted individuals raised in Sweden support this tail phenomenon hypothesis. Most transnationally adopted individuals in these studies did not report serious psychological problems (e.g., suicide attempts, substance abuse) (Hjern, Lindblad, & Vinnerljung, 2002; Lindblad, Hjern, & Vinnerljung, 2003). However, the adopted individuals were more likely to report these problems, as well as other maladjustment indicators (e.g., unemployment, alcohol and drug abuse), when compared to their non-adopted peers. These higher rates of suicide ideation and attempts among transnationally adopted adults have been replicated elsewhere (e.g., Keyes, Malone, Sharma, Iacono, & McGue, 2013). Notably, the odds for suicide attempt and death by suicide were greater for the transnationally adopted sample than the within-country adopted sample (von Borczyskowski, Hjern, Lindblad, & Vinnerljung, 2006). Further, transnationally adopted individuals, who were all from Asia or Latin America, reported similar or worse levels of mental distress as non-adopted immigrant adolescents from these same regions (Hjern et al., 2002). Combined, these findings suggest that race-based discrimination is a likely cause of distress.

These studies present two important points to understanding the development of adopted individuals. First, the tail distribution phenomenon suggests that adopted individuals might be at greater risk for adjustment problems than their non-adopted peers. Second, cultural, ethnic, and racial experiences likely play a significant yet under-studied role in the well-being and adjustment of transnationally adopted individuals. This argument corresponds with that of other adoption scholars who have noted the need to further study the cultural, ethnic, and racial experiences of transnationally, transracially adopted individuals (e.g., Kim, 2010; Park Nelson, 2016). In the next section, we advance a new framework for adoption studies that privileges the adopted persons' experiences and directly considers the importance of culture, race, and ethnicity in untangling the relation between adoption and mental health.

A critical adoption studies and Asian Americanist integrative approach to adoption studies

We integrate a critical adoption studies framework with an Asian Americanist perspective to understand the experiences of adopted individuals and their families. Both approaches developed out of critical race theory, yet they present distinct perspectives that individually acknowledge and contest systems of power and oppression (Homans et al., 2018; Lee et al., 2016b). An integration of these approaches recognizes that transnational, transracial adoption is driven by the global adoption complex and is impacted by systemic racism, and highlights the importance of considering these systems to understanding the experiences of transnational, transracial adopted individuals.

Critical adoption scholarship considers the role of the global adoption complex in creating and sustaining adoption as a practice, as well as the pivotal roles that power and privilege play in who is adopted, who is allowed to adopt, and how birth families are treated. Critical adoption studies complicates adoption research by critiquing and questioning the dominant narratives of adoption, such as adoption as an act of rescue – ignoring that "orphans" have been created as an act of supply and demand (Condit-Shrestha, 2018); adoption as a win-win – ignoring the loss, trauma, and stress associated with both abandonment and adoption (Brodzinsky, 1990); and adoption as a singular event – ignoring that coming to terms with one's adoption is a life-long process (Grotevant, 1997). Ultimately, critical adoption studies forces us to consider *how* we know what we know about adoption (e.g., by asking whose voices are represented in adoption research) (Homans et al., 2018).

We apply an Asian Americanist lens to critical adoption studies in order to critically approach the ethnic and racial aspects of the experiences of transnationally adopted Koreans. Applying a critical race and ethnic studies approach (Lee et al., 2016b), an Asian Americanist lens reveals and critiques dominant racial and cultural narratives in adoption studies (e.g., those that Orientalize and homogenize the stories of birth parents and sending countries) and calls for psychology to consider history and context as they reveal systems of oppression. This approach also centers the experiences of transnationally, transracially adopted Korean Americans, emphasizing the agentic nature of these individuals in constructing their lives. Therefore, we use this integrated framework to serve as the interpretive lens for our program of research throughout this chapter.

The historical and cultural context of Korean adoption

Transnational adoption from South Korea began in the wake of the Korean War as a way to care for children born to Korean mothers and foreign military fathers (Pate, 2014). Due to a combination of economic, political, and social factors, adoption from Korea became a routine child welfare practice. Simultaneously, demand for infants in countries such as the United States outpaced the availability of domestic adoptions, leading many families to pursue transnational adoption (Kim, 2010). In total, more than 160,000 Korean-born individuals have been adopted by parents outside of South Korea (Kim, 2010), the vast majority of whom were adopted by White parents in the United States (Kreider & Lofquist, 2014).

The transnational and transracial context of these adoptions positions adopted Koreans at the intersection of two distinct paradoxical experiences as ethnic *and* racial minorities. The *transnational adoption paradox* describes the loss of birth culture that accompanies adoptive family socialization (Lee & Miller, 2009). The early socialization experiences of adopted Korean children and youth are largely based around a White cultural frame, and so they quickly lose contact with their ethnic heritage. This replacement of birth culture with White American culture can create a feeling of otherness from non-adopted Koreans. One adult adopted Korean American noted, "there is discrimination that we [adopted Koreans] are second-class Koreans because we have been raised in White society, in American society. We don't know about our own heritage, and we don't know our language" (Meier, 1999, p. 28). Consequently, some individuals report feeling excluded from the broader Korean American community (Hoffman & Peña, 2013; Kim, Hynes, & Lee, 2017).

The *transracial adoption paradox* (distinct from the *transnational* adoption paradox) describes a set of experiences wherein the non-White adopted individual is treated as being White by their adoptive family and their experiences as racial minorities are downplayed (Lee, 2003); yet this treatment of the adopted individual as White does not extend beyond the family (Hoffman & Peña, 2013). Instead, adopted Korean Americans are situated within a racist system in which they are subject to the oppressive narratives that are applied to Asian Americans, including the assumption of being a foreigner and the expectations of being a model minority (Kim, 1999). This process, known as racialization, manifests early on in life (e.g., Meier, 1999). These contradictory racialized experiences are particularly troubling as adopted Koreans are often not taught how to deal with race-based bias and are not adequately supported in the wake of discriminatory experiences.

These two paradoxes provide the context for why cultural socialization, discrimination, and identity often become important developmental issues to adopted Korean individuals across the lifespan (e.g., Kim et al., 2017). With this historical, cultural, and developmental context in mind, we review research on the experiences of adopted Koreans. This review is split into four overlapping themes: discrimination, ethnic-racial identity, cultural socialization, and self-directed cultural engagement.

Review of research

Perceived discrimination

We start our review by focusing on the role of discrimination on the mental health and adjustment of adopted Korean Americans. As noted above, adoption scholars have largely focused on pre-adoption adversity, such as institutionalization, as the explanation for later life developmental and adjustment problems. However, these approaches objectify adopted individuals to reinforce narratives that frame adoptive parents as saviors and that require adopted individuals to be grateful (Homans et al., 2018). Further, these approaches perpetuate a racial colorblindness ideology by denying the salience of race for adopted Koreans raised by White parents. In our research, we shift the narrative to acknowledge the relevance and impact of race on the development and adjustment of transnationally and transracially adopted children and youth.

We have demonstrated in a series of studies with multiple samples that race-based discrimination experienced by adopted Korean Americans is associated with child developmental outcomes above and beyond pre-adoption adversity. In a study of the impact of discrimination on the adjustment of transnationally adopted children and adolescents, we found that American adoptive parents[1] of children and adolescents who were adopted from Asia (63 percent of whom were adopted from Korea) and Latin America reported that their children experienced more discrimination than individuals adopted from Eastern Europe (Lee, 2010). Further, internalizing and externalizing problems were predicted by discrimination over and above pre-adoption adversity, but only for individuals adopted from Asia and Latin America. While this study was one of the first large-scale studies to empirically document the detrimental impacts of discrimination in transnationally adopted youth, it was limited by a reliance on adoptive parent-report of the adopted individual's experience.

Focusing on the perspective of the adopted individual, we found support for the impact of discrimination on the adjustment of adopted Korean Americans in childhood, adolescence, and young adulthood. In one study, discrimination was negatively related to the well-being of adopted Korean adults (Lee, Yoo, & Roberts, 2004). Further, two studies using separate samples of adopted Korean American adolescents found a positive correlation between adolescent-report of discrimination and measures of distress and maladjustment, over and above pre-adoption adversity (Lee, Lee, Hu, & Kim, 2015) and parent-report of childhood distress and maladjustment (Qin, Kim, Su, Hu, & Lee, 2017). These findings are consistent with past work on non-adopted minority populations (e.g., Lee & Ahn, 2011; Pascoe & Smart Richman, 2009).

In order to understand developmental effects, we examined the effects of racial discrimination on adolescent adjustment after controlling for childhood behavioral problems (Qin et al., 2017) and the effects of racial discrimination on behavioral development across three waves of data from adolescence to emerging adulthood (Schires et al., 2019). In this latter study, we used cross-lagged analyses to show that depression and externalizing behaviors at wave three were predicted by discrimination at wave two. Further, discrimination at wave two was not related to depression or externalizing behaviors at wave one, suggesting a causal impact of discrimination on future maladjustment.

Ethnic-racial identity

First-person accounts by transnationally, transracially adopted Korean Americans highlight the many ways in which culture, ethnicity, and race inform their identity development. Early work by adoption scholars acknowledged that adopted Koreans were likely to experience ethnic-racial teasing, identity confusion, and questions about their ethnic heritage and racial background (e.g., Cederblad, Höök, Irhammar, & Mercke, 1999); yet these issues are often viewed as secondary to abandonment-related trauma and the individual's relationship with their adoptive family, and overlooked completely (Lee, 2003). Instead, we argue that these narratives from adopted Koreans illustrate that ethnicity and race play a central role in their sense of self. Notably, these individuals recognize early on that they are ethnically and racially different from their parents and peers, and negotiate the meaning of these differences as they develop a sense of self (Meier, 1999).

This understanding of the self in relation to an ethnic-racial group has been described as an ethnic-racial identity (ERI; Umaña-Taylor et al., 2014). ERI captures the cognitive, affective, and behavioral components of belonging to an ethnic-racial group. The cognitive dimension taps into clarity and understanding around the meaning of group membership. The affective dimension taps into pride in group membership and positive emotions toward the group. These two dimensions of cognition and affect are often combined to capture identity commitment (e.g., Roberts et al., 1999). Finally, the behavioral dimension includes actions that help an individual learn more about their group and its relevance to the individual, as well as participation in group-based actions.

Our early studies on ERI examined the direct effect of ERI on adjustment for adopted Koreans across a variety of operationalizations of ERI and outcome measures. For instance, using a unidimensional measure of ERI that captured a combined sense of pride, clarity, and searching behaviors, we found ERI was unrelated to well-being in a sample of adopted Korean American college students (Lee, Yun, Yoo, & Park Nelson, 2010). In another study that operationalized ERI as consisting of individual dimensions of pride in being Korean, active engagement in learning about being Korean, and a sense of clarity about what it means to be Korean (American) (see Lee & Yoo, 2004), we found that ERI engagement was positively related to well-being in a sample of adopted Korean American adults, while ERI pride and clarity were unrelated to well-being (though the effect sizes suggest a possible positive relation between ERI pride and well-being) (Lee et al., 2004). These mixed findings suggest that the dimensions of ERI may differentially relate to adjustment. Therefore, we focused specifically on the ERI dimensions of pride, clarity, and engagement in order to further explicate our understanding of the ERI-adjustment relation (Lee et al., 2015). Controlling for pre-adoption adversity, ERI clarity was negatively related to internalizing problems, ERI pride was negatively related to externalizing problems, and ERI engagement was positively related to internalizing problems and substance use.[2]

Recognizing that their adoptive status is also likely to be salient to adopted individuals, we examined how an individual's adoptive identity (AI) – clarity and understanding around being adopted – might relate with their ERI, and how those patterns might relate to adjustment (Beaupre, Reichwald, Zhou, Raleigh, & Lee, 2015). We used a person-centered approach with a sample of adopted Korean adolescents[3] to derive six identity profiles based on combinations of ERI commitment and AI commitment: (1) strong ERI commitment, weak AI commitment; (2) weak ERI commitment, strong AI commitment; (3–6) four profiles that ranged from very uncommitted to very committed on both identity domains. Next, we examined how these profiles predicted mental health and adjustment. The profiles generally did not differ from each other across a wide variety of outcomes. However, individuals who were especially weakly committed to both their ERI and AI reported less life satisfaction and less school belonging. These findings highlight the heterogeneity of the experiences of adopted Koreans and suggest that extreme disidentification may be problematic.

These studies highlight the general relevance of ERI to many adopted Koreans. The mixed nature of these findings also advances a more complicated understanding of adopted Koreans. Rather than existing as a monolithic group with homogenous experiences, adopted Koreans engage with their adoption and ethnic heritage in a variety of ways, most of which are not pathological in nature. Further, these findings indicate the importance of considering the operationalization of ERI in interpreting the extant literature.

ERI as a protective factor

Beyond instilling a positive sense of self and relating directly to adjustment, ERI has been theorized to function as a protective factor against the negative impact of discrimination. Therefore, we examined the role of ERI as a moderator in the discrimination–adjustment relation (Lee et al., 2015). We found that discrimination was positively related to externalizing problems for individuals high in ERI pride, but not for individuals low in ERI pride. Additionally, discrimination was positively related to substance use for individuals high in ERI engagement, but not for individuals low in ERI engagement. Therefore, rather than functioning as a protective factor, ERI functioned as an exacerbating agent for adopted Koreans. This aligns with research with non-adopted samples that highlights mixed findings between different identity dimensions, outcomes, and sample characteristics (e.g., Pascoe & Smart Richman, 2009), and points to the need for future research to investigate the moderating role of ERI.

Parental cultural socialization

Early research on the adoptive family environment investigated the quality of parent–child relationships (e.g., attachment style) (Haugaard & Hazan, 2003), but they overlooked the adopted individual's experiences as an ethnic and racial minority within their household and society. Those studies that did examine the ethnic and racial experiences of these individuals highlighted cultural assimilation – the internalization of the dominant culture coupled with the loss of the adopted individual's heritage culture – as the dominant outcome of early socialization experiences (Baden, Treweeke, & Ahluwalia, 2012; Lee, 2003). Rejecting an assimilationist framework, we argue that while it is important that adopted individuals are able to develop positive relationships with adoptive parents and families, it is also necessary for adoptive parents to address the challenges and experiences that their adoptive children might face as ethnic and racial minorities.

Parental cultural socialization refers to the process through which parents teach their children how to function as ethnic-racial minorities within an oppressive context (Hughes &

Chen, 1997). Cultural socialization is conceptualized as addressing two distinct domains: ethnic socialization and racial socialization (Lee, Grotevant, Hellerstedt, & Gunner, 2006). Ethnic socialization emphasizes pride in their ethnic heritage and includes passing on the traditions and belief systems of their heritage culture. Racial socialization efforts focus on teaching the individual how to function as a racial minority. This includes preparing the individual to face discrimination, as well as providing them with tools to negotiate these experiences. While these practices are common among parents of color within the US (e.g., Hughes & Chen, 1997), less is known about how White adoptive parents engage in cultural socialization practices that are oriented toward the adopted individual's ethnic heritage and racial group (e.g., Korean culture, being Asian American), which the adoptive parents do not experience themselves.

As a first approach to understanding the cultural socialization practices of adoptive parents, we asked adoptive families to discuss a series of topics, including ethnicity and race (Kim, Reichwald, & Lee, 2013). When prompted to discuss the role that ethnicity and race play in their family, we found that adoptive parents had frequently failed to respond to instances of discrimination. For instance, one adopted Korean American adolescent told her adoptive mother, "We've mentioned it to you before and you blow it off" (Kim et al., 2013, p. 85). This unwillingness, or inability, to address issues of race coincides with adoptive parents' colorblind attitudes (Lee et al., 2006; Shiao & Tuan, 2008), as captured by a White adoptive mother telling her adopted son, "See when I look at you I don't see Asian, or White, or whatever, I just see you" (Kim et al., 2013, p. 80).

These discussions also revealed that adoptive parents and adopted individuals often disagreed on the amount of cultural socialization that the adoptive parents engaged in (Kim et al., 2013). Critically, we found that only reports of past cultural socialization from adopted individuals aligned with the in-lab conversations, and that adoptive parents over-reported the amount of cultural socialization that they engaged in. Further, reports of parental ethnic socialization and racial socialization were lower for adopted Korean Americans than their non-adopted peers (Seol, Yoo, Lee, Park, & Kyeong, 2016).[4] Despite these differences, adoptive parents generally report believing that cultural socialization is important (Lee et al., 2006). Therefore, we also examined how adoptive parents *do* engage in cultural socialization.

Further analyzing the discussions that adoptive families had around ethnicity and race, we found that their cultural socialization efforts tended to focus on explicit, isolated activities (Kim et al., 2013). These cultural socialization efforts typically included going out to eat at a Korean restaurant or attending Korean culture camps. Notably absent from these cultural socialization efforts were the more subtle, daily means of cultural socialization, such as using conversations with others that indicate the importance of Korean culture (ethnic socialization) or demonstrating how to respond to instances of discrimination (racial socialization). Finally, adoptive parents tended to place the onus for these different forms of cultural socialization on the adopted individual, expecting the adopted individual to indicate when they wanted to engage in cultural socialization, or to show positive feedback to parental cultural socialization efforts.

Cultural socialization and ethnic-racial identity

Cultural socialization is meant to instill a positive view of the self as a member of a particular ethnic-racial group. Using a seven-year two-wave study, we found that parental ethnic socialization predicted adolescent ERI participation and resolution seven years later (Hu, Zhou, & Lee, 2017), supporting the theoretical causal impact of cultural socialization. This aligns with cross-sectional studies that found positive ethnic socialization-ERI relations (Ferrari, Hu, Rosnati, & Lee, 2017; Hu, Anderson, & Lee, 2015).[5]

Cultural socialization and psychological outcomes

Beyond instilling a sense of identity, parental cultural socialization efforts are meant to help adolescents be productive and well-adjusted members of society. For instance, we found that ethnic socialization was positively related to a sense of school engagement for both adopted and non-adopted Korean American adolescents (Seol et al., 2016). We also found a curvilinear relation between racial socialization and school adjustment for both samples. Specifically, a moderate amount of racial socialization yielded the highest school adjustment.

In another study, we examined socialization through direct conversations about ethnicity and race that adopted adolescents had with their adoptive families, and found three ways in which they understood their within-family ethnic and racial differences (Anderson, Lee, Rueter, & Kim, 2015). More than half of the families disagreed on whether there were within-family ethnic and racial differences, roughly one-third of the sample acknowledged differences, and a minority of families rejected within-family differences. Further, adoptive parents in families that acknowledged differences were more likely to engage in ethnic socialization. We found that adopted adolescents whose families held discrepant views of racial differences reported significantly more delinquent behaviors (e.g., cutting classes at school) than adopted adolescents in families who agreed about within-family ethnic and racial differences (either acknowledging or rejecting these differences). This highlights the importance of a mutual understanding of the role of race and ethnicity within the adoptive family, and, when considered with the findings from Seol et al. (2016), points to the importance of cultural socialization for positive adjustment.

Cultural socialization as a protective factor

Past research with non-adopted samples has suggested that socialization should act as a protective factor against the effects of discrimination (Hughes et al., 2006). Therefore, we tested the moderating effect of cultural socialization across adopted and non-adopted Korean Americans (Seol et al., 2016). We found a significant three-way interaction between adoptive status, ethnic socialization, and perceived discrimination on school belonging. Discrimination was negatively related to school belonging. However, for non-adopted individuals, this negative relation persisted under low levels of ethnic socialization, but was non-significant under high levels of ethnic socialization; yet this buffering effect was not found for the adopted sample. In contrast, for the adoptive sample, under conditions of low ethnic socialization, the discrimination–school belonging relation was non-significant, yet under conditions of high ethnic socialization racial discrimination was negatively related to school belonging. This difference by adoptive status points to the need for further examination of the moderating role of socialization on the discrimination–adjustment relation for adopted individuals.

Self-directed cultural engagement

The ethnic heritage and racial erasure highlighted by the transnational and transracial adoption paradoxes prompts another question: how do adopted Koreans personally engage with their heritage culture, ethnicity, and race? We have begun to examine this question across a series of studies. A grounded theory analysis of a sample of adopted Korean adults revealed seven themes describing their cultural engagement (Song & Lee, 2009).[6] The themes ranged from a focus on exploring Korea/Korean culture and developing co-ethnic relationships, to navigating the complexities of birth family, and understanding the racial and multicultural aspects of living within the United States. Further, we found that these experiences of cultural exploration and engagement were related to ERI if they occurred in adulthood, but not in adolescence or earlier. This aligns with reculturation theory, which emphasizes the role of adopted individuals in being the drivers of their own cultural exploration (Baden et al., 2012). Finally, awareness of race-related issues was the least-reported theme, and was not present at all in childhood accounts, further supporting our finding that colorblindness is a prominent theme in the socialization practices of adoptive families (Kim et al., 2013).

Following up on these dimensions of cultural engagement, we examined the ways in which adopted Korean adults navigate their identity as they develop a coherent life narrative (Grotevant, 1997). Assessing a sample of adopted Korean American adults, we found that participants consistently reported a continual negotiation of intra- and interpersonal connection and understanding (Kim et al., 2017). Individuals reported navigating a sense of authentic connection to "their own story or identity" (p. 240) as well as to their adoptive and birth families. For instance, one individual described feeling like a "living doll" (p. 242) in their adoptive family, while simultaneously feeling an unequivocal sense of belonging to that family. Further, an individual who had reconnected with their birth family described this relationship as "deeply gratifying" (p. 241), yet they also felt insecure about their relationship with their birth family, fearing what they perceived as a second rejection. These vacillations between conflict and resolution represent the work that individuals put into coming to terms with their cultural and familial connections.

As with our quantitative studies of identity (e.g., Beaupre et al., 2015), participants varied in how they incorporated experiences with their adoption and Korean heritage into their sense of self. Some individuals purposely worked to ignore, or even distance themselves from, their ethnic-racial and adoptive identities, while other individuals actively explored these aspects of the self. For some, this exploration led to coherence and connection, with one individual noting that their engagement with the diaspora of transnationally adopted Koreans helped them "[put] the pieces together of my life" (Kim et al., 2017, p. 243). Others noted how exploration had brought about interpersonal and emotional challenges. One individual described feeling "a deep ache and the feeling of anguish and pain" (Kim et al., 2017, p. 242) after visiting Korea. This individual came out of visiting Korea feeling "thrown away" and unwanted (Kim et al., 2017, p. 242).

These two studies highlight the heterogeneity of the adopted experience, and more fully exemplify our integration of an Asian Americanist lens with critical adoption studies. By giving adopted individuals the space to voice their opinions in an open-ended format, we found distinct ways in which they navigate their cultural connection and develop a sense of self. Though these experiences are not without struggles, they also point to unique areas of resilience, such as a sense of belonging with the community of adopted Koreans. Finally, these studies highlight that adopted children grow up and become adults with agency.

Policy and practice implications

Because the goal of adoption is to find permanent, safe, and nurturing family home environments for children, child welfare advocates and practitioners understandably prioritize the needs of the child. An integrated critical adoption and Asian Americanist perspective on transracial and transnational adoption does not dispute this prioritization of the child. Rather, it complicates traditional ways of understanding what the fundamental needs of the child are by re-centering the narrative on the whole experience of the adopted individual, which includes culture, ethnicity, and race, and reinforces the role and responsibility of adoptive parents to acknowledge and address these issues and experiences. In this section, we highlight a few ways this reframing of adoption affects policy and practices directed toward adopted Koreans and their adoptive families. We specifically build on the policy and practice implications that have been advanced previously by Baden and Wiley (2007) (see also Grotevant, 2003; Lee, 2003).

While adoption can provide children with a full and enriched life, it is critically important to understand and challenge the rescue narrative within adoption, which privileges the actions of the adoptive family (e.g., parents as saviors) and the larger adoption system (e.g., by not acknowledging the economy of adoption). This problematic rescue narrative (Briggs, 2003) overlooks the cultural, racial, and ethnic challenges of transnational and transracial adoption that adopted individuals face, neglects the rights of the birth family, and perpetuates a system of child welfare that does not fully hold accountable the sending country. In the case of South Korea, which now has one of the largest economies in the world, it is no longer a developing country that needs to rely on transnational adoption as a means to address the lack of a systemic social welfare. In fact, it has been argued that transnational adoption has been used to avoid addressing larger human rights issues in South Korea (McKee, 2016). Nevertheless, South Korea remains a sending country for transnational adoption, and is one of the few signatory nations to still not ratify the Hague Convention on Protection of Children and Co-operation in Respect of Intercountry Adoption.

Our scholarship also documents the importance and impact of transracial and transnational experiences and challenges on development across the lifespan. These research findings have been used to inform how adoption agencies work with prospective adoptive parents as they prepare for transracial and transnational adoption and how adoption agencies develop and offer post-adoption services for adopted individuals and adoptive families. Adoption agencies are more aware of the need to inform and educate adoptive families around ethnic heritage and birth family, racism and discrimination, and raising children with positive and strong ethnic-racial identities.

Further, adoptive parents should consider the tact, timing, and dosage of how they address these transracial and transnational aspects of adoption. Adopted youth benefit from everyday conversations and activities that positively promote their ethnic heritage and help them understand how to navigate racial differences and racism. At the same time, these socialization efforts must be developmentally appropriate and responsive to the context. Our research highlights the overall importance of ethnic socialization for ERI development and its beneficial impact on well-being and adjustment. Similarly, racial socialization is developmentally important and impactful, but these conversations about race and racial differences must be constructive, and the ways to respond to discrimination must be modeled and reinforced appropriately by parents. In the end, all members of the adoptive family need to buy into being a multicultural *and* multiracial family, acknowledging and actively engaging with ethnic and racial differences within the family.

Finally, we highlight two important post-adoption experiences directly affecting adopted individuals and adoptive families that need to be addressed now and in the future by adoption policymakers, practitioners, and scholars. The first is the greater risk for suicide attempts among adopted youth and adults (e.g., von Borczyskowski et al., 2006). More basic science using rigorous study designs is needed to better elucidate the factors (e.g., racism and discrimination) that contribute to and might prevent suicide ideation and attempts. Additionally, evidence-based preventive intervention tailored to the unique experiences and issues of transracially and transnationally adopted individuals and their families is needed to reduce these high odds. The second is the rapid adoption and use of medical and direct-to-consumer genetic testing to identify health risks and disease and to find and confirm birth family (May et al., 2016). Adoptive families and adopted individuals, as well as birth family, are increasingly interested in genetic testing to address the lack of birth family information. This desire for more knowledge must be considered in the context of the privacy rights and other bioethical concerns (Lee, Kim, & Lee, 2016a).

Discussion

In this review, we presented a framework that integrates an Asian Americanist perspective and a critical adoption studies perspective to review, interpret, and critique the theoretical and empirical literature on transnational, transracial adoption. Individually, these approaches draw on largely distinct bodies of interdisciplinary literature that acknowledge and contest systems of power and oppression as they relate to race and adoption. Our integrated Asian Americanist and critical adoption studies framework highlights how these two forces act on and influence each other through systems of oppression. These systems privilege White prospective adoptive parents and make non-White children from "third-world" countries globally "available" (Ngabonziza, 1991).

We applied this integrated framework to examine research on the cultural, ethnic, and racial experiences of adopted Koreans. Research on race-based discrimination suggests that discrimination has lasting negative impacts on mental health beyond pre-adoption adversity and early childhood experiences. Research on ethnic-racial identity found that ERI is relevant to adopted Koreans, and yet adopted Koreans approach their identities in a wide variety of ways – most of which are not inherently pathological. Research on parental cultural socialization indicates that adoptive parents engage in limited cultural socialization efforts, often relying on a "child-choice" approach that relies on the adopted individual to be an active driver of cultural socialization. Finally, research on adopted individuals as agents of self-directed cultural engagement found that adopted Koreans engaged with their adoption – including navigating birth family – and their relation to Korea in a wide variety of ways. As a whole, these studies suggest that adopted Koreans are not merely *kyopo*.[7] Rather, adopted Koreans navigate a "third space" (Hübinette, 2004, p. 23) between their countries of birth and adoption, and in so doing create their own sense of self and community.

Future research

We propose four directions for future research inspired by our integrated framework. First, more research needs to consider the adoption experience throughout the lifespan. As adopted individuals age, how do their experiences with, and understanding of, discrimination, ERI, and cultural engagement change? Further, researchers must investigate how the aging process impacts adopted individuals' relationships with their adoptive and birth families, and with adoption as a whole. This includes the quality and continued development of the adoptive parent–adopted individual relationship, as well as what drives the dissolution or strengthening of these relationships. Similarly, does the process of becoming parents themselves have ramifications for how they think about their birth, relinquishment, and adoption?

Second, future research needs to further consider how adopted individuals understand their sense of self. Narratives from adopted individuals indicate struggling with a personal sense of belonging and self-understanding that are tied to their transnational and transracial upbringing (e.g., Kim et al., 2017). Extant literature primarily draws on ERI development to study this sense of self. However, ERI and its measurement were developed for and with non-adopted samples. To date, there is no study demonstrating measurement invariance between adopted and non-adopted ethnic-racial minority samples. Given their differential patterns of cultural socialization and feelings of belonging to their ethnic-racial group, we could reasonably expect that adopted and non-adopted individuals might derive meaning from their ethnic-racial group differently, and therefore might read items that tap into ERI differently. That this measurement possibility cannot be refuted by extant literature should be cause for concern.

There is also a general lack of measures that can capture concepts particular to the adoption experience. For instance, ERI – regardless of how it is measured – and AI do not fully capture the adoption-related experiences that adopted Koreans might build their identities around. Future research needs to dedicate resources to ground-up operationalizations of constructs specific to the experiences of adopted individuals, including how they integrate aspects of migration, race, and adoption, and how they relate to their birth family, including imagined understandings of the birth family.

Third, we must consider the unique experiences and well-being of birth families, and not merely as controls to understand the impacts of adoption as a natural experiment. Importantly, as most birth families come from communities that fall outside of the typical focus of modern psychology (i.e., are non-White and non-Western), this work needs to be careful to not impose its own worldview on the communities being studied. Rather, researchers should work with the communities to develop research questions and theories, and should be cognizant about the bias that the research team brings to study.

Fourth, adoption research as a whole needs to recognize that researchers' identities and positionalities (e.g., adoptive parents, White, male) have a meaningful impact on the research process. This influence includes directing the topics that are studied, the perspective from which they are studied, how the studies are designed, and the interpretations of the findings. Individuals from all positions within the triad occupy unique positionalities that could be related to bias. To date, White adoptive parents have largely dominated the research literature as both advocates and researchers, leading to research that has privileged the voices of adoptive parents and has been limited in scope. As more adopted individuals enter the academy, we need to recognize their positionality as a strength and not as a source of bias. Just as adoptive parent perspectives on adoptive parenthood can be a place of strength, so called "me-search" conducted by adopted individuals can provide a new set of topics, approaches, and interpretations of the experiences of adopted individuals.

In closing, by reviewing adoption research through an integrated Asian Americanist and critical adoption studies framework, we critiqued the ways in which adoption research – and adoption as a whole – has been practiced. Through this critique, we hope to add nuance and a more critical understanding of the psychology of Korean adoption that better serves those individuals living with adoption.

Notes

1 1,552 of the 1,579 parents in the sample identified as White (98.3 percent).

2 The main effects for ERI pride and ERI engagement in Lee et al. (2015) are accompanied by interactions with discrimination and need to be interpreted in this context. See "Ethnic-racial identity as a protective factor" for further discussion.

3 Beaupre et al. (2015) and Lee et al. (2015) used the same dataset, but Lee et al. (2015) only included participants with matched adoptive parent data in their sample (n = 136) whereas Beaupre et al. (2015) did not screen for matched adoptive parent data; therefore Beaupre et al. (2015) had a larger sample size (n = 189) that overlapped with the Lee et al. (2015) sample.
4 The adopted individuals in this study partially overlap with the samples from Beaupre et al. (2015) and Lee et al. (2015).
5 The adopted adolescents in Hu et al. (2017) were the younger siblings of the adopted adolescents in Ferrari et al. (2017) and Hu et al. (2015).
6 This study used the same sample as Lee et al. (2004).
7 *Kyopo* is the Korean term for overseas Koreans.

References

Anderson, K. N., Lee, R. M., Rueter, M. A., & Kim, O. M. (2015). Associations between discussions of racial and ethnic differences in internationally adoptive families and delinquent behavior among Korean adopted adolescents. *Children and Youth Services Review*, *51*, 66–73. doi:10.1016/j.childyouth.2015.02.001

Baden, A. L., Treweeke, L. M., & Ahluwalia, M. K. (2012). Reclaiming culture: Reculturation of transracial and international adoptees. *Journal of Counseling & Development*, *90*, 387–399. doi:10.1002/j.1556-6676.2012.00049.x

Baden, A. L., & Wiley, M. O. (2007). Counseling adopted persons in adulthood: Integrating practice and research. *The Counseling Psychologist*, *35*(6), 868–901. doi:10.1177/0011000006291409

Beaupre, A., Reichwald, R., Zhou, X., Raleigh, E., & Lee, R. (2015). Korean adoptee identity: Adoptive and ethnic identity profiles of adopted Korean Americans. *New Directions for Child and Adolescent Development*, *150*, 47–61. doi:10.1002/cad.20124

Briggs, L. (2003). Mother, child, race, nation: The visual iconography of rescue and the politics of transnational and transracial adoption. *Gender & History*, *15*(2), 179–200. doi:10.1111/1468-0424.00298

Brodzinsky, D. M. (1990). A stress and coping model of adoption adjustment. In D. M. Brodzinsky & M. D. Schechter (Eds.), *The psychology of adoption* (pp. 3–24). New York, NY: Oxford University Press.

Buchanan, J. P., McGue, M., Keyes, M., & Iacono, W. G. (2009). Are there shared environmental influences on adolescent behavior? Evidence from a study of adoptive siblings. *Behavior Genetics*, *39*(5), 532–540. doi:10.1007/s10519-009-9283-y

Cederblad, M., Höök, B., Irhammar, M., & Mercke, A. (1999). Mental health in international adoptees as teenagers and young adults. An epidemiological study. *Journal of Child Psychology and Psychiatry*, *40*(8), 1239–1248. doi:10.1111/1469-7610.00540

Condit-Shrestha, K. (2018). South Korean and adoption's ends: Reexamining the numbers and historicizing market economies. *Adoption & Culture*, *6*(2), 364–400. doi:10.26818/adoptionculture.6.2.0364

Ferrari, L., Hu, A. W., Rosnati, R., & Lee, R. M. (2017). Ethnic socialization and perceived discrimination on ethnic identity among transracial adoptees: A cross-cultural comparison between Italy and the United States. *Journal of Cross-Cultural Psychology*, *48*(10), 1507–1521. doi:10.1177/0022022117728338

Grotevant, H. D. (1997). Coming to terms with adoption: The construction of identity from adolescence into adulthood. *Adoption Quarterly*, *1*(1), 3–27. doi:10.1300/J145v01n01_02

Grotevant, H. D. (2003). Counseling psychology meets the complex world of adoption. *The Counseling Psychologist*, *31*(6), 753–762. doi:10.1177/0011000003258388

Haugaard, J. J. (1998). Is adoption a risk factor for the development of adjustment problems?. *Clinical Psychology Review*, *18*(1), 47–69. doi:10.1016/S0272-7358(97)00055-X

Haugaard, J. J., & Hazan, C. (2003). Adoption as a natural experiment. *Development and Psychopathology*, *15*(4), 909–926. doi:10.1017/S0954579403000427

Hjern, A., Lindblad, F., & Vinnerljung, B. (2002). Suicide, psychiatric illness, and social maladjustment in intercountry adoptees in Sweden: A cohort study. *The Lancet*, *360*(9331), 443–448. doi:10.1016/S0140-6736(02)09674-5

Hoffman, J., & Peña, E. V. (2013). Too Korean to be white and too white to be Korean: Ethnic identity development among transracial Korean American adoptees. *Journal of Student Affairs Research and Practice*, *50*(2), 152–170. doi:10.1515/jsarp-2013-0012

Homans, M., Phelan, P., Ellerby, J. M., Walker, E., Balcom, K., Myers, K., … Yngvesson, B. (2018). Critical adoption studies: Conversation in progress. *Adoption & Culture*, *6*(1), 1–49. doi:10.26818/adoptionculture.6.1.0001.

Hu, A. W., Anderson, K. N., & Lee, R. M. (2015). Let's talk about race and ethnicity: Cultural socialization, parenting quality and ethnic identity development. *Family Science (Special Section: Family Relationships and Well-being within Adoptive families), 6*, 87–93. doi:10.1037/dev0000421

Hu, A. W., Zhou, X., & Lee, R. M. (2017). Ethnic socialization and ethnic identity development among internationally adopted Korean American adolescents: A seven-year follow-up. *Developmental Psychology, 53*(11), 2066–2077. doi:ezp1.lib.umn.edu/10.1037/dev0000421

Hübinette, T. (2004). Adopted Koreans and the development of identity in the "third space". *Adoption & Fostering, 28*(1), 16–24. doi:10.1177/030857590402800104

Hughes, D., & Chen, L. (1997). When and what parents tell children about race: An examination of race-related socialization among African American families. *Applied Developmental Science, 1*, 200–214. doi:10.1207/s1532480xads0104_4

Hughes, D., Rodriguez, J., Smith, E. P., Johnson, D. J., Stevenson, H. C., & Spicer, P. (2006). Parents' ethnic-racial socialization practices: A review of research and directions for future study. *Developmental Psychology, 42*(5), 747–770. doi:10.1037/0012-1649.42.5.747

Juffer, F., & van IJzendoorn, M. H. (2005). Behavior problems and mental health referrals of international adoptees: A meta-analysis. *JAMA, 293*(20), 2501–2515. doi:10.1001/jama.293.20.2501

Keyes, M. A., Malone, S. M., Sharma, A., Iacono, W. G., & McGue, M. (2013). Risk of suicide attempt in adopted and nonadopted offspring. *Pediatrics, 132*(4), 639–646. doi:10.1542/peds.2012-3251

Kim, C. J. (1999). The racial triangulation of Asian Americans. *Politics & Society, 27*(1), 105–138. doi:10.1177/0032329299027001005

Kim, E. (2010). *Adopted territory: Transnational Korean adoptees and the politics of belonging*. Durham, NC: Duke University Press.

Kim, O. M., Hynes, K. C., & Lee, R. M. (2017). Searching for connection – Finding resolution: A grounded theory analysis of writings of Korean American adopted adults. *Asian American Journal of Psychology, 8*(3), 235–247. doi:ezp1.lib.umn.edu/10.1037/aap0000082

Kim, O. M., Reichwald, R., & Lee, R. M. (2013). Cultural socialization in families with adopted Korean adolescents: A mixed-method, multi-informant study. *Journal of Adolescent Research, 28*, 69–95. doi:10.1177/0743558411432636

Kreider, R. M., & Lofquist, D. A. (2014). *Adopted children and stepchildren: 2010 (Current Population Reports, P20–572)*. Washington, DC: US Census Bureau.

Lee, D. L., & Ahn, S. (2011). Racial discrimination and Asian mental health: A meta-analysis. *The Counseling Psychologist, 39*(3), 463–489. doi:10.1177/0011000010381791

Lee, J. P., Lee, R. M., Hu, A. W., & Kim, O. M. (2015). Ethnic identity as a moderator against discrimination for transracially and transnationally adopted Korean American adolescents. *Asian American Journal of Psychology, 6*(2), 154–163. doi:10.1037/a0038360

Lee, R. M. (2003). The transracial adoption paradox: History, research, and counseling implications of cultural socialization. *The Counseling Psychologist, 31*(6), 711–744. doi:10.1177/0011000003258087

Lee, R. M. & The Minnesota International Adoption Project Team. (2010). Parental perceived discrimination as a postadoption risk factor for internationally adopted children and adolescents. *Cultural Diversity and Ethnic Minority Psychology, 16*(4), 493–500. doi:10.1037/a0020651.

Lee, R. M., Grotevant, H. D., Hellerstedt, W. L., & Gunner, M. R. & The Minnesota International Adoption Project Team. (2006). Cultural socialization in families with internationally adopted children. *Journal of Family Psychology, 20*(4), 571–580. doi:10.1037/0893-3200.20.4.571.

Lee, R. M., Kim, O. M., & Lee, H. (2016a). Unpacking reasons for genetic testing of adoptees. *The American Journal of Bioethics, 16*(12), 39–40. doi:10.1080/15265161.2016.1239793

Lee, R. M., Kim, A. Y. J., & Zhou, X. (2016b). Commentary: An Asian Americanist perspective on child development. *Child Development, 87*(4), 1061–1065. doi:10.1111/cdev.12575

Lee, R. M., & Miller, M. J. (2009). History and psychology of adoptees in Asian America. In N. Tewari & A. N. Alvarez (Eds.), *Asian American psychology: Current perspectives* (pp. 337–363). New York, NY: Psychological Press.

Lee, R. M., & Yoo, H. C. (2004). Structure and measurement of ethnic identity for Asian American college students. *Journal of Counseling Psychology, 51*(2), 263–269. doi:10.1037/0022-0167.51.2.263

Lee, R. M., Yoo, H. C., & Roberts, S. (2004). The coming of age of Korean adoptees: Ethnic identity development and psychological adjustment. In I. J. Kim (Ed.), *Korean Americans: Past, present, and future* (pp. 203–224). Elizabeth, NJ: Hollym International Corporation.

Lee, R. M., Yun, A. B., Yoo, H. C., & Park Nelson, K. (2010). Comparing the ethnic identity and well-being of adopted Korean Americans with immigrant/US-born Korean Americans and Korean international students. *Adoption Quarterly, 13*(1), 2–17. doi:10.1080/10926751003704408

Lindblad, F., Hjern, A., & Vinnerljung, B. (2003). Intercountry adopted children as young adults – A Swedish cohort study. *American Journal of Orthopsychiatry, 73*(2), 190–202. doi:10.1037/0002-9432.73.2.190

May, T., Strong, K. A., Zusevics, K. L., Jeruzal, J., Farrell, M. H., LaPean Kirschner, A., … Grotevant, H. D. (2016). Does lack of "genetic-relative family health history" represent a potentially avoidable health disparity for adoptees? *The American Journal of Bioethics, 16*(12), 33–38. doi:10.1080/15265161.2016.1240255.

McKee, K. D. (2016). Monetary flows and the movements of children: The transnational adoption industrial complex. *Journal of Korean Studies, 21*(1), 137–178. doi:10.1353/jks.2016.0007

Meier, D. I. (1999). Cultural identity and place in adult Korean-American intercountry adoption. *Adoption Quarterly, 3*(1), 15–48. doi:10.1300/J145v03n01_03

Ngabonziza, D. (1991). Moral and political issues facing relinquishing countries. *Adoption & Fostering, 15*(4), 75–80. doi:10.1177/030857599101500413

Park Nelson, K. (2016). *Invisible Asians: Korean American adoptees, Asian American experiences and racial exceptionalism*. New Brunswick, NJ: Rutgers University Press.

Pascoe, E. A., & Smart Richman, L. (2009). Perceived discrimination and health: A meta-analytic review. *Psychological Bulletin, 135*(4), 531–554. doi:10.1037/a0016059

Pate, S. (2014). *From orphan to adoptee: US empire and genealogies of Korean Adoption*. Minneapolis, MN: University of Minnesota Press.

Qin, Y., Kim, A. Y., Su, J. C., Hu, A. W., & Lee, R. M. (2017). Does emotion regulation moderate the discrimination-adjustment link for adopted Korean American adolescents? *Asian American Journal of Psychology, 8*(3), 190–199. doi:10.1037/aap0000081

Roberts, R. E., Phinney, J. S., Masse, L. C., Chen, Y. R., Roberts, C. R., & Romero, A. (1999). The structure of ethnic identity of young adolescents from diverse ethnocultural groups. *The Journal of Early Adolescence, 19*(3), 301–322. doi:10.1177/0272431699019003001

Rutter, M. (1998). Developmental catch-up, and deficit, following adoption after severe global early privation. *The Journal of Child Psychology and Psychiatry and Allied Disciplines, 39*(4), 465–476. doi:10.1017/S0021963098002236

Schires, S. M., Buchanan, N. T., Lee, R. M., McGue, M., Iacono, W. G., & Burt, S. A. (2019). Discrimination and ethnic-racial socialization among youth adopted from South Korea into White American families. *Child Development*. Advance online publication. doi: 10.1111/cdev.13167

Seol, K. O., Yoo, H. C., Lee, R. M., Park, J. E., & Kyeong, Y. (2016). Racial and ethnic socialization as moderators of racial discrimination and school adjustment of adopted and nonadopted Korean American adolescents. *Journal of Counseling Psychology, 63*(3), 294–306. doi:10.1037/cou0000120

Shiao, J. L., & Tuan, M. H. (2008). Korean adoptees and the social context of ethnic exploration. *American Journal of Sociology, 113*(4), 1023–1066. doi:10.1086/522807

Song, S. L., & Lee, R. M. (2009). The past and present cultural experiences of adopted Korean American adults. *Adoption Quarterly, 12*(1), 19–36. doi:10.1080/10926750902791946

Umaña-Taylor, A. J., Quintana, S. M., Lee, R. M., Cross, W. E., Jr., Rivas-Drake, D., & Schwartz., S. J. & Ethnic and Racial Identity in the 21st Century Study Group. (2014). Ethnic and racial identity during adolescence and into young adulthood: An integrated conceptualization. *Child Development, 85*(1), 21–39.

van IJzendoorn, M. H., & Juffer, F. (2006). The Emanuel Miller memorial lecture 2006: Adoption as intervention. Meta-analytic evidence for massive catch-up and plasticity in physical, socio-emotional, and cognitive development. *Journal of Child Psychology and Psychiatry, 47*(12), 1228–1245. doi:10.1111/j.1469-7610.2006.01675.x

von Borczyskowski, A., Hjern, A., Lindblad, F., & Vinnerljung, B. (2006). Suicidal behavior in national and international adult adoptees: A Swedish cohort study. *Social Psychiatry and Psychiatric Epidemiology, 41*(2), 95–102. doi:10.1007/s00127-005-0974-2

10

A NATIONALLY REPRESENTATIVE COMPARISON OF BLACK AND WHITE ADOPTIVE PARENTS OF BLACK ADOPTEES

Elizabeth Raleigh and Rose M. Kreider

In 1972, the National Association of Black Social Workers (NABSW) released a statement in strong opposition to the transracial adoption of Black children by White adoptive parents. Decrying "the placement of Black children in White homes for any reason," the NABSW undertook the position that Black children should only be adopted into Black families where they belonged physically, psychologically, and culturally (National Association of Black Social Workers, 1972, p. 1). The publication of the statement spurred a national debate over the merits of the NABSW's argument that Black adoptive children in White homes were hindered from healthy development of themselves as Black people (National Association of Black Social Workers, 1972, p. 1). Supporters of the NABSW's position rallied against the notion that the only alternative to transracial adoption was foster care, countering that there were ample Black families eager to adopt who faced unreasonable hurdles and systematic discrimination by White social workers (Briggs, 2012; Hollingsworth, 1997). For example, Schwartz and Austin assert, "Black children can be placed in Black homes because, much to contrary belief, Black families do adopt" (2011, p. 164).

Despite the NABSW's call to only racially match Black children with Black adoptive parents, over the subsequent decades there was a marked shift toward race-neutral, colorblind adoption attitudes, policies, and practices. Proponents of transracial adoption pointed to research that found high levels of social and personal adjustment among Black transracial adoptees (Grow & Shapiro, 1974; Simon & Alstein, 1994). Legislators used this data to support the passage of the 1994 Multi-Ethnic Placement Act which prohibited federally funded adoption agencies from using race to delay or deny the placement of a child with an adoptive family (Jennings, 2006). This legislation was undertaken to more easily facilitate the transracial placement of Black children in White homes.

Even though the numbers of transracial adoptions grew alongside its increasing acceptance, it is important to keep in mind that most adoptions involve matching children and parents of the same race (Ishizawa & Kubo, 2014; Raleigh, 2012). For example, in a population-based study of adoptive families, Raleigh (2012) found that 95% of Black adoptive parents adopt a child of the same race. However, because Black same-race adoptive families are not as visible – nor as controversial – as transracial adoptive families, White adoptive families have received more attention from social scientists than Black same-race adoptions. The goal of this chapter is to shift the focus by providing a nationally representative profile of parents who have adopted Black children. We seek to bridge an important gap in the literature by identifying and describing key national benchmarks about Black adopted children raised by either White or Black adoptive parents. Our research questions focus on providing a profile of White, non-Hispanic (from this point on, referred to as White) and Black adoptive parents of Black children. We examine two questions:

1. What are the demographic characteristics of White and Black adoptive parents of Black children?
2. How do White and Black adoptive parents with Black children compare with each other?

By providing a national population-based snapshot of Black adoptees, we seek to contribute information that might be useful to policy makers as they consider the placement needs of Black children and Black adoptive families.

Literature review

There was a dearth of nationally representative data on adoptive families prior to Census 2000, which included an option to identify the respondent's children as biological, adopted, foster, or stepchildren, creating a data source on adopted children in US households (Kreider, 2003). Since then, there has been a growth of population-based research studying adoptive families in general (Amato & Cheadle, 2008; Hamilton, Cheng, & Powell, 2007) and transracial adoptive families in particular (Ishizawa, Kenney, Kubo, & Stevens, 2006; Raleigh & Kao, 2013; Selman, 2009). Yet, much of this literature only includes Black adoptees who were transracially adopted by White parents, with little or no attention to Black children adopted by Black parents.

The relatively recent release of the results from the 2007 National Survey of Adoptive Parents (NSAP) enabled researchers to paint a more detailed national picture of adoption, especially about the type of adoptions (e.g., foster care, domestic, or international) parents pursue (Vandivere, Malm, & Radel, 2009). However, a limitation of NSAP data, when investigating Black adoptive families, is that more than a third of the families in the sample used transnational adoption (Vandivere et al., 2009). We know that parents who adopt internationally are disproportionately White (Ishizawa et al., 2006). In contrast, Black parents are more likely to adopt from foster care (Vandivere et al., 2009). One reason for this difference might be that adopting internationally is often more costly. In fact, a recent report compiled by the US Department of State found that the median cost of an international adoption was over $31,000 (2015b). In the US, Black people are likely to have lower incomes and wealth compared to White people (Oliver & Shapiro, 2006), making it more difficult for a large proportion of would-be Black parents to adopt internationally. Thus, a drawback of the NSAP data is that the sample includes a sizeable proportion of transnational adoptive parents, which means the composition of parents is disproportionately White. Moreover, since White parents tend to have a strong preference for White, Asian, and Hispanic children (Raleigh, 2012), there are relatively few Black adoptive parents or Black adopted children in the sample (Ishizawa & Kubo, 2014, p. 649; Vandivere et al., 2009).

Jacobson and colleagues also used the NSAP in conjunction with a 5% subsample of the US Census to examine the racial composition of transracial adoptive families (2012). Their work establishes some interesting national benchmarks about transracial adoption, showing how transracial adoption is associated with higher income and education levels among adoptive parents, but only for White parents with Asian and Hispanic children and not White parents with Black children. In addition, they find that Black children are among the least likely to be adopted by White parents, "suggesting that much of the adoption of Black children is by Black families" (Jacobson et al., 2012, p. 80). These findings indicate that it would be beneficial to conduct a separate investigation examining the demographics of Black adopted children. Yet since the authors' focus was on transracial adoption, their study omits an analysis of Black adoptive parents.

Of note, the majority of the literature on Black adoptive parents is from a social work perspective and tends to be based on convenience samples. Hairston and Williams (1989) conducted a study based on 53 Black adoptive families and found that Black parents' reasons for adopting were quite similar to those of White parents in that infertility was a driving factor. Moreover, these families shared a similar demographic background with White adoptive parents since most of their respondents were college educated. It is unclear whether these findings would be reflected in national data or if they are only a result of the small snowball sample.

Since these initial studies, two main topics have emerged in the handful of studies focused on Black adoptive families. The first is an examination of Black children's outcomes in same-race adoptive families (Alexander, Hollingsworth, Morrison Dore, & Hoopes, 2004; Gillum & O'Brien, 2010; Smith-McKeever, 2006). Alexander and colleagues (2004) found that, similar to White adoptive parents, Black adoptive parents (mostly mothers) cited grappling with recognizable issues surrounding adoptive parenthood such as when and how to disclose their children's adoptive status, and how to respect and incorporate their children's birth history. In addition, Smith-McKeever examined parental satisfaction among 83 Black adoptive parents who adopted an older child (over age four) from one of two private agencies specializing in the placement of Black children who had been removed from their biological families. Although these children, given their relatively older age (compared to infant adoptions), would have been considered "special needs" or harder to place, Smith-McKeever's findings were encouraging in that "the vast majority (80%) of the African-American private agency adoptive families described themselves as being extremely satisfied with their adoptions and described their child as being a perfect fit for their families (84%)" (2006, p. 838). As these smaller-scale qualitative studies suggest, Black same-race adoptive families are present and thriving, even if not often acknowledged in the scholarly literature.

Another vein of research is analyses of best practices for promoting adoption among African Americans (Hollingsworth, 1997; McRoy, Oglesby, & Grape, 1997). McRoy and colleagues point to the mismatch between many White-led adoption agencies who "have a large number of approved Caucasian families but a limited supply of approved waiting African American adoptive families" (1997, p. 89). The authors point to the need for more "culturally competent" policies since many African American families "have considered adopting but have been screened out of the process" (McRoy et al., 1997, p. 89). Likewise, Hollingsworth finds "active and ongoing efforts to recruit and retain adoptive families of color should be increased so that the pool of available families equals or surpasses the numbers of children of color who are available for non-kin adoption" (1997, p. 114).

Given the disproportionate number of Black children in foster care awaiting adoption, most of these studies tend to focus on publicly funded adoptions of children from foster care, rather than private infant adoption (Gillum & O'Brien, 2010; see Smith-McKeever & McRoy, 2005 for an exception). For example, Schwartz and Austin profiled an agency with a longstanding mission of moving Black children out of foster care and into permanent homes (2011). The authors detail how the agency deliberately worked to recruit Black adoptive parents by widening their scope to include "non-traditional" families "by delivering services to many different types of families such as single adults and couples, working and retired parents, homeowners and home renters, [and] families with diverse levels of income" (2011, p. 162). Understanding how to potentially recruit more of these families is particularly important because prior research suggests that Black adoptive parents may be more likely to adopt monoracial Black children, who can be harder to place compared to multiracial Black children.

Multiracial Black adoptees

While there is more research on Black adopted children than Black adoptive parents, scholars tend to treat Black adoptees as a monolithic group, ignoring potential differences between multiracial and monoracial Black children. This practice reflects the legacy of hypodescent: until the late 20th century, persons with "one drop" of Black heritage were considered Black (Davis, 1991). In line with the finding that Black parents are more likely to identify their (biologically related) multiracial Black children as Black (Lee & Bean, 2010), it could be that Black adoptive parents are likely to racially identify their children as Black regardless of whether they have multiracial ancestry. We know from sociological research that Black parents are the least likely to indicate that their multiracial children have an additional racial ancestry (Rockquemore & Brunsma, 2007; Tafoya, Johnson, & Hill, 2004). This approach to racial identification is so dominant that research indicates between 75% to 90% of African Americans could identify themselves as more than one race, but only a fraction choose to do so (Lee & Bean, 2010). In contrast, qualitative research suggests that White adoptive parents do not abide by the same model. In previous work, Raleigh (2016) has shown how White adoptive parents differentiate between biracial (part-White) children and "full" Black children, such that the former are perceived to be more desirable than the latter. Thus, it could be that White transracial adoptive parents are more likely to adopt a Black child identified as more than one race, whereas Black adoptive parents might be more likely to seek out monoracial Black children.

Gaps in the literature

In sum, much of the literature on Black adoptive families is fairly outdated (i.e. based on data collected in the 1990s) and was based on smaller convenience samples. Taken together, there are two main points. First, Black parents do adopt, but they face additional hurdles. Second, for those Black parents who do manage to adopt, these adoptive families are extremely satisfied with their placements, even when adopting older children, who in adoption parlance were often referred to as special needs or harder to place (Herman, 2008). Contextualizing these studies, in a review of the literature on Black families who adopt Black children, Gillum surmises there is still much work to be done, since these inquiries are sporadically published and not easily replicable (2011, p. 327). Notably, Gillum ends her review with a call for research focusing on Black adoptive families, arguing that an expanded knowledge about these families can "provide data that can be used in addressing their needs" (2011, p. 328). Importantly, these studies posit that single and working class Black adoptive parents could be a beneficial pool from which to recruit adoptive families. Undoubtedly, it would have been helpful for these authors to be able to point to population-based data that documented that these families already existed, but due to data limitations, investigators lacked the empirical power to examine these questions further.

Missing from these analyses is a comprehensive nationally generalizable description of Black adopted children and their adoptive families. This chapter attends to some gaps in the literature by providing a detailed description of the demographic composition of parents who adopt Black children. We do not seek to weigh in on the contentious debate surrounding transracial adoption, rather, our goal is to provide a national benchmark of Black adoptive parents so that researchers have a better understanding of these families, particularly Black adoptive parents of Black children. Mainly, we seek to illuminate the fact that Black families do adopt Black children, yet they are not the privileged (highly educated, fully employed, high income) nuclear families that comprise the majority of White adoptive families. We show how, unlike many White adoptive parents who seek out more expensive forms of transnational private adoption, the vast majority of Black adoptive parents opt to adopt US-born children. Additionally, our findings suggest that Black adoptive families are more likely to identify their Black child as monoracially Black. Since monoracial Black children, compared to mixed-race Black children, are seen as some of the hardest to place (Raleigh, 2016), our findings could be particularly important for policy makers tasked with formulating best practices to place and support these children.

Methods

The US Census Bureau has replaced the long-form census with continuous sampling in the form of the American Community Survey (ACS). Data informing this description of Black adoptees are from the 2010–2014 (ACS) 5-year data. Since we are analyzing a relatively small population – White or Black householders who report an adopted child who is Black alone or Black multiracial – the internal five-year file is the most appropriate available data because it provides a larger sample than the Public Use Microdata Sample data (US Census Bureau, 2018).

For the descriptive statistics we compare three distinct groups of parents who have an adopted child under 18 in their household who is identified as Black alone or Black in combination with another race or races: White alone householders (group 1), Black alone householders (group 2), and interracial couples in which a White parent has a spouse who is other than White (group 3). However, since the group of White interracial parents was quite small, they were combined with the White adoptive parents for the logistic regression models predicting whether adoptive parents of Black children are White or Black. The models are not causal but allow us to see which characteristics are more common for Black adoptive parents compared with White adoptive parents. As stated earlier, we are using "White" to refer to White non-Hispanic, yet "Black" does include Black Hispanics. Although people who are neither White nor Black (e.g. Asian) do adopt Black children, this occurs infrequently (Ishizawa et al., 2006). We exclude these groups from this analysis since we expect they will be too small to be meaningful in the context of controlling for multiple characteristics of the parent/family.

One limitation of the ACS data is that respondents are simply reporting a living arrangement and the data do not include details about whether the adoption occurred through the public foster care system, was privately arranged, or whether the parent was related to the child before they were adopted (e.g., grandchild or stepchild). Thus the "adopted" category also includes some children who started out as stepchildren or are the biological child of the householder's unmarried partner, and they report the child as their adopted son or daughter. Additionally, the race and ethnicity data are self-reported and minor-aged adoptees' categorizations are likely to be reported by their adoptive parents.

Independent variables

To examine demographic differences between White and Black adoptive parents, we focus on four key variables regarding the adopted child: sex, disability, multiracial identification, and immigration status. To evaluate whether there are differences in child's sex across these groups, we create a sex ratio that measures the proportion of adopted girls to boys. Based on the research indicating that adoptive parents prefer girls (Chandra, Abma, Maza, & Bachrach, 1999; Ward-Gailey, 2010), we hypothesize that adoptive parents, regardless of race, will be more likely than their counterparts with biological children to have adopted a daughter versus a son. Also, given prevalence of gendered stereotypes associating Black male youth with delinquent behavior (Rios, 2011), we hypothesize that White parents who adopt transracially will be the most likely to adopt girls. While we show the sex ratio in the descriptive table, we do not add it to the models, since it is a group-level characteristic rather than an individual one.

Regarding adoptees with disabilities, we hypothesize that White parents will be more likely to adopt a child with a disability than Black parents adopting Black children, or at least more likely to have identified their child as having a disability (Bramlette, 2010; Kreider & Cohen, 2009; McManus, Carle, & Rapport, 2014; Ong-Dean, 2009). In the model, we operationalize this measure by identifying parents who have adopted at least one Black child who has at least one disability. We include a dummy variable for those who have only children under age five, who are out of universe for the disability questions.

Since research has shown Black parents are the least likely of all racial-ethnic groups to identify their multiracial children as more than one race (Rockquemore & Brunsma, 2007; Tafoya et al., 2004), it is possible that this trend is carried out among Black adoptive parents as well. In contrast, White adoptive parents with Black children might want to emphasize their children's multiracial heritage and might be more likely to identify their son or daughter as more than one race. Thus, we might over-estimate the differences in the prevalence of Black multiracial children in Black versus White adoptive families when we hypothesize that there will be a higher proportion of multiracial Black children living with White adoptive parents than with Black adoptive parents. Since we are comparing parents, and not children, the measure we use is whether the parent has at least one adopted Black child who is identified as multiracial.

We code immigration status to indicate parents who have at least one Black adopted child who was not born in the US. The combined 2010–2014 ACS data are well situated to capture the increase in transnational adoptions from Africa and the Caribbean that occurred at the turn of the millennium (US Department of State, 2015a, 2015b). We hypothesize that the Black children of White parents are more likely to have been internationally adopted than the Black children of Black adoptive parents.

Last, to help us better understand the profiles of parents with Black adopted children, we include a series of control variables including current living arrangements (e.g., married, with an unmarried partner), marital history, educational attainment, labor force participation, home ownership, and geographic region of residence. The models are not causal but allow us to compare White and Black adoptive parents of Black children in a multivariate context.

Results

Table 10.1 provides estimates for descriptive characteristics of adoptive parents of Black children for the three groups of parents. White parents are more likely to have a spouse present – 73% compared with 44% of Black parents. All of the White interracially married parents are married, by definition. Black mothers with no spouse or partner present (44%) are more than twice the proportion of White mothers with no spouse or partner present (18%). Black parents (28%) are more likely than White parents (24%) to have been married more than once, neither of which differ statistically from the percentage of White interracial parents (27%) who have been married more than once.

Since adoptive parents tend to have higher levels of education than the general US population (Kreider & Lofquist, 2014), we show "graduate or professional school degree" as a category separate from "bachelor's degree" in Table 10.1. However, for a more basic comparison, we add the two categories together and find that, on average, White adoptive parents have higher levels of education than Black adoptive parents, with 53% having at least a bachelor's degree, compared with 25% for Black parents. The difference between White interracial adoptive parents and White adoptive parents is smaller than that between Black and White parents (47% of White interracial parents have at least a bachelor's degree). In comparison to the US population according to the 2014 Current Population Survey, the proportion of Black adoptive parents with at least a bachelor's degree (25%) is higher than the percentage for all Black adults aged 25 and over (22%). The proportion of White adoptive parents with at least a bachelor's degree (53%) is higher than for all White adults aged 25 and over (36%), a difference (17%) that is greater than the difference identified between Black adoptive parents and Black adults (3%) (US Census Bureau, 2014).

The contrasts in labor force participation among the three groups of adoptive parents show a pattern similar to educational attainment. The difference between White (79.4%) and White interracial adoptive parents (77.0%) is not statistically significant, although both groups differ significantly from Black parents (67.9%). The percentage of Black parents who are unemployed (9.7%) is more than twice that of White (4.1%) or White intermarried parents (3.9%). These differences in labor force participation are reflected in the poverty levels for the groups. While only 9% of White adoptive parents' households and 6% of White interracial adoptive parents' households are below the poverty level, more than one quarter (28%) of Black adoptive parents' households were below the poverty level. This economic gap is also found in homeownership, with 50% of Black parents renting their homes, while just 17% of White parents and 23% of White interracial parents live in rented homes.

The analysis of the sex of the Black adoptees revealed that the ratio of adopted girls to boys varied little across the three groups, with a ratio of 0.9 for White parents, and 1.1 for Black parents, and 1.0 for White intermarried parents. There were no statistically significant differences between any of the groups.

White and White interracial adoptive parents were more likely to have at least one Black adopted child identified as multiracial – 43% for White parents and 48% for White

Table 10.1 Characteristics of adoptive parents of Black children[1]

	White non-Hispanic parent			*Black alone parent*			*White non-Hispanic intermarried parent*		
	Number	*Percent*	*Margin of error*[2]	*Number*	*Percent*	*Margin of error*[2]	*Number*	*Percent*	*Margin of error*[2]
Total adoptive parents	69,619	100.0	X	115,851	100.0	X	7,379	100.0	X
Living arrangement of the parent									
Married couple households	50,857	73.1	0.92	51,276	44.3	1.03	7,379	100.0	X
Male – no spouse present	3,925	5.6	0.53	10,338	8.9	0.61	X	X	X
With an unmarried partner	1,383	2.0	0.32	2,896	2.5	0.34	X	X	X
No unmarried partner present	2,542	3.7	0.44	7,442	6.4	0.52	X	X	X
Female – no spouse present	14,837	21.3	0.93	54,237	46.8	1.03	X	X	X
With an unmarried partner	2,476	3.6	0.53	3,843	3.3	0.37	X	X	X
No unmarried partner present	12,361	17.8	0.82	50,394	43.5	0.99	X	X	X
Parent has been married more than once[3]	14,886	23.9	1.07	22,799	27.5	1.09	2,022	27.4	3.46
Educational attainment of the parent									
Less than high school	2,155	3.1	0.44	12,341	10.7	0.62	244	3.3	1.07
High school graduate	10,174	14.6	0.82	29,018	25.0	0.86	977	13.2	2.29
Some college	20,556	29.5	1.17	46,046	39.7	0.98	2,665	36.1	3.73
Bachelor's degree	19,460	28.0	1.26	16,161	13.9	0.77	1,833	24.8	3.18
Graduate or professional school degree	17,274	24.8	1.12	12,285	10.6	0.60	1,660	22.5	3.13
Labor force participation of the parent[4]	69,619	100.0	X	115,797	100.0	X	7,379	100.0	X
In labor force	58,120	83.5	0.90	89,821	77.6	0.87	5,967	80.9	3.15

(*Continued*)

Table 10.1 (Cont.)

	White non-Hispanic parent			*Black alone parent*			*White non-Hispanic intermarried parent*		
	Number	*Percent*	*Margin of error*[2]	*Number*	*Percent*	*Margin of error*[2]	*Number*	*Percent*	*Margin of error*[2]
Employed	55,277	79.4	1.01	78,571	67.9	1.03	5,680	77.0	3.35
Unemployed	2,843	4.1	0.49	11,250	9.7	0.60	287	3.9	1.64
Not in labor force	11,499	16.5	0.90	25,976	22.4	0.87	1,412	19.1	3.15
Household income[5]									
$0 or less	196	0.3	0.12	2,220	1.9	0.29	1	0.0	0.02
$1–$24,999	5,478	7.9	0.73	30,252	26.1	0.97	297	4.0	1.48
$25,000–$49,999	10,731	15.4	0.87	30,032	25.9	1.03	1,007	13.6	2.44
$50,000–$99,999	24,677	35.4	1.43	31,888	27.5	1.00	2,345	31.8	4.04
$100,000–$199,999	22,150	31.8	1.11	17,937	15.5	0.83	2,980	40.4	3.99
$200,000 or more	6,387	9.2	0.66	3,522	3.0	0.31	749	10.2	2.32
Below the poverty level	6,333	9.1	0.76	32,421	28.0	0.97	459	6.2	1.86
Tenure									
Owns with a mortgage	50,124	72.0	1.02	49,832	43.0	1.20	5,222	70.8	4.31
Owns free and clear	7,407	10.6	0.77	8,723	7.5	0.51	438	5.9	1.76
Rents home[6]	12,088	17.4	0.98	57,296	49.5	1.26	1,719	23.3	3.99
Region									
Northeast	11,368	16.3	0.83	18,754	16.2	0.72	977	13.2	2.27
Midwest	22,757	32.7	1.07	24,532	21.2	0.68	1,579	21.4	3.17
South	20,511	29.5	1.02	62,145	53.6	1.08	2,644	35.8	3.63
West	14,983	21.5	0.93	10,420	9.0	0.65	2,179	29.5	4.38
Characteristics of householder's adopted children[7]									
Age of youngest child									
0–5 years	23,100	33.2	1.18	27,746	23.9	1.02	2,411	32.7	3.27
6–11 years	25,592	36.8	1.23	39,436	34.0	1.00	2,676	36.3	3.44
12–17 years	20,927	30.1	1.06	48,669	42.0	0.92	2,292	31.1	3.89
Ratio of adopted girls to adopted boys for the group	0.9	X	0.2	1.1	X	0.2	1.0	X	0.7
At least one child identified as multiracial	29,925	43.0	1.15	6,558	5.7	0.47	3,553	48.2	3.96

(Continued)

Table 10.1 (Cont.)

	White non-Hispanic parent			*Black alone parent*			*White non-Hispanic intermarried parent*		
	Number	*Percent*	*Margin of error*[2]	*Number*	*Percent*	*Margin of error*[2]	*Number*	*Percent*	*Margin of error*[2]
At least one foreign-born child	9,520	13.7	0.75	3,951	3.4	0.34	514	7.0	1.77
At least one child aged 5 and over	54,357	100.0	X	99,369	100.0	X	5,787	100.0	X
At least one child with a disability[8]	7,426	13.7	0.79	11,129	11.2	0.78	846	14.6	3.27
Unweighted total	6,647	X	X	7,825	X	X	627	X	X
(X) – not applicable.									

Notes:

1 All relationships are collected with reference to the householder, so adoptive parents shown in this table are the householder – someone who owns or rents the home and has at least one Black alone or in combination adopted child under 18 present in the household.
2 This figure, added to, or subtracted from the percent, provides the 90% confidence interval.
3 Percentage is shown out of all those who have ever been married.
4 The universe for this question is the population aged 16 and over.
5 Estimates shown for adjusted household income.
6 Rents or occupies without payment.
7 Only the Black alone or in combination adopted children under 18 are included when constructing these estimates.
8 Only shown for parents with at least one child aged 5 and over, since some of the disability questions only apply to those aged 5 and over.

Source: US Census Bureau, ACS, 2010– 2014. For information on confidentiality protection, sampling error, nonsampling error, and definitions, see www2.census.gov/programs-surveys/acs/tech_docs/accuracy/MultiyearACSAccuracyofData2014.pdf

interracial parents. Yet only 6% of Black adoptive parents had a Black adoptee they identified as multiracial.

White adoptive parents have the highest percentage of internationally adopted Black children, with at least one child born outside of the US (14%). They are followed by White interracial parents (7%), and Black parents had the fewest internationally adopted Black children (3%).

For parents with at least one Black adopted child aged 5 and over, 15% of White interracial adoptive parents have at least one child with a disability. This is not statistically different from White adoptive parents (14%). Black adoptive parents have a lower percentage of Black adoptees with a disability (11%), and the difference between Black parents and the other groups is statistically significant.

The multivariate model in Table 10.2 allows us to compare groups of adoptive parents while simultaneously controlling for various characteristics. As previously explained, since the group of White interracially adoptive parents is small, they are combined with the other White parents. This consolidation provides a more nuanced picture of which of the apparent differences between Black and White parents remain after we control for demographic and socioeconomic characteristics. The logistic regression model is "predicting" which parents are Black, and essentially compares characteristics against those of White parents. It is not a causal

Table 10.2 Comparison of Black adoptive parents with White adoptive parents[1]

	Model 1		
	Black parent vs. White parent		
	Estimate	*Standard error*	*Odds ratio*
Living arrangement			
Married couple	(reference)		
Female, no spouse or partner	0.6637	0.2746	1.94*
Male, no spouse or partner	0.5368	0.5440	1.71
Marital history			
Never married	(reference)		
Married once	–0.3960	0.3368	0.67
Married twice or more	–0.4167	0.4654	0.66
Educational attainment			
Less than high school	0.5130	0.4820	1.67
High school graduate or some college	(reference)		
Bachelor's degree	–0.7318	0.3244	0.48*
Graduate or professional degree	–0.7893	0.2767	0.45**
Labor force participation			
Employed	(reference)		
Unemployed	0.3467	0.5646	1.41
Not in labor force	0.0177	0.3312	1.02
In poverty	0.3301	0.4013	1.39
Tenure			
Own	–0.9723	0.3221	0.38**
Rent	(reference)		
Region			
Northeast	(reference)		
Midwest	–0.3932	0.3211	0.67
South	0.6836	0.2902	1.98*
West	–0.8073	0.4440	0.45
Has at least one multiracial Black adopted child	–2.6243	0.3354	0.07***
Has at least one foreign-born Black adopted child	–1.4821	0.3830	0.23***
Has at least one Black adopted child with a disability	–0.5187	0.3314	0.60
Has no Black adopted child 5 years old and over	–0.6205	0.3221	0.54

Note: Significance is noted as follows: *(<0.05), **(<0.01), ***(<0.001).

1 Adoptive parents include only White non-Hispanic, and Black alone householders. White non-Hispanic householders with spouses who are not White non-Hispanic are included with White householders. Black adopted children include those who reported Black alone or in combination with other race groups.

Source: ACS, 2010–2014. For information on confidentiality protection, sampling error, nonsampling error, and definitions, see http://www2.census.gov/programs-surveys/acs/tech_docs/accuracy/MultiyearACSAccuracyofData2014.pdf

model. A model (not shown) excluding the White intermarried parents provides essentially the same results.

As expected, the gaps seen in Table 10.1 for several characteristics also hold in the model. Black adoptive parents are significantly more likely to be a mother without a spouse or partner, and less likely to have a bachelor's or professional degree than White adoptive parents. They are less likely to own their home and more likely to live in the South. The difference in percent in poverty is not significant. This is likely due to other related characteristics, such as education, home ownership, and labor force participation, outweighing the percentage in poverty in the multivariate context. Black parents are less likely than White adoptive parents to have a multiracial child or an internationally adopted child. The difference in the proportion of Black and White adoptive parents with at least one child with a disability is not significant.

Discussion

This chapter presents some of the first national benchmarks of Black children in adoptive families. Although some of our results are not surprising (e.g., Black adoptive parents on average hail from lower socioeconomic status households), other findings did not align with our original hypotheses. For example, even though prior research has found that prospective adoptive parents often have a preference for girls (Chandra et al., 1999; Ward-Gailey, 2010), the results do not support this, and there are not significant differences in gender ratios among these groups of adoptive parents. Regarding disability, it was interesting to see that the proportion of White and Black adoptive parents with at least one child with a disability is not significantly different in the multivariate model. Together, these findings indicate that White parents who transracially adopt Black children are roughly as likely to adopt boys or to have children with a disability as the other groups of parents. However, since the disability data only pertains to children aged 5 and over, and we do not have information on when the child was adopted, it is unclear whether these parents adopted a child with an identified disability, or whether the child was diagnosed after the adoption was finalized.

Although we expected Black parents to be less likely to have at least one Black adopted child who is identified as multiracial, the extent of observed differences between White and Black adoptive parents was substantial. We find White adoptive parents are approximately seven times more likely to say they have a multiracial Black adopted child compared to Black adoptive parents, who are much more likely to categorize their Black adopted child as monoracial. Data limitations do not allow us to untangle how much of this phenomenon can be attributed to whether Black parents are more likely to seek out monoracial Black children (versus White parents seeking out multiracial Black children), or whether Black parents are more likely to identify their children as monoracially Black regardless of whether they could claim a mixed-race heritage. However, our findings do suggest that Black adoptive parents perceive themselves as a monoracial family, even if their children could "technically" be considered of multiracial descent. Interestingly, White interracial adoptive parents are the most likely to report having a multiracial child. It could be that intermarried adoptive parents have a desire for their adoptive family to adhere to the "as if begotten model" of adoption, such that the adopted child can racially pass as the parents' would-be biological child (Modell, 1994). For these families, there might be more of an incentive on the part of the interracially married adoptive parents to adopt a child who would theoretically resemble a biological child.

The multivariate model also confirms our hypothesis that Black adoptive parents are less likely than White adoptive parents to have an adopted child born outside of the US. This finding reaffirms previous research indicating that international adoption is largely utilized by White parents and that it is less accessible to parents of color (Ishizawa et al., 2006). Indeed, results from the NSAP show that 92% of international adoptive parents are White (Vandivere et al., 2009). In contrast, Black parents are more likely to adopt from foster care (Vandivere et al., 2009). As stated previously, international adoption is often quite costly (US Department of State, 2015b). Given the lower socioeconomic status shown in the descriptive estimates in Table 10.1, it is perhaps not surprising that Black parents are less likely to have a foreign-born child.

Conclusion

Using ACS 5-year data, this chapter takes a closer look at the demographic profile of Black adoptive parents who adopt Black children. These families are often overlooked as researchers, adoption specialists, and policy makers often prefer to focus on the placement of Black children in White homes. There have been a handful of small qualitative studies examining Black adoptive families, but before the ACS, few datasets were large enough to examine this group at the national level.

Given the volume of the debate on transracial adoption, it might be surprising to learn that there are more Black children adopted by Black parents than White parents. Although the demographic finding is relatively straightforward, there are important implications because this statistic will hopefully remind child welfare workers and adoption researchers to recognize and focus on a sizeable group of adoptive families. Because others cannot easily identify monoracial Black adoptive families, these families often go unnoticed. Of course, White monoracial adoptive families are not obvious either, but since White adoptive parents are disproportionately represented in the population (Kreider & Lofquist, 2014), they dominate the image of adoptive parents.

Whereas prior research has found that White adoptive parents are more privileged than White parents raising biological children (Hamilton et al., 2007), our findings indicate that Black adoptive parents do not share the same privileged socioeconomic status. In this study we find that they are less likely to be highly educated, own their homes, or be in the labor force. They are also more likely to be raising children as single mothers, and more than a quarter (28%) of Black adoptive parents live below the poverty line. These findings are in line with national trends on racial disparities, on average,

These results suggest that on average, Black adoptive parents may not traverse the same pathway to adoption as many White adoptive parents. Given Black families' lower average socioeconomic status, it is likely that fewer of these parents utilized private adoption, which is much more expensive than public foster care adoption (Vandivere et al., 2009). From our results, it is clear that only a minuscule number of Black adoptive parents pursue transnational private adoption. Our findings allow us to rule out transnational adoption as a common pathway to adoptive parenthood for Black parents; however, the data do not allow us to distinguish between other forms of adoption.

These findings raise some important implications for child well-being. Considering that many child welfare advocates agree that there is benefit to Black children being adopted by Black parents, it is our hope that these population-based results might help identify potential demographic profiles from which to recruit Black families. Given that among adoptive parents, Blacks are the most likely to adopt US-born children, these families could represent an untapped resource. However, it could be that, in line with McRoys and colleagues' findings (1997), Black applicants still get screened out of the pool since many of these prospective adoptive parents might be single applicants who might not have comparable socioeconomic status levels to White prospective parents.

Thus, our conclusions raise more questions than are answered. Whereas the modal family structure for White transracial adoptive parents is a married household, our findings indicate that the story is not as straightforward for Black adoptive parents. Considering that a large proportion of Black adoptive parents report being married more than once, it is unclear which of these adoptive families are kinship and/or second parent adoptions and which ones represent the more conventional adoption of a previously unrelated child. Yet our findings suggest that there are likely other potential Black adoptive parents who fit similar profiles to those who have already adopted. By providing a national benchmark of White and Black adoptive parents of Black children, these findings could be helpful to adoption workers and policy makers by raising the visibility of Black adopted children and their families.

Author note

The views expressed on statistical or methodological issues are those of the authors and not necessarily those of the US Census Bureau.

References

Alexander, L., Hollingsworth, L., Morrison Dore, M., & Hoopes, J. (2004). A family of trust: African American parents' stories of adoption disclosure. *American Journal of Orthopsychiatry*, *74*(4), 448–455. doi:10.1037/0002-9432.74.4.448

Amato, P., & Cheadle, J. (2008). Parental divorce, marital conflict & children's behavior problems: A comparison of adopted and biological children. *Social Forces*, *86*(3), 1139–1161. doi:10.1353/sof.0.0025

Bramlett, M. (2010). When stepparents adopt: Demographic, health and health care characteristics of adopted children, stepchildren and adopted stepchildren. *Adoption Quarterly*, *13*, 248–267. doi:10.1080/10926755.2010.537954

Briggs, L. (2012). *Somebody's children: The politics of transracial and transnational adoption*. Durham, NC: Duke University Press.

Census Bureau, U. S. (2014). Retrieved from www.census.gov/hhes/socdemo/education/data/cps/2014/Table percent201-04.xlsx

Chandra, A., Abma, J., Maza, P., & Bachrach, C. (1999). Adoption, adoption seeking, and relinquishment for adoption in the United States. *Advance data from vital and health statistics*, no. 306. Hyattsville, Maryland: National Center for Health Statistics.

Davis, J. (1991). *Who is black? One nation's definition*. University Park, PA: Penn State University Press.

Gillum, N. (2011). Review of research on Black families who formally adopted Black children. *Families in Society – the Journal of Contemporary Social Services*, *92*(3), 324–328. doi:10.1606/1044-3894.4136

Gillum, N., & O'Brien, M. (2010). Adoption satisfaction of Black adopted children. *Children & Youth Services Review*, *32*(12), 1656–1663. doi:10.1016/j.childyouth.2010.07.005

Grow, L., & Shapiro, D. (1974). *Black children, White parents: A study of transracial adoption*. New York: Research Center, Child Welfare League of America.

Hairston, C., & Williams, V. (1989). Black adoptive parents – How they view agency adoption practices. *Social Casework-Journal of Contemporary Social Work*, *70*(9), 534–538. doi:10.1177/104438948907000902

Hamilton, L., Cheng, S., & Powell, P. (2007). Adoptive parents, adaptive parents: Evaluating the importance of biological ties for parental investment. *American Sociological Review*, *72*(1), 95–116. doi:10.1177/000312240707200105

Herman, E. (2008). *Kinship by design: A history of adoption in the modern United States.* Chicago, IL: University of Chicago Press.

Hollingsworth, L. (1997). Effect of transracial/transethnic adoption on children's racial and ethnic identity and self-esteem: A meta-analytic review. *Marriage and Family Review, 25*(1–2), 99–130. doi:10.1300/J002v25n01_07

Ishizawa, H., Kenney, C., Kubo, K., & Stevens, G. (2006). Constructing interracial families through intercountry adoption. *Social Science Quarterly, 87*(5), 1207–1224. doi:10.1111/j.1540-6237.2006.00424.x

Ishizawa, H., & Kubo, K. (2014). Factors affecting adoption decisions: Child and parental characteristics. *Journal of Family Issues, 35*(5), 627–653. doi:10.1177/0192513X13514408

Jacobson, C., Nielsen, L., & Hardeman, A. (2012). Family trends and transracial adoption in the United States. *Adoption Quarterly, 15*(2), 73–87. doi:10.1080/10926755.2012.681591

Jennings, P. (2006). The trouble with the multiethnic placement act: An empirical look at transracial adoption. *Sociological Perspectives, 49*(4), 559–581. doi:10.1525/sop.2006.49.4.559

Kreider, R. (2003). Adopted children and stepchildren: 2000. *Census 2000 Special Reports*, CNSR-6RV, Washington, DC, US: US Department of Commerce. Retrieved from www.census.gov/prod/2003pubs/censr-6.pdf

Kreider, R., & Cohen, P. (2009). Disability among internationally adopted children in the United States. *Pediatrics, 124*(5), 1311–1318. doi:10.1542/peds.2008-3206

Kreider, R., & Lofquist, D. (2014). Adopted children and stepchildren: 2010. *Current Population Reports*: 20–572, Washington, DC, US: US Department of Commerce. Retrieved from www.census.gov/prod/2014pubs/p20-572.pdf

Lee, J., & Bean, F. (2010). *The diversity paradox: Immigration and the color line in twenty-first century America.* New York: Russell Sage.

McManus, B., Carle, A., & Rapport, M. (2014). Classifying infants and toddlers with developmental vulnerability: Who is most likely to receive early intervention?. *Child: Care, Health, and Development, 40*(2), 205–214. doi:10.1111/cch.12013

McRoy, R., Oglesby, Z., & Grape, H. (1997). Achieving same-race adoptive placements for African American children: Culturally sensitive practice approaches. *Child Welfare, 76*(1), 85–104.

Modell, J. (1994). *Kinship with strangers.* Berkeley, CA: University of California Press.

National Association of Black Social Workers. (1972). *Position statement on trans-racial adoptions.* New York, NY.

Oliver, Melvin L. & Shapiro, Thomas. (2006). *Black wealth, White wealth: A new perspective on racial inequality.* Second Edition. New York, NY: Routledge.

Ong-Dean, C. (2009). *Distinguishing disability: Parents, privilege and special education.* Chicago: University of Chicago Press.

Raleigh, E. (2012). Are same-sex and single adoptive parents more likely to adopt transracially? A national analysis of race, family structure, and the adoption marketplace. *Sociological Perspectives, 55*(3), 449–471. doi:10.1525/sop.2012.55.3.449

Raleigh, E. (2016). The color line exception: The transracial adoption of foreign-born and biracial black children. *Women, Gender, and Families of Color, 4*(1), 86–107. doi:10.5406/womgenfamcol.4.1.0086

Raleigh, E., & Kao, G. (2013). Is there a (transracial) adoption achievement gap?: A national longitudinal analysis of adopted children's educational performance. *Children and Youth Services Review, 35*(1), 142–150. doi:10.1016/j.childyouth.2012.09.019

Rios, V. (2011). *Punished: Policing the lives of Black and Latino boys.* New York: New York University Press.

Rockquemore, K., & Brunsma, D. (2007). *Beyond Black: Biracial identity in America.* Second Edition. New York: Rowman & Littlefield.

Schwartz, S., & Austin, M. (2011). Black adoption placement and research center at 25: Placing African-American children in permanent homes (1983–2008). *Journal of Evidence-Based Social Work, 8*(1–2), 160–178. doi:10.1080/15433714.2011.542397

Selman, P. (2009). The rise and fall of intercountry adoption in the 21st century. *International Social Work, 52*(5), 575–594. doi:10.1177/0020872809337681

Simon, R. J., & Alstein, H. (1994). *The case for transracial adoption.* Lanham, MD: The American University Press.

Smith-McKeever, C. (2006). Adoption satisfaction among African-American families adopting African-American children. *Children and Youth Services Review, 28*(7), 825–840. doi:10.1016/j.childyouth.2005.08.009

Smith-McKeever, C., & McRoy, R. (2005). The role of private adoption agencies in facilitating African American adoptions. *Families in Society – the Journal of Contemporary Social Services, 86*(4), 533–540. doi:10.1606/1044-3894.3458

Tafoya, S., Johnson, H., & Hill, L. (2004). Who chooses to choose two?: Multiracial identification and Census 2000. New York: Russell Sage Foundation and Population Reference Bureau. Retrieved December 2, 2015, from www.prb.org

US Census Bureau. (2018). Retrieved from www.census.gov/programs-surveys/acs/guidance/estimates.html

US Department of State. (2015a). Intercountry Adoption Statistics. Bureau of Consular Affairs. Retrieved December 2, 2015 from http://travel.state.gov/content/adoptionsabroad/en/about-us/statistics.html

US Department of State. (2015b). FY 2014 Annual Report on Intercountry Adoption. Washington DC, US: Bureau of Consular Affairs. Retrieved November 5, 2015 from http://travel.state.gov/content/dam/aa/pdfs/fy2014_annual_report.pdf

Vandivere, S., Malm, K., & Radel, L. (2009). Adoption USA: A chartbook based on the 2007 National Survey of Adoptive Parents. Washington, DC, US: Department of Health and Human Services. Retrieved December 2, 2015 from http://aspe.hhs.gov/report/adoption-usa-chartbook-based-2007-national-survey-adoptive-parents

Ward-Gailey, C. (2010). *Blue-ribbon babies and labors of love: Race, class, and gender in US adoption practice.* Austin, TX: University of Texas Press.

11

RACIAL AND GENDER PREFERENCES AMONG POTENTIAL ADOPTIVE PARENTS

Kathryn A. Sweeney

When discussing potential adoptive parents' preferences for children of a specific race or gender it is important to remember that even though adoptive parents have individual agency in choosing children to adopt, these choices are also shaped by policies, practice, structural limitations (such as finances), and cultural social norms (Ishizawa, Kenney, Kubo, & Stevens, 2006; Stolley, 1993). Larger shifts in economic stability, access to education, available contraception, acceptance of single motherhood, and child welfare policies have all contributed to patterns in the availability of children placed for adoption in the US and around the world (Briggs, 2012; Melosh, 2002). Additionally, global and country-specific policies implement further restrictions and regulations on adoption, for example limiting adoption to parents who fit specific health, marital status, and age requirements (US Department of State – Bureau of Consular Affairs, 2018a). Research has found that within these restrictions, prospective adoptive parents still have choices about the child they would like to adopt, and tend to prefer to form families that resemble those formed biologically, which typically means of the same race (Ishizawa & Kubo, 2014); however, some are willing to adopt transnationally and/or transracially, with varied preferences for the child, such as gender, age, health, ability, and nationality. This chapter reviews the roles policy, structure, and culture play in impacting adoptive parent preferences. It then focuses on preferences regarding the child's gender and race. It concludes with a discussion of implications for policy and practice.

The influence of policy and practice

Historically, adoption agency practice in the US revolved around trying to "match" adoptive parents with children on as many characteristics as possible (e.g., hair texture and skin color) in an attempt to create perceived mono-racial families (Melosh, 2002). While transracial placement was not illegal, race matching was the norm. In 1948, the Child Welfare League of America changed their professional guidelines to encourage social workers and adoption agencies to consider transracial adoption. Within this environment, programs emerged focusing on specific groups, such as the Indian Adoption Project (1958–67) which promoted the placement of Native American children into White families (Crofoot & Harris, 2012; Hollinger, 1988; Mannes, 1995). With the exception of these Native American children being placed with White families, the tendency for same-race placement persisted until there was a brief increase in transracial placements of Black children with White parents in the 1960s. This change prompted concerns of forced assimilation of Black and Native American children into White culture. Backlash surrounding the disproportionate and forced removal of Native children from their homes, families, and tribal communities eventually led to the passing of the 1978 Indian Child Welfare Act (ICWA) (Briggs, 2012; Mannes, 1995). ICWA provides specific guidelines and provisions for practitioners regarding placement of Native American children and designates legal rights to tribes and communities to shape decisions regarding foster care and adoption placement when a birth parent is a tribal citizen (Bussey & Lucero, 2013). This law recognizes the role and rights of sovereign tribal nations, but it is not always followed or upheld. The IWCA is regularly legally challenged, and Native American children continue to be removed from their families and communities at disproportionate rates compared to other racial/ethnic groups in the US (Crofoot & Harris, 2012).

While ICWA encourages recognition and preservation of Native nationality in regard to children available for adoption (see Nagel (2000) for discussion on defining Native American), later US policies focused on deprioritizing race in adoption placement decisions (Fogg-Davis, 2002). For example, the Multiethnic Placement Act (MEPA) passed in 1994 and amended in 1996, restricted the use of race in adoption placement, making placement across race lines easier. In addition, the 1997 Adoption and Safe Families Act provided incentives for adoptions of foster children labeled as "special needs," which included children of color who were considered "hard to place" (McRoy & Griffin, 2012; Melosh, 2002).

All of these laws and regulations shape the options available to prospective adoptive parents and are intertwined with their stated preferences. Internationally, the United Nations Convention on the Rights of Children (referred to as the Hague Convention) mandates that countries prioritize placement within country before transnational adoption and directly consider culture, ethnicity, and religion in placement decisions (Freundlich, 2000). About 75 countries have agreed to follow the Hague Convention, including the US (Vandivere, Malm, & Radel, 2009). This contributes to shifts and changes in sending countries, because if the ability of a sending country to follow the rules of the Hague Convention is in question, receiving countries may halt adoptions from that country. For example, Guatemala went from sending the largest number of children to the US for adoption in 2007 to bringing international adoptions to a close in 2008. This change occurred after the US Department of State announced it would no longer process adoptions of children from Guatemala due to concern that the Hague guidelines were not being followed. Shortly thereafter Guatemala decided not to process new adoption cases (Vandivere et al., 2009, p. 4).

Country-specific rules

Along with the Hague Convention guidelines, individual countries regulate who can adopt based on characteristics such as marital status, health, and age. For example, since 2007, China has required potential adoptive parents to be at least 30 years of age with limits placed on age differences between parent and adoptee. Different-sex married couples need to be married at least two years to be considered, with additional conditions for time married if a spouse has previously divorced. There are further detailed requirements for single women, including not having more than two children under 18 in the home and their youngest child must be at least six years old. Income and wealth guidelines dictate that families earn at least \$10,000 per family member. Couples need to have a net worth of at least \$80,000 and single parents are required to have a minimum net worth of \$100,000. All prospective adoptive parents must also meet health guidelines that include having a body mass index below 40 and not having specific diseases (e.g., being HIV positive, having lupus, or epilepsy), being diagnosed with mental illness (e.g., depression or schizophrenia), or having certain physical limitations (e.g., paralysis, loss of limbs, and blindness) (US Department of State – Bureau of Consular Affairs, 2018b). Each country has their own prerequisites, thus limiting where prospective adoptive parents are eligible to adopt and which avenues and children they consider and pursue.

Agency practice

Prospective adoptive parent options are also affected and influenced by agency practice. While agencies work within the boundaries of laws and policies (which also vary by state in the US), practice does not always meet state or federal mandates. For instance, research indicates that the goals of MEPA have not been met regarding removing barriers to adoption or increasing Black foster child placements into permanent homes (see discussion in McRoy & Griffin, 2012). Agencies also continue to categorize children in ways that perpetuate the idea that Black children have "special needs" (Quiroz, 2007) or are not as healthy or desirable as other children. Research by Quiroz (2008) illustrates how the methods used by private adoption agencies influence which children are deemed more or less "attractive" to adopt. Programs that are race-based or that organize available children into racial categories, reinforce a racialized system that places White infants at the top of the hierarchy and Black children at the bottom (Quiroz, 2008, p. 260).

Hall and Whipple (2017) argue that prevalent prioritizing of light skin in society contributes to discriminatory placement practices against darker skinned children by social workers. Similarly, Brooks and James (2003) found that experiences with agencies and workers influenced prospective adoptive parent decisions; adoptive parents who reported discouragement from adoption and agency workers were less likely to adopt Black children. In other cases, research indicates that agencies try to *encourage* transracial adoption, influencing adopter preferences in an effort to find permanent homes for "hard to place" children, such as those who are Black, older, or have disabilities, by doing such things as offering discounted fees or stressing shorter wait times (Fedders, 2014; Raleigh & Rothman, 2014). These varied policies and practices influence the choices available to parents as they consider which children to adopt, and consequently, their stated preferences regarding child characteristics. Ultimately these policies and practices influence which children are eventually adopted into particular families.

Structural opportunities and constraints

Regardless of type of adoption sought (i.e., domestic public, domestic private, or international) and whichever child characteristics prospective adoptive parents prefer, available adoption options differ depending on individual potential adoptive parent characteristics, the political climate, and various local and federal policies, rules, and regulations regarding adoption (Briggs, 2012; Downing, Richardson, Kinkler, & Goldberg,

2009; Gailey, 2010; Ishizawa & Kubo, 2014; Raleigh, 2012). For these reasons, it is difficult to fully differentiate preferences from the lived reality of limited possibilities as adoptive parents work within the systems and options available to them. When the idealized child is not an option, prospective adoptive parents often have to choose certain child aspects over others, as some characteristics must be prioritized in the adoption process. For example, Jennings (2006) found that transracial adoption was considered by White affluent infertile women in the sample only after realizing the difficulties and extended length of time it would take to adopt a White infant. Ishizawa and Kubo (2014) found that those with greater financial resources were better able to be matched with a child of their preference, through either international or private domestic adoption, compared to those who were less well-off who typically used public adoption via foster care in the US.

When faced with choosing between child characteristics, research has found that prospective parents tend to prioritize child age and health over child race (Ishizawa et al., 2006; Vandivere et al., 2009). Scholars theorize that this concentration on health may stem from the experiences of White adoptive families who prioritized Whiteness in the past and struggled parenting children with physical or mental challenges that they were not prepared to raise (Raleigh & Rothman, 2014). For example, many parents who adopted children from Russia and Romania in the 1990s were unprepared for the attachment issues, developmental delays, and behavior problems their children experienced associated with fetal alcohol syndrome and institutionalization prior to adoption (Farina, Leifer, & Chasnoff, 2004; Shapiro, Shapiro, & Paret, 2001).

The adoption marketplace

Regardless of reasons for prospective parent priorities, ideas of preference are situated in the reality of available possibilities. For instance, qualitative work by Downing et al. (2009) illustrates how the type of adoption (i.e., domestic public, domestic private, or international) chosen by male same-sex couples was dictated both by options available and desired child characteristics. Some of the gay men in the sample chose domestic private adoption, preferring a shorter wait time for a White infant, others specifically used public adoption for older children and open adoptions (i.e., contact with birth mothers), and still others chose international adoption because they thought it provided greater assurance and security of a successful placement and adoption. However, all of these choices were mediated by finances and expenses, as well as laws restricting same-sex couple and single male adoption in various countries (Downing et al., 2009).

While the highest demand in the US adoption "market" has historically been for White infants, Black children are disproportionately available which has resulted in a system where the financial cost of adopting a White child is much higher than adopting a Black child (Baccara, Collard-Wexler, Felli, & Yariv, 2014; Fedders, 2014). Research has found that most of the variation in adoption costs can be attributed to child characteristics with older, Black, and special needs children being the least expensive (Skidmore, Anderson, & Eiswerth, 2016). Some of these differences are explained by supply and demand in the adoption marketplace: child availability (i.e., supply) and adoptive parent preferences (i.e., demand). A large proportion of those adopting are White. Due to social norms of mono-racial families, they often desire White children. However, there are disproportionately larger numbers of Black and Brown children available in foster care in comparison to the portion of Black and Brown potential adoptive parents. Thus, White children are a disproportionately small number of the supply of children available for adoption, yet the most in demand by most potential adoptive parents. White parents prioritizing White children for adoption has in part contributed to Black and Brown children from the US being adopted transnationally (i.e., people in other countries adopting US-born Brown and Black children) (Engel, Phillips, & Della Cava, 2015).

Adoption type and child characteristics

As noted, expenses, expected wait time, child age, and level of contact or openness with the biological family all shape preferences of prospective adoptive parents (Ishizawa & Kubo, 2014). Even though adoption through foster care in the US is free or has minimal costs, adoptive parents might not know how long they will have to wait for the child of their choice depending on wants regarding gender, age, ability, and race (Maldonado, 2006). They might also be wary of biological family involvement or perceive greater health and behavioral risks commonly associated with public adoption (Briggs, 2012; Gailey, 2010; Kubo, 2010; Zhang & Lee, 2011). However, while private domestic adoption increases the odds of adopting an infant and placement of a child who meets other desired characteristics, it tends to be expensive. Additionally, placement is typically based on birth mother choice, introducing various challenges for prospective parent possibilities and available options, particularly for those prospective adoptive parents who are older, single, or gay. The third adoption route available is international adoption, which tends to be the most expensive avenue and involves country-specific limitations on who can adopt (Maldonado, 2006). Each of these methods (domestic public, domestic private, or international) is also linked to likely race of the adoptee, so choosing a certain avenue both reflects and affects priorities (Ishizawa & Kubo, 2014). Analysis of data from the 2007 National Survey of Adoptive Parents finds that

> children adopted from foster care [are] most likely to be Black (35 percent) and those adopted internationally least likely to be Black (3 percent). Children adopted privately from the US are most likely to be White (50 percent); those adopted internationally are least likely to be White (19 percent).
>
> *(Vandivere et al., 2009, p. 13)*

Over time, changes leading to fewer healthy White infants available internationally have contributed to a shift from international adoption being used by White parents in the US to adopt White infants to a process where placements tend to be transracial of non-infant "waiting" children with physical medical conditions deemed minor and "fixable," such as a cleft palate or a lazy eye (Raleigh & Rothman, 2014). Raleigh and Rothman argue that "now that babies of all racial groups are increasingly rare on the adoption market, we move into a new form of stratification by stigma, as physical stigma comes into play," further shaping preferences within availability (Raleigh & Rothman, 2014, p. 46).

Cultural social norms

Stigma that contributes to the stratification of the adoption process is shaped by societal norms and expectations. While choices regarding which children to incorporate into families via adoption are viewed as individual decisions, they are not only made in the context of larger constraints and options available but are also based on social norms.

Sex/gender preference

International adoption often becomes coded, with specific countries being associated with children of a particular gender and race despite the varied make-up of each country. For example, the one-child policy in China led to a disproportionate number of girls available for adoption and thus choosing to adopt from China effectively meant choosing to adopt a girl (Gailey, 2010; Vandivere et al., 2009). In fact, most of the difference in gender (i.e., more girls adopted than boys) among internationally adopted children is explained by the influx of adoptive girls from China (Ishizawa et al., 2006; Kreider, 2003).

Some research has found that prospective parents prefer girls, particularly among women considering adoption (Chandra, Abma, Maza, & Bachrach, 1999; Jones, 2008). Yet, in general, the sex of a child is not found to be one of the more important factors in adoptive parent choices. Even though studies typically include child sex in their models analyzing prospective parent preference, most do not find significant differences, meaning people report similar willingness to adopt a girl or a boy (Brooks, James, & Barth, 2002). Because sex tends to be insignificant, or not as strong of a predictor as other factors in adoption choices, it has not been the focus of much of the adoption literature. Although interestingly, Gibby and Thomas's (2018) analysis of nationally representative data from the 2016 American Community Survey found that adoption may be used as means to balance out the sex of siblings in a family, especially when adopting girls. However, it is unclear how much of the effect is due to availability or a real preferencing of girls (Gibby & Thomas, 2018, p. 9).

Research has also noted that choices regarding gender are intertwined with race, evidenced by Black boys being sought after less than Black girls. Differences are explained in part by the perception that boys have a greater likelihood of unseen health or behavior issues (Baccara et al., 2014, p. 152). Additionally, gender preferences have found to be associated with characteristics of potential adoptive parents. Baccara et al. (2014) learned that gay, lesbian, and single potential adopters had higher preference for girls, with the highest preference held by lesbian adopters. Additional research is needed to better understand how parent and child characteristics intersect to influence ideas of which children are preferred, and thus which type of adoption is pursued.

Racial preferences

Similarly, certain countries are deemed "White" or not (Gailey, 2010; Quiroz, 2014; Treitler, 2014). For instance, even though there are a range of racial/ethnic groups in various Central and South American countries who may be considered Black in the US, people perceive those countries and possible children adopted from them to be Latino/Hispanic (Gailey, 2010). Similarly, presumptions are made that children from Eastern European countries such as Romania and Russia are considered White.

It has been found that even with supposed colorblind or race-neutral placement and policies deprioritizing race (e.g., MEPA), adoptive parents, social workers, and birth mothers all make decisions and operate within a larger system influenced by societal norms. Choices are shaped by the history and context of race in the US, racial stereotypes, anti-transracial arguments, and concerns about racial identity, forced migration, and forced assimilation (Briggs, 2012; Fedders, 2014). Most of the research on adoptive parent priorities focuses on White parents, in part because most adoptions in the US are by White people (Ishizawa et al., 2006; Marr, 2017; Vandivere et al., 2009). Although research has found that

19 percent of children adopted privately in the US and 27 percent of those adopted via foster care are adopted by Black parents (Vandivere et al., 2009, p. 13), there are fewer studies focusing on adoptive and prospective adoptive parents of color.

While the majority of those seeking to adopt state a willingness to adopt across race lines, preference is for children of the same race (Jones, 2008), followed by additional preferences by White adopters for children with perceived or known partial White heritage versus "fully Black" ancestry (Samuels, 2009). Research has shown that it is not just a tendency of White people to prefer to adopt White babies, but there is a greater willingness to adopt children who are specifically *not* Black (Baccara et al., 2014; Brooks et al., 2002; Jennings, 2006; Khanna & Killian, 2015; Sweeney, 2013). For example, Baccara et al. (2014) found bias of potential adoptive parents against Black children, but not against Hispanic children. Jones (2008) found that most (84 percent) White prospective adoptive mothers stated willingness to adopt a Black child, yet a larger percentage (95 percent) said they were willing to adopt a non-Black child of color. In comparison, the majority (93 percent) of Black prospective parents were willing to adopt a child of another race and most (75 percent) stated willingness to adopt a White child (Jones, 2008, p. 16). These findings are further supported by a range of qualitative work looking at how adoptive parents understand and rationalize their choices in the adoption process. For example, Khanna and Killian's (2015) analysis of in-depth interviews illustrates how even when most White adoptive parents in their sample were willing to adopt children of color, some potential adoptive parents were unwilling to adopt Black children, especially those who were African American. These children were considered to be "too different" culturally and physically from their White, middle class families. Potential adoptive parents were concerned about their ability to provide adequate racial socialization, particularly in regard to preparation for racism, and also about how family and people in their White social networks would respond to and treat an African American child. This, in part, led to their decisions to adopt internationally instead of domestically, and a prioritizing of children who were not Black (Khanna & Killian, 2015).

The preference for non-Black children is influenced by ideas about race in society and is shaped by agency practice. Multiracial and foreign-born Black children are both portrayed by agencies and viewed by White parents as distinct, special, and less raced, or not "really Black," compared to those children identified as African American (Quiroz, 2007; Raleigh, 2016; Sweeney, 2013). Samuels (2009) argues that the distinction for biracial or multiracial children might be in part because White parents think they will have more in common with a child who is "part White."

Ideas about which children are considered acceptable to adopt or "easier" to incorporate into White families are also tied to common stereotypes of various racial/ethnic groups. Preferring and choosing children who are Asian and Hispanic could be because these racial-ethnic groups are associated with positive stereotypes while Black children might be associated with negative stereotypes (Briggs, 2012; Gailey, 2010; Khanna & Killian, 2015; Kubo, 2010). Kubo's (2010) analysis illustrates how parents fall back on dominant stereotypes of Asians as smart (i.e., the model minority) and African American children and birth families as deficient when discussing their willingness to adopt across race lines via international versus domestic adoption. Jennings (2006) found that White women's views of birth mothers influenced ideas of which children they preferred to adopt. Potential adoptive White women often pictured White birth mothers as college students who had made a mistake and were selfless in placing their child, while they saw Black birth mothers and poor White women as delinquent deviants. Fears of low-income women extorting them, or fears of transmitted health or genetic problems also influenced their decisions and preferences. Briggs (2012) notes how these ideas are linked to the history of the "war on drugs" in the US where the perception of "crack babies" and deviant Black women led to increased numbers of Black and Brown children in the foster care system available for adoption.

Parents have also expressed concerns that a Black child would stand out more, or not fit in well with their family or community (Kubo, 2010). Certain children may be seen as easier to integrate into their White segregated lives. Dorow (2006) found that parents who chose international adoption did so in part because of perceptions of rescuing children in need, and the impression that international adoption was less complicated as the result of physical distance from birth families. White parents who chose to adopt from China also focused on the idea of *racial flexibility* that they thought was not available when adopting Black children domestically in the US. They perceived an Asian child as more similar, being White, than adopting a Black child and thus more easily "fitting into" their lives with few necessary changes or challenges (Dorow, 2006). Quiroz (2014) aligns adoption trends with Dorow's (2006) concept of racial flexibility and Bonilla-Silva's (2004) three-tiered racial hierarchy of Whites, "honorary Whites," and "collective Blacks." Quiroz (2014) argues that adoptees from Russia and Eastern European countries are considered White, with difference that is not visible. Adoptees from Asian and Central American countries, as well as multiracial adoptees, are viewed as "honorary Whites" with flexibility in their ethnic identity. Whereas, dark skinned Asians and Latinos and Black children are part of the "collective Black" category viewed with restricted "unalterable" difference that is limited to derogatory ideas of Blackness rooted in stereotypes of neglect, abuse, and drug addiction. Thus, White parents prioritize White children. Then those who are perceived as part of the "honorary White" category are typically chosen by White adoptive parents before children who are Black or African American since Blackness is viewed as having less racial flexibility and being further from Whiteness.

In general, those who express willingness to adopt Black children have been found to be open to a wider range of adoptee characteristics (including age and physical or mental needs) than those who were unwilling to adopt a Black child (Brooks & James, 2003). Raleigh (2012) found that single parents and same-sex couples were more likely than different-sex couples to adopt children of color in general, and more specifically Black children. Goldberg and Smith (2009) concluded that those who were younger, lesbian, and perceived their neighborhood as racially diverse, were more willing to adopt Black children in particular. Similarly, Baccara et al. (2014) determined that the general preference for a child who is not African American is not as strong for gay, lesbian, and single potential parents; gay, lesbian, and single potential parents express interest in adopting Black children at higher rates compared to different-sex couples. It is difficult to parse out the role of structure influencing these attitudes and behaviors since those potential adoptive parents that are younger and lesbian may have fewer options available. Raleigh theorizes that prospective adoptive parents who are the most marginalized, are the most likely to be matched with, and adopt, children with marginalized status (Raleigh, 2012, p. 466). Yet the perception of neighborhood racial make-up may indicate perceived support among potential adoptive parents for conscientious racial socialization (in terms of access to role models and community preparation for racism) and thus a greater willingness and readiness to adopt a Black child.

Implications for policy and practice

This chapter conveys the complexities in investigating and understanding prospective adoptive parent preferences regarding sex and race, showing how various preferences are intertwined and related to policies, practice, parent characteristics, and social norms. Research has found that potential adoptive parents and those who end up adopting tend to prefer children that would match those formed biologically but, given limitations in availability and access to particular children, priorities often shift and change in the adoption process (Ishizawa & Kubo, 2014; Jones, 2008). Preferences are influenced by a wide range of structural limitations (such as finances and regulations) as well as cultural norms and agency practice. Policies have tried to regulate adoption practice in terms of race, Native belonging, and time to placement. Yet these mandates face challenges and may, for the most part, be ignored with little consequence (McRoy & Griffin, 2012). Research indicates the need for additional oversight and compliance, particularly that MEPA and ICWA regulations should be upheld and greater efforts made to recruit Black prospective adoptive parents. Additionally, future research should include adoptive parents of color.

The research also suggests that the role of agencies in shaping prospective parent choices should be reviewed and potentially revised to remove the categorization of children by race and eliminate programs that provide incentives to adopt certain children. Agencies often present children in ways that might make them more desirable, emphasizing possible shorter wait times for adopting "harder to place" children (who tend to be older, Black, and/or male), offering lower fees for adopting those deemed special needs, and putting Black children into the special needs category (Quiroz, 2008). Fedders (2014) argues that agencies should stop offering financial incentives for adopting children of color because it contributes to false notions of inferiority. Findings outlined in this chapter suggest that in order to reduce the influence of agencies in potentially presenting Black children as deficient, or in possibly pushing people to adopt "hard to place" children, various programs should be re-evaluated to reduce this bias: this includes eliminating financial discounts, incentives that may pressure potential adoptive parents to adopt certain children, and to stop organizing programs or presenting children by race.

Raleigh and Rothman (2014) maintain that agencies should not downplay difference and potential difficulties in order to place children; rather they should better prepare prospective parents. Thus, the focus should be on making sure there are prepared and well-informed parents to better serve the best interest of children waiting for permanent placements. Improved pre-adoption counseling could help prospective adoptive parents better understand the realities of raising children whose birth families are of different nationalities or racial or ethnic groups than their own. Additional focus is needed to help prospective adoptive parents make educated choices about which children they are able to raise, and then stronger post-adoption support is needed as they grapple with various challenges. This may require changes in educating social workers on racism and programs to teach prospective parents how to talk about race, given the tendency to rely on coded language and a lack of understanding of racism (Sweeney, 2013).

In addition, as Quiroz (2008) notes, more research is needed that incorporates the voices of everyone in the adoption triad (birth mother/family, adoptee, and adoptive parents) as well as agency workers in order to determine best practices and inform social worker training, programs for prospective parents, post-adoption services, and agency compliance with rules and regulations.

While there are legitimate reasons for concern regarding transracial adoptee racial socialization, that concern should not necessarily be the reason for White prospective adoptive parents to rule out adopting Black children. Until changes are made to reduce the number of children removed from their birth families, of whom there are disproportionately large numbers who are Black and Brown (Gailey, 2010), we are left with the reality of children waiting for permanent homes. If the consensus is that permanent placement (regardless of race) is a better alternative to remaining in foster care, then greater education is needed to inform parents of actual concerns and possible realities they will face versus false ideas rooted in racism left unchallenged. Such false ideas include the stereotypical notion that Black children will be more likely than children of other racial/ethnic groups (whether relinquished at birth or removed from birth parents) to be addicted to drugs or have behavioral problems. Additional concerns arise from findings in the literature that prospective adoptive parents who have the financial means often choose international adoption because they fear birth mother/family involvement or even extortion (Khanna & Killian, 2015; Zhang & Lee, 2011). This suggests the need for education about the various types of contact or levels of "openness," which conveys the potential benefits of open adoptions for adoptees, birth mothers, and adoptive parents (see Jones (2016) for discussion). Furthermore, research on racial socialization suggests the need for consideration of prospective parent social networks, school composition, and other factors that can improve adoptee racial socialization when being raised by White parents (see Sweeney (2018) for further discussion).

Along with the deprioritizing of Black children, prospective parent preferences for children who are "closer to White" indicates a need that may be addressed by social workers and agencies. The ideas that children who are "closer to White" in the racial/ethnic hierarchy (those who are Hispanic, Asian, and multiracial) will not face racism or will more easily fit into White parents' lives is false and neglects the research that shows otherwise (see for example Samuels, 2009). Sweeney's (2013) qualitative research indicates that some of the White parents in the sample who had adopted a multiracial child were specifically looking to adopt a second child perceived as Black because they learned that their multiracial child faced racism they were not prepared to address and that their child felt alone in their White family. Addressing the false notion that race will not be significant in the lives of adoptees may start with training social workers to better understand the role of race and racism in society. This will ultimately better prepare prospective adoptive parents so that less of the learning about race by adoptive parents comes after the fact, and hopefully, reduce learning at the expense of the adoptee.

In addition, research has found that gay, lesbian, and single prospective adoptive parents are more willing to adopt Black children or other children deemed "hard to place" (Baccara et al., 2014). Thus, it is important to address and push back against any measures to limit access of potential adoptive parents by government as well as individual agencies working for the government. For example, the practice of conservative religiously affiliated agencies not facilitating foster placement or adoptions from foster care to gay and lesbian parents, which is currently legal but under question ethically, is being challenged legally.

Adoptive and prospective adoptive parent preferences are complicated by their own characteristics, including financial resources, marital status, and health, all of which determine which adoption types and children are options for them. Availability, wait times, and child characteristics (e.g., child race, age, and health) further shift and shape prospective parent preferences and ultimately decisions of which children they adopt. Even so, White adoptive parents continue to preference children who are considered "closer to White" and particularly those who are not Black, especially African American. The complexity of this issue calls for continued empirical examination and potential revisions to policies, social worker training, and prospective parent education to reduce bias. Structural opportunities (e.g., financial barriers and legal limits on who can adopt), agency practice, social worker interactions and influence, and prospective parent training are not fixed; they can and should be informed by relevant scholarly research.

References

Baccara, M., Collard-Wexler, A., Felli, L., & Yariv, L. (2014). Child-adoption matching: Preferences for gender and race. *American Economic Journal: Applied Economics*, *6*(3), 133–158. doi:10.1257/ap.6.3.133

Bonilla-Silva, E. (2004). From bi-racial to tri-racial: Towards a new system of racial stratification in the USA. *Ethnic and Racial Studies*, *27*(6), 931–950. doi:10.1080/0141987042000268530

Briggs, L. (2012). *Somebody's children: The politics of transnational and transracial adoption*. Durham, NC: Duke University Press.

Brooks, D., & James, S. (2003). Willingness to adopt black foster children: Implications for child welfare policy and recruitment of adoptive families. *Children and Youth Services Review*, *25*(5–6), 463–489. doi:10.1016/S0190-7409(03)00031-8

Brooks, D., James, S., & Barth, R. P. (2002). Preferred characteristics of children in need of adoption: Is there a demand for available foster children? *Social Service Review*, *76*(4), 575–602. doi:10.1086/342996

Bussey, M., & Lucero, N. M. (2013). Re-examining child welfare's response to ICWA: Collaborating with community-based agencies to reduce disparities for American Indian/Alaska Native children. *Children and Youth Services Review*, *35*(3), 394–401. doi:10.1016/j.childyouth.2012.12.021

Chandra, A., Abma, J., Maza, P., & Bachrach, C. (1999). *Adoption, adoption seeking, and relinquishment for adoption in the United States*. (No. 306). Hyattsville, MD: US Department of Health and Human Services, Centers for Disease Control and Prevention, National Center for Health Statistics.

Crofoot, T. L., & Harris, M. S. (2012). An Indian child welfare perspective on disproportionality in child welfare. *Children and Youth Services Review*, *34*(9), 1667–1674. doi:10.1016/j.childyouth.2012.04.028

Dorow, S. (2006). Racialized choices: Chinese adoption and the "white noise" of blackness. *Critical Sociology*, *32*(2–3), 357–379. doi:10.1163/156916306777835277

Downing, J., Richardson, H., Kinkler, L., & Goldberg, A. (2009). Making the decision: Factors influencing gay men's choice of an adoption path. *Adoption Quarterly*, *12*(3–4), 247–271. doi:10.1080/10926750903313310

Engel, M. H., Phillips, N. K., & Della Cava, F. A. (2015). Inter-country adoption of children born in the United States. *Sociology between the Gaps: Forgotten and Neglected Topics*, *1*(1), 1–13.

Farina, Lana, Leifer, Myra, & Chasnoff, Ira J. (2004). Attachment and behavioral difficulties in internationally adopted Russian children. *Adoption and Fostering*. *28*(2), 38-49. doi.org/10.1177%2F030857590402800206

Fedders, B. (2014). Race and market values in domestic infant adoption. In V. Treitler (Ed.), *Race in transnational and transracial adoption* (pp. 49–69). London: Palgrave Macmillan.

Fogg-Davis, H. G. (2002). *The ethics of transracial adoption*. Ithaca, NY: Cornell University Press.

Freundlich, M. (2000). *Adoption and ethics: The market forces in adoption*. Washington, DC: Child Welfare League of America.

Gailey, C. W. (2010). *Blue-ribbon babies and labors of love: Race, class, and gender in US adoption practice*. Austin, TX: University of Texas Press.

Gibby, A. L., & Thomas, K. J. (2018). Adoption: A strategy to fulfill sex preferences of US parents. *Journal of Marriage and Family*, *81*(2), 531–541. doi:10.1111/jomf.12541

Goldberg, A. E., & Smith, J. Z. (2009). Predicting non-African American lesbian and heterosexual preadoptive couples' openness to adopting an African American child. *Family Relations*, *58*(3), 346–360. doi:10.1111/j.1741-3729.2009.00557.x

Hall, R. E., & Whipple, E. E. (2017). The complexion connection: Ideal light skin as vehicle of adoption process discrimination vis-à-vis social work practitioners. *Journal of Human Behavior in the Social Environment*, *27*(7), 669–677. doi:10.1080/10911359.2017.1321511

Hollinger, J. H. (1988). Beyond the best interests of the tribe: The Indian child welfare act and the adoption of Indian children. *University of Detroit Mercy Law Review, 66*, 451–501.

Ishizawa, H., Kenney, C. T., Kubo, K., & Stevens, G. (2006). Constructing interracial families through intercountry adoption. *Social Science Quarterly, 87*(5), 1207–1224. doi:10.1111/j.1540-6237.2006.00424.x

Ishizawa, H., & Kubo, K. (2014). Factors affecting adoption decisions: Child and parental characteristics. *Journal of Family Issues, 35*(5), 627–653. doi:10.1177/0192513X13514408

Jennings, P. K. (2006). The trouble with the Multiethnic Placement Act: An empirical look at transracial adoption. *Sociological Perspectives, 49*(4), 559–581. doi:10.1525/sop.2006.49.4.559

Jones, C. (2016). Openness in adoption: Challenging the narrative of historical progress. *Child & Family Social Work, 21*(1), 85–93. doi:10.1111/cfs.12113

Jones, J. (2008). Adoption experiences of women and men, and demand for children to adopt by women ages 18–44 in the United States, 2002. *National Center for Health Statistics, Vital Health Stat, 23*(27), 1–36.

Khanna, N., & Killian, C. (2015). "We didn't even think about adopting domestically": The role of race and other factors in shaping parents' decisions to adopt abroad. *Sociological Perspectives, 58*(4), 570–594. doi:10.1177/0731121415572688

Kreider, R. M. (2003). *Adopted children and stepchildren: 2000, Census 2000 Special Reports, CENSR-6RV*. Washington, DC: US Census Bureau.

Kubo, K. (2010). Desirable difference: The shadow of racial stereotypes in creating transracial families through transnational adoption. *Sociology Compass, 4*(4), 263–282. doi:10.1111/j.1751-9020.2010.00274.x

Maldonado, S. (2006). Discouraging racial preferences in adoptions. *UC Davis Law Review, 39*, 1415–1480.

Mannes, M. (1995). Factors and events leading to the passage of the Indian Child Welfare Act. *Child Welfare, 74*(1), 264–282.

Marr, E. (2017). US transracial adoption trends in the 21st Century. *Adoption Quarterly, 20*(3), 222–251. doi:10.1080/10926755.2017.1291458

McRoy, R., & Griffin, A. (2012). Transracial adoption policies and practices: The US experience. *Adoption & Fostering, 36*(3-4), 38–49. doi:10.1177/030857591203600305

Melosh, B. (2002). Adoption Stories: Autobiographical Narrative and the Politics of Identity. In E. Carp (Ed.), *Adoption in America: Historical perspectives* (pp. 218–246). Ann Arbor: University of Michigan Press.

Nagel, J. (2000). False faces: Ethnic identity, authenticity, and fraud in Native American discourse and politics. In J. E. Davis (Ed.), *Identity and social change* (pp. 81–106). New Brunswick: Transaction Publishers.

Quiroz, P. A. (2007). *Adoption in a color-blind society*. Lanham, MD: Rowman & Littlefield.

Quiroz, P. A. (2008). From race matching to transracial adoption: Race and the changing discourse of US adoption. *Critical Discourse Studies, 5*(3), 249–264. doi:10.1080/17405900802131777

Quiroz, P. A. (2014). Adoptive parents e-racing adopted children by choosing, keeping, avoiding, and purchasing identity. In V. Treitler (Ed.), *Race in transnational and transracial adoption* (pp. 133–154). London: Palgrave Macmillan.

Raleigh, E. (2012). Are same-sex and single adoptive parents more likely to adopt transracially? A national analysis of race, family structure, and the adoption marketplace. *Sociological Perspectives, 55*(3), 449–471. doi:10.1525/sop.2012.55.3.449

Raleigh, E. (2016). The color line exception: The transracial adoption of foreign-born and biracial black children. *Women, Gender, and Families of Color, 4*(1), 86–107. doi:10.5406/womgenfamcol.4.1.0086

Raleigh, E., & Rothman, B. K. (2014). Disability is the new black: The rise of the "cleft lip and palate program" in transracial international adoption. In V. Treitler (Ed.), *Race in transnational and transracial adoption* (pp. 33–48). London: Palgrave Macmillan.

Samuels, G. M. (2009). "Being raised by White people": Navigating racial difference among adopted multiracial adults. *Journal of Marriage and Family, 71*(1), 80–94. doi:10.1111/j.1741-3737.2008.00581.x

Shapiro, V., Shapiro, J., & Paret, I. (2001). International adoption and the formation of new family attachments. *Smith College Studies in Social Work, 71*(3), 389–418. doi:10.1080/00377310109517637

Skidmore, M., Anderson, G., & Eiswerth, M. (2016). The child adoption marketplace: Parental preferences and adoption outcomes. *Public Finance Review, 44*(2), 163–196. doi:10.1177/1091142114547412

Stolley, K. S. (1993). Statistics on adoption in the United States. *The Future of Children, 3*(1), 26–42. doi:10.2307/1602400

Sweeney, K. A. (2013). Race-conscious adoption choices, multiraciality, and color-blind racial ideology. *Family Relations, 62*(1), 42–57. doi:10.1111/j.1741-3729.2012.00757.x

Sweeney, K. A. (2018). White parents of transracial adoptees navigating race, NCFR report magazine, family focus. *National Council on Family Relations.*

Treitler, V. B. (2014). Introduction: Race is a fiction … Coloring children and parents nonetheless. In V. Treitler (Ed.), *Race in transnational and transracial adoption* (pp. 1–29). London: Palgrave Macmillan.

US Department of State – Bureau of Consular Affairs. (2018a). *Intercountry adoption: Country information.* Retrieved January 7, 2019, from https://travel.state.gov/content/travel/en/Intercountry-Adoption/Intercountry-Adoption-Country-Information.html

US Department of State – Bureau of Consular Affairs. (2018b). *Intercountry adoption: Country information: China: People's Republic of China.* Retrieved January 7, 2019, from https://travel.state.gov/content/travel/en/Intercountry-Adoption/Intercountry-Adoption-Country-Information/China.html

Vandivere, S., Malm, K., & Radel, L. (2009). *Adoption USA: A chartbook based on the 2007 National Survey of Adoptive Parents.* Washington, DC: US Department of Health and Human Services: Office of the Assistant Secretary for Planning and Evaluation.

Zhang, Y., & Lee, G. R. (2011). Intercountry versus transracial adoption: Analysis of adoptive parents' motivations and preferences in adoption. *Journal of Family Issues, 32*(1), 75–98. doi:10.1177/0192513X10375410

12

ADOPTIVE FAMILIES HEADED BY LGBTQ PARENTS

Rachel H. Farr and Cassandra P. Vázquez

Many lesbian, gay, bisexual, transgender, and queer (LGBTQ) individuals desire to become parents, and adoption is often a preferred route to parenthood among LGBTQ adults (dickey, Ducheny, & Ehrbar, 2016; Farr & Patterson, 2009; Riskind & Tornello, 2017; Stotzer, Herman, & Hasenbush, 2014). In the United States and around the world, many LG[1] adults are already adoptive parents (Gates, 2013; Patterson & Tornello, 2011). In recent years, the numbers of LG adoptive parents have doubled (Gates, 2011), and same-sex couples are seven times more likely than other-sex couples to parent adopted children (Goldberg & Conron, 2018). Yet controversy continues to surround LGBTQ parent adoption in the US and many other countries (Carroll & Mendos, 2017; Farr & Goldberg, 2018). An increasingly large literature over the last 20 years about LGBTQ adoptive parent families has addressed questions at the center of these debates, of which we provide a summary in this chapter.

In providing an overview of recent research about LGBTQ adoptive parent families, we include inclusive descriptions of LGBTQ experiences wherever possible. Much of the existing literature, however, has focused more so on LG parent families as compared with BTQ parent families (Goldberg, Gartrell, & Gates, 2014; Moore & Stambolis-Ruhstorfer, 2013; Patterson, 2017). Here, we review research on LGBTQ adoptive parent families using an interdisciplinary, international, and intersectional framework. Although research about LGBTQ adoptive parents and their children has generally been conducted within clinical and developmental psychology, studies from fields such as demography, economics, education, family science, law, medicine, social work, and sociology are also informative. We use developmental, family systems, and ecological perspectives in considering the experiences of LGBTQ parent adoptive families, and where possible, we evaluate how intersecting identities, such as those based on sexuality, gender, race, ethnicity, class, as well as sociopolitical contexts and legal landscapes result in varied experiences among LGBTQ adoptive parents and their children. We consider work regarding pathways to adoption for LGBTQ adults, as well as the experiences of LGBTQ individuals and couples during the adoption process. We review studies sampling LGBTQ adoptive parent families and findings about psychosocial experiences and adjustment outcomes for children, parents, couples, and whole families. We discuss similarities and differences between LGBTQ and cisgender heterosexual adoptive parent families throughout the chapter. Finally, we offer recommendations for future research, practice, and policy.

Debate about adoption by LGBTQ people

The issue of LGBTQ parent adoption has been controversial around the world, including in the US (Davis, 2013; Farr & Goldberg, 2018; Patterson & Goldberg, 2016). Generally, there is information regarding adoption law and policy for sexual minority adults, but less for gender minority adults (i.e., transgender and gender-nonconforming, or TGNC, individuals; Farr & Goldberg, 2018). As of 2017, joint adoption by married same-sex couples was permitted in 26 countries worldwide (17 in Europe; Carroll & Mendos, 2017). Options for legal adoptive parenthood expanded in the US with the 2015 Supreme Court ruling on federal marriage equality (*Obergefell* v. *Hodges*). Adoption laws, however, remain regulated on the state level in the US, creating variation in the experiences of LGBTQ people who pursue adoption (Farr & Goldberg, 2018). Today, married same-sex couples can petition for joint and step-parent adoption (i.e., recognized as legal parents) in all 50 US states and DC (MAP, 2018b), and LG parents can pursue second-parent adoption in 15 states and DC[2] (MAP, 2018b). Although there do not exist specific legal obstacles to adoption in the US at this time for TGNC adults (dickey et al., 2016; Farr & Goldberg, 2018), currently there are ten states with religious "freedom" or "exemption" laws. These laws allow state-licensed child welfare agencies to refuse services to LGBTQ prospective parents based on religious belief (MAP, 2018a). At the federal level, the US House of Representatives considered a federal appropriations bill in 2018 called the Aderholt Amendment. If it had passed, state-funded child welfare agencies could have rejected otherwise qualified LGBTQ applicants based on religious belief. Moreover, federal funding would have been cut in states with anti-discrimination laws and policies related to sexual orientation and gender identity and expression (SOGIE) protecting children in foster care (MAP, 2018a). Only three states (California, New Jersey, and Rhode Island) and DC protect parents from discrimination in matters of adoption based on SOGIE, and five additional states (Maryland, Massachusetts, New York, Oregon, and Wisconsin) do so based on sexual orientation only (MAP, 2018b).

Research on families headed by LGBTQ adoptive parents

How and why LGBTQ people adopt children

How and why do LGBTQ adults become adoptive parents? First, LG and heterosexual adoptive parents appear to be similar demographically: they are often well-educated, affluent, older, and White (Davis, 2013; Farr, Forssell, & Patterson, 2010a; Gates, 2011; Goldberg, 2009a, 2009b), but there is limited information available among bisexual, queer, and transgender adoptive parent families as well as adoptions among unmarried same-sex parents or single LGBTQ adults (Davis, 2013; Gates, 2013). Despite demographic similarities, LGBTQ people may pursue adoption for similar and dissimilar reasons as compared to cisgender heterosexual adults (Goldberg, 2012; Goldberg et al., 2014; Mallon, 2011; Tornello & Bos, 2017). Across studies in the United States and United Kingdom, LG adoptive parents appear less motivated than heterosexual adoptive parents to have biologically related children, and heterosexual adoptive couples report attempts to conceive more so than do LG adoptive couples (Farr & Patterson, 2009; Goldberg, Downing, & Richardson, 2009; Goldberg & Smith, 2008; Jennings, Mellish, Tasker, Lamb, & Golombok, 2014). Furthermore, biological parenthood may be particularly challenging for gay men to achieve in terms of practical constraints and/or cost (Goldberg, 2012; Goldberg et al., 2014). For these reasons, many scholars have noted that LGBTQ adoptive parents appear more likely than cisgender heterosexual adoptive parents to choose adoption as a "first choice" route to parenthood (dickey et al., 2016; Farr & Goldberg, 2018; Mallon, 2011; Tornello & Bos, 2017).

Another way that LGBTQ adoptive parents may be distinct from cisgender heterosexual adoptive parents is in their likelihood to adopt children with a different racial-ethnic identity than their own. LG couples have been found to be more likely to express openness to, or to actually have completed, a transracial adoptive placement (Farr & Patterson, 2009; Goldberg, 2009a; Lavner, Waterman, & Peplau, 2012; Raleigh, 2012). In contrast, in a recent large sample of approximately 1,000 LG and heterosexual parents in the US, there were no differences as a function of parental sexual orientation in rates of transracial adoption (Brodzinsky & Goldberg, 2016). These mixed findings could reflect different pathways to adoptive parenthood across studies (i.e., international vs. domestic, public vs. private adoption), but more research is needed to examine this possibility. There are a few reasons why LGBTQ adults might be more likely to complete transracial placements in the US. First, more so than other-sex couples, same-sex couples are interracial, and interracial couples complete more transracial adoptions than do same-race couples (Farr & Patterson, 2009; Raleigh, 2012). Second, LGBTQ parent families tend to live in areas characterized by racial-ethnic diversity (Gates, 2013), which could be relevant to greater interracial contact and openness to transracial adoption. Finally, openness to transracial adoption among LGBTQ adults may also reflect their lower commitment to achieving biological parenthood, as described earlier (dickey et al., 2016; Farr & Patterson, 2009; Goldberg et al., 2009; Jennings et al., 2014).

Related to preferences for child gender, LGBTQ adoptive parents may also be dissimilar from, but also similar to, cisgender heterosexual adoptive parents. Among a sample of LG and heterosexual prospective adoptive couples in the US, about half expressed gender preferences: women tended to prefer girls while men tended to prefer boys (regardless of parental sexual orientation), but heterosexual men were the least likely to express a preference and gay men were the most likely (Goldberg, 2009b). These findings are consistent with research regarding preferences for child gender among similar adoptive samples in the US and Europe, as well as among parents pursuing donor insemination (Baccara, Collard-Wexler, Felli, & Yariv, 2014; Herrmann-Green & Gehring, 2007). The reason might be related to concerns about heterosexism and gender socialization (Goldberg, 2009b), but more research is necessary to address this question.

One dynamic unique to adoptive parenthood is the possibility for openness arrangements (e.g., contact and information sharing between birth and adoptive families; Farr & Goldberg, 2015). Compared with other-sex adoptive couples, same-sex adoptive couples appear to express greater openness to contact with their children's birth family (Goldberg, Kinkler, Richardson, & Downing, 2011), and in some cases, describe more positive relationships with birth family members (Brodzinsky & Goldberg, 2016). Similar to earlier interpretations, this pattern of results could reflect the lower emphasis that LGBTQ adults place on heteronormativity, especially as related to family relationships (Farr, Ravvina, & Grotevant, 2018). Although LGBTQ parents might express preferences related to children's racial-ethnic background, gender, and openness arrangement with birth relatives, additional factors include consideration of children's age, health, and particular pathways to adoption (Downing, Richardson, Kinkler, & Goldberg, 2009).

What is the transition to adoptive parenthood like for LGBTQ adults? Although this topic has been studied more extensively among heterosexual couples, some information exists about the transition among LG adoptive couples. Aligned with studies about the general transition to parenthood, Goldberg, Smith, and Kashy (2010) found that relationship quality decreased for LG and heterosexual couples (in the US) across the transition to adoptive parenthood, regardless of parental sexual orientation. This was particularly the case for women in general, and for those in relationships with women. Among the same sample, however, all parents reported perceived increases in parenting skill across this transition, which were hampered by expectations of more childcare and relational conflict (Goldberg & Smith, 2009). These same couples also benefited in terms of better mental health across the transition to adoptive parenthood if they enjoyed greater couple relationship quality and social support, consistent with the broader adoption literature (Goldberg & Smith, 2008, 2011). Unique to LG parents in this sample, those who lived in areas with less favorable legal climates regarding LG adoption and with higher internalized homophobia also had the steepest increases in symptoms of anxiety and depression across the transition (Goldberg & Smith, 2011). Also potentially unique to LGBTQ adoptive parents across the transition to parenthood is the experience of how to choose their child's last name. In one study, although heterosexual couples tended to follow patronymic conventions, LG couples tended to hyphenate parents' last names (Patterson & Farr, 2017). Taken together, the factors that seem to contribute most strongly to positive well-being and couple relationships among LG adoptive parent families across the transition to parenthood are social support, family processes broadly, and their child's age, rather than parents' SOGIE (Goldberg, Kinkler, Moyer, & Weber, 2014; Lavner, Waterman, & Peplau, 2014; Sumontha, Farr, & Patterson, 2016).

Challenges and strengths of LGBTQ adoptive parents

Are there unique challenges and strengths for LGBTQ adults who adopt? Every adoptive parent undergoes many steps to adopt, including a rigorous application process, workshops and training, and an in-depth home study evaluation (Mallon, 2011). LGBTQ parents, however, often face additional challenges related to variations in sociopolitical climate (e.g., not all child welfare agencies and/or employees openly work with or have accurate knowledge in working with LGBTQ clients; Brodzinsky, 2011; Farr & Goldberg, 2018). In the US, Brodzinsky (2011) found that the religious affiliations and program focus (if applicable) of adoption agencies were relevant to the number of children placed with LG parents each year. These factors also related to whether agencies accepted applications from openly LG parents, were interested in training geared toward working with LG parents, and actively recruited LG adoptive parents. Agencies with conservative religious affiliations (e.g., fundamentalist Christian churches) were least likely to work with LG applicants. Relatedly, beyond intersecting with discrimination throughout the adoption process, LG adoptive parents have also described having few role models to guide them (Brown, Smalling, Groza, & Ryan, 2009). Indeed, around the world, social resistance to LGBTQ parent adoption is commonplace, especially among conservative groups, and discrimination is a regular theme (Brodzinsky, 2015; Mallon, 2011; Messina & D'Amore, 2018; Perry, 2017; Pyne, 2012; Stotzer et al., 2014). As an example, among 96 mothers in Sweden who completed a second-parent adoption with their same-sex partner, many described their social workers as asking inappropriate questions about sexuality and expressing heterosexist bias regarding family (e.g., "children should have a mother and father"; Malmquist, 2015). Thus, LGBTQ prospective parents face numerous attitudinal and institutional obstacles in the adoption process.

Despite challenges, LGBTQ adoptive parents may also possess unique strengths. Among their sample of LG and heterosexual adoptive couples in the US, Farr and Patterson (2013) found that LG couples were more likely to share childcare equally (for their preschool-age children), and this dynamic was connected with greater relationship satisfaction. In this same sample, lesbian mothers were observed to be more supportive of one another in the context of family interaction than were gay fathers or heterosexual parents, and supportive coparenting was significantly associated with fewer behavior problems among children. Another strength of LG adoptive couples may be resilience to adoption stigma. Goldberg, Kinkler, and Hines (2011) found that LG couples (in the US) internalized adoption stigma (i.e., feeling biological parenthood is superior to adoptive parenthood) less often than did heterosexual adoptive couples, and those who generally described less stigma internalized also had fewer depressive symptoms. Indeed, several additional studies in the US and UK have described positive characteristics unique to LGBTQ adoptive parents that may be advantageous to their children (Golombok et al., 2014; Perry, 2017). Last, many LGBTQ adoptive parents report satisfaction in their experiences, as well as receiving greater-than-expected amounts of family support and enjoying being a role model to other parents (Brown et al., 2009; Goldberg & Smith, 2014; Lavner et al., 2014).

Individual outcomes for members of LGBTQ parent families

What do we know about child development in LGBTQ adoptive parent families, as well as broader outcomes for parents, couples, and whole families? Much of the controversy on adoption by LGBTQ adults has focused on whether the sexual orientation and gender identity of these parents affect children's development. Studies on parents diverse in sexual orientation has demonstrated that children with LGB parents develop on par with children of heterosexual parents (Biblarz & Stacey, 2010; Moore & Stambolis-Ruhstorfer, 2013; Patterson, 2017). More recent research has begun to explore child development in adoptive families headed by LGBTQ parents. This collective body of research demonstrates that factors such as family relationship quality are more relevant to the development of children than the sexual orientation of their parents.

Behavioral adjustment has been a child outcome of great interest in studies of LGBTQ adoptive parent families. In the US, numerous studies have indicated that adopted children's behavior problems are unrelated to parental sexual orientation, even after controlling for family income, child age, and sex (Averett, Nalavany, & Ryan, 2009; Farr, 2017; Farr et al., 2010a; Farr & Patterson, 2009; Goldberg & Smith, 2013; Tan & Baggerly, 2009). In the UK, Golombok et al. (2014) found that young children with LG parents showed fewer behavior problems than did those with heterosexual parents. Therefore, children adopted by LG parents appear to show healthy behavioral adjustment, at least equivalent to that of children with heterosexual parents.

Children's gender development has also been a topic of interest among studies of LGBTQ adoptive parent families, and studies in this area have generally revealed few differences as a function of parental sexual orientation. In one sample of LG and heterosexual adoptive parent families in the US, children exhibited gender-typical preferences for toys and activities (observed and parent-reported) across early to middle childhood, regardless of parental sexual orientation (Farr et al., 2018, 2010a). In another similar sample from the US, children adopted by lesbian mothers demonstrated less gender-typical play compared with those with gay fathers or heterosexual parents over time (Goldberg & Garcia, 2016), perhaps as a result of more flexible attitudes about gender among LGBTQ versus cisgender heterosexual adults (Biblarz & Stacey, 2010). Relatedly, among that first sample of LG and heterosexual adoptive parent families described in this paragraph, Sumontha, Farr, and Patterson (2017) found that children with LG parents had more flexible attitudes about gender when their parents also had flexible attitudes and divided childcare equally. Research using multiple methods and longitudinal data collection in the future could bring to light possible associations between children's gender development, related family processes, and parental sexual orientation. Generally, it appears that factors such as parents' attitudes and behaviors (i.e., divisions of family labor) are better predictors of children's gender development within LGBTQ adoptive parent families than is parental sexual orientation.

The perspectives of children adopted by LGBTQ parents are also critical to consider. In a study examining adoptees in middle childhood, children noted that they experienced some bullying due to their parents' sexual orientation, but they generally displayed positive feelings toward their family and were open to speaking about them (Farr, Crain, Oakley, Cashen, & Garber, 2016; Farr, Oakley, & Ollen, 2016). Among racially diverse adopted adolescents and young adults, Gianino, Goldberg, and Lewis (2009) qualitatively described disclosure practices about parental sexual orientation and adoption status with friends, peers, and at school. Adolescents used a diversity of approaches, from telling others openly to complete secrecy. Some of these participants noted a necessity to disclose their adoptive status because of the visibility of their family structure (e.g., transracial same-sex parents), but many were hesitant to speak about their families. Despite this hesitancy, most adolescents had positive experiences in disclosing their adoption. Adolescents adopted through foster care by LG parents have also reported positive feelings about diversity because of having same-sex parents (Cody, Farr, McRoy, Ayers-Lopez, & Ledesma, 2017).

Socialization around children's and parents' identities (e.g., sexual orientation, race) may help children feel comfortable in speaking about their families (Gianino et al., 2009). Little research has yet specifically explored the processes of minority identity socialization within LGBTQ parent adoptive families and how children interpret such experiences. A few studies, however, have shown that LG adoptive parents (generally with preadolescent children) indeed value and utilize such socialization practices around identities such as race and ethnicity, parental sexual orientation, and children's adoptive status (Goldberg & Smith, 2016; Oakley, Farr, & Scherer, 2017; Wyman Battalen, Farr, Brodzinsky, & McRoy, 2018).

Studies (in the US unless noted) have also examined individual parent, couple, and family-level outcomes in adoptive families headed by LG parents. In terms of individual mental and emotional health, LG adoptive parents tend to report few depressive symptoms (Goldberg & Smith, 2011). Lesbian, gay, and heterosexual adoptive parents also describe low or normative levels of parenting stress, with no differences uncovered as a function of parental sexual orientation (Farr et al., 2010a; Tornello, Farr, & Patterson, 2011). In a study of prospective adoptive couples, no differences in levels of overall well-being were found among lesbian and heterosexual couples (Goldberg & Smith, 2008). In a study in the UK, Golombok et al. (2014) found that gay adoptive fathers reported higher well-being than lesbian or heterosexual adoptive parents. Longitudinal studies have also supported similar findings, demonstrating that levels of parenting stress among lesbian, gay, and heterosexual adoptive parents do not vary by parental sexual orientation over time (Farr, 2017; Goldberg & Smith, 2014; Lavner et al., 2014). Research has also supported the effective parenting practices of LG adoptive parents as compared with heterosexual adoptive parents through self-report and observational data (e.g., Farr et al., 2010a; Farr & Patterson, 2013; Goldberg & Smith, 2009; Golombok et al., 2014).

Regarding couple relationship dynamics, research has revealed that LG adoptive parents in same-sex couples appear to show, on average, low conflict, high relationship satisfaction, and secure attachment relationship quality in long-term relationships (Farr et al., 2010a; Farr, Forssell, & Patterson, 2010b; Goldberg & Smith, 2009). They also describe being satisfied with divisions of childcare labor, which they tend to divide in an egalitarian manner over time (Farr & Patterson, 2013; Sumontha et al., 2017). Interestingly, across these samples, couple dissolution rates were lower among gay and heterosexual couples and higher among lesbian couples (Farr, 2017; Goldberg & Garcia, 2015). Given that these are among the first studies in this area, more research is needed to investigate longitudinal couple relationship dynamics among LGBTQ adoptive parent couples.

Aligned with the broader literature, quality of parenting and family relationships appear to be more important to child outcomes than parental sexual orientation. In one study of LG and heterosexual adoptive parent families in the US, high-quality parenting, family functioning, and couple relationships were significantly correlated with fewer parent-reported child behavior problems over time, while parental sexual orientation was not linked with any child outcomes (Farr, 2017; Farr et al., 2010a; Farr & Patterson, 2013). Among another US sample of LG and heterosexual adoptive families, parent–adolescent relationship qualities were unrelated to parental sexual orientation, but were associated with adolescents' self-reported life satisfaction (Erich, Kanenberg, Case, Allen, & Bogdanos, 2009). In contrast, among a sample of LG and heterosexual adoptive parent families in the UK, more positive parent–child relationships were reported among gay fathers versus heterosexual parents (Golombok et al., 2014). Although few significant associations between parental sexual orientation and family relationships have emerged, results tend to favor LGBTQ parent families.

Implications for future research, policy, and practice

Extant research about LGBTQ adoptive families is informative, yet also in its infancy. As such, further study is needed as related to theory, methods, and implications for law, policy, and practice. Greater interdisciplinary integration, across diverse fields such as family science, social work, psychology, sociology, economics, law, and demography, would enrich our understanding of the social, psychological, and economic aspects of LGBTQ adoptive parent family life. Recent reviews have also underscored the general lack of purposeful theoretical frameworks in studies of LGBTQ parent families; instead, many studies appear motivated by public and policy debate (Farr, Tasker, & Goldberg, 2017; van Eeden-Moorefield, Few-Demo, Benson, Bible, & Lummer, 2018). Regarding methodology, engaging a greater diversity of research strategies would be advantageous (Fish & Russell, 2018). Existing research has often been based on cross-sectional designs incorporating self-report data, yet longitudinal designs using multiple or mixed methods (e.g., observational data; qualitative and quantitative data) and multiple informants (such as from people outside the family, e.g., peers, teachers) would contribute to the knowledge base. Samples more diverse in racial-ethnic and socioeconomic background, as well as international context, would be valuable, given that the experiences of families likely vary based on these factors. Furthermore, fewer studies in this area have attended to the experiences of bisexual or transgender adoptive parents as compared with LG adoptive parents, although this is beginning to change. Thus, more inclusive samples of sexual and gender minority adoptive parents, with attention to other aspects of intersectionality, as well as more rigorous theoretical frameworks and research designs, would advance our understanding of the experiences of diverse adoptive family systems.

Research should include the perspectives of adopted children of LGBTQ parents wherever possible. It is important to understand how contextual and environmental factors might shape adopted children's experiences based on their parents' SOGIE status. As noted previously, these children generally have positive developmental outcomes despite facing possible adversity due to their parents' sexual orientation (Cody et al., 2017; Farr, Crain et al., 2016). Indeed, future work in this area can help shed light on the factors that adopted children of LGBTQ parents describe as most influential to their development and that contribute to resilience.

Future work should consider all contextual and sociopolitical forces with which LGBTQ adoptive families might interact. Social, economic, and legal factors all influence the choices that LGBTQ parent adoptive families make (e.g., where to live; adoption pathway) and their overall family functioning (e.g., minority stress related to stigmatized identities; Farr & Goldberg, 2018). As such, variability in attitudes, laws, and policies toward LGBTQ adoptive parents across the US and in many countries around the world deems it necessary for continued research into how these broader contextual factors influence these families and their interactions with the world around them (Patterson, 2013).

Related to connections with policy and legal domains, research about LGBTQ adoptive parent families can be informative. For instance, state-level religious exemption laws in the US allow for open discrimination of qualified LGBTQ prospective adoptive parents when they apply to state-funded child welfare agencies, and the projected impact is that many children in the US child welfare system will "pay the price" (MAP, 2018a; MAP/FEC, 2018). There is no empirical justification for such legislation; rather, research clearly establishes the efficacy of LGBTQ parents in raising adopted children and does not support such legislation as beneficial to children or families (Patterson, 2013).

Approximately 443,000 children are in the US child welfare system; about a quarter of these children (123,000) are awaiting adoption (US Department of Health & Human Services, 2018). In a policy brief co-authored by the Movement Advancement Project (MAP) and the Family Equality Council (FEC), current religious exemption laws in ten states discriminate against not only LGBTQ youth in care, but also prospective LGBTQ parents (as well as single parents and interfaith couples; MAP/FEC, 2018). In contrast, research supports the effectiveness of LGBTQ parents in fostering and adopting children. In one study, results showed no differences among LG and heterosexual parent families who had adopted children from care, despite children with LG parents having significantly higher biological and environmental risk (e.g., prenatal substance exposure, birth complications, or neglect and abuse) prior to placement than did children with heterosexual parents (Lavner et al., 2012). To avoid unintentional harm to the many children awaiting adoptive placement in the US, MAP and FEC advocate passage of the federal "Every Child Deserves a Family Act." This law would prohibit discrimination by federally funded child welfare agencies based on SOGIE or marital status (MAP/FEC, 2018).

Moreover, a perceived shortage of available adoptive parents compounds the challenge of meeting the needs of children awaiting adoption in the US. If child welfare agencies employed recruitment strategies that specifically targeted prospective LGBTQ parents, it is possible that more waiting children would be placed with permanent, "forever" families in the US and perhaps elsewhere too (Brodzinsky, 2011). In the US, it is in this vein that the Human Rights Campaign (HRC) began an initiative called "All Children–All Families" (HRC, 2018). In an effort to find permanent placements for more children, participating child welfare agencies receive support in working with prospective and current LGBTQ parents. In completing the HRC's training, agencies can become recognized as an affirming agency to LGBTQ people seeking adoption services (Farr & Goldberg, 2018; HRC, 2018).

Conclusion

In sum, LGBTQ parents in the US and many other places in the world are adopting a growing number of children. Although LGBTQ adults do face potential challenges along the way, members of LGBTQ adoptive parent families tend to be well-adjusted and have positive family relationships. The time is ripe to continue learning about the diverse community represented by LGBTQ adoptive parent families, and how their experiences are shaped by their social and cultural contexts.

Notes

1 Please note we use acronyms to accurately reflect the sexual and gender identities of participants represented in previous research.
2 Step-parent adoption requires parents to be in a legally recognized relationship (e.g., marriage); second-parent adoption does not (MAP, 2018a).

References

Averett, P., Nalavany, B., & Ryan, S. (2009). An evaluation of gay/lesbian and heterosexual adoption. *Adoption Quarterly, 12*, 129–151. doi:10.1080/10926750903313278

Baccara, M., Collard-Wexler, A., Felli, L., & Yariv, L. (2014). Child-adoption matching: Preferences for gender and race. *American Economic Journal: Applied Economics, 6*(3), 133–158. doi:10.1257/ap.6.3.133

Biblarz, T. J., & Stacey, J. (2010). How does the gender of parents matter? *Journal of Marriage and Family, 72*, 3–22. doi:10.1111/j.1741-3737.2009.00678.x

Brodzinsky, D. M. (2011). Adoption by lesbians and gay men: A national survey of adoption agency policies and practices. In D. Brodzinsky & A. Pertman (Eds.), *Adoption by lesbians and gay men: A new dimension in family diversity* (pp. 62–84). New York: Oxford University Press.

Brodzinsky, D. M. (2015). *The modern adoptive families study: An introduction.* New York: Evan B. Donaldson Adoption Institute.

Brodzinsky, D. M., & Goldberg, A. E. (2016). Contact with birth family in adoptive families headed by lesbian, gay male, and heterosexual parents. *Children and Youth Services Review, 62*, 9–17. doi:10.1016/j.childyouth.2016.01.014

Brown, S., Smalling, S., Groza, V., & Ryan, S. (2009). The experiences of gay men and lesbians in becoming and being adoptive parents. *Adoption Quarterly, 12*, 226–246. doi:10.1080/10926750903313294

Carroll, A., & Mendos, L. R. (2017). *State-sponsored homophobia 2017: A world survey of sexual orientation laws: Criminalisation, protection and recognition.* International Lesbian, Gay, Bisexual, Trans and Intersex Association. Retrieved from https://ilga.org/downloads/2017/ILGA_State_Sponsored_Homophobia_2017_WEB.pdf

Cody, P. A., Farr, R. H., McRoy, R. G., Ayers-Lopez, S. J., & Ledesma, K. J. (2017). Youth perspectives on being adopted from foster care by lesbian and gay parents: Implications for families and adoption professionals. *Adoption Quarterly, 20*(1), 98–118. doi:10.1080/10926755.2016.1200702

Davis, M. A. (2013). Demographics of gay and lesbian adoption and family policies. In A. K. Baumle (Ed.), *International handbook on the demography of sexuality* (pp. 383–401). Dordrect, The Netherlands: Springer. doi:10.1007/978-94-007-5512-3_19

dickey, L. M., Ducheny, K. M., & Ehrbar, R. D. (2016). Family creation options for transgender and gender nonconforming people. *Psychology of Sexual Orientation and Gender Diversity, 3*(2), 173–179. doi:10.1037/sgd0000178

Downing, J., Richardson, H., Kinkler, L., & Goldberg, A. (2009). Making the decision: Factors influencing gay men's choice of an adoption path. *Adoption Quarterly, 12*, 247–271. doi:10.1080/10926750903313310

Erich, S., Kanenberg, H., Case, K., Allen, T., & Bogdanos, T. (2009). An empirical analysis of factors affecting adolescent attachment in adoptive families with homosexual and straight parents. *Children & Youth Services Review, 31*, 398–404. doi:10.1016/j.childyouth.2008.09.004

Farr, R. H. (2017). Does parental sexual orientation matter? A longitudinal follow-up of adoptive families with school-age children. *Developmental Psychology, 53*, 252–264. doi:10.1037/dev0000228

Farr, R. H., Bruun, S. T., Doss, K. M., & Patterson, C. J. (2018). Children's gender-typed behavior from early to middle childhood in adoptive families with lesbian, gay, and heterosexual parents. *Sex Roles, 78*, 528–541. doi:10.1007/s11199-017-0812-5

Farr, R. H., Crain, E. E., Oakley, M. K., Cashen, K. K., & Garber, K. J. (2016). Microaggressions, feelings of difference, and resilience among adopted children with sexual minority parents. *Journal of Youth and Adolescence, 45*, 85–104. doi:10.1007/s10964-015-0353-6

Farr, R. H., Forssell, S. L., & Patterson, C. J. (2010a). Parenting and child development in adoptive families: Does parental sexual orientation matter? *Applied Developmental Science, 14*, 164–178. doi:10.1080/10888691.2010.500958

Farr, R. H., Forssell, S. L., & Patterson, C. J. (2010b). Lesbian, gay, and heterosexual adoptive parents: Couple and relationship issues. *Journal of GLBT Family Studies, 6*, 199–213. doi:10.1080/15504281003705436

Farr, R. H., & Goldberg, A. E. (2015). Contact between birth and adoptive families during the first year post-placement: Perspectives of lesbian, gay, and heterosexual parents. *Adoption Quarterly, 18*(1), 1–24. doi:10.1080/10926755.2014.895466

Farr, R. H., & Goldberg, A. E. (2018). Sexual orientation, gender identity, and adoption law. *Family Court Review, 56*(3), 374–383. doi:10.1111/fcre.12354

Farr, R. H., Oakley, M. K., & Ollen, E. W. (2016). School experiences of young children and their lesbian and gay adoptive parents. *Psychology of Sexual Orientation and Gender Diversity, 3*(4), 442. doi:10.1037/sgd0000187

Farr, R. H., & Patterson, C. J. (2009). Transracial adoption by lesbian, gay, and heterosexual parents: Who completes transracial adoptions and with what results? *Adoption Quarterly, 12*, 187–204. doi:10.1080/10926750903313328

Farr, R. H., & Patterson, C. J. (2013). Coparenting among lesbian, gay, and heterosexual couples: Associations with adopted children's outcomes. *Child Development, 84*(4), 1226–1240. doi:10.1111/cdev.12046

Farr, R. H., Ravvina, Y., & Grotevant, H. (2018). Birth family contact experiences among lesbian, gay, and heterosexual adoptive parents with school-age children. *Family Relations, 67*(1), 132–146. doi:10.1111/fare.12295

Farr, R. H., Tasker, F., & Goldberg, A. E. (2017). Theory in highly cited studies of sexual minority parent families: Variations and implications. *Journal of Homosexuality, 64*(9), 1143–1179. doi:10.1080/00918369.2016.1242336

Fish, J. N., & Russell, S. T. (2018). Queering methodologies to understand queer families. *Family Relations, 67*(1), 12–25. doi:10.1111/fare.12297

Gates, G. J. (2011). Family formation and raising children among same-sex couples. *National Council of Family Relations*. Retrieved from https://escholarship.org/uc/item/5pq1q8d7

Gates, G. J. (2013). *LGBT parenting in the United States*. The Williams Institute. Retrieved from https://escholarship.org/uc/item/9xs6g8xx

Gianino, M., Goldberg, A., & Lewis, T. (2009). Disclosure practices among adopted youth with gay and lesbian parents. *Adoption Quarterly, 12*, 205–228. doi:10.1080/10926750903313344

Goldberg, A. E. (2009a). Lesbian and heterosexual preadoptive couples' openness to transracial adoption. *American Journal of Orthopsychiatry, 79*, 103–117. doi:10.1037/a0015354

Goldberg, A. E. (2009b). Heterosexual, lesbian, and gay preadoptive parents' preferences about child gender. *Sex Roles, 61*, 55–71. doi:10.1007/s11199-009-9598-4

Goldberg, A. E. (2012). *Gay dads: Transitions to adoptive fatherhood*. New York: NYU Press.

Goldberg, A. E., Downing, J. B., & Richardson, H. B. (2009). The transition from infertility to adoption: Perceptions of lesbian and heterosexual preadoptive couples. *Journal of Social & Personal Relationships, 26*, 938–963. doi:10.1177/0265407509345652

Goldberg, A. E., & Garcia, R. (2015). Predictors of relationship dissolution in lesbian, gay, and heterosexual adoptive parents. *Journal of Family Psychology, 29*(3), 394–404. doi:10.1037/fam0000095

Goldberg, A. E., & Garcia, R. L. (2016). Gender-typed behavior over time in children with lesbian, gay, and heterosexual parents. *Journal of Family Psychology, 30*(7), 854. doi:10.1037/fam0000226

Goldberg, A. E., Gartrell, N. K., & Gates, G. J. (2014). Research report on LGB-parent families. *The Williams Institute*. Retrieved from https://escholarship.org/uc/item/7gr4970w

Goldberg, A. E., Kinkler, L. A., & Hines, D. A. (2011). Perception and internalization of adoption stigma among gay, lesbian, and heterosexual adoptive parents. *Journal of GLBT Family Studies, 7*, 132–154. doi:10.1080/1550428X.2011.537554

Goldberg, A. E., Kinkler, L. A., Moyer, A. M., & Weber, E. (2014). Intimate relationship challenges in early parenthood among lesbian, gay, and heterosexual couples adopting via the child welfare system. *Professional Psychology*, *45*(4), 221. doi:10.1037/a0037443

Goldberg, A. E., Kinkler, L. A., Richardson, H. B., & Downing, J. B. (2011). Lesbian, gay, and heterosexual couples in open adoption arrangements: A qualitative study. *Journal of Marriage and Family*, *73*(2), 502–518. doi:10.1111/j.1741-3737.2010.00821.x

Goldberg, A. E., & Smith, J. Z. (2008). Social support and psychological well-being in lesbian and heterosexual preadoptive couples. *Family Relations*, *57*, 281–294. doi:10.1111/j.1741-3729.2008.00500.x

Goldberg, A. E., & Smith, J. Z. (2009). Perceived parenting skill across the transition to adoptive parenthood among lesbian, gay, and heterosexual couples. *Journal of Family Psychology*, *23*, 861–870. doi:10.1037/a0017009

Goldberg, A. E., & Smith, J. Z. (2011). Stigma, social context, and mental health: Lesbian and gay couples across the transition to adoptive parenthood. *Journal of Counseling Psychology*, *58*, 139–150. doi:10.1037/a0021684

Goldberg, A. E., & Smith, J. Z. (2013). Predictors of psychological adjustment in early placed adopted children with lesbian, gay, and heterosexual parents. *Journal of Family Psychology*, *27*(3), 431. doi:10.1037/a0032911

Goldberg, A. E., & Smith, J. Z. (2014). Predictors of parenting stress in lesbian, gay, and heterosexual adoptive parents during early parenthood. *Journal of Family Psychology*, *28*(2), 125. doi:10.1037/a0036007

Goldberg, A. E., & Smith, J. Z. (2016). Predictors of race, adoption, and sexual orientation related socialization of adoptive parents of young children. *Journal of Family Psychology*, *30*(3), 397. doi:10.1037/fam0000149

Goldberg, A. E., Smith, J. Z., & Kashy, D. A. (2010). Preadoptive factors predicting lesbian, gay, and heterosexual couples' relationship quality across the transition to adoptive parenthood. *Journal of Family Psychology*, *24*, 221–232. doi:10.1037/a0019615

Goldberg, S. K., & Conron, K. J. (2018). How many same-sex couples in the US are raising children? *The Williams Institute*. Retrieved from https://williamsinstitute.law.ucla.edu/research/parenting/how-many-same-sex-parents-in-us/

Golombok, S., Mellish, L., Jennings, S., Casey, P., Tasker, F., & Lamb, M. E. (2014). Adoptive gay father families: Parent-child relationships and children's psychological adjustment. *Child Development*, *85*(2), 456–468. doi:10.1111/cdev.12155

Herrmann-Green, L. K., & Gehring, T. M. (2007). The German lesbian family study: Planning for parenthood via donor insemination. *Journal of GLBT Family Studies*, *3*, 351–395. doi:10.1300/J461v03n04_02

Human Rights Campaign. (2018). *All children—All families: List of participating agencies*. Retrieved from www.hrc.org/resources/all-children-all-families-list-of-participating-agencies

Jennings, S., Mellish, L., Tasker, F., Lamb, M., & Golombok, S. (2014). Why adoption? Gay, lesbian, and heterosexual adoptive parents' reproductive experiences and reasons for adoption. *Adoption Quarterly*, *17*(3), 205–226. doi:10.1080/10926755.2014.891549

Lavner, J. A., Waterman, J., & Peplau, L. A. (2012). Can gay and lesbian parents promote healthy development in high-risk children adopted from foster care? *American Journal of Orthopsychiatry*, *82*(4), 465. doi:10.1111/j.1939-0025.2012.01176.x

Lavner, J. A., Waterman, J., & Peplau, L. A. (2014). Parent adjustment over time in gay, lesbian, and heterosexual parent families adopting from foster care. *American Journal of Orthopsychiatry*, *84*(1), 46. doi:10.1037/h0098853

Mallon, G. P. (2011). The home study assessment process for gay, lesbian, bisexual, and transgender prospective foster and adoptive families. *Journal of GLBT Family Studies*, 7(1–2), 9–29. doi:10.1080/1550428X.2011.537229

Malmquist, A. (2015). A crucial but strenuous process: Female same-sex couples' reflections on second-parent adoption. *Journal of GLBT Family Studies*, *11*(4), 351–374. doi:10.1080/1550428X.2015.1019169

Messina, R., & D'Amore, S. (2018). Adoption by lesbians and gay men in Europe: Challenges and barriers on the journey to adoption. *Adoption Quarterly*, *21*(2), 59–81. doi:10.1080/10926755.2018.1427641

Moore, M. R., & Stambolis-Ruhstorfer, M. (2013). LGBT sexuality and families at the start of the twenty-first century. *Annual Review of Sociology*, *39*, 491–507. doi:10.1146/annurev-soc-071312-145643

Movement Advancement Project. (2018a). *Creating a license to discriminate: 2018 federal child welfare amendment (Issue Brief)*. Retrieved from www.lgbtmap.org/file/AderholtAmendmentAnalysis.pdf

Movement Advancement Project. (2018b). *Foster and adoption laws*. Retrieved from www.lgbtmap.org/equality-maps/foster_and_adoption_laws/

Movement Advancement Project & Family Equality Council. (2018). *Kids pay the price (Issue Brief)*. Retrieved from www.lgbtmap.org/file/Brief-Kids-Pay-Price-Two-Pager-Sept-2018.pdf

Oakley, M. K., Farr, R. H., & Scherer, D. G. (2017). Same-sex parent socialization: Understanding gay and lesbian parenting practices as cultural socialization. *Journal of GLBT Family Studies*, *13*(1), 56–75. doi:10.1080/1550428X.2016.1158685

Patterson, C. J. (2013). Children of lesbian and gay parents: Psychology, law, and policy. *Psychology of Sexual Orientation and Gender Diversity*, *1*(S), 27–34. doi:10.1037/2329-0382.1.S.27

Patterson, C. J. (2017). Parents' sexual orientation and children's development. *Child Development Perspectives*, *11*, 45–49. doi:10.1111/cdep.12207

Patterson, C. J., & Farr, R. H. (2017). What shall we call ourselves? Last names among lesbian, gay, and heterosexual couples and their adopted children. *Journal of GLBT Family Studies*, *13*, 97–113. doi:10.1080/1550428X.2016.1169239

Patterson, C. J., & Goldberg, A. E. (2016). *Lesbian and gay parents and their children. (Policy Brief)*. Minneapolis, MN: National Council on Family Relations.

Patterson, C. J., & Tornello, S. L. (2011). Gay fathers' pathways to parenthood: International perspectives. *Zeitschrift Für Familienforschung (Journal of Family research)*, 7, 103–116.

Perry, J. R. (2017). *Promising practices for serving transgender & non-binary foster & adoptive parents*. Washington, DC: The Human Rights Campaign Foundation.

Pyne, J. (2012). *Transforming family: Trans parents and their struggles, strategies, and strengths*. Toronto: LGBTQ Parenting Network, Sherbourne Health Clinic.

Raleigh, E. (2012). Are same-sex and single adoptive parents more likely to adopt transracially? A national analysis of race, family structure, and the adoption marketplace. *Sociological Perspectives*, *55*(3), 449–471. doi:10.1525/sop.2012.55.3.449

Riskind, R. G., & Tornello, S. L. (2017). Sexual orientation and future parenthood in a 2011–2013 nationally representative United States sample. *Journal of Family Psychology*, *31*(6), 792–798. doi:10.1037/fam0000316

Stotzer, R. L., Herman, J. L., & Hasenbush, A. (2014). *Transgender parenting: A review of existing literature*. The Williams Institute. Retrieved from https://escholarship.org/uc/item/3rp0v7qv

Sumontha, J., Farr, R. H., & Patterson, C. J. (2016). Social support and coparenting among lesbian, gay, and heterosexual adoptive parents. *Journal of Family Psychology*, *30*(8), 987–996. doi:10.1037/fam0000253

Sumontha, J., Farr, R. H., & Patterson, C. J. (2017). Children's gender development: Associations with parental sexual orientation, division of labor, and gender ideology. *Psychology of Sexual Orientation and Gender Diversity*, *4*, 438–450. doi:10.1037/sgd0000242

Tan, T. X., & Baggerly, J. (2009). Behavioral adjustment of adopted Chinese girls in single-mother, lesbian-couple, and heterosexual-couple households. *Adoption Quarterly*, *12*, 171–186. doi:10.1080/10926750903313336

Tornello, S. L., & Bos, H. (2017). Parenting intentions among transgender individuals. *LGBT Health*, *4*(2), 115–120. doi:10.1089/lgbt.2016.0153

Tornello, S. L., Farr, R. H., & Patterson, C. J. (2011). Predictors of parenting stress among gay adoptive fathers in the United States. *Journal of Family Psychology*, *25*(4), 591–600. doi:10.1037/a0024480

US Department of Health & Human Services. (2018). *Trends in foster care and adoption, FY 2008–FY 2017*. Retrieved from www.acf.hhs.gov/sites/default/files/cb/trends_fostercare_adoption_08thru17.pdf

van Eeden-Moorefield, B., Few-Demo, A. L., Benson, K., Bible, J., & Lummer, S. (2018). A content analysis of LGBT research in top family journals 2000-2015. *Journal of Family Issues*, *39*(5), 1374–1395. doi:10.1177/0192513X17710284

Wyman Battalen, A., Farr, R. H., Brodzinsky, D. M., & McRoy, R. G. (2018). Socializing children about family structure: Perspectives of lesbian and gay adoptive parents. *Journal of GLBT Family Studies*. Advance online publication. doi: 10.1080/1550428X.2018.1465875

13

POST-INSTITUTIONALIZED ADOPTED CHILDREN

Effects of prolonged institutionalization and adoption at an older age

Megan M. Julian

The first months and years of a child's life serve as the foundation for the rest of development. When a child's early years are characterized by sensitive and responsive care from a small number of committed caregivers, their developmental potential is maximized. Children who are adopted typically reside in relatively high-resourced homes with dedicated parents after adoption, but their experience before adoption is highly variable. At one extreme, some children are placed at birth with foster parents who go on to adopt them. At the other extreme, some children experience abuse or neglect in their family of origin and are involuntarily relinquished, and subsequently placed in an institution where they experience social-emotional neglect before being adopted into a family. Because pre-adoption experiences are so highly variable and adoptive parents often do not have detailed and accurate information about their child's pre-adoption history, there is little research available on the effects of specific components of adopted children's early life experience. In order to best illustrate how pre-adoptive experiences can impact children's ongoing development, this chapter discusses the development of adopted children who have a history of prolonged institutional care and were adopted at a relatively older age. Consistent with the literature on post-institutionalized adopted children, an "older" age at adoption is conceptualized as older than approximately six months of age in conditions of severe neglect, or 12–18 months of age in qualitatively better institutions.

Early caregiving relationships

In the first months and years of life, young children's development progresses rapidly, and this is the developmental period during which experience has the greatest impact on the course of a child's later development (Fox, Levitt, & Nelson, 2010). Both environmental and genetic factors interact to shape the way neural structures in the brain are built, so experiences in these early years are an integral part of how the brain becomes wired (Fox et al., 2010; Roth & Sweatt, 2011). Infants and young children are heavily dependent on their caregivers to support their development, and caregivers shape and guide their interactions with other people and objects in the environment. Based on a young child's experiences, certain neural connections are either strengthened or pruned, essentially tailoring a child's brain to the specific environment they are living in. Animal models have also shown that parental care (i.e., licking and grooming) is linked to changes in the epigenome that are, in turn, associated with changes to gene expression and behavior (Meaney, 2010). Early caregiving relationships are a central and critical component of a young child's early experience and play an integral role in shaping their neural development; when children's early caregiving relationships are deficient due to prolonged institutional rearing, their developmental outcomes are likely to be negatively affected.

For children who are adopted, especially children adopted at older ages, it is not uncommon for their early years to be marked by neglect, ruptured attachments, a complete lack of early attachments, or abuse. A later age at adoption nearly always means a longer period of time in which a child resides in an environment that is not optimal for their development. In fact, in a study of children adopted from Russian institutions, children who were adopted at an older age (>18 months of age) were more likely than earlier-adopted children to have spent time in a family before entering an institution, but they were also more likely to have been involuntarily relinquished and to have experienced abuse or neglect (Hawk et al., 2012). In other words, while early family care is more common among later-adopted children, many of these children experience maltreatment within family care which leads to their eventual removal. Early abuse and neglect are widely known to be associated with negative behavioral (Cecil, Viding, Fearon, Glaser, & McCrory, 2017; Doyle & Cicchetti, 2017) and neurobiological outcomes (Cicchetti, Rogosch, & Toth, 2011; Glaser, 2000), and this is true even for children who go on to be adopted into supportive families (van der Vegt, van der Ende, Ferdinand, Verhulst, & Tiemeier, 2009). Further, children adopted at a relatively later age are likely to have had more placement instability early in life relative to those placed in an adoptive home soon after birth. While research on the effect of placement instability on developmental outcomes in post-institutionalized adopted children is limited, research on children in the foster care system suggests that when children experience more placement transitions, they are likely to go on to experience more emotional and behavior problems (Rubin, O'Reilly, Luan, & Localio, 2007).

Quality of care in institutions

Though institutions are broadly thought to be non-optimal rearing environments, they vary greatly in quality. Globally depriving institutions are those that provide inadequate medical care, nutrition, sanitation, stimulation, and material resources, in addition to having many and changing caregivers who provide insensitive and unresponsive care (Gunnar, 2001). Institutions from 1990s' Romania, which gained significant media attention for their unfortunate conditions, would fall within this category (Smyke, Dumitrescu, & Zeanah, 2002; Zeanah et al., 2003). Psychosocially depriving institutions are those that generally meet children's needs with respect to medical care, nutrition, sanitation, and material resources, yet still fail to meet children's social-emotional needs. In these institutions, despite having adequate care in some respects, children rarely see the same caregiver from one day to the next, and the care they receive is often performed in a perfunctory or business-like manner, making it rare for attachment relationships to develop. Institutions in St. Petersburg, Russian Federation, typically fall within this category (The St. Petersburg-USA Orphanage Research Team, 2005). Some institutions, such as those in South Korea and parts of western Europe, provide care that is developmentally appropriate in most respects, including sensitive and responsive care from caregivers (Lee, Seol, Sung, & Miller, 2010; Tizard & Rees, 1975). But caregivers often have irregular work schedules and rotate frequently between different wards of children, resulting in limited opportunity to develop ongoing relationships with resident children. Thus, across many different types of institutions of varying quality, institutionalized children typically lack the kind of long-term adult–child relationships that are typical in family contexts, and so fundamental to human development.

Development of post-institutionalized adopted children

In general, adopted children who spent some of their early months and years in institutional care experiencing early social-emotional neglect are at a higher risk for a variety of problems, including difficulties in attachment, disinhibited social behavior, peer relationships, physical/growth development, sensory functioning, emotion regulation, externalizing behaviors, inattention/overactivity, and executive functioning (for more detail in these areas, refer to Chapters 14, 24–28 in the current volume). Importantly, these behavioral differences in attention, executive function, and emotion regulation have also been linked to neuroanatomical and neural activation differences in post-institutionalized youth (see Chapter 26, especially). There is some evidence that longer duration of early institutional care is associated with greater differences in brain morphology (Hodel et al., 2015).

Researchers have proposed that the "core" deficits associated with institutional care, which are unique to the specific nature of deprivation experienced in institutions, include quasi-autism, disinhibited attachment, cognitive impairment, and inattention/overactivity (Rutter et al., 2010). In particular, executive function and attention problems have been identified as one of the most consistent outcomes linked to prolonged institutional care (Julian, 2013; Kreppner, O'Connor, Rutter, & The English and Romanian Adoptees Study Team, 2001), and may mediate the effect of age at adoption on disinhibited social behavior (Bruce, Tarullo, & Gunnar, 2009). While only limited research has thus far examined the effects of prolonged institutional care into adulthood, compared to those not exposed to early institutional rearing, post-institutionalized individuals show evidence of experiencing lower educational attainment, and higher unemployment and mental health service use (Sonuga-Barke et al., 2017).

The institutional environment is typically experienced as quite stressful for young children, in large part because the relationships with caregivers that infants and young children rely so heavily upon are deficient. Young children do not yet have the capacity to regulate their stress response on their own, and instead depend on a sensitive and responsive caregiver to help them do so (Gunnar & Quevedo, 2007). The hypothalamic-pituitary-adrenal (HPA) axis plays a central role in the body's stress response, and early adversity such as that experienced by institutionalized children is associated with changes to the diurnal cortisol activity; related to this, institutionalized children can experience behavioral and emotional problems as well as health problems associated with inflammation later on (see Chapter 26 for a detailed discussion of this issue). Of note, it has been hypothesized that the transition between middle childhood and adolescence might constitute an additional sensitive period for the development of the stress response system; among post-institutionalized youth, those who had both earlier adoption and increased time in an adoptive home demonstrated some recovery in their diurnal cortisol slopes as they grew older (Flannery et al., 2017).

A key contributor to the heterogeneity among post-institutionalized adopted children is the vast variability between children in the degree and duration of deprivation that they experienced. Overall, children who were adopted from qualitatively better institutions, such as those in parts of China or South Korea, tend to have more moderate levels of problems, and are commonly reported to have some difficulty with behavior problems, social problems, and attention problems (Dalen, 2001; Tan & Marfo, 2016; Tan, Marfo, & Dedrick, 2010). Children adopted from psychosocially depriving institutions such as those in St. Petersburg, Russian Federation are associated with a relatively higher level of problems, with executive function problems, externalizing behavior problems, and social problems most common (Julian & McCall, 2016; Merz & McCall, 2010; Merz, McCall, & Groza, 2013). Children who were adopted from globally depriving institutions such as those of 1990s' Romania tend to have the most significant and lasting problems, including quasi-autistic behaviors and stunted physical growth, in addition to behavior problems, inattention/overactivity, and attachment and social difficulties (Rutter et al., 2010). Additionally, within a given country of origin, measures of pre-adoption adversity have been found to associate with rate of behavior problems reported over time, again pointing to the critical role of quality of pre-adoptive care in predicting children's outcomes (Tan & Marfo, 2016).

Importantly, when the quality of social-emotional care within an institution has been improved, the development of children residing in those institutions improves as well (McCall et al., 2010; Smyke et al., 2002; The St. Petersburg-USA Orphanage Research Team, 2008), and some of these developmental improvements are maintained after children are adopted into families (Julian et al., 2019; McCall et al., 2016). Substantial improvements in children's development are also observed when children are moved from globally depriving institutions into foster care (Smyke, Zeanah, Fox, Nelson, & Guthrie, 2010), or from institutions into adoptive homes (van IJzendoorn, Bakermans-Kranenburg, & Juffer, 2007; van IJzendoorn & Juffer, 2006). As this research demonstrates, the quality of care a child experiences – while residing in an institution or elsewhere – has a considerable impact on their developmental outcomes.

The effect of prolonged institutionalization on a young child's development is thus intimately connected to the quality of care experienced in the institution. Broadly, a young child might be able to withstand a year or more of institutionalization in a qualitatively better institution with few apparent lasting effects, but a matter of months in a globally depriving institution can prove detrimental. Interestingly, however, the effect of duration of institutionalization – often estimated by the proxy measure of age at adoption – is for most outcomes not continuous, but rather a step function. Specifically, there is often a "cut-off" age at adoption such that children adopted before that cut-off age are similar to parent-reared children with respect to the nature and extent of problems they experience, but children adopted after that cut-off age have an elevated rate of problems (Julian, 2013). As age at adoption increases beyond that specified "cut-off" age, however, there are typically no further increases in problems. The age when the step function occurs tends to vary across studies, but is generally in line with the severity of institutional deprivation experienced by a given sample. For example, for children adopted from the globally depriving institutions of 1990s' Romania, there is often a step function at approximately six months of age at adoption (Beckett et al., 2002; Kreppner et al., 2007; Stevens et al., 2008). For children adopted from socially-emotionally depriving institutions in St. Petersburg, Russian Federation, a similar step function is seen at approximately 18 months of age at adoption (Julian & McCall, 2016; Merz & McCall, 2010, 2011).

Resilience

While problems such as those discussed above are known to be more common among post-institutionalized adopted children than among parent-reared non-adopted children, only some children who experience institutional care go on to experience these problems as they grow older. Even among children adopted after six months of age from globally depriving Romanian institutions, up to 20% reach adulthood without reporting any significant emotional or behavioral difficulties (Sonuga-Barke et al., 2017). There are numerous factors that might contribute to some children demonstrating resilience in the face of institutional rearing. It is possible, for instance, that individual differences in quality of care within the institution contribute to differences in outcomes, as youth who are "favorites" in the institution might receive more sensitive and responsive care than those less favored by caregivers (Smyke et al., 2007). While it would also be prudent to consider whether some children had positive experiences prior to institutional care that buffered them from the effects of institutionalization, most children enter institutional care soon after birth, with later-arriving children more likely to have experienced abuse or neglect in their family of origin (Hawk et al., 2012). Factors such as birthweight and prematurity have also largely not accounted for differences in outcomes among post-institutionalized children (Kreppner et al., 2007; Merz & McCall, 2010, 2011; Sonuga-Barke et al., 2008), but other prenatal factors including prenatal stress, nutrition, and substance exposure have not been sufficiently examined in the literature. Genetic factors have been identified as critical in predicting children's degree of responsivity to environmental factors (National Scientific Council on the Developing Child, 2005). Children who show the most resiliency might be those who are genetically least vulnerable to environmental effects (Brett et al., 2015; Rutter, 2003; Rutter, Moffitt, & Caspi, 2006), or interaction of genotype with the duration of institutionalization may predict problems in some domains such as attention or emotional problems (van IJzendoorn et al., 2011).

Sleeper effects

While it might generally be expected for the effects of a given experience – such as institutionalization – to be most prominent proximal to that experience, the effects of prolonged institutionalization are often most apparent later on in development (see review in Julian, 2013). In multiple independent samples of post-institutionalized youth, effects of age at adoption were less apparent in early childhood, and more notable in adolescence (Merz & McCall, 2010; Rutter et al., 2010; Smyke et al., 2012; Verhulst, Althaus, & Versluis-Den Bieman, 1990; Wolkind, 1974), with most types of problems persisting into young adulthood (Sonuga-Barke et al., 2017). This pattern suggests that the problems that post-institutionalized children experience are likely not behaviors that were acquired through learning, because if that were the case, they would be expected to be most pronounced immediately after adoption. Instead, this "sleeper effect" suggests that institutionalization may have effects on certain basic skills, the effects of which are not apparent until later on in development (Zeanah, Gunnar, McCall, Kreppner, & Fox, 2011). For post-institutionalized children, it could also be that the increased social and behavioral demands and expectations of adolescence prove particularly challenging, making their deficits more apparent. Support and guidance from parents and other caring adults might help post-institutionalized youth to meet social and behavioral expectations earlier in childhood, but when that support naturally fades as children enter adolescence, and the social environment becomes increasingly complex, post-institutionalized children may experience more difficulty.

Timing of institutionalization and sensitive periods

Most post-institutionalized children entered institutional care soon after birth, rendering it impossible to disentangle the effects of duration of institutionalization from the timing of institutionalization. However, given that the first two years of life are known to be critical in children's development of attachment relationships (Bowlby, 1969), there is reason to think that institutionalization during these years might have a particularly negative impact on children's development. In fact, studies of social deprivation in primates have demonstrated that earlier social deprivation proves much more detrimental than later social deprivation (Harlow & Novak, 1973; Suomi, 2003). The data are more limited in the human literature, but here too, evidence points to institutionalization having particularly prominent effects when it occurs in the first two years of life (Lee et al., 2010; Wolkind, 1974). Specifically among institutionalized youth, entry into institutional care before the first birthday is associated with increased risk of insecure attachment (Lionetti, Pastore, & Barone, 2015).

This increased propensity for problems among children who were institutionalized during the first two years of life, and the tendency for the age at adoption effect for many outcomes to be in the form of a step function rather than a linear function, suggests that sensitive periods might contribute to these effects. Traditionally, sensitive periods are thought of as distinct periods of time in development during which individuals are especially susceptible to the effects of experience. Sensitive periods are typically understood to be universal for a given species, but our current understanding suggests that the temporal boundaries of a sensitive period can be somewhat flexible, especially in the context of early deprivation (Knudsen, 2004; Zeanah et al., 2011). The existence of a step function for age at adoption – a rather abrupt distinction between those with a lower versus higher risk for problems – suggests that some kind of intraorganismic change may have taken place (Kreppner et al., 2007). Epigenetic changes are hypothesized to be a potential biological mechanism behind these behavioral trends, as stress elevations are linked to epigenetic changes and associated changes to the biological stress response, brain architecture and brain chemistry, and behavior in animal models (National Scientific Council on the Developing Child, 2010; Shonkoff, Boyce, & McEwen, 2009). Epigenetic processes have recently been identified as a key pathway linking adversity during early sensitive or critical periods to behavioral and biological outcomes much later in life in humans as well (Vaiserman & Koliada, 2017). It is possible that epigenetic changes might be triggered by a shorter amount of time residing in a globally depriving institution (e.g., 6 months), or a longer amount of time residing in a socially-emotionally depriving institution (e.g., 18 months).

While research has not yet examined these specific timing-related hypotheses related to age or duration of deprivation, research has begun to examine whether there is evidence of epigenetic changes among post-institutionalized children. For instance, some differences in DNA methylation patterns have been detected between post-institutionalized adopted children and non-adopted parent-reared children, particularly in stress-related genes, though more research is needed to replicate these findings (Esposito et al., 2016; Non et al., 2016). Importantly, one study suggests that increased time in institutional care was linked to lower DNA methylation at two sites of stress-related genes (Non et al., 2016). Telomeres, which are found at the end of chromosomes, shorten in response to environmental stress exposure and are linked to negative health outcomes when shortened (Price, Kao, Burgers, Carpenter, &

Tyrka, 2013). Recent research has found that early institutional rearing is associated with accelerated telomere shortening, with duration of deprivation predicting the degree of shortening, and with transfer into a more supportive caregiving environment ineffective in reversing these changes (Humphreys et al., 2016). This, too, points to a potential sensitive period early in life such that among children who were exposed to deficient social-emotional care in an institution throughout their first months or years of life, permanent cellular changes may occur, contributing to later health and behavioral problems.

Practice and policy implications

A wide body of research demonstrates that prolonged early institutionalization is associated with significant and lasting effects on children's development. While some children exhibit remarkable resiliency in the face of incredibly challenging early circumstances, the unfortunate truth is that as little as six months in a globally depriving institution or 18 months in a socially-emotionally depriving institution is associated with a notable increase in risk of later problems (Julian, 2013). Literature on the effects of improving institutions or transferring children into qualitatively better foster care or adoptive homes makes clear that the quality of social-emotional care children receive on a day-to-day basis is a crucial predictor of their later functioning. For children without permanent parents who are placed in institutions, early transfer into family care is in their best interest as developmental outcomes are notably better for children who are adopted or in foster care relative to those who remain in institutions (Julian & McCall, 2011), and a later age at adoption is associated with higher risk of later problems (Julian, 2013).

However, early outplacement is not always feasible due to children having unclear status (e.g., abandoned or no birth certificate), delays in obtaining signed relinquishment from biological parents, and lengthy administrative and judicial procedures. For children who must remain in the child welfare system, foster care placement might serve as a more developmentally supportive placement alternative. Foster care is not widely implemented in many low-resource countries in which institutionalization is common, so there could be numerous barriers to implementation. However, foster care programs have been developed and implemented in countries where it was previously not widely available, and children who were randomly assigned to transfer from institutional care into foster care showed improved developmental outcomes (Zeanah, Humphreys, Fox, & Nelson, 2017).

While placement of children into family care should be a priority, it is likely that despite our best efforts, many children will remain in institutional care due to the high numbers of orphaned and abandoned children in many countries and the limited resources some countries are able to devote to family care. For those who must remain in institutional care, it is critical that efforts are made to improve the quality of social-emotional care within institutions. When a more family-like environment is created within an institution, and caregivers are trained to provide more sensitive and responsive care, children in turn show improvements in their development (Cohen's $d = 1.05$) that are comparable in magnitude to the effect size of adoption (Cohen's $d = 1.17$; Bakermans-Kranenburg, van IJzendoorn, & Juffer, 2008; The St. Petersburg-USA Orphanage Research Team, 2008). The extant research suggests that the most critical aspect of institutional care with regard to young children's developmental outcomes is the quality of the social-emotional relationships between caregivers and resident children, so it is this aspect of care that should be at the forefront of attention when designing and implementing interventions within institutions (Barone, Dellagiulia, & Lionetti, 2016).

When children who have experienced prolonged institutional care are adopted into families, they experience rapid catch-up growth (van IJzendoorn et al., 2007), but remain at elevated risk for later problems in domains including attention and executive function problems, attachment and social relationship difficulties, and externalizing and internalizing behavior problems (Julian, 2013; Rutter et al., 2010). Importantly, for many children, childhood is a time of positive functioning, and problems only emerge or become clinically significant as they reach adolescence. Research has made clear connections between the problems that post-institutionalized adopted youth typically experience and their early life adversity, but it is common for adoptive parents to blame themselves when problems emerge, and to be reluctant to seek support services (Alessia & Roufeil, 2012). It is therefore critical that adoption agencies provide adoptive families with psychoeducational material about the various ways that post-institutionalized youth's early experiences might affect their development not only in early childhood, but throughout their school years, adolescence, and young adulthood.

When clinical services are indicated, a trauma-informed lens is crucial, as many of the difficulties that post-institutionalized youth experience are known to be a consequence of their early life adversity. In line with a wide body of work on children who have experienced trauma, clinical interventions that bolster the parent–child relationship are likely to be most effective (Julian, Lawler, & Rosenblum, 2017). A secure parent–child attachment relationship helps to buffer a young child's stress response (Gunnar & Quevedo, 2007) and helps a child to develop the capacity for self-regulation (Calkins & Johnson, 1998). Specifically among post-institutionalized children and their adoptive parents, improving attachment relationships is associated with improvement in social-emotional adjustment, even for children who were adopted at a relatively later age (Barone, Lionetti, & Green, 2017). There is also evidence that parents' mental state language (e.g., using words like *think*, *feel*, *know*, *remember*, *happy*, and *angry*) relates to outcomes among post-institutionalized adopted children (Tarullo et al., 2016). Specifically, adoptive parents who use more mental state language have children who have greater emotion understanding. Greater emotion understanding is in turn related to fewer internalizing and externalizing problems. Thus, helping parents of post-institutionalized adopted children to use more mental state language could be one way to help later-adopted youth to gain skills that will ultimately help them to achieve better outcomes.

Further, interventions that target interpersonal relationships, particularly those tailored for youth with histories of deficient early relationships, are likely to prove beneficial. For instance, Child Parent Psychotherapy for preschool-aged and younger children (Lieberman & Van Horn, 2004), Interpersonal Therapy for Adolescents (IPT-A; Mufson, Weissman, Moreau, & Garfinkel, 1999), and Skills Training in Affective and Interpersonal Regulation for Adolescents (STAIR-A; Gudiño, Leonard, & Cloitre, 2016) are likely to meet the needs of children who were adopted at a relatively older age from institutional care (Doyle & Cicchetti, 2017).

This line of work studying children adopted following prolonged institutional care clearly demonstrates the lasting impact of deficient early caregiving relationships on children's development. It is fitting then that this work also points to several routes for future intervention work. First, caregiving relationships must be improved for young children in the child welfare system, whether they must remain in institutional care or if they transition into a family care setting. Second, after adoption, interventions must also focus on bolstering adoptees' (and parents') attachment relationships and interpersonal skills as healthy relationships are foundational to physical and mental health and resilience.

References

Alessia, K., & Roufeil, L. (2012). "It's quite a journey": Australian parents' experience of adopting older children from overseas orphanages. *Children Australia, 37*(04), 161–169. doi:10.1017/cha.2012.37

Bakermans-Kranenburg, M. J., van IJzendoorn, M. H., & Juffer, F. (2008). Earlier is better: A meta-analysis of 70 years of intervention improving cognitive development in institutionalized children. *Monographs of the Society for Research in Child Development, 73*(3), 279–293. doi:10.1111/j.1540-5834.2008.00498.x

Barone, L., Dellagiulia, A., & Lionetti, F. (2016). When the primary caregiver is missing: Investigating proximal and distal variables involved in institutionalised children's adjustment. *Child Abuse Review, 25*(6), 454–468. doi:10.1002/car.2365

Barone, L., Lionetti, F., & Green, J. (2017). A matter of attachment? How adoptive parents foster post-institutionalized children's social and emotional adjustment. *Attachment & Human Development, 19*(4), 323–339. doi:10.1080/14616734.2017.1306714

Beckett, C., Bredenkamp, D., Castle, J., Groothues, C., O'Connor, T. G., & Rutter, M.; The English and Romanian Adoptees Study Team. (2002). Behavior patterns associated with institutional deprivation: A study of children adopted from Romania. *Journal of Developmental and Behavioral Pediatrics, 23*(5), 297–303.

Bowlby, J. (1969). *Attachment and loss: Attachment.* New York: Basic Books.

Brett, H., Humphreys, K. L., Smyke, A. T., Gleason, M. M., Nelson, C. A., Zeanah, C. H., ... Drury, S. S. (2015). Serotonin transporter linked polymorphic region (5-HTTLPR) genotype moderates the longitudinal impact of early caregiving on externalizing behavior. *Development and Psychopathology, 27*(1), 7–18. doi:10.1017/S0954579414001266

Bruce, J., Tarullo, A. R., & Gunnar, M. R. (2009). Disinhibited social behavior among internationally adopted children. *Development and Psychopathology, 21*(1), 157–171. doi:10.1017/S0954579409000108

Calkins, S. D., & Johnson, M. C. (1998). Toddler regulation of distress to frustrating events: Temperamental and maternal correlates. *Infant Behavior and Development, 21*(3), 379–395. doi:10.1016/S0163-6383(98)90015-7

Cecil, C. A. M., Viding, E., Fearon, P., Glaser, D., & McCrory, E. J. (2017). Disentangling the mental health impact of childhood abuse and neglect. *Child Abuse & Neglect, 63*, 106–119. doi:10.1016/j.chiabu.2016.11.024

Cicchetti, D., Rogosch, F. A., & Toth, S. L. (2011). The effects of child maltreatment and polymorphisms of the serotonin transporter and dopamine D4 receptor genes on infant attachment and intervention efficacy. *Development and Psychopathology, 23*(2), 357–372. doi:10.1017/S0954579411000113

Dalen, M. (2001). School performances among internationally adopted children in Norway. *Adoption Quarterly, 5*(2), 39–58. doi:10.1300/J145v05n02_03

Doyle, C. M., & Cicchetti, D. (2017). From the cradle to the grave: The effect of adverse caregiving environments on attachment and relationships throughout the lifespan. *Clinical Psychology: Science and Practice, 24*(2), 203–217. doi:10.1111/cpsp.12192.

Esposito, E. A., Jones, M. J., Doom, J. R., MacIsaac, J. L., Gunnar, M. R., & Kobor, M. S. (2016). Differential DNA methylation in peripheral blood mononuclear cells in adolescents exposed to significant early but not later childhood adversity. *Development and Psychopathology, 28*(4pt2), 1385–1399. doi:10.1017/s0954579416000055

Flannery, J. E., Gabard-Durnam, L. J., Shapiro, M., Goff, B., Caldera, C., Louie, J., ... Tottenham, N. (2017). Diurnal cortisol after early institutional care - Age matters. *Developmental Cognitive Neuroscience, 25*, 160–166. doi:10.1016/j.dcn.2017.03.006

Fox, S. E., Levitt, P., & Nelson, C. A. (2010). How the timing and quality of early experiences influence the development of brain architecture. *Child Development, 81*(1), 28–40. doi:10.1111/j.1467-8624.2009.01380.x

Glaser, D. (2000). Child abuse and neglect and the brain – A review. *Journal of Child Psychology and Psychiatry and Allied Disciplines, 41*(1), 97–116. doi:10.1111/1469-7610.00551

Gudiño, O. G., Leonard, S., & Cloitre, M. (2016). STAIR-A for girls: A pilot study of a skills-based group for traumatized youth in an urban school setting. *Journal of Child & Adolescent Trauma, 9*(1), 67–79. doi:10.1007/s40653-015-0061-0

Gunnar, M. R. (2001). Effects of early deprivation: Findings from orphanage-reared infants and children. In C. A. Nelson & M. Luciana (Eds.), *Handbook of developmental cognitive neuroscience* (pp. 617–629). Cambridge, MA: MIT Press.

Gunnar, M. R., & Quevedo, K. (2007). The neurobiology of stress and development. *Annual Review of Psychology, 58*, 145–173. doi:10.1146/annurev.psych.58.110405.085605

Harlow, H. F., & Novak, M. A. (1973). Psychopathological perspectives. *Perspectives in Biology and Medicine, 16*(3), 461–478.

Hawk, B., McCall, R. B., Groark, C. J., Muhamedrahimov, R. J., Palmov, O. I., & Nikiforova, N. V. (2012). Age at adoption: A measure of time in the orphanage or child-specific factors?. *Adoption Quarterly, 15*(1), 18–34. doi:10.1080/10926755.2012.661331

Hodel, A. S., Hunt, R. H., Cowell, R. A., Van Den Heuvel, S. E., Gunnar, M. R., & Thomas, K. M. (2015). Duration of early adversity and structural brain development in post-institutionalized adolescents. *NeuroImage, 105*, 112–119. doi:10.1016/j.neuroimage.2014.10.020

Humphreys, K. L., Esteves, K., Zeanah, C. H., Fox, N. A., Nelson, C. A., & Drury, S. S. (2016). Accelerated telomere shortening: Tracking the lasting impact of early institutional care at the cellular level. *Psychiatry Research, 246*, 95–100. doi:10.1016/j.psychres.2016.09.023

Julian, M. M. (2013). Age at adoption from institutional care as a window into the lasting effects of early experiences. *Clinical Child and Family Psychology Review, 16*(2), 101–145. doi:10.1007/s10567-013-0130-6

Julian, M. M., Lawler, J. M., & Rosenblum, K. L. (2017). Caregiver-child relationships in early childhood: Interventions to promote well-being and reduce risk for psychopathology. *Current Behavioral Neuroscience Reports, 4*(2), 87–98. doi:10.1007/s40473-017-0110-0

Julian, M. M., & McCall, R. B. (2011). The development of children within alternative residential care environments. *International Journal of Child & Family Welfare, 14*(3–4), 119–147.

Julian, M. M., & McCall, R. B. (2016). Social skills in children adopted from socially-emotionally depriving institutions. *Adoption Quarterly, 19*(1), 44–62. doi:10.1080/10926755.2015.1088106

Julian, M. M., McCall, R. B., Groark, C. J., Muhamedrahimov, R. J., Palmov, O. I., & Nikiforova, N. V. (2019). Development of children adopted to the United States following a social–emotional intervention in St. Petersburg (Russian Federation) institutions. *Applied Developmental Science, 23*, 273–293. doi:10.1080/10888691.2017.1420480

Knudsen, E. I. (2004). Sensitive periods in the development of the brain and behavior. *Journal of Cognitive Neuroscience, 16*(8), 1412–1425. doi:10.1162/0898929042304796

Kreppner, J. M., O'Connor, T. G., Rutter, M., & The English and Romanian Adoptees Study Team. (2001). Can inattention/overactivity be an institutional deprivation syndrome?. *Journal of Abnormal Child Psychology, 29*(6), 513–528.

Kreppner, J. M., Rutter, M., Beckett, C., Castle, J., Colvert, E., Groothues, C., … Sonuga-Barke, E. J. S. (2007). Normality and impairment following profound early institutional deprivation: A longitudinal follow-up into early adolescence. *Developmental Psychology, 43*(4), 931–946. doi:10.1037/0012-1649.43.4.931

Lee, R. M., Seol, K. O., Sung, M., & Miller, M. J. The Minnesota International Adoption Project Team. (2010). The behavioral development of Korean children in institutional care and international adoptive families. *Developmental Psychology, 46*(2), 468–478. doi:10.1037/a0017358

Lieberman, A. F., & Van Horn, P. (2004). *Don't hit my mommy: A manual for child parent psychotherapy with young witnesses of family violence*. Washington, DC: Zero to Three Press.

Lionetti, F., Pastore, M., & Barone, L. (2015). Attachment in institutionalized children: A review and meta-analysis. *Child Abuse & Neglect, 42*, 135–145. doi:10.1016/j.chiabu.2015.02.013

McCall, R. B., Groark, C. J., Fish, L., Harkins, D., Serrano, G., & Gordon, K. (2010). A socioemotional intervention in a Latin American orphanage. *Infant Mental Health Journal, 31*(5), 521–542. doi:10.1002/imhj.20270

McCall, R. B., Muhamedrahimov, R. J., Groark, C. J., Palmov, O. I., Nikiforova, N. V., Salaway, J. L., & Julian, M. M. (2016). The development of children placed into different types of Russian families following an institutional intervention. *International Perspectives in Psychology: Research, Practice, Consultation, 5*(4), 255–270. doi:10.1037/ipp0000060

Meaney, M. J. (2010). Epigenetics and the biological definition of gene x environment interactions. *Child Development, 81*(1), 41–79. doi:10.1111/j.1467-8624.2009.01381.x

Merz, E. C., & McCall, R. B. (2010). Behavior problems in children adopted from psychosocially depriving institutions. *Journal of Abnormal Child Psychology, 38*(4), 459–470. doi:10.1007/s10802-009-9383-4

Merz, E. C., & McCall, R. B. (2011). Parent ratings of executive functioning in children adopted from psychosocially depriving institutions. *Journal of Child Psychology and Psychiatry, 52*(5), 537–546. doi:10.1111/j.1469-7610.2010.02335.x

Merz, E. C., McCall, R. B., & Groza, V. K. (2013). Parent-reported executive functioning in postinstitutionalized children: A follow-up study. *Journal of Clinical Child & Adolescent Psychology, 42*(5), 726–733. doi:10.1080/15374416.2013.764826

Mufson, L., Weissman, M. M., Moreau, D., & Garfinkel, R. (1999). Efficacy of interpersonal psychotherapy for depressed adolescents. *Archives of General Psychiatry, 56*(6), 573–579.

National Scientific Council on the Developing Child. (2005). Excessive stress disrupts the architecture of the developing brain: Working paper #3. Retrieved November 2, 2018, from www.developingchild.net

National Scientific Council on the Developing Child. (2010). Persistent fear and anxiety can affect young children's learning and development: Working paper #9. Retrieved November 2, 2018, from www.developingchild.net

Non, A. L., Hollister, B. M., Humphreys, K. L., Childebayeva, A., Esteves, K., Zeanah, C. H., … Drury, S. S. (2016). DNA methylation at stress-related genes is associated with exposure to early life institutionalization. *American Journal of Physical Anthropology, 161*(1), 84–93. doi:10.1002/ajpa.23010

Price, L. H., Kao, H. T., Burgers, D. E., Carpenter, L. L., & Tyrka, A. R. (2013). Telomeres and early-life stress: An overview. *Biological Psychiatry, 73*(1), 15–23. doi:10.1016/j.biopsych.2012.06.025

Roth, T. L., & Sweatt, J. D. (2011). Annual research review: Epigenetic mechanisms and environmental shaping of the brain during sensitive periods of development. *Journal of Child Psychology and Psychiatry and Allied Disciplines, 52*(4), 398–408. doi:10.1111/j.1469-7610.2010.02282.x

Rubin, D. M., O'Reilly, A. L. R., Luan, X., & Localio, A. R. (2007). The impact of placement stability on behavioral well-being for children in foster care. *Pediatrics, 119*(2), 336–344. doi:10.1542/peds.2006-1995

Rutter, M. (2003). Genetic influences on risk and protection: Implications for understanding resilience. In S. S. Luthar (Ed.), *Resilience and vulnerability: Adaptation in the context of childhood adversities* (pp. 489–509). New York: Cambridge University Press.

Rutter, M., Moffitt, T. E., & Caspi, A. (2006). Gene-environment interplay and psychopathology: Multiple varieties but real effects. *Journal of Child Psychology and Psychiatry, 47*(3–4), 226–261. doi:10.1111/j.1469-7610.2005.01557.x

Rutter, M., Sonuga-Barke, E. J. S., Beckett, C., Castle, J., Kreppner, J. M., Kumsta, R., … Bell, C. A. (2010). Deprivation-specific psychological patterns: Effects of institutional deprivation. *Monographs of the Society for Research in Child Development, 75*(1), vii-ix, 1–252.

Shonkoff, J. P., Boyce, W. T., & McEwen, B. S. (2009). Neuroscience, molecular biology, and the childhood roots of health disparities: Building a new framework for health promotion and disease prevention. *The Journal of the American Medical Association, 301*(21), 2252–2259. doi:10.1001/jama.2009.754

Smyke, A. T., Dumitrescu, A., & Zeanah, C. H. (2002). Attachment disturbances in young children. I: The continuum of caretaking casualty. *Journal of the American Academy of Child and Adolescent Psychiatry, 41*(8), 972–982. doi:10.1097/00004583-200208000-00016

Smyke, A. T., Koga, S. F., Johnson, D. E., Fox, N. A., Marshall, P. J., & Nelson, C. A.; The BEIP Core Group. (2007). The caregiving context in institution-reared and family-reared infants and toddlers in Romania. *The Journal of Child Psychology and Psychiatry and Allied Disciplines, 48*(2), 210–218.

Smyke, A. T., Zeanah, C. H., Fox, N. A., Nelson, C. A., & Guthrie, D. (2010). Placement in foster care enhances quality of attachment among young institutionalized children. *Child Development, 81*(1), 212–223. doi:10.1111/j.1467-8624.2009.01390.x

Smyke, A. T., Zeanah, C. H., Gleason, M. M., Drury, S. S., Fox, N. A., Nelson, C. A., & Guthrie, D. (2012). A randomized controlled trial comparing foster care and institutional care for children with signs of reactive attachment disorder. *American Journal of Psychiatry, 169*(5), 508–514. doi:10.1176/appi.ajp.2011.11050748

Sonuga-Barke, E. J. S., Beckett, C., Kreppner, J. M., Castle, J., Colvert, E., Stevens, S. E., … Rutter, M. (2008). Is sub-nutrition necessary for a poor outcome following early institutional deprivation?. *Developmental Medicine and Child Neurology, 50*(9), 664–671. doi:10.1111/j.1469-8749.2008.03065.x

Sonuga-Barke, E. J. S., Kennedy, M., Kumsta, R., Knights, N., Golm, D., Rutter, M., … Kreppner, J. M. (2017). Child-to-adult neurodevelopmental and mental health trajectories after early life deprivation: The young adult follow-up of the longitudinal English and Romanian Adoptees study. *The Lancet, 6736*(17), 1–10. doi:10.1016/S0140-6736(17)30045-4

The St. Petersburg-USA Orphanage Research Team. (2005). Characteristics of children, caregivers, and orphanages for young children in St. Petersburg, Russian Federation. *Journal of Applied Developmental Psychology, 26*(5), 477–506. doi:10.1016/j.appdev.2005.06.002

The St. Petersburg-USA Orphanage Research Team. (2008). The effects of early social-emotional and relationship experience on the development of young orphanage children. *Monographs of the Society for Research in Child Development, 73*(3), vii-viii, 1–297. doi:10.1111/j.1540-5834.2008.00483.x

Stevens, S. E., Sonuga-Barke, E. J. S., Kreppner, J. M., Beckett, C., Castle, J., Colvert, E., ... Rutter, M. (2008). Inattention/overactivity following early severe institutional deprivation: Presentation and associations in early adolescence. *Journal of Abnormal Child Psychology, 36*(3), 385–398. doi:10.1007/s10802-007-9185-5

Suomi, S. J. (2003). Gene-environment interactions and the neurobiology of social conflict. *Annals of the New York Academy of Sciences, 1008*, 132–139. doi:10.1196/annals.1301.014

Tan, T. X., & Marfo, K. (2016). Pre-adoption adversity and behavior problems in adopted Chinese children: A longitudinal study. *Journal of Applied Developmental Psychology, 42*, 49–57. doi:10.1016/j.appdev.2015.11.006

Tan, T. X., Marfo, K., & Dedrick, R. F. (2010). Early developmental and psychosocial risks and longitudinal behavioral adjustment outcomes for preschool-age girls adopted from China. *Journal of Applied Developmental Psychology, 31*(4), 306–314. doi:10.1016/j.appdev.2010.04.002

Tarullo, A. R., Youssef, A., Frenn, K. A., Wiik, K., Garvin, M. C., & Gunnar, M. R. (2016). Emotion understanding, parent mental state language, and behavior problems in internationally adopted children. *Development and Psychopathology, 28*(02), 371–383. doi:10.1017/S095457941500111X

Tizard, B., & Rees, J. (1975). The effect of early institutional rearing on the behaviour problems and affectional relationships of four-year-old children. *Journal of Child Psychology and Psychiatry and Allied Disciplines, 16*(1), 61–73. doi:10.1111/j.1469-7610.1975.tb01872.x

Vaiserman, A. M., & Koliada, A. K. (2017). Early-life adversity and long-term neurobehavioral outcomes: Epigenome as a bridge?. *Human Genomics, 11*(1), 1–15. doi:10.1186/s40246-017-0129-z

van der Vegt, E. J. M., van der Ende, J., Ferdinand, R. F., Verhulst, F. C., & Tiemeier, H. (2009). Early childhood adversities and trajectories of psychiatric problems in adoptees: Evidence for long lasting effects. *Journal of Abnormal Child Psychology, 37*(2), 239–249. doi:10.1007/s10802-008-9272-2

van IJzendoorn, M. H., Bakermans-Kranenburg, M. J., & Juffer, F. (2007). Plasticity of growth in height, weight, and head circumference: Meta-analytic evidence of massive catch-up after international adoption. *Journal of Developmental and Behavioral Pediatrics, 28*(4), 334–343. doi:10.1097/DBP.0b013e31811320aa

van IJzendoorn, M. H., & Juffer, F. (2006). The Emanuel Miller memorial lecture 2006: Adoption as intervention. Meta-analytic evidence for massive catch-up and plasticity in physical, socio-emotional, and cognitive development. *Journal of Child Psychology and Psychiatry, 47*(12), 1228–1245. doi:10.1111/j.1469-7610.2006.01675.x

van IJzendoorn, M. H., Palacios, J., Sonuga-Barke, E. J. S., Gunnar, M. R., Vorria, P., McCall, R. B., ... Juffer, F. (2011). I. Children in institutional care: Delayed development and resilience. *Monographs of the Society for Research in Child Development, 76*(4), 8–30. doi:10.1111/j.1540-5834.2011.00626.x

Verhulst, F. C., Althaus, M., & Versluis-Den Bieman, H. J. M. (1990). Problem behavior in international adoptees: II. Age at placement. *Journal of the American Academy of Child and Adolescent Psychiatry, 29*(1), 104–111. doi:10.1097/00004583-199001000-00016

Wolkind, S. N. (1974). The components of "affectionless psychopathy" in institutionalized children. *Journal of Child Psychology and Psychiatry and Allied Disciplines, 15*(3), 215–220. doi:10.1111/j.1469-7610.1974.tb01246.x

Zeanah, C. H., Gunnar, M. R., McCall, R. B., Kreppner, J. M., & Fox, N. A. (2011). VI. Sensitive periods. *Monographs of the Society for Research in Child Development, 76*(4), 147–162. doi:10.1111/j.1540-5834.2011.00631.x

Zeanah, C. H., Humphreys, K. L., Fox, N. A., & Nelson, C. A. (2017). Alternatives for abandoned children: Insights from the Bucharest Early Intervention Project. *Current Opinion in Psychology, 15*, 182–188. doi:10.1016/j.copsyc.2017.02.024

Zeanah, C. H., Nelson, C. A., Fox, N. A., Smyke, A. T., Marshall, P., Parker, S. W., & Koga, S. (2003). Designing research to study the effects of institutionalization on brain and behavioral development: The Bucharest Early Intervention Project. *Development and Psychopathology, 15*(4), 885–907. doi:10.1017.S0954579403000452

14

ADOPTEES WITH DISABILITIES OR MEDICALLY INVOLVED CHILDREN

A multidisciplinary approach for preparing parents, assessing the child, and supporting successful family formation

Dana E. Johnson, Judith Eckerle, Megan Bresnahan, and Maria Kroupina

Background

Intentionally adopting a child with a recognized or potential disability, once a rare event in the US, has now become the norm. This chapter traces the evolution of adoption practice over the past century and reviews advances in knowledge that inform us on the nature of disabilities in contemporary adoptees. Finally, we discuss the process of parent preparation, post-arrival medical evaluation, and mental health consultation, because most children currently being placed for adoption have risk factors for medical, developmental, and mental health problems.

Children with disabilities have long faced significant challenges surviving, much less thriving, in society. Historically, since disabilities in offspring were commonly believed to be due to parental transgression of social mores or religious teachings, children with obvious physical imperfection were regularly abandoned and often died from exposure (Boswell, 1988). Through much of history, this moral censure, lack of treatment options, and the economic burden that accompanied acceptance of a child with a disability into a family, limited the likelihood that such abandoned children would find permanence through formal or informal adoption. For those who survived, exclusion from mainstream society was a common fate. Until the late 20th century, children with disabilities were segregated in institutions where physical and social neglect, the closed environment, and lack of robust protections inherent in institutional living placed them at risk for severe developmental sequelae, physical or sexual abuse, and violation of fundamental human rights (Carr, Duff, & Craddock, 2018).

While improving, the current outlook for disabled children worldwide is mixed. In economically advanced countries, medical care, sophisticated support services for families, and enlightened government policies have supported integration of affected children into educational systems and the workforce, enabling a greater participation in society. However, where such services are lacking or the basic causes of childhood disabilities remain shrouded in superstition, families continue to face a decision whether to parent or forsake their child. Consequently, whether social services are institution- or family-based, disability remains an important driver for entry into the child protection system where adoption might be the only way to achieve permanence. Human Rights Watch has found an "overrepresentation" of children with disabilities in orphanages in India, Japan, Serbia, and Russia. In Serbia, 80 percent of children in orphanages were identified as having a disability (Rau Barriga, Buchanan, Ćerimović, & Sharma, 2017). Children with disabilities are overrepresented in foster care. In the US, 31.1 percent of children and youth 0–18 years of age in the foster care system were determined to have a disability in contrast with 5.8–6.2 percent of children of similar age in the general population (Kraus, 2017; Waldrop & Stern, 2003).

Adoption of children with disabilities

In 1909, a US Conference for the Care of Dependent Children developed recommendations on the importance of family-based vs. institutional care, establishing the foundation for child welfare and adoption practice in the United States (Children's Bureau, 1967). By the 1930s, adoption was an established method of building a family for White, married couples. During this "first wave" of adoption in the US, adoption practice focused on finding children for families rather than families for children, rigidly adhering to racial boundaries, and employing secrecy to avoid stigma and social sanctions for both birth and adoptive parents. Since virtually all families willing to consider adoption sought White, healthy infants, children with characteristics that positioned them outside this prized group were more difficult to place and were labeled as having "special needs," e.g., older age, racial differences, sibling groups, known sexual or physical abuse, or a disability. These children were commonly considered unadoptable (Bohman, 1970).

The second wave: International and special needs adoption

In 1968 an estimated 86,300 unrelated adoption placements occurred, but by 1975 the total number had dropped precipitously to 47,700 (Placek, 1999). This change coincided with an era that saw both increasing social tolerance and financial support for unmarried mothers and enhanced reproductive control through reliable contraception and increased availability of legal abortion services. The net result was that fewer infants were born to single mothers and even fewer were relinquished for adoption. Prior to 1973, the percentage of infants relinquished for adoption by never-married women less than 45 years old was 8.7 percent. From 1989–95, the figure was 0.9 percent (Miller & Coyl, 2000).

The shortfall between the ongoing demand and decreasing supply was filled with children adopted from abroad and children with special needs. During the same period when domestic adoptions decreased 46 percent, international adoption more than tripled from 1,612 to 5,663 (Altstein & Simon, 1991). Concurrently, the adoption of children with special needs also increased. Professional practice in adoption began to focus on permanence and the best interest of children (Baker, 2007). In the case of children with disabilities, the shrinking pool of available children as well as changes in adoption practice may have catalyzed the initial rise in the number of placements. However, additional factors, such as medical advances that improved outcomes (e.g., effective HIV treatment), a more inclusive view of the contributions of individuals with disabilities to society (as exemplified in the Americans with Disabilities Act of 1990), simple altruism, establishment of adoption agencies that specialized in placing children with disabilities, as well as follow-up studies showing that children with disabilities could be successfully integrated into adoptive families, also contributed to growth in this field (Baker, 2007).

The third wave: At-risk and medically complex children

The 1990s saw not only a quantitative increase in international adoptees to the US, but also a qualitative change in their overall well-being. From 1972 through 1990, more than 50 percent of international adoptees were from Korea (Altstein & Simon, 1991). These children were relinquished by generally healthy women stigmatized by single parenthood, raised in foster families, provided a high level of medical care, and adopted as infants. In contrast, adoptees from Eastern Europe who began arriving in large numbers in the early 1990s were more likely to be abandoned by poorly nourished, destitute mothers who had often abused alcohol or intravenous drugs. These children were housed in orphanages where they received inadequate medical care (Johnson, 2000). The 1990s also brought a deeper understanding of how early childhood experiences in a developmental environment characterized by prenatal risk and postnatal social, nutritional, and medical deprivation profoundly affected brain development (Shonkoff & Phillips, 2000). Children from these environments experience unbuffered periods of stress, generally referred to as "toxic stress," which exacts a toll in most developmental areas and is associated with a dose-dependent negative effect on physical and mental health in later life (Centers for Disease Control and Prevention, 2018; Danese & McEwen, 2012; Dozier, Roben, Caron, Hoye, & Bernard, 2018; Shonkoff & Garner, 2012). Considering the profound adversity experienced within institutional care settings in terms of abuse, neglect, and exposure to violence, the findings that these experiences were associated with important medical problems as well as both acute and persistent developmental, emotional, and behavioral disabilities in post-institutionalized adoptees were not surprising (Kumsta et al., 2015; McCall, van IJzendoorn, Juffer, Groark, & Groza, 2011; Nelson, Fox, & Zeanah, 2014). Based on 2000 US census data, disabilities in international children adopted to the US (11.7 percent) were similar to domestic adoptees (12.2 percent) but the odds of disability, relative to domestic adoptees, were twice as large or more in adoptees from Romania, Bulgaria, and other Eastern European countries (Kreider & Cohen, 2009).

The incidence of significant medical issues as well as long-term disabilities in international adoptees continues to increase, as illustrated by the evolution in adoptions from China, the principal sending country to the US since 2004. Following gradual relaxation and then termination of the one-child policy in 2015 (Buckley, 2015), domestic placements through the Chinese social welfare system have grown to outnumber international placements almost 6:1 (Ministry of Civil Affairs, 2018). Following the pattern in nascent domestic adoption programs worldwide, Chinese families seeking to adopt prefer healthy, young children. Of those children available for adoption that remain institutionalized, 98 percent are categorized as being disabled (Vanderklippe, 2018). Therefore, Chinese children currently available for international adoption all have medical or mental disabilities that range from minor to extremely complex (Crary, 2010; Curry, 2018). These children are also older. In 2004,

94 percent of children adopted from China were 2 years of age or younger vs. only 17 percent in 2017 (US Department of State-Bureau of Consular Affairs, 2018). Consequently, adoptees from China now experience longer periods within institutional care and are at substantially increased risk of secondary cognitive, emotional, and behavioral sequelae related to prolonged social deprivation (Tan & Robinson, 2018). Similar changes have been observed in most sending countries over the past decade.

Recapitulating the abrupt decrease in White infant adoptions in the late 1960s, the number of international adoptions to the US have fallen 79 percent since 2004, returning to levels (4,714 in FY 2017) not seen since the 1970s (Altstein & Simon, 1991; US Department of State-Bureau of Consular Affairs, 2018). The reasons behind this decline include issues that decreased both demand (e.g., improved infertility treatments) and availability (e.g. Russia banning US citizens from adopting in 2013) (Budiman & Lopez, 2017; Westerman, 2018). In contrast, adoptions from foster care in the US have increased over the past 20 years. Following passage of the Adoption and Safe Families Act of 1997 – legislation designed to speed placement of waiting children into permanent homes – the number of adoptions from foster care rose 54 percent from 36,650 in 1998 to 53,549 in 2015 (Johnston, 2017). However, as with institutionalized children, the dose-dependent impact of adversity on children prior to and after entering foster care has been increasingly recognized (Turney & Wildeman, 2017).

Parent preparation

A high percentage of children now being placed through international adoption or from foster care have either recognized medical problems and/or risk factors that increase the likelihood of developmental, emotional, and behavioral disabilities (O'Dell, McCall, & Groark, 2015). Even children placed as infants through private adoption might share such risks due to intrauterine drug or alcohol exposure or maternal stress during pregnancy (Mulder et al., 2002). Thus, it is critically important to fully and accurately inform adoptive parents about issues they will likely face when parenting a specific child.

Medical providers play a crucial role in parent education and should be fully integrated into the adoption preparation process. Establishing appropriate expectations is critical as expectations minus reality equals disappointment – a state that can contribute to adoption dissatisfaction and disruption (Coakley & Berrick, 2008; Palacios, Sánchez-Sandoval, & Lee, 2006). Unpublished data from the Minnesota International Adoption Project (Hellerstedt et al., 2008) confirmed that families who spoke with a medical provider during the preadoption period reported fewer negative feelings about adoption and fewer incorrect expectations.

Discussions with medical providers can begin even before a specific child is identified. Many agencies have families complete a checklist indicating which medical conditions they are willing to consider. The goal of consultation at this, or any point in the adoption process, is to help parents knowledgeably ascertain whether their financial and emotional resources, social network, marriage, and family structure are congruent with the likely needs of a particular child.

While a full exploration of the process for evaluating referral information is beyond the scope of this chapter, a list of information helpful in assessing a child's condition (Table 14.1), general guidelines for interpreting this information (Table 14.2), and a list of factors that increase the risk of developmental, behavioral, and emotional problems (Table 14.3) which can help families establish appropriate expectations, were created based on over 30 years of experience with over 25,000 referrals.

Table 14.1 Information helpful in assessing a child prior to adoption

- History, including perinatal risk factors, particularly maternal alcohol use
- Birth and current measurements (height, weight, and head circumference)
- Laboratory tests with dates (hepatitis B and C, syphilis, HIV, and hemoglobin)
- Developmental information (particularly if standardized testing can be obtained)
- Detailed information about the child's disability or medical condition
    - On what information did they base the diagnosis?
- Photographs of child's face (close up, looking directly at the camera, mouth closed and not smiling) to look for facial features diagnostic of fetal alcohol spectrum disorder
- Video demonstrating developmental milestones (five minutes or longer with the child in minimal clothing [i.e., infants in only diaper] playing and interacting with peers/caregivers in their customary environment)
- Photographs and video of the specific disability or condition

Table 14.2 Interpreting information

- Growth (use World Health Organization curves)
    - Most foster care: normal growth
    - Most institutional care: growth impairment
- Development
    - Foster care: gross motor delays up to age 8–10 months (no "tummy time")
    - Institutional care:
        - Gross and fine motor delays until age 8–9 months and then catch-up with most children walking by 18 months
        - Language delays that become more significant with greater time in institutional care
        - Social:
            - Indiscriminate friendliness
            - Institutional quasi-autistic behavior (stereotypies) in profoundly deprived children can be confused with true autism spectrum disorders
- Interpretation of laboratory tests
    - Date of testing needed for appropriate interpretation of most laboratory tests
- Actual vs. reported age
    - Almost impossible to determine the true age of a child vs. the reported age unless height, dental, bone, or developmental age are significantly advanced over reported age. Most children experiencing adversity will be behind in these areas.

The accuracy of a potential adoptee's medical and social information varies widely depending on the capabilities of the medical system in the country of origin, the quality of translations, as well as the training, experience, and personal biases of the professionals responsible for collecting and reporting referral information. The experience of health care professionals familiar with the issues in adoption medicine can help families accurately interpret the often-confusing referral information and realistically gauge whether additional information should, or even could, be obtained. While asking for more information rarely imperils the child's eventual placement, prolonging the decision-making process with repeated attempts to obtain every scrap of data is rarely in the best interests of either the

Table 14.3 Factors that increase the risk of identifying developmental and mental health problems after placement (risks are additive)

- Institutional care
- Age at arrival (> 2 years)
- Birthweight < 2.5 kg
- ≥ 2 caregiving disruptions
- Head circumference < –3 SD
- Severe developmental delays (developmental age/chronologic age × 100 ≤ 50) or clear autistic behavior

child or the adoptive family. Delays prolong the period of adversity and, irrespective of how much additional information is obtained, risk will never be completely eliminated, and some questions will never be answered. Factors to consider when requesting additional information include how long it will take and whether the results will alter the medical opinion or make a difference in the parent's decision to adopt. Almost all families who adopt internationally have health insurance (Hellerstedt et al., 2008) and children adopted from the foster care system often qualify for government-sponsored long-term medical assistance. Nevertheless, families must consider the range of services that their child might require as not all might be available in their community or adequately covered by insurance.

While the goal in most cases is simply to provide information to assist the family in their decision-making process, additional exploration of parental expectations is warranted in situations where there is a high likelihood of severe family stress or disruption, such as adoption of a child with fetal alcohol spectrum disorder (FASD), a history of sexual or severe physical abuse, large sibling groups with multiple risk factors, and children with profound cognitive delays or signs of autism spectrum disorder. In such situations, there is a chance that the child might never achieve complete independence and the family must consider whether they have the desire as well as the financial, social, and personal resources to parent a child who requires life-long medical care and direct supervision.

The comprehensive assessment for foster/adopted children

The remainder of the chapter will focus on how a multidisciplinary team focused on adopted children with complex problems can help ease the transition of a child into their new family. While actual and potential disabilities must be addressed, this process should give equal attention to the strengths of the child and family, recognizing how powerful adoptive families can be in promoting recovery from illness and adversity. An initial examination is recommended two to three weeks after a child arrives in their adoptive home. Assuming the child is not acutely ill, this brief hiatus between arrival and first visit allows the family and child to adapt to one another, improves child cooperation during the initial assessment, and permits the family to formulate specific questions.

Medical assessment

The first visit includes testing for major infectious diseases, vaccination status, growth delays, and nutritional deficiencies. Not only is this evaluation important for the adopted child's health, but undiagnosed infectious diseases can be transmitted to members of the adoptive family (Sciauvaud et al., 2014). Specific recommendations will vary depending on review of the child's medical records and the physical examination, but a variety of testing regimens have been proposed (Adoption Medicine Clinic, 2018; Eckerle, Howard, & John, 2013; Jones & Committee On Early Childhood, Adoption, & Dependent Care, 2012). Since the risk of hearing and vision problems is much higher in these children, arrangements should be made for testing through pediatric ophthalmologists and audiologists (Eckerle et al., 2014). Developmental and mental health assessments are a critical part of this initial visit and will be discussed below in detail. Finally, specific referrals for medical specialty consultation as well as dental care are arranged. It is important to note that a variety of conditions, previously unknown, are often diagnosed after arrival (Miller & Hendrie, 2000).

Children should be rescreened six months post-placement. At this time, growth trajectory is assessed and necessary infectious disease and health screening tests are finalized (Adoption Medicine Clinic, University of Minnesota, 2018). Catch-up growth is usually so robust that most children are now within the normal range in height, weight, and head circumference. If not, further diagnostic work-up is warranted, often in consultation with a pediatric endocrinologist. Calorie intake is an important factor in catch-up growth (Miller et al., 2010) and feeding problems are common in children with sensory-motor problems or a history of adverse early feeding experiences (Rowell, 2012). Thus, referral to a dietician and/or feeding specialist might be helpful in these cases. This is also a good time to evaluate family adjustment, as the "honeymoon period" may be waning and issues with sleep, eating, attachment, tantrums, rocking, or other self-stimulating behaviors may be emerging. Parents know much more about their child at this point and are better able to integrate discussions on further medical referrals, developmental and behavioral interventions, and other parenting practices.

Regular visits to the pediatrician should continue throughout childhood and adolescence. School age children will encounter ever increasing expectations for academics, attention, and behavior, and children who initially did well in the early grades might begin to experience challenges. It is also important to monitor for signs of early or rapidly advancing puberty, which is more common in adopted children, particularly girls (Johnson & Gunnar, 2011). Further screening should be done at several time points for signs of FASD as children with prenatal alcohol exposure are at higher risk (Astley, Stachowiak, Clarren, & Clausen, 2002; Landgren, Svensson, Stromland, & Andersson Gronlund, 2010).

Developmental assessment

Many factors aside from medical conditions contribute to delays in development among children currently being placed for adoption. Lack of developmental stimulation leads to delays due to a lack of opportunity, while sensory deprivation contributes to delays particularly for sensory processing skills. If a child is not exposed to normal sensory input (e.g. is not held, rocked, provided with eye contact, etc.) or has sensory end organ dysfunction (e.g. deafness, reduced vision), important neural pathways that process and respond to sensory input might not develop appropriately. Additionally, substance exposure *in utero* (e.g., alcohol, drugs) can impact the progression of a child's development skills due to consequent change in brain architecture. Children experiencing drug withdrawal might be hospitalized for long periods of time, removed from a nurturing environment that promotes normal development. Also, a child who is born prematurely is at risk for delays in development skills due to illness, prolonged hospitalization, and the vulnerability of important sensory systems, such as vision and hearing. Often, adopted children experience multiple transitions prior to placement in the adoptive home. In this situation, the child does not have the opportunity to learn routines and experience a stable environment which enhances the progression of development skills. Finally, malnutrition, with resulting weakness, can also play a significant role in altering development.

When initially assessing an adoptee with a history of deprivation or with known medical or physical disabilities, occupational, physical, and speech therapists contribute to a child's comprehensive evaluation in several critical areas. The first is to document the child's baseline developmental status (Table 14.4). This initial assessment can then be used to ascertain the rate of improvement over time. In all cases, understanding the child's background is essential for the correct assessment of a child's development status, as both social adversity and ill health can significantly delay achievement of skills (Table 14.2). Most children adopted internationally or from foster care will have a range of developmental deficits, which usually improve upon entering a nurturing adoptive family. Rapid catch-up usually bodes well for more complete recovery, while persistent delays could be an indicator that intervention or further evaluation is needed.

Another important contribution is to establish whether intervention is needed immediately or can be safely deferred until the rate of recovery within the adoptive family can be determined. Developmental delays do not always require immediate professional intervention. For children where delays are associated with deprivation, joining a competent family might be sufficient initial "therapy" as the child is now living in an environment where they can undertake appropriate developmental activities and experience normal sensory input. Parents should be encouraged to be patient and sensitive to their child's reactions, to be aware of their own response, and to adapt to the child's lead. It can be helpful for parents and therapist to try to identify situations or settings that cause problems for a child and structure the home environment and daily routines accordingly. For children with severe or organically based delays (e.g. a developmental age less than half the child's chronologic age, cerebral palsy, etc.), an early medical- or school-based intervention program might be beneficial.

Table 14.4 Items included in an initial developmental assessment for adoptees with disabilities or medical disorders

- Motor skills
- Strength
- Range of motion
- Muscle tone
- Cognition
- Psychosocial skills
- Self-care skills
- Feeding skills
- Sensory processing
- Reflexes
- Receptive and expressive language

Sensory processing assessment

According to Ayres, sensory integration is the organization of sensation for use (Ayres, 1972). A child with sensory processing disorder (SPD) often has not experienced a normal variety of sensory input during development and consequently has a difficult time processing and responding appropriately to ordinary sensory stimuli (Dunn, 2014; Kranowitz, 2005; Yack, Sutton, & Aquilla, 1998). A biological basis for this diagnosis is supported by studies showing that children affected with SPD have quantifiable differences in brain white matter microstructure, compared to typically developing children, in areas that subserve sensory processing and integration (Chang et al., 2015). Sensory processing difficulties can be categorized into four groupings: sensory seeking, sensory sensitivity, low registration, and sensory avoiding. Some children seek sensory input at a higher rate than others and require a greater amount of sensory input in their day. Children can be more sensitive to sensory input than others. There are also children who have low registration; it takes a high amount of sensory input for the child to notice it. Children might also avoid sensory input depending on the nature of the stimulus. Signs of SPD can vary significantly among children, and combinations of challenges in these groupings are commonly encountered.

Sensory processing or sensory integration concerns are frequent among children who have been adopted. For example, several studies involving children who experienced prolonged institutionalization demonstrated higher levels of reactivity to sensation and more aversion and approach to sensory stimuli than other groups (Lin, Cermak, Coster, & Miller, 2005; Wilbarger, Gunnar, Schneider, & Pollak, 2010). This is likely related to conditions children experience during institutionalization, such as restricted vestibular and visual stimulation due to lying stationary in a crib and looking primarily at the ceiling. Consequently, these children will not always have an accurate or reliable perception of their body or environment and, as a result, misperceive the world.

It should be noted that sensory processing problems and developmental delays commonly impact behavior, which is discussed in the next section on mental health. Children averse to touch might recoil when a parent attempts to hug them. Those who seek sensation might appear hyperactive. If there are language delays, a child might not be able to communicate and could become easily frustrated. Occupational, physical, and speech-language therapists play a critical role in reframing these behaviors for parents and initiating therapy that can help resolve these issues. In such cases, collaboration with mental health professionals can be the key to avoiding misidentifying a child as having a behavior disorder and embarking on a course of treatment that fails to address the underlying issues.

Mental health assessment and support

As previously mentioned, most adoptees have been exposed to a diverse range of pre- and postnatal risk factors. Not only are each of these risk factors individually capable of derailing a child's developmental trajectory, but in combination, they can produce a unique pattern of mental health issues. Furthermore, risk factors impact mental health and neurodevelopment in different ways at different ages. As a result, the prevention of long-term mental health and neurodevelopmental issues in adopted children *requires* a comprehensive, multidimensional, and longitudinal approach that assumes that ongoing intervention is required to address the full range of a child's potential problems. This is critically important to family adjustment as behavior problems are the most challenging for families adopting special needs children (Nalavany, Glidden, & Ryan, 2009).

The initial evaluation must include assessments for all potential risk factors and, given their differential impact at different stages of development, integrate this information with the timing of exposure. Second, once a full picture of the child's history is acquired, focus must shift to the protective factors, or absence thereof, in their environment. It is critical for parents and providers to understand that these protective factors, more so than any history of risk, are likely to determine the child's developmental outcome. Current research emphasizes the protective role that adoptive parents play in a child's life by building a safe and secure emotional relationship (McLaughlin, Zeanah, Fox, & Nelson, 2012). These relationships allow adoptive parents to play an important role in buffering the inevitably high levels of stress experienced by a child. This buffering is critical to preventing the negative outcomes associated with excessive stress levels (toxic stress) early in life (Shonkoff & Garner, 2012). Children with risk factors such as premature birth, prenatal drug exposure, or compromised health status are particularly sensitive to the effects of buffering relationships (Treyvaud et al., 2009). Not only is a buffering relationship with adoptive parents important in preventing toxic stress in the moment; this kind of interaction also provides a scaffold for the child to develop their own stress-regulation skills. These skills, in turn, are central to long-term outcomes as the child becomes independent of their adoptive parents and begins to encounter stressors on their own.

Providing this crucial buffering relationship is far from easy. Given a lack of stable relationships early in life, adopted children might not have learned how to effectively signal their emotional needs. As a result, these children might have difficulty developing a connection with their parents and thus the ability to signal a need for comfort when they are in distress (Stovall-McClough & Dozier, 2004). Instead, children in this population can appear impulsive, overactive, aggressive, or shut down emotionally when they are distressed. Such problems are unfortunately common. Research from the Adoption Medicine Clinic at the University of Minnesota revealed that of over 100 adopted children referred, 60 percent demonstrated difficulties signaling distress, despite the fact that all but one child in the sample did not meet the full criteria for Reactive Attachment Disorder. As a result, adoptive parents often struggle to interpret what might seem like chaotic behavior from their new child. Children who have a history of multiple foster care placements and histories of abuse and neglect are at particular risk (Zeanah, Chesher, Boris, & American Academy of Child and Adolescent Psychiatry Committee on Quality Issues, 2016). Addressing these difficulties in early parent–child communication is critical to establishing the kind of buffering relationship essential for normalizing the developmental trajectory of adopted children.

Previous research has also pointed to other factors that might impact the emergence and quality of a buffering relationship. These include an adoptive parent's own issues such as a history of trauma, mental health status, or current stressors. Thus, in addition to identifying communication difficulties in the adopted child, any intervention program must include screening for parental risk factors that could impact the development of a buffering relationship. Failure to identify, at the outset, risk factors from either the child's or parent's side of the relationship is liable to result in the parent being unable to completely buffer a child's stress, with all attendant negative developmental outcomes.

To address this complex set of issues, a two-step clinical model has been developed. The first step is mental health screening during the initial medical exam, which helps determine if a referral is needed. The main focus of this evaluation is observing how a child signals and communicates with their parent during times of distress and how parents read these signals. A child who is confident and curious to explore and who will seek out their caregiver for comfort when they are distressed will probably do well. However, a child who is overwhelmed by fear and does not explore their environment, has a difficult time signaling distress, freezes during the stressful experience, and does not reach for, or even shows fear toward their caregiver is likely a child at-risk who would benefit from ongoing mental health intervention and support.

As discussed above, there are several key pieces to consider when making a referral as a result of an initial screening. These include: a child's ability to signal their needs to their parents, whether or not the parent is able to interpret the needs of their child accurately, information obtained about the quality of the parent buffer, the parent's mental health (e.g. screening for depression), the family's resources, and the child's social/emotional status. Once it is determined that a referral is needed, it is imperative to proceed quickly given the importance of early intervention. Neurodevelopment during early childhood is a rapid process and identified risk factors are more likely to have significant negative effects the longer a buffering relationship is absent.

Once a child is referred, the second step of the model involves a full evaluation which includes formal developmental testing (e.g., social-communication, cognitive, and motor capacities), parental interview, and assessment of the quality of parent–child interactions in the new family environment. The clinical observation will assess how a child plays with their parent(s), toys, and a new adult, and how they respond to a series of separations and reunions in a novel environment. The parent interview consists of the parent(s) discussing concerns as well as assessment of parental reflective capacity. Based on the results of this evaluation and the child's age, specific evidenced-based, relationship-focused interventions are recommended. These include Child Parent Psychotherapy (Lieberman, Ghosh Ippen, & Van Horn, 2006), Circle of Security (Mercer, 2015), Attachment Bio-Behavioral Catch-Up (Dozier et al., 2018), or Trauma-Focused Cognitive Behavioral Therapy (for children aged 4 years and older) (Deblinger, Mannarino, & Cohen, 2018). Collaboration with pediatric occupational, physical, and speech therapists is critical not only for diagnostic services for the child but to provide additional information and support for parents.

Ultimately, interventions must consider future developmental challenges, including entering the school system and dealing with more complex social relationships during adolescence. Neuropsychological testing prior to entering school is an adjunct that can help to delineate academic strengths or weaknesses and help the family and the school to understand a child's potential needs. Special education services might be appropriate and instituting such programs early can help improve academic achievement, mental health, and self-esteem.

Children require careful follow-up as not all mental health problems will be apparent within the first few months after adoption and parents might not seek out services due to normalizing abnormal behavior. Since earlier intervention almost always yields superior outcomes, a follow-up mental health and developmental assessment one year after adoption is strongly recommended for all children regardless of their initial status.

Conclusion

Most children now adopted have known disabilities or have risk factors for short- or long-term problems. While generally rewarding, adoption can also present families with unexpected medical, developmental, behavioral, and emotional challenges. Preadoption counseling and review are of utmost importance to uncover any previously undetected medical or developmental issues, setting appropriate expectations, and assisting families in identifying resources to address their child's problems. Health care professionals also play a key role in comprehensively assessing a child's physical, developmental, and mental health status after arrival and developing therapeutic plans with appropriate medical specialists and community resources that will enable the child to succeed.

References

Adoption Medicine Clinic, University of Minnesota. (2018). *Screening protocols.* Retrieved from https://adoption.umn.edu/postadoption/child-development-transition-and-mental-health/screening-protocols

Altstein, H., & Simon, R. J. (1991). Introduction. In H. Altstein & R. J. Simon (Eds.), *International adoption: A multinational perspective* (pp. 1–20). New York: Praeger.

Astley, S. J., Stachowiak, J., Clarren, S. K., & Clausen, C. (2002). Application of the fetal alcohol syndrome facial photographic screening tool in a foster care population. *Journal of Pediatrics, 141*(5), 712–717. doi:10.1067/mpd.2002.129030

Ayres, A. J. (1972). *Sensory integration and the child.* Los Angeles: Western Psychological Services.

Baker, C. (2007). Disabled children's experience of permanancy in the looked after system. *British Journal of Social Work, 37,* 1173–1188. doi:10.1093/bjsw/bcl082

Bohman, M. (1970). *Adopted children and their families: A follow-up study of adopted children, their background, environment and adjustment.* Stockholm: Proprius.

Boswell, J. (1988). *The kindness of strangers: The abandonment of children in Western Europe from late antiquity to the renaissance.* New York: Pantheon.

Buckley, C. (2015). *China ends one-child policy, allowing families two children.* New York Times. Retrieved from www.nytimes.com/2015/10/30/world/asia/china-end-one-child-policy.html

Budiman, A., & Lopez, M. H. (2017). *Amid decline in international adoptions to US, boys outnumber girls for the first time.* Retrieved from www.pewresearch.org/fact-tank/2017/10/17/amid-decline-in-international-adoptions-to-u-s-boys-outnumber-girls-for-the-first-time/

Carr, A., Duff, H., & Craddock, F. (2018). A systematic review of the outcome of child abuse in long-term care. *Trauma Violence Abuse,* 1–18. Retrieved from doi:https://doi.org/10.1177/1524838018789154

Centers for Disease Control and Prevention. (2018). *Adverse childhood experiences (ACEs).* Retrieved from www.cdc.gov/violenceprevention/acestudy/index.html

Chang, Y. S., Gratiot, M., Owen, J. P., Brandes-Aitken, A., Desai, S. S., Hill, S. S., ... Mukherjee, P. (2015). White matter microstructure is associated with auditory and tactile processing in children with and without sensory processing disorder. *Frontiers in Neuroanatomy, 9,* 169. doi:10.3389/fnana.2015.00169

Children's Bureau. (1967). *The story of the White House conferences on children and youth.* Retrieved from https://files.eric.ed.gov/fulltext/ED078896.pdf

Coakley, J. F., & Berrick, J. D. (2008). Research review: In a rush to permanency: Preventing adoption disruption. *Child & Family Social Work, 13,* 101–112. doi:10.1111/j.1365-2206.2006.00468.x

Crary, D. (2010). *Adopting China's special-needs kids.* Children's health on NBCNEWS.com. Retrieved from www.nbcnews.com/id/36037857/ns/health-childrens_health/t/adopting-chinas-special-needs-kids/#.XBlGRy2ZNp8

Curry, E. (2018). Want to adopt a baby from China? *adoption.com.* Retrieved from https://adoption.com/want-to-adopt-a-chinese-baby-6-things-you-should-know

Danese, A., & McEwen, B. S. (2012). Adverse childhood experiences, allostasis, allostatic load, and age-related disease. *Physiology & Behavior, 106*(1), 29–39. doi:10.1016/j.physbeh.2011.08.019

Deblinger, E., Mannarino, A. P., & Cohen, J. A. (2018). Trauma-focused cognitive behavioral therapy for children and families. *Psychotherapy Research, 28*(1), 47–57.

Dozier, M., Roben, C. K. P., Caron, E., Hoye, J., & Bernard, K. (2018). Attachment and biobehavioral catch-up: An evidence-based intervention for vulnerable infants and their families. *Psychotherapy Research, 28*(1), 18–29. doi:10.1080/10503307.2016.1208375

Dunn, W. (2014). *Sensory profile 2 user's manual.* Bloomington, MN: PsychCorp.

Eckerle, J. K., Hill, L. K., Iverson, S., Hellerstedt, W., Gunnar, M., & Johnson, D. E. (2014). Vision and hearing deficits and associations with parent-reported behavioral and developmental problems in international adoptees. *Maternal and Child Health Journal, 18*(3), 575–583. doi:10.1007/s10995-013-1274-1

Eckerle, J. K., Howard, C. R., & John, C. C. (2013). Infections in internationally adopted children. *Pediatric Clinics of North America, 60*(2), 487–505. doi:10.1016/j.pcl.2012.12.010

Hellerstedt, W. L., Madsen, N. J., Gunnar, M. R., Grotevant, H. D., Lee, R. M., & Johnson, D. E. (2008). The international adoption project: Population-based surveillance of Minnesota parents who adopted children internationally. *Maternal and Child Health Journal, 12*(2), 162–171. doi:10.1007/s10995-007-0237-9

Johnson, D. E. (2000). Medical and developmental sequelae of early childhood institutionalization in Eastern European adoptees. In C. A. Nelson (Ed.), *The effects of early adversity on neurobehavioral development: The Minnesota symposia on child psychology* (pp. 113–162). Mahwaw, NJ: Lawrence Erlbaum Associates.

Johnson, D. E., & Gunnar, M. R. (2011). IV. Growth failure in institutionalized children. *Monographs of the Society for Research in Child Development, 76*(4), 92–126. doi:10.1111/j.1540-5834.2011.00629.x

Johnston, W. R. (2017). *Historical statistics on adoption in the United States, plus statistics on child population and welfare.* Retrieved from www.johnstonsarchive.net/policy/adoptionstats.html

Jones, V. F. Committee On Early Childhood, Adoption, & Dependent Care. (2012). Comprehensive health evaluation of the newly adopted child. *Pediatrics, 129*(1), e214–223. doi:10.1542/peds.2011-2381

Kranowitz, C. S. (2005). *The out of sync child.* New York: Berkley.

Kraus, L. (2017). *2016 Disability statistics annual report.* Durham, NH: University of New Hampshire.

Kreider, R. M., & Cohen, P. N. (2009). Disability among internationally adopted children in the United States. *Pediatrics, 124*(5), 1311–1318.

Kumsta, R., Kreppner, J., Kennedy, M., Knights, N., Rutter, M., & Sonuga-Barke, E. (2015). Psychological consequences of early global deprivation: An overview of findings from the English & Romanian adoptees study. *European Psychologist, 20*, 138–151. doi:10.1027/1016-9040/a000227

Landgren, M., Svensson, L., Stromland, K., & Andersson Gronlund, M. (2010). Prenatal alcohol exposure and neurodevelopmental disorders in children adopted from Eastern Europe. *Pediatrics, 125*(5), e1178–1185. doi:10.1542/peds.2009-0712

Lieberman, A. F., Ghosh Ippen, C., & Van Horn, P. (2006). Child-parent psychotherapy: 6-month follow-up of a randomized controlled trial. *Journal of the American Academy of Child and Adodoescent Psychiatry, 45*(8), 913–918. doi:10.1097/01.chi.0000222784.03735.92

Lin, S. H., Cermak, S., Coster, W. J., & Miller, L. C. (2005). The relation between length of institutionalization and sensory integration in children adopted from Eastern Europe. *American Journal of Occupational Therapy, 59*(2), 139–147. doi:10.5014/ajot.59.2.139

McCall, R. B., van IJzendoorn, M. H., Juffer, F., Groark, C. J., & Groza, V. (2011). Children without permanent parents: Research, practice, and policy. *Monographs of the Society for Research in Child Development, 6*(4), 1–281. doi:10.1111/j.1540-5834.2011.00634.x

McLaughlin, K. A., Zeanah, C. H., Fox, N. A., & Nelson, C. A. (2012). Attachment security as a mechanism linking foster care placement to improved mental health outcomes in previously institutionalized children. *Journal of Child Psychology and Psychiatry, 53*(1), 46–55. doi:10.1111/j.1469-7610.2011.02437.x

Mercer, J. (2015). Examining circle of security™: A review of research and theory. *Research on Social Work Practice, 25*(3), 382–392. doi:10.1177/1049731514536620

Miller, B. C., & Coyl, D. D. (2000). Adolescent pregnancy and childbearing in relation to infant adoption in the United States. *Adoption Quarterly, 4*, 3–25. doi:10.1300/J145v04n01_02

Miller, B. S., Kroupina, M. G., Mason, P., Iverson, S. L., Narad, C., Himes, J. H., … Petryk, A. (2010). Determinants of catch-up growth in international adoptees from Eastern Europe. *International Journal of Pediatric Endocrinology, 2010*(107252), 1–8. doi:10.1155/2010/107252

Miller, L. C., & Hendrie, N. W. (2000). Health of children adopted from China. *Pediatrics, 105*(6, E76. 1-6. 10.1542/peds.105.6.e76

Ministry of Civil Affairs, People's Republic of China. (2018). *Data of Chinese children adoption (2010–2016).* Retrieved from www.mca.gov.cn

Mulder, E. J., Robles de Medina, P. G., Huizink, A. C., Van den Bergh, B. R., Buitelaar, J. K., & Visser, G. H. (2002). Prenatal maternal stress: Effects on pregnancy and the (unborn) child. *Early Human Development, 70*(1–2), 3–14. doi:10.1016/S0378-3782(02)00075-0

Nalavany, B. A., Glidden, L. M., & Ryan, S. D. (2009). Parental satisfaction in the adoption of children with learning disorders: The role of behavior problems. *Family Relations, 58*, 621–633. doi:doi.org/10.1111/j.1741-3729.2009.00579.x

Nelson, C. A., Fox, N. A., & Zeanah, C. H. (2014). *Romania's abandoned children: Deprivation, brain development, and the struggle for recovery*. Cambridge: Harvard University Press.

O'Dell, K. E., McCall, R., & Groark, C. (2015). Supporting families through the international special needs adoption process. *Children and Youth Services Review, 59*, 161–170.

Palacios, J., Sánchez-Sandoval, Y., & Lee, E. (2006). International adoption disruptions in Spain. *Adoption Quarterly, 9*, 35–55.

Placek, P. J. (1999). National adoption data. In C. Marshner & W. L. Pierce (Eds.), *Adoption Factbook III* (pp. 24–68). Alexandria, VA: National Council for Adoption.

Rau Barriga, S., Buchanan, J., Ćerimović, E., & Sharma, K. (2017). *Children with disabilities: Deprivation of liberty in the name of care and treatment*. Retrieved from www.hrw.org/news/2017/03/07/children-disabilities-deprivation-liberty-name-care-and-treatment#_ftn2

Rowell, K. (2012). *Love Me, Feed Me*. St. Paul, MN: Feeding Dynamics.

Sciauvaud, J., Rigal, E., Pascal, J., Nourrisson, C., Poirier, P., Poirier, V., … Lesens, O. (2014). Transmission of infectious diseases from internationally adopted children to their adoptive families. *Clinical Microbiology and Infection, 20*(8), 746–751. doi:10.1111/1469-0691.12454

Shonkoff, J. P., & Garner, A. S.; Committee on Psychosocial Aspects of Child and Family Health, Committee on Early Childhood, Adoption and Dependent Care, Section on Developmental and Behavioral, Pediatrics. (2012). The lifelong effects of early childhood adversity and toxic stress. *Pediatrics, 129*(1), e232-246.

Shonkoff, J. P., & Phillips, D. A. (2000). *From neurons to neighborhoods: The science of early childhood development*. Washington: National Academy Press.

Stovall-McClough, K. C., & Dozier, M. (2004). Forming attachments in foster care: Infant attachment behaviors during the first 2 months of placement. *Development and Psychopathology, 16*(2), 253–271. doi:10.1017/S0954579404044505

Tan, T. X., & Robinson, E. A. X. (2018). Institutionalized Chinese children with congenital medical conditions: Placement delay, developmental issues at arrival and current wellbeing. *Children and Youth Services Review, 88*, 380–386. doi:10.1016/j.childyouth.2018.03.032

Treyvaud, K., Anderson, V. A., Howard, K., Bear, M., Hunt, R. W., Doyle, L. W., … Anderson, P. J. (2009). Parenting behavior is associated with the early neurobehavioral development of very preterm children. *Pediatrics, 123*(2), 555–561. doi:10.1542/peds.2008-0477

Turney, K., & Wildeman, C. (2017). Adverse childhood experiences among children placed in and adopted from foster care: Evidence from a nationally representative survey. *Child Abuse & Neglect, 64*, 117–129. doi:https://doi.org/10.1016/j.chiabu.2016.12.009

US Department of State-Bureau of Consular Affairs. (2018). *Adoption statistics*. Retrieved from https://travel.state.gov/content/travel/en/Intercountry-Adoption/adopt_ref/adoption-statistics.html

Vanderklippe, N. (2018). *The tragic tale of China's orphanages: 98% of abandoned children have disabilities*. The Globe and Mail. Retrieved from www.theglobeandmail.com/news/world/the-tragic-tale-of-chinas-orphanages-98-of-abandoned-children-have-disabilities/article17625887/

Waldrop, J., & Stern, S. M. (2003). *Disability status: 2000*. Washington, DC: US Census Bureau.

Westerman, A. (2018). *Why international adoption cases in the US have plummeted*. NPR. Retrieved from www.npr.org/2018/06/25/623114766/why-international-adoption-cases-in-the-u-s-have-plummeted

Wilbarger, J., Gunnar, M., Schneider, M., & Pollak, S. (2010). Sensory processing in internationally adopted, post-institutionalized children. *Journal of Child Psychology and Psychiatry, 51*(10), 1105–1114. doi:10.1111/j.1469-7610.2010.02255.x

Yack, E., Sutton, S., & Aquilla, P. (1998). *Building bridges through sensory integration: Occupational therapy for children with autism and other pervasive developmental disorders*. Toronto: Print Three.

Zeanah, C. H., Chesher, T., & Boris, N. W.; American Academy of Child & Adolescent Psychiatry (AACAP) Committee on Quality Issues (CQI). (2016). Practice parameter for the assessment and treatment of children and adolescents with reactive attachment disorder and disinhibited social engagement disorder. *Journal of the American Academy of Child and Adolescent Psychiatry, 55*(11), 990–1003.

15

ADOPTION IN THE CONTEXT OF NATURAL DISASTER

Peter Selman

Adoption rates are influenced by a multitude of factors. At the micro level, individuals' decisions to place their child for adoption or to adopt a non-relative child are affected by larger, structural forces that shape those smaller choices. At the broader macro level, connections can be made between major historical events (e.g., war, poverty, affluence, political policies and manoeuvres, and natural disasters) and an individual's opportunity and ability to participate in the adoption process. The aim of this chapter is to examine international adoptions after the natural disaster of the 2010 earthquake in Haiti and to provide insight into why these adoption practices did not occur in similar disasters in richer countries or in previous disasters affecting poor countries, such as the South Asian tsunami. Consideration will also be given to other types of natural disasters, such as famine and flood, which have affected many poor countries in Africa and Asia. The chapter begins with a brief overview of international adoption statistics, a discussion of how availability of children for adoption has been shaped by large historical events, as well as how media coverage has impacted people's eagerness to adopt. The concept of adoption as a form of rescue is explored prior to an examination of adoption after the 2010 Haitian earthquake. The chapter concludes with policy and practice implications.

Trends in international adoption

In the 70 years since the ending of the Second World War, over one million children have been placed for adoption in countries other than those in which they were born (Selman, 2017). The annual number of international adoptees rose to 20,000 by 1987, driven largely by adoptions from South Korea following the ending of the Korean War (Selman, 2012c). However, in the late 1980s, annual numbers of international adoptions declined. South Korea began to reduce the number of such adoptions as a response to adverse publicity during the 1988 Olympics in Seoul, when their government was accused of being unwilling to care for their own children while claiming to be a leading industrialized nation (Ellingson, 2007). In 1989 the South Korean government introduced a policy to end international adoption by 1995, prompting Altstein and Simon (1991) to ask, "Are we witnessing the beginning of the end of wide-scale ICA [Intercountry Adoption]?" (Altstein & Simon, 1991, p. 191).

Yet in the 1990s, this downward trend was dramatically reversed after a surge in international adoptions following the overthrow of the Romanian dictator Ceauşescu in 1990. Altstein and Simon (1991) characterized the increasing availability of Romanian orphans as a "momentary addition" to the world's pool of children available for adoption by foreigners; however, their prediction was incorrect due to other countries beginning to allow their children to be adopted internationally. The dissolution of the Soviet Union in 1991 led to a huge increase in adoptions from Russia and other eastern European countries. During the same year, the People's Republic of China began to allow intercountry adoption of their available children (Selman, 2009; Simon & Altstein, 2000, pp. 9–12). The greater number of children available to adopt globally increased the numbers of children adopted internationally.

Annual international adoption numbers peaked in 2004 when more than 45,000 children (half of them from China and Russia) were adopted abroad to 24 receiving countries. Since then numbers have fallen dramatically to under 10,000 in 2017 (Selman, 2018), the lowest figure recorded since the late 1970s. During these 13 years there was a sharp reduction in the number of children sent by China and Russia. These decreases, however, were somewhat offset by a temporary increase in adoptions from Africa and a doubling of adoptions from Haiti in 2010 following the January earthquake (Selman, 2012b, 2015).

The number of international adoptions is not only impacted by the availability of children to adopt, but also the desire among potential adoptive parents to adopt internationally, the impact of media presentations of the suffering of children in orphanages, and the call to rescue children from intolerable conditions. These depictions were central to the surge in adoptions from Romania following the fall of Ceauşescu. UNICEF estimated that more than 10,000 children were taken from the country between January 1990 and July 1991. Yet a nine-month moratorium was imposed leading to the eventual permanent discontinuance of Romanian adoptions due to emerging information that many of these children were taken by Western couples travelling to Romania to save poor children, yet many of the children taken were not older children rescued from orphanages, but infants "bought" from poor parents (Defence for Children International, 1991; Reich, 1990).

The media's impact on encouraging prospective adoptive parents to adopt internationally was also a factor in China. In the 1980s, few children were adopted from China. Kane (1993) estimates a decade total of 94 children, most of whom were adopted by parents in the US. In the early 1990s, the annual number of international adoptions rose as China relaxed its opposition to the practice, faced with a growing number of abandoned infants in already overcrowded orphanages. In 1992, China passed a law "officially granting foreigners the right to adopt and setting up protocols for doing this" (Evans, 2000, p. 17). Three years later in 1995, a television documentary, *The Dying Rooms: Asia's Darkest Secret*, painted a frightening picture of Chinese government-run orphanages where abandoned girls were left to die (Johnson, 2016; Munroe & Rigsby, 1996). Annual numbers of adoptions from China were already rising – from under 200 in 1991 to an estimated 1,500 in 1994, but thereafter estimated annual numbers increased to 7,500 in 2001 and 14,500 in 2005 (Selman, 2009, 2019).

Thus, large structural, political, cultural, economic, and communication changes have a great impact on the number of children available globally to adopt, the desire among individuals to adopt, and the places from which children are mostly likely adopted. When major events such as natural disasters, war, and genocide create a situation in which children need parents, a common response has been for individuals to seek to address the need through international adoption. This will be discussed in more detail in the next section.

Adoption as rescue

The idea of rescuing children affected by war or natural disaster has a long history in international adoption (Bergquist, 2012). Altstein and Simon (1991, p. 1) wrote that international adoption "began primarily as a North American philanthropic response to the devastation of Europe in World War II," when many displaced children were said to be "adopted" during the ensuing chaos of the summer and autumn of 1945. However, many of these adoption arrangements proved to be only temporary and ended with the child being abandoned and passed to the United Nations Relief and Rehabilitation Administration thus not the definition of "adoption" used in the later-half of the 20th century (Taylor, 2017).

However, there is some evidence of international adoption prior to the Second World War. "Kindertransport" was a movement of children from Germany who were not orphans but were being rescued from an impending genocide with the knowledge and consent of their parents, most of whom subsequently died under the Holocaust (Hodge, 2012). After the end of the Second World War, thousands of German children – many the offspring of American GIs and German women – were adopted to the US and other Western countries (Textor, 1991). There were also future occurrences of adoption to the US from German orphanages during the Cold War (Dodds, 1997).

Examples of adoption as rescue can be also be seen in the aftermath of the Korean War in 1956, when many mixed-race children of American soldiers were adopted to the US and European countries (Hubinette, 2006). Additionally, in response to the Vietnam War, approximately 2,000–3,000 children from South Vietnam were flown to the US (Bergquist, 2012, p. 44). The first of these "babylifts" occurred on April 5, 1975, with a disastrous beginning in which 180 Vietnamese orphans died when the first flight crashed soon after take-off. However, babylifts continued until April 26, a few days prior to the fall of Saigon on April 30, 1975 (Martin, 2000).

These kinds of "rescue" adoptions have been increasingly challenged by the sending countries' home governments as unsuitable for the needs of child victims of disasters. For example, in the aftermath of the Rwandan genocide of April–June 1994, when an estimated 800,000 Rwandan Tutsis died, an Italian agency allegedly rescued 122 orphans who were later found to have a living parent. Many of these children returned to Rwanda when the Tutsis became the government, but others were adopted by families in the Brescia region. These adoptions were clearly not in accord with the 1993 Hague Convention (designed to address illegalities and abductions in international adoption), which Italy signed in 1995 and ratified in 2000. Six years later, the Rwandan government demanded the return of 41 of the adoptees (BBC News, 2000; Frenkiel, 2001). The Italian government eventually agreed to return the children to Rwanda with their adoptive families in order to apply for a properly documented adoption, if the birth parents consented, or to establish that the children were genuinely orphans.

Africa has also experienced many natural disasters, such as the 1984 famine in Ethiopia. In the 1980s, international adoption from Africa was rare. Kane (1993) reports that less than 400 children were adopted from Ethiopia between 1980 and 1989 – and there is no evidence that international adoption was viewed as a possible solution to the famine. Yet in the 21st century, the number of Ethiopian children adopted internationally grew rapidly. This was not as a response to disasters, but rather to the increased demand for children to adopt due to the 2004 closure of many existing sources of adoptive children in Latin America and Asia. We have more recently learned that many of those adopted from African orphanages were not orphans (Davis, 2017) and that many orphanages were funded by overseas charities for which releasing children for adoption helped to ensure future funding (Mezmur, 2009b).

In 2005, the Indian, Indonesian, and Sri Lankan governments, backed by UNICEF and the US State Department, took steps to ensure that intercountry adoption was not considered a solution to the South Asian tsunami of December 2004 (McGinnis, 2005; Selman, 2010). Adoption agencies around the world had been flooded with phone calls from people with good intentions wishing to adopt children orphaned by the disaster, but experts and aid agencies warned these potential adoptive parents that they were likely to be disappointed since the children were unlikely to be available for international adoption. The government of Indonesia, a predominantly Muslim nation, placed a ban on any child under the age of 16 leaving the Aceh district without their parents, and also banned adoptions therein. Many receiving countries also stressed that their citizens should not adopt in the aftermath of the tsunami (McGinnis, 2005: Selman, 2010). The result was that few, if any, orphans from the affected areas were adopted by parents internationally. This was confirmed by the statistics on international adoptions from these countries between 2003 and 2006, the years prior to and following the catastrophe (Table 15.1).

All four of these countries had a tradition of international adoption going back many years, but by 2004, before the tsunami, numbers in India and Thailand were falling and Indonesia, a country that had sent 3,307 children to the Netherlands between 1970 and 1985 (Hoksbergen, 1986), had virtually ended all international adoptions. There was also a dramatic fall in numbers in Sri Lanka, which had sent 7,000 children to be adopted in countries overseas in the 1980s. This was largely driven by growing awareness of corruption in governments, some non-governmental organizations, and some adoption agencies, as some children who were not orphans were being sold, a scandal only fully revealed much later (ColomboPage, 2017; The Guardian, 2017). A much smaller tsunami in 2018 passed without any suggestion that adoption could be a solution.

The issue of international adoption was raised in Pakistan in July 2004 following the earthquake and floods, but was firmly rejected by its government. The Minister for Social Welfare, Zubaida Jalal, told the National Assembly, "We have decided to look after the thousands of orphans. We have imposed a complete ban on adoption of these children" (Masood, 2005).

In quite different circumstances, two years later in 2007, six members of the French charity organization Zoe's Ark (founded in 2005 to aid victims of the South Asian tsunami) were accused of child trafficking as they attempted to fly 103 children out of Chad. Although they were sentenced to eight years' hard labor (BBC News, 2007; Duval Smith & Rolley, 2007; Mezmur, 2009a), they were subsequently pardoned by the Chadian president and released from prisons in France in 2008 (Chrisafis, 2008; Selman, 2010).

Table 15.1 International adoptions before and after the South Asian tsunami of December 2004

State of origin	*Pre-tsunami*			*Post-tsunami*		
	1980–89	*2003*	*2004*	*2005*	*2006*	*2017*
India	15,325	1,172	1,083	873	847	578
Indonesia	442	5	8	4	5	1
Sri Lanka	6,815	46	55	59	57	13
Thailand	858	490	501	465	419	225

The 2010 Haitian earthquake

The natural disaster that has been the focus of most attention in international adoption research is the 2010 Haitian earthquake (Lindsey, 2010; Rotabi & Bergquist, 2010; Selman, 2012a). It was also the starting point for *The Child Catchers*, an exploration of the impact of conservative Christians' participation in international adoption by K. Joyce (2013). Joyce was one of the first to explicitly describe the role of religion in the ethnocentric ideology of adoption as a form of rescue by explaining that the Christian adoption movement has prioritized "the global 'orphan crisis': the idea that there are hundreds of millions of orphaned children across the world who are in need of American help and waiting to be adopted" (Joyce, 2013, p. xiii).

On January 10, 2010, a 7.0 Richter magnitude earthquake hit Haiti, the poorest country in the Western Hemisphere. A quarter of a million homes in Port-au-Prince were destroyed. The death toll – estimated as over 222,000 by International Social Service (Dambach & Baglietto, 2010) – is similar to that resulting from the South Asian tsunami in 2004, which was estimated to have killed at least 225,000 (McGinnis, 2005). A million families were made homeless, with many children separated from their parents and some orphaned as a result of losing both mother and father.

In the years immediately prior to the January 2010 earthquake, the number of children sent from Haiti for intercountry adoption had fluctuated between 700 and 1,400 a year with the majority going to just three countries: Canada, the US, and France. During this period, Haiti had one of the highest rates of intercountry adoption: 5.0 per 1,000 live births in 2008, compared with 0.33 in China and 2.7 in Russia in the same year (Selman, 2012a). With the suspension of adoptions from Guatemala in 2009 due to their failure to comply with the Hague Convention, Haiti became a prime target for agencies in the US seeking new sources of children for those waiting to adopt. Thus, there were many prospective adopters in the US at the beginning of 2010 who had been approved by an agency and were waiting for a child from Haiti, many of whom had not received a final decision from Haitian courts. In the aftermath of the earthquake, the media focused on these prospective adoptive parents' fear that they would not be able to adopt the child with whom they had been matched (see Gray, 2010). During this period, there were also many new applications received from would-be adopters offering to save the children orphaned by the earthquake.

Soon after the earthquake on January 19, 2010, 54 Haitian-born children arrived in Pittsburgh on a flight with Pennsylvanian governor Ed Rendell. It was later revealed that most of them were not orphans and 12 of the children were not in the process of adoption (Rotabi, Armistead, & Monico, 2015; Thompson, 2010). Ten days later, ten members of an Idaho-based Baptist charity were arrested for trying to take 33 Haitian children across the border into the Dominican Republic without proper paperwork (Clark, 2010; Crary, 2010). It was subsequently found that all 33 children had parents, with whom they were eventually reunited at a camp run by *SOS Children's Villages* based in Austria (Bajak, 2010; Radnege, 2010). Other groups of children – not all of whom had legal proof of adoption – were taken by air to Canada, France, Germany, and the Netherlands in the weeks following the earthquake. This raised concerns reminiscent of previous times of crisis in which adoption was used as a form of rescue.

The international response to the plight of children after the earthquake

As early as January 15, 2010 – a few days after the earthquake – concern was being expressed over children already approved for adoption by the agencies, and in the process of being approved by Haiti. Dixie Bickel, director of *God's Littlest Angels* orphanage just outside Port-au-Prince, argued that emergency visas and passports could help push through adoptions that were stalled after the earthquake. This would open up beds for children who had lost their parents in the disaster (Gray, 2010). Bickel stressed that the request was only for those children who had been legally adopted but were still living in Haiti because their cases were going through a lengthy government approval process that could take anywhere from six months to two years. This complex situation was exacerbated by the destruction of government organization and agencies that could regulate and monitor events. The US government responded by announcing a special program to give humanitarian visas in such cases. Conversely, there is little evidence that US migration policy was used to help adult Haitians whose lives had also been destroyed by the earthquake (Clements & Farrell, 2011).

During this time, many international organizations spoke out against the movement of children from Haiti, and the Haitian government issued a warning that child traffickers might take advantage of the ensuing chaos to prey on vulnerable children. On January 18, 2010, the International Social Service (ISS) – a network of international legal and social work professionals who help to carry out the Hague Convention – stated that intercountry adoptions should not take place in a situation of war or natural disaster when it was impossible to verify the personal and family situations of children (ISS, 2010). On January 21, Carolyn Miles of *Save the Children*, an international charity founded in the United Kingdom, was quoted as saying that "[t]he vast majority of the children currently on their own still have family members alive who will be desperate to be reunited with them and will be able to care for them with the right support" (Schapiro, 2010). Later that year, *Save the Children* published a detailed report informing workers in the field of international humanitarian welfare on how to make the right decision for children in emergencies (Doyle, 2010).

Increases in international adoption in the year after the earthquake

If the humanitarian visas are included in the US figures for adoption from Haiti, the total number of Haitian adoptions to countries worldwide in 2010 can be estimated to be over 2,500 – more than double the total for 2009 – with significant rises in the number of children going to the US, Canada, France, and the Netherlands (Table 15.2).

These four countries had been the most involved in adoption from Haiti prior to the earthquake and seem clearly to have encouraged expediting the adoptions already in hand as well as accepting some new applications. In contrast, Spain, which had received 100 children from Haiti in the previous five years, took no children as its intercountry adoption legislation does not permit adoption from countries in crisis (International Social Service, 2010).

For many years France had been the main destination for children adopted internationally from Haiti, with more than 4,000 adopted since 2000. At the beginning of 2010, more than 900 French families were in the process of applying to adopt from Haiti, and 276 were already matched with a child. On January 14, France stated that it would not "expedite" adoptions, but on January 17 many of the prospective adoptive parents held a demonstration in front of the Quai d'Orsay demanding that procedures be hastened. In response, the French Central Authority announced that any child with serious medical needs or in the process of adoption would be evacuated from Haiti. In the next six weeks, a series of Air France flights brought out 489 children (Dambach & Baglietto, 2010, p. 44). A similar number were brought to France in the latter part of 2010 following a special agreement with the Haitian government to expedite adoption judgements.

Table 15.2 Adoptions from Haiti 2004–2017 (with peak year in bold)

	2000	*2004*	*2005*	*2007*	*2008*	*2009*	*2010*	*2011*	*2014*	*2017*
US	130	356	231	190	302	330	**1,223**[a]	33	464	227
France	167	507	475	403	731	651	**992**	34	23	70
Canada	127	**159**	115	89	148	141	135	77	33	24
Netherlands	59	42	51	28	91	60	**108**	0	13	15
Germany	n/a	46	27	11	36	45	13[b]	**78**	11	25
Spain	0	**36**	24	22	27	13	0	0	0	0
Italy	0	9	**13**	2	0	0	0	0	1	31
All countries	533	1,170	949	783	1,310	1,210	**2,501**	239	572	397

a US fiscal year data – includes 1,090 "humanitarian" visas (Reitz, 2010), but it remains unclear how many were adopted and whether these are recorded additionally in later years.

b ISS (2010) estimated 62 adoptions to Germany in Jan–Feb 2010. The German Central Authority totals of 78 (in 2011) and 102 (in 2012) indicate when the children were formally adopted.

Although in response to the 2004 South Asian tsunami, the US Department of State mandated that it would not be possible for US citizens to adopt children who had been orphaned, the response to the earthquake in Haiti five years later was somewhat different, largely because of the number of adoptions in process. Within days of the disaster, the US Department of State announced that orphaned children from Haiti would be allowed to enter the US temporarily on a case-by-case basis to ensure they received proper care (Reitz, 2010; USCIS, 2010).

Under the plan, entry into the US would be granted to children who had been legally confirmed as orphans eligible for intercountry adoption by the government of Haiti and were being adopted by US citizens, or to children who had been previously identified by an adoption service provider or facilitator as eligible for intercountry adoption and had been matched to a US citizen as a prospective adoptive parent (Lindsey, 2010; Reitz, 2010). However, there were concerns that documentation in Haiti might lie buried beneath rubble, making previous adoption details difficult to determine, thus creating vulnerability to fraud, abuse, and trafficking.

This program was ended three months later on April 13, 2010 at the request of the Haitian government (Baker, 2010), but by that time 1,090 such visas had been issued. These humanitarian visas were not recorded as adoption visas in the US Department of State's annual report for 2010, which then indicated that the number of adoptions from Haiti in 2010 had *fallen* after the earthquake.

Similar to the US, the Netherlands announced on January 15, 2010 that it would facilitate the transfer of children for whom an adoption judgement had been made. Soon after, they extended this policy to those where adoptive parent/child matching had occurred. On January 17, it was decided that nine children who had not been matched with adoptive parents would be brought in (Dambach & Baglietto, 2010). Within weeks of the earthquake, a Dutch flight brought 106 children from quake-ravaged Haiti to the Netherlands and Luxembourg. Three other adoptees died in an air crash alongside their prospective adoptive parents who had flown to Haiti to collect them. Many of these children flown from Haiti were in the process of being adopted before the quake, but the move had not been approved by a Haitian judge (Adams, 2010). The number of children taken to the Netherlands in the two months after the quake was larger than it was for the entire year of 2009.

Between 2001 and 2009, Canadians adopted nearly 1,000 children from Haiti, a policy that had not been without problems. Following the coup against Jean-Bertrand Aristide in Haiti on February 29, 2004, the Canadian Department of Foreign Affairs warned prospective adoptive parents against travelling to Haiti, a warning repeated at various times in the next three years. However, in the early months of 2010, some Canadian adoptions in progress were fast tracked and emergency airlifts were arranged for children already matched. The government of Haiti gave permission for 217 children who were already in the adoption process at the time of the earthquake to go to Canada. This was more than the total number of Haitian children adopted to Canada in 2009. By the end of February, 203 children had arrived in their new country (Selman, 2012a), but the total registered by Canada as adopted in 2010 was 135, and the number registered in 2011 was 77, fewer than the annual totals recorded in each of the preceding ten years.

Adoption from Haiti in the years after the earthquake

Nine years after the earthquake, it is now possible to see what actually occurred and how this affected the number of adoptions from Haiti worldwide, in particular, those countries that had taken substantial numbers of Haitian adoptees in the past. Table 15.2 shows the figures for the full year of 2010 as reported by the receiving countries involved.

In April 2010, the Haitian government announced that it would allow the completion of adoptions started prior to the earthquake and consider new applications for any child who was genuinely an orphan. In January 2011, the US Department of State reported that Haiti's adoption authority, the *Institut du Bien-être Social et de Recherches*, had informed the US government that they were accepting new adoption applications for children who were documented as orphans or who had been relinquished by their birth parent(s) (Selman, 2012a).

On March 2, 2011, Haiti signed the 1993 *Hague Convention on Protection of Children and Cooperation in Respect of Intercountry Adoption*. France and other countries viewed this as a step toward a resumption of adoption with safeguards to ensure it is in the best interests of the child. In June 2011 there was a meeting in Port-au-Prince of the "Montreal Group" of nine receiving countries to encourage early ratification and a resumption of adoptions. Consequently, although the number of international adoptions from Haiti in 2011 and 2012 fell much lower than the numbers in 2010, there was an increase in following years of 2013 and 2014. Yet since 2014, the annual number of adoptions has fallen again and remains below 500, less than half the total recorded international adoptions from Haiti in 2004, and less than one-fifth of the total estimated for 2010 (Table 15.2). Nevertheless, in 2017 the number of Haitian children adopted internationally was similar to international adoptions from South Korea and Vietnam, and more than Russia (Selman, 2018).

Reflections on the policy of expediting adoptions

In the days following the earthquake, a considerable number of children left Haiti, and most were said to be in the process of being legally adopted. Rotabi and Bergquist (2010) estimate the number to be well over 1,000, and ISS proposed a figure of over 2,000 in the first two months of 2010 (Dambach & Baglietto, 2010). What could not be established, however, was how many of these children were orphans; how many were taken without full legal investigation; and whether any can be said to have been trafficked, given that there was an existing history of trafficking to or via the Dominican Republic for child labor, sex, or selling to US adopters (Smolin, 2004).

In retrospect what is clear is that the fast-tracking of adoptions made it impossible to ensure that all procedures were followed appropriately, and the normal process of placement was disrupted. This meant that some children were able to travel to the receiving countries with their new parents who were often ill prepared for the sudden placement, and that many of the children, already traumatized by the earthquake, were subjected to additional stress resulting from such a hasty transition (Dambach & Baglietto, 2010; Rotabi & Bergquist, 2010).

There have been many concerns over the process of expediting adoptions from Haiti after the earthquake, even when the adoptions were in process. The ISS report (Dambach & Baglietto, 2010) details these concerns using case studies of the countries involved.

In late January 2010, the Hague Conference requested that all contracting states apply the same safeguards and standards as would be required if Haiti had ratified the 1993 Convention. An information note published on January 20 (Hague Conference on Private International Law, 2010a) stated:

> [I]n a disaster situation, like that brought about by the earthquake, efforts to reunite a displaced child with his or her parents or family members must take priority. Premature and unregulated attempts to organise the adoption of such a child abroad should be avoided and resisted.
>
> *(Hague Conference on Private International Law, 2010b, p. 5)*

It was also determined that it was justifiable to expedite the process if a child's identity was verified and a court decision for adoption made, while stressing that a disaster could not be a reason for bypassing essential safeguards for safe adoption, especially when child protection services had broken down.

Natural disasters since the Haitian earthquake

A year after the Haitian earthquake, an even more powerful earthquake hit Japan, with an estimated 20,000 deaths and many children orphaned. Many people offered to adopt these children, but Tazuru Ogaway, director of the Japanese adoption agency, *Across Japan*, responded that "such … emails make Japanese people very uncomfortable, because for us, it sounds like someone who is looking for 'what I want' from our terrible disaster" (Macedo, 2011). In this case, offers to adopt were not limited to the US, and reports indicate that many Chinese families offered to take in children. Japan has sent between 30 and 40 adopted children a year to the US over the past decade, but the US State Department indicated that there was no intention to expedite any "pipeline" children – those in the process of being adopted but with no final court decision – as this would not have been acceptable under adoption procedures in that country. Macedo (2011) also notes that many people – including leading adoption agencies – felt uneasy about the response to Haiti and did not want this repeated in the case of Japan. What happened to the children orphaned by the Japanese earthquake is unclear. Macedo reports Tom DeFilipo of Joint Council on International Children's Services as explaining that Japan has around 400 children's homes caring for over 25,000 unparented children, and that there is no tradition of domestic adoption for such children.

The reaction in Japan to other countries' offers to adopt Japanese children reflects the position typical of an affluent country which deems that it does not need or want such help in a crisis. There would likely be a similar reaction in most developed countries. For example, how would Americans feel if Mexico had offered to adopt their children after Hurricane Katrina?

In making international comparisons, it is worth noting that the issue of adoption was not raised after the floods in Pakistan later in 2010. This was not only because of memories of the firm rejection of international adoption following their 2005 earthquake (Masood, 2005), but also because of lessons learned from the Haitian earthquake.

More recently, in 2015, Nepal suffered a 7.9 magnitude earthquake and there were fears that there would be a similar response of rescue given the concerns over illegal adoption in the country in previous years (UNICEF & Terre des Hommes, 2008). Yet child protection organizations united to ensure that separated children were quickly reunited with their families. Nepal had signed the Hague Convention in April 2009, and in November of the same year, a group of experts were sent to Nepal to advise on how to help these children (Hague Conference on Private International Law, 2009). The response of the international community also owed much to lessons learned from previous natural disasters (van Doore, 2015, 2016). International adoptions from Nepal had peaked at 452 in 2006 but fell to eight in 2012 following a review of procedures. By 2014 the annual total had fallen to four and there was no increase in the years after the earthquake.

Conclusion: policy and practice implications

Six months after the Haitian earthquake, the 10th Special Commission of the HCCH was held June 17–25, 2010. Included in the *Conclusions and Recommendations* section of the statement in *Response to disaster situations* was advice repeated in its earlier information note recognizing that premature and unregulated attempts to organize adoption abroad should be avoided and resisted. It further stated that "No new adoption applications should be considered in the period after the disaster or before the authorities in that State are in a position to apply the necessary safeguards" (Hague Conference on Private International Law, 2010b, p. 5) and called for government authorities in all countries to seek a common approach based on lessons learned.

Nine years later, this view of adoption in the context of disaster seems to have a wide consensus among international bodies. Mellon, from the National Council for Adoption, outlined five reasons international adoption was not the appropriate response to a natural disaster, war, or other crisis (Mellon, 2016). In Montgomery and Powell's recent book *Saving International Adoption* (2018), they argue for a reversal of the current decline in international adoption. The authors assert that it is vital to separate the two sides of the Haiti adoptions: the "pipeline" cases – which they do not see as problematic – from the children removed without proper parenthood or parent permission as a result of the chaos existing after a crisis, which should not be allowed. The account of international adoption from Haiti after the earthquake shows that this was not a clear division and that expediting adoptions was used to fast track new adoptions and often involved cases with inadequate paperwork.

A report from Terre des Hommes (Cantwell, 2017) also raised concerns over the process of expedition, noting the involvement of many private individuals (e.g., lawyers, intermediaries, and prospective adoptive parents) whose interests might be prioritized over the best interests of the children. Fronek and Cuthbert (2012) further argued that the literature on the psychosocial care of children in post-disaster contexts demonstrates that expatriation of children in such situations is often against the best interests of the child. However, recent reports on Haiti's orphanages found that at least 30,000 children (a number that increased in the aftermath of the earthquake) are living in poor conditions, that most are not orphans, and that many adoption agencies are run for profit (even if funded by church and other non-profit organizations) mainly from the US (Cohen, 2018). In this case there seems to be an urgent need for foster care and local adoption.

New stories of children moved from Rwanda during and after the genocide have emerged, including those mistakenly registered as orphans and adopted abroad (Kanamugire, 2017), but there is also more evidence on the rise in the number of orphanages for the majority who stayed in the country. This has been recognized as a significant problem, and the Rwandan government announced plans to close all its orphanages by 2020 (Cruddas, 2015), a project that has proved hard to achieve (Bakker, 2016). This is reflective of problems throughout African countries as the continuing demand for intercountry adoption has raised concerns over pressures from orphanages funded by Western agencies to provide children for adoption, as well as concern for those exploited by child traffickers (African Child Policy Forum, 2012).

From the aftermath of the Korean and Vietnam wars to the response to the Haitian earthquake, we have learned how international adoption has been one response to war and natural disaster, and how often these responses have retrospectively been viewed as "misguided kindness" (Doyle, 2010) with negative consequences for some of the children rescued. International responses to recent natural disasters seem to indicate that lessons have been learned, but there remains a need to be vigilant and to explore alternatives that enable children affected to remain in the land of their birth without the equally misguided response of orphanages funded by rich countries.

References

Adams, G. (2010, January 19). Adoption agencies warned off Haiti's orphans. *The Independent*. Retrieved April 15, 2019, from www.independent.co.uk/news/world/americas

African Child Policy Forum. (2012). *Intercountry adoption alternatives and controversies*. Proceedings of the Fifth International Policy Conference on the African Child, Addis Ababa, 29–30 May, 2012. Retrieved April 17, 2019, from https://bettercarenetwork.org

Altstein, H., & Simon, R. (1991). *Intercountry adoption: A multinational perspective*. New York, NY: Praeger.

Bajak, F. (2010, February 27). Baptists' "orphans" all have families. *Sydney Morning Herald*. Retrieved May 13, 2019, from www.theage.com.au/world/baptists-orphans-all-have-families-20100221-onzu.html

Baker, M. D. (2010, April 9). *USCIS to end special humanitarian parole program for Haiti orphans at Haitian government's request*. Law Office of Michael D, Baker. Retrieved May 15, 2019, from https://mikebakerlaw.wordpress.com/2010/04/09/uscis-to-end-special-humanitarian-parole-program-for-haitian-orphans-at-haitian-governments-request/

Bakker, P. (2016, January 21). *Closure of Rwanda genocide orphanages exacts heavy toll*. AlJazeera, Retrieved April 17, 2019, from www.aljazeera.com/indepth/features/2015/12/closure-rwanda-genocide-orphanages-exacts-heavy-toll-151215114710827.html

BBC News. (2000, November 14). Rwanda accuses Italy over orphans. *BBC*. Retrieved April 17, 2019, from http://news.bbc.co.uk/1/hi/world/africa/1022875.stm

BBC News. (2007, October 29). Profile: Zoe's ark. *BBC News*. Retrieved April 27, 2019, from http://news.bbc.co.uk/2/hi/europe/7067374.stm

Bergquist, K. (2012). Implications of the Hague Convention on the humanitarian evacuation and "rescue" of children. In J. L. Gibbons & K. S. Rotabi (Eds.), *Intercountry adoption: Policies, practices, and outcomes* (pp. 43–54). Surrey, UK: Ashgate Press.

Cantwell, N. (2017). *The sale of children and illegal adoption*. Den Haag: Terre des Hommes.

Chrisafis, A. (2008, April 1). Chad president pardons French charity workers. *The Guardian*. Retrieved May 14, 2019, from www.guardian.co.uk/world/2008/apr/01/france.internationalaidanddevelopment

Clark, M. (2010, February 1). Haiti "orphan" rescue mission: Adoption or child trafficking? *The Christian Science Monitor*. Retrieved April 16, 2019 from www.csmonitor.com/World/GlobalNews/2010/0201/Haiti-Americans-accused-of-child-trafficking-could-be-tried-in-US/

Clements, M., & Farrell, K. (2011). *Beyond aid: Migration as a tool for disaster recovery*. Washington, DC: Center for Global Development.

Cohen, L. (2018, March 2). How traffickers exploit children in Haiti's orphanages. *CNN*. Retrieved April 16, 2019 from https://edition.cnn.com/2017/11/20/health/haiti-orphanages/index.html

ColomboPage (2017, Sep 25) *Netherlands launch investigation into irregularities on adoptions from Sri Lanka*. Retrieved May 15, 2019, from www.colombopage.com/archive_17B/Sep25_1506354712CH.php

Crary, D. (2010, February 2). Arrest of US Baptists trying to remove Haitian orphans deepens international adoption debate. *Cleveland.com*. Retrieved May 15, 2019 from www.cleveland.com/world/2010/02/arrest_of_us_baptists_trying_t.html

Cruddas, S. (2015, March 12). Rwanda outgrows its genocide orphanages. *BBC News*. Retrieved from www.bbc.co.uk/news/world-africa-31830220

Dambach, C., & Baglietto, C. (2010). *Haiti: "Expediting" intercountry adoptions in the aftermath of a natural disaster*. Geneva: ISS. Retrieved April 14, 2019, from https://resourcecentre.savethechildren.net/library/haiti-expediting-intercountry-adoptions-aftermath-natural-disaster-preventing-future-harm

Davis, J. (2017, October 14). The "orphan" I adopted from Uganda already had a family. *CNN Opinion*. Retrieved April 16, 2019 From https://edition.cnn.com/2017/10/13/opinions/adoption-uganda-opinion-davis/index.html

Defence for Children International. (1991). *Romania; The adoption of Romanian children by foreigners*. Geneva: DCI/ISS.

Dodds, P. (1997). *Outer search inner journey: An orphan and adoptee's quest*. Washington: Aphrodite Publishing Company.

Doyle, J. (2010). *Misguided kindness. Making the right decisions for children in emergencies*. London: Save the Children UK.

Duval Smith, A., & Rolley, S. (2007, November 4). Did they plot to steal Africa's orphans of war? Retrieved from www.guardian.co.uk/world/2007/nov/04/france.sudan

Ellingson, L. B. (2007). Creating a climate for "best interests"; Recognizing intercountry adoptions as a disfavored placement under the Hague Convention. In K. Park Nelson, E. Kim, & L. M. Peterson (Eds.), *Proceedings of the First International Korean Adoption Studies Symposium*. Seoul, South Korea, July 2017.

Evans, K. (2000). *The lost daughters of China*. New York: Tarcher.

Frenkiel, O. (2001, April 12). Rwanda's tug-of-war children. *BBC News*. Retrieved April 20, 2019 from http://news.bbc.co.uk/1/hi/programmes/crossing_continents/africa/1271890.stm

Fronek, P., & Cuthbert, D. (2012). History repeating … Disaster-related intercountry adoption and the psychosocial care of children. *Social Policy & Society*, *121*, 429–442.

Gray, M. (2010, January 16). Orphanage: Adoption plan needed for Haitian children. *CNN*. Retrieved April 17, 2019, from http://edition.cnn.com/2010/WORLD/americas/01/15/haiti.orphanage

The Guardian. (2017, September 20). There were a lot of baby farms: Sri Lanka to act over adoption racket claims. Retrieved May 15, 2019, from www.theguardian.com/global-development/2017/sep/20/baby-farms-sri-lanka-admits-adoption-racket-claims

Hague Conference on Private International Law. (2009). Intercountry adoption technical assistance programme – Report of mission to Nepal (23–27 November, 2009) Retrieved April 23, 2019 from https://assets.hcch.net/upload/wop/nepal_rpt09.pdf.

Hague Conference on Private International Law. (2010a, January 20). *Information note to states and central authorities: Haiti earthquake and intercountry adoption of children*. The Hague: HccH. Retrieved April 17, 2019 from www.hcch.net/index_en.php?act=events.details&year=2010&varevent=183

Hague Conference on Private International Law. (2010b). *Conclusions and recommendations of the special commission of june 2010*. The Hague: HccH. Retrieved April 16, 2019 from www.hcch.net/upload/wop/adop2010concl_e.pdf

Hodge, D. (2012). *Rescuing the children; The story of the Kindertransport*. Toronto: Penguin Random House.

Hoksbergen, R. (1986). *Adoption in worldwide perspective*. Lisse: Swets & Zeutlinger.

Hubinette, T. (2006). From orphan trains to babylifts: Colonial trafficking, empire building and social engineering. In J. Trenka, J. Oparah, & S. Y. Shin (Eds.), *Outsiders within: Writing on transracial adoption* (pp. 139–149). Cambridge, MA: South End Press.

International Social Service. (2010). *Earthquake in Haiti: Intercountry adoption cases*. Geneva: ISS. Retrieved April 15, 2019 from http://iss-blog.iss-usa.org/earthquake-in-haiti-intercountry-adoption-cases

Johnson, K. (2016). *China's hidden children*. Chicago: The University of Chicago Press.

Joyce, K. (2013). *The child catchers: Rescue, trafficking and the new gospel of adoption*. New York: Public Affairs.

Kanamugire, J. (2017, October 31). Father finally re-united with daughter lost in chaos of Rwanda's 1994 genocide. *The Guardian*. Retrieved April 16, 2019, from www.theguardian.com/global-development/2017/oct/31/father-finally-reunited-with-daughter-lost-in-chaos-of-rwanda-1994-genocide

Kane, S. (1993). The movement of children for international adoption: An epidemiological perspective. *The Social Science Journal*, *30*(4), 323–339. doi:10.1016/0362-3319(93)90012-K

Lindsey, M. (2010). Examining intercountry adoption after the earthquake in Haiti. *Adoption Advocate no. 28*. Retrieved May 1, 2019, from www.adoptioncouncil.org/resources/adoption-advocate

Macedo, D. (2011, March 22). Foreigners looking to adopt Japanese earthquake orphans need not apply. *Fox News*. Retrieved April 17, 2019, from www.foxnews.com/world/foreigners-looking-to-adopt-japanese-earthquake-orphans-need-not-apply

Martin, A. (2000). The legacy of operation babylift. *Adoption Today*, *2*(4). Retrieved April 17, 2019 from www.adoptvietnam.org/adoption/babylift.htm

Masood, A. (2005, December 16). Pakistan bans adoption of quake orphans. *Arab News*. Retrieved April 17, 2019, from www.arabnews.com/node/277457

McGinnis, H. (2005). *Intercountry adoption in emergencies: The tsunami orphans*. NY: The Evan B. Donaldson Adoption Institute. Retrieved April 17, 2019, from www.adoptioninstitute.org/wp-content/uploads/2013/12/2005_Brief_ICA_In_Emergencies_April.pdf

Mellon, J. (2016, November 6). 5 reasons international adoption is not the appropriate response to a natural disaster, war or other crisis. Retrieved April 16, 2019, from https://adoption.com/

Mezmur, B. (2009a). From Angelina (to Madonna) to Zoe's ark: What are the "A-Z" lessons for intercountry adoption in Africa?. *International Journal of Law, Policy and the Family*, *23*, 145–173. doi:10.1093/lawfam/ebn013

Mezmur, B. (2009b). Intercountry adoption as a measure of last resort in Africa: Advancing the rights of a child rather than the right to a child. *Sur-International Journal of Human Rights*, *6*(10), 83–104. doi:10.1590/S1806-64452009000100005

Montgomery, M., & Powell, I. (2018). *Saving international adoption*. Nashville: Vanderbilt University Press.

Munroe, R., & Rigsby, J. (1996). *Death by default: A policy of fatal neglect in China's state orphanages*. New York: Human Rights Watch.

Radnege, A. (2010, February 21). Found: The parents of all 33 Haiti earthquake "orphans". *Metro*. Retrieved from http://metro.co.uk/news/world/814188-found-the-parents-of-all-33-haiti-earthquake-orphans

Reich, D. (1990). Children of the Nightmare. *Adoption & Fostering*, *14*(1), 9–14.

Reitz, W. A. (2010). Reflections on the special humanitarian parole program for Haitian orphans. *New York Law School Law Review*, *55*, 791–798.

Rotabi, K., Armistead, L., & Monico, C. (2015). Sanctioned government intervention, "misguided information" and child abduction activities of US citizens in the midst of disaster. In Ballard, R. L., Goodno, N. H., Cochran, R. F. and Milbrandt, J. A. (Eds.), *The intercountry adoption debate* (pp. 629–650). Newcastle upon Tyne, UK: Cambridge Scholars Publishing.

Rotabi, K., & Bergquist, K. (2010). Vulnerable children in the aftermath of Haiti's earthquake of 2010: A call for sound policy and processes to prevent international child sales and theft. *Journal of Global Social Work Practice*, *3*(1), 1–5.

Schapiro, R. (2010, January 21). Haiti earthquake: Groups urge adoption freeze, believing kids' kin may be alive. *New York Daily News*. Retrieved from www.nydailynews.com/news/world/haiti-earthquake-groups-urge-adoption-freeze-believing-kids-kin-alive-article-1.459850

Selman, P. (2009). From Bucharest to Beijing: Changes in countries sending children for international adoption. In G. Wrobel & E. Neil (Eds.), *International advances in adoption research for practice* (pp. 41–70). Chichester, UK: Wiley-Blackwell.

Selman, P. (2010). Intercountry adoption as globalised motherhood. In W. Chavkin & J. Mather (Eds.), *The globalisation of motherhood* (pp. 79–105). London: Routledge.

Selman, P. (2012a). Intercountry adoption after the Haiti earthquake; Rescue or robbery? *Adoption & Fostering*, *35*(4), 41–49. doi:10.1177/030857591103500405

Selman, P. (2012b). The rise and fall of intercountry adoption in the 21st century: Global trends from 2001 to 2010. In J. L. Gibbons & K. S. Rotabi (Eds.), *Intercountry adoption: Policies, practices, and outcomes* (pp. 7–28). Surrey, UK: Ashgate Press.

Selman, P. (2012c). The global decline of intercountry adoption: What lies ahead? *Social Policy & Society*, *11*(3), 381–397. doi:10.1017/S1474746412000085

Selman, P. (2015). Global trends in intercountry adoption: 2003–2013. In Ballard, R. L., Goodno, N. H., Cochran, R. F. and Milbrandt, J. A. (Eds.), *The intercountry adoption debate* (pp. 9–48). Newcastle upon Tyne, UK: Cambridge Scholars Publishing. Retrieved from www.newcastle.academia.edu/PeterSelman

Selman, P. (2017). One million children moving, reflections on 70 years of international adoption since the end of World War II. Paper presented at *Conference on the History and Practices of International Adoption*. November 17–18. University of Kassel, Germany. (Convenor – Silke Hackenesch).

Selman, P. (2018). *Global statistics for intercountry adoption: Receiving states and states of origin 2004–17*. Retrieved April 16, 2019, from https://assets.hcch.net/docs/a8fe9f19-23e6-40c2-855e-388e112bf1f5.pdf

Selman, P. (2019). *International adoptions from the People's Republic of China to 16 receiving states, 1992–2017*. Retrieved from www.newcastle.academia.edu/PeterSelman

Simon, R. J., & Altstein, H. (2000). *Adoption across borders: Serving the children in transracial and intercountry adoptions*. Lanham, MD: Rowman & Littlefield Publishers, Inc.

Smolin, D. (2004). Intercountry adoption as child trafficking. *Valparaiso Law Review*, *39*, 281–325. Retrieved April 18, 2019, from http://works.bepress.com/david_smolin/3/

Taylor, L. (2017). *In the children's best interests: Unaccompanied displaced children in American-occupied Germany, 1945–1952*. Toronto: University of Toronto Press.

Textor, M. R. (1991). International adoption in West Germany; a private affair. In H. Altsein& & R. Simon (Eds.), *Intercountry adoption: A multinational perspective* (pp. 109–126). New York: Praeger.

Thompson, G. (2010, February 23). Questions surface after Haitian airlift. *The New York Times*. Retrieved from www.nytimes.com/2010/02/24/world/americas/24orphans.html

UNICEF, & Terre des Hommes. (2008). *Adopting the rights of the child: A study on intercountry adoption and its influence on child protection in Nepal*. Kathmandu: Terre des Hommes Foundation.

US Citizenship & Immigration Services. (2010). Special humanitarian parole program for Haitian orphan fact sheet. Retrieved April 29, 2019, from www.ilw.com/immigrationdaily/news/2010,0407-haitian.shtm

van Doore, K. (2015, May 5). Earthquake orphans – What Nepal can learn from Haiti. *Child Rights International Network, The Conversation*. Retrieved from http://theconversation.com/earthquake-orphans-what-nepal-can-learn-from-haiti-41165

van Doore, K. (2016). Paper orphans: Exploring child trafficking for the purpose of orphanages. *International Journal of Children's Rights*, *24*, 378–407. doi:10.1163/15718182-02402006

PART III
Lived experience

16

BIRTH MOTHERS' OPTIONS COUNSELING AND RELINQUISHMENT EXPERIENCES

Elissa E. Madden, Donna M. Aguiniga, and Scott Ryan

This chapter offers important insight into the experiences of women who relinquished a child for adoption: birth mothers. The data collected by the authors for a report on counseling experiences in adoption published by the Donaldson Adoption Institute (DAI), were analyzed to provide a broader overview of the thoughts, considerations, and experiences of birth mothers who relinquished a child during the era of open adoptions (i.e., biological parents continue some type of contact with adoptive parents) beginning in the late 1980s. It begins with a brief overview of relinquishment in US adoption history and important aspects of the relinquishment process. The methodology of the research project is then described, followed by the findings regarding access to information on relinquishment, factors considered, sources of support, sources of pressure, and birth mothers' reflections on the decision to relinquish. It concludes with a discussion of the results and related recommendations for practice and policy.

Relinquishment

Relinquishment of infants at birth has become an increasingly rare event in the US (Coleman & Garratt, 2016). The percentage of parents who place a child for adoption has steadily declined over the past 40–50 years for myriad reasons, including an increase in access to birth control, the legalization of elective abortion, and a decrease in stigma attached to unwed single parenting (Coleman & Garratt, 2016; Jones, 2008). Jones and Placek (2017) estimated that in 2014, one-half of one percent of all live births and 1.1 percent of births to unmarried women in the US resulted in the infants being relinquished for adoption.

Prior to the 1970s, unmarried women who became pregnant (referred to therein as expectant mothers) were pressured to relinquish parental rights and place their child for adoption while being given little to no information about possible alternatives (Castle, 2014; Ellison, 2003; Fisher, 2012; Johnson & Faase, 2012; McAdoo, 1992). Under the threat of intense social stigma, mothers who placed a child for adoption during this era (referred to therein as birth mothers) generally had little input in the adoption process (Castle, 2014; Donaldson Adoption Institute [DAI], 2007; Wegar, 1997). Furthermore, attachment theory, the presiding theory guiding placements by the 1950s, prescribed that mothers be separated from their infants as soon after birth as possible to enable the children to begin the bonding process with the adoptive parents (Ellison, 2003).

Beginning in the 1960s, advocates for expectant mothers' rights began calling for increased protections for expectant and birth mothers, including, but not limited to, the time required before a mother is allowed to relinquish her parental rights after the birth and a revocation period in which a mother can change her mind without having to prove to the courts that it is in the best interest of the child (Child Welfare Information Gateway [CWIG], 2017; DAI, 2007). Currently, at least 30 US states and the District of Columbia now require a mandated waiting period before a relinquishment of maternal rights can be signed (CWIG, 2017). The specific waiting period varies widely from state to state, ranging from the ability to sign during the pregnancy available in Alabama, to a mandated minimum waiting period of 15 days after the birth in Rhode Island (CWIG, 2017). Of the 30 states that require waiting periods, Kansas has the shortest waiting period at 12 hours; however, the average waiting period required by law is 72 hours after the birth (CWIG, 2017). Currently, 16 states specify a minimum waiting period of 72 hours. The legislation establishing these waiting periods, however, has been found to be limited, and sometimes vague. Some advocates argue that these measures are insufficient and do not ensure adequate protections for expectant and birth parents (DAI, 2007).

Globally, a number of countries have longer waiting periods than the US. For instance, New Zealand requires a minimum waiting period of 12 days for birth mothers (New Zealand Government, 2018). Germany mandates that relinquishment papers cannot be signed before the infant is eight weeks old (Bürgerliches Gesetzbuch [BGB] §1747).

Another important consideration is the revocation period during which birth mothers can nullify their decision to relinquish their parental rights. Samuels (2005) noted that in a number of first-world countries (e.g., many European countries and Australia), consent to terminate parental rights does not become irrevocable for as many as six weeks. However in the US, only a handful of states and the District of Columbia have laws that recognize a time period after the relinquishment papers have been signed in which the birth mother can nullify the contract without having to prove fraud, duress, coercion, or that it would be in the best interest of the child (CWIG, 2017; Samuels, 2005). In these states the time periods range from three days in Maine to 30 days in Pennsylvania (CWIG, 2017). There are also cases where birth parents are able to contest the contract based on the best interest of the child. Yet, since the adoptive parents are generally more affluent, established, and have usually had custody of the child since its birth, they are likely to have the legal upper hand (DAI, 2007; Zill, 2015).

Birth parents' response to the relinquishment process

Research has shown that the decision to relinquish parental rights of a child for adoption is a difficult process for many parents and one that can be fraught with conflicted feelings of grief, loss, shame, isolation, and guilt (Freundlich, 2002; Wiley & Baden, 2005; Winkler, Brown, van Keppel, & Blanchard, 1988). While there is general consensus among researchers regarding the immediate impact that placing a child for adoption can have on mothers, research regarding the long-term effects of relinquishing a child for adoption for mothers is less clear. Based upon a review of 1980s' and 1990s' adoption research, Freundlich (2002) suggested that two opposing, though not mutually exclusive, standpoints could be found in the literature: (1) the belief that relinquishing a child for adoption is a traumatic and life-altering experience that can have lasting emotional and interpersonal impact for birth mothers, and (2) the belief that relinquishing a child provides beneficial gains, primarily in terms of economic and educational attainment, for mothers who find themselves in an unplanned/crisis pregnancy. Askren and Bloom (1999) noted a theme of persistent grief that negatively impacted various aspects of birth mothers' lives in their meta-analysis of published studies on the post-relinquishment experiences of birth mothers. More recently, Coleman and Garratt (2016) concluded that mothers in their study experienced prolonged and ambiguous grief following their decision to relinquish their child for adoption. However, a longitudinal analysis of 127 birth mothers 12–20 years post-placement by Henney, Ayers-Lopez, McRoy, and Grotevant (2007) found that birth mothers' grief was somewhat attenuated by time. Furthermore, Henny and colleagues noted that other factors appear to play a role in grief, including the birth mother's life stage, their situation at the time, and the amount of satisfaction the mother has with her contact arrangement.

Services and support during the relinquishment process

For expectant parents experiencing a crisis or unintended pregnancy, the decision to relinquish their child for adoption often occurs without adequate access to services and support during their decision-making process. Most advocates agree that expectant parents should be presented with accurate information that enables them to weigh the advantages and disadvantages of all possible options for the pregnancy (Johnson & Faase, 2012; Simmonds & Likis, 2005; Singer, 2004). While ethical and best practice guidelines require that expectant parents be informed of all their options, free from the agency, attorney, or counselor's bias, some advocates have observed that expectant parents are not always provided with clear and non-directive information about all options and resources available to them, or the implications associated with each decision (DAI, 2007; McAdoo, 1992; Wiley & Baden, 2005). Currently, fewer than half of the states in the US include counseling in adoption-related statutes. Of those, most merely advise, rather than mandate, that expectant parents be made aware that counseling is available (CWIG, 2017; DAI, 2007). Among states that do mandate or advise that counseling be made available to expectant parents, only a small number provide explicit guidance for adoption professionals regarding the range of information that must be shared, the duration and number of required sessions (including post-relinquishment), or who may provide counseling services (DAI, 2007; Johnson & Faase, 2012).

In addition to inadequate or absent counseling services, expectant parents in most states do not have access to independent legal representation to advise them of their state's laws and the implications of these laws for both them and their child. Currently, only two states, Louisiana and New Hampshire, mandate that birth parents be provided with independent counsel to protect their interests pre- and post-relinquishment (CWIG, 2017).

This chapter shares findings from the DAI's Options Counseling Study. Findings presented in this chapter represent a portion of the findings from the overall study that specifically pertain to birth mothers' experiences and satisfaction with their decision to place their child for adoption. It should be noted that the term "birth mother" is used throughout the presentation of the findings, as the study surveyed women who had voluntarily relinquished parental rights to an infant for adoption in the US post-1989.

Methodology

Recruitment and procedures

Potential participants for the online survey were recruited through a number of different methods with the intent of maximizing the number of responses. Women who had relinquished a child for adoption in the US after 1989 were invited to participate in the survey. The time frame was established to limit the sample to birth mothers for whom open adoption arrangements were an option. Additionally, based on policies implemented by many agencies during the early 1990s, we believed that there would be more uniformity in experiences of women who relinquished a child for adoption during this time frame compared to those who relinquished when closed adoptions were more pervasive. Birth fathers who had relinquished a child for adoption in the US during the last 25 years (after 1989) were also invited to participate in the survey; however, only six birth fathers responded. The comparatively low number of responses from birth fathers (n=6) prohibited us from drawing meaningful conclusions about their experiences.

The study was publicized through various adoption-related websites and monthly newsletters. Online interest, advocacy and support groups, blogs, and listservs were also used to recruit participants. In addition to the above recruitment methods, some participants were recruited for the study through snowball sampling; that is, respondents were asked to forward information about the survey to other potential participants. Survey data were collected between November 2015 and July 2016 via Qualtrics, a secure web-based tool for conducting online surveys. The final sample size for analysis was 223 birth mothers. Since the snowball sampling technique prohibited counting the number of potential participants, a response rate cannot be determined.

Sample

Table 16.1 provides a demographic overview of birth mother characteristics at the time they completed the survey. Birth mothers were between the ages of 19.3 and 53.5 years old at the time of study (M=34.5, SD=8.7). Almost half (48.9 percent) of the birth mothers reported having some college or technical training while slightly more than one-third (39.4 percent) reported having a bachelor's degree or higher. Over half of the birth mothers reported full-time employment (52.0 percent) while 16.1 percent reported their employment status as "stay-at-home parent." Almost two-thirds of birth mothers (n=142, 64.0 percent) reported an annual household income below the 2016 median household income of $57,617 (Guzman, 2017). The majority (60.1 percent) of birth mothers reported being married or living with a partner while a little more than one-quarter (28.7 percent) reported their relationship status as "single."

Measure

Since no existing surveys addressed the range of issues examined, an original survey was developed for this study. Survey questions were included based on existing literature about the experiences of expectant parents and birth parents. The survey covered a wide range of topics, including basic demographic information about respondents and their child(ren); when they first considered adoption; whether they received clear, unbiased information about their options; the types and format of information provided to them; the context in which adoption was addressed with the birth parent (i.e., where, when, and by whom); the various influences that were

Table 16.1 Birth mother demographics at time of survey (n=223)

Variable	*M*	*SD*
Age at time of survey (years) (range 19.26–53.50 years)	34.5	8.7
Number of individuals in household (range 1–8)	3.0	1.6
Number of children relinquished for adoption (range 1–3+)	1.1	0.3
Number of children parented (range 0–6+)	1.3	1.4
	n	**%**
Education	1	<1.0
Less than high-school		
High-school graduate or GED	25	11.2
Some college or technical training	109	48.9
Completed bachelor's degree	44	19.7
Some graduate training beyond a bachelor's degree	12	5.4
Completed master's degree or higher	32	14.3
Employment status		
Employed full-time	116	52.0
Employed part-time	32	14.3
Stay-at-home parent	36	16.1
Unemployed, but looking	16	7.1
Other	23	10.3
Annual household income[a]		
Less than $20,000	50	22.4
$20,000–$39,999	54	24.2
$40,000–$59,999	38	17.0
$60,000–$79,999	24	10.8
$80,000–$99,999	17	7.6
$100,000–$119,999	12	5.4
$120,000 or more	27	12.1
Unknown	1	<1.0
Relationship status		
Single	64	28.7
Married or living with partner	134	60.1
Separated or divorced	22	9.9
Other	3	1.3

Notes: Percentages might not add to 100.0 percent due to rounding.
[a] n=222

present, whether positive or negative, on their decision-making process; services available to them before and after placement, as well as their utilization of these services; and their overall satisfaction with their decision to place their child for adoption. Zimet and colleagues' (1988) Multidimensional Scale of Perceived Social Support was adapted for use in this study to assess birth mothers' perceptions of support from three sources: family, friends, and a significant other. The scale, comprised of a total of 12 items, has been determined to have good internal reliability as well as moderate construct validity (Zimet et al., 1988).

Once an initial draft of the instrument was created, further commentary and revision were sought from birth parents knowledgeable about survey research methods and the scope and intent of the study. The panel was asked to review the instrument with an eye for clarity, bias, and content validity. Based on the feedback from the expert reviewers, some items were altered to further clarify intent.

Data analysis

Univariate statistics were used to examine questions on the survey. An analysis of missing data revealed no significant patterns; therefore, data were assumed to be missing at random. Missing data were not imputed or replaced.

Results

Sample at the time of relinquishment

Women and men who had relinquished a child for adoption in the US during the last 25 years (i.e., after 1989) were eligible to participate in the survey. Birth mothers were asked a series of questions about their circumstances at the time that they signed a relinquishment of parental rights for their child. Average age of birth mothers was 22.6 years old (SD=5.85) at the time of the relinquishment (see Table 16.2). Ninety-nine birth mothers (n=44.4 percent) reported having a high-school diploma/GED or less at the time of their relinquishment and almost one-third (n=73, 32.7 percent) reported that they had some college or an Associate's degree. Thirty birth mothers (13.5 percent) reported having a college degree or higher at the time of their relinquishment. Slightly less than one-third of birth mothers reported that they experienced mental health issues at the time of their relinquishment. Additionally, a small proportion of respondents (n=14, 6.3 percent) reported experiencing some substance use or addiction issues at that time in their lives.

With regard to relationship status, the vast majority of birth mothers (n=151, 67.7 percent) reported being single at the time of their relinquishment, followed by living with a partner (n=39, 17.5 percent). The remaining birth mothers reported being married (n=9, 4.0 percent), divorced (n=8, 3.6 percent), separated (n=5, 2.2 percent), or "Other" (n=11, 4.9 percent). Almost two-thirds of respondents (n=140, 62.8 percent) reported living with a relative (n=92, 41.3 percent) or on their own/with a roommate (n=48, 21.5 percent) at the time of the relinquishment. A small proportion of birth mothers reported living with a "host" family that was sponsored by the agency or their attorney (n=7, 3.1 percent), living in a maternity home (n=6, 2.7 percent), or living with the prospective adoptive family (n=3, 1.3 percent).

Consideration of adoption

Birth mothers identified the different options that they considered during their decision-making process. Almost one-third (n=70, 31.4 percent) of birth mothers shared that they did not strongly consider alternatives other than adoption for their child. Of the 153 birth mothers who reported they considered options other than adoption, the largest group of birth mothers (n=134, 87.6 percent) considered parenting their child. The next most common alternatives to adoption identified by birth mothers were termination of the pregnancy (n=60, 39.2 percent) and "marrying my child's birth father and raising the child" (n=34, 22.2 percent). The one birth mother (<1 percent) who identified "Other" reported that she had a "forced adoption after termination of pregnancy did not happen."

Table 16.2 Birth mother demographics at time of relinquishment (n=223)

Variable	*M*	*SD*
Age at relinquishment (years)	22.63	5.85
	n	%
Education	36	16.1
Less than high-school		
High-school graduate or GED	63	28.3
Some college or technical training	94	42.2
Completed bachelor's degree	19	8.5
Some graduate training beyond a bachelor's degree	6	2.7
Completed master's degree or higher	5	2.2
Relationship status		
Single	151	67.7
Married or living with partner	48	21.5
Separated or divorced	13	5.8
Other	11	4.9
Living arrangements		
Lived alone or with a roommate (non-romantic)	48	21.5
Lived with a spouse or a partner	44	19.7
Lived with my children	22	9.9
Lived with a relative (including parents)	92	41.3
Lived with the prospective adoptive family for my child	3	1.3
Lived in a maternity home or with a family sponsored by the agency or an attorney	13	5.6
I don't know/I can't remember	1	<1.0
Mental health issues		
Yes	68	30.5
No	115	51.6
Maybe/I'm not sure	40	17.9
Substance use or addiction issues		
Yes	14	6.3
No	206	92.4
Maybe/I'm not sure	3	1.3

Notes: Percentages may not add to 100 percent due to rounding.

Birth mothers were asked at what point in the process they first considered placing their child for adoption. Ninety (40.3 percent) birth mothers considered adoption as soon as they learned they were pregnant; another 89 (39.9 percent) considered adoption a few months after they found out they were pregnant. A small number of birth mothers (n=5, 2.2 percent) reported that adoption was identified as an option immediately after the baby's birth.

Influences on relinquishment decision

Birth mothers considering relinquishment of their child shared information about a variety of factors that influenced their decision. This section explores the types of information and support, or lack thereof, that birth mothers reported experiencing at the time they were making a decision regarding their pregnancy.

Access to information

Birth mothers reported on their access during their decision-making process to a variety of information sources. Pamphlets and other written materials on adoption were the only source of information identified as accessible by more than half of the birth mothers (n=142, 63.7 percent). While nearly half (n=66, 46.5 percent) found the information somewhat helpful, birth mothers' responses were split between "very helpful" (n=30, 21.1 percent) and "not helpful" (n=29, 20.4 percent).

Adoption-related websites (n=101, 45.3 percent), information from birth parents who had placed a child for adoption (n=98, 43.9 percent), and books on adoption (n=97, 43.5 percent) were the next most common sources of information for which birth mothers had access. Resources with information about parenting were some of the least accessible. Specifically, these parenting resources included videos on parenting (n=42, 18.8 percent), information from birth parents who considered adoption but chose to parent (n=46, 20.6 percent), and parenting-related websites (n=61, 27.4 percent). Figure 16.1 indicates the various information sources birth mothers were asked about and the proportion that indicated "yes" or "no."

The helpfulness of videos on adoption was also somewhat mixed. Of those who had access to videos about adoption, 24 (38.1 percent) reported they were "somewhat helpful," while 16 (25.4 percent) reported that they "did not use" the videos. Birth mothers tended to view adoption-related websites as either "very helpful" (n=39, 38.6 percent) or "somewhat helpful" (n=37, 36.6 percent). Information from other expectant parents and birth parents appeared to be the most helpful resource for these birth mothers. Information from other expectant parents considering adoption was reported to be "very helpful" by 21 (36.2 percent) birth mothers and "somewhat helpful" by 27 (46.6 percent) of the birth mothers who received this information. Furthermore, of the respondents who spoke to a birth parent about their experience with placing a child, over two-thirds (n=77, 78.9 percent) reported the information they received to be "very helpful" or "somewhat helpful."

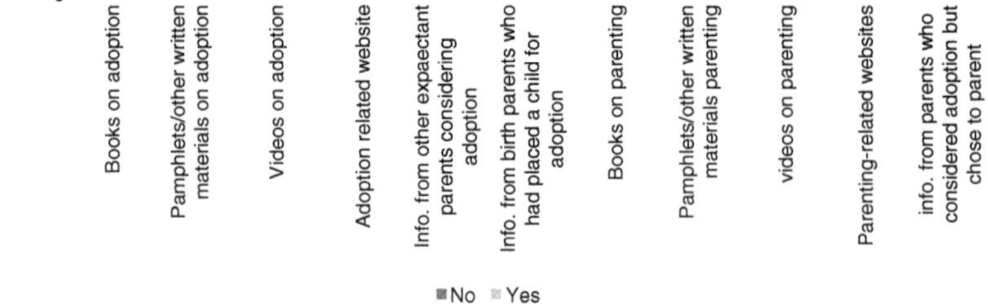

Figure 16.1 Access to sources of information

Access to services

Birth mothers were asked to indicate if they had access to various services when contemplating their decision for their child. Figure 16.2 indicates the various services birth mothers were asked about and the proportion that indicated "yes" or "no." Two services, adoption agency professional/caseworker services and prenatal care services, were identified as accessible by more than half of the birth mothers (n=177, 79.4 percent and n=188, 84.3 percent, respectively). Three services were identified as accessible by fewer than a quarter of the birth mothers: (1) an independent attorney solely for the birth mother (n=43, 19.3 percent), (2) counseling services with an independent licensed practitioner (n=49, 22.0 percent), and (3) a support group for expectant parents (n=43, 19.3 percent).

Birth mothers were asked to indicate the overall helpfulness of the various services to which they had access when making their final decision. Access to services in most cases was reported to be either "very helpful" or "somewhat helpful." Of the 70 birth parents who reported having access to an attorney representing the agency and/or the adoptive parents, 21 (30.0 percent) found the agency/adoptive parents' attorney to be "very helpful" while (n=8, 11.4 percent) stated the person was "somewhat helpful." Among the mothers who had access to this resource, the largest proportion reported that their attorney was "not helpful" (n=25, 35.7 percent). Among the 43 birth mothers who had access to an attorney who represented just their interests and not those of the agency or adoptive parents, slightly more than one-third (n=15, 34.9 percent) reported that the attorney was "very helpful" while 12 reported the attorney was "not helpful" (n=12, 27.9 percent).

Among those who had access to counseling services, over half (n=26, 56.5 percent) reported counseling services with an independent licensed practitioner were "very helpful." Another 11 birth parents (23.9 percent) found them "somewhat helpful." Four birth mothers (8.7 percent) found the service "not helpful" while five (10.9 percent) stated they "did not use" the service. Other services that were rated as "very helpful" include prenatal care services (n=98, 52.4 percent), informal counseling services (e.g., religious leader, teacher, mentor) (n=37, 48.1 percent), counseling services with an agency/attorney affiliated licensed practitioner

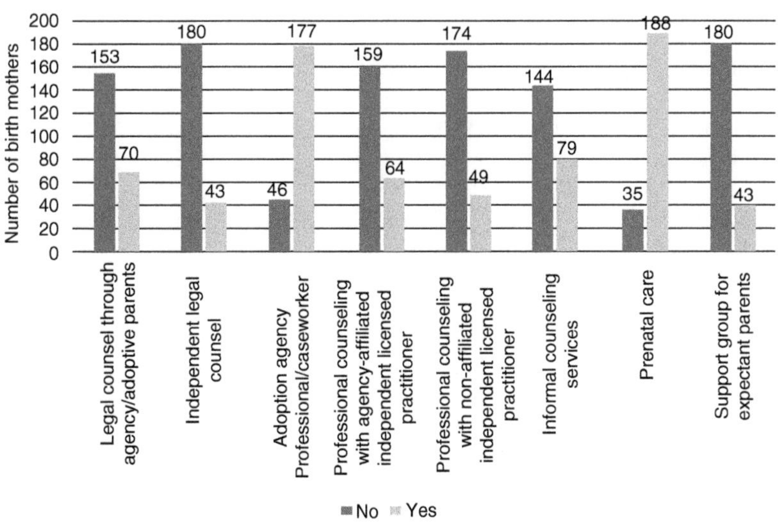

Figure 16.2 Access to services (n=223)

(n=30, 46.9 percent), and support groups for expectant parents (n=20, 47.6 percent). Additionally, almost half of the birth parents surveyed reported that having access to an adoption agency professional/caseworker was "very helpful" (n=79, 45.4 percent).

Sources of social support

Birth mothers were asked to assess the different types of support to which they had access when making their decision using a seven-point Likert scale to rate the support they had available (see Table 16.3). Responses ranged from "very strongly disagree" (i.e., no support

Table 16.3 Support available when making a decision about placing child for adoption (n=223)

Variable	*Very strongly disagree*	*Strongly disagree*	*Mildly disagree*	*Neither agree nor disagree*	*Mildly agree*	*Strongly agree*	*Very strongly agree*
	n (%)	***n (%)***	***n (%)***	***n (%)***	***n (%)***	***n (%)***	***n (%)***
There was a special person who was around when I was in need	54 (24.2)	24(10.8)	11 (4.9)	13 (5.8)	29 (13.0)	46 (20.6)	46 (20.6)
There was a special person with whom I could share joys and sorrows	57 (25.6)	25 (11.2)	13 (5.8)	17 (7.6)	29 (13.0)	33 (14.8)	49 (22.0)
My family really tried to help me	78 (35.0)	24 (10.8)	17 (7.6)	18 (8.1)	28 (12.6)	24 (10.8)	34 (15.2)
I got the emotional help and support I needed from my family	88 (39.5)	32 (14.2)	15 (6.7)	20 (9.0)	25 (11.2)	19 (8.5)	24 (10.8)
I had a special person who was a real source of comfort to me	61 (27.4)	15 (6.7)	12 (5.4)	15 (6.7)	37 (16.6)	38 (17.0)	45 (20.2)
My friends really tried to help me	59 (26.5)	20 (9.0)	28 (12.6)	22 (9.9)	43 (19.3)	26 (11.7)	25 (11.2)
I could count on my friends when things went wrong	61 (27.4)	25 (11.2)	36 (16.1)	25 (11.2)	34 (15.2)	22 (9.9)	20 (9.0)
I could talk about my problems with my family	97 (43.5)	28 (12.6)	23 (10.3)	14 (6.3)	24 (10.8)	16 (7.2)	21 (9.4)
I had friends with whom I could share my joys and sorrows	53 (23.8)	26 (11.7)	23 (10.3)	17 (7.6)	50 (22.4)	28 (12.6)	26 (11.7)
There was a special person in my life who cared about my feelings	56 (25.1)	16 (7.2)	14 (6.3)	15 (6.7)	36 (16.1)	35 (15.7)	51 (22.9)
My family was willing to help me make decisions	81 (36.3)	25 (11.2)	16 (7.2)	26 (11.7)	24 (10.8)	16 (72.0)	35 (15.7)
I could talk about my problems with my friends	59 (26.5)	22 (9.9)	31 (13.9)	20 (9.0)	37 (16.6)	27 (12.1)	27 (12.1)

available) to very "strongly agree" (i.e., significant support available). Lack of support from family was an area of significant concern for many birth mothers. Over half (n=125, 56.1 percent) of birth mothers reported either "very strongly disagreed" or "strongly disagreed" that they could talk about their problems with their family. Additionally, 120 (53.7 percent) birth mothers "very strongly disagreed" or "strongly disagreed" that they get emotional help from their family. Birth mothers reported similar trends regarding the lack of support from friends. Eighty-six (38.6 percent) indicated that they "very strongly disagreed" or "strongly disagreed" that they could count on friends when things went wrong. While many birth parents indicated a lack of support from family and/or friends, 92 (41.3 percent) respondents either "strongly agreed" or "very strongly agreed" that they had at least one special person in their life who was around when they were in need. A similarly high number also "strongly agreed" or "very strongly agreed" that they had access to at least one person who was a real source of comfort to them during this time (n=83, 37.2 percent) and/or access to someone with whom they could share their joys and sorrows (n=82, 36.8 percent).

Birth mothers were asked to rate the influence of various individuals on their decision to place their child for adoption. A little more than half of birth mothers (n=122, 54.8 percent) reported that their parents either had "some" or "a lot" of influence on their decision to place their child for adoption. Almost half (n=110, 49.4 percent) of birth mothers reported that the prospective adoptive family had "some" or "a lot" of influence on their decision. Additionally, the child's birth father appeared to be very influential in the decision-making process for many birth mothers: 108 (48.4 percent) respondents reported that the child's father had "some" or "a lot" of influence on their decision.

Sources of pressure

Birth mothers were asked if at any point in their decision-making process they felt pressured to place their child for adoption. Slightly more than half of birth mothers (n=117, 52.5 percent) responded in the affirmative. When asked who or what pressured them to place their child for adoption, the most common responses included: "my immediate family members" (n=74, 63.2 percent), "my financial circumstances" (n=70, 59.8 percent), "my housing situation at the time" (n=50, 42.7 percent) and "my child's birth father" (n=45, 38.5 percent). Figure 16.3 presents the various sources from whom birth mothers reported feeling pressure to place their child.

With the exception of two birth mothers, all indicated that they felt pressured to place their child for adoption and provided additional information about the various ways in which they felt pressured. Almost two-thirds (n=84, 73 percent) of birth mothers reported concerns about possible loss of emotional or social support. Birth mothers also expressed concerns about possible loss of financial support (n=66, 57.4 percent), possible loss of their housing (n=64, 55.7 percent), the possibility that they would owe money to the adoptive agency or the adoptive parents (n=24, 20.5 percent), and possible loss of custody of the child (n=6, 5.1 percent). In the "Other" category, 10 (8.7 percent) explicitly stated hurting or disappointing the adoptive family as a form of pressure and four (3.5 percent) respondents identified religious beliefs.

Information and time

Many birth mothers reported receiving insufficient information and time from the various professionals with whom they worked to help them adequately process and weigh their

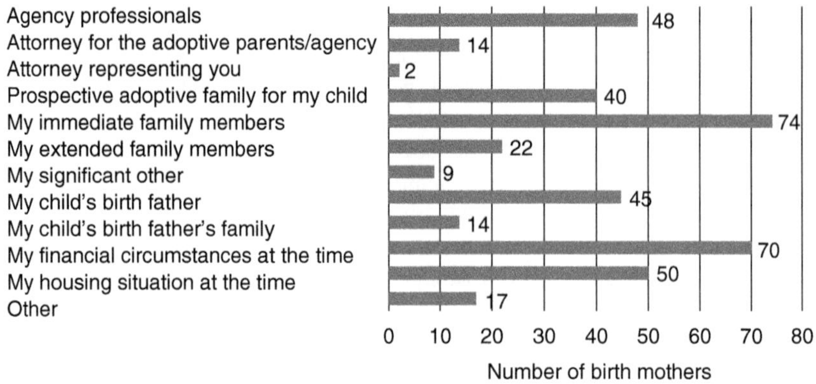

Figure 16.3 Pressure on birth mother during the decision-making process

decisions. Birth mothers were asked if they felt like they had enough opportunities to talk through their decision with others. About half (n=113, 50.7 percent) reported "no" to this question. When asked if they were provided with enough information about different options for their child by the various parties involved in their situation, slightly more than half (n=117, 52.5 percent) reported "no."

Birth mothers were asked what information they would like to have known more about during their decision-making process. A majority (n=100, 85.4 percent) of birth mothers indicated that they would like to have known more about local, state, and federal parenting resources available to assist them should they opt to parent their child. Additionally, 91 (77.8 percent) birth mothers reported that they would like to have known more about the long-term implications, for themselves and for their child, of their decision to place their child for adoption. Eighty-two (70.1 percent) birth mothers reported that they would like to have known more about their options for legal independent counsel to protect their interests during the relinquishment process. Finally, 77 (65.8 percent) birth mothers indicated a desire for additional information about the complete continuum of openness and all the potential options associated with this type of adoption (i.e., frequency and types of contact, which parties would be involved).

Relinquishment decision

This section shares details of the birth mothers' relinquishment decision, including the timeframe that birth mothers had between giving birth and signing relinquishment of parental rights documents, their reasons for relinquishment, and their overall level of satisfaction with their decision.

Relinquishment timeframe

Birth mothers were asked when they signed the relinquishment of parental rights documents. Almost one-third (n=70, 31.4 percent) of birth mothers reported that they signed relinquishment documents within one to two days after the birth of their child. Sixty-one (27.4 percent) signed the documents seven or more days after the birth. In contrast, a small percentage (n=9, 4.0 percent) signed relinquishment documents while pregnant, and 15 (6.7 percent) signed the documents within a few hours of their child's birth. Relinquishment documents were most commonly signed in the hospital (n=91, 40.8 percent), followed by an agency or other office-type setting (n=57, 25.6 percent), court house (n=36, 16.1 percent), or the mother's home (n=17, 7.6 percent). Twenty-two (9.9 percent) birth mothers selected "Other" location, including restaurants, churches, and hotel rooms.

Birth parents were asked if they believed they had sufficient time to review the relinquishment of parental rights documents prior to signing. Of the 222 participants who responded to the question, slightly more than one-third (n=86, 38.7 percent) reported they felt that they did not have sufficient time to review documents, while the remaining birth mothers (n=136, 61.3 percent) indicated they felt they had sufficient time to review relinquishment documents.

Reasons for relinquishment

Respondents were asked to select all of the reasons they had for relinquishing their child for adoption. Figure 16.4 presents the various reasons that birth mothers were asked to choose from and the number of birth mothers who selected each answer. The most common reasons selected included "financial concerns" (n=183, 82.1 percent), their "relationship status" with the child's father (n=133, 59.6 percent), "lack of social support" (n=114, 51.1 percent), and "felt unprepared to be a parent" (n=113, 50.7 percent).

In addition to the constellation of reasons birth mothers reported for why they relinquished their child for adoption, they were also asked to choose one of these as their primary reason for their decision to relinquish their child for adoption. An overwhelming majority of birth mothers reported that the primary reason they relinquished their child was concerns about finances (n=183, 82.1 percent). The next most frequently selected reason was "felt unprepared to be a parent" (n=36, 16.1 percent), followed by the "circumstances in my life were not conducive to parenting" (n=34, 15.2 percent). Twenty-nine (13 percent) birth mothers reported that the primary reason they made the decision to relinquish was pressure from family members.

Birth mothers were asked the extent to which their decision to relinquish was based on their own wishes. Almost one-fourth of the birth mothers (n=54, 24.3 percent) reported

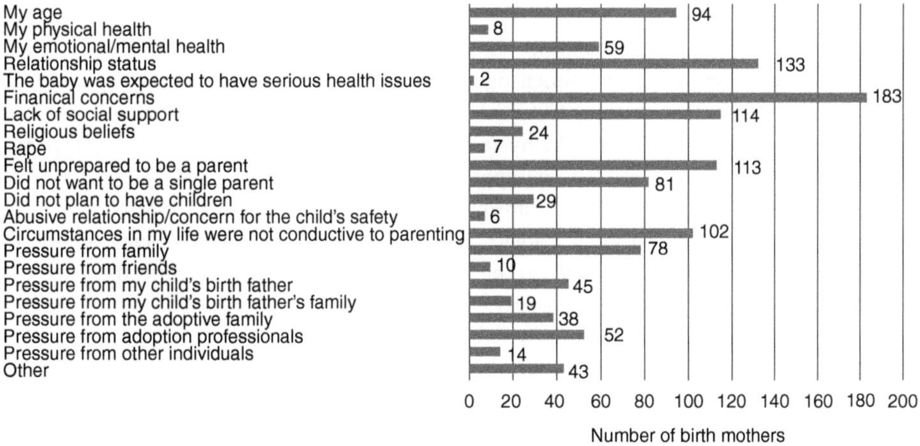

Figure 16.4 Reasons for relinquishing child for adoption

that the decision was "not at all" based on their wishes. Seventy-three (32.9 percent) birth mothers indicated that the decision was based either "a little" or "some" on their wishes. The highest proportion of birth mothers in the study (n=95, 42.8 percent) reported that the decision was based "a lot" on their own wishes for the situation.

Satisfaction with decision

Using a five-point Likert scale, birth mothers were asked to rank their overall satisfaction with the decision to relinquish their child for adoption. Almost half (n=103, 46.2 percent) reported that they were either "very satisfied" or "satisfied" with the decision. Fifty (20.2 percent) birth mothers reported having "mixed/ambivalent" feelings about the decision to relinquish their child, while the remaining 75 (33.6 percent) birth mothers reported feeling "dissatisfied" or "very dissatisfied." Respondents were asked a follow-up question to understand if they have ever regretted their decision to relinquish their parental rights to their child. Almost half (n=103, 46.2 percent) reported that they have regretted their decision in some capacity. Sixty-four (28.7 percent) birth mothers indicated that they have not ever regretted their decision to relinquish their parental rights to their child. When asked how well they have adjusted to their decision to relinquish their child, a majority (n=134, 60.1 percent) of birth mothers reported "very well" or "somewhat well." Twenty-four (10.8 percent) birth mothers reported they have not adjusted well at all, while 21 (9.4 percent) reported feeling "neutral" about their adjustment. Forty (17.9 percent) birth mothers responded "I don't know" to this question.

Birth mothers were asked what impact the adoption has had on their life. Responses from birth mothers were very mixed. Fifty-nine (26.5 percent) birth mothers reported that the adoption has had an "overall negative impact," while the same number of birth mothers (n=59, 26.5 percent) reported that the experience has had an "overall positive impact." Slightly more than one-third (n=85, 38.1 percent) of birth mothers reported that the adoption has had a "mixed impact" on their life. Two respondents (<1 percent) reported the adoption had a "positive impact at first, but more negative impact now" while one (<1 percent) indicated that the adoption had "no impact" on their life.

Post-relinquishment support

Birth mothers were also asked to identify the types of services and supports available to them since the relinquishment of their parental rights to their child for adoption (See Figure 16.5). The majority (n=160, 71.7 percent) of birth mothers reported having access to postnatal care services after their child's delivery. Many (n=136, 61 percent) birth mothers also reported having access to family and friends to support them post-relinquishment. Generally, birth parents reported having little access to informal supports, such as informal counseling services (n=147, 65.9 percent) or informal contact with other birth parents in their community (n=124, 55.6 percent). Birth mothers also reported difficulty accessing other informal supports such as online support groups or listservs for members of the adoption triad (n=145, 65.0 percent) or those targeted specifically to birth parents (n=139, 62.3 percent).

Helpfulness of informal and formal supports

For each of the services and supports they accessed, birth parents were asked to indicate how helpful each was to them post-relinquishment. Generally, most birth mothers in the

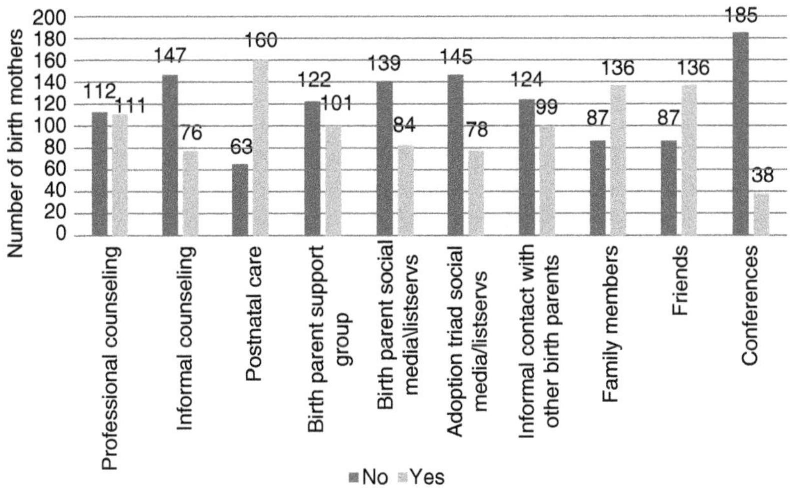

Figure 16.5 Access to post-relinquishment services and support

study reported that all of the services were "very helpful" or at least "somewhat helpful." However, support groups, online or face-to-face, appeared to be the most beneficial to birth parents. More than three-fourths (n=174, 78.2 percent) of birth parents reported that support groups were either "very helpful" or "somewhat helpful." While all of the services and supports that were listed were rated fairly positively, the support provided by family appeared to be the least helpful for some respondents. Forty-seven (21.3 percent) birth mothers reported that family members were "not helpful."

Using a five-point Likert scale, birth parents were asked to indicate their overall satisfaction with the level of post-placement support available to them to address issues surrounding the relinquishment of their child. Ninety-six birth mothers (43 percent) reported that they were "not at all satisfied" with the level of support available to them after the placement of their child. Responses for the remaining 127 respondents were somewhat mixed. Slightly more than one-fourth (n=64, 28.7 percent) of birth mothers reported that they were "considerably satisfied" or "completely satisfied," while the remaining 63 (28.2 percent) birth mothers indicated they were "a little satisfied" or "moderately satisfied" with the services and supports available to them after their child's placement.

Limitations

This study is the first to examine the type and nature of information provided to expectant parents who are considering plans to place their child for adoption. Nevertheless, all studies have inherent limitations. As the results of this study are based on respondents who learned of the survey and then chose to participate, it is important to note that it is not possible to know the extent to which the survey participants are representative of all birth mothers. As participants were recruited through support and interest groups, they might be more likely to share their experiences and/or might be experiencing a more acute need for support than the general population of birth mothers.

Relatedly, despite our best efforts to recruit a diverse sample for the survey, the sample was significantly skewed toward White women. That said, the composition of birth mothers in this study is consistent with prior literature that has found White women relinquish infants for adoption at higher rates than women of color (Wiley & Baden, 2005).

Another limitation pertains to the wide variation of time frames during which participants relinquished their children for adoption. At least one participant in the sample relinquished her child within three months of completing the survey, while at least 18 relinquished in 1990. This study relied on retrospective data from participants. Recall bias is common among retrospective studies that rely on self-reported information. Recall bias occurs when participants' recollections of specific past events are distorted by the knowledge of how things have turned out (Rubin & Babbie, 2010). For example, it is possible that some participants' memories about their experiences with options counseling and relinquishment were positively or negatively influenced by their perspective of whether things "worked out" or not following the relinquishment. While there are some limitations, the current study represents a significant step forward in the research on the relinquishment experiences of birth mothers.

Discussion

This study provides further insight into the experiences and perceptions of birth mothers who placed their child for adoption. The birth mothers in this study had much to say about the experience of placing their child and the various services and supports that were and were not available to them during the decision-making and placement process. While the findings of this study cannot be generalized, the information reported by birth mothers in the study represents a full continuum of experiences and outcomes. Furthermore, this study adds to the existing body of literature on relinquishment and provides a more updated and nuanced picture of the experiences of women who have placed a child for adoption in the US in the last 25 years.

The findings of this study are consistent with prior literature on relinquishment that suggests that despite some advancements in how adoption is approached and framed by agencies and other adoption professionals, the experiences of women who place a child for adoption are often punctuated by limited information and resources, external pressures, and lack of financial and social support (DAI, 2007). Birth mothers reported notable deficits in their experiences during their pregnancy and decision-making process in terms of access to information, services, and unbiased support from those around them, which might have influenced their decision to place their child for adoption. Birth mothers reported less access to different types of source materials about parenting than comparable materials on adoption, suggesting that the options counseling they received was slanted toward the benefits of adoption. In addition, 81 percent of the birth mothers reported that they did not have access to their own independent counsel to advise them regarding their legal rights or help them navigate the relinquishment process. Additionally, 78 percent of birth mothers reported not having access to counseling services with a licensed practitioner to help them adequately process their decision and weigh the pros and cons of each option.

A lack of emotional and social support also contributed to many of the birth mothers' decisions to relinquish. Loss of emotional and social support was a pressure experienced by almost two-thirds (73 percent) of birth mothers as they made decisions, as well as a deciding factor in their decision to relinquish their child. Similarly, financial and housing concerns also acted both as pressures and deciding factors, with more than 80 percent of birth mothers citing financial concerns as a reason they chose to place their child. For the 100 mothers in this study who reported that they would have liked more information about services to help them parent, the incomplete nature of the information they received about available parenting education, financial, and housing services was likely a contributing factor in their final decision to relinquish their rights to the child for adoption. The lack of broader community supports available to those who find themselves in a crisis pregnancy may leave some expectant mothers vulnerable to people and circumstances that pressure them to consider and, ultimately, choose adoption.

The findings indicate that this pressure is experienced from a variety of sources. As birth mothers reported about the available people in their personal life who could provide support, a common theme that emerged was one of isolation. Over half of the birth mothers in this study reported that during their pregnancy they lacked family or friends with whom they could share their problems and feelings. However, given that the most common pressure experienced by birth mothers was from immediate family members, the isolation that birth mothers experienced did not necessarily mean that families were absent from their day-to-day lives. Rather, the responses of birth mothers suggest that they felt their families were unable to support them emotionally or to help them make a decision regarding their pregnancy in a way that would allow for thoughtful consideration of other alternatives, specifically parenting their child. This experience of isolation during the decision-making process was likely compounded by the feeling that many birth mothers had of professionals (i.e., attorneys, agency professionals, caseworkers, and/or counselors) working with them who failed to advocate for their interests.

It is important to note that the choice to place their child was at the time of relinquishment, and now during post-relinquishment, considered to be the best and most appropriate option for many of the women in this study. Slightly less than half of the birth mothers reported satisfaction with their relinquishment decision, and more than a quarter indicated they have not experienced any regret about their decision. What is critical is that adequate, unbiased services and supports are offered to expectant mothers exploring their options so that they can make an informed decision and reduce the likelihood of future regret.

Practice and policy recommendations

- *Provide expectant parents with access to unbiased and independent legal representation*: Birth mothers expressed a repeated desire for access to legal representation and information regarding the short- and long-term legal implications of their decision. While adoptive parents and adoption agencies typically have legal staff that represent the agencies' interests, it was not uncommon for birth mothers to report that they did not have access or support focused on ensuring that they fully understood applicable adoption statutes and their personal legal rights. It is imperative that expectant mothers have access to unbiased legal representation who can educate, support, and advocate for expectant parents as they deliberate their options and – for those who choose adoption – navigate the relinquishment process.
- *Establish best practice guidelines regarding access to independent licensed counselors*: Half of the birth mothers (50.7 percent) reported access to an independent or agency-affiliated licensed counselor helped them carefully consider their options and explore each available alternative. The enormity of the decision that expectant mothers are weighing necessitates that agencies and adoption professionals ensure that parents have access to unbiased counsel that will allow the parent to carefully weigh the pros and cons of each option. Furthermore, it is recommended that birth mothers be provided access to an independent licensed counselor post-relinquishment for a minimum of one year to help

them process their decision and confront feelings of grief and loss that might emerge in the weeks and months following the placement.

- *Increase expectant parents' access to support groups and other parents*: Isolation was a common experience for many of the birth mothers. However, only a small percentage were referred to support groups for expectant parents and there was no universal access to support groups post-adoption. Yet, birth mothers who participated in these groups tended to find them a valuable source of support. Therefore, adoption professionals, particularly agency professionals/caseworkers who provide access to information and services, should prioritize the use of support groups involving birth parents who have placed a child, as well as those with other expectant parents who are considering adoption, during the decision-making and post-adoption phases of the process. These groups could help reduce the isolation and ambivalence that expectant mothers experience and provide a safe venue for exploration of their options among those with a shared experience.
- *Establish national standards regarding the development and provision of evidence-based options counseling materials*: To help ensure that expectant mothers receive information that can help them make an informed decision, it is recommended that national standards are established regarding the development and provision of counseling materials explaining evidence-based options. These materials can be tailored to incorporate local and state services and supports. In addition to written materials, national regulations should also be developed that provide expectant mothers with access to independent legal and counseling professionals. Together, these new standards could help ensure that expectant mothers have access to neutral resources as they explore their options. Currently, there is wide variation in state policies around the waiting period to sign relinquishment paperwork. A minimum wait period should be established at the federal level to help guide states in their efforts to mitigate the influence of external pressures birth mothers might be experiencing upon delivery and during the immediate post-delivery recovery period.

Authors' note

Funding for this study was provided by the Donaldson Adoption Institute's Lynn Franklin Fund. This chapter is an adaptation of a report released by the Donaldson Adoption Institute (DAI) in fall 2016. The excerpted materials were published on the DAI website as: Madden, E., Ryan, S., Aguiniga, D., & Crawford, M. (2016). *Understanding options counseling experiences in adoption: A quantitative analysis of birth parents and professionals*. New York City: Donaldson Adoption Institute. The authors retain the copyrights to all materials contained in this report.

References

Askren, H. A., & Bloom, K. C. (1999). Postadoption reactions of the relinquishing mother: A review. *Journal of Obstetric, Gynecological & Neonatal Nursing*, *28*(4), 395–400. doi:10.1111/j.1552-6909.1999.tb02008.x

Bürgerliches Gesetzbuch. [BGB] [German Civil Code], § 1747.

Castle, P. (2014). The experience of choice in voluntary relinquishment. *Family Matters*, *14*, 53–57.

Child Welfare Information Gateway [CWIG]. (2017). *Consent to adoption*. Washington, DC: US Department of Health and Human Services, Children's Bureau.

Coleman, P. K., & Garratt, D. (2016). From birth mothers to first mothers: Toward a compassionate understanding of the life-long act of adoption placement. *Issues in Law & Medicine*, *31*(2), 139–163.

Donaldson Adoption Institute [DAI]. (2007). *Safeguarding the rights and well-being of birth parents in the adoption process*. Retrieved from www.adoptioninstitute.org/old/publications/2006_11_Birthparent_Study_All.pdf

Ellison, M. (2003). Authoritative knowledge and single women's unintentional pregnancies, abortions, adoption, and single motherhood: Social stigma and structural violence. *Medical Anthropology Quarterly, 17*, 322–347. doi:10.1525/maq.2003.17.3.322

Fisher, J. (2012). *How birth mothers fare: A qualitative study of their long-term adjustment* (Unpublished doctoral dissertation). New York University, NY.

Freundlich, M. (2002). Adoption research: An assessment of empirical contributions to the advancement of adoption practice. *Journal of Social Distress and the Homeless, 11*(2), 143–166. doi:10.1023/A:1014363901799

Guzman, G. G. (2017). *Household income: 2016* (Report No. ACSBR/16-02). US Census Bureau. Retrieved from www.census.gov/content/census/en/library/publications/2017/acs/acsbr16-02.html

Henney, S. M., Ayers-Lopez, S., McRoy, R. G., & Grotevant, H. D. (2007) Evolution and resolution: Birthmothers' experience of grief and loss at different levels of adoption openness. *Journal of Social and Personal Relationships, 24*(6), 875–889. doi:org/10.1177%2F0265407507084188

Johnson, C., & Faase, K. (2012). Birthparent counseling in policy and practice. *Adoption Advocate, 45*, 1–10.

Jones, J. (2008). Adoption experiences of women and men and demand for children to adopt by women 18–44 years of age in the United States, 2002. *Vital and Health Statistics, 23*(27), 1–36.

Jones, J., & Placek, P. (2017). *Adoption by the numbers*. Retrieved from https://indd.adobe.com/view/4ae7a823-4140-4f27-961a-cd9f16a5f362

McAdoo, L. (1992). *Birth mothers: The forgotten link in the adoption triad* (Unpublished doctoral dissertation). University of New Mexico, Albuquerque, NM.

New Zealand Government. (2018). *Placing a child for adoption*. Retrieved from: www.govt.nz/browse/family-and-whanau/adoption-and-fostering/placing-a-child-for-adoption/

Rubin, A., & Babbie, E. R. (2010) *Essential Research Methods for Social Work* (7th ed.). Belmont, CA: Brooks/Cole.

Samuels, E. (2005). Time to decide? The laws governing mothers' consents to the adoption of their newborn infants. *Tennessee Law Review, 72*, 509–572.

Simmonds, K. E., & Likis, F. E. (2005). Providing options counseling for women with unintended pregnancies. *Journal of Obstetric, Gynecologic, & Neonatal Nursing, 34*, 373–379. doi:10.1177/0884217505276051

Singer, J. (2004). Options counseling: Techniques for caring for women with unintended pregnancies. *Journal of Midwifery & Women's Health, 49*, 235–242. doi:10.1016/j.jmwh.2004.01.002

Wegar, K. (1997). In search of bad mothers: Social constructions of birth and adoptive motherhood. *Women's Studies International Forum, 20*, 77–86. doi:10.1016/S0277-5395(96)00097-0

Wiley, M. O. L., & Baden, A. L. (2005). Birth parents in adoption research, practice, and counseling psychology. *The Counseling Psychologist, 33*, 13–50. doi:10.1177/0011000004265961

Winkler, R. C., Brown, D. W., van Keppel, M., & Blanchard, A. (1988). *Clinical practice in adoption*. New York: Paragon Press.

Zill, N. (2015). *The paradox of adoption*. Retrieved from https://ifstudies.org/blog/the-paradox-of-adoption/

Zimet, G. D., Dahlem, N. W., Zimet, S. G., & Farley, G. K. (1988). The multidimensional scale of perceived social support. *Journal of Personality Assessment, 52*, 30–41. doi:10.1207/s15327752jpa5201_2

17

TRANSRACIAL ADOPTEES

The rewards and challenges of searching for their birth families

Danielle Godon-Decoteau and Patricia Ramsey

> My whole life since I was little girl I had so many questions … [about] what my life was like before I was adopted … I think going into this [search for birth parents] there is always a moment of apprehension and some underlying fear too, like are they going to accept me, how are they going to react towards me?
>
> (Goldstein, 2013, p. 47)

"Do you want to find your 'real' parents?" This common query, often addressed to adoptees, along with countless romanticized stories about reunification with birth parents, reflect society's value of biological connections. However, beyond these assumptions and sensational stories, what do we really know about the search motivations and experiences of adopted individuals from their own perspectives? Early seminal research on search and reunion experiences was conducted in the UK and mainly focused on domestic in-race adoptions (i.e., child adopted by parents of their same racial group) (e.g., Aumend & Barrett, 1983, 1984; Howe & Feast, 2001; Sachdev, 1992; Triseliotis, Feast, & Kyle, 2005). However, we know less about the search and reunion processes for transracial adoptees (TRAs; i.e., child is adopted by parents of a different racial group than their own), who may be adopted domestically or internationally (i.e., adopted to the US from other countries such as China, Ethiopia, Guatemala) (Kirton, Feast, & Howe, 2000; Müller & Perry, 2001; Tieman, van der Ende, & Verhulst, 2008).

Transracial adoptions occur under a wide range of circumstances and in many different places, both domestically and internationally. TRAs represent different racial and cultural groups, their life experiences vary across adoptive families and communities, and, regardless of context, individuals develop unique views and perspectives. Although TRAs include everyone who is racially different from their adoptive parents (Silverman, 1993), the overwhelming majority of TRAs are people of color, including African, Latinx, Native, and Asian Americans who are raised by White families (Baden, 2007; Lee, 2003). In this chapter, we focus on TRAs in a variety of stages of the process of deciding whether or not to search, conducting a search, and, in some cases, contacting or spending time with their birth families. This does not include TRAs adopted from foster care, whose search and reunification experiences might be qualitatively different, yet we believe its contribution to the scholarship on search and reunion provides insight into the experience and informs future research involving all TRAs.

It is important to explore the search and reunion experiences of TRAs because policies and attitudes about transracial adoption, as well as racial, ethnic, and cultural stereotypes related to racism, might make searches and reunions potentially more pressing yet challenging for TRAs than they are for in-race adoptees. TRAs typically grow up in predominantly White communities. Thus, they might be highly motivated to locate their birth families in order to connect with others who are racially similar to them, especially as they explore and navigate their racial and ethnic identities (Godon, Green, & Ramsey, 2014). Yet if they decide to search, TRAs can encounter daunting obstacles, particularly those adopted from different countries who will need to face unfamiliar bureaucracies, languages, and cultures (Tieman et al., 2008).

Currently, many studies that examine adult TRAs' search and reunion experiences focus on Asian children adopted to the US, particularly people adopted from South Korea, who were adopted between the 1950s and 1980s and now represent the largest adult group of transracial international adoptees in the US (McGinnis, Smith, Ryan, & Howard, 2009). Many adoptees are now adoption researchers (including the first author of this chapter), writers, activists, and clinicians (Kalb & Tucker, 2019; McGinnis, Baden, Kim, & Kim, 2019). Given that TRAs' experiences of race and racism likely differ depending on the history and specific stereotypes associated with each racial group, we hope that the future research will represent and inform our understandings of TRAs from a variety of racial and nationality backgrounds.

In the following section, we describe what is known about motivation to search in general, and elaborate on the context of transracial adoption in particular. Müller and Perry (2001) developed three theoretical models of search motivation: searching in the context of sociocultural norms that surround adoption and family life in general; searching as a normative process; and searching that is motivated by psychological difficulties. Using these three models as a framework, this chapter reviews the existing literature on the topic as well as findings from our own research. In later sections, we discuss searching strategies and reunion processes and conclude with implications and recommendations for practice.

Motivations to search

Sociocultural context of searching

The desire to search occurs in a sociocultural context and history. All adoptees who search do so in the context of *sociocultural norms* about adoption (Müller & Perry, 2001), which may motivate searching. Western society tends to value blood ties and often stigmatizes adoption as second best (Fisher, 2003; Palacios, 2009). Many movies and TV series have featured romantic stories and images of reunions, often misrepresenting the lived experience of adoptees and birth families (Choy & Choy, 2006) and potentially creating unrealistic fantasies and hopes. This social cultural norm of valuing of blood ties may draw attention to physical and temperamental differences between adoptees and their families. (Brodzinsky, 2011). Studies have shown that in-race adoptees' perceptions of dissimilarity with their adoptive parents have been a predictor of search interest (Hollingsworth, 1998).

Feeling dissimilar from their adoptive families can be especially acute for TRAs because of visible racial differences (Brodzinsky, 2011; Triseliotis et al., 2005). TRAs and their adoptive families are not able to hide their non-biological relationship and are vulnerable to being perceived and judged against social norms that highly value biological connections and devalue people of color. This is evident in a Korean TRA's reflection that, "while growing up, I thought I was White unless I walked past a mirror and then it's like, 'Oh yea, that's why people are staring at us [family]'" (Godon, 2012). Additionally, Korean TRAs frequently discussed experiencing intrusive questions that reflected ignorance about adopted people in general, and transracial families in particular (Godon-Decoteau & Ramsey, 2018). Thus, TRAs might have particularly strong motivations to search due to feeling dissimilar with their adoptive families and communities (Kirton et al., 2000).

In addition to sociocultural values about adoption, race and racism play a role in every transracial adoption. Racism comes in different forms, from individual prejudice to institutional and systemic discrimination. It also varies in intensity and clarity from subtle microaggressions to blatant threats and violence. TRAs inevitably encounter racist attitudes and incidents, especially in predominantly White settings (McGinnis et al., 2009). As children they might be teased by peers and, as adults, have to face stereotypes and intrusive questions.

> My early memories of discrimination were gestures. People tried to copy my eyes and mimic Chinese to me as a joke. … [Now] strangers randomly will ask me in public, "Where are you from?" I hate answering that question. I would feel OK to mention the neighborhood I live in, but most people press for birth country … If I pressed them for the country of their family's heritage, they would think I am being rude, nosy, and awkward. That's not fair. I want the right to be ignored and not asked this question.
>
> *33 year old Korean American transracial adoptee (Godon, 2012)*

Unlike children of color who grow up in families from the same racial group, TRAs often face the pervasive racism on their own. Growing up in predominantly White communities and with family members who have never personally experienced racism can lead to feelings of racial isolation. Unfortunately, even well-meaning White parents cannot fully appreciate the impact of these slights and often dismiss or overlook their children's concerns (Docan-Morgan, 2011; Samuels, 2009). These factors, in turn, might give rise to a desire to search for birth families in order to find social environments where they feel less racially conspicuous. One TRA noted, "my visit to Korea and meeting my birth parents made me see Asian people in another way and therefore myself too" (Godon, 2012).

On the other hand, TRAs might, consciously or unconsciously, deal with racial isolation by trying to assimilate into the White community, minimizing their racial background, and distancing themselves from their birth racial group. For example, a 23-year-old man adopted from India said:

> I have never really experienced racism. Growing up, [town] was predominantly White, and as far as I was and am concerned, I, too, am White. Culturally, socially … everything about me is White, Irish, Catholic, with the slight exception that my skin is brown.
>
> *(Green, 2009)*

These feelings, which develop during childhood and adolescence, can result in TRAs' disinterest in, or even averse feelings toward, searching for their birth families. For example, the man adopted from India quoted above went on to say, "As far as I am concerned, they [birth family] are just strangers that I probably will not like who I just happen to share mitochondrial DNA with" (Green, 2009).

Countless racial stereotypes reflect the long history of oppression of different groups in our society and potentially affect the way that TRAs view themselves and are perceived by others. Common images of dangerous Black men, exotic and foreign Asian American women, and Latinx gang members are just a few of the many stereotypes that permeate media, institutions, and interpersonal relationships. Due to historical and current racial privilege, White adoptive families are more likely to have access to financial resources, high-quality healthcare and education, and safe neighborhoods. Being raised in White families, however, does not protect TRAs from exposure to racism, especially when they move away from home. For example, Chad Goller-Sojourner, a Black transracial adoptee, writer, and performer, discussed what it was like to be a dark-skinned Black man who was raised by White parents in episode six of the documentary series *Adoptees in the Wild* (Sanvidge, 2014). Goller-Sojourner explained that in a society that is afraid of dark-skinned Black men, TRAs "age out" of their honorary White status and "suburban privilege" when they leave their adoptive family's home and experience more blatant racism. He poignantly recounted how he was initially surprised, but eventually grew accustomed to, being pulled over by police officers on his way to college.

In summary, sociocultural norms about family, adoption, and race may affect TRAs' interest in connecting with their birth family. While being raised in White adoptive families might provide some privilege and sheltering from discrimination, TRAs are still affected by race and racism. They respond to their racial environment in a variety of ways, from actively resisting racist ideologies to internalizing racism and denying or being unaware of how it affects them. Regardless of their responses, racism affects their lives, opportunities, well-being, and quite likely, their interests in connecting with their birth family.

Normative aspects of searching

Deciding whether or not to search for their birth family is a *normative process* for all adopted individuals (Müller & Perry, 2001) that often affects identity development. It is usually a gradual process with many motivations that fluctuate in their relative importance over time. Some factors in deciding whether or not to search are related to adoptive parent support (both perceived and actual); stories about other adoptees' searching experiences; chance opportunities (e.g., unexpectedly learning about a homeland trip or an organization that helps locate birth parents); and expectation of success (e.g., adoptees who assume that they cannot find their birth family might have less interest in initiating a search).

Often adoptees indicate that they are motivated because they want to obtain medical information related to life events (e.g., experiencing health issues, considering biological reproduction). A quest for medical information may provide a more acceptable or easily approachable reason to search. Also, the desire to search may ebb and flow as adoptees go through different life phases. For example, when adoptees are more independent and no longer living at home, they might feel freer to explore and express their interests in their birth families (Kryder, 1999).

Another motivation to search is to gain information that will aid identity formation and development of a coherent and more complete sense of self (Baden & Wiley, 2007; Grotevant, 1997; Howe, 2009; Howe & Feast, 2001). It is often prompted by curiosity about birth parents and other family members, family traits, and reasons for being placed for adoption (Hamilton, Samek, Keyes, McGue, & Iacono, 2015; Wrobel & Dillon, 2009; Wrobel, Grotevant, & McRoy, 2004). McGinnis et al. (2009) noted that for adoptees, "gaining information about their origins is not [only] a matter of curiosity, but a matter of gaining the raw materials needed to fill in the missing pieces of their lives and to derive an integrated sense of self" (p. 50). In a study of Norwegian TRAs, Darnell, Johansen, Tavakoli, and Brugnone (2017) found that each adoptee's story included curiosity about their history and ties with their birth parents.

Ethnic identity and racial identity are additional normative developmental factors that might influence search interest for TRAs. Whereas all adoptees might be curious about their particular birth families, many TRAs – especially those adopted internationally – might have little knowledge about their birth group and culture, making it more difficult to develop coherent identities that can embody both their adoptive and birth selves. In one study, Korean-born adoptees identified their unfamiliarity with Korean culture as a negative aspect of transracial adoption (Godon-Decoteau & Ramsey, 2018). Often, adoptive parents try to support their children's ethnic identity development by providing information and experiences about their birth culture through culture camps and celebrations. These efforts, however, often fall short (McGinnis et al., 2009), because most adoptive parents do not have the skills and "insider knowledge" to socialize their children into their birth culture and to raise them bi-culturally (Tessler, Gamache, & Liu, 1999, p. xi).

As adolescent and adult TRAs engage in identity development, they might want to learn about the background of their birth group (e.g., studying birth country and language or joining organized groups of racially or ethnically similar people in college or informal groups in the community; McGinnis et al., 2009). In a study of Korean adoptees, Song and Lee (2009) found that, as young adults, they expand and deepen their explorations by traveling to South Korea and possibly searching for their birth family. In these cases, interest in searching might reflect normative ethnic identity development. Godon et al. (2014) found that birth group ethnic identity was higher for TRAs who were searching for their birth families or had made contact with them compared to TRAs with no interest in searching.

Despite their efforts to learn about their birth culture, some TRAs face obstacles trying to join ethnic groups (Godon-Decoteau & Ramsey, 2018; Ramsey & Mika, 2011). An adoptee from India felt that she was often rejected by other Indians in the Midwest community where she was raised. This exclusion contributed to her feeling as if she were an incomplete jigsaw puzzle where "you're always trying to put the pieces together and … there are always pieces missing … and you ask yourself why the hell you even had to do a puzzle" (Green, 2009).

Given that most TRAs are people of color, *normative processes* may also include racial identity development and what it means to be a person of color in a White family and, typically, a predominantly White community. Studies have suggested that many TRAs have thought that they were White or wanted to be White at some point in their lives, particularly during childhood (Langrehr, Yoon, Hacker, & Caudill, 2015; McGinnis et al., 2009). As they grow up and begin to experience racism, some TRAs seek racially similar groups and feel a sense of belonging perhaps for the first time. As one Korean adoptee said about joining a Korean church, "I never realized how uncomfortable I was until I was comfortable" (Godon et al., 2014, p. 17).

To summarize, interest in searching is related to normative developmental tasks, including identity formation. For TRAs, racial and ethnic identity development are additional normative factors. Searching might prompt more interest in ethnic and racial backgrounds, amplifying those aspects of identity; or, conversely, as adoptees begin to explore their backgrounds, they might begin to wonder about their birth families and embark on a search.

Psychological aspects of searching

Müller and Perry (2001) noted that desire to search also may be motivated by what they referred to as *psychopathology*: a sense of loss, adjustment difficulties, and discontent with adoption and adoptive family. Findings are mixed, with older studies suggesting that adoptees who searched for birth families had more negative self-concepts and attitudes toward their adoptive parents than non-searchers (Aumend & Barrett, 1983, 1984; Sobol & Cardiff, 1983; Tieman et al., 2008). However, some researchers have critiqued these assumptions. Tieman et al. (2008) noted that, despite searchers in their study having more problems and being more likely to meet criteria for psychiatric disorders, the majority of searchers were well adjusted. Likewise, Müller and Perry (2001) pointed out that later studies indicated that most searchers are content with their adoptive parents and their lives in general. In a study of TRAs headed by the first author of this chapter, searchers and non-searchers had similar scores on measures of self-esteem and self-reported success in academics, social life, and family relationships; and presence/absence of significant emotional and behavioral problems (Godon et al., 2014).

While we should not assume that all searchers are motivated by mental health issues and discontent with their adoption, we do need to acknowledge that searches can involve considerable psychological stress. Most searchers, to some extent, will encounter uncertainty during the process of searching and multiple emotions related to the prospect of meeting their birth family. They may also feel torn between their adoptive and birth families. For TRAs, the additional stressors of racial isolation, discrimination, and identity confusion can exacerbate psychological distress (Basow, Lilley, Bookwala, & McGillicuddy-DeLisi, 2008; Samuels, 2009) and factor into their desire to search.

In summary, searching is a highly individual decision, and adoptees' interest in searching varies throughout stages of development and by their past and current experiences. Some adoptees might have no interest in searching, and that is also normative. Whatever the motivation, a birth family search is a way to make meaning of the story of their life. At the same time, it involves many logistics and practical steps that we will describe in the next section on searching strategies.

Searching strategies

In previous decades, domestic, in-race adoptees struggled to gain access to records, to learn current locations of birth families, and to track down family members who might be reluctant to respond. Adoptees are likely unaware that there might be authorization forms that allow the adoption agency to contact them if their birth parents seek them out. All these challenges are relevant to TRAs who search who might also encounter additional hurdles. For instance, international TRAs have to learn how to manage cultural and language differences and find their way through unfamiliar bureaucracies. Despite these difficulties, McGinnis et al. (2009) found that 30 percent of the Korean adoptees in their study had made contact with their birth families.

Because of their large adult cohort, Korean adoptees have been pioneers in advocating for birth family reunions as well as finding and developing resources for searchers. The Children's Home Society and Family Services (as cited in Goldstein, 2013) has a manual for Korean searchers that contains advice that is relevant to a wide range of international adoptees. It cautions adoptees that the search process is unpredictable and can take years. It also describes various methods of initiating a birth family search in South Korea, such as hiring private detectives, getting as much information as possible from both the US and Korean adoption agencies, asking these agencies for help to locate birth parents, and appearing on adoption-related shows on KBS (Korean Broadcasting System) television, where they can publicize the information they have about their Korean families. Based on their experiences, Korean adoptees have set up networks and groups to assist fellow adoptees in their efforts to locate birth parents. One example, Nafziger (2006), went to South Korea in the 1990s to search for her family and struggled to find social and economic support while there; despite many attempts, she was unable to locate her birth family. She subsequently established Global Overseas Adoptees' Link (GOA'L), an organization that provides resources and support for Korean adoptees, including assistance with birth family search and post-reunion support.

Recent technological and social developments have provided new search strategies for adoptees. The proliferation of social media and online information sources has created additional avenues to finding and contacting birth parents, siblings, and extended families (Black, Moyer, & Goldberg, 2016). Additionally, burgeoning genetic research and increased access to inexpensive at-home DNA kits have opened doors for adoptees to find their extended birth families (Volkman, 2009). "Records, research, and DNA are changing the whole nature of birth search," said Katherine Kim, President and Secretary of 325KAMRA, a non-profit organization, started in 2015 and primarily run by volunteers (personal communication, May 14, 2019). The organization distributes free DNA kits to Korean adoptees in the hopes of filling in biological and family medical history (325kamra.org/). It also helps adoptees search through genetic genealogy if they have a DNA match of approximately a 2nd cousin or closer biological relationships. The organization is also available to facilitate connection with birth families, which might include photos, medical history, and reunions. To date, 325KAMRA has helped 90 Korean adoptees identify and reunite with birth cousins, siblings, and parents. Kim explains that, given the possibility that adoption records might be missing, inaccurate, or falsified, DNA and genetic genealogy provides a new avenue for adoptees – some of whom had been searching for over 20 years – to locate birth families. Kim foresees the utilization of DNA kits as a method of birth search proliferating in other communities of international adoptees (e.g., people adopted from China).

Inspired by the advocacy of Korean and other international adult adoptees, several organizations offer homeland trips to adoptees from many sending countries (Wilson & Summerhill-Coleman, 2013). These usually include a tour of the birth country with visits to places of particular personal interest to specific adoptees, such as the birth mother's village or town, the spot where the child was found, or the orphanage or foster family where the child stayed while awaiting adoption. Some homeland trips also include assistance in finding birth parents. First Trip Home is an annual program organized by GOA'L for Korean adoptees who want to return to Korea for the first time since adoption; during the trip, adoptees are able to meaningfully immerse themselves in Korean culture and conduct an intensive birth family search (goal.or.kr). The TIES Program (adoptivefamilytravel.com) arranges homeland visits for international adoptees to a wide range of countries, including several in Latin America, Asia, Europe, and Africa. Initially, homeland trips were geared for adults, but recently adoptive parents have started a new trend by taking their pre-teen and adolescent children on homeland tours.

These parent-initiated searches for younger adoptees have introduced a new aspect of searching which has only recently become the focus of research efforts. In a study of children and families participating on homeland tours, Wang, Ponte, and Ollen (2015) found that adoptive parents were motivated by the wish to verify children's origins and the desire to help their children resolve feelings of loss related to their birth parents. These parent-initiated searches were complicated, and most "unfolded in stages spread over several years, involving many false starts and stops" (Wang et al., 2015, p. 63). Using accounts of pre-teen and teen adoptees on homeland trips to Russia, Guatemala, China, and Cambodia, Wilson and Summerhill-Coleman (2013) described some of the challenges of these trips but concluded that overall they helped adoptees in several ways: connecting with other adoptees from the same country, creating a more coherent adoption story, learning about and empathizing with birth parents (even if they did not meet them), exploring their ethnic/racial heritage and starting to see how they might develop a more complete identity, and creating a sense of belonging. As one adolescent said about her return to Cambodia, "When I got off the plane in [my birth country], the first thing I thought was, 'Wow, everyone looks like me!' and then I realized how much my parents stood out, and it made me smile" (Wilson & Summerhill-Coleman, 2013, p. 270).

Ponte, Wang, and Fan (2010), who studied six Chinese adoptees (ages 8–11) and their parents (all part of a homeland trip to China), were a bit more cautionary in their conclusions, noting that many emotional complexities arise. They also found that all the parents were happy with the trip and felt that it increased their family intimacy, but their children focused more on the difficult and emotional parts of the trip. They recommended that parents be clear about their own motivations and reactions and not assume that their children feel the same.

Contact and reunions

Contact or reunions with the birth families might or might not occur as a result of search; however, anticipating them is central to the search process (Henderson, Sass, & Carlson, 2007; Sobol & Cardiff, 1983). Earlier studies of in-race White adoptees showed that reunion outcomes were generally positive (Campbell, Silverman, & Patti, 1991). These reunions with birth family did not undermine relationships with adoptive parents (Sachdev, 1992), and even made some adoptees more appreciative of their adoptive families (Howe & Feast, 2001). Many adoptees continued to stay in contact with their birth parents who became friends rather than parents (Howe & Feast, 2001). Some of the adoptees who had close bonds and open communication with adoptive parents tended to form positive connections with birth parents (Farr, Grant-Marsney, & Grotevant, 2014), whereas the reverse was true for adoptees who had felt alienated from their adoptive parents (Howe, 2009). This latter pattern may be due to difficulty making close family connections, or unrealistic hopes that their birth parents would compensate for their disappointments with their adoptive family.

Despite the generally positive outcomes of reunions, some searchers had negative experiences reuniting due to personality clashes and lack of common social and/or cultural backgrounds (Howe & Feast, 2001). Müller, Gibbs, and Ariely (2003) also noted that adoptees felt more negative about their contact experiences when their birth mother was less interested in having a relationship than the adoptee was, when the two had different lifestyles and values, or when the relationship was "shrouded in secrecy" (p. 22).

The fact that in-race reunions were more successful if adoptees and birth parents shared similar values and lifestyles suggests that TRA reunions might be more challenging because they inevitably involve crossing racial, cultural, language, economic, and/or values lines. Ironically, feeling physically different from their adoptive parents might intensify TRAs' desire for contact, but these other factors might make their birth family contacts and subsequent relationships more difficult and disappointing (Tieman et al., 2008). One adoptee from Haiti (Green, 2009) described the difficulties of economic differences. She stays in touch with members of her birth family but is not comfortable with them because they expect her to give them money, and she feels guilty that she has many more opportunities than they do. However, some TRAs have had positive experiences despite these difficulties. One young Filipino man found that, despite language barriers and some cultural and financial conflicts (his birth mother expected him to send her money), being with his birth mother "filled like a gap, or a void … Having a picture of her and being with her really, um, really healed up patches that were missing in my life" (Godon et al., 2014, p. 19). After getting to know her and members of his extended birth family, he had more direction in his life, returned to school, and became active in the Filipino-American community.

Reunions provide opportunities for TRAs to meet people who look like them, which can lead to feelings of connection. One adoptee was looking through a photo album with her birth family and noticed how much she looked like her brother and sister, and observed, "so that was one of the most surreal moments, having these other people that look like me in world and, like, having it in front of me" (Goldstein, 2013, p. 56). Another adoptee described a photograph, taken during her first reunion, that embodied the connection between her and both of her families.

> I had my arms looped with both my sisters, then my father, I had, like, um, uh, I had my [birth] step father and uncle, um, he had his arms looped with … my adoptive dad, and my [birth and adoptive] mothers were both holding hands.
>
> *(Goldstein, 2013, p. 55)*

Reunions might also satisfy some questions for TRAs about why they were relinquished and how their birth parents felt about the adoption. Sometimes they discovered that their birth parents were not the ones who made the decision to give them up for adoption. For example, one Korean adoptee learned that her birth aunt, who was 21 years older than the birth mother, decided to give her [the adoptee] up for adoption in order "to give her a 'better life'" (Goldstein, 2013, p. 52).

In addition to meeting their families, TRAs also describe feeling uplifted by spiritually connecting with the land of their ancestors. In a beautiful poem about her return to Africa, Oparah (2006) describes how she feels renewed when "the red earth claims me … and the dark coils of unspoken bitterness loosen their grip" (p. 249). White Hawk (2006), an indigenous TRA, speaks of how she was healed after a lifetime of abuse from her adoptive mother by returning to the reservation where she was born and re-connecting with the land and her extended family. This experience led her to organize First Nations Orphan Association (wearecominghome.com) to advocate for and support all indigenous adoptees and fostered individuals and help them re-connect with their Native families and cultural traditions.

After the reunion, maintaining relationships with birth families can be challenging. The lack of a common language and culture can make it difficult to build relationships. Trenka's book, *The language of blood* (2003), is a compelling account of her childhood as a Korean adoptee in a Midwest rural area, her trips to Korea, and her evolving relationship with her birth family – all in the context of racial prejudice and language and cultural challenges. Even though they do not usually involve different languages, domestic reunions can be complicated if they cross economic and/or values lines. For example, a Pakistani-Scottish domestic TRA described how his relationship with his birth mother was complicated by her addiction and their very different lifestyles and values (McLay, 2006).

Wang et al. (2015) described how some parent-initiated searches have resulted in reunions between adoptees and their birth parents; however, they note that often the adoptive parents and their children are not adequately prepared for this meeting. In contrast to the romanticized media depictions of birth family reunions, they characterize initial meetings as "emotionally charged, highly unpredictable events … that brought myriad unforeseen emotional challenges as both children and adoptive parents tried to reconcile their expectations with reality" (Wang et al., 2015, p. 63). Young children were sometimes confused about why their birth mother (whom they perceived to be a stranger) wanted to hold or touch them. Some birth parents were overcome by guilt and shame at relinquishing their children. On the positive side, birth parents were able to answer questions about relinquishment and to introduce children and adoptive parents to other family members. Like adult searchers, adoptive parents were challenged by trying to stay in touch with the birth parents, but they were committed to these relationships, even if their children were not interested in maintaining contact at this time. Wang et al. (2015) note that one advantage of these early reunions is the potential for developing a parent–child relationship between adoptees and their birth parents. Although this outcome is very different from those of most adult adoptee reunions, the authors conclude that these early connections with birth parents help children make easier post-reunion transitions and strengthen their bonds with their adoptive parents.

Last, challenges can arise when searches result in identification of birth family but do not culminate with in-person meetings. In some cases, birth parents might be deceased or not wish to be contacted. For instance, Kim of 325KAMRA was able to identify birth family through genetic genealogy. In a personal communication, Kim said, "I feel blessed to have my puzzle pieces. I have photos and some history and I know that is so much more than what most [international] adoptees have." At the time of this writing, Kim explained that despite DNA evidence, her birth mother refused to acknowledge their biological relationship. She describes her pain by stating:

> All that I want is for her [Korean mother] to simply say "yes, I am that person and I hope you had a good life."… Our connections to our mothers are our first loves and it is incredibly painful to be rejected once again … I am not angry that she relinquished me for adoption, but I am angry that she denies she is my mother.
>
> *(K. Kim, personal communication, May 14, 2019)*

At the same time, Kim recognizes that "it happens and I know I am not the only one." Kim, who searched for 30 years, is currently connected with her younger half-sister and plans to continue that relationship.

In summary, reunions with birth family members are typically the goals of most searches, yet they are unpredictable. Some result in satisfying and close ties between adoptees and birth families, and others are rife with conflicts and miscommunications. Most reunions fall somewhere in between, with wonderful moments laced with frustrations due to language, cultural, economic, and value differences. Whatever the outcome, they provide adoptees with new information and a chance to create a more coherent narrative about their adoption and, thus, themselves. Many adoptees report that after their reunions, they are more settled and focused in their lives, as they are not as distracted by unanswered questions and feelings of loss.

Implications for practice

Each person involved in an adoption has a unique journey and varied reactions to different phases and outcomes. Thus, while we can use research and general guidelines to frame our work with clients, we try to avoid making assumptions about individuals. The following suggestions are grounded in the research reviewed in this chapter with the goal of providing informed practice that should be guided by the interests, desires, and circumstances specific to the individuals involved.

Practitioners working with TRAs need to be aware of the larger sociocultural context of their clients, particularly in regard to racism. They should encourage TRAs and their adoptive parents to explore how race, culture, identity, and racism affect all aspects of TRAs' lives, including their interests in searching for birth parents. Also, practitioners should be aware of the cultural, economic, and values differences that can complicate searching and reunions.

Given that the decision to search is highly individualized, clinicians should validate and normalize TRAs' interest (or lack of interest) in searching for and having contact with birth family. As part of these discussions, they can encourage TRAs to explore their personal motivations for searching or not searching. They may ask TRAs to consider whether search/reunion interest is related to other social, emotional, or developmental needs and goals. They should also encourage the TRAs to reflect whether their decision to not search is related to internalized negative beliefs about their group and, if so, explore how these beliefs relate to themselves as members of that group.

Search interest may fluctuate within individuals over time. Some adoptees might have always had a desire to connect with their birth families, whereas others might carefully calculate the pros and cons. For many, the so-called "decision" to seek contact with birth family occurs over time, organically, and sometimes unintentionally (e.g., birth family reaches out to the adoptee, a relative is unexpectedly discovered through a DNA match).

The following lists of suggestions have been written for clinicians working with adult TRAs who are in the process of deciding about a search or have already embarked on it. Many are also applicable to adoptive parents who are initiating searches on their children's behalf. Depending on the age of the adoptee and other factors, clinicians will need to decide when to meet with adoptive parents and children together or separately.

Prior to searching, practitioners should help and encourage adoptees to:

- Clarify their hopes and expectations for the search and possible reunions while, at the same time, staying open to a wide range of possibilities. What happens *after* the reunion? What if the search does not result in a reunion for various reasons (e.g., unavailable information, death, birth family does not want a reunion)?
- Consider and communicate needs with their adoptive family and other significant people in their life.
- Connect with other TRAs (especially those from the same country/background) who have searched. Various TRA groups and social networks exist, both in person and online. TRA communities can provide support and a realistic sense of what to expect in terms of conducting a search and managing contacts and reunions. By communicating with many

individuals, adoptees will also learn about the variability in search attitudes, experiences, and outcomes.

- Consider how language and cultural differences could affect the search and communication with birth family members.
- Consider how economic differences might affect relationships with birth families and communities.
- If a reunion is made, explore long-term plans and hopes related to their birth family. Do they envision just meeting their birth parents, or do they hope to build a long-term relationship? Do they desire to meet extended birth family members?
- Think through the emotional consequences of the possible outcomes and how they will feel if they do not find their birth parents or if the reunion is disappointing. Imagine the reactions of their birth parents and how they [TRAs] might feel in the potential face of birth parents' guilt, unrealistic expectations, unreciprocated desire to meet, and other possible negative reactions.
- View this search as part of a larger quest for identity and affiliation that can be met in many ways, including close connections with their birth culture and community, other adoptees, and friends who come from a wide range of racial and cultural backgrounds.
- Explore technical assistance on searching, including adoptee-led organizations as well as agencies, lawyers, and other resources.

After the search and, if applicable, the reunion, counselors can encourage adoptees to:

- Process what occurred and how they feel. What went well? What was hard? How did they feel at different points during the search and reunion? How do they feel now? How do they feel if a reunion was not possible?
- Accept what happened – the good and the bad – and recognize how they have learned from the full experience.
- Consider what kind of support they desire going forward, especially if they seek to maintain an ongoing relationship with their birth family.
- Talk with adoptive parents and other family members about their search and, if applicable, their reunion and how these experiences have changed their views and feelings about their adoption and relationships with their adoptive family.
- Process the reactions of adoptive family members and others to the search and reunion.
- Consider how their identity has changed/is changing as a result of searching.
- Reflect on their quest for affiliation and what individuals and groups they are currently feeling drawn to.
- Reflect on their overall feelings about their adoption and consider what comes next.
- Explore how the search and reunion experiences are incorporated into their ongoing adoption narrative.

Conclusion

Searching is a normative process that is influenced by sociocultural factors, especially racial and ethnic experiences for TRAs. Just as the desire to search for birth family is normative, the decision not to search is also normal. While there might be some common elements in search and reunion experiences of TRAs, there are many unpredictable events, connections, and barriers that may influence interest in searching and affect the outcome. Likewise, what occurs during and after contact with birth families is highly variable. It is critical that practitioners understand the larger context of TRAs' lives, as well as their individual experiences as they support their clients' explorations about searching and contact.

References

Aumend, S. A., & Barrett, M. C. (1983). Searching and non-searching adoptees. *Adoption & Fostering*, 7 (2), 37–42. doi:10.1177/030857598300700212

Aumend, S. A., & Barrett, M. C. (1984). Self-concept and attitudes toward adoption: A comparison of searching and nonsearching adult adoptees. *Child Welfare: Journal of Policy, Practice, and Program*, *63*(3), 251–259.

Baden, A. L., & Wiley, M. O. (2007). Counseling adopted persons in adulthood: Integrating practice and research. *The Counseling Psychologist*, *35*(6), 868–901. doi:10.1177/0011000006291409

Basow, S. A., Lilley, E., Bookwala, J., & McGillicuddy-DeLisi, A. (2008). Identity development and psychological well-being in Korean-born adoptees in the US. *American Journal of Orthopsychiatry*, *78*, 473–480. doi:10.1037/a0014450

Black, K. A., Moyer, A. M., & Goldberg, A. E. (2016). From face-to-face to Facebook: The role of technology and social media in adoptive family relationships with birth family members. *Adoption Quarterly*, *19*, 307–332. doi:10.1080/10926755.2016.1217575

Brodzinsky, D. M. (2011). Children's understanding of adoption: Developmental and clinical implications. *Professional Psychology: Research and Practice*, *42*(2), 200–207. doi:10.1037/a0022415

Campbell, L. H., Silverman, P. R., & Patti, P. B. (1991). Reunions between adoptees and birth parents: The adoptees' experience. *Social Work*, *36*(4), 329–335.

Choy, G. P., & Choy, C. C. (2006). What lies beneath. In J. J. Trenka, J. C. Oparah, & S. Y. Shin (Eds.), *Outsiders within: Writing on transracial adoption* (pp. 189–198). Cambridge, MA: South End Press.

Darnell, F. J., Johansen, A. B., Tavakoli, S., & Brugnone, N. (2017). Adoption and identity experiences among adult transnational adoptees: A qualitative study. *Adoption Quarterly*, *20*, 155–166. doi:10.1080/10926755.2016.1217574

Docan-Morgan, S. (2011). "They don't know what it's like to be in my shoes": Topic avoidance about race in transracially adoptive families. *Journal of Social and Personal Relationships*, *28*, 336–354. doi:10.1177/0265407510382177

Farr, R. H., Grant-Marsney, H. A., & Grotevant, H. D. (2014). Adoptees' contact with birth parents in emerging adulthood: The role of adoption communication and attachment to adoptive parents. *Family Process*, *53*, 656–671. doi:10.1111/famp.12069

Fisher, A. P. (2003). Still "not quite as good as having your own?" Toward a sociology of adoption. *Annual Review of Sociology*, *29*, 335–361. doi:10.1146/annurev.soc.29.010202.100209

Godon, D. E. (2012). Negotiating sense of belonging and sense of exclusion in Korean transracial adoptees. Unpublished raw data.

Godon, D. E., Green, W. F., & Ramsey, P. G. (2014). Transracial adoptees: The search for birth family and the search for self. *Adoption Quarterly*, *17*, 1–27. doi:10.1080/10926755.2014.875087

Godon-Decoteau, D., & Ramsey, P. G. (2018). Positive and negative aspects of transracial adoption: An exploratory study from Korean transracial adoptees' perspectives. *Adoption Quarterly*, *21*, 17–40. doi:10.1080/10926755.2017.1387209

Goldstein, K. E. (2013). *Birth family searching and meaning: A Korean transracial adoptee perspective* (Masters thesis). Retrieved from http://sophia.stkate.edu/msw_papers/181

Green, W. F. (2009). Identity formation in transracial adoptees. Unpublished raw data.

Grotevant, H. D. (1997). Coming to terms with adoption: The construction of identity from adolescence into adulthood. *Adoption Quarterly*, *1*, 3–27. doi:10.1300/J145v01n01_02

Hamilton, E., Samek, D. R., Keyes, M., McGue, M. K., & Iacono, W. G. (2015). Identity development in a transracial environment: Racial/ethnic minority adoptees in Minnesota. *Adoption Quarterly*, *18*, 217–233. doi:10.1080/10926755.2015.1013593

Henderson, D. B., Sass, D. A., & Carlson, J. (2007). Adoptees' and birth parents' therapeutic experiences related to adoption. In R. A. Javier, A. L. Baden, F. A. Biafora, & A. Camacho-Gingerich (Eds.), *Handbook of adoption: Implications for researchers, practitioners, and families* (pp. 379–397). Thousand Oaks, CA: Sage.

Hollingsworth, L. D. (1998). Adoptee dissimilarity from the adoptive family: Clinical and research implication. *Child and Adolescent Social Work Journal*, *15*, 303–319. doi:10.1023/A:1025163912090

Howe, D. (2009). Nature, nurture and narratives. In G. M. Wrobel & E. Neil (Eds.), *International advances in adoption research* (pp. 3–16). Malden, MA: Wiley-Blackwell.

Howe, D., & Feast, J. (2001). The long-term outcome of reunions between adult adopted people and their birth mothers. *British Journal of Social Work, 31*(3), 351–368. doi:10.1093/bjsw/31.3.351

Kalb, S., & Tucker, A. (2019). How adoptees are shaping post-adoption services. Retrieved from www.umass.edu/ruddchair/sites/default/files/rudd.kalb.pdf

Kirton, D., Feast, J., & Howe, D. (2000). Searching, reunion and transracial adoption. *Adoption & Fostering, 24*, 6–18. doi:10.1177/030857590002400303

Kryder, S. (1999). Self and alma mater: A study of adopted college students. *Child and Adolescent Social Work Journal, 16*, 355–372. doi:10.1023/A:1022395612530

Langrehr, K. J., Yoon, E., Hacker, J., & Caudill, K. (2015). Implications of transnational adoption status for adult Korean adoptees. *Journal of Multicultural Counseling and Development, 43*, 6–25. doi:10.1002/j.2161-1912.2015.00061.x

Lee, R. M. (2003). The transracial adoption paradox: History, research, and counseling implications of cultural socialization. *The Counseling Psychologist, 31*, 711–744. doi:10.1177/0011000003258087

McGinnis, H., Smith, S. L., Ryan, S., & Howard, J. A. (2009). *Beyond cultural camp: Promoting healthy identity formation in adoption*. New York: Evan B. Donaldson Adoption Institute. Retrieved from https://adoptioninstitute.org/old/publications/2009_11_BeyondCultureCamp.pdf

McGinnis, H. A., Baden, A. L., Kim, A. Y., & Kim, J. (2019). Generational shifts: Adult adoptee scholars' perspective on future research and practice. Retrieved from www.umass.edu/ruddchair/sites/default/files/rudd.mcginnis.pdf

McLay, R. (2006). From victim to survivor. In J. J. Trenka, J. C. Oparah, & S. Y. Shin (Eds.), *Outsiders within: Writing on transracial adoption* (pp. 189–198). Cambridge, MA: South End Press.

Müller, U., Gibbs, P., & Ariely, S. G. (2003). Adults who were adopted contacting their birthmothers: What are the outcomes, and what factors influence these outcomes? *Adoption Quarterly, 7*, 7–25. doi:10.1300/J145v07n01_02

Müller, U., & Perry, B. (2001). Adopted persons' search for and contact with their birth parents: Who searches and why? *Adoption Quarterly, 4*, 5–37. doi:10.1300/J145v04n03_02

Nafziger, A. I. (2006). Proud to be me. In J. J. Trenka, J. C. Oparah, & S. Y. Shin (Eds.), *Outsiders within: Writing on transracial adoption* (pp. 233–247). Cambridge, MA: South End Press.

Oparah, J. C. (2006). Praise song for Ala. In J. J. Trenka, J. C. Oparah, & S. Y. Shin (Eds.), *Outsiders within: Writing on transracial adoption* (pp. 249–250). Cambridge, MA: South End Press.

Palacios, J. (2009). The ecology of adoption. In E. Neil (Ed.), *International advances in adoption research for practice* (pp. 71–94). West Sussex: Wiley-Blackwell.

Ponte, I. C., Wang, L. K., & Fan, S. P. S. (2010). Returning to China: The experience of adopted Chinese children and their parents. *Adoption Quarterly, 13*, 100–124. doi:10.1080/10926755.2010.481039

Ramsey, P. G., & Mika, K. (2011). Identity of transracial adoptees: Outsiders looking in? *Anales de Psocologia, 27*, 611–624. doi:10.1037/t06009-000

Sachdev, P. (1992). Adoption reunion and after: A study of the search process and experience of adoptees. *Child Welfare: Journal of Policy, Practice, and Program, 71*, 53–68.

Samuels, E. (2009). Being raised by White people: Navigating racial difference among adopted multiracial adults. *Journal of Marriage and Family, 71*(1), 80–94. doi:10.1111/j.1741-3737.2008.00581.x

Sanvidge, J. C. (2014). *Adoptees in the wild: Gazillion voices*. Retrieved from https://adoptionstar.com/adoptees-wild-gazillion-voices

Silverman, A. (1993). Outcomes of transracial adoption. *The Future of Children, 3*, 104–118. doi:10.2307/1602405

Sobol, M. P., & Cardiff, J. (1983). A sociopsychological investigation of adult adoptees' search for birth parents. *Family Relations, 32*, 477–483.

Song, S. L., & Lee, R. M. (2009). The past and present cultural experiences of adopted Korean American adults. *Adoption Quarterly, 12*, 19–36. doi:10.1080/1092675090279194

Tessler, R., Gamache, G., & Liu, L. (1999). *West meets east: Americans adopt Chinese children*. Westport, CT: Bergin & Garvey.

Tieman, W., van der Ende, J., & Verhulst, F. C. (2008). Young adult international adoptees' search for birth parents. *Journal of Family Psychology, 22*(5), 678–687. doi:10.1037/a0013172

Trenka, J. J. (2003). *The language of blood: A memoir*. Saint Paul, MN: Minnesota Historical Society Press.

Triseliotis, J., Feast, J., & Kyle, F. (2005). *The adoption triangle revisited: A study of adoption, search and reunion experiences*. London: British Association for Adoption and Fostering (BAAF).

Volkman, T. A. (2009). Seeking sisters: Twinship and kinship in an age of internet miracles and DNA technologies. In D. Marre & L. Briggs (Eds.), *International adoption: Global inequalities and the circulation of children* (pp. 283–301). New York: New York University Press.

Wang, L. K., Ponte, I. C., & Ollen, E. W. (2015). Letting her go: Western adoptive families' search and reunion with Chinese birth parents. *Adoption Quarterly, 18*, 45–66. doi:10.1080/10926755.2014.945703

White Hawk, S. (2006). Generation after generation we are coming home. In J. J. Trenka, J. C. Oparah, & S. Y. Shin (Eds.), *Outsiders within: Writing on transracial adoption* (pp. 291–301). Cambridge, MA: South End Press.

Wilson, S. L., & Summerhill-Coleman, L. (2013). Exploring birth countries: The mental health implications of heritage travel for children/adolescents adopted internationally. *Adoption Quarterly, 16*, 262–278. doi:10.1080/10926755.2013.790865

Wrobel, G. M., & Dillon, K. (2009). Adopted adolescents: Who and what are they curious about? In G. M. Wrobel & E. Neil (Eds.), *International advances in adoption research for practice* (pp. 217–244). London: Wiley-Blackwell.

Wrobel, G. M., Grotevant, H. D., & McRoy, R. G. (2004). Adolescent search for birthparents: Who moves forward? *Journal of Adolescent Research, 19*, 132–151. doi:10.1177/0743558403258125

18

COMMUNICATION ABOUT ADOPTION IN FAMILIES

Lindsey J. Thomas and Kristina M. Scharp

Communication is often a taken-for-granted part of life, yet it is imperative to everyday lived experiences and the construction and even dissolution of family relationships. In adoptive families in particular, communication has been studied both as predictive and outcome variables in models/theories as well as being positioned as the ongoing process through which families continually (re)create identities and boundaries. This chapter first provides an overview of several family communication and sensemaking theories that are salient to the study of adoptive families and communication. Next, the chapter puts forth an overview of the importance of communication in and around adoptive families and details empirical contributions of scholars who study communication and related phenomena in adoptive families. Finally, the chapter concludes with implications for practice and policy.

Models and theories of adoption-related family communication

One way that communication has been used in studies pertaining to adoption is as a variable in models. Typically, communication, or a particular communication practice, is positioned as a predictive, or independent, variable when modeling family-centered or adopted youth outcomes. However, there are occasions when communication variables, such as disclosure, might serve as a dependent variable. For example, researchers have positioned communication within the family as positively influencing adopted youth adjustment and attachment. In particular, open communication practices that acknowledge, rather than deny, differences in experience for adoptive families are associated with positive outcomes for adopted children (e.g., Brodzinsky, 2006).

In addition to models in which communication is a variable, other theoretical frameworks take a constitutive approach, positing that communication does not just impact relationships; communication is what creates relationships and identities and renders experiences meaningful. Although there are numerous communication-centered theories and models that are relevant to the study of adoptive families and adoption outcomes, this chapter covers five theoretical frameworks/models that are particularly salient – the family adoption communication model, family communication patterns theory, narrative theories, relational dialectics theory, and the perspective of families as discourse dependent – before turning to a discussion of more emergent communication challenges and connections.

Family adoption communication model: theorizing change

The family adoption communication model (FAC) (Wrobel, Kohler, Grotevant, & McRoy, 2003) highlights communication about adoption as an ever-changing process that impacts the family environment as a whole. The FAC emphasizes that at any time, children can acquire adoption-related information when: (a) parents share unsolicited information; (b) parents answer a child's questions; and/or (c) children independently seek information. As children grow, parents might share more information, children might ask and receive nuanced answers to deeper and broader questions, and many children eventually directly seek and garner information, taking control of the information-gathering process. For example, a study by Skinner-Drawz, Wrobel, Grotevant, and Von Korff (2011) confirmed the FAC-based assumption that information seeking and communication in regards to adoption tend to shift over time. Specifically, nearly two-thirds (62%) of the adoptee participants experienced an increase in information seeking over time, and open, flexible communication about adoption within the adoptive family emerged as important to supporting adoptees and their information seeking during adolescence and into emerging adulthood. Nelson (2017) further suggests that the FAC can be adapted and fruitfully applied to the context of foster care and foster adoption. Couched in FAC and family communication patterns theory (see below) it was found that ongoing, open dialogue is important to adoptees, and perceiving one's family as engaging open communication was associated with less preoccupation about one's adoption.

Family communication patterns theory: exploring cohesion

Like the FAC, family communication patterns theory (FCP) (e.g., Koerner & Fitzpatrick, 2002) attends to the ways in which communication within the family shapes the family environment. Specifically, FCP highlights family cohesion, or shared social reality, by examining two process orientations that families engage: conversation and conformity. Families high in conversation allow for the participation of all members in constructing social reality and encourage free-flowing communication among members. Families high in conformity encourage those in roles of authority (e.g., parents) to put forth the beliefs, values, and attitudes that family members are expected to share. Mapping a family as either high or low in regards to conversation and conformity orientation produces one of four family types: laissez-faire (low conformity, low conversation); pluralistic (low conformity, high conversation); protective (high conformity, low conversation); or consensual (high conformity, high conversation). Using FCP as a framework for investigating adolescent adjustment, Reuter and Koerner (2008) found that families with adopted and non-adopted children were similar in regards to FCP. However, the authors also found that adopted adolescents in laissez-faire and protective families – those configurations low in regards to conversation orientation – were more at risk for adjustment issues than their non-adopted peers (Reuter & Koerner, 2008). Further bolstering understandings of the importance of conversation orientation is Horstman, Colaner, and Rittenour's (2016) work. In addition to finding that perceiving one's family as engaging open communication, as well as that ongoing, open dialogue was important to adoptees, and that these aspects were associated with less preoccupation about one's adoption, Horstman et al. found that conversation orientation alone significantly predicted adoptees' perceptions of their adoptive parents' adoption openness (i.e., how open, honest, and approachable adoptees perceive their parents to be in regards to adoption issues).

Narrative theories: Illuminating sensemaking and identity

Narrative theories provide the foundation of a vast array of empirical work, from normative studies to interpretive explorations, critical essays, and dialogic examinations. The commonality of narrative theories is an assumption that humans socially tell/perform stories, and stories help individuals and groups to construct identities and make sense of events and experiences (e.g., Becker, 1997; Langellier & Peterson, 2004; Riessman, 2008). One particular genre of adoption-related narrative that has garnered the attention of communication scholars is the entrance narrative, or the story that a family tells about how a child came to be a member of the family. Entrance narratives often contain themes of fate and choice, rescue, and the forever-ness of family. Aligning with the underpinnings of narrative theories, research suggests that entrance narratives are important to family and individual identity, influencing how children, in particular, perceive themselves, their adoptive families, and their birth families.

Entrance narratives vary across storytellers (e.g., adoptee; parent) and contexts (e.g., adoptive families; foster families) and are associated with a variety of outcomes. For example, adoptees have been found to tell stories with themes of openness and deception, fate, and rescue, as well as being a chosen child, experiencing difference, and reconnection (Kranstuber & Koenig Kellas, 2011). The latter three themes in particular – chosen child, difference, and reconnection – were found to significantly predict differences in adoptees' self-concept (Kranstuber & Koenig Kellas, 2011). In one early study of entrance narratives told by adoptive parents, researchers found similar themes of rescue and destiny, in addition to themes of dialectical tensions, compelling connection, and legitimacy (Krusiewicz & Wood, 2001). In a later study of themes found in adoptive parents' entrance narratives about a child's open adoption, rescue, fate, and forever-ness again emerged, in addition to chosen parents, birth parents as family, and adoption making a family (Hays, Horstman, & Colaner, 2016). Overall, open adoption entrance narratives emphasized the fluidity of adoption relationships. Indeed, adoptive parents' satisfaction with birth parents influenced storytelling; in turn, storytelling was linked to adoptees' perceptions of birth parents. Thus, adoptive parents – adoptive mothers in particular – were found to be the gatekeepers of ever-changing family constructions and relationships (Hays et al., 2016). In addition to adoption, scholars have also begun to illuminate the importance of entrance narratives in the context of foster care, finding them similar to those found in adoption entrance narratives. Themes such as forever-ness and being better off, themes of birth parent consequences and untold learning, deep connection, specialness, pragmatics, and temporariness emerge from foster parents' entrance narratives about children in foster care (Nelson & Horstman, 2017). As with adoption entrance narratives, themes in foster entrance narratives were found to be associated with individual adjustment outcomes, including parents' perceptions of foster child adjustment and closeness between foster parents and foster children (Nelson & Horstman, 2017). Overall, research couched in narrative theories covers a wide range of adoption-related topics. Narrative theories can be used to investigate themes, empirically link themes with outcomes, and/or critically examine competing understandings of what family is and can be. Those who take a constitutive approach to communication, assuming that communicative interactions are what make life understandable and meaningful, further posit that narratives do not just reflect experiences, they create meaning and identities. In family communication, including studies of adoption, researchers who take a constitutive approach often draw on the framework of families as discourse dependent which is detailed in the following subsection.

Relational dialectics theory: Competing for meaning-making

One of the most prominent frameworks that family communication scholars use to explore adoption is relational dialectics theory (RDT; Baxter, 2011). RDT posits that meaning is made in the competition of discourses (i.e., cultural ideologies); some of those discourses are widely circulated in the culture and others are less legitimated. This theory is particularly useful in illustrating the ways stigmatized or disenfranchised family members resist the ideologies that marginalize them. In the context of adoption, researchers have explored the meaning of (foster) adoption (Baxter, Suter, Thomas, & Seurer, 2015), the process of adoption (e.g., Norwood & Baxter, 2011), members of the adoption triad (e.g. Baxter, Scharp, Asbury, Jannusch, & Norwood, 2012b), adoptive and foster family (Baxter, Norwood, Asbury, & Scharp, 2014; Thomas, Jackl, & Crowley, 2017; Thomas & Scharp, 2017), and adoption reconnection (Scharp, 2013). In many of these findings, researchers identify the ways in which the culture views adoption as second best to biological child rearing; ultimately illuminating the taken-for-granted assumption that biological families are the only way to be a good family. By doing so, this research holds implications for, and speaks to, other family-related practices such as the experience of infertility and the choice to be child-free.

Discourse dependency: Communicating complexities, challenges, and connections

Alongside narrative theories and RDT, many scholars who study communication in and surrounding adoptive families position family relationships and identities as what Galvin (2006, 2014) calls discourse dependent. Discourse dependency offers a framework for understanding the ways that communication can help to construct – or challenge – family configurations. Scholars who study families as discourse dependent position communication as a driving force in creating, maintaining, dissolving, and explaining family relationships and drawing family boundaries. In other words, communication helps both family members and non-family members to know their roles and understand the family. Furthermore, a discourse dependent approach helps to illustrate how some families carry more burden than others in explaining and legitimating their family status, because certain ways of being and doing family are more readily understood by the culture at large. For example, in the US, families are often thought of as biologically related, being legally tied, and sharing a residence (Baxter, 2014). Family configurations that fulfill, or appear to fulfill, all three of these expectations require less explanation than those that exist outside of these understandings.

According to Galvin (2006, 2014), although these processes can happen simultaneously, families manage boundaries to continually (re)create and reify (non)membership in both internal and external communication and interaction. Internally, within families and among family members, family communication marks inclusive membership through practices of naming, discussing, narrating, and ritualizing. Naming involves choosing/using familial titles (e.g., instructing a fostered youth to "Call me Papa"; telling a friend who has become family, "You're my unbiological sister"). Discussing includes talk about how to navigate being a family, including roles (e.g., caregiving duties) and routes to family development (e.g., deciding to adopt a child). Narrating involves the ongoing construction of family stories that (re)create family background, identity, and values (e.g., a family formed through adoption might include as part of their narrative: "Your dad and I always wanted to provide care and guidance for fostered youth; when you came along, we knew our family was meant to be"). Enacting rituals helps to tie family members to one another and the family to the broader culture (e.g., families formed through adoption might annually celebrate a child's adoption, or "gotcha," day). Externally, families mark (non-)members via labeling, explaining, legitimizing, and defending. Labeling is a corollary to naming, marking the titles that family members use with outsiders to mark the ties they have with other family members (e.g., a child introducing her two fathers: "This is my dad and my papa"). Explaining involves telling outsiders how a family operates and is family-like (e.g., "Instead of a mom and dad, I have a dad and a papa"). Legitimizing draws on commonly understood/accepted configurations of family to render a family understandable (e.g., "I was adopted by two dads, like Lily on the TV show *Modern Family*"). Defending justifies or validates a family in an interaction in which an outsider has challenged or attacked a family form (e.g., "They're BOTH my real dads – they both love me and care for me!" in response to an outsider with a follow-up inquiry of, "OK, but which one is your real dad?"). Families use any or all of these communicative practices to construct familial identities and roles, creating a sense of who is, and is not, family. Much of the research on family construction and sensemaking in the following empirical findings section draws on Galvin's work to frame (adoptive) families as discourse dependent.

Adoption decisions, pathways, and experiences: empirical findings

Although all families rely on communication, as mentioned, families face different complexities and challenges when it comes to creating, maintaining, conveying, and even dissolving a sense of identity among family members and with outsiders. One way to examine these varying complexities and challenges is by looking at the role that communication plays in a variety of adoption-related decisions, pathways, and experiences. The following subsections detail communication and experiences surrounding (pre-) adoption decisions, the importance of entrance narratives, primary pathways of adoptive family formation and their related opportunities and challenges, and adoption reunion expectations and outcomes.

(Pre-)adoption decisions

Even before an adoptive family comes into being, communication is an important factor in its creation. Birth parents/birth mothers must choose to place a child for adoption or, in the case of foster care adoption, parental rights must be relinquished or terminated, and adoptive parents must come to a decision to adopt and choose a path – and child – for adoption. Norwood and Baxter (2011) discuss the letters some families write birth mothers describing the types of parents they expect to be. Holman Jones (2005) further speaks to the dialectical tensions surrounding the decision to proceed with adoption: in every adoption, there is both gain and loss, often for all involved parties. For birth parents/birth mothers, the loss of relinquishing a child is often positioned as a potential gain of a better life for the child. For children, losing a family of origin and biological connection coexists with gaining an adoptive family. For adoptive parents, coming to terms with the loss of potential biological reproduction often precedes gaining a child via adoption. Indeed, numerous scholars have pointed to the cultural expectation of biological relatedness among family members, the prevalence of which renders adoption an ideologically "second-best" path toward creating a family, assumed to be undertaken only in the absence of ability or opportunity to biologically procreate (e.g., Baxter et al., 2014).

Research suggests that parents who identify as part of the LGBTQ+ (lesbian, gay, bisexual, transgender, queer) community might have additional considerations when deciding to adopt and as (adoptive) parents. For example, lesbian and gay couples often face mixed responses and potential discrimination in interactions with foster/adoption agencies, legal systems and judicial decisions, birth parents/biological family members, and even potential adoptees (e.g., Bergen, Suter, & Daas, 2006; Downing, Richardson, Kinkler, & Goldberg, 2009; Patrick, 2006). Although many married LGBTQ+ couples likely have a less burdensome adoption experience since *Obergefell* v. *Hodges* ensured equal marriage rights for lesbian and gay couples, unmarried couples still face barriers to adoption (e.g., Paulsen, 2018). However, some scholars have also illuminated openness in acceptable foster adoptive family configurations. For example, in examining how "ideal" families are constructed in online photolistings that promote youth from foster care, Thomas and Scharp (2017) found that a variety of family forms, including single-parent and two-mother households, were noted as preferred adoptive families for some of the featured children.

Primary pathways

After deciding to adopt, there are several routes that adoptive parents might navigate as primary pathways to adoption. Specifically, domestic private adoption, domestic adoption through the foster care system, and international adoption are paths to adoptive family formation that each present different communicative opportunities and challenges.

Domestic (private) adoption

When children are adopted domestically, a primary consideration is the degree of openness of the adoption (see Grotevant & McRoy, 1998). Closed, or confidential, adoptions, wherein children's biological parent(s) have no involvement with an adoptive family or child once an adoption was completed, were once common in the US. However, more recently, adoptions have become increasingly open. Adoption openness refers to the depth and breadth with which adoption is discussed in an adoptive family, as well as the amount of information that is exchanged among biological and adoptive families and the prevalence of involvement and interaction between biological parents and adoptive families and/or adopted children (see Brodzinsky, 2006; Grotevant & McRoy, 1998). Although it is possible for any adoptive family to practice some degree of openness, domestic adoption increases the opportunities for openness and even ongoing contact among birth and adoptive family members. Research has illustrated, however, that those involved with adoption, such as adoption practitioners, birth families, adoptive families, and adoptees, recognize the complexities that come with openness. These studies suggest that having an open adoption relationship is complex and facilitates opportunities as well as presents challenges.

Increased openness surrounding adoption can create both connections and challenges. For example, connections with biological family create opportunities in regards to health communication and allowing adoptive families a better understanding of a child's background and hereditary risks. Openness is also perceived as allowing children more nuanced connections for identity-building and providing more closure for biological families, especially birth mothers (Colaner & Scharp, 2016; Haugaard, West, & Moed, 2000). In addition to these connections, the presence of biological family members can also present challenges, as families navigate the depth and breadth of adoptive–biological interactions and relationships (Colaner & Scharp, 2016; Haugaard et al., 2000). Ongoing contact between adoptive and birth family members also varies regarding outcomes, with, for example, satisfaction of contact better predicting adoptee adjustment than contact quantity or quality alone (Grotevant, McRoy, Wrobel, & Ayers, 2013). In light of these nuances, it becomes apparent that communication is central to navigating these challenges.

Communication scholars who study the intricacies of domestic adoption often reference the adoption triad: (1) the adopted child(ren); (2) biological relatives to the adopted child(ren), most often birth mothers; and (3) adoptive family members, most often the adoptive parent(s). Research on the adoption triad, particularly that which examines narratives authored by adoption triad members, indicates that experiences and sensemaking of adoption among triad members differ greatly. Specifically, in studies of adoption sensemaking and narrative coherence (in which studies are examined to see how well narrators make sense of the adoption experience, which is often positively correlated with benefits in regards to psychological wellbeing), adoption triad members are overall unlikely to tell highly coherent stories, but members vary across different dimensions of coherence. For example, birth mothers tend to tell emotionally congruent stories that rebuff the cultural ideology of intensive mothering that often positions birth mothers as bad mothers (Baxter, Norwood, Asbury, Jannusch, & Scharp, 2012a; Baxter et al., 2012b). The ideology of intensive mothering positions birth mothers as bad mothers by dictating that placing a child for adoption violates the expectations that good mothers perform unconditional love and self-sacrifice for children (see Hays, 1996). In light of these expectations, birth mothers put forth the ways that they are good mothers (e.g., chose self-sacrificing adoption to give a child a better life) or not mothers at all (e.g., biological carrier rather than mother) (Baxter et al., 2012b). Although birth mothers tend to tell both highly emotional stories (i.e., stories heavily laden with emotion) and emotionally appropriate stories (i.e., stories that illustrate emotions that are fitting given the content and context), adoptive parents are the members of the adoption triad most likely to tell an overall coherent story, when examining chronology, setting and actor details, and providing accounts of why experiences and events took place (Baxter et al., 2012a).

Foster adoption

One subset of domestic adoption, often separated from domestic adoption via private agencies in extant literature, is adoption through the foster care system. Children in foster care are the most at-risk youth group in the US (e.g., Kools, Paul, Norbeck, & Robbins, 2009; Zill, 2011), and formerly fostered youth's narratives construct a variety of identities, from victim to survivor to victor over the foster care system (Thomas, 2014). To promote wellbeing and minimize negative outcomes, those involved with the foster care system strive to find fostered youth permanent placements with caring families, either through reunification with the family of origin or via adoption (Children's Bureau, 2018). At present, approximately 100,000 children, nearly one-quarter of the youth in foster care, are available for adoption in the US (Children's Bureau). In comparison with domestic private adoption, foster care adoption presents additional communicative challenges and opportunities for parents and children alike. In addition, fostered (adopted) youth often keep in contact with members of their family of origin, including birth parents, biological siblings, and extended relatives such as grandparents (e.g., Cossar & Neil, 2013; Leathers, 2003; Linares, Rhodes, & Montalto, 2010). Thus, foster adoption tends to engage varying levels of openness in regards to communication among adoptive families, adopted children, and families of origin; as such, foster adoptive families tend to require communicative navigation of a variety of familial ties.

Communication scholars to date have studied the narratives and sensemaking of both foster adoptive parents and youth adopted through foster care. Adoptive parents' narratives draw on two understandings of foster adoption: adoption through the foster care system as a way to build and/or complete one's family, and foster adoption as a way to provide long-term care for a child in need (Baxter et al., 2015). Foster adoptive parents' narratives also show an understanding that biological ties are often culturally privileged, yet everyday care and unconditional love are what matter to foster adoptive family identity (Suter, Baxter, Seurer, & Thomas, 2014). Foster adopted youth have illustrated similar narrative sensemaking of family, in recognizing the culturally privileged position of biological relatedness while putting forth the importance of ongoing care and love, regardless of biology (Thomas et al., 2017). The emphasis on care and love not only operates to construct family relationships in the absence of biological ties, it also assists individuals in dissolving culturally assumed family ties, such as biological ties that lack care and love (Thomas et al., 2017).

International adoption

In addition to communication in and about families created through domestic adoption, a large body of communication-centered literature focuses on international adoption. In particular, much of the international adoption communication research focuses on family communication, constructions, and challenges surrounding visible adoption. Visible adoption refers to situations in which children and parents, and sometimes other siblings, look physically different from one another, as is common in transracial adoptive families, thus calling attention to the absence of assumed biological ties. Visible adoption can lead to a variety of external interactions that are less commonly faced by adoptive families who pass as potentially biological (see Brodzinsky (2006), for discussion of passing in the context of adoption). Although visible adoption can also occur in domestic private and foster care adoptions, it is especially common for international adoptions. In the field of family communication studies, scholars have been particularly interested in the often intrusive interactions and communication practices of both adoptees and parents in internationally adoptive families.

For example, in one study, Korean adoptees reported a variety of negative experiences in interactions with others, including negative comments about appearance, derogatory remarks regarding ethnicity, and even physical attacks (Docan-Morgan, 2011). In particular, Korean adoptees found comments and questions about family relatedness, compliments, stares, mistaken identities, and interactions that adoptees experienced in the absence of their families to be intrusive (Docan-Morgan, 2010). Docan-Morgan's (2011) work also emphasizes the importance of internal communication in light of these external interactions: although adoptees often expressed reluctance to discuss negative external interactions with their parents out of self-protection or anticipated parental unresponsiveness, some adoptees described openness and support when talking with parents about negative experiences. Adoptive, predominantly White, parents with Chinese children also found several interactions to be particularly intrusive and difficult to navigate in external interactions (Suter, 2008). Questions about China's history or culture, stereotypes about Asians, and savior talk (i.e., describing a parent as good for "saving" their adopted child) marked interactions that required parents to develop identity-affirming responses. Parent participants reported that responses depended on several criteria, including the commenter's identity, the comment or question itself, child-related factors (e.g., child's age), the interaction's timing and setting, and the adoptive parent's disposition (Suter & Ballard, 2009). Parents reported some positive external interactions, such as compliments about their child or their parenting, comments that affirmed family relations and identity – including comments on a child's similarities to parents or other siblings, and interest in better understanding the adoption process. Yet there were also some particularly negative questions that parents reported refusing to answer, such as intrusive questions about the adoption decision and the child's China story, inquiries about a child's cost, and the ways in which the adoptive family was rendered more visible (Suter & Ballard, 2009).

Adoption reunions

Sometimes adoptees seek (re)connection with a member of their biological family, attempting what is known as an adoption reunion. Specifically, Scharp and Steuber (2014) found that adult adoptees who had not taken part in an adoption reunion would, if they reconnected with a biological family member, seek information about biological family relationships (e.g., birth parent information; extended family information), context (e.g., birth mother and adoption circumstances), and adoptee identity, including health information. Given that adoption reunions are often sought when adoptees feel uncertainty about their adoption (Powell & Afifi, 2005), one might assume that adoption reunions would be negatively associated with adoptive parent/family relationships. However, research has illustrated that, although adoption reunions can be complicated, they can also be neutral or beneficial. For example, in an early study of adoption reunion experiences, Sachdev (1992) found that adoptees' relationships with adoptive parents were often either not affected or were reported as improving after adoptees took part in an adoption reunion.

In the context of domestic adoption reunions, which comprises the bulk of adoption reunion research, adoptees describe competing experiences of reconnecting with biological family members (Scharp, 2013). The experience can be either – or both – romantic or pragmatic. Romantic reconnection, reminiscent of love at first sight, emphasizes desires for shared physical resemblance and immediate connection upon reunifying. Pragmatic reconnection sits in stark contrast with romantic experiences and expectations, emphasizing the practicality of a reunion (e.g., a desire to reconnect for health information; stating that connection is never a guarantee) and a framing that birth family members, despite being biological relatives, are nonetheless strangers. These competing ideologies of what reunions can mean for adoptees put forth a vast array of understandings of the domestic adoption reunion experience (Scharp, 2013).

Although much literature on adoption reunion experiences focuses on domestic adoptees, some research does examine the context of international adoption reunions. For example, Tieman, van der Ende, and Verhulst (2008) found that among international adoptees in the Netherlands, fewer participants than anticipated were searching for their birth families, and those who were searching were more prone to problematic behaviors and psychiatric disorders than those who were not searching for their birth parents. The authors speculate that this might in part be due to constraints surrounding one's ability to search internationally and emphasize that it is more likely that problems (e.g., family functioning; loss-related stress) led to searching than vice-versa. In addition to Tieman et al.'s comparisons of (non)searchers, Docan-Morgan has examined international adoption reunion experiences among American adoptees from Korea. Overall, adoptees wanted to share positive post-adoption experiences with their birth families and emphasized that they did not want birth family members to feel guilty, whereas birth family members tended to share information surrounding the adoption circumstances (Docan-Morgan, 2014). Adoptees also reported engaging in a variety of rituals during their adoption reunion, including engaging in extended touch with birth family members, exchanging gifts, partaking in outings, exchanging culture, and participating in symbolic family activities (Docan-Morgan, 2014). Research also indicates that international adoption reunions might differ from domestic adoption reunions in regards to cultural perceptions and the impact of cultural perceptions on feelings of closeness to one's birth family. In particular, Korean international adoptees perceived cultural differences in family roles and expectations, standards for beauty and femininity, expectations for interactions, and past and present circumstances. Thus, some adoptees reported feeling closer to their birth families and others reported feeling like they did not belong in their birth family.

Implications for practice and policy

Taken together, extant literature that focuses on communication in and about adoptive families emphasizes the importance of nuance: there is no single correct way to talk about or perform family. However, practitioners, policy makers, adoptive family members, adoptees, and even birth family members alike might benefit from keeping in mind the positive outcomes associated with open and ongoing communication, even if that can be challenging at times. Indeed, all five of the theoretical frameworks surveyed at the beginning of this chapter examine communication as a fluid process that can promote positive outcomes, strengthen the family system, create family boundaries, and construct members' senses of identity and belonging. In addition, empirical work illustrates that different pathways are prone to varying connections, complexities, and challenges. Although some interactions might hold potential to be perceived as threatening relationships within an adoptive family (e.g., when outsiders make intrusive comments; when an adoptee seeks to reunify with a birth family member), many experiences also hold the potential to strengthen individual and relational identities (e.g., when replying to an outsider affirms an adoptee's belonging; when an adoption reunion bolsters both an adoptee's identity and relationships in their adoptive family). As it happens, fostering a positive communication environment early on, and especially in the case of open adoption, could alleviate complications later on in life.

In culmination, the preceding chapter holds implications for both adoption practice and policy. Drawing on the importance of open communication highlighted in studies that employ FAC and/or FCP, practitioners might consider implementing communication education sessions for (potential) adoptive parents. Such sessions might focus on age-appropriate conversation topics, offer guidance in regards to discussing adoption and birth families, and provide assurance that curiosity about – even interactions with – one's biological relatives need not undermine the identity and cohesion of the adoptive family. In addition, drawing on narrative theories and RDT, education sessions might emphasize the importance of entrance narratives, and particular themes such as specialness and (adoptive) family as legitimate and forever, in building family members' roles and identities. Finally, understanding families as in flux and dependent upon communication highlights the importance of recognizing that policy can both enable and constrain families and children's wellbeing. Policy makers should keep in mind that there is no single correct path to ensure healthy, happy children and families. Thus, implementing policies that attend to not only quantity of interactions (e.g., the openness of an adoption/amount of information exchanged) but also the quality of interactions (e.g., periodically revisiting how satisfied children and families are with ongoing birth-adoptive family contact) might bolster wellbeing.

References

Baxter, L. A. (2011). *Voicing relationships*. Thousand Oaks, CA: Sage Publications.

Baxter, L. A. (2014). Introduction to the volume. In L. A. Baxter (Ed.), *Remaking "family" communicatively* (pp. 3–16). New York: Peter Lang Publishing.

Baxter, L. A., Norwood, K. M., Asbury, B., Jannusch, A., & Scharp, K. M. (2012a). Narrative coherence in online stories told by members of the adoption triad. *Journal of Family Communication, 12*, 265–283. doi:10.1080/15267431.2012.686944

Baxter, L. A., Norwood, K. M., Asbury, B., & Scharp, K. M. (2014). Narrating adoption: Resisting adoption as "second best" in online stories of domestic adoption told by adoptive parents. *Journal of Family Communication, 14*, 253–269. doi:10.1080/15267431.2014.908199

Baxter, L. A., Scharp, K. M., Asbury, B., Jannusch, A., & Norwood, K. M. (2012b). "Birthmothers are not bad people": A dialogic perspective of online birth mother narratives. *Qualitative Communication Research, 1*, 53–82. doi:101525/qcr.2012.1.1.53

Baxter, L. A., Suter, E. A., Thomas, L. J., & Seurer, L. M. (2015). The dialogic construction of "adoption" in online foster adoption narratives. *Journal of Family Communication, 15*, 193–213. doi:10.1080/15267431.2015.1043431

Becker, G. (1997). *Disrupted lives: How people create meaning in a chaotic world*. Berkeley, CA: University of California Press.

Bergen, K. M., Suter, E. A., & Daas, K. L. (2006). "About as solid as a fish net": Symbolic construction of a legitimate parental identity for nonbiological lesbian mothers. *Journal of Family Communication, 6*, 201–220. doi:10.1207/s15327698jfc0603_3

Brodzinsky, D. (2006). Family structural openness and communication openness as predictors in the adjustment of adopted children. *Adoption Quarterly, 9*(4), 1–18. doi:10.1300/j145v09n04_01

Children's Bureau of the United States Department of Health and Human Services. (2018). Child welfare information gateway: Foster care statistics 2016. Retrieved from www.childwelfare.gov/pubs/factsheets/foster.pdf

Colaner, C. W., & Scharp, K. M. (2016). Maintaining open adoption relationships: Practitioner insights on adoptive parents' regulation of adoption kinship networks. *Communication Studies, 67*, 359–378. doi:10.1080/10510974.2016.1164208

Cossar, J., & Neil, E. (2013). Making sense of siblings: Connections and severances in post-adoption contact. *Child & Family Social Work, 18*, 67–76. doi:10.1111/cfs.12039

Docan-Morgan, S. (2010). Korean adoptees' retrospective reports of intrusive interactions: Exploring boundary management in adoptive families. *Journal of Family Communication, 10*, 137–157. doi:1080/15267431003699603

Docan-Morgan, S. (2011). "They don't know what it's like to be in my shoes": Topic avoidance about race in transracially adoptive families. *Journal of Social and Personal Relationships, 28*, 226–255. doi:10.1177/0265407510382177

Docan-Morgan, S. (2014). "They were strangers who loved me": Discussion, narratives, and rituals during Korean adoptees' initial reunions with birth families. *Journal of Family Communication, 14*, 352–373. doi:10.1080/15267431.2014.946033

Downing, J., Richardson, H., Kinkler, L., & Goldberg, A. (2009). Making the decision: Factors influencing gay men's choice of an adoption path. *Adoption Quarterly, 12*, 247–271. doi:/10.1080/10926750903313310

Galvin, K. M. (2006). Diversity's impact on defining the family: Discourse-dependence and identity. In L. H. Turner & R. West (Eds.), *The family communication sourcebook* (pp. 3–20). Thousand Oaks, CA: Sage Publications.

Galvin, K. M. (2014). Blood, law, and discourse: Constructing and managing family identity. In L. A. Baxter (Ed.), *Remaking "family" communicatively* (pp. 17–32). New York: Peter Lang Publishing.

Grotevant, H. D., & McRoy, R. G. (1998). *Openness in adoption: Exploring family connections*. Thousand Oaks, CA: Sage Publications.

Grotevant, H. D., McRoy, R. G., Wrobel, G. M., & Ayers, L. S. (2013). Contact between adoptive and birth families: Perspectives from the Minnesota/Texas Adoption Research Project. *Child Development Perspectives*, 7, 193–198. doi:10.1111/cdep.12039

Haugaard, J. J., West, N. M., & Moed, A. M. (2000). Open adoptions. *Adoption Quarterly*, *4*, 89–99. doi:10.1300/J145v04n02_05

Hays, A. H., Horstman, H. K., & Colaner, C. W. (2016). "She chose us to be your parents": Exploring the content and process of adoption entrance narratives told in families formed through open adoption. *Journal of Social and Personal Relationships*, *33*, 917–937. doi:10.1177/0265407515611494

Hays, S. (1996). *The cultural contradictions of motherhood*. New Haven, CT: Yale University Press.

Holman Jones, S. (2005). M(o)thering loss: Telling adoption stories, telling performativity. *Text and Performance Quarterly*, *25*, 113–135. doi:10.1080/10462930500122716

Horstman, H. K., Colaner, C. W., & Rittenour, C. E. (2016). Contributing factors of adult adoptees' identity work and self-esteem: Family communication patterns and adoption-specific communication. *Journal of Family Communication*, *16*, 263–276. doi:10.1080/15267431.2016.1181069

Koerner, A. F., & Fitzpatrick, M. A. (2002). Understanding family communication patterns and family functioning: The roles of conversation orientation and conformity orientation. *Communication Yearbook*, *26*, 37–69. doi:10.1080/23808985.2002.11679010

Kools, S., Paul, S. M., Norbeck, J. S., & Robbins, N. R. (2009). Dimensions of health in young people in foster care. *International Journal of Adolescent Medicine and Health*, *21*, 221–233. doi:10.1515/IJAMH.2009.21.2.221

Kranstuber, H. A., & Koenig Kellas, J. (2011). The relationship between adoption entrance narratives and adoptees' self-concept. *Communication Quarterly*, *59*, 179–199. doi:10.1080/01463373.2011.563440

Krusiewicz, E. S., & Wood, J. T. (2001). "He was our child from the moment we walked in that room": Entrance stories of adoptive parents. *Journal of Social and Personal Relationships*, *18*, 785–803. doi:10.1177/0265407501186003

Langellier, K. M., & Peterson, E. E. (2004). *Storytelling in daily life*. Philadelphia, PA: Temple University Press.

Leathers, S. J. (2003). Parental visiting, conflicting allegiances, and emotional and behavioral problems among foster children. *Family Relations*, *53*, 53–63. doi:10.1111/j.1741-3729.2003.00053.x

Linares, L. O., Rhodes, J., & Montalto, D. (2010). Perceptions of coparenting in foster care. *Family Process*, *49*, 530–542. doi:10.1111/j.1545-5300.2010.01338.x

Nelson, L. R. (2017). The evolving nature and process of foster family communication: An application and adaptation of the family adoption communication model. *Journal of Family Theory & Review*, *9*, 366–381. doi:10.1111/jftr.12204

Nelson, L. R., & Horstman, H. K. (2017). Communicated meaning-making in foster families: Relationships between foster parents' entrance narratives and foster child well-being. *Communication Quarterly*, *65*, 144–166. doi:10.1080/01463373.2016.1215337

Norwood, K. M., & Baxter, L. A. (2011). "Dear birth mother": Addressivity and meaning-making in online adoption-seeking letters. *Journal of Family Communication*, *11*, 198–217. doi:10.1080/15267431.2011.554751

Patrick, D. (2006). The story of a gay foster parent. *Child Welfare*, *85*, 123–132. Retrieved from www.californiacasa.org/wp-content/uploads/2015/04/gay_foster_parent.pdf

Paulsen, B. S. (2018). A stranger in the eyes of the court: How the judicial system is failing to protect nonbiological LGBTQ parents. *Illinois Law Review*, *5*, 311–344.

Powell, K. A., & Afifi, T. D. (2005). Uncertainty management and adoptees' ambiguous loss of their birth parents. *Journal of Social and Personal Relationships*, *22*, 129–151. doi:10.1177/0265407505049325

Reuter, M. A., & Koerner, A. F. (2008). The effect of family communication patterns on adopted adolescent adjustment. *Journal of Marriage and Family*, *70*, 715–727. doi:10.1111/j.1741-3737.2008.00516.x

Riessman, C. K. (2008). *Narrative methods for the human sciences*. Thousand Oaks, CA: Sage Publications.

Sachdev, P. (1992). Adoption reunion and after: A study of the search process and the experience of adoptees. *Child Welfare*, *71*, 53–70.

Scharp, K. M. (2013). Making meaning of domestic adoption reunion in online narratives: A dialogic perspective. *Departures in Critical Qualitative Research*, *2*, 301–325. doi:101525/qcr.2013.2.3.301

Scharp, K. M., & Steuber, K. R. (2014). Perceived information ownership and control: Negotiating communication preferences in potential adoption reunions. *Personal Relationships*, *21*, 515–529. doi:10.1111/pere.12046

Skinner-Drawz, B. A., Wrobel, G. M., Grotevant, H. D., & Von Korff, L. (2011). The role of adoption communicative openness in information seeking among adoptees from adolescence to emerging adulthood. *Journal of Family Communication, 11*, 181–197. doi:10.1080/15267431003656587

Suter, E. A. (2008). Discursive negotiations of family identity: A study of families with adopted children from China. *Journal of Family Communication, 8*, 126–147. doi:10.1080/15267430701857406

Suter, E. A., & Ballard, R. L. (2009). "How much did you pay for her?": Decision-making criteria underlying adoptive parents' responses to inappropriate remarks. *Journal of Family Communication, 9*, 107–125. doi:10.1080/15267430902773253

Suter, E. A., Baxter, L. A., Seurer, L., & Thomas, L. J. (2014). Discursive constructions of the meaning of "family" in online narratives of foster adoptive parents. *Communication Monographs, 81*, 59–78. doi:10.1080/03637751.2014.880791

Thomas, L. J. (2014). "Once a foster child": Identity construction in former foster children's narratives. *Qualitative Research Reports in Communication, 15*, 84–91. doi:10.1080/17459435.2014.955596

Thomas, L. J., Jackl, J. A., & Crowley, J. L. (2017). "Family? Not just blood": Discursive constructions of "family" in adult former foster children's narratives. *Journal of Family Communication, 17*, 238–253. doi:10.1080/15267431.2017.1310728

Thomas, L. J., & Scharp, K. M. (2017). "A family for every child": Discursive constructions of "ideal" adoptive families in online foster adoption photolistings that promote adoption of children from foster care. *Adoption Quarterly, 20*, 44–64. doi:10.1080/10926755.2016.1263261

Tieman, W., van der Ende, J., & Verhulst, F. C. (2008). Young adult international adoptees' search for birth parents. *Journal of Family Psychology, 22*, 678–687. doi:10.1037/a0013172

Wrobel, G. M., Kohler, J. K., Grotevant, H. D., & McRoy, R. G. (2003). The family adoption communication (FAC) model. *Adoption Quarterly*, 7(2), 53–84. doi:10.1300/j145v07n02_04

Zill, N. (2011). Better prospects, lower cost: The case for increasing foster care adoption. *Adoption Advocate, 35*, 1–7.

19
OPEN ADOPTION

Harold D. Grotevant

Since the 1970s and 80s, there has been a major shift in how adoption is viewed and practiced. Prior to that time, adoption was seen as a way to build a family by effectively subtracting a child from one family and adding that child to another, with the child losing membership in his or her family of birth and gaining membership in a new adoptive family. Identifying information was not shared among birth and adoptive family members about each other, and contact between them was prevented through policies that sealed adoption records and altered birth certificates.

Over the succeeding decades, conceptualizations and practices have changed dramatically. Now, adoption is viewed as the creation of an adoptive kinship network, in which adopted children connect their families of birth and adoption (Grotevant & McRoy, 1998; Reitz & Watson, 1992). The psychological connections in this network are viewed as real, and personal contact can be facilitated by the sharing of identifying information between adoptive and birth family members. Although official statistics on this topic are not kept, a relatively recent nationally representative sample of US adoptive parents revealed that approximately two-thirds of children adopted through private agency domestic adoptions in the US maintain some form of contact with birth relatives (Vandivere, Malm, & Radel, 2009). Open adoptions are increasing because growing numbers of adoptive parents and professionals in the field feel that it is in the best interests of the child to have contact (Siegel & Smith, 2012). In contrast, closed adoptions are becoming increasingly difficult to maintain, due to the ability to search for relatives through the internet (Whitesel & Howard, 2013) and the ability to find relatives through genetic testing services that are publicly available (Rosenbaum, 2018). For detailed discussions about the history of open adoption, see Carp (1998), Grotevant and McRoy (1998), and Siegel and Smith (2012).

This chapter reviews the growing body of knowledge about open adoption, differentiating among experiences in the three major forms of adoption in the United States: domestic private adoptions, adoptions from the child welfare system, and international adoptions. Both family dynamics and child outcomes will be addressed. Because important national and cultural differences exist in adoption policies and practices, the main focus of the chapter will be experiences within the United States. However, relevant literature from other countries with similar practices, especially in Western Europe, Australia, and New Zealand, will be included where relevant.

For this chapter, open adoption is defined as any kind of contact that occurs between birth and adoptive family members. Open adoptions can vary in terms of type of contact. Direct contact includes the sharing of identifying information and thus can include exchange of letters, photos, gifts, and face-to-face meetings, as well as technology-mediated contact that involves e-mail, texting, Skype, and social media. Indirect contact (sometimes referred to as mediated or letterbox) involves exchange of information through a go-between, typically the adoption agency, which removes identifying information before transmitting the communication. Open adoptions can also involve different people: sometimes contact is just between the child's birth mother and adoptive parent(s); typically (but not always) it includes the child; and sometimes it includes many members of the birth and adoptive family networks. Open adoptions also differ in frequency and intensity of contact. Adding complexity to the picture, openness is dynamic and changes across time as individuals, relationships, and circumstances change (Grotevant, Wrobel, Fiorenzo, Lo, & McRoy, 2019).

Domestic infant adoptions

Family dynamics

The Minnesota Texas Adoption Research Project (MTARP: Grotevant & McRoy, 1998; Grotevant, McRoy, Wrobel, & Ayers-Lopez, 2013) has followed 190 adoptive families and 169 birth mothers over four waves of measurement spanning 30 years. Illustrating the diversity in dynamics of contemporary domestic adoptions, four major trajectories of contact were observed: one group consistently had no contact between birth and adoptive family members from placement into adulthood; a second group had contact that stopped at some point in time; a third group had ongoing contact, but it was limited in the extent and/or frequency of contact; and the fourth had ongoing contact among an extensive number of adoptive and birth family members (Grotevant et al., 2019). The research team is planning to conduct more detailed analyses of factors contributing to these varying patterns as well as differential outcomes for adopted persons as a function of trajectory group membership.

Since the families in MTARP were pioneers in open adoption relationships, most agreements about contact were developed and maintained informally among the adults. In more recent years, agencies have promoted the use of written post-adoption contact agreements (PACAs) in order to make mutual expectations clear (e.g., Allisan, 2019). Legal requirements around PACAs vary from state to state, and in some states, PACAs are legally enforceable (Child Welfare Information Gateway, 2014). Research is needed to examine short- and long-term consequences of PACAs. PACAs are now routinely used in open adoptions in the Australian state of New South Wales, discussed in the section on domestic adoptions from the child welfare system.

Interviews with study participants over time have revealed that openness trajectories emerge as a function of interpersonal processes among the participants, especially emotional distance regulation (Grotevant, 2009). In cases where birth and adoptive family members develop trusting relationships based on empathy as well as commitment to the child's dual connection to both families, contact is likely to increase and flourish. When, for a variety of reasons, that trusting relationship has not developed or has been compromised, it is more likely that contact will decrease and might even stop.

Mutually satisfying relationships depend on the participants' communication skills, ability to maintain boundaries, flexibility in day-to-day interaction, and commitment to the relationships (Grotevant, 2009). Because of the highly personalized nature of maintaining such relationships, most existing studies have shown that the degree of contact can fluctuate somewhat over time. Nevertheless, it is important to note that the skills used in maintaining open relationships can be learned, and that contact can be supported through informal, psychoeducational, and therapeutic means (Grotevant et al., 2013).

As adopted children grow up they typically take on more responsibility for determining the pattern of birth family contact (Dunbar et al., 2006); however, their relationships with their adoptive parents continue to be important. During emerging adulthood (late teens through 20s), adoptees in the MTARP study were more satisfied with their openness arrangements when their communication with their adoptive parents was also open and sensitive (Farr, Grant-Marsney, & Grotevant, 2014).

Contact after adoption has also played an important role in adoptions to lesbian and gay couples. In Farr's (2017) longitudinal study with young children adopted through private agencies, having contact has been the norm rather than the exception (Farr, Ravvina, & Grotevant, 2018). The status of contact did not differ by family type (lesbian, gay, heterosexual) when the children were in middle childhood, and most parents were satisfied with the contact they were having (Farr et al., 2018).

Longitudinal research is beginning to reveal dynamics of intergenerational relationships followed over time. Battalen, Sellers, McRoy, and Grotevant (2019) reported that, when birth mothers have contact with the children they placed for adoption who are now adults, and their birth grandchildren, they report the interactions as positive and adding joy to their lives, even if the contact is limited by distance and time. However, the lack of clear societal expectations for this new role (birth grandmother) means that family members need to develop ways of making their relationships work. Nevertheless, there seem to be considerable potential benefits to continued contact for the adopted adults, their children, and birth grandparents.

Outcomes for adoptive kinship network members

A major question for guiding practice and policy is how contact affects those participating in it. In the early days of open adoptions, concerns were expressed that it would be confusing for children, which could lead to identity problems and adjustment difficulties; it would harm adoptive parents' sense of entitlement to serve as the child's full parents; and it would exacerbate grief felt by birth parents (e.g., Kraft et al., 1985). None of these fears have been borne out in the research literature; however, the effects of contact have not been straightforward to describe, because "contact" can be experienced and evaluated in different ways by its participants.

Contact with the child's birth parent(s) certainly provides a source for communication of potentially important information about family health history, which is otherwise unknown in closed adoptions (see May, Lee, & Evans, 2018 for examples and discussion). It also provides children with a reality-based understanding of who their birth parents are (e.g., Siegel, 2012) and an avenue for obtaining answers to the many questions they might have as they are growing up. Wrobel and Dillon (2009) found that adolescents most wanted to gain an adult understanding of why they were placed for adoption. In contrast, emerging adults, who were beginning to enter into committed relationships and think about starting their own families, most wanted to understand their genetic and family health histories (Wrobel & Grotevant, 2019).

Birth relative contact per se was not directly associated with variations in adjustment outcomes for adolescent or young adult adoptees (e.g., Ge et al., 2008; Von Korff, Grotevant, & McRoy, 2006). However, family members' satisfaction with their openness arrangements was associated with adjustment. Those who were more satisfied with their contact arrangements showed better adjustment outcomes (Grotevant, Rueter, Von Korff, & Gonzalez, 2011). The effect of contact on adoptive identity development in adolescence and emerging adulthood was mediated by the presence of adoption-related conversation within the adoptive family. Families experiencing contact talked about birth relatives' roles in the family and their involvement in daily life, stimulating thinking about the meaning of adoption and the construction of adoptive identity. In closed adoptions, little or no new information was available for discussion, and the construction of adoptive identity seemed less dynamic (Von Korff & Grotevant, 2011).

Adoptive parents also make meaning of their relationships in the adoptive kinship network, and those attitudes and values shape and are shaped by their contact. For example, at Wave 1 in MTARP (when the children were 8 years of age, on average), adoptive parents' fear that the birth mother might try to reclaim her child varied significantly as a function of contact. The highest rating of fear (coded from both adoptive mothers' and fathers' interviews) was found among those who had no contact and no identifying information about their child's birth parents; the fear was based on stereotypes about birth parents in general, which were often fueled by negative media portrayals of birth parents who wanted their children back. The least fear was found among adoptive parents who had ongoing direct contact with their child's birth mother; in many cases, the birth and adoptive parents had spoken directly about this issue, and birth parents assured them that they would not attempt to reclaim their child (Grotevant, McRoy, Elde, & Fravel, 1994). When their children were adolescents, adoptive parents with contact were also more satisfied with their contact arrangements than were those with no contact (Grotevant et al., 2011).

Findings from MTARP also contradicted assumptions that birth mothers with contact would experience high levels of unresolved grief, preventing them from moving on with their lives. Interviews with birth mothers, both when their placed children were in middle childhood and in adolescence, revealed that those in fully disclosed adoptions had the lowest levels of unresolved grief, whereas those in confidential adoptions or those in which contact had stopped had the highest levels (Christian, McRoy, Grotevant, & Bryant, 1997; Henney, Ayers-Lopez, Mack, McRoy, & Grotevant, 2007). MTARP findings also contradicted the assumption that birth mothers would not welcome contact from the children they placed for adoption. Among birth mothers who thought their adolescent child would search for them if they lost contact, 80 percent of them felt positively about being contacted, 5 percent felt neutral, 15 percent felt ambivalent, and none of them felt negatively about a search the child might initiate (Ayers-Lopez, Henney, McRoy, Hanna, & Grotevant, 2008).

Domestic adoptions from the child welfare system

When children are removed from their homes and placed in foster care, one of the key goals of the child welfare system is family reunification; thus, contact with birth family is an important aspect of the foster care experience. In these cases, when contact with birth parents can be arranged that assures the safety of the child, it can be beneficial in terms of psychological adjustment (McWey & Cui, 2017). However, when efforts at reunification are ended and parental rights are terminated, the child can be placed for adoption.

Even following of termination of parental rights and subsequent adoption, contact in the case of adoptions from the public child welfare system is becoming more common (Neil, Beek, & Ward, 2015). In contrast to the case of private domestic adoptions where placements typically occurred in infancy, the average age of children adopted with public agency involvement in the US is 6.3 years (USDHHS, 2018). Most children are adopted by a foster parent (51 percent) or relative (35 percent); only 14 percent by a non-relative. During the years prior to adoption, the child might have experienced maltreatment by parents (neglect and parental drug abuse are the most common reasons for child removal; USDHHS, 2018) and may have experienced one or more placements in foster homes. Thus, determinations about whether contact is in the child's best interest must take into consideration the child's safety in order to prevent retraumatization; it must also consider birth parents' capacity to participate in helpful ways.

Until fairly recently, it was thought that the child's best interests would not be served by maintaining contact with birth relatives. However, despite termination of birth parents' rights, many children desire contact with family members, including parents, grandparents, siblings, and extended family. A key question for future research is how the child's safety and well-being can be assured while permitting continued contact.

In the United Kingdom, domestic infant adoptions and international adoptions are rare; most adoptions are through the public care system. Most children are adopted from care under the age of five. When contact occurs, it might occur through the exchange of letters ("letterbox contact" through the agency), through meetings with biological siblings from whom they have been separated, or (for less than 20 percent) through meetings with biological parents or grandparents (Neil, 2019).

Neil's longitudinal research has concluded that "staying in touch with birth relatives can be positive for adopted children when arrangements carry minimal conflict and where the child's place in their adoptive and birth family are both respected" (Neil, 2019, p. 1). Three considerations are particularly important for child welfare professionals working with these families: making individualized decisions rather than "one size fits all" policies, considering the quality of the contact, and offering support when needed (Neil, 2019).

Although face-to-face contact is less common in the UK than is letterbox contact through the agency, direct contact appears to be more lasting and satisfying (Neil et al., 2015). Some study participants felt that letters did not convey a real sense of the individual, making it more difficult to feel a sense of real connection. A significant advantage of having direct contact is that children have a better understanding of their families of origin and reasons for placement; this helps them feel more at ease with their adoption story as a result (Neil et al., 2015). However, "how the adults think about and manage contact is vital to the child's experience" (Neil, 2019, p. 3). Contact seemed to work better when the adoptive mother displayed high levels of communicative openness and when the child's birth relatives accepted the finality of the placement. Relationships were more difficult when the birth relatives were unable to come to terms with the permanence of the placement (Neil, 2009).

In the Australian state of New South Wales (NSW), children in foster care can only be adopted by their foster parents, and arrangements permitting face-to-face contact are required by law (del Pozo de Bolger, Dunstan, & Kaltner, 2018). A legally enforceable post-adoption contact plan is agreed upon by the parties in advance of the adoption and must be approved by the court. The most frequent types of contact are with biological siblings, grandparents, and mothers (del Pozo de Bolger, Dunstan, & Kaltner, 2017). A three-fold benefit for adopted children was envisioned in promoting contact: reassurance (for the child, the birth parents, and the adoptive parents), identity, and continuity (Wright, 2018).

Early reports from research in progress in NSW suggests that open arrangements can be positive if it is safe for the child. However, beyond safety, a positive experience requires that all participating adults are able to acknowledge the child's connections to two families, maintain appropriate boundaries, communicate effectively, and demonstrate mutual respect (del Pozo de Bolger et al., 2018). These conclusions are consistent with results of other studies of open adoption, including Grotevant et al. (2013), Neil (2009), and Siegel (2012).

Evidence is also beginning to accrue about outcomes of open adoptions from care in NSW for adolescents and young adults who were adopted before the age of five. A qualitative study reporting on identity development in nine adoptees (age 9–23) revealed that the continuity created through foster parents adopting contributed to adoptees' sense of belonging with their adoptive family (Luu, de Rosnay, Wright, & Tregeagle, 2018). The young people reported that contact with birth relatives allowed them to understand their birth parents and their histories; they uniformly spoke about the importance of being in contact with their biological siblings. As was noted earlier in the MTARP study, frequency and type of contact changed over time.

Interviews with the adoptees also underscored the important role that adoptive parents play in supporting their quest for knowledge about and contact with birth relatives. Interviews also suggested that communicative openness (openness to discussion about adoption within the adoptive family) could even be more important than contact, but further research is needed about whether communicative openness and direct contact play distinctive or coordinated roles. Consistent with results from MTARP, communicative openness within the adoptive family (Brodzinsky, 2006) was viewed as supporting adoptive identity development (Luu et al., 2018; see also Von Korff & Grotevant, 2011).

A recent review of 11 studies of children adopted from care in the UK concluded that where contact occurred, child outcomes depended on certain moderating variables. Outcomes of contact were positive when there was a collaborative relationship between the birth and adoptive parents, and were poorest when children had contact with birth parents who had maltreated them (Boyle, 2017). It is clear that contact has the potential to be positive for children. However, further research is needed to clarify the conditions under which contact can be beneficial and the support that might be needed for families who have contact.

International adoptions

Because contact in international adoptions is still quite rare, much less empirical evidence is available to evaluate its impact. We do know, however, that contact between adoptive and birth family members in international adoptions is more difficult than in domestic adoptions, but increasing (e.g., Baden, 2013).

For some children, accurate identification of their birth parents is difficult or impossible to obtain. Despite the safeguards put in place through legislation implementing the Hague Convention on Intercountry Adoption, birth records might be missing entirely (e.g., in the case of abandoned children) or might have been falsified at some stage in the process to obscure evidence of child laundering (Smolin, 2010).

Cultural differences in people's basic understanding of the meaning of adoption can also work against contact. Roby's work in the Marshall Islands (Roby & Matsumura, 2002) revealed that birth mothers, despite what they might have read or been told, assumed that their children would return to them and their community once they were adults. In this communal culture, the western idea of termination of parental rights is difficult to comprehend, since they consider a child always to be a part of his or her family, even if all the family members do not live together. Likewise, detailed accounts of interactions between Finnish adoptive mothers and South African birth mothers portrayed the complex dynamics within the child's adoptive kinship network, exacerbated by cultural differences in understanding of adoption (Högbacka, 2016). Thus, incompatible views of the permanence of adoption can make establishment of post-adoption contact quite problematic.

In addition, in some cultures, pregnancy outside of marriage or the placement of a child for adoption might bring stigma to the birth mother and shame to her family (e.g., Rotabi & Gibbons, 2012). Thus, placements are often hidden, even from close family members (e.g., Docan-Morgan, 2016). Contact with her birth child would unmask her secret, possibly exposing her to social stigma or even danger.

Even if birth parents are willing to have contact, some adoptive parents might have opted for international rather than domestic adoption so that they would not need to deal with the possibility of contact (Baden, 2013). Their decisions might have been rooted in views predominating in the 1960s and 1970s, holding that contact would be harmful for adopted children, adoptive parents, and birth parents alike (Kraft et al., 1985).

Finally, contact in international adoption involves logistical challenges, including possible language barriers between birth and adoptive family members, long distances, and travel difficulties. Large economic disparities between birth and adoptive parents can also complicate social interaction (Högbacka, 2016).

New Zealand provides a useful context for studying open international adoptions, because, in general, the country is quite accepting of the concept of contact in domestic adoptions. Scherman and Hawke (2010) studied 73 New Zealand families who had adopted internationally, mostly from Russia and Romania. Approximately one-half of the families had attempted contact, and half of those had succeeded. Positive outcomes for the child included having more and accurate information about birth family members and establishing personal relationships that can continue into the future. Difficult aspects were distance, pain of separation, additional unanswered questions, and seeing birth relatives living in poverty. Despite the complexities of contact, a number of adoptive parents viewed making early contact as important, so that birth family information does not "dry up" or become impossible to obtain.

Although ongoing contact from an early age is still rare, the recent Modern Adoptive Families project (MAF: Brodzinsky & Goldberg, 2017) examined contact in international adoptions for children adopted by heterosexual (N=479) and female sexual minority (N=38) parents in the United States. Although the children's birth countries were quite varied, contact was more likely to occur when the child came from Africa (especially Ethiopia) than from other regions. Sexual minority parents were more likely to have had contact than heterosexual parents, but most contact was indirect and occurred once a year or less. Most parents reported a neutral to positive relationship with birth family members. Among families with no contact, most were unsure about whether they would seek it in the future, with about one-third indicating that they would and less than 25 percent indicating that they would not. The results from MAF were consistent with those of Goldberg, Kinkler, Richardson, and Downing (2011), who noted that lesbian and gay parents in general had positive attitudes toward open adoption, consistent with their beliefs about openness concerning their sexual orientation (Brodzinsky & Goldberg, 2017).

In addition to increasing rates of contact during the childhood years, there are increasing numbers of international reunions with birth families that occur after the adopted person reaches adulthood. In one interview study of Korean adoptees post-reunion, participants noted a number of cultural differences: family roles and expectations, standards for beauty and femininity, expectations for social interactions, and past and present circumstances, including secrecy about the adoption (Docan-Morgan, 2016). The 19 participants had strikingly varied reactions to these differences, with some feeling a deep sense of belonging in birth family and culture and others feeling estranged. Further research is needed to identify circumstances that would best facilitate positive contact, both during the adopted person's early years and as an adult experiencing reunion.

The number of children being adopted internationally worldwide has been decreasing for over a decade. It is possible that international adoption rates will continue to fall, or that the practice might cease (Baden, 2019). Nevertheless, Selman (2009) has noted that between the end of World War II and 2010, approximately one million children had been adopted across national boundaries worldwide. Many of the impediments to contact that had been cited in the past are being circumvented by widespread use of the internet and genetic testing services (Rosenbaum, 2018; Whitesel & Howard, 2013). Thus, research on contact in intercountry adoptions will continue to be important as these children come of age.

Conclusions

Taken together, what can we conclude from the small, but rapidly growing body of evidence about open adoption? The following conclusions apply equally to domestic infant, child welfare, and international adoptions; however, each type of adoption carries its own unique set of issues which must also be taken into account, as reviewed in the previous sections.

1 Open adoption is not inherently harmful to adopted children, adoptive parents, or birth parents.
2 Open adoption can provide a very positive set of relationships and experiences for adopted children, adoptive parents, and birth parents.
3 Open adoption implies a fundamental expansion in one's concept of family, from a smaller, traditional nuclear family to a broader adoptive kinship network.
4 Open adoption requires understanding that individuals and relationships change over time, and that families change as members are added and depart. Thus, open adoptions are dynamic and complex, and change over time should be expected.
5 In order for open adoption to work, several things must occur:

   a The safety and well-being of the adopted child must be paramount. If these criteria are not given precedence, direct contact can be counter-productive.
   b As children grow, their wishes and thoughts about contact might change and should be taken into account by adults.
   c The relevant adults – the birth parents and the adoptive parents – must be committed to entering into this family situation and making it work over time by communicating openly and keeping agreements.
   d Their commitment means honest engagement, undergirded by empathy for one another, effective communication, and flexibility in day-to-day interaction.
   e Family members should be resourceful and open to seeking help when needed, with the realization that, at the present time, open adoption is neither universally understood nor accepted.

Recommendations for practice and policy

Several recommendations for practice and policy follow from the set of conclusions listed above.

1. Adoption intermediaries who are arranging placements or counseling birth or adoptive family members before or after placement must develop competence in understanding the dynamic nature of open adoptions. This should be a key component of any training for adoption competence for social workers or mental health professionals.
2. Adoption professionals should have deep understanding of typical and abnormal child and adolescent development, and in particular, children's growing understanding of adoption and complex families.
3. Agencies must find ways to provide support and services to birth and adoptive families in an ongoing way, realizing that counsel might be needed at unanticipated times. Cost of services should not be a barrier to access.
4. Agencies must ensure that full and complete information about medical and health histories are collected from birth parents and shared with the adoptive family.
5. One size does not fit all. Each adoptive kinship network is unique in some ways, and the uniqueness of the family composition and dynamics must be taken into account in guiding practice and policy.

Recommendations for future research

The following recommendations for future research follow from the literature reviewed above:

1. Additional longitudinal, culturally sensitive research is needed on open adoptions for a variety of situations: domestic infant placements, child welfare adoptions, international adoptions, adoptions by sexual minority parents, and adoptions by single persons. Inclusion of large-scale quantitative, in-depth qualitative, and mixed-methods approaches will contribute to a more thorough understanding of open adoptions.
2. Research is essential to identifying best practices for use of PACAs. That research should become the foundation upon which practice and policy recommendations about PACAs are made.
3. Research should address sibling relationships more comprehensively, with acceptance of the reality that adopted siblings growing up together will likely have different types of contact with birth relatives and that the presence of parents' biological child(ren) could complicate family dynamics.
4. Researchers who are adopted persons or birth parents should be encouraged to contribute to this growing literature, and the growing number of memoirs and videos produced by adopted persons and birth parents should inform the research literature.
5. Further research is needed into the role of social media and new technologies in open adoptions.
6. In regard to international adoptions, the United States is both a country of destination and a country of origin ("outgoing" international adoption). Many outgoing international adoptions involve contact between birth and adoptive family members, but research on these adoptive kinship networks is needed.

7 Researchers interested in openness in adoption should inform their work by studying other family forms across cultures in which children grow up with multiple adults who take on different biological and social roles in their lives, including customary and indigenous models of adoption, child circulation, guardianship, long-term foster care, and contact in the case of families created through assisted reproductive technologies.

References

Allisan, M. R. (2019). Foundation for love: General principles for post-adoption communication agreements. *Rudd Adoption Research Program Publication Series: The Future of Adoption*. University of Massachusetts Amherst.

Ayers-Lopez, S., Henney, S., McRoy, R. G., Hanna, M., & Grotevant, H. D. (2008). Openness in adoption and the impact on birthmother plans for search and reunion. *Families in Society*, *89*(4), 551–561. doi:10.1606/1044-3894.3815

Baden, A. (2013, April). *Contact in international adoptions*. Presentation at the New Worlds of Adoption Conference: Rudd Adoption Research Program. Amherst, MA: University of Massachusetts Amherst. Retrieved from www.umass.edu/ruddchair/adoption-conference/past-conferences/conference-2013/videos

Baden, A. (2019). Intercountry adoption: The beginning of the end. *Rudd Adoption Research Program Publication Series: The Future of Adoption*. University of Massachusetts Amherst.

Battalen, A., Sellers, C. M., McRoy, R. G., & Grotevant, H. D. (2019). Birth mothers now birth grandmothers: Intergenerational relationships in open adoptions. *Adoption Quarterly*. Advance online publication.

Boyle, C. (2017). "What is the impact of birth family contact on children in adoption and long-term foster care?" A systematic review. *Child and Family Social Work*, *22*, 22–33.

Brodzinsky, D. M. (2006). Family structural openness and communication openness as predictors in the adjustment of adopted children. *Adoption Quarterly*, *9*, 1–18. doi:10.1300/j145v09n04_01

Brodzinsky, D. M., & Goldberg, A. E. (2017). Contact with birth family in intercountry adoptions: Comparing families headed by sexual minority and heterosexual parents. *Child and Youth Services Review*, *74*, 117–124. doi:10.1016/j.childyouth.2016.01.014

Carp, E. W. (1998). *Family matters: Secrecy and disclosure in the history of adoptions*. Cambridge: Harvard University Press.

Child Welfare Information Gateway. (2014). *Postadoption contact agreements between birth and adoptive families*. Washington, DC: US Department of Health and Human Services, Children's Bureau. Retrieved from www.childwelfare.gov/pubPDFs/cooperative.pdf

Christian, C. L., McRoy, R. G., Grotevant, H. D., & Bryant, C. (1997). Grief resolution of birthmothers in confidential, time-limited mediated, ongoing mediated, and fully disclosed adoptions. *Adoption Quarterly*, *1*(2), 35–58. doi:10.1300/J145v01n02_03

del Pozo de Bolger, A., Dunstan, D., & Kaltner, M. (2018). Open adoptions of children from foster care in New South Wales Australia: Adoption process and post-adoption contact. *Adoption Quarterly*, *21*(2), 82–101. doi:10.1080/10926755.2018.1448915

del Pozo de Bolger, A., Dunstan, D. A., & Kaltner, M. (2017). Descriptive analysis of foster care adoptions in New South Wales, Australia. *Australian Social Work*, *70*, 477–490. doi:10.1080/0312407X.2017.1335759

Docan-Morgan, S. (2016). Cultural differences and perceived belonging during Korean adoptees' reunions with birth families. *Adoption Quarterly*, *19*(2), 99–118. doi:10.1080/10926755.2015.1088109

Dunbar, N., van Dulmen, M. H. M., Ayers-Lopez, S., Berge, J. M., Christian, C., Gossman, G., … McRoy, R. G. (2006). Processes linked to contact changes in adoptive kinship networks. *Family Process*, *45*, 449–464. doi:10.1111/j.1545-5300.2006.00182.x

Farr, R. H. (2017). Does parental sexual orientation matter? A longitudinal follow-up of adoptive families with school-age children. *Developmental Psychology*, *53*, 252–264. doi:10.1037/dev0000228

Farr, R. H., Grant-Marsney, H. A., & Grotevant, H. D. (2014). Adoptees' contact with birthparents in emerging adulthood: The role of adoption communication and attachment to adoptive parents. *Family Process*, *53*, 656–671. doi:10.1111/famp.12069

Farr, R. H., Ravvina, Y., & Grotevant, H. D. (2018). Birth family contact experiences among lesbian, gay, and heterosexual adoptive parents with school-age children. *Family Relations, 67*, 132–146. doi:10.1111/fare.12295

Ge, X., Natsuaki, M. N., Martin, D. M., Leve, L. D., Neiderhiser, J. M., Shaw, D. S., … Reiss, D. (2008). Bridging the divide: Openness in adoption and postadoption psychosocial adjustment among birth and adoptive parents. *Journal of Family Psychology, 22*(3), 529–540. doi:10.1037/a0012817

Goldberg, A. E., Kinkler, L. A., Richardson, H. B., & Downing, J. B. (2011). Perceptions and experiences of open adoption among lesbian, gay, and heterosexual couples: A qualitative study. *Journal of Marriage and Family, 73*, 502–518. doi:10.1016/j.ecresq.2014.07.008

Grotevant, H. D. (2009). Emotional distance regulation over the life course in adoptive kinship networks. In G. Wrobel & E. Neil (Eds.), *International advances in adoption research for practice* (pp. 295–316). Chichester, UK: Wiley.

Grotevant, H. D., & McRoy, R. G. (1998). *Openness in adoption: Exploring family connections*. Thousand Oaks, CA: Sage.

Grotevant, H. D., McRoy, R. G., Elde, C., & Fravel, D. L. (1994). Adoptive family system dynamics: Variations by level of openness in the adoption. *Family Process, 33*, 125–146. doi:10.1111/j.1545-5300.1994.00125.x

Grotevant, H. D., McRoy, R. G., Wrobel, G. M., & Ayers-Lopez, S. (2013). Contact between adoptive and birth families: Perspectives from the Minnesota/Texas adoption research project. *Child Development Perspectives*, 7, 193–198. doi:10.1111/cdep.12039

Grotevant, H. D., Rueter, M., Von Korff, L., & Gonzalez, C. (2011). Post-adoption contact, adoption communicative openness, and satisfaction with contact as predictors of externalizing behavior in adolescence and emerging adulthood. *Journal of Child Psychology and Psychiatry, 52*, 529–536. doi:10.1111/j.1469-7610.2010.02330.x

Grotevant, H. D., Wrobel, G. M., Fiorenzo, L., Lo, A. Y. H., & McRoy, R. G. (2019). Trajectories of birth family contact in domestic adoptions. *Journal of Family Psychology, 33*, 54–63. doi:10.1037/fam0000449

Henney, S. M., Ayers-Lopez, S., Mack, J. M., McRoy, R. G., & Grotevant, H. D. (2007). Birth mothers' perceptions of their parented children's knowledge of and involvement in adoption. *Adoption Quarterly, 10*(3–4), 103–129. doi:10.1080/10926750802163212

Högbacka, R. (2016). *Global families, inequality and transnational adoption: The de-kinning of first mothers*. London: Palgrave Macmillan.

Kraft, A. D., Palombo, J., Mitchell, D. L., Woods, P. K., Schmidt, A. W., & Tucker, N. G. (1985). Some theoretical considerations on confidential adoptions. Part III: The adopted child. *Child and Adolescent Social Work Journal, 2*, 139–153. doi:10.1007/BF00758065

Luu, B., de Rosnay, M., Wright, A. C., & Tregeagle, S. (2018). Identity formation in children and young people in open adoptions from out-of-home care in New South Wales, Australia. *Adoption Quarterly, 21*(2), 120–139. doi:10.1080/10926755.2018.1468371

May, T., Lee, R., & Evans, J. (Eds.). (2018). Healthcare challenges faced by adopted persons lacking family health history information. *Narrative Inquiry in Bioethics, 8*, 2. doi:10.1353/nib.2018.0036

McWey, L. M., & Cui, M. (2017). Parent-child contact for youth in foster care: Research to inform practice. *Family Relations, 66*, 684–695. doi:10.1111/fare.12276

Neil, E. (2009). The corresponding experiences of adoptive parents and birth relatives in open adoptions. In G. M. Wrobel & E. Neil (Eds.), *International advances in adoption research for practice* (pp. 269–293). Chichester: Wiley-Blackwell.

Neil, E. (2019). Planning and supporting birth family contact when children are adopted from care. *Rudd Adoption Research Program Publication Series: The Future of Adoption*. University of Massachusetts Amherst.

Neil, E., Beek, M., & Ward, E. (2015). *Contact after adoption: A longitudinal study of post adoption contact arrangements*. London: CoramBAAF.

Reitz, M., & Watson, K. W. (1992). *Adoption and the family system: Strategies for treatment*. New York: Guilford Press.

Roby, J. L., & Matsumura, S. (2002). If I give you my child, aren't we family? A study of birthmothers participating in Marshall Islands-US adoptions. *Adoption Quarterly, 5*(4), 7–31. doi:10.1300/J145v05n04_02

Rosenbaum, S. I. (2018, August 4). The twilight of closed adoptions. *Boston Globe*. Retrieved from www.bostonglobe.com/ideas/2018/08/04/the-twilight-closed-adoptions/1Iu4c5da4W5qNbIPn5IEmL/story.html?event=event12

Rotabi, K. S., & Gibbons, J. L. (2012). Does the Hague convention on intercountry adoption adequately protect orphaned and vulnerable children and their families? *Journal of Child and Family Studies, 21*, 106–119. doi:10.1007/s10826-011-9508-6

Scherman, R., & Hawke, W. (2010, July). *Openness and intercountry adoption*. Paper presented at the Third International Conference on Adoption Research (ICAR3), Leiden, The Netherlands.

Selman, P. (2009). From Bucharest to Beijing: Changes in countries sending children for international adoption 1990 to 2006. In G. M. Wrobel & E. Neil (Eds.), *International advances in adoption research for practice* (pp. 41–70). Chichester: Wiley-Blackwell.

Siegel, D. (2012). Growing up in open adoption: Young adults' perspectives. *Families in Society, 93*, 133–140. doi:10.1606/1044-3894.4198

Siegel, D. H., & Smith, S. L. (2012). *Openness in adoption: From secrecy and stigma to knowledge and connections*. New York: Evan B. Donaldson Adoption Institute. Retrieved from http://adoptioninstitute.org/publications/2012_03_OpennessInAdoption.pdf

Smolin, D. M. (2010). Child laundering and the Hague convention on intercountry adoption: The future and past of intercountry adoption. *University of Louisville Law Review, 48*, 441–498. Retrieved January 25, 2019, from https://works.bepress.com/david_smolin/8/

US Department of Health and Human Services. (2018). Adoption and foster care analysis and reporting system (AFCARS) reports. Retrieved from www.acf.hhs.gov/sites/default/files/cb/afcarsreport25.pdf

Vandivere, S., Malm, K., & Radel, L. (2009). *Adoption USA: A chartbook based on the 2007 National Survey of Adoptive Parents*. Washington, DC: US Department of Health and Human Services, Office of the Assistant Secretary for Planning and Evaluation. Retrieved from https://aspe.hhs.gov/system/files/pdf/75911/index.pdf

Von Korff, L., & Grotevant, H. D. (2011). Contact in adoption and adoptive identity formation: The mediating role of family conversation. *Journal of Family Psychology, 25*, 393–401. doi:10.1037/a0023388

Von Korff, L., Grotevant, H. D., & McRoy, R. G. (2006). Openness arrangements and psychological adjustment in adolescent adoptees. *Journal of Family Psychology, 20*, 531–534. doi:10.1037/0893-3200.20.3.531

Whitesel, A., & Howard, J. A. (2013). *Untangling the web II: A research-based roadmap for reform*. New York: Donaldson Adoption Institute. Retrieved from www.adoptioninstitute.org/wp-content/uploads/2013/12/2013_12_UntanglingtheWeb2.pdf

Wright, A. C. (2018, March). *Permanency reforms in NSW child protection*. Presentation to SCWK4003 – Violence Against Women and Children, Sydney, Australia.

Wrobel, G. M., & Dillon, K. (2009). Adopted adolescents: Who and what are they curious about? In G. Wrobel & E. Neil (Eds.), *International advances in adoption research for practice* (pp. 217–244). Chichester, UK: Wiley.

Wrobel, G. M., & Grotevant, H. D. (2019). Adoption-related curiosity at emerging adulthood. *Adoption Quarterly*. Advance online publication.

20

HOW ADOPTIVE PARENTS THINK ABOUT THEIR ROLE AS PARENTS

Albert Y.H. Lo and Krystal K. Cashen

Literature on adoptive parenting has focused heavily on how parents can promote successful adoptee and family outcomes. Through this work, it has been found that specific parenting processes are generally more predictive of positive development than are group differences in aspects such as level of birth family contact or demographic characteristics of the parents (Grotevant & Lo, 2017). Traditionally, research examining adoptive parenting processes has largely revolved around observing parenting behavior, such as adoption-related communication within the family (e.g. Brodzinsky, 2006; Wrobel, Kohler, Grotevant, & McRoy, 2003). Less common are investigations of processes not as readily visible, specifically the thoughts, feelings, and other cognitive beliefs that adoptive parents might hold about themselves, their child, and ultimately, their role as parents. The cognitive processes of parents have already repeatedly been shown to have important developmental implications for all parents (e.g. Bornstein, Putnick, & Suwalsky, 2018; Meins, 2013). The current chapter addresses the questions: (1) What cognitive processes are specifically relevant to adoptive parents as they think about their role as parents? and (2) How might these processes relate to adoptee development and family functioning? We then present implications of the extant literature on these topics for agency and clinical practices. To begin, we focus on an early theory of adoptive parenting that has informed decades of adoption research and practice.

Parent role and Shared Fate Theory

Kirk's (1984) Shared Fate Theory has been influential in shaping how we conceptualize how adoptive parents make sense of their roles as parents. Kirk argues that the dominant cultural scripts around how to parent and what it means to be a parent are centered around the assumption that parents are raising biological children. For example, when a child is born to biological parents, the parents can bring the baby home and be reasonably certain that the baby will be a part of their family forever. For adoptive parents, there is a period of uncertainty between the time when the child is placed in their home and the adoption is legally finalized, during which the child could be removed from their family for a number of reasons. Because cultural parenting scripts do not necessarily map on to the experiences of adoptive parents, Kirk argues that adoptive parents experience a role handicap. In other words, adoptive parents' inability to rely on cultural scripts presents a barrier to competent performance as parents. Kirk argues that adoptive parents can respond to this role handicap in one of two ways: they can reject the fact that their experiences are different from those of biological families and follow the scripts as much as possible, or they can acknowledge the differences between their family and biological families.

According to Kirk (1984), whether parents choose to acknowledge or reject these differences can have lasting implications for the parent–child relationship. Rejecting differences might provide parents with a means of coping, for example, with feelings of loss and pain experienced before the adoption due to infertility or difficulties during the adoption process. By taking the view that their family is just like a biological family, adoptive parents might attempt to put the experience of the adoption process behind them and focus on being a parent. Acknowledging differences, in contrast, positions adoptive parents to experience greater empathy for the experiences of their adopted child. Acknowledging that their family is different from biological families allows adoptive parents to recognize that their child will have unique experiences stemming from the adoption. This empathy translates into more open communication about the adoption within the family. Open communication about adoption, in turn, facilitates the development of trusting relationships between the adoptive parents and adopted child. A longitudinal examination of these constructs has found some support for Kirk's theory, with acknowledgment of differences positively predicting later empathy and openness in communication (Cashen, Lo, & Grotevant, 2018).

When thinking about Kirk's social role theory, it is important to acknowledge the social context in which it was developed. At the time when the first edition of Kirk's (1964) book *Shared Fate* was released, the prevailing social context around adoption was characterized by secrecy. The majority of formal adoptions were confidential adoptions of infants born to unwed mothers by married, heterosexual, White parents. When placing children with families, adoption professionals emphasized matching children with families on physical characteristics so that the family would be able to pass as biological families (Kirk, 1984). Social stigma around being born out of wedlock was a major reason for these practices. In the last few decades, however, this social context around adoption has shifted. Open adoption arrangements have become more common, and norms around premarital sex have shifted (McRoy, Grotevant, & White, 1988).

Shared Fate Theory as adoptive parenting cognitions

Although not framed as such in its original conceptualization, adoptive parents' acknowledgment of differences is a cognitive process. Specifically, adoptive parents think about their own roles as parents to their adopted children and decide the degree to which these roles must differ from those of nonadoptive parents. Through this cognition, adoptive parents decide the degree to which they acknowledge the adopted status of the child and the unique experiences that the child might have due to being adopted. Such thinking and decision making might not necessarily be deliberate or done independently. For example, some adoptive parents might model their decisions after others they have seen, or their decisions might be driven by agency recommendations or their own assumptions about adoption.

Many of the unique experiences of adopted children are internal and not readily apparent to others, including rumination about birth family origins or navigating feelings of difference from adoptive family members and peers (Farr, Crain, Oakley, Cashen, & Garber,

2016; Grotevant, Lo, Fiorenzo, & Dunbar, 2017). Thus, adoptive parents might be unaware of these experiences unless they willingly take their child's perspective as an adopted child in a bionormative society. This approach is contingent on adoptive parents thinking of the adoption as integral to their role as parents and potentially influential to their child's experiences. Without first engaging in these thought processes, such perspective and role-taking are not possible, and the child's adoption-related experiences and struggles might be ignored (Kirk, 1984).

When Kirk's (1964) Shared Fate Theory was first conceptualized, there existed limited theoretical framework on parents' ability for perspective-taking and understanding a child's mental states, both within and outside the context of adoption. More recently, however, there has been emphasis on these social cognitive and mentalization aspects of parenting for all parents, with examinations of how they manifest and how they relate to the child's developmental and relational outcomes. Constructs that emerged from this emphasis include mind-mindedness (Meins, 1997), parental insightfulness (Oppenheim & Koren-Karie, 2002), and parental reflective functioning (Fonagy, Steele, Steele, Moran, & Higgitt, 1991). Though these constructs differ in name, they are similar in their focus on parents being attuned to the mental process of the child, seeing things from the perspective of the child, and understanding how a child's mental state might be motivating their behaviors.

Overall, cognitive processes outlined in Shared Fate Theory overlap with these more contemporary constructs in terms of general perspective-taking. They differ in that acknowledgment of differences is specific to the adoption context, and adoptive parents might need to acknowledge differences before accurate perspective-taking can occur. Nevertheless, specific parallels can be drawn in their shared attention to accurately interpreting the motivations underlying the child's behavior. A core tenet of parental insightfulness is parents' "insight into the child's motives" (Oppenheim & Koren-Karie, 2002, p. 593), whereas mind-mindedness places importance on parents being attuned to the child's internal state (Meins, 2013). Similarly, Shared Fate Theory describes how adoptive parents who reject differences are distracted by their fear of acknowledging the adoption, leading them to misinterpret the reasoning behind their child's behaviors. For example, an adoptive parent might mistake the child's silence regarding adoption as a lack of interest as opposed to a feeling that adoption-related discussions are not welcome within the family. A closely related parallel exists in parents' ability to navigate their own emotional distress for the sake of empathizing with the child and placing the child's need above their own, an ability important to parental reflective functioning (Rutherford, Booth, Luyten, Bridgett, & Mayes, 2015; Rutherford, Goldberg, Luyten, Bridgett, & Mayes, 2013). Adoptive parents who acknowledge differences between adoptive and nonadoptive experiences often find such acknowledgment distressing. Not only must they understand that they might experience unique parenting challenges, they might also willingly confront difficult memories and insecurities regarding the adoption process (Kirk, 1984). Examples include loss and grief associated with infertility, feelings of uncertainty and powerlessness leading up to the adoption, and stigma over choosing adoption as a way to form a family. Adoptive parents who acknowledge differences are thus tasked with holding this distress as they navigate raising their adopted children.

Given these similarities, the cognitive processes relayed in Shared Fate Theory fit into an existing framework of parental role-taking, perspective-taking, and attunement, and can be considered adoptive parenting cognitions. In addition to being particularly relevant to adoptive families, these adoptive parenting cognitions differ from existing constructs in that adoptive parents must first engage in specific adoption-related cognitive processes before the perspective-taking can take place, namely acknowledging that their roles as parents might differ from nonadoptive parents and that their children might have experiences specifically related to adoption.

Implications of adoptive parenting cognitions

Notable aspects of parenting cognitions such as mind-mindedness, parental insightfulness, and reflective functioning, are their implications for the parent–child relationship. Specifically, such constructs have been repeatedly found to be predictive of child attachment security (Koren-Karie, Oppenheim, Dolev, Sher, & Etzion-Carasso, 2002; Meins, Fernyhough, Fradley, & Tuckey, 2001; Slade, Grieneberger, Bernbach, Levy, & Locker, 2005). The importance of parenting cognitions is such that they might be stronger predictors of parent–child attachment than parental sensitivity as it is traditionally measured (Koren-Karie et al., 2002; Meins et al., 2012). The predictive effect of parenting cognitions extends to the context of adoptive families (Colonnesi et al., 2012), and there is some evidence to suggest that adoptive parents display particularly adaptive mentalizing abilities, such as is the case for parents of previously institutionalized children (Palacios, Román, Moreno, & León, 2009).

Given the similarities between parenting cognitions and the cognitive, mentalizing aspects of Shared Fate Theory, it could be hypothesized that adoptive parents' acknowledgment of differences, or how they view their role as adoptive parents, are also positively linked with parent–child attachment security. Many past examinations of parenting cognitions generally involved the parents of infants and toddlers (e.g. Meins et al., 2001), as those time periods are often considered the formative years of attachment security, and children of that age cannot easily verbalize their own intentions and mental states. However, children do not develop the cognitive capacity to comprehend adoption and its implications for their lives until middle childhood (approximately 6–12 years old) and adolescence (approximately 13–18 years old; Brodzinsky, 2011). Such understandings might include the biological connectedness (or lack thereof) between family members, the awareness of adoption-related stigma, and the circumstances of birth parents who place children for adoption. Therefore, one would expect adoptive parenting cognitions to play a particularly important role in the parent–child relationship beyond infancy and toddlerhood. Fortunately, there is evidence that general parenting cognitions could have positive implications for the development of pre-adolescents and adolescents (Benbassat & Priel, 2012; Scopesi, Rosso, Viterbori, & Panchieri, 2015). General parenting cognitions have also been examined in adoptive parents, with aspects of reflective functioning being identified as having positive implications for interactions between the parent and child (León, Steele, Palacios, Román, & Moreno, 2018). Such findings further provide a theoretical framework for the predictive effect of acknowledgment of differences.

Early findings on implications of acknowledgment of differences for the parent–child bond did not necessarily fit within the modern parenting cognition framework. For example, Kaye (1990) determined that higher levels of parental acknowledgment of differences, as measured through observations of parent–child conversations, were linked to more problems in adoptive families. Similarly, Sobol and colleagues (1994) measured parental acknowledgment of differences through retrospective reports of adult adoptees and determined that higher acknowledgment of differences was related to lower feelings of adoptees' closeness to their parents. Of note, these studies did not measure aspects of Shared Fate Theory as cognitive processes that tap into adoptive parents' roles as parents, instead relying on parenting behaviors and perceptions of the adopted person.

Another reason for these findings might be the hypothesis that acknowledgment of differences might have a curvilinear (concave down) relationship with positive family functioning. Specifically, parents' over-emphasis on the adoption (termed insistence-of-differences) is associated with children not being fully integrated into the family (Brodzinsky, 1987). Parents who insist on differences might see such differences as the reason that parent–child and broader family conflicts occur (Brodzinsky, 1987). One example of such insistence presented by Brodzinsky (1987) is parents attributing behavioral/emotional difficulties to the child's genetic history ("bad blood"). Thus, it is possible that the adoption might influence parents' perceptions of their roles as parents to a degree that interferes with their abilities to parent effectively. Some evidence for this curvilinear relationship was found in a study in which higher acknowledgment of differences was cross-sectionally related to lower quality parent–child communication about adoption and lower child emotion regulation ability (Soares, Barbosa-Ducharne, Palacios, & Pacheco, 2017). Of note, the measure of acknowledgment of differences used in the study potentially pulled for parents' feelings of having family difficulties resulting from the child's adoptive backgrounds, in line with insistence-of-differences. Specifically, items on the measure included: "Is it necessary to develop extra competences in adoptive parenting?" and "Is it more difficult to be an adoptive parent than a nonadoptive one?" Last, parent–child conflict has been observed being associated with parents' perceptions of incompatibility between their own traits and the characteristics of the child (McRoy, Grotevant, & Zurcher, 1988). In these situations, parents' acknowledgment of differences might be a reaction to the child's behaviors as opposed to thoughts of how the adoption influences their role as parents.

Recently, adoptive parents' acknowledgment of differences was found to have longitudinal implications from middle childhood to adolescence, in that it positively predicted adolescents' perceptions of closeness to their adoptive parents (Lo & Grotevant, in press). In this study, acknowledgment of differences was measured through parents' self-reports of their thought processes regarding the child's birth history and their acknowledgment of the child's adoptive background. This positive predictive effect seemed to appear most prominently under certain circumstances. Specifically, adoptive parents' acknowledgment of differences had positive implications when their child expressed not liking to talk about adoption or having mixed feelings about talking about adoption. Such findings suggest that it might be particularly important for adoptive parents to reflect on their role of parenting an adopted child when the child has less than positive feelings about the adoption. By doing so, they might be able to successfully navigate these complicated emotions and respond in an appropriately sensitive way. In addition, parent acknowledgment of differences was predictive of attachment in closed adoptions and fully disclosed adoptions. Closed adoptions, in which there is little to no information about the birth family available to the adopted child, were the context in which acknowledgment of differences was first conceptualized (Kirk, 1984), and adoptive parents' understanding of their role as adoptive parents might allow them to be more thoughtful in processing this information gap with their child. In the case of fully disclosed adoptions where contact with the birth family is direct and sometimes frequent, the attunement that comes with acknowledging the adoption might allow parents to accurately adjust levels of contact in ways that are satisfactory to their child. Although consistent with general parenting cognitions, these findings require replication, and specific mechanisms from acknowledgment of differences to parent–child attachment within these different contexts remain to be explored.

Overall, cognitive processes first introduced in Shared Fate Theory (Kirk, 1964) emphasize how adoptive parents view their role as parents of adopted children, specifically their decision to acknowledge or reject the specific ways adoption influences their families. Acknowledgment of differences, in the context of Shared Fate Theory, fits within the broader parenting cognition literature in that it might be an essential precursor to attunement and perspective-taking within the adoptive family. Current evidence points to this adoption-specific parenting cognition as having positive implications for parent–child attachment, a construct also emphasized in the more general parenting cognition literature. However, existing literature also suggests that certain forms of this acknowledgment might be less beneficial. As a cognition specific to adoption, acknowledgment of differences could be sensitive to the heterogeneity of experiences seen in adoption. Its implications under different circumstances and the specific mechanisms that lead to positive outcomes remain important aspects to be explored.

Parental role in ethnic-racial socialization

When Kirk first conceptualized about the role of adoptive parents in the 1960s, most adoptions were within-race and involved infants placed at birth. Also prominent was the idea that adoptive families should be indistinguishable from their nonadoptive counterparts (Kirk & McDaniel, 1984), and adoption agency staff made efforts to phenotypically "match" children to parents. Thus, the primary difference that adoptive parents potentially considered was that of being an adoptive family versus a nonadoptive family. Since then, adoptions have become more racially diverse and have involved the placement of children with parent(s) of a different race. With this diversity has come the idea that adoptive parents must not only acknowledge that their parenting experiences will differ due to the child not being biologically their own, but also that the child may have racial and ethnic experiences the parents do not share (Kirk, 1984). As the experiences of transracial and international adoptees and their families is discussed elsewhere in this handbook, the following section will provide a brief overview of how parents in these families think about their role in raising children who are of a different race and ethnicity than themselves.

Many adoptive parents of transracially and internationally adopted children must decide the extent to which they acknowledge differences in race, ethnicity, and culture between parent and child. In line with Shared Fate Theory, this cognitive process can result in adoptive parents acknowledging or rejecting such differences (Kirk, 1984; Lee, 2003). When adoptive parents acknowledge racial and ethnic differences, they recognize that the child's racial and ethnic background have important implications for the child and the family; in contrast, adoptive parents who reject differences discount the importance of the child's ethnic-racial background, and they might instead opt for a "color-blind" view or emphasize shared humanity (Bebiroglu & Pinderhughes, 2012; Crolley-Simic & Vonk, 2011; DeBerry, Scarr, & Weinberg, 1996; Lee, Grotevant, Hellerstedt, Gunnar, & the Minnesota International Adoption Project Team, 2006).

In the context of parents' roles, attitudes toward ethnic-racial differences are related to how adoptive parents navigate these differences behaviorally, such as through ethnic-racial socialization. For example, parents who acknowledge racial-ethnic differences might see it as their role to provide their children with the values, beliefs, and customs of their birth cultures, often referred to as cultural socialization (Bebiroglu & Pinderhughes, 2012; Lee et al., 2006). White parents who acknowledge difference might also see it as their role to prepare their children of color for the racial and ethnic discrimination and biases that proliferate within a White-dominant society, termed preparation-for-bias (Hughes et al., 2006; Pinderhughes, 2018). Ethnic-racial socialization might require a certain level of perspective-taking by adoptive parents; specifically, by seeing these differences through the eyes of the child and attempting to understand the challenges of being a person of color in a White family (Crolley-Simic & Vonk, 2011; Pinderhughes, 2018). In this sense, the road toward ethnic-racial socialization shares aspects of attunement that are seen in the cognitive processes initially suggested in Shared Fate Theory (Kirk, 1984).

Studies have examined other ways that adoptive parents think about their role as parents of transracially and internationally adopted children. In addition to attitudes toward ethnic-racial differences, Pinderhughes (2013) identified attitudes toward the importance of providing ethnic-racial socialization as well as conceptualization of the ethnic/racial identity of the family as a whole. Adoptive parents who place more importance on providing exposure to birth culture or on preparing children for racism and discrimination have been found to display more cultural socialization and preparation-for-bias, respectively (Berbery & O'Brien, 2011). Concerning family identity, adoptive parents who view their families as more multicultural might also be more likely to engage in cultural socialization behaviors (Pinderhughes, Zhang, & Agerbak, 2015). Overall, how parents of transracially and internationally adopted children view their role as parents appears highly related to parental behaviors in navigating race, ethnicity, and culture. Such findings remain important, as the presence of ethnic-racial socialization has been related to more positive mental health outcomes in adopted persons (Leslie, Smith, Hrapczynski, & Riley, 2013; Manzi, Ferrari, Rosnati, & Benet-Martinez, 2014).

Adoptive parents' feelings of entitlement

Developing a sense of entitlement has been discussed as one of the core issues facing adoptive parents (Timm, Mooradian, & Hock, 2011). Reitz and Watson (1992) define entitlement as a parent's sense of their legal and emotional right to parent their child. One study found that 30 percent of adoptive mothers reported facing challenges around entitlement (Timm et al., 2011). While this concept applies to both biological and adoptive parents (Cohen, Coyne, & Duvall, 1996), the context of adoption may pose unique challenges to developing a sense of entitlement for adoptive parents. These challenges might stem from the nature of the adoption process itself (Kirk, 1964; Miall, 1996). For one, there is a period of time between when the child is placed in the adoptive parents' home and the adoption is finalized in which the adoptive parents' legal rights to the child are uncertain (Daniluk & Hurtig-Mitchell, 2003). Additionally, undergoing thorough screening and home study processes intended to evaluate the qualifications of potential adoptive parents might make them doubt those very qualifications and therefore question their emotional right to parent their child (Miall, 1996). Another challenge to adoptive parents' sense of entitlement comes from social beliefs that adoptive families are less legitimate than biological families (Daniluk & Hurtig-Mitchell, 2003; Kirk, 1964). If adoptive parents are exposed to doubts of their legitimacy as the child's real parents, they might doubt their right to parent the child.

Within adoptive families, researchers have noted several characteristics that might be associated with adoptive parents' levels of entitlement. For one, adoptive parents of children who are older at the time of adoption show lower levels of entitlement (Cohen et al., 1996). There is also some evidence that experiences of contact with birth families might shape adoptive parents' feelings of entitlement. For example, some adoptive parents report that approval from the birth mother helps assure them of their right to parent the child

(Sykes, 2001). Others report that contact with birth families reminds them that the child was not originally theirs, which leads them to question their own legitimacy as parents (Sykes, 2001). Finally, length of time since placement is associated with entitlement. Lower levels of entitlement are expressed following placement with increasing levels of entitlement over time (Goldberg, Moyer, & Kinkler, 2013).

Entitlement is an essential concept to understand because of its associations with important family and child outcomes. Challenges in entitlement may also be associated with challenges in bonding with the adopted child (Goldberg et al., 2013). However, we also see resilience in the face of difficulties with entitlement, as many adoptive mothers report that dealing with these challenges has strengthened their marriage (Timm et al., 2011). Research also suggests that parents' sense of entitlement might be associated with behavior problems in the adopted child. Lower levels of entitlement are observed in adoptive families who have been referred for clinical services as compared to adoptive families who have not (Cohen et al., 1996). Some researchers suggest that entitlement could affect problem behaviors through parents' ability to effectively discipline their children, as parents who doubt their right to parent the child might be more likely to use inconsistent or permissive discipline techniques (Cohen et al., 1996; Reitz & Watson, 1992). However, others suggest that dealing with problematic behaviors can lead adoptive parents to doubt their ability and thus their right to parent their adoptive child (Tan, Mahoney, Jackson, & Rice, 2017).

More research is needed to understand how adoptive parents develop a sense of entitlement in contemporary adoptive families and how it changes over time. With a few exceptions (e.g. Goldberg et al., 2013; Tan et al., 2017), the majority of research on entitlement has focused on White heterosexual couples who adopted children of the same race. Goldberg and colleagues (2013) found few differences between heterosexual parents and lesbian and gay parents in challenges related to entitlement. However, to our knowledge, no studies have compared entitlement in adoptive parents who completed transracial adoptions to those who adopted a child of the same race. More research is needed to understand how experiences unique to transracial adoptions might shape adoptive parents' experiences of entitlement.

Implications for practice

Informing agencies

The findings reviewed in this chapter suggest several implications for adoption agency practices. Adoption agency professionals play an important role in preparing adoptive parents for their transition to adoptive parenthood. As such, they are well positioned to provide support to parents as they are developing a sense of their parental role both indirectly through their conversations with the adoptive parents and more directly through support services. In conversations with adoptive parents, adoption professionals should use language that supports the adoptive parent's sense of entitlement in parenting the child (Goldberg et al., 2013). For example, adoption professionals should refer to the child as "your child" when speaking with adoptive parents.

It is important that adoption professionals acknowledge that while the context of adoption provides unique challenges to adoptive parents, many of the parenting challenges discussed in this chapter are also experienced by those who are parenting biological children. Many nonadoptive parents experience challenges with feeling entitled to parent their child (Cohen et al., 1996). While nonadoptive parents might not need to practice taking their child's perspective specifically around the experience of being an adoptee, they will still need to practice taking their child's perspective around a host of other experiences (e.g. Sharp & Fonagy, 2008). Nonadoptive parents also engage in cultural socialization (Hughes et al., 2006). In this way, adoptive parents are taking on many of the same parenting tasks as other parents, but are doing so within a unique set of circumstances. Normalizing these challenges as part of parenthood broadly rather than adoptive parenthood specifically might better position adoptive parents to cope with these challenges.

There have been many calls for increased availability of supports for adoptive families that extend beyond placement (Cashen, Altamari, Grotevant, & McRoy, in press; Waid & Alewine, 2018). The research reviewed in this chapter adds to these calls by showing that parenting challenges do not end when the adoption is finalized. Adoptive parents' parenting cognitions can have lasting implications for parent–child relationships (Lo & Grotevant, in press; Sobol et al., 1994). Importantly, these studies have found associations between adoptive parents' parenting cognitions and outcomes for the adopted child that extend past childhood to adolescence and beyond. Furthermore, the adopted person's sense of identity as an adoptee (and/or as a person of color in the case of transracial adoption) and desire for, or amount of, contact with their birth family may shift over the course of development (Brodzinsky, 2011; Grotevant, Dunbar, Kohler, & Esau, 2000; Grotevant, McRoy, Wrobel, & Ayers-Lopez, 2013; Samuels, 2009). These shifts might challenge the way adoptive parents think about their role as parents. Adoption agencies should therefore be prepared to support adoptive parents in developing their parenting cognitions throughout the course of development and not just during the transition to adoptive parenthood.

Informing clinical work

In addition to agency practices, literature and theory on how adoptive parents view their roles as parents can inform mental health services for adopted persons and their families. Clinical care that is informed by adoption research and implemented by providers well-versed with adoption issues remains essential, particularly because adopted persons are largely over-represented in mental health services (Juffer & Van IJzendoorn, 2005). In addition, some adoptees experience difficulties specific to being adopted, including identity development and issues related to birth family members (Baden & O'Leary Wiley, 2007).

To begin, findings outlined in this chapter stress the importance of thoughtfully incorporating adoptive parents when working with adopted persons. The cognitive processes of adoptive parents could have implications for the relational and mental health outcomes of their children. Examples include the association between acknowledging differences and later parent–child attachment (Lo & Grotevant, in press) as well as the link between parents' attitudes toward preparing children toward bias and racial socialization behaviors that can be protective (Berbery & O'Brien, 2011; Leslie et al., 2013). Thus, clinical work with adoptive parents might need to extend beyond information-gathering and behavioral interventions. Instead, such work might necessitate focus on underlying beliefs that adoptive parents hold (such as on adoption, parenting, race, and culture), as these beliefs potentially have significant downstream effects on child functioning. Even in cases where the directionality between parent cognitive processes and adoptee adjustment is unclear, as in the case of entitlement (Cohen et al., 1996; Tan et al., 2017), full exploration of parental beliefs in clinical settings might clarify how the two are related in the family and provide potential areas of intervention for mental health providers.

While focus on the multiple adoption-related thoughts and beliefs that adoptive parents hold might be beneficial, mental health providers must remain conscious of individual differences observed in these cognitive constructs. Adoptive parents vary widely in their adoption-related cognitions. For example, difficulties with entitlement might present more prominently in several situations, such as for parents of children who were adopted when they were older and for some adoptive families with birth family contact (Cohen et al., 1996; Sykes, 2001), and many adoptive parents might not display such difficulties at all (Timm et al., 2011). Thus, mental health providers must ensure they do not assume all adoptive parents experience difficulties with their roles as parents, and, by extension, pathologize the adoption.

In line with this focus on individual differences, providers must also not assume that parent role variables are always related to the reasons adopted persons and their families seek mental health services. To begin, acknowledgment of differences was found to be predictive of the parent–child relationship only under certain circumstances related to the child's own attitudes and openness arrangements (Lo & Grotevant, in press). In a similar vein, the importance of acknowledgment of differences might fluctuate depending on the age of the child (Brodzinsky, 1987). Thus, clinicians must be careful to not have generalized beliefs or approaches to adoptive parents regarding how parent role variables might be affecting presenting issues.

References

Baden, A. L., & O'Leary Wiley, M. (2007). Counseling adopted persons in adulthood: Integrating practice and research. *The Counseling Psychologist, 35*, 868–901. doi:10.1177/0011000006291409

Bebiroglu, N., & Pinderhughes, E. E. (2012). Mothers raising daughters: New complexities in cultural socialization for children adopted from China. *Adoption Quarterly, 15*, 116–139. doi:10.1080/10926755.2012.681596

Benbassat, N., & Priel, B. (2012). Parenting and adolescent adjustment: The role of parental reflective function. *Journal of Adolescence, 35*, 163–174. doi:10.1016/j.adolescence.2011.03.004

Berbery, M., & O'Brien, K. (2011). Predictors of White adoptive parents' cultural and racial socialization behaviors with their Asian adopted children. *Adoption Quarterly, 14*, 284–304. doi:10.1037/e702742011-001

Bornstein, M. H., Putnick, D. L., & Suwalsky, J. T. (2018). Parenting cognitions → parenting practices → child adjustment? The standard model. *Development and Psychopathology, 30*, 399–416. doi:10.1017/s0954579417000931

Brodzinsky, D. M. (1987). Adjustment to adoption: A psychosocial perspective. *Clinical Psychology Review, 7*, 25–47. doi:10.1016/0272-7358(87)90003-1

Brodzinsky, D. M. (2006). Family structural openness and communication openness as predictors in the adjustment of adopted children. *Adoption Quarterly, 9*, 1–18. doi:10.1300/j145v09n04_01

Brodzinsky, D. M. (2011). Children's understanding of adoption: Developmental and clinical implications. *Professional Psychology: Research and Practice, 42*, 200–207. doi:10.1037/a0022415

Cashen, K. K., Altamari, D., Grotevant, H. D., & McRoy, R. G. (in press) Hearing the voices of emerging adult adoptees: Perspectives on adoption agency practices. *Child Welfare.*

Cashen, K. K., Lo, A. Y. H., & Grotevant, H. D. (2018). Examining Kirk's social role theory: Revisiting shared fate in a contemporary adoptive sample. Presentation at the Sixth International Conference on Adoption Research (ICAR 6), Montreal, Quebec.

Cohen, N. J., Coyne, J. C., & Duvall, J. D. (1996). Parents' sense of "entitlement" in adoptive and nonadoptive families. *Family Process, 35*, 441–456. doi:10.1111/j.15455300.1996.00441.x

Colonnesi, C., Wissink, I. B., Noom, M. J., Asscher, J. J., Hoeve, M., Stams, G. J. J. M., & Kellaert-Knol, M. G. (2012). Basic trust: An attachment-oriented intervention based on mind-mindedness in adoptive families. *Research on Social Work Practice, 23*, 179–188. doi:10.1177/1049731512469301

Crolley-Simic, J., & Vonk, M. E. (2011). White international transracial adoptive mothers' reflections on race. *Child & Family Social Work, 16*, 169–178. doi:10.1111/j.1365-2206.2010.00729.x

Daniluk, J. C., & Hurtig-Mitchell, J. (2003). Themes of hope and healing: Infertile couples' experiences of adoption. *Journal of Counseling & Development, 81*, 389–399. doi:0.1002/j.1556-6678.2003.tb00265.x

DeBerry, K. M., Scarr, S., & Weinberg, R. (1996). Family racial socialization and ecological competence: Longitudinal assessments of African-American transracial adoptees. *Child Development, 67*, 2375–2399. doi:10.1111/j.1467-8624.1996.tb01863.x

Farr, R. H., Crain, E. E., Oakley, M. K., Cashen, K. K., & Garber, K. J. (2016). Microaggressions, feelings of difference, and resilience among adopted children with sexual minority parents. *Journal of Youth and Adolescence, 45*, 85–104. doi:10.1007/s10964-015-0353-6

Fonagy, P., Steele, M., Steele, H., Moran, G. S., & Higgitt, A. C. (1991). The capacity for understanding mental states: The reflective self in parent and child and its significance for security of attachment. *Infant Mental Health Journal, 12*, 201–218. doi:10.1002/1097-0355(199123)12:3<201::aid-imhj2280120307>30.co;2-7

Goldberg, A. E., Moyer, A. M., & Kinkler, L. A. (2013). Lesbian, gay, and heterosexual adoptive parents' perceptions of parental bonding during early parenthood. *Couple and Family Psychology: Research and Practice, 2*, 146–162. doi:10.1037/a0031834

Grotevant, H. D., Dunbar, N., Kohler, J. K., & Esau, A. M. L. (2000). Adoptive identity: How contexts within and beyond the family shape developmental pathways. *Family Relations, 49*, 379–387. doi:10.4135/9781412976633.n6

Grotevant, H. D., & Lo, A. Y. H. (2017). Adoptive parenting. *Current Opinion in Psychology, 15*, 71–75. doi:10.1016/j.copsyc.2017.02.020

Grotevant, H. D., Lo, A. Y. H., Fiorenzo, L., & Dunbar, N. D. (2017). Adoptive identity and adjustment from adolescence to emerging adulthood: A person-centered approach. *Developmental Psychology, 53*, 2195–2204. doi:10.1037/dev0000352

Grotevant, H. D., McRoy, R. G., Wrobel, G. M., & Ayers-Lopez, S. (2013). Contact between adoptive and birth families: Perspectives from the Minnesota/Texas Adoption Research Project. *Child Development Perspectives, 7*, 193–198. doi:10.1111/cdep.12039

Hughes, D., Rodriguez, J., Smith, E. P., Johnson, D. J., Stevenson, H. C., & Spicer, P. (2006). Parents' ethnic-racial socialization practices: A review of research and directions for future study. *Developmental Psychology, 42*, 747–770. doi:10.1037/0012-1649.42.5.747

Juffer, F., & Van IJzendoorn, M. H. (2005). Behavior problems and mental health referrals of international adoptees: A meta-analysis. *The Journal of the American Medical Association, 293*, 2501–2515. doi:10.1001/jama.293.20.2501

Kaye, K. (1990). Acknowledgement or rejection of differences?. In D. M. Brodzinsky & M. D. Schechter (Eds.), *The psychology of adoption* (pp. 121–143). New York, NY: Oxford University Press.

Kirk, H. D. (1964). *Shared fate: A theory and method of adoptive relationships*. New York: Free Press.

Kirk, H. D. (1984). *Shared fate: A theory and method of adoptive relationships*. Port Angeles, WA: Ben-Simon Publications.

Kirk, H. D., & McDaniel, S. A. (1984). Adoption policy in great Britain and North America. *Journal of Social Policy, 13*, 75–84. doi:10.1017/s0047279400022832

Koren-Karie, N., Oppenheim, D., Dolev, S., Sher, E., & Etzion-Carasso, A. (2002). Mothers' insightfulness regarding their infants' internal experience: Relations with maternal sensitivity and infant attachment. *Developmental Psychology, 38*, 534–542. doi:10.1037/0012-1649.38.4.534

Lee, R. M. (2003). The transracial adoption paradox: History, research, and counseling implications of cultural socialization. *The Counseling Psychologist, 31*, 711–744. doi:10.1177/0011000003258087

Lee, R. M., Grotevant, H. D., Hellerstedt, W. L., & Gunnar, M. R. the Minnesota International Adoption Project Team. (2006). Cultural socialization in families with internationally adopted children. *Journal of Family Psychology, 20*, 571–580. doi:10.1037/0893-3200.20.4.571

León, E., Steele, M., Palacios, J., Román, M., & Moreno, C. (2018). Parenting adoptive children: Reflective functioning and parent-child interactions. A comparative, relational and predictive study. *Children and Youth Services Review, 95*, 352–360. doi:10.1016/j.childyouth.2018.11.009

Leslie, L. A., Smith, J. R., Hrapczynski, K. M., & Riley, D. (2013). Racial socialization in transracial adoptive families: Does it help adolescents deal with discrimination stress?. *Family Relations, 62*, 72–81. doi:10.1111/j.1741-3729.2012.00744.x

Lo, A. Y. H., & Grotevant, H. D. (in press) Adoptive parenting cognitions: Acknowledgement of differences as a predictor of adolescent's attachment to parents. *Parenting: Science and Practice.*

Manzi, C., Ferrari, L., Rosnati, R., & Benet-Martinez, V. (2014). Bicultural identity integration of transracial adolescent adoptees: Antecedents and outcomes. *Journal of Cross-Cultural Psychology, 45*, 888–904. doi:10.1177/0022022114530495

McRoy, R. G., Grotevant, H. D., & White, K. L. (1988). *Openness in adoption: New practices, new issues.* New York, NY: Praeger.

McRoy, R. G., Grotevant, H. D., & Zurcher, L. A., Jr. (1988). *Emotional disturbance in adopted adolescents: Origins and development.* New York, NY: Praeger.

Meins, E. (1997). *Security of attachment and the social development of cognition.* Hove, UK: Psychology Press. doi:10.4324/9780203775912

Meins, E. (2013). Sensitive attunement to infants' internal states: Operationalizing the construct of mind-mindedness. *Attachment & Human Development, 15,* 524–544. doi:10.1080/14616734.2013.830388

Meins, E., Fernyhough, C., de Rosnay, M., Arnott, B., Leekam, S. R., & Turner, M. (2012). Mind-mindedness as a multidimensional construct: Appropriate and nonattuned mind-related comments independently predict infant-mother attachment in a socially diverse sample. *Infancy, 17,* 393–415. doi:10.1111/j.1532-7078.2011.00087.x

Meins, E., Fernyhough, C., Fradley, E., & Tuckey, M. (2001). Rethinking maternal sensitivity: Mother's comments on infants' mental processes predict security of attachment at 12 months. *Journal of Child Psychology and Psychiatry, 42,* 637–648. doi:10.1017/s0021963001007302

Miall, C. E. (1996). The social construction of adoption: Clinical and community perspectives. *Family Relations, 45,* 309–317. doi:10.2307/585503

Oppenheim, D., & Koren-Karie, N. (2002). Mothers' insightfulness regarding their children's internal worlds: The capacity underlying secure child-mother relationships. *Infant Mental Health Journal, 23,* 593–605. doi:10.1002/imhj.10035

Palacios, J., Román, M., Moreno, C., & León, E. (2009). Family context for emotional recovery in internationally adopted children. *International Social Work, 52,* 609–620. doi:10.1177/0020872809337679

Pinderhughes, E. E. (2013, July). The complexities of ethnic-racial socialization among transracial adoptive families. Presentation at the Fourth International Conference on Adoption Research (ICAR4), Bilbao, Spain.

Pinderhughes, E. E. (2018). Cultural socialization and preparation-for-bias: Critical tasks facing adoptive parents in promoting the well-being of their transracially adopted children. Presented at the 2018 Rudd Adoption Conference, Amherst, Massachusetts.

Pinderhughes, E. E., Zhang, X., & Agerbak, S. (2015) "American" or "multiethnic"? Family ethnic identity among transracial adoptive families, ethnic-racial socialization, and children's self-perception. *New Directions for Child and Adolescent Development, 150,* 5–18. 10.1002/cad.20118

Reitz, M., & Watson, K. W. (1992). *Adoption and the family system: Strategies for treatment.* New York, NY: Guilford Press.

Rutherford, H. J., Booth, C. R., Luyten, P., Bridgett, D. J., & Mayes, L. C. (2015). Investigating the association between parental reflective functioning and distress tolerance in motherhood. *Infant Behavior and Development, 40,* 54–63. doi:10.1016/j.infbeh.2015.04.005

Rutherford, H. J., Goldberg, B., Luyten, P., Bridgett, D. J., & Mayes, L. C. (2013). Parental reflective functioning is associated with tolerance of infant distress but not general distress: Evidence for a specific relationship using a simulated baby paradigm. *Infant Behavior and Development, 36,* 635–641. doi:10.1016/j.infbeh.2013.06.008

Samuels, G. M. (2009). "Being raised by White people": Navigating racial difference among adopted multiracial adults. *Journal of Marriage and Family, 71,* 80–94. doi:10.1111/j.1741-3737.2008.00581.x

Scopesi, A. M., Rosso, A. M., Viterbori, P., & Panchieri, E. (2015). Mentalizing abilities in preadolescents' and their mothers' autobiographical narratives. *The Journal of Early Adolescence, 35,* 467–483. doi:10.1177/0272431614535091

Sharp, C., & Fonagy, P. (2008). The parent's capacity to treat the child as a psychological agent: Constructs, measures and implications for developmental psychopathology. *Social Development, 17,* 737–754. doi:10.1111/j.1467-9507.2007.00457.x

Slade, A., Grieneberger, J., Bernbach, E., Levy, D., & Locker, A. (2005). Maternal reflective functioning, attachment, and the transmission gap: A preliminary study. *Attachment & Human Development, 7,* 283–298. doi:10.1080/14616730500245880

Soares, J., Barbosa-Ducharne, M., Palacios, J., & Pacheco, A. (2017). Adopted children's emotion regulation: The role of parental attitudes and communication about adoption. *Psicothema, 29,* 49–54. doi:10.7334/psicothema2016.71

Sobol, M. P., Delaney, S., & Earn, B. M. (1994). Adoptees' portrayal of the development of family structure. *Journal of Youth and Adolescence, 23,* 385–401. doi:10.1007/bf01536726

Sykes, M. R. (2001). Adoption with contact: A study of adoptive parents and the impact of continuing contact with families of origin. *Journal of Family Therapy, 23*, 296–316. doi:10.1177/030857590002400205

Tan, T., Mahoney, E., Jackson, A., & Rice, J. (2017). East meets west: Adopted Chinese girls' nighttime sleep problems and adoptive parents' self-judgment about parenting. *Behavioral Sleep Medicine, 15*, 242–255. doi:10.1080/15402002.2015.1120204

Timm, T. M., Mooradian, J. K., & Hock, R. M. (2011). Exploring core issues in adoption: Individual and marital experience of adoptive mothers. *Adoption Quarterly, 14*, 268–283. doi:10.1080/10926755.2011.628264

Waid, J., & Alewine, E. (2018). An exploration of family challenges and service needs during the post-adoption period. *Children and Youth Services Review, 91*, 213–220. doi:10.1016/j.childyouth.2018.06.017

Wrobel, G. M., Kohler, J. K., Grotevant, H. D., & McRoy, R. G. (2003). The family adoption communication (FAC) model: Identifying pathways of adoption-related communication. *Adoption Quarterly, 7*, 53–84. doi:10.1300/J145v07n02_04

21

RELIGIOSITY AND ADOPTION

Emily Helder and Elisha Marr

In the US, religious groups are regularly called upon to consider adopting in order to provide a home for a child in need (ABBA, n.d; Daly, 2015; One Church One Child, 2019). While Jewish and Islamic religious traditions accept child adoption (al-Azhary Sonbol, 1995; Yarden, 2012), at this point most of the literature on adoption in the US has focused on adoption in the Christian tradition. Research reported in this chapter will have a predominantly Christian sample unless otherwise noted. Clearly articulated or implicitly insinuated is the message that the issue of the large number of children in need of homes can be addressed by the acts of a few individuals/families who are willing to open their home. There is a notable amount of literature dedicated to examining religious theology, ethics, culture, organizations, and movements, particularly on the topic of encouraging and mobilizing Christians to adopt a child (Coburn & Smith, 1999; Joyce, 2013; Perry, 2017; Smolin, 2012). However, there is less scientifically sound research on the relationship between religiosity and the adoption practices of these individuals (Perry, 2017), and the existing information is relatively decentralized. The broader, more macro-level perspectives on religion and adoption need to be complemented with more comprehensive and thorough micro-level understandings of the religiosity of individuals involved in the adoption process.

This chapter focuses on potential and current adoptive parents because adoptive parents have the most decision-making power in the adoption process. Acknowledging that adoption is shaped by many factors (e.g., number of children available, domestic and international laws), potential and current adoptive parents' willingness to adopt is central, and fundamentally essential, to the adoption of a child. Adoption begins as a voluntary act by potential adoptive parents' consideration of adoption, followed by seeking of information, applying, completing an adoption, and raising a non-relative child. Undeniably, adoption greatly impacts the lives of adoptees, their birth parents, their adoptive families, and adoption professionals involved in the matching, yet adoptive parents are the catalysts of the adoption process. The role of religion in their experiences is an important, yet under researched area. In fact, all of the research studies cited in the next section analyze potential and current adoptive parents with only one-quarter additionally including information on birth parents who are not the central focus of their projects (see section on religion and willingness to adopt).

This chapter contributes to the scholarship on religion and adoption by compiling what is known about the relationship between religiosity and the activities of potential and current adoptive parents, concluding with a consideration of the ways this information can better inform pre- and post-adoption practice. Areas of future research are also identified that could provide insight into whether micro-level adoption activities among the religious can be connected with more macro-level efforts among religious groups to encourage their congregants to adopt. The chapter begins with a review of the literature on the relationship between self-identified measures of religiosity and willingness to adopt, which is followed by an examination of self-professed religious motivations to adopt among adoptive parents and how these might impact parenting and child outcomes. Finally, it proceeds to explore how adoptive families use religiosity and spirituality to give meaning to their adoption experiences and ends with a discussion of the implications of this information for adoption research, policy, and practice.

Religion and willingness to adopt

Much of the nationally representative research providing insight into how religion might impact a person's willingness to adopt has been demographic analyses of those who have considered adopting a child. When a national survey includes questions about whether the participants (which have predominantly been women) have ever considered, taken steps toward, or adopted a child, those who have responded affirmatively are examined to identify patterns in age, marital status, fecundity, and religious identity and practices. The National Survey of Family Growth (NSFG) has been the main source of this information for almost 50 years (1973–present). Participants are asked a series of questions about the ways in which people create families involving topics such as marriage, cohabitation, birth control, biological reproduction, and adoption. Some of the adoption questions focus on a woman's decision to place her child for adoption. The other adoption questions focus on the extent to which the participant has considered or taken steps to grow their family by adopting a child. Thus, this data source provides a breadth of information about those who have considered adoption, yet regarding religion, the information has been limited to the participants' self-identified religious affiliation, their frequency in attendance at religious services, and the importance they place on religion.

The other major source of information on the role of religion in propensity to adopt is the National Survey of Fertility Barriers (NSFB) which collected two waves of data since its inception in the early 21st century. The survey includes questions regarding the participants' consideration of adopting a child as well as religious practices (e.g., frequency of prayer) and religious beliefs (e.g., level of closeness to God). The NSFB also includes questions about the participants' attitudes toward children and parenting (e.g., importance of motherhood, ideal number of children).

Since neither of these two national representative surveys, nor a few other large data sources (e.g., Bausch, 2006; Vandivere, Malm, & Radel, 2009), include self-professed motivations to adopt that are explicitly about religion, the nationally generalizable research on willingness to adopt focuses on the relationship between the consideration and/or act of adopting and religious identity/affiliation or religious attitudes and practices. There are also a notable number of studies that examine the impact of demographic factors on willingness to adopt yet do not include religious measures (Chandra, Abma, Maza, & Bachrach, 1999; Malm & Welti, 2010).

Religious identity/affiliation

Bonham's (1977) analysis of NSFG data from 1973 to determine which demographic factors were associated with higher willingness to adopt a child is the earliest research currently known to the authors that attends to the role of religion and adoption. At that time questions about adoption were only asked of married women who indicated that they intended to have more children. Half of the Protestant women in this group considered adopting (50.0 percent). This was a slightly greater proportion than Catholics (45.3 percent) and other religions (46.1 percent) who also considered adopting (Bonham, 1977). These proportions were similar to those among the White women in this group (51.7 percent Protestant, 45.9 percent Catholic, 49.0 percent other religions). Black women, however, were less likely to consider adoption than White women in every religious category: however, Protestant Black women were still the most likely (36.9 percent), followed by Catholic Black women (30.9 percent), and Black women from other religious groups were the least likely to consider adopting a child (18.9 percent) (Bonham, 1977).

Bernal, Hu, Moriguchi, and Nagypal's (2007) work on historical determinants of adoption included a table on the characteristics of adoptive women during the first six cycles of the NSFG from 1973 to 2002 (Bernal et al., 2007, Table 7). One characteristic included was religious affiliation of adoptive mothers for each of the six years. The most distinct pattern gleaned from this table is that in each surveyed year, women who identified as Protestant were the majority of adoptive mothers (range of 53.9 percent in 1995 to 74.7 percent in 1988) followed by Catholics (range 16.1 percent in 1988 to 31.9 percent in 1982 and 1995). An additional observation is that in 1973, there were small proportions of adoptive mothers who identified with a religion that is not Protestant or Catholic (2.6 percent) or did not identify with any religion (1.6 percent). Yet over the 30-year period, more adoptive mothers fell into these categories, with 5.2 percent identifying as a religion that is not Protestant or Catholic and 8.6 percent identifying as not having a religion in 2002 (Bernal et al., 2007).

We hypothesized that these longitudinal patterns in the religious affiliation of adoptive mothers could be partially explained by overarching trends in religious affiliation in the US, for which there has been a decrease in the proportion of those who identify as Protestant and an increase in those who do not identify with a religion. We then decided to complete an original analysis to (1) compare the religious affiliation of adoptive mothers in 1995 and 2002 with the religious affiliations of the US population and (2) add information about the religious affiliation of adoptive mothers since 2002, the last year included in Bernal et al.'s (2007) table. Our initial discovery was that the percentages in Bernal et al.'s (2007) table were not weighted, which is necessary for more accurate national estimates (National Center for Health Statistics [NCHS], 2016). Additionally, Bernal et al. (2007) categorized any female respondent who indicated that she had adopted a child as an adoptive mother. Since this chapter focuses on the adoption of unrelated children, opposed to the adoption of a stepchild or relative, women who adopted related children were excluded from our analysis. The comparison of our analysis with Bernal et al.'s (2007) table revealed that for 1995, Bernal's 53.9 percent of Protestant adoptive mothers was 2 percent more than the weighted Protestant adoptive mothers of unrelated children (51.4 percent) in our analysis (Table 21.1). Bernal et al. (2007) also had 2 percent fewer Catholic adoptive women at 31.9 percent than our result of 33.6 percent (Table 21.1). There were no differences in the "other religion" and "no religion" categories for 1995 (Bernal et al., 2007). The differences between Bernal et al.'s (2007)

Table 21.1 Comparison of religious proportion of adoptive mothers and US population

Adoptive mothers of unrelated children by percentage of religious affiliation each year				
	1995	2002	2006–2010	2013–2015
Protestant	51.4%	57.8%	86.3%	72.7%
Catholic	33.6%	37.3%	12.5%	9.5%
Other	8.0%	2.4%	1.2%	10.0%
None	6.9%	2.4%	0.0%	7.6%
US population by percentage of religious affiliation each year				
	1995	2002	2008	2014
Protestant	58.4%	55.6%	53.3%	48.6%
Catholic	26.9%	25.5%	25.5%	25.6%
Other	5.7%	5.1%	4.4%	5.2%
None	9.0%	13.8%	16.8%	20.6%
Difference in proportion between adoptive mothers and US population each year				
	1995	2002	2008	2014
Protestant	–7.0%*	2.2%	33.0%**	24.0%**
Catholic	6.7%*	11.8%**	–13.1%**	–16.0%**
Other	2.3%	–2.7%*	–3.3%**	4.9%**
None	–2.1%	-11.4%**	–16.8%**	–13.0%**

* statistically significant at the .05 level
** statistically significant at the .01 level
Data on adoptive mothers from the National Survey of Family Growth
Data on US population from the General Social Survey

table and our analysis for 2002 were starker. The unweighted proportion of Protestant adoptive women in Bernal et al.'s (2007) table was 62.1 percent, which is over a 4 percent difference from the weighted proportion of Protestant adoptive women of unrelated children of 57.8 percent in our analysis (Table 21.1). For Catholic adoptive women the difference was slightly over 13 percent, with 24.1 percent in Bernal et al.'s (2007) table and 37.3 percent in our analysis (Table 21.1). Those belonging to other religious groups (5.2 percent unweighted in Bernal et al.'s 2007 table) and those who did not identify with a religion (8.6 percent unweighted) each comprised 2.4 percent of adoptive mothers of unrelated children in 2002 (Table 21.1). We concluded that although Bernal et al.'s (2007) table provides some insight into overarching longitudinal trends about the religious affiliation of adoptive mothers, it is not as useful when seeking more precise figures on the nationally representative religious affiliation of adoptive mothers.

After analyzing the 1995 and 2002 NSFG data for the religious affiliation of adoptive mothers of unrelated children, we obtained more current NSFG data on adoptive mothers of unrelated children from the periods of 2006–2010 and 2013–2015 (the NSFG began continuous interviewing in 2006 to provide public use data on a more frequent and timelier basis; NCHS, 2016). We also obtained data from the General Social Survey (Smith, Davern, Freese, & Hout, 2018) for the years 1995, 2002, 2008, and 2014 about religious identification in the US. We completed a two-tailed t-test for difference in proportions to learn whether the religious proportions of adoptive mothers for each year are similar to the religious proportion of the US to test our hypothesis.

Table 21.1 shows that there are statistically significant differences during each sampled year. In 1995, the proportion of Protestant women who had adopted unrelated children was 7 percent less than the proportion of Protestants in the US, overall. Conversely, 6.7 percent more Catholic women had adopted unrelated children than the proportion of Catholics in the US. In 2002, although 13.8 percent of people in the US did not identify with a religion, they comprised only 2.4 percent of adoptive women. Again, Catholic women are a greater portion of adoptive women (37.3 percent) than the proportion of Catholics in the US (25.5 percent). Although 5.1 percent of the US identified with a religion that was not Protestant or Catholic in 2002, adoptive mothers affiliated with these other religions were half of that proportion at 2.4 percent.

The majority of the adoptive mothers of unrelated children during 2006–2010 and 2013–2015 were Protestant (86.3 percent and 72.5 percent, respectively, Table 21.1) despite fewer people in the US identifying as Protestant during the same time periods. The statistically significant differences between Protestant adoptive women and people in the US of 33.0 percent in the 2006–2010 time period and 24.0 percent in the 2013–2015 time period indicate that Protestant women are highly overrepresented among adoptive women of unrelated children in the 21st century. Although Catholics consistently comprise slightly more than 25 percent of the US from 1995–2005, their proportion of adoptive women decreases over time resulting in a difference of about 13 percent in the 2006–2010 time period and 16 percent in the 2013–2015 time period. Whereas Catholics were overrepresented as adoptive mothers in 1995 and 2002, they are highly underrepresented as adoptive mothers in 2006–2010 and 2013–2015.

Adoptive mothers of unrelated children who identify as a religion other than Protestant or Catholic have no discernible pattern over time. Comprising a little more or less than 5 percent of the US throughout these sampled years, they are underrepresented as a portion of adoptive mothers in 2006–2010 (–3.3 percent) and overrepresented in 2013–2015 (4.9 percent; Table 21.1). The proportion of those in the US who do not identify with a religion has increased throughout the 1995–2015 time period. Yet similar to the religious others, their proportion of adoptive mothers varies over time, with no adoptive mothers identifying as no religion in 2006–2010 despite being 16.8 percent of the US and 7.6 percent of adoptive mothers in 2013–2015, and despite one-fifth of the US not identifying with a religion (Table 21.1).

Thus, our conclusions do not support our hypothesis that changes over time in the proportions of adoptive mothers of unrelated children are explained by changes in religious identification in the US. A project seeking to explore an additional hypothesis of the changes in the proportion of religion among adoptive mothers being a factor of the choices of birth parents was abandoned after a quick analysis of the NSFG data on women who surrendered a child for adoption during the same time periods revealed that a large proportion did not identify with a religion (25 percent in 2002, 43 percent in 2013–2015) while the percentage who identified as Protestant or Catholic dwindled (35.6 percent Protestant, 12.5 percent Catholic in 2013–2015).

Some have noted that those who are not religious experience discrimination in their efforts to adopt children in a highly privatized and religious system of adoption (ABBA, n.d; Perry, 2017). Since faith-based adoption agencies are predominantly Protestant or Catholic, as private organizations they have the ability to determine which parents are able to adopt the children in their care.

The current most plausible explanation for Protestants being overrepresented as adoptive mothers is the orphan care movement among evangelicals, a branch of

Protestantism. Books, conferences, and organizations have been promoting adoption and foster care among evangelicals to show God's love to vulnerable children. In his 2017 book *Growing God's family: The global orphan care movement and the limits of evangelical activism*, S. Perry dedicates much of the first chapter to examining trends in adoption and foster care to determine whether adoptions are increasing due to the efforts of evangelicals. Acknowledging the scarcity of nationally representative data on adoption, he reviews information from the US Children's Bureau, the Adoption and Foster Care Analysis and Reporting System, and even previously published data from the NSFG, to determine that adoptions have been on the decline since 2005, and at the time of publication, there was no reliable evidence that evangelicals are adopting and fostering at higher rates than in the past or more than other Americans. Our findings do not provide any insight into foster care, yet provide some evidence that when adoption of unrelated children is occurring, the women are much more likely to be Protestant. Future research should seek to provide insight into whether there is a connection between the evangelical social movement and the decisions of potential adoptive mothers. Additionally, religious affiliation and identification have been found to be important aspects to consider when learning about motivations to adopt.

Measures of religiosity

The NSFG has also been a primary source of information about the relationship between the propensity to consider adopting a child and measures of religion that are not limited to identification and/or affiliation with a particular religious group. In addition to current religious affiliation, the NSFG survey also includes questions about the religion within which the respondent was raised, how frequently the respondent currently attends religious services, as well as the frequency of their attendance when they were 14 years old. The participant is also asked, "Currently, how important is religion in your daily life?" and given a three-point Likert scale with responses ranging from "very important" to "not important." Studies on religiosity and adoption that examine NSFG data use one or more of these measures of religiosity in their analyses of women who have ever considered, taken steps, and/or adopted a child.

Bonham's (1977) analysis of the 1973 NSFG data only included a consideration of religious affiliation. Bachrach, London, and Maza's (1991) analysis of the 1988 NSFG data, however, did include the respondent's religious participation at age 14. They determined that of women aged 15–44 who ever took steps to adopt (e.g., contacted a lawyer or agency to explore adopting a child), the proportion who regularly attended religious services at 14 was only slightly higher than the proportion who attended religious services less than weekly at the time of the survey (Bachrach et al., 1991). Specifically, approximately 3.8 percent of White women (which they refer to as "Nonblack") regularly attended religious services at age 14 and sought to adopt, whereas a smaller 2.8 percent of White women had lower rates of attending religious services at age 14 and sought to adopt. Similarly, 4.0 percent of Black women who sought to adopt were more regular attenders of religious services at age 14 than the 2.1 percent who were less frequent attenders. Frequency in religious participation at age 14 was not a statistically significant predictor of having taken steps to adopt for Black women or White women in the logistic regression models (Bachrach et al., 1991).

Hollingsworth (2000) used the importance of religion variable in the analysis of women who took steps to adopt in the 1995 NSFG data. Extrapolating from the numbers and percentages describing the various characteristics of women 18–44 who ever sought to adopt, approximately 70 percent of all women, 66 percent of White women, and 77 percent of Black women seeking to adopt considered religion to be "very important" (Hollingsworth, 2000). The logistic regression revealed that all women and White women who considered religion to be "very important" were 1.95 times and 2.67 times, respectively, more likely to seek to adopt than those who considered religion "not important." Importance of religion was not a statistically significant predictor of Black women's propensity to adopt (Hollingsworth, 2000).

Although Hollingsworth (2000) and Bachrach et al. (1991) examined the differences between White women and Black women in their analyses, Lamb (2008) sought to understand the difference between Hispanic women's and non-Hispanic White women's propensity to seek to adopt a child using the 2002 NSFG data. Of the women who took steps to adopt, almost three-fourths (71.3 percent) of Hispanic women with partners (married or cohabiting) and two-thirds of all Hispanic women (67.8 percent) considered religion to be "very important" (Lamb, 2008). These proportions are higher than non-Hispanic White women who took steps to adopt, of which slightly over half of all women and those who were partnered considered religion to be "very important" (54.2 percent and 55.1 percent, respectively). The differences between Hispanic women and non-Hispanic White women in regard to frequency of religious attendance were less stark, with slightly more than half of Hispanic women, partnered or not, indicating that they attend services weekly (54.4 percent partnered Hispanic women, 51.1 percent all Hispanic women). Approximately 44.2 percent of partnered non-Hispanic White women and 42.5 percent of all non-Hispanic women attended services weekly. The logistic regression analysis revealed that the only statistically significant variable for predicting propensity to adopt was religious attendance for non-Hispanic White women. Those non-Hispanic White women who attended religious services weekly, opposed to less than weekly, increased the odds of having sought adoption by 28 percent for partnered women and 25 percent for all women (Lamb, 2008). Thus, neither religious attendance nor religious importance were statistically significant indicators of Hispanic women's propensity to seek to adopt.

Bachrach et al. (1991), Hollingsworth (2000), and Lamb (2008) focused on women who took steps to adopt yet did not compare them with women who had adopted. Marr and Hoeksema's (2019) analysis of the 2013–2015 NSFG continuous cycle data compared those who never considered adoption to anyone who considered adopting, compared those who considered adopting but did not take steps to anyone who took steps to adopt a child, and compared those who took steps but did not adopt a child with women who had adopted. Measuring religiosity as frequency in attendance at religious services and importance of religion to respondent, the findings revealed that those with those higher levels of religiosity were more likely to consider adopting opposed to not considering adopting a child. Higher religiosity was also found among those who took steps to adopt compared with those who had or were considering adopting but had not yet taken steps. This pattern did not hold when comparing those who took steps to adopt, yet did not, and those who adopted. One of the measures of religiosity, attendance at religious services, was higher among those who took steps to adopt, yet did not, than it was for those who adopted. There was not a statistically significant difference in importance of religion between the groups of women who adopted and women who had taken steps to adopt but did not. Marr and Hoeksema (2019) suggest future research explore why there are higher levels of religiosity among women who consider and take steps to adopt a child than there are among the women who adopt a child. They note that this information will be important to adoption professionals who seek to cultivate adoptive parents who will complete the process.

In addition to frequency of attendance at religious services and importance of religion, the NSFB included more measures of religion than the NSFG, specifically frequency of prayer, closeness to God, and how much religious beliefs influence the respondents' daily life (Park & Wonch Hill, 2014; Van Laningham, Scheuble, & Johnson, 2012). Van Laningham et al. (2012) analyzed the pilot data for the NSFB collected in the spring of 2002. Although their study did not include religious affiliation or identity, they did acknowledge that Christianity was likely the predominant religion of the representative probability sample of Midwestern women ages 25–50 (they reference the Pew Forum on Religion and Public Life's estimate that almost 80 percent of people in the Midwest, and the overall US, identify as Christian) (Van Laningham et al., 2012). They created a scale of religiosity using the mean score of three variables: frequency of prayer, influence of religious beliefs, and closeness to God, with higher numbers indicating higher levels of religiosity. They learned that considering adopting a child (i.e., considered adopting yet did not take steps) was significantly correlated with these higher levels of religiosity in comparison to those who did not consider adopting. In fact, for each unit increase in religiosity, women were 1.3 times more likely to consider adoption. However, religiosity was not a statistically significant predictor of which women were likely to take steps to adopt a child (e.g., contact an adoption agency or lawyer) in comparison to those who merely considered but did not take steps and those who did not consider adoption at all. They note that since religiosity affects considering adoption, but not taking steps, future research should be done to learn about how pro-adoption, anti-abortion attitudes might not result in adoption-seeking behaviors. Additionally, they explain that their conclusions find "support for involving churches and other religious organizations in the education and recruitment of potential adoptive families, with the goal of encouraging those who may already be considering adoption to move forward in the process" (Van Laningham et al., 2012, p. 17).

Park and Wonch Hill's (2014) research on childless women from the 2004–2007 NSFB data also included a scale of religiosity compiling the variables regarding frequency of prayer, importance of religion, and closeness to God. They also included frequency of attending religious services as a variable separate from the religiosity scale. The bivariate analysis showed that those with higher levels of church attendance (mean 2.86) were more likely to be currently considering adoption than formerly considering adoption (2.63) or had never considered adopting a child (2.46). Similarly, those with higher levels of religiosity (mean 3.84) were more likely to be currently considering adoption, than formerly (3.60) or never (3.47) (Park & Wonch Hill, 2014). The multinomial regression analysis showed that for every unit increase in church attendance there was a 25 percent increase in the odds that someone is currently considering adoption opposed to never having considered adoption. The religiosity scale was not a statistically significant predictor of consideration of adoption in the multinomial regression analysis. They concluded that both frequency of attendance at religious services (which they refer to as church attendance) and the religiosity scale were associated with a greater likelihood of currently considering adoption, yet there were few differences between those who formerly considered and those who never considered adopting a child (Park & Wonch Hill, 2014).

One of the other nationally representative surveys on adoption, the 2007 National Survey of Adoptive Parents (NSAP; Vandivere et al., 2009), only included one measure of religion, yet it applied to adopted children rather than adoptive parents: child attends religious services at least monthly. Approximately 78 percent of adopted children ages 0–17 attend religious services monthly, which is a statistically significant difference from the 70 percent of all children in the US. Children in foster care are the most likely to attend religious services monthly (87 percent), followed by domestic adoptees (77 percent), and international adoptees (66 percent; Vandivere et al., 2009, p 34). This ratio of approximately four out of five adoptive children regularly attending religious services is consistent with the ratio of four out of five adoptive mothers associating with a religious identity in the 2006–2010 NSFG continuous cycle data as mentioned in the first section of this chapter.

In summary, several measurements of religiosity, spanning from frequency of attendance at religious services to closeness the respondent feels to God, have been found to be predictors of whether women consider or take steps to adopt a child. However, no specific measures of religiosity are consistently found throughout the literature to impact a woman's willingness to adopt. Nor are religious measures statistically significant predictors of willingness to adopt among all of the racial and/or ethnic groups in the analysis. In general, women of color who seek to adopt are found to be more religious than non-Hispanic White women; however, there is some evidence that level of religiosity plays a greater role in non-Hispanic White women's propensity to seek to adopt than it does among Black and Hispanic women.

Religion not included

A survey of the scholarship on nationally representative research on willingness to adopt reveals that although levels of religiosity are included in some analyses, a similar number of studies do not include religious variables. Some of these studies that do not include religious variables acknowledge the importance of religion in shaping adoption decisions. Yet whether it was due to the lack of religious variables collected for their data set, or their own decisions prioritizing and choosing relevant variables to consider, these projects reviewed literature on religion and adoption, yet did not include religion in their analysis. Other studies did not include a consideration of the role of religion in willingness to adopt in their literature reviews, analyses, or discussion. Following is a review of the literature currently known to the authors on willingness to adopt that do not include any religious variables in their analyses.

Ishizawa and Kubo's (2014) examination of factors affecting adoption decisions acknowledges that religion is commonly cited as a motivating factor for adopting a child. They note that potential adoptive parents' decision-making process often involves seeking a child with traits similar to their own and indicate that religion is on the list of traits; however, religion is not a part of their analysis. The literature review in Malm and Welti's (2010) article on motivations to adopt includes a section on altruism and religiosity summarizing results from studies in which prospective and current adoptive parents indicate religious, spiritual, and humanitarian beliefs as their reason for considering adopting a child. Their analysis of data from the 2007 NSAP includes altruistic independent variables (e.g., to provide a permanent home for a child, to help child avoid foster care), yet none specific to religion. Bausch (2006) analyzed data collected from 185 randomly sampled married adults in the Midwest, as well as 47 individuals in the process of adoption at a local agency, to identify which demographic and attitudinal factors were predictors of willingness to adopt a child. Although the survey included questions regarding pronatalist beliefs, there was not a direct connection to religious beliefs, nor were there any other religious aspects in the literature review or the analysis (Bausch, 2006).

US Department of Health and Human Services reports on adoption from the NSFG cycles four (conducted in 1995) and five (conducted in 2002) also do not include any information on how religion could be a factor in willingness to adopt. Chandra, Abma, Maza, and Bachrach's (1999) analysis of the 1995 data considers whether those who are currently seeking to adopt, or have previously sought to adopt, preferred to adopt a child of their own religion (e.g., Protestant women preferring to adopt children born to a Protestant birth mother), yet in their analysis of which demographic factors increased a woman's propensity to seek to adopt no measures of religion were included. Jones' (2008) analysis of the 2002 data did not include the preferences of the religion of an adoptive child nor a consideration of religious affiliation or practices on propensity to adopt

Religious motivations to adopt among adoptive parents

In addition to examining ways that religious affiliation and religiosity impact the consideration of adoption and taking steps to adopt, research has also directly measured the frequency of religious motivation among adoptive and foster parents and the ways that this motivation is associated with choices families make, parenting practices, and outcomes. This research has found that a substantial minority of adoptive families endorse religious motivations in their choice to adopt. Specifically, Brooks and James (2003) reported that 24 percent of their sample of domestic adopters in California reported that religious or humanitarian motivations were present in their decision to adopt. Similarly, Berry, Barth, and Needell (1996) found that religious and humanitarian motivations were present for 27 percent of their sample of US parents who had domestically adopted. Among studies including participants with higher levels of religiosity, religious motivation is reported even more frequently. Belanger, Copeland, and Cheung (2008) reported that 64 percent of families adopting domestically in areas of Texas and Louisiana stated that their faith was essential in their decision to adopt, with only 5 percent of the sample indicating that their faith was not associated with their adoption decision. The presence of religious motivation has also been examined frequently within the context of foster care. Studies in the US that utilized nationally representative datasets of current and former foster parents have found that religious motivations to foster were endorsed by 11 percent (Rhodes, Cox, Orme, & Coakley, 2006) and 13 percent (Howell-Moroney, 2014) of families. Among Canadian foster parents, 15 percent reported that they chose to foster due to their religious calling (Rodger, Cummings, & Leschied, 2006). Additionally, in smaller samples recruited through child welfare agencies, religious reasons were among the top five most commonly selected motivations to foster across several studies (De Maeyer, Vanderfaeillie, Vanschoonlandt, Robberechts, & Van Holen, 2014; Gillis-Arnold, Crase, Stockdale, & Shelley, 1998). Among the general population who has not adopted, Tyebjee (2003) also found that religious motivation for US families open to adopting was frequently reported. Specifically, among those in the sample that expressed an openness to considering adoption, motivation to adopt due to religious beliefs about caring for children was endorsed by the majority of participants (57 percent definitely applied, 29 percent somewhat applied). Additionally, 22 percent (Dave Thomas Foundation for Adoption, 2017) of those considering becoming foster parents in the US stated that they are motivated to do so by their religious faith. While these motivations are frequently endorsed by adoptive and foster families, it is important to acknowledge that they are often not the sole motivation endorsed and it is common for families to simultaneously express multiple motivations (Berry et al., 1996). Additionally, Perry (2017) has critiqued research on self-professed religious motivation to adopt by suggesting that expressed religious motivations can also be viewed, at times, as "vocabularies of motive" which religious individuals might use when describing their actions in particular contexts where self-interested motivations might be less socially acceptable to endorse.

Research has also been conducted to examine the ways that religious motivation affects the decisions that adoptive families make while taking steps to adopt. Adoptive families with higher levels of religious motivation are more likely to adopt children with special needs, such as severe behavioral and emotional difficulties (Belanger, Cheung, & Cordova, 2012) or cognitive or developmental disabilities (Glidden, 1985; Jennings, 2010). Families with greater religious motivations have also been reported to have larger family sizes, adopting more children and/or adopting children in addition to biological children already in the home (Belanger et al., 2012; Helder, Timmermans, & Gunnoe, 2019). Additionally, families who endorse religious motivations to adopt are more open to adopting transracially (Brooks & James, 2003). Among the general population this holds true as well, as individuals who report higher levels of religious practice (more frequent prayer, reading of religious texts, and service attendance) were more supportive of the practice of transracial adoption (Perry, 2010). However, research examining the link between approval of transracial adoption and self-identified religious affiliation suggests a more complex relationship, with Protestants in the general population less supportive of transracial adoption than Catholics and those identifying as non-religious (Perry, 2010). Similarly, among social workers, Fenster (2003) found that White Protestant social workers were less supportive of transracial adoption than White social workers who identified as Catholic, Jewish, or other. Among Black social workers, Fenster (2003) did not find a relationship between religious affiliation and views on transracial adoption.

Several studies have also examined whether religious motivations to adopt might be associated with parenting practices. Across both domestic (Reilly & Platz, 2003) and international (Helder et al., 2019) adoption samples, families who were more religious or endorsed religious motivations to adopt tended to be stricter and place a higher emphasis on obedience in their parenting practices. Reilly and Platz (2003) additionally found that adoptive parents with higher levels of religiosity were more likely to support the use of corporal punishment.

Additionally, a small body of literature has examined the link between religiosity, religious motivations to adopt, and outcomes for children and families. With regard to child outcomes of behavioral adjustment, studies that have examined parent-reported religiosity and support from religious communities found that higher religious support was associated with fewer behavioral problems among adopted children (Belanger et al., 2012). This is consistent with research outside of the adoption context which has linked greater parent religiosity with fewer child behavior problems and less adolescent risk-taking, even when controlling for demographic factors and other predictors, such as peer relationships (summarized in Bridges & Moore, 2002). However, research that has examined religious motivations to adopt and their longitudinal relationship with later child behavioral outcomes, reports that religious motivations are not a significant predictor of child behavioral adjustment after controlling for relevant demographic factors (Helder et al., 2019). Similarly, Kumsta, Rutter, Stevens, and Sonuga-Barke (2010) also found that types of motivation in their study (e.g., infertility vs. altruism) were unrelated to child behavioral outcomes. Child attachment outcomes and their relationship with initial parent motivations have also been examined. In the context of foster care, Cole (2005) reported higher levels of insecure attachment among infants whose foster parents endorsed religious motivations to foster. However, this was not replicated when examined within an international adoption context, with both Helder et al. (2019) and Kumsta et al. (2010) reporting no links between parent motivation type and child attachment quality.

Research examining the link between religious motivations and parent outcomes is similarly mixed in terms of its findings. Belanger et al. (2008) reported that higher levels of religiosity and the presence of religious motivations to adopt were associated with lower parenting stress. However, Smith (2011) and Helder et al. (2019) found that religious motivation to adopt was unrelated to parenting stress when controlling for age at adoption.

Very little research exists that examines the impact of religiosity on outcomes such as adoption dissolution, though what does exist finds that parents who agree that "the adoption was part of God's plan" had a reduced incidence of adoption dissolution (Belanger et al., 2012). Relatedly, in a qualitative study of foster parents, Buehler, Cox, and Cuddeback (2003) reported that 80 percent of foster families cited faith or church support as a contributor to their success in caring for their foster children.

To summarize, religious motivations to adopt are present in a number of families who adopt children. Research consistently suggests that religious motivations impact choices adoptive parents make, such as an increased willingness to adopt children with special needs and to have larger families. The literature that examines the relationships between religious motivations and parenting practices and outcomes is quite small at this time. Findings consistently suggest that higher religiosity and religious motivation to adopt predict stricter discipline approaches. Yet among studies examining child and parent outcomes findings are quite mixed, which is likely due to significant methodological differences among studies, including whether the analysis examined religiosity more generally or religious motivations to adopt specifically, variability in sample characteristics, and differences in approaches to operationalizing religiosity and religious motivations. This last issue could be especially important in explaining differences in findings, as several researchers have pointed out that religious motivation is not a monolithic concept and likely can be subdivided into several types of religious motivation, some of which might result in positive outcomes (Firmin, Pugh, Markham, Sohn, & Gentry, 2017b). For example, religious motivations that are primarily driven by a sense of obligation, duty, or external pressures from a religious community (see Cole, 2005) might be differentially associated with poorer outcomes compared to intrinsic religious motivations, such as adoption due to an outflow of personal faith values, relationship with God, and calling (described in Marx, 1990). Additionally, many of the outcome studies are cross-sectional in design (Belanger et al., 2008, 2012; Cole, 2005; Reilly & Platz, 2003; Smith, 2011) and ask parents to retrospectively report on religious motivations, which limits the ability to make strong conclusions about the impact of religious motivations over time. Much more research, especially longitudinal studies that operationalize religious motivation consistently, is needed to better understand the link between religious motivations to adopt and outcomes for adopted children and their families.

Religious meaning-making in adoption

Beyond examining religious motivations to adopt, several studies have also examined ways that adoptive families utilize religiosity and spirituality to frame and give meaning to their adoption experiences and vice versa. Thus far, all of the existing research has focused on the adoptive parents' perspective, rather than adopted individuals themselves, and the majority of the studies have been qualitative in nature. Recently, Wrobel et al. (2018) examined interview responses of 15 adoptive mothers from the Minnesota-Texas Adoption Research Project (Grotevant & McRoy, 1998; Grotevant, McRoy, Wrobel, & Ayers-Lopez, 2013) regarding religious meaning associated with the adoption of their children. All adoptive mothers identified as Christian and were religiously active. Within the four domains identified (Prayer, Influence of Religious/Church Community, God's Plan, Religious Importance for the Family), the most frequent categories endorsed by the mothers as influencing religious meaning were: (1) God had an active role in the adoption process (e.g., felt God was in control and had a plan, God provided an avenue for adoption after infertility) and (2) discussion of adoption with other religious individuals (e.g., clergy, other church members).

Among common themes emerging across other studies examining this issue, one was that adoptive parents found that their faith provided them with hope for the future in the context of their adoption process (Belanger et al., 2008; Foli, Hebdon, Lim, & South, 2017; Marx, 1990). Belanger et al. (2008) suggested that this might be evident in their finding that higher religiosity was linked with lower parenting stress. A second theme was that participants' faith played an important role in coping with uncertainty (Foli et al., 2017), disappointments (Jennings, 2010), and fear (Marx, 1990) that adoptive parents experienced throughout the adoption process and in their family life post-adoption. Third, several studies found that participants described that faith was central to developing trust in God's will, such that challenges they encountered as a part of the adoption were a part of life (Foli et al., 2017) or "God's plan" (Firmin, Pugh, Markham, Sohn, & Gentry, 2017a; Marx, 1990) and that God would provide (Firmin et al., 2017a; Foli et al., 2017) and/or God's plan would prevail (Marx, 1990). A fourth theme raised across several studies was that faith communities provided significant support in the adjustment of adoptive families, both initially and after adoptions were finalized (Belanger et al., 2012; Firmin et al., 2017a; Foli et al., 2017; Wrobel et al., 2018). Last, Firmin et al. (2017a) reported on ways that evangelical Christian participants reported that the adoption experience gave greater meaning and depth to their faith, specifically that they formed a more mature faith because of experiences related to the adoption and developed a deeper understanding of faith concepts, such as God's grace and unconditional love.

Implications for policy and practice

The findings described in this chapter have a number of relevant implications for researchers, adoption agencies, and practitioners serving adoptive families and adoptees. Among adoption scholars, more research is needed to examine the association between religious affiliation, religiosity, and considering, taking steps, and adopting a child. Much of the literature that has provided insight into these relationships explores how a variety of fertility and demographic factors influence a woman's propensity to initiate and progress in the adoption process. Since the more macro-level work on adoption explores how certain religious cultures frame adoption as a way to honor God, and how faith-based adoption agencies work with specific denominations and churches to motivate individuals to adopt, it is important to examine if and how that is playing out in the micro-level decisions of religious and non-religious people. Additionally, the inconsistent findings in regard to the influence of race and socioeconomic status on individuals considering or taking steps to adopt illustrate that not only should they be a focus of future research, but specific attention should be given to how they interact with religious affiliation and religiosity to provide insight into adoptive behaviors.

Furthermore, while a number of studies document that religious motivations to adopt or foster are present for a significant number of families, there is a dearth of research examining the ways that these motivations influence parenting and outcomes for adoptees and adoptive families. What little research does exist has used widely varying methods to assess religious motivations and religiosity, making drawing conclusions across studies quite difficult. Notably, there is little literature on this topic from the adopted individuals' perspective. Researchers could examine outcomes from the adoptees' perspective when their adoptive parents endorsed religious motivations. Additionally, it would be valuable to explore how adopted persons do or do not use religious themes in understanding and framing their narratives of their own adoption. Since adoptive parents and adoptees make choices within structural and cultural contexts, it would be interesting to determine the extent to which their self-described experiences, perspectives, opinions, and activities reflect the values and actions encouraged by their religious communities and institutions.

The findings summarized above can also inform adoption agencies seeking to find adoptive homes for children. It is important to provide empirical, scientifically sound data because conclusions from projects that lack validity or accuracy might be used to incorrectly inform adoption agency practices, funding, and legislation (see Perry's critique of Barna Frames' research, 2017, pp. 57–59). Religious individuals are more likely to consider adopting, though not necessarily to complete an adoption. Agencies looking to recruit potential foster and adoptive caregivers could focus attention on these religious communities and the factors that could move them from considering to completing adoption. However, the strength of the relationship between religiosity and considering adoption varies by race and ethnic group, so this might not be as effective a strategy for recruiting adoptive families of color. Within the research on religious motivations to adopt, families adopting who endorsed religious motivations were more likely to adopt difficult-to-place children and utilize existing social networks (such as faith communities) to provide support. This is important recruitment information for agencies looking to place older children and children with more significant care needs.

It is hard to draw firm conclusions about outcomes for adopted individuals and families when religious motivations are present, due to the dearth of research and the variability in methods. At the very least, religious motivations are generally not found to be related to poorer outcomes for adopted children and their parents. More research is needed, but at this point agencies and adoption practitioners should not be concerned that parents endorsing religious motivations to adopt (especially intrinsic religious motivations) are at risk for negative outcomes.

References

ABBA Fund. (n.d.). Home page. Retrieved from www.abbafund.org

al-Azhary Sonbol, A. (1995). Adoption in Islamic society: A historical perspective. In E. Warnock Fernea (Ed.), *Children in the Muslim Middle East* (pp. 45–67). Austin, TX: University of Texas Press.

Bachrach, C. A., London, K. A., & Maza, P. L. (1991). On the path to adoption: Adoption seeking in the United States, 1988. *Journal of Marriage and Family*, *53*(3), 705–718. Retrieved from: www.jstor.org/stable/352745

Bausch, R. S. (2006). Predicting willingness to adopt a child: A consideration of demographic and attitudinal factors. *Sociological Perspectives*, *49*(1), 47–65. doi:10.1525/sop.2006.49.1.47

Belanger, K., Cheung, M., & Cordova, W. (2012). The role of worker support and religious support in African American special needs adoption: The Bennett Chapel experience. *Adoption Quarterly*, *15*(3), 185–205. doi:10.1080/10926755.2012.700299

Belanger, K., Copeland, S., & Cheung, M. (2008). The role of faith in adoption: Achieving positive adoption outcomes for African American children. *Child Welfare, 87*(2), 99–123.

Bernal, R., Hu, L., Moriguchi, C., & Nagypal, E. (2007). *Child adoptions in the United States: Historical trends and the determinants of adoption demand and supply 1951–2002.* Unpublished manuscript. Retrieved from http://faculty.wcas.northwestern.edu/~cmo938/adoptAEA.pdf

Berry, M., Barth, R. P., & Needell, B. (1996). Preparation, support, and satisfaction of adoptive families in agency and independent adoptions. *Child and Adolescent Social Work Journal, 13*(2), 157–183. doi:10.1007/BF01876644

Bonham, G. S. (1977). Who adopts: The relationship of adoption and social-demographic characteristics of women. *Journal of Marriage and Family, 39*(2), 295–306. Retrieved from: www.jstor.org/stable/351125

Bridges, L. J., & Moore, K. A. (2002). *Religious involvement and children's well-being: What research tells us (and what it doesn't).* Child Trends Research Brief. Retrieved from www.childtrends.org/wp-content/uploads/2002/09/ReligiosityRB.pdf

Brooks, D., & James, S. (2003). Willingness to adopt Black foster children: Implications for child welfare policy and recruitment of adoptive families. *Children and Youth Services Review, 25*(5–6), 463–489. doi:10.1016/S0190-7409(03)00031-8

Buehler, C., Cox, M. E., & Cuddeback, G. (2003). Foster parents' perceptions of factors that promote or inhibit successful fostering. *Qualitative Social Work, 2*(1), 61–83. doi:10.1177/1473325003002001281

Chandra, A., Abma, J., Maza, P. L., & Bachrach, C. A. (1999). Adoption, adoption seeking, and relinquishment for adoption in the United States. *Advance data from vital and health statistics* (Vol. 306). Hyattsville, MD: National Center for Health Statistics. https://pdfs.semanticscholar.org/28b8/53b807cffb0fcaddc130e659b060db07fb45.pdf?_ga=2.199394350.1247636183.1573245483-2087845013.1573245483

Coburn, C. K., & Smith, M. (1999). *Spirited lives: How nuns shaped Catholic culture and American life, 1836–1920.* Chapel Hill, NC: University of North Carolina Press.

Cole, S. A. (2005). Foster caregiver motivation and infant attachment: How do reasons for fostering affect relationships? *Child and Adolescent Social Work Journal, 22*, 441–457. doi:10.1007/s10560-005-0021-x

Daly, J. (2015, September 4). Let's make this headline happen: "Church wipes out foster care adoption list". *DailyFocus.*

Dave Thomas Foundation for Adoption. (2017). *2017 US adoption attitudes survey.* Retrieved from www.davethomasfoundation.org/wp-content/uploads/2018/02/2017-adoption-attitudes-survey-us.pdf

De Maeyer, S., Vanderfaeillie, J., Vanschoonlandt, F., Robberechts, M., & Van Holen, F. (2014). Motivation for foster care. *Children and Youth Services Review, 36*, 143–149. doi:10.1016/j.childyouth.2013.11.003

Fenster, J. (2003). Race, religion, altruism, and the transracial adoption debate: A survey of Catholic, Protestant, and Jewish social workers. *Social Thought, 22*(1), 45–61. doi:10.1080/15426432.2003.9960325

Firmin, M. W., Pugh, K. C., Markham, R. L., Sohn, V. A., & Gentry, E. N. (2017a). Outcomes of adoption for Christian adoptive parents: A qualitative study. *Journal of Psychology and Christianity, 36*, 16–28. Retrieved from https://search.proquest.com/docview/1925376896?accountid=9844

Firmin, M. W., Pugh, K. C., Markham, R. L., Sohn, V. A., & Gentry, E. N. (2017b). Perspectives regarding motivations for adoption by Christian adoptive parents: A qualitative study. *Journal of Psychology and Theology, 45*(1), 58–68. doi:10.1177/009164711704500105

Foli, K. J., Hebdon, M., Lim, E., & South, S. C. (2017). Transitions of adoptive parents: A longitudinal mixed-method analysis. *Archives of Psychiatric Nursing, 31*, 483–492. doi:10.1016/j.apnu.2017.06.007

Gillis-Arnold, R., Crase, S. J., Stockdale, D. F., & Shelley, M. C. (1998). Parenting attitudes, foster parenting attitudes, and motivations of adoptive and nonadoptive foster parent trainees. *Children and Youth Services Review, 20*, 715–732. doi:10.1016/S0190-7409(98)00033-4

Glidden, L. M. (1985). Adopting mentally handicapped children: Family characteristics. *Adoption & Fostering, 9*(3), 53–56. doi:10.1177/030857598500900314

Grotevant, H. D., & McRoy, R. G. (1998). *Openness in adoption: Exploring family connections.* Thousand Oaks, CA: Sage.

Grotevant, H. D., McRoy, R. G., Wrobel, G. M., & Ayers-Lopez, S. (2013). Contact between adoptive and birth families: Perspectives from the Minnesota/Texas Adoption Research Project. *Child Development Perspectives, 7*, 193–198. doi:10.1111/cdep.12039

Helder, E. J., Timmermans, H., & Gunnoe, M. L. (2019). Religious motivation to adopt as a predictor of adoptive family structure, parental discipline, and outcomes. Under review.

Hollingsworth, L. D. (2000). Who seeks to adopt a child? *Adoption Quarterly, 3*(3), 1–23. doi:10.1300/J145v03n03_01

Howell-Moroney, M. (2014). The empirical ties between religious motivation and altruism in foster parents: Implications for faith-based initiatives in foster care and adoption. *Religions, 5*(3), 720. doi:10.3390/rel5030720

Ishizawa, H., & Kubo, K. (2014). Factors affecting adoption decisions: Child and parental characteristics. *Journal of Family Issues, 35*(5), 627. doi:10.1177/0192513X13514408

Jennings, P. K. (2010). "God had something else in mind": Family, religion, and infertility. *Journal of Contemporary Ethnography, 39*(2), 215–237. doi:10.1177/0891241609342432

Jones, J. (2008). Adoption experiences of women and men and demand for children to adopt by women. *Vital health statistics* (Vol. 23). National Center for Health Statistics.

Joyce, K. (2013). *The child catchers: Rescue, trafficking, and the new gospel of adoption*. New York: Public Affairs.

Kumsta, R., Rutter, M., Stevens, S., & Sonuga-Barke, E. J. (2010). Risk, causation, mediation, and moderation. *Monographs of the Society for Research in Child Development, 75*(1), 187–211. doi:10.1111/j.1540-5834.2010.00556.x

Lamb, K. A. (2008). Exploring adoptive motherhood: Adoption-seeking among Hispanic and Non-Hispanic White women. *Adoption Quarterly, 11*(3), 155–175. doi:10.1080/10926750802421974

Malm, K., & Welti, K. (2010). Exploring motivations to adopt. *Adoption Quarterly, 13*, 185–203. doi:10.1080/10926755.2010.524872

Marr, E., & Hoeksema, S. (2019). Who adopts? Characteristics of women in the process of adoption. Under review.

Marx, J. (1990). Better me than somebody else: Families reflect on their adoption of children with developmental disabilities. *Journal of Children in Contemporary Society, 21*(3–4), 141–174.

National Center for Health Statistics (NCHS). (2016). 2013–2015 National Survey of Family Growth public use data and documentation. *Center for Disease Control National Center for Health Statistics*. Hyattsville, MD. Retrieved from http://cdc.gov/nchs/nsfg/nsfg_2013_2015_puf.htm

One Church, One Child. (2019). About us. Retrieved April 30, 2019 from www.nationalococ.org/about.html

Park, N. K., & Wonch Hill, P. (2014). Is adoption an option? The role of importance of motherhood and fertility help-seeking in considering adoption. *Journal of Family Issues, 35*(5), 601. doi:10.1177/0192513X13493277

Perry, S. (2010). The effects of race, religion, and religiosity on attitudes towards transracial adoption. *Journal of Comparative Family Studies, 41*(5), 837–853. doi:10.3138/jcfs.41.5.837

Perry, S. L. (2017). *Growing God's family: The global orphan care movement and the limits of evangelical activism*. New York: New York University Press.

Reilly, Thom and Platz, Laurie. (2003) Characteristics and challenges of families who adopt children with special needs: An empirical study. *Children and Youth Services. 25*(10), 781–803.

Rhodes, K., Cox, M. E., Orme, J. G., & Coakley, T. (2006). Foster parents' reason for fostering and foster family utilization. *Journal of Sociology and Social Welfare, 33*, 105–126.

Rodger, S., Cummings, A., & Leschied, A. W. (2006). Who is caring for our most vulnerable children?: The motivation to foster in child welfare. *Child Abuse & Neglect, 30*(10), 1129–1142. doi:10.1016/j.chiabu.2006.04.005

Smith, K. M. (2011). *Intercountry adoptive parents and parental stress: Are religious faith and empathy supportive factors?* (Doctoral Dissertation). Retrieved from ProQuest Dissertations Publishing. (Accession no. 3465514).

Smith, T. W., Davern, M., Freese, J., & Hout, M. (2018). General social surveys, 1972–2016 [machine-readable data file]. Chicago, IL: NORC. Data accessed from the GSS Data Explorer website at gssdataexplorer.norc.org.

Smolin, D. M. (2012). Of orphans and adoption, parents and the poor, exploitation and rescue: A scriptural and theological critique of the evangelical Christian adoption and orphan care movement. *Regent Journal of International Law, 8*(2), 267–324.

Tyebjee, T. (2003). Attitude, interest, and motivation for adoption and foster care. *Child Welfare, 82*(6), 685–706.

Van Laningham, J. L., Scheuble, L. K., & Johnson, D. R. (2012). Social factors predicting women's consideration of adoption. *Michigan Family Review, 16*(1), 1–21. doi:10.3998/mfr.4919087.0016.101

Vandivere, S., Malm, K., & Radel, L. (2009). *Adoption USA: A chartbook based on the 2007 National Survey of Adoptive Parents*. Washington, DC: The US Department of Health and Human Services, Office of the Assistant Secretary for Planning and Evaluation.

Wrobel, G. M., Hook, C., Magnusson, S., Ruff, M., Nelson, T., Sybrant, S., & Thorison, M. (2018, July). Adopted mother's religious meaning regarding adoption. In E. Helder (Chair). *Explorations of family processes in adoptive families from childhood to adulthood*. Symposium conducted at the 6th International Conference on Adoption Research, Montreal, Canada.

Yarden, O. (2012). Adoption in Judaism. *Dialog: A Journal of Theology*, *51*(4), 276–283. doi:10.1111/j.1540-6385.2012.007

22

ADOPTIVE MICROAGGRESSIONS

Historical foundations, current research, and practical implications

Karin Garber[1]

Although adoption is becoming more prominent and accepted in society as a means for building a family (Fisher, 2003), adoptive individuals and families may continue to experience negative sociocultural experiences that dismiss and degrade their kinship ties (March, 1995; March & Miall, 2000; Wegar, 2000). While, historically, degrading messages have been expressed more intensively and obviously, currently many marginalized groups continue to experience a subtler and concealed form of prejudice from the more powerful dominant group (Sue, 2010b). The microaggressions framework conceptualizes the different types of slights that can occur to marginalized individuals (Sue et al., 2007). More recently, this framework has been used to delineate and study adoptive individuals' and families' experiences of prejudice in the context of a bionormative society where biological ties are more valued and perceived as more legitimate compared to other types of kinship networks (Baker, 2008). Underlying these microaggressions are values and expectations around family, historical practices of adoption, and stigmatizing narratives linked with adoption triad members. This chapter focuses on the history and evolution of adoptive microaggressions and their significance in describing experiences of more covert adoption-related stigma; then it presents the most current research on adoptive microaggressions and offers practical implications. While the adoptive microaggressions literature converges with the more general microaggressions field in some aspects, it also illuminates experiences and contexts unique to adoption.

The historical context of adoption

Adoption is a sociolegal practice where adoptive parents incur parental rights and responsibilities after they have been terminated by biological parents (Siegel & Smith, 2012). The "adoption triad" is comprised of three main parties: the adopted person, the adoptive parent(s), and the biological parent(s). While awareness of adoption has increased and forming families through adoption has become more socially acceptable (Fisher, 2003), various contexts shape the way that society perceives adoption today. Adoption has a complicated history punctuated by controversy, and therefore its practices have shifted with the current of the sociopolitical times and cultural values. Adoptive practices and history can exemplify how secrecy and concerns related to bionormativity created an environment in which stigma could proliferate.

Although adoption has informally existed for centuries, its specific legal practices and social contexts have changed over the years (Carp, 1998). Adoption in the US first became a recognized legal practice in the late 1800s. In the US, adoption was seen primarily as a pragmatic practice that could resolve social issues for children born out of wedlock (Zamostny, O'Brien, Baden, & Wiley, 2003). As adoption became legalized and regulated, closed adoptions predominated, where birth parents did not have contact with the adoptive family. To aid in secrecy, social workers "matched" children with their families according to their physical appearance, which allowed families to disguise the fact that the child was not biologically related to the adoptive parents (Zamostny et al., 2003). Adoption professionals, believing that confidentiality was necessary to protect adoptive children and families, also reinforced concealment by not allowing adoptive families to view records of court proceedings (Carp, 1998). While eventually adoptive parents were allowed access to proceedings, information was limited, and the decision to disclose about the adoption to the child remained with the adoptive parents (Carp, 1998).

Generally, Carp (2009) identifies the 1950s as a time when adoptions in several countries burgeoned due to war and ensuing socioeconomic dynamics, culminating in changes to secrecy in adoption. For example, in England, the Adoption of Children Act of 1926 solidified the practice of legal adoptions in England through the Tomlin Committee, which mandated open adoptions between adoptive parents and birth parents (Carp, 2009). This decision allowed for access to birth records for all triad members. However, an era of secrecy was later ushered in by the Adoption of Children Act in 1949, when birth parents lost legal power to obtain information about the adoptive parents, and adoptees' access to birth records was only obtainable through a court order (Carp, 2009). New Zealand also had open access to adoption records from 1881–1915. However, in 1915, New Zealand became the first country to use amended birth certificates, where an adoptee's original birth certificate would be altered to include their adoptive parents' names instead of their biological parents' identities (Carp, 2009). By 1955, the Adoption Act in New Zealand was passed, guaranteeing legislative reform enforcing closed birth records (Carp, 2009).

The majority of significant policy and cultural changes shaping the practice of adoption has occurred mostly in the late 20th century (Zamostny et al., 2003). Generally, changes in more open communication about adoption coincided with researchers delving into the psychological consequences of secrecy. Early studies discovered that adoptive families felt that instead of trying to mask dissimilarities in the family, they would rather unite in sharing a "same fate" together through having discussions about the struggles they endured as adoptive families (Kirk, 1964). In the 1970s, adoption practices in the US were advanced by social movements started by adoptees pushing for further openness in communication about adoption, access to original birth certificates, and increased awareness of adoptive issues (Grotevant & McRoy, 1998). Similar movements were occurring in Australia in the 1970s where adoption advocates championed open access to records, which later led to practice reform between the 1980s–1990s (Higgins, 2012).

Even in the last few decades, confidentiality and "openness" remain substantial and relevant concerns in adoption. Grotevant and McRoy (1998) outlined more current justifications in the field for maintaining confidentiality among triad members, including the interest of the birth mother so that she can fully grieve the loss of her child, the adoptive parents so they can independently raise their child, and the adopted individual such that serious identity issues could be avoided. However, many researchers argue that often all adoption triad members can benefit from levels of openness, as this might lead to greater understanding and less confusion for everyone involved (Grotevant & McRoy, 1998; Neil, 2009). These findings can reorient the adoption field's conceptions of the "goodness" or "badness" of openness in adoption arrangements, which can aid in reducing the secrecy around adoption.

The stigmatization of adoption

Despite trends in openness, adoption still remains stigmatized due to its history of secrecy and shame, as well as sociopolitical and cultural contexts (Wegar, 2000; Zamostny et al., 2003). This secrecy has led to ignorance about adoption, which has affected societal attitudes and awareness of adoption over time. In the absence of education about adoption, stigmatizing historical narratives have formed the bedrock of collective prejudicial ideas that society has regarding adoptees, adoptive parents, and birth parents.

The birth mother narrative is a portrait of a young, poor woman with no scruples who had sex outside of marriage and birthed an "illegitimate" child (Garber & Grotevant, 2015; Wegar, 2000); birth fathers are often exempt altogether from this picture. Historically, birth mothers who had children out of wedlock and then placed the child for adoption were seen as deviant. If a woman was unable to fulfill her social role as a mother, she was considered morally inadequate and socially abnormal (Wegar, 1997). Furthermore, since the late 19th century, those in the adoption field and policy makers alike in the US and England viewed birth mothers as helpless, neurotic, or sexualized women needing to be controlled (Carp, 2009; Wegar, 1997). While before World War II, women who had children out of wedlock in the US were expected to keep their babies for religioethical reasons, after the war, birth mothers who had "sinned" could redeem themselves through terminating their parental rights (Wegar, 1997). In Catholic Ireland in the 1950s, religious dogma about women, sexuality, and family encouraged closed adoptions such that women could hide illegitimate children that brought shame upon the individual, the family, and the state (Kelly, 2009). Thus, patterns of sociopolitical and religious norms have all contributed to the stigmatization of birth mothers throughout the history of adoption.

The social norms of motherhood and parenthood also affected adoptive parents who were disparaged by their communities and seen in a critical and unfavorable light. Adoptive parents were often portrayed as infertile couples who were unable to biologically conceive (Wegar, 2000). Childless married couples were rebuffed by society for violating social norms in either being "selfish" in choosing to not have children, or seen as defective and inadequate for not having the ability to biologically conceive (Miall, 1987; Wegar, 2000). If a childless couple did decide to adopt a child, their status as parents was not seen as completely legitimate because their family still violated fertility and kinship norms (Miall, 1987). Miall (1987, p. 35) described a kinship system as one that "defines which individuals in a society are related to one another and how they should behave toward one another." In the US, the foundation of kinship systems is considered to be blood or biological ties (Miall, 1987). Because adoption violates kinship and fertility norms, adoptive parents have been stigmatized and viewed as deviant due to the lack of consanguinity, or sharing the same blood, in their ties with their child (Kressierer & Bryant, 1996). Society's belief in the importance of consanguinity is perpetuated and normalized in everyday language when people express the notion that the adoptive parents are not the "real" parents of their adopted child, or that adoption is a secondary choice to having a biological child (Fisher, 2003; Miall, 1987).

Due to these historical narratives and values around kinship ties, children who were conceived out of wedlock were considered "illegitimate" or "bastards," and were perceived as coming from inferior backgrounds (Kressierer & Bryant, 1996; Wegar, 2000; Zamostny et al., 2003). Bionormative perspectives have emphasized the idea that adoptees come from disadvantaged backgrounds and are genetically inferior to those who have biological ties to parents (Wegar, 2000). Adopted children were believed to be plagued with identity issues, developmental delays, and other psychological concerns (Wegar, 2000). Empirical studies in psychology have reinforced this notion as they have historically tended to examine adoptees in clinical contexts from a more psychopathological framework in looking for behavioral and psychosocial disorders, substance abuse, identity issues, and attentional/learning symptoms that differentiated them from their non-adopted peers (Brodzinsky, 2008).

Psychological frameworks of adoption have also concentrated heavily on the idea of loss as being inherent to adoption, whether it is the adoptee losing a birth parent, the birth parent losing a child, or the adoptive parents' physical or psychological loss of a birth child (Leon, 2002). However, Leon (2002) has argued that loss might not be quite as inherent to adoption as the field once suggested, because feelings of loss might not apply to all adoptive situations, and loss could be strongly exacerbated by societal stigmatization of adoption. Framing loss as the sole lens for understanding adoption might be informative for some adoptive experiences, but it can also maintain stigmatization or only provide a unidimensional view of adoption; indeed, adoption can also include positive and meaningful gain of familial bonds.

While studies that look at the internal psychopathology of adopted children have been prominent over the years, studies investigating sociocultural values imparted to adopted people and families in the form of stigma and prejudice have been relatively scant. March's (1995) study found that the stigma of adoption motivated adult adoptees, who were aware of differences they had with their adoptive families, to search for their birth parents in order to feel a sense of normalcy and wholeness after being reunited.

The US media has also transmitted and perpetuated particular cultural values around adoption. Out of the 292 news stories related to adoption between 2001 and 2004, the media covered and depicted more negative than positive stories related to adoption. Although there were positive stories about adoptive *families* reported, news about adopted *individuals* tended to propagate negative claims about their emotional issues such as feelings of loss, antisocial behaviors, and identity issues (Kline, Karel, & Chatterjee, 2006).

Despite adoption being depicted in a more favorable way in society (Fisher, 2003), some adoptive families continue to experience prejudice, stigma, and feelings of non-normativity (Wegar, 2000). These seemingly contradictory findings could possibly be explained by consulting the social psychological literature on implicit bias. Implicit bias occurs when one openly espouses anti-discrimination rhetoric and opposes stereotyping, but might still unconsciously hold negative connotations or associations of particular groups (e.g., Dasgupta, 2008). Thus, although people might express positive sentiments about a group, they could still hold negative prejudices. These prejudices then become apparent when negative messages about adoption are coded in language used to describe adoption and adoptive families.

Historical, sociopolitical, cultural, and religious contexts all shape the way society perceives adoption and adoptive families currently. Over the years, studies in the adoption literature have consistently reported that the stigmatization of adoption persists as well as notions of adoption being an inferior family structure (March & Miall, 2000; Wegar, 2000; Zamostny et al., 2003). As it becomes less permissible to express openly derogatory comments, microaggressions have become a vehicle for communicating and reinforcing historically oppressive narratives about a marginalized group in a more socially acceptable mode of expression. Thus, the microaggressions literature has evolved into a relevant framework that underscores how subtle instances of prejudice, discrimination, and stigma continue to be communicated to people in marginalized social groups.

Research on racial microaggressions

Microaggressions, as defined by Sue et al. (2007, p. 271), are "Brief and commonplace daily verbal, behavioral, or environmental indignities, whether intentional or unintentional, that communicate hostile, derogatory, or negative … slights and insults towards people of color." Chester Pierce was the first person to coin and define the term (Pierce, Carew, Pierce-Gonzalez, & Willis, 1977), and Derald Wing Sue has garnered awareness around this concept to describe covert discriminatory experiences that people of color encounter. Sue et al. (2007) described that microaggressions can be organized into three different forms. He postulated that *microassaults* are the most overt and conscious form of microaggressions that aim to injure marginalized people through openly derogatory language and oppressive behaviors. *Microinsults* devalue a marginalized person's identity, background, or sociodemographic group (Sue et al., 2007). Although the initiator might not be aware of communicating a negative message toward the recipient, the message still contains a negative slight. A microinsult can be exemplified by a White American stating to a Black American, "You are so articulate." Although the White person might be trying to express a compliment, this message conveys the expectation that all Black Americans are less intelligent or ineloquent, and that Black Americans are a monolithic group with no variation in how they express themselves. *Microinvalidations* are often considered the subtlest form of microaggressions that nullify and undermine the worldview and experiences of people of color (Sue et al., 2007). For example, color blindness, which is the idea that race cannot be seen or perceived, can obfuscate the reality of racism and negate the racialized lived experiences of people of color.

Sue (2010a, 2010b) has written extensively on different microaggressive themes that occur to major racial groups in the US. Sue (2010b) hypothesized that each racial group will often experience certain themes of microaggressions specific to that group's historical narrative and ensuing societal perceptions of that particular race. For example, Latinx and Asian Americans might experience more microaggressions related to the theme *Alien in One's Own Land*, as Asians and Latinx individuals are regularly viewed as foreigners and their status as Americans is often questioned.

Furthermore, there is a growing literature on how the intersectionality of identities can influence the way that microaggressions are experienced. This research shows that those who identify with more than one marginalized group can experience microaggressions through the contexts of their multiple identities. For example, Asian and Latinx women in engineering programs, which are often dominated by men, reported experiences wherein their gender was experienced through the lens of their race/ethnicity (Camacho & Lord, 2011). Studies with adoptive individuals and families continue to extend Sue et al.'s (2007) microaggressions work by shaping unique theories significant to a new population.

Adoptive microaggressions research

The adoptive microaggression literature is in its nascent stages with only a few empirical studies conducted. Adoptive microaggressions reported by White adolescent adoptees in same-race families have been evidenced in empirical qualitative (Garber & Grotevant, 2015) and quantitative (Garber, 2014) studies. In Garber and Grotevant's (2015) study, all adoptive microaggressive themes were connected with adoption's stigmatized history and marginalizing narratives of all members of the adoption triad (i.e., birth parents being perceived as "rejecting" of their children, adoptive parents being portrayed as not "real" parents of their adopted child, and adopted individuals as being non-normative, marginalized, or inferior). Their typology of adoptive microaggressive themes was found to map onto Sue et al.'s (2007) categories of microinvalidations, microinsults, and microassaults.

Microinvalidations about adoption were similar to Sue et al.'s (2007) in that they negated or excluded a person's identity, thoughts, or feelings about adoption. Garber and Grotevant's (2015) themes such as *Silence about Adoption* and *Unacknowledged Identity Status* illuminated how adoption can fail to be validated, recognized, or discussed. For example, when a teacher assigns a family tree or genetic family history assignment, their lack of awareness of adoptive families might lead an adopted student to feel unseen and invalidated as they are unable to complete such a project. *Questioning Authenticity* was a more intense form of negation where open disbelief or willful rejection of an adopted person's identity occurred. These microinvalidations were connected to the historical roots of adoption, where secrecy, shame, and confidentiality were norms in the field and in families.

The absence of open communication and education about adoption, coupled with the cultural stigmatization of adoption, has led to ignorance and misinformation about adopted individuals and families; this was the foundation for microinsults. Microinsults formed the largest group of microaggressions in Garber and Grotevant's (2015) study, and included themes that communicated insensitivity, ignorance, or degrading messages related to adoption. Adoptive microinsult themes included *Overly Intrusive Questions* about an adoptee's personal adoptive history; *Assumptions of Bionormativity* that relayed biological familial ties were superior to adopted kinship networks; and *Being the Spokesperson for Adoption*, where adopted individuals were made to represent all adoptees or the "adoptive experience." Other microinsult themes were *Public "Outing,"* related to moments when adopted individuals had their adoptive status or details of their adoption publicly disclosed by a non-adopted person without permission, and *Adoptees as Non-Normative* where adopted individuals were viewed as strange, dysfunctional, or apart from those of "normal" biological families. It should be noted that adoptive microaggressions toward an adopted individual could be initiated from family members (including extended family, parents, and siblings), mentors, and peers (Baden, 2016; Garber, 2014). The microinsult theme *In-House Divisions within the Adoptive Family* occurred when the adopted person was made to feel unwanted, slighted, or separate from the adoptive family. For example, slights were relayed when adoptive parents did not respect the pace at which adopted individuals wished to discuss adoption, or when adoptive parents did not provide the adoptee with information about adoption when requested. The remaining microinsult themes were *Sensitivity*, where pity by non-adopted people was expressed due to their underlying assumptions that adoption was a "sensitive," taboo, or challenging topic for the adopted individual, *Recurring Confusion or Ignorance Regarding Adoption*, *Adoptees as Orphans*, *Negative Societal Portrayal of Adoption*, and *Negative Stereotypes about Birth Parents* (Garber & Grotevant, 2015). The last major category of microaggressions in Garber and Grotevant's (2015) study included a more overt microassault theme, *Using Adoption*, which was when a non-adopted person co-opted adoption and utilized it as a means for harming and demeaning the adoptee.

Other studies have drawn more from media, literature, and theory to conceptualize how microaggressions might manifest toward adopted individuals. Baden (2016) theorized an adoptive microaggressions framework that included microassaults, microinsults, and microinvalidations, as well as the important category of microfictions. Microfictions occur when an adopted individual's adoption history or process is altered, falsified, or omitted in a way that subverts the person's actual narrative and identity (Baden, 2016). Microfictions can also result when an adopted person's adoptive identity is hidden from them by their families or agencies. Much of Baden's (2016) conceptual framework converged with content in Garber and Grotevant's (2015) study, including themes such as *Biology Is Best/Normative*, *Bad Seed Adoptees*, and *Shameful/Inadequate Birth/First Parents*. Baden's (2016) and Garber and Grotevant's (2015) research also showed divergences related to which microaggressions are labeled as microinsults versus microinvalidations or microassaults. As adoptive microaggression research develops and expands, it would be beneficial to find a more consistent overarching framework for the field.

Baden's (2016) theory explicated microaggressive themes that occur to all members of the adoption triad, whereas Garber and Grotevant's (2015) study was conducted solely from the perspective of the adopted individual. According to Baden (2016), adoptees are considered by society to be "lucky" because their adoption "saved" them from perceived catastrophic or impoverished conditions (*Grateful Adoptees*); international adoptees also received messages that they should feel grateful or "special" to be adopted into Western countries with more "opportunities" (*Cultural Philanthropy*). Another adoptee-specific theme included *Cultural Limbo and Invalidation of Heritage*, which emphasized how racial/cultural identity can add complex layers to the experience of microaggressions for transracial adoptees. Adoptive parents were perceived as deficient in terms of their parenting skills due to their choice to adopt (*Pseudo/Inadequate Adoptive Parents*), or they were viewed as "rescuing" their children (*Altruistic Rescuers*). Birth parents, on the other hand, were often no longer believed to play a part in adoption after relinquishing their child (*Phantom Birth/First Parents*).

Baden's (2016) themes that more broadly touched on several triad members were *Adoption Is a Win-Win Situation*, related to the idea that adoption results in only positive outcomes for all involved in the adoption triad; *Commerce in Adoption*, which portrayed adopted individuals as commodities to be "bought" and adoptive parents as people who "purchase" their children; *Love Will Conquer All*, where love was considered to erase all challenges and issues that arise in adoption; and *Infantilizing Adoptees and Birth Parents*, which exemplified how adopted individuals were perpetually represented as children and birth parents as infantile or stunted. Other research also focused on the microaggressive experiences that adoptive parents reported due to their family structure. MacDonald (2016) discussed the "extraordinary" lens through which adoptive parents could be viewed, where society simultaneously praised parents for their efforts in raising "someone else's child" while also degrading the familial connection and relegating adoption to a less legitimate form of kinship.

The intersectionality of multiple identities in the context of adoptive microaggressions

Similar to the racial microaggressions literature, adoptive microaggressions research is beginning to exhibit how intersectionality influences the experience of microaggressions in relation to a person's multiple identities. Research on the intersectionality of identities is indispensable to the adoptive microaggressions literature in that it emphasizes the dimensionality and fluidity of identity, thus further humanizing the lived experience of individuals. Farr, Crain, Oakley, Cashen, and Garber (2016) studied how microaggressions and feelings of difference were reported by adopted children ages 6–11 years old with sexual minority parents. In this study, microaggression themes such as *Public Outing, Spokesperson, Questioning Legitimacy of Family, Stereotypes and Discrimination,* and *Teasing and Bullying* mirrored similar themes present in the adoptive literature (Garber & Grotevant, 2015) and further delineated microaggressions related to their family structure and parents' marginalized identities as sexual minorities. Microaggressive themes related to the children's family structure included *Heterosexism, Uncomfortable Disclosing, Fear of Rejection, Guard Up and Need for Security, Awareness of Difference in Own Family,* and *Internalized Stigma.* The adoptive microaggressions literature highlights that the questioning of legitimacy of adoption for an individual or family is salient across many current studies. Farr et al.'s (2016) study reaffirms this recurring finding and displays the problematic bionormative and heteronormative conceptualizations of what is a "family." Farr et al. (2016) also contributed themes of resiliency to their framework including *Resilience, Positive Feelings about Family,* and *Positive Feelings Specific to Lesbian and Gay Families* as an important reminder that resiliency, reframing, and building strong coping skills can still occur in the context of stigmatizing sociocultural values related to family and identity. Other investigations into the microaggressive experiences of adopted children in families headed by sexual minority parents also revealed that younger children tended to describe these events as occurring at a "low intensity" compared to older children, and several children displayed "neutrality" when discussing these events (Crain & Farr, 2014). This finding reflects similar adoptive microaggressions research with adolescents who report "neutral" emotional feelings toward microaggressive experiences (Garber, 2014). Reasons for feelings of neutrality in response to adoptive microaggressions can be related to differing developmental understandings of microaggressions, resiliency (Crain & Farr, 2014), or a desire to "fit in" with peers and family (Garber, 2014).

The intersection of adoptive and racial microaggressions that transracial adoptees experience is another growing area of investigation. Baden, Pinderhughes, Harrington, and Waddell (2013) analyzed microaggressive experiences that were reported by adoptive parents of Chinese children aged 6–10 years old using Baden's (2016) conceptual adoption microaggressions themes and Sue et al.'s (2007) racial microaggression framework. Harrington et al. (2014) advanced this work by discovering that Chinese adoptees tended to experience more adoptive microaggressions compared to racial microaggressions, indicating that race might be a more taboo subject in interpersonal interactions compared to adoption. They also recognized that the White adoptive parents in the study were both receivers of microaggressions from others (i.e., being perceived as "pseudo/inadequate parents"), as well as initiators of microaggressions to their children (i.e., relaying themes that "severed" the children's connection with birth parents).

Contextual variables might also influence the experience of microaggressions for transracial adoptees. Zhang, Zhang, and Pinderhughes' (2019) study showed that while transracial adoptees growing up in communities with a high level of diversity had greater awareness of racial microaggressions, they ultimately reported fewer racial microaggressions compared to transracial adoptees growing up in communities with less diversity. The authors suggested that living in a community with greater diversity, therefore, might be a protective factor for transracial adoptees.

This research also indicated that transracial adoptees are often navigating multiple microaggressive events at once, related to both their racial and adoptive identities. This can culminate in confusing and complex messages that are difficult to process. The authors concluded that developmental level can also be related to the perception of microaggressions, especially racial microaggressions (E. Zhang et al., 2019). Additionally, a study has relayed that cognitive developmental stage can also be related to children's ability to report on their experiences with adoptive microaggressions (DeBenedetto & Pinderhughes, 2016).

Parental racial socialization is also a factor that can be associated with transracial adoptees' understanding of microaggressions. Researchers revealed that parents who engaged with their transracially adopted children in more "empowering" discussions related to adoption and race tended to report fewer microaggressions (X. Zhang et al., 2019). While parental socialization about microaggressions in adoptive families might be beneficial, parents are not always able to perceive microaggressions or proactively intercede or collaborate with their children in responding to such events (Dolan, 2015; X. Zhang et al., 2018). However, when adoptive parents have increased awareness of their stigmatized "difference" due to their status as an adoptive family, they may further be able to recognize microaggressions that occur to their transracially adopted children (Morgan & Langrehr, 2018).

Other upcoming areas of research address how transracial adoptees might not only experience microaggressions from the dominant White culture, but also from others of the same race/ethnicity who were not adopted. Garber's (2016) research addresses the complicated interpersonal exchanges that occur between Korean American transracially adopted individuals and their Asian non-adopted peers. Intraracial/intraethnic microaggressions provide insight into the multiple spheres and contexts that a transracial adoptee is navigating. With further development in this area, the field can gain a more comprehensive picture of the differing environments, relationships, and cultures that transracially adopted people navigate.

Conclusion and practice implications

The research on adoptive microaggressions shows that stereotypes, prejudices, and expectations about adoption are still upheld by stigmatizing bionormative narratives that have become repackaged and propagated over time. Though the adoptive microaggressions literature is in its infancy, there are convergences in findings as well as unique differences highlighted by the various methods and participants. It is clear from the current adoptive microaggressions literature that these slights can occur across a wide range of development, from school aged children to adolescents to adults. Furthermore, adoptive microaggressions can occur to adopted people in different cultural contexts and environments, and by an array of other non-adopted individuals in their lives. While these experiences might be perceived, expressed, or understood in varying ways, at different intensities, and by various initiators, adoptive microaggressions continue to be a pervasive experience for adopted individuals and families.

In possessing a developmental lens for these microaggressions, those who work with adoptive individuals and families should understand that navigating these slights could be a long-term process and not necessarily a short-term concern. Being able to provide education to prospective adoptive families that emphasizes appropriate socialization and continued collaboration with their children throughout their development could be an important tool in proactively defending against microaggressions. When microaggressions do occur, modeling how to respond to them and then debriefing how the situation went for the adopted person could also be beneficial. It might be helpful to develop "stock answers" that families can decide to use in a given microaggressive situation, or, if an adopted person wishes to not confront these situations, parents can show support through respecting this decision (Garber & Grotevant, 2015). Responses to microaggressions might evolve based on development, resiliency and coping strategies, awareness of microaggressions, relationship of the initiator to the recipient, or desire in the moment to engage or disengage with the initiator.

Furthermore, adoptive parents should be taught about the themes in microaggressions frameworks such that they can raise awareness regarding moments when they or other family members or friends might initiate microaggressions. With this knowledge, parents could have discussions with non-adopted siblings, extended family members, mentors, teachers, neighbors, or peers about how these slights can reinforce negative stigma around adoption. Indeed, when families feel united in a "familial adoptive identity" and have a greater awareness of adoption stigma, members might be more motivated to perceive and interrupt negative messages perpetuated about adoption (Garber, 2014; Morgan & Langrehr, 2018). Parents could also find adoptive mentors for their children who can openly discuss and model how to navigate microaggressive experiences (Garber & Grotevant, 2015; Garber, French, & Grotevant, 2015; X. Zhang et al., 2019).

As fielding questions about adoption in interpersonal situations can be challenging and exhausting at times for adoptive individuals and families, it is helpful to have trainings on a more widespread scale that can educate many different types of practitioners about adoption to aid in preventing adoptive microaggressions. Researchers encourage the integration of adoption curriculum or training in educational spheres to prevent harmful messages from burgeoning in classrooms or other professional settings (Garber & Grotevant, 2015; E. Zhang et al., 2019). Trainings and educational systems can be a starting place for spreading more realistic narratives of adoption and adoptive families. In schools, this can additionally be a way to discuss, change, prevent, or substitute class projects that could be microaggressive to adopted people (e.g., a family tree assignment; see Chapter 33 for more information and resources). In a sociocultural sense, greater awareness of not only group-level identity and diversity (e.g., race, gender, sexual orientation, religion, etc.), but also familial diversity (e.g., adoption, intergenerational, single parent, etc.) can be an important addition to education.

Although microaggressive communications might be subtle, the pervasiveness can have resounding repercussions. For example, adoptive microaggressions can have an association with higher levels of negative perceptions of one's own adoption (Garber, 2014). The implications of adoptive microaggressions as they relate to mental health should be further investigated to understand the psychological and emotional toll constituted by these slights. With greater knowledge about the harm related to these slights, practitioners in health and social welfare fields should receive training specific to adoptive families in order to develop competence in this area (Baden, 2016). Crafting intake forms or initial consultations to ask about family background questions without conveying bionormative assumptions is an important first step in building positive relationships with adoptive families (Garber & Grotevant, 2015). Ceasing the use of bionormative language such as "real parents" or "your own children" and learning the preferred language of the client through open discussion can aid in ensuring that the practitioner is entering the client's world in a meaningful way. For practitioners, exploring and gaining more insight into one's own bionormative biases and assumptions can also challenge narratives about the desires, actions, thoughts, and feelings that adopted individuals, adoptive families, and birth parents are thought to have (Baden, 2016; Garber & Grotevant, 2015). Therapists and social workers should be aware if microaggressive language or themes are being enacted and reinforced in sessions, in an individual's family, or in other areas of an adopted person's life. Furthermore, practitioners working with adoptive families may also be vigilant if microfictions (Baden, 2016) are present or actively proliferating in sessions to conceal or alter information about an adopted person.

The idea of "control" (Garber, 2014; Garber & Grotevant, 2015) in the context of adoptive microaggressions is an overarching concept of all the current research in the field. Whether adopted individuals and families are being overlooked, outed, silenced, invalidated, questioned, or asked to be spokespersons for adoption, microaggressions evoke situations where the narrative of one's adoption and identity are taken out of the control of the adopted person or family and co-opted by others who repurpose these experiences within their expected and valued notion of what "family" is and who adoptees "are" or "should be" (Garber & Grotevant, 2015). Practitioners should be able to aid a member of the adoption triad in exploring their own beliefs and feelings around self-definition. In this way, the person might be able to retain control and dignity over their experiences and identities. Being flexible and adept in conceptualizing intersectionality in context in a way that allows for both exploration and consolidation is key to acquiring a greater sense of the client. In some contexts, certain identities might intermix or fade or become salient, and discussing the nuance of these situations and how a client responds to each one is helpful for conceptualization and intervention. Family therapists may also be mindful that conversations about adoption allow for open communication among family members, with particular attention around supporting the adoptive person.

Last, it is necessary to discuss voices that are not yet present in the adoptive microaggressions literature. Further studies about the experiences of adoptive parents and birth families need more inquiry. While much of the adoptive microaggressions research conveys themes that are related to these groups, studies that center on the nuanced experiences of adoptive and birth parents warrant a more complex lens as it is likely conceptualizations will be augmented or revised. Birth fathers, for example, are almost completely omitted from the current adoptive microaggressions literature. Importantly, more research on intersectionality of adoptive identity in relation to other identities is imperative for further understanding the complex lived experience of adopted individuals. There are identities (e.g., ability, religious, sexual orientation of the adopted person, ethnic diversity) that are not yet represented in the current adoptive microaggressions literature that are required to have a fuller understanding of how these slights manifest.

Note

1 This author received financial support for the research of this chapter from the William T. Grant Foundation (Grant No. 7146) and the Rudd Family Foundation Chair in Psychology at the University of Massachusetts Amherst.

References

Baden, A. L. (2016). "Do you know your *real* parents?" and other adoption microaggressions. *Adoption Quarterly, 19*(1), 1–25. doi:10.1080/10926755.2015.1026012

Baden, A. L., Pinderhughes, E. E., Harrington, E. S., & Waddell, J. (2013). *Racial and adoption microaggressions: Recognizing them and dealing with them.* Workshop presented at the International Conference on Adoption Research 4, Bilbao, Spain.

Baker, K. K. (2008). Bionormativity and the construction of parenthood. *Georgia Law Review, 42*, 649–697.

Brodzinsky, D. M. (2008). Adoptive parent preparation project phase I: Meeting the mental health and developmental needs of adopted children. Retrieved from www.adoptioninstitute.org/publications/2008_02_Parent_Preparation.pdf

Camacho, M. M., & Lord, S. M. (2011). Microaggressions in engineering education: Climate for Asian, Latina, and White women. Paper presented at *2011 Frontiers in Education Conference*, Rapid City, SD: IEEE.

Carp, E. W. (1998). *Family matters: Secrecy and disclosure in the history of adoption.* Cambridge, Massachusetts: Harvard University Press.

Carp, E. W. (2009). How tight was the seal? A reappraisal of adoption records in the United States, England, and New Zealand, 1851-1955. In G. M. Wrobel & E. Neil (Eds.), *International advances in adoption research for practice* (pp. 17–39). Chichester, UK: Wiley & Sons Ltd.

Crain, E. E., & Farr, R. H. (2014, April). *Experiences of microaggressions and resiliency among children with same-sex parents.* Poster presented at the New Worlds of Adoption Conference 2014, Amherst, MA.

Dasgupta, N. (2008). Color lines in the mind: Unconscious prejudice, discriminatory behavior, and the potential for change. In A. Grant-Thomas & G. Orfield (Eds.), *21st century color lines: Exploring the frontiers of America's multicultural future.* Retrieved from people.umass.edu/kyogeesw/Dasgupta_Color LinesChapter.pdf

DeBenedetto, A., & Pinderhughes, E. E. (2016, May). *The role of developmental comprehension in understanding microaggressions in transracially-adopted children.* Poster presented at the New Worlds of Adoption and Foster Care: Thriving on the Frontline 2016, Amherst, MA.

Dolan, J. H. (2015). How white adoptive parents of Asian born youth talk about racism within the family. *Journal of Social Distress and the Homeless, 24*(2), 81–92. doi:10.1179/1053078915Z.00000000025

Farr, R. H., Crain, E. E., Oakley, M. K., Cashen, K. K., & Garber, K. J. (2016). Microaggressions, feelings of difference, and resilience among adopted children with sexual minority parents. *Journal of Youth and Adolescence, 45*(1), 85–104. doi:10.1007/s10964-015-0353-6

Fisher, A. P. (2003). Still "Not quite as good as having your own"? Toward a sociology of adoption. *Annual Review of Sociology, 29*, 335–361. doi:10.1146/annurev.soc.29.010202.100209

Garber, K. J. (2014). *"YOU were adopted?!": An exploratory analysis of microaggressions experienced by adolescent adopted individuals.* (Unpublished Master's thesis). Amherst, MA: University of Massachusetts Amherst.

Garber, K. J. (2016). *Intraracial and intraethnic microaggressions experienced by Korean American internationally and transracially adopted persons.* (Unpublished Dissertation). Amherst, MA: University of Massachusetts Amherst.

Garber, K. J., French, Q. Y. S., & Grotevant, H. D. (2015). Participation in the Adoption Mentoring Partnership: Mentors' experiences of ethnic identity. In E. E. Pinderhughes & R. Rosnati (Eds.), *Special issue: Adoptees' ethnic identity within family and social contexts. New directions for child and adolescent development* (pp. 77–89). Hoboken, NJ.: Wiley.

Garber, K. J., & Grotevant, H. D. (2015). "YOU were adopted?!": Microaggressions toward adolescent adopted individuals in same-race families. *The Counseling Psychologist, 43*(3), 435–462. doi:10.1177/0011000014566471

Grotevant, H. D., & McRoy, R. G. (1998). *Openness in adoption: Exploring family connections.* Thousand Oaks, CA: Sage.

Harrington, E. S., Kimball, J., Kitchen, A., Mazza, J., Shaw, Z., Stephens, J., ... Pinderhughes, E. (2014). *A qualitative study of racial and adoption microaggressions experienced by adoptive families with children.* Poster presented at the New Worlds of Adoption Conference 2014, Amherst, MA.

Higgins, D. (2012). *Past and present adoptions in Australia.* (Fact Sheet 2012). Melbourne, VIC: Australian Institute of Family Studies.

Kelly, R. (2009). Emerging voices: Reflections on adoption from the birth mother's perspective. In G. M. Wrobel & E. Neil (Eds.), *International advances in adoption research for practice* (pp. 245–268). KG: Chichester, UK: Wiley & Sons Ltd.

Kirk, D. H. (1964). *Shared fate.* New York, NY: Free Press.

Kline, S. L., Karel, A. I., & Chatterjee, K. (2006). Covering adoption: General depictions in broadcast news. *Family Relations, 55*(4), 487–498. doi:10.1111/j.1741-3729.2006.00417.x

Kressierer, D. K., & Bryant, C. D. (1996). Adoption as deviance: Socially constructed parent-child kinship as a stigmatized and legally burdened relationship. *Deviant Behavior, 17*, 391–415. doi:10.1080/01639625.1996.9968037

Leon, I. G. (2002). Adoption losses: Naturally occurring or socially constructed? *Child Development, 73*(2), 652–663. doi:10.1111/1467-8624.00429

MacDonald, M. (2016). Public openness, difference, and microaggressions: "Different but the same.". In *Parenthood and open adoption* (pp. 67–88). London: Palgrave Macmillan.

March, K. (1995). Perception of adoption as social stigma: Motivation for search and reunion. *Journal of Marriage and Family, 57*(3), 653–660. doi:10.2307/353920

March, K., & Miall, C. (2000). Adoption as a family form. *Family Relations, 49*(4), 359–362. doi:10.1111/j.1741-3729.2000.00359.x

Miall, C. E. (1987). The stigma of adoptive parent status: Perceptions of community attitudes toward adoption and the experience of informal social sanctioning. *Family Relations, 36*(1), 34–39.

Morgan, S. K., & Langrehr, K. J. (2018). Transracially adoptive parents' colorblindness and discrimination recognition: Adoption stigma as moderator. *Cultural Diversity and Ethnic Minority Psychology*, Aug 16. doi:10.1037/cdp0000219

Neil, E. (2009). Post-adoption contact and openness in adoptive parents' minds: Consequences for children's development. *British Journal of Social Work, 39*(1), 5–23. doi:10.1093/bjsw/bcm087

Pierce, C. M., Carew, J. V., Pierce-Gonzalez, D., & Willis, D. (1977). An experiment in racism: TV commercials. *Education and Urban Society, 10*(1), 61–87. doi:10.1177/001312457701000105

Siegel, D. H., & Smith, S. L. (2012). Openness in adoption: From secrecy and stigma to knowledge and connections. Retrieved from www.adoptioninstitute.org/publications/2012_03_OpennessInAdoption.pdf

Sue, D. W. (Ed.). (2010a). *Microaggressions and marginality: Manifestation, dynamics, and impact.* New Jersey: Wiley.

Sue, D. W. (Ed.). (2010b). *Microaggressions in everyday life: Race, gender, and sexual orientation.* New Jersey: Wiley.

Sue, D. W., Capodilupo, C. M., Torino, G. C., Bucceri, J. M., Holder, A. M. B., Nadal, K. L., & Esquilin, M. (2007). Racial microaggressions in everyday life: Implications for clinical practice. *American Psychologist, 62*(4), 271–286. doi:10.1037/0003-066X.62.4.271

Wegar, K. (1997). In search of bad mothers: Social constructions of birth and adoptive motherhood. *Women's Studies International Forum, 20*(1), 77–86. doi:10.1016/S0277-5395(96)00097-0

Wegar, K. (2000). Adoption, family ideology, and social stigma: Bias in community attitudes, adoption research, and practice. *Family Relations, 49*(4), 363–370. doi:10.1111/j.1741-3729.2000.00363.x

Zamostny, K. P., O'Brien, K. M., Baden, A. L., & Wiley, M. O. (2003). The practice of adoption: History trends, and social context. *The Counseling Psychologist, 31*(6), 651–678. doi:10.1177/0011000003258061

Zhang, E., Zhang, X., & Pinderhughes, E.E. (2019). "Your skin's not as good as us": Microaggressions among transracially-adopted children from China. *Adoption Quarterly, 22*(4), 284–306. doi: 10.1080/10926755.2019.1675837.

Zhang, X., Cinney, A., DeBenedetto, A., Nealon-Shapiro, C., Shin, H.R., Zhang, E., … Pinderhughes, E.E. (2016). *Out of the mouths of babes: Developmental differences in microaggressions conveyed by young children and relations with parent-child discussions.* Poster presented at the New Worlds of Adoption and Foster Care: Thriving on the Frontline Conference 2016, Amherst, MA.

Zhang, X., Shin, R., Kimura, A., Cinney, A., Boland, K., Jurca, A., … Pinderhughes, E. (2018). *How is parent-reported family race/ethnicity related to parents' understanding and explanation of adoption bias?* Poster presented at The Rudd Adoption Research Program Conference 2018, Amherst, MA.

23

MALTREATMENT OF ADOPTEES IN ADOPTIVE HOMES

Jessica A.K. Matthews

Maltreatment in adoptive homes is not a well-recognized, researched, or understood phenomenon. This is perhaps because the very idea is anathema to the entire purpose of adoption as a system of family formation, one with the intention of promoting a family environment, safety, and permanence for children. Parents pursuing any type of adoption are subject to pre-placement evaluations that are intended to prevent children from entering unsafe or unstable circumstances (Child Welfare Information Gateway, CWIG, 2015a). Given the rigor of the pre-placement screening of adoptive parents, we would expect that adoptive families have fewer issues and less risk for maltreatment than in biological families. Many child maltreatment researchers are likely to assert that, by default, maltreatment is more likely in biological homes (e.g. van IJzendoorn, Euser, Prinzie, Juffer, & Bakermans-Kranenburg, 2009). However logical this claim might seem, very few studies compare rates of maltreatment perpetration between adoptive and biological parents. In fact, maltreatment in adoptive homes has never been specifically investigated (Mohanty, Chokkanathan, & Park, 2019). At the time of the writing of this chapter there is only one known article, which reported on the deaths of 18 internationally adopted children in the US due to maltreatment by their adoptive parents (Miller, Chan, Tirella, Reece, & Pertman, 2007). A simple review of the news media reveals hundreds of stories of adoptive parents accused or responsible for the abuse, neglect, or even death of adopted children in their care, yet no other scientific research efforts provide information about the prevalence of maltreatment among US adoptive families in general. Recognizing that maltreatment is occurring in these families that were created with the intention of increasing safety for the adoptee, this topic warrants a more scientifically sound examination. This chapter reviews the little that is known about maltreatment in adoptive families and follows up with information on maltreatment in biological families and foster care (the most comparable family form to adoption) to provide context.

Maltreatment of children

Adoptive families

As mentioned previously, no study has specifically focused on maltreatment in the adoptive home; however, a handful of studies on other topics provide relevant information. For example, research on tribal reunification among Native American/First Nation children removed from their families and tribal communities and placed into adoptive and foster homes learned that many of these adults reported experiencing chronic and many types of maltreatment (described as poly-victimization) during their time in foster and adoptive families (Landers, Danes, & White Hawk, 2015). Though the research focus was reunification, this finding is extremely important when analyzing the experience of adopted and fostered children, particularly with respect to race and culture.

Other studies have also noted high rates of maltreatment experience reported retrospectively by adult adoptees. For example, a secondary analysis of the Fact-Finding Survey on Korean International Adoptees determined that many adults adopted from Korea as children experienced maltreatment in their adoptive homes (Mohanty et al., 2019). Specifically, 47% of adoptees reported experiencing emotional abuse, 37.8% experienced physical abuse, and 7.6% experienced sexual abuse (Mohanty et al., 2019). Furthermore, in a study addressing the experience of adoptees who experienced discontinuity in their adoption histories, Kim (2018) found that nearly her entire sample of adoptees (n=15) reported experiences with physical and emotional abuse perpetrated by their adoptive parents.

Some research indicates that many children experience maltreatment perpetrated by people other than their parents, which might also be true for adoptees. The National Child Abuse and Neglect Data System (NCANDS) files list 12 different potential perpetrators, including parent, other relative, group home staff, non-relative foster parent, unmarried partner of parent, legal guardian, friend or neighbor, foster parent, relative foster parent, other professional, child daycare provider, and other. Some foster children are maltreated by other children (whether fostered or biological) in the home (Tittle, Poertner, & Garnier, 2001). There is no reason to think that non-parent perpetrators would prey exclusively on children living with biological parents.

Since maltreatment in adoptive homes has been identified in studies primarily focused on other adoption experiences, there are limitations to our ability to understand and interpret this phenomenon for the wider population of adopted children. For example, all studies that have reported on adoptee maltreatment are retrospective in nature. Though this does not mean the experiences should be discounted, it does complicate interpretation and extrapolation. Additionally, the focus of these studies can create sampling biases that prevent more widespread generalization. For example, Kim's study (2018) recruited adults with adoption discontinuity histories, which is not a typical characteristic of adoptees.

Matthews (2018), who focused specifically on the maltreatment experience of previously adopted children (PAC) in foster care, identifies a number of deeply troubling findings. PAC are those currently in the foster care system who have experienced an adoption, such as children who have had disrupted adoptions who have been placed in foster care, as well as children removed from adoptive homes into foster care. Data were analyzed from the NCANDS Restricted Child File, and the two 2009 Adoption and Foster Care Analysis and Reporting System (AFCARS) datasets which include information on children placed in temporary foster homes or permanently adopted through public government agencies. Maltreatment reports (both substantiated and unsubstantiated) on PAC were identified. Within their reports on maltreatment, Matthews found that 878 (of 3,595) children had experienced substantiated maltreatment perpetrated by the adoptive parent. Adoptive parents represented two-thirds of the parent perpetrators (also including biological and step-parents) within the 2009 dataset (Matthews, 2018).

Matthews (2018) work on PAC in care also explores how the family's status as an adoptive family affects recognized issues in the reporting, investigation, and assessment of maltreatment. Data show that many children report cases of child maltreatment, but over half are unsubstantiated (n=1,861 of 3,595 PAC in 2009) even though that child is in foster care. There are a number of theories for this phenomenon. Perhaps social workers and other authorities are more sensitive to the idea of maltreatment in adoptive homes, such that any hint of maltreatment leads to removal. Alternatively, we might see incidences being reported but deemed unsubstantiated due to the investigator's faith in pre-screening and desire to preserve permanency of the family. Unfortunately, more information is needed to understand what is actually occurring in these cases.

Biological families

To provide context for the risk posed to adopted children, base rates of child maltreatment in biological families should be reviewed. Over 6 million children (8% of US children, ChildTrends, 2018) are involved as victims in reports to Child Protective Services (CPS), and more cases are known yet unreported (Institute of Medicine & National Research Council of the National Academies [IOM & NRC], 2013) each year. Underreporting is a common issue in child maltreatment for many reasons, including children's inability to understand what constitutes maltreatment, professionals' failure to report, or family deciding to deal with maltreatment in informal ways (see IOM & NRC (2013) for a more thorough discussion of underreporting). Almost 75% of these cases are classified as neglect, 15% as physical abuse, and 10% as sexual abuse. Most involve children under the age of five, as the highest rates of maltreatment occur among the very youngest children (IOM & NRC, 2013). Each year, more than 3 million reports of child maltreatment are made, and multiple children may be included on a single report (Oliver & Washington, 2009). The perpetrators of this maltreatment are predominately parents (80%), 87% of whom are biological parents, and slightly more than half are female (IOM & NRC, 2013).

Rates of child maltreatment peaked in 1993 (ChildTrends, 2018) reaching 15 cases per 1,000 children. Periodically, Congress mandates a research effort to assess child abuse and neglect nationally, though the last effort was conducted in 2010 (the Fourth National Incidence Study of Child Abuse and Neglect [NIS-4]; Sedlak et al., 2010). At the time, the NIS-4 showed a significant decline in the frequency of child sexual abuse, and a marginal decline in child physical and emotional abuse. After a peak in 1993, child maltreatment and victimization decreased by 40–70% to 12 cases per 1,000 children in 2004 (Finkelhor & Jones, 2006) and continued to decline to a rate of 9.1 cases per 1,000 children in 2012. The rate and number of children has remained relatively steady since 2012 and was measured at 9.1 per 1,000 children in 2016 (ChildTrends, 2018).

There are multiple factors that might have contributed to the overall decline since 1993, including increased funding and attention to child maltreatment in the community and criminal justice system during the 1980s and 1990s (Jones & Finkelhor, 2003), increased use of psychiatric medication by would-be perpetrators (Del Vecchio, Eckardt Erlanger, & Slep, 2013), or a change in awareness and/or decreasing societal tolerance of physical and sexual abuse of children. However, in shorter term studies and more localized studies, reports from individual US states and research studies vary as to whether rates of child neglect are increasing, decreasing, or remaining constant (IOM & NRC, 2013). Local areas might not be reflective of national trends, and there are tremendous differences in the measurement approaches. Additionally, studies that examine the incidence of child maltreatment officially reported within a single year time frame will show drastically lower rates than studies that ask adults about their personal histories experiencing maltreatment. Last, studies also vary in whether they differentiate between types of abuse or neglect, affecting rates they report.

For example, in 2017, there were roughly 3,501,000 cases of maltreatment reported to the various state child welfare and CPS agencies and compiled within the NCANDS by the National Data Archive on Child Abuse and Neglect (NDACAN) housed at Cornell University. In 2009, there were 3,582,717 cases reported and 3,658 of these cases listed an adoptive parent as perpetrator, or 0.7% of all parent perpetrators. Adoptive parents make up a very small fraction of all perpetrators of child maltreatment (less than 1% of parent perpetrators), which is consistent with Dutch families assessed by van IJzendoorn et al. (2009) who found 0.12% of adoptees were maltreated by adoptive parents.

Foster care

A number of studies describe the former and current experience of maltreatment in foster care living situations, which, as the other type of family in which children live with non-biological parents, is the most comparable situation to adoptive children. The issue is complex, and a full discussion is beyond the scope of this chapter; however, there might be similarities between maltreatment of foster children by foster parents and of adoptees by adoptive parents.

Many adoptees have a pre-placement history of maltreatment, especially since the largest proportion of adoptees are adopted directly from foster care (Jones & Placek, 2017). Studies have shown that children in the foster care system can continue to experience maltreatment (Poertner, Bussey, & Fluke, 1999; Tittle et al., 2001); however, rates of maltreatment in foster care vary widely by study. The Administration for Children and Families (2010) reports that maltreatment rates for children in foster care range from 0.00–2.33%, with a median of 0.35%, though these rates might be underestimates due to underreporting. Newer studies using interviews of foster care alumni in three states suggest that the rates of maltreatment in care are as high as 33% of the course of their entire history in care (Katz, Courtney, & Novotny, 2016).

Poertner and colleagues (1999) found that 1.7–2.3% of foster children experienced maltreatment in a single year period, usually perpetrated by the foster parent (31%) or by a primary caregiver (25%). Given the more rigorous pre-adoption evaluation processes, we would expect that the rates of adoptees from care who experience maltreatment are even lower than those of foster children. Not enough is known about why certain children continue to experience maltreatment in care, where they are ostensibly meant to be safe and protected, but studies have attempted to describe related factors and predictors.

Individual child and ecological factors have been identified as contributing to the experience of continued maltreatment, though these factors undoubtedly interact (Zuravin, Benedict, & Somerfield, 1993). For the purposes of this chapter, only characteristics potentially analogous to the adoptee experience are described: of the foster caregivers, foster children, and agencies. The author would like to note the older age of many of the study results presented here. McFadden and Ryan (1986) found that foster caregivers might be triggered to maltreat by foster children's disobedience, aggression, and use of foul language. Some research suggests that male foster children, who exhibit more externalizing problems (Leadbeater, Kuperminc, Blatt, & Hertzog, 1999), are more likely to be physically abused, resulting in marks or injuries (McFadden & Ryan, 1986). Benedict, Zuravin, Somerfield, and Brandt (1996) found that foster children in care who were sexually abused were more likely to be female, in a foster family environment, and to have problems related to mental health and development. Thus, age, gender, mental health, and behavioral issues are all risk factors to consider in the maltreatment of adoptees. In the only study on the topic, McFadden and Ryan (1986) identified certain agency practices that might contribute to maltreatment of foster children, including issues with matching children to a foster family's abilities or preferences, insufficient home visiting by social workers, and insufficient foster parent training. These issues are often also faced by adoptive families, and thus could be similar risk factors with respect to the maltreatment of adoptees.

The most common forms of maltreatment reported by foster youth include physical and sexual abuse and neglect (Benedict et al., 1996; McFadden & Ryan, 1986); however, results are mixed with respect to prevalence of maltreatment types within foster placement types. Some studies suggest neglect is most common in family and kinship foster care (Poertner et al., 1999), while Benedict et al. (1996) found that sexual abuse, followed by physical abuse and neglect, were the most prevalent forms of maltreatment. These results are troubling, given that foster children are removed from their families of origin, usually due to maltreatment, with the goal of promoting their safety and security. These findings also suggest that methodological and other issues prevent a clear understanding of these experiences.

Maltreatment type, using latent class analysis (LCA), differentiated foster children and predicted future maltreatment experience (Katz et al., 2016). Using 2,600 foster alumni interviews, Katz and colleagues (2016) found children with high neglect and physical abuse backgrounds were significantly more likely to experience neglect by foster parents in care than those with low maltreatment backgrounds. Research suggests that re-victimization experiences represent the highest risk for continued placement instability and re-victimization (Katz et al., 2016; Orsi, 2015), and the maltreatment type in care might be of particular importance to predicting these outcomes. Thus, adoptees with more complex pre-placement histories could be the most susceptible to re-victimization. Though we would like to believe that the risk of maltreatment does not extend to adoptive families, we know that not to be the case, evidenced by the little that is known about adoptee maltreatment. The better we understand the experiences of maltreated foster children, the more prepared we are to understand the experiences of adoptees maltreated in adoptive homes and to prevent those experiences in the future.

It is important to note that there are a number of limitations with respect to how rates of maltreatment are measured in studies of youth in foster care. First, much of the research evidence we have on maltreatment in foster care is up to three decades old. Second, many administrative reports measure rates based on indicated reports over a single year period (Katz et al., 2016). A single year in foster care might not be representative of the full experiences of children who often spend many years in care. Third, many studies rely on youth self-report of maltreatment, which can be problematic. Children in care might fear retribution for reporting, might feel their reports might not be heard or validated by system officials, or might be unaware of or unable to acknowledge what constitutes maltreatment. These underreporting issues could certainly apply to maltreated adoptees.

Understanding of maltreatment

The next section addresses why child maltreatment occurs and how our theories apply to adoptive families.

Etiology of child maltreatment

Prevention of child maltreatment must come through an evidence-based understanding of why it occurs in the first place. Though there are multiple theories that attempt to explain the etiology of child maltreatment, these theories have yielded relatively low predictive power. Our best research on child maltreatment identifies risk factors at various ecological levels. A full discussion of the etiology of child maltreatment is beyond the scope of this chapter, though a brief introduction to the overarching theories is given here. (For additional information, see Del Vecchio et al., 2013.)

Family- and community-level theories

Family risk factors have been implicated in the etiology of child maltreatment, including early motherhood, poverty, and lower educational attainment – none of which are likely to apply to most adoptive families, who tend to be older, more affluent, and better educated (Malm, Vandivere, & McKlindon, 2011). With respect to parental age, studies have mixed results; young mothers might have slightly increased risk for the commission of physical abuse and neglect (Stith et al., 2009), for more severe abuse (Gil, 1971), or no significant association (Chaffin, Kelleher, & Hollenberg, 1996). Other studies have found no significant relation between parent age and child neglect (Stith et al., 2009) or sexual abuse (Allen & Pothast, 1994). This suggests that our understanding of these family-level risk factors is incomplete and that more research is necessary to unpack these associations.

Poverty is often linked to physical abuse and neglect (e.g., Chaffin et al., 1996; Gil, 1971). Although prospective adoptive parents (PAPs) are screened to ensure a level of financial stability, there are ranges in the socioeconomic status of PAPs and PAPs could experience poverty in the future. In their meta-analysis of 155 studies, Stith et al. (2009) found that unemployment was moderately related to neglect, but minimally related to child physical abuse. With respect to severity, studies show mixed results: Chaffin et al. (1996) found no association with poverty, but severe injuries were more likely among low-income families (Gil, 1971; Sedlak & Broadhurst, 1996). Mixed results could be due to methodological issues, such as failing to differentiate between maltreatment types. Also, severity is often measured by retrospective accounts from adult survivors of child maltreatment, not specifically measured by recorded frequency (e.g., in number of investigations by child welfare services, or hospitalizations).

Furthermore, it is likely that stressors associated with poverty, such as educational level, single-parent status, and psychopathology (Allen & Pothast, 1994; Gil, 1971; Milner & Chilamkurti, 1991), mediate the association between poverty and abuse (Pianta, 1984). Gil (1971) found a connection between maltreatment and larger families, with higher numbers of maltreatment more common among larger, low-income families. Chaffin and colleagues (1996) found no significant relation between severity and single-parent status, but other studies (e.g., Ethier, Couture, & Lacharite, 2004; Sedlak & Broadhurst, 1996) have shown a connection between single parenthood and the incidence and chronicity of maltreatment. These mixed results again suggest that the ecology of child maltreatment is complex and cannot be attributed to a single factor.

Stress and anger models

Many researchers have explored the relation of stress and anger to child maltreatment. High-risk and abusive parents report more life stress and more parenting stress (e.g.,

Holden, Willis, & Foltz, 1989; Whipple & Webster-Stratton, 1991). However, it is not the case that all stressed parents abuse their children. Abusive mothers, when compared to non-abusive mothers, report more defensiveness and aggressiveness, seek less support, and are lonelier (Egeland, Breitenbucher, & Rosenberg, 1980; Milner & Robertson, 1990). It has been posited that abusive parents have fewer available resources. Studies have found that receipt of social support distinguishes abusive from non-abusive parents (Corse, Schmid, & Trickett, 1990; Pianta, Egeland, & Erickson, 1989) and not availability of social support (Chaffin et al., 1996). PAP social support should be evaluated in the home study, yet, could be a risk factor for adoptive parents.

Maladaptive coping skills might contribute to abusive parenting. Studies have suggested that negative coping methods including drinking, hostility, behavioral or mental disengagement through withdrawing caregiving behavior, using mental distractors to avoid stressors, rumination, and venting are all related to neglectful or physically abusive parents (Hillson & Kuiper, 1994; Pianta, 1984). A number of studies have also demonstrated that maltreating parents have childrearing and childcare-related problem-solving skill deficits (Azar, Robinson, Hekimian, & Twentyman, 1984; Dawson, de Armas, McGrath, & Kelly, 1986). In a more recent meta-analytic review, Stith and colleagues (2009) found that parent anger consistently predicted both child physical abuse and neglect. Studies have shown that adoptive families generally have less stress than biological families (Palacios & Sánchez-Sandoval, 2006), but this depends on many factors, such as the child's age at adoption (Goldberg & Smith, 2014) and level of special needs (McGlone, Santos, Kazama, Fong, & Mueller, 2002).

Individual-level theories

In psychopathological models, attention is paid to parents' mental health as the etiological factor for maltreatment. Two mental health disorders in particular are consistently associated with perpetration: depression and substance abuse (Black & Mayer, 1980; Chaffin et al., 1996; Murphy et al., 1991; Stith et al., 2009). Murphy and colleagues (1991) found that 43% of cases of serious maltreatment in a juvenile court involved at least one parent with substance abuse issues. In a study of alcohol and opiate addicts, 41% of addicts had children who met criteria for serious neglect and/or abuse, though all experienced some degree of neglect (Black & Mayer, 1980). In an Ontario survey of population mental health, parental substance abuse was associated with a more than twofold increase in the risk of childhood physical and sexual abuse (Walsh, MacMillan, & Jamieson, 2003). Even though many studies demonstrate a connection between substance abuse, depression, and child maltreatment, the psychopathological model cannot account for the fact that neither substance abuse nor depression are either necessary or sufficient for child maltreatment. Additionally, PAPs would hopefully be screened for active substance abuse and mental health issues; though substance abuse and mental health issues might only be flagged in a home study if there is a criminal conviction (CWIG, 2015c), and these issues could arise after the placement of the adoptee.

Theories of child maltreatment often focus on single predictors, such as specific characteristics of child, parent, or context; however, the theoretical models cannot provide sufficient explanation for why certain risk combinations result in child maltreatment in certain families, but not in others. No single identified factor is either necessary or sufficient for the perpetration of child maltreatment. This means that operationalizing these theories in order to protect children could prevent a number of otherwise safe PAPs from adopting. For example, a strict guideline could reject all PAPs with a history of depression, which could prevent healthy, stable people from adopting. Additionally, many of these risk factors are going to operate as common-sense exclusionary criteria for a licensed social worker conducting a home study (CWIG, 2015b). For example, it is highly unlikely that a PAP with an active substance abuse disorder, or untreated mental illness would pass a home study. Thus, these potential risk factors are, theoretically, already exclusionary, and then cannot explain the perpetration of child maltreatment by adoptive parents. It is clear, however, that child maltreatment is a complex issue that is not the result of a single factor in isolation, and more research is needed to understand the complexities of child maltreatment for both adoptive and non-adoptive families.

Consequences of child maltreatment

The consequences of child maltreatment are myriad, including effects on current and future behavioral and emotional functioning, and on cognitive and neurological functioning (IOM & NRC, 2013). Child maltreatment has an impact on every level of child development, and these impacts extend to society as a whole (IOM & NRC, 2013). In 2012, Gelles and Perlman estimated that the entire network of costs associated with child maltreatment in the US was over 80 billion dollars annually. For children who have been adopted and already impacted by the disruption and loss of one family, there could be additionally complicated effects from maltreatment within the adoptive home. The next section of this chapter addresses implications of this phenomenon and potential recommendations.

Policy and practice recommendations

Home studies

Given the evidence that some adoptees are maltreated by adoptive parents, the question of eligibility to adopt is raised. Every state in the US requires that PAPs pass a home study, wherein a licensed social worker enters the home and evaluates the family on a number of characteristics. Though parents must pass, there are no federal regulations concerning what a home study must entail, as these are set by each state (CWIG, 2015c). In fact, home study guidelines can vary between each child welfare agency. Some adoption agencies employ licensed social workers able to perform home studies, and others contract out to specific home study agencies. This variability prevents standardization of the quality of the pre-adoption approval process across states, counties, or agencies, even where requirements appear similar across states. Though this does not mean that home studies are not rigorous, it means that there could be cracks in this system that allow unfit PAPs to slip through at the pre-placement level.

That some children are subject to maltreatment at the hands of pre-screened parents indicates that home studies are not guaranteed measures of child protection. However, more stringent home studies might not increase prevention of maltreatment of adoptees. Our current theoretical understanding of the etiology of maltreatment only allows for the creation of sweeping exclusion criteria, based on single factors such as age, education, or income. This would likely create as many problems as it solves by preventing even greater numbers of PAPs from adopting, and potentially increasing the unregulated or illegal acquisition of children. More stringent home study guidelines would likely disproportionately affect people of color, reducing an already woefully small pool of these PAPs. However, federal regulation of home studies, ensuring uniformity of approval, could be one important step in shoring up cracks in the home study system. Currently, there is no delineation of essential aspects or topics that should be reviewed in every home study. Each state, perhaps even each county, has different guidelines (CWIG, 2015b). Each agency may have different semi-structured interview protocols, and each individual social worker has discretion about the topics they review and the depth into which they are explored. For example, one social worker might consider mental health history extremely important and collect many details; whereas another might simply ask more basic and general questions, gathering minimal information. These differences in home studies could lead to greater variability among families that pass or do not pass a home study, leading to increasingly complex realities for researchers to capture during studies of adoption maltreatment. Regulation of these guidelines at the federal level would simplify the home study process for both child welfare agencies responsible for conducting studies and the families submitting to studies. We could institute uniform training protocols for social workers conducting home studies and disseminate these protocols throughout the country. Uniform protocols would, at the very least, provide better grounds for the evaluation of the home study process, and reduce the number of variables explored in cases of adoption maltreatment.

Pre-placement training and education

All families, whether adoptive or foster, should receive better pre-placement training – particularly with respect to trauma and adoption. All adoptees have experienced a disruption in care, even if only at birth. Indeed, adoption comes with an additional layer of complexity for normative developmental tasks (Brodzinsky, 1993). Children removed from their homes, either permanently or temporarily, have suffered a trauma due to placement instability. Further, children removed due to maltreatment have also been victimized. For this population of children, the trauma is compound and complex. Both families adopting and families fostering these children should be thoroughly educated and trained in both adoption and trauma. This training requirement should doubly hold for families who will be the second adoptive home for a child.

Matching

Matching children with adoptive parents is often touted as the most important factor for success in adoptive homes (Hanna & McRoy, 2011), and is always questioned when issues arise in the adoptive family. In fact, a common issue in foster care is that of "stretching" – where a foster family is encouraged to accept a child who has characteristics the family was not prepared to tackle or expressly identified as unacceptable. However, much caution is necessary in this line of inquiry with respect to prevention of maltreatment. Certainly, more research on matching is needed to increase success and determine best practices, but citing poor match as a reason for maltreatment might result in victim blaming. In other countries, PAPs and foster parents are trained for, and then only matched to, children meeting specific gender, age, and need criteria. (e.g., parents trained to accept high-school-age boys are only matched to high-school-age boys). Adopting this type of system and training could not only make current foster or adoptive parents more equipped and capable, but might also increase trust in the system, such that recruiting additional parents would be easier and more successful.

Post-placement supports

If any of the stress and coping theories of child maltreatment have credence, we need to refocus our attention on post-placement support for adoptive families. Every policy and practice implications section on adoptive family issues includes the recommendation that we increase our awareness and support of adoptive families after the adoption, not limited to the first six months to a year (CWIG, 2018). Adoptive families need ongoing support beyond the initial adjustment period (Pinderhughes, Matthews, Deoudes, & Pertman, 2013). Families need access to adoption-specific services and adoption-competent professionals (See Chapter 31 this volume), either free through their adoption agencies, or covered through their health insurance. Any family at risk of child maltreatment requires ongoing support, but especially in the context of adoption. The needs of an adoptive family are not necessarily greater than non-adoptive families, but awareness of risk factors should be increased when adoptees have already experienced disruption in care and, in some cases, maltreatment.

Financial

The final set of policy and practice recommendations take into account the tremendous cost of foster care, adoption, and child maltreatment. Adoption and child welfare together are a multi-billion-dollar industry (Miller, 2018), not including the even greater costs associated with child maltreatment. The ideal recommendation is a financial overhaul of the entire system, where funds are focused on family preservation, prevention of issues, and ongoing support to families.

A more practical first step might be to reconsider the federal Adoption Tax Credit. Currently the tax credit is a non-refundable credit, making the benefits available only to families with sufficient federal income tax liability. The federal Multi-Ethnic Placement Act requires that every effort be made to place children with families that are as diverse as the population of children; however, the child welfare system struggles to find available minority parents. Families of color should be more strongly incentivized to foster and adopt. A practical way to address the recruitment of families of color would be to change the federal Adoption Tax Credit policy from a non-refundable credit to a refundable credit. This refundable credit would ease the burden of costs associated with the adoption and allow families completing adoptions to receive tax refunds that go a long way for families of color, who are disproportionately lower-income (Povich, Roberts, & Mather, 2014–2015).

Conclusion

Maltreatment in adoptive homes is a violation of children's rights, the law, and US values. Adopted children are not a large population, but their families are formed not through blood, but through law and promises. Adoption is meant to provide children a second chance to a family. That they might suffer harm within those families is a heinous violation of our morals and values. Better understanding of maltreatment would allow us to spend time, money, and effort on other issues, but beyond any practical argument, we have a moral obligation to invest in research and prevent maltreatment from occurring. We cannot shy away from the topic of maltreatment in adoptive homes as too limited, or too political, because adopted children need safe and permanent families.

References

Administration for Children and Families. (2010). *Child welfare outcomes 2007–2010: Report to Congress.* Washington, DC: US Department of Health and Human Services, Children's Bureau.

Allen, C. M., & Pothast, H. L. (1994). Distinguishing characteristics of male and female child sex abusers. *Journal of Offender Rehabilitation, 21*, 73–88.

Azar, S. T., Robinson, D. R., Hekimian, E., & Twentyman, C. T. (1984). Unrealistic expectations and problem-solving ability in maltreating and comparison mothers. *Journal of Consulting and Clinical Psychology, 52*, 687–691.

Benedict, M., Zuravin, S., Somerfield, M., & Brandt, D. (1996). The reported health and functioning of children maltreated while in family foster care. *Child Abuse & Neglect, 20*(7), 561–571.

Black, R., & Mayer, J. (1980). Parents with special problems: Alcohol and opiate addiction. *Child Abuse & Neglect, 4*, 45–54.

Brodzinsky, D. M. (1993). Long-term outcomes in adoption. *The Future of Children, 3*(1), 153–166.

Chaffin, M., Kelleher, K., & Hollenberg, J. (1996). Onset of physical abuse and neglect: Psychiatric, substance abuse, and social risk factors from prospective community data. *Child Abuse & Neglect, 20*, 191–203.

Child Welfare Information Gateway. (2015a). *Background checks for prospective foster, adoptive and kinship caregivers.* Washington DC: US Department of Health and Human Services, Children's Bureau.

Child Welfare Information Gateway. (2015b). *Home study requirements for prospective parents in domestic adoption.* Washington DC: US Department of Health and Human Services, Children's Bureau.

Child Welfare Information Gateway. (2015c). *The adoption homestudy process.* Washington, DC: US Department of Health and Human Services, Children's Bureau.

Child Welfare Information Gateway. (2018). *Providing adoption support and preservation services.* Washington, DC: US Department of Health and Human Services, Children's Bureau.

ChildTrends. (2018). Number of children. Bethesda, MD: Author. Retrieved: www.childtrends.org/indicators/number-of-children.

Corse, S. J., Schmid, K., & Trickett, P. K. (1990). Social network characteristics of mothers in abusing and nonabusing families and their relationships to parenting beliefs. *Journal of Community Psychology, 18*, 44–59.

Dawson, B., de Armas, A., McGrath, M. L., & Kelly, J. A. (1986). Cognitive problem-solving training to improve the child-care judgment of child neglectful parents. *Journal of Family Violence, 1*, 209–226.

Del Vecchio, T., Eckardt Erlanger, A. C., & Slep, A. M. S. (2013). Theories of child abuse. In M. A. Fine & F. D. Fincham (Eds.), *Handbook of family theories: A content-based approach* (pp. 208–227). New York: Routledge.

Egeland, B., Breitenbucher, M. C., & Rosenberg, M. S. (1980). Prospective study of the significance of life stress in the etiology in child abuse. *Journal of Consulting and Clinical Psychology, 48*, 195–205.

Ethier, L. S., Couture, G., & Lacharite, C. (2004). Risk factors associated with the chronicity of high potential for child abuse and neglect. *Journal of Family Violence, 19*, 13–24.

Finkelhor, D., & Jones, L. M. (2006). Why have child maltreatment and child victimization declined?. *Journal of Social Issues, 62*, 685–716.

Gelles, R. J., & Perlman, S. (2012). *Estimated annual cost of child abuse and neglect.* Chicago, IL: Prevent Child Abuse America.

Gil, D. G. (1971). *Violence against children: Physical abuse in the United States.* Cambridge, MA: Harvard University Press.

Goldberg, A. E., & Smith, J. Z. (2014). Predictors of parenting stress in lesbian, gay, and heterosexual adoptive parents during early parenthood. *Journal of Family Psychology, 28*(2), 125–137.

Hanna, M. D., & McRoy, R. G. (2011). Innovative practice approaches to matching in adoption. *Journal of Public Child Welfare, 5*(1), 45–66.

Hillson, J. M. C., & Kuiper, N. A. (1994). Stress and coping model of child maltreatment. *Clinical Psychology Review, 14*, 261–285.

Holden, E. W., Willis, D. J., & Foltz, L. (1989). Child abuse potential and parenting stress: Relationships in maltreating parents. *Psychological Assessment, 1*(1), 64–67.

Institute of Medicine & National Research Council of the National Academies (IOM & NRC). (2013). *New directions in child abuse and neglect research: Committee on child maltreatment research, policy, and practice for the next decade: Phase II: Board on children, youth, and families.* Washington, DC: The National Academies Press.

Jones, J., & Placek, P. (2017). *Adoption: By the numbers.* Alexandria, VA: National Council for Adoption.

Jones, L. M., & Finkelhor, D. (2003). Putting together evidence on declining trends in sexual abuse: A complex puzzle. *Child Abuse & Neglect, 27*, 133–135.

Katz, C. C., Courtney, M. E., & Novotny, E. (2016). Pre-foster care maltreatment class as a predictor of maltreatment in foster care. *Child Adolescent Social Work Journal, 11*, 1–15.

Kim, J. (2018). *Intercountry adopted adults with adoption discontinuity histories*. Paper presented at the International Conference on Adoption Research, July 8–12, 2018, Montreal, Quebec, Canada.

Landers, A. L., Danes, S. M., & White Hawk, S. (2015). Finding their way home: The reunification of First Nations adoptees. *First Peoples Child & Family Review, 10*(2), 18–30.

Leadbeater, B. J., Kuperminc, G. P., Blatt, S. J., & Hertzog, C. (1999). A multivariate model of gender differences in adolescents' internalizing and externalizing problems. *Developmental Psychology, 35*(5), 1268–1282.

Malm, K., Vandivere, S., & McKlindon, A. (2011). *Children adopted from foster care: Child and family characteristics, adoption motivation, and well-being*. APSE Research Brief, Office of the Assistant Secretary for Planning and Evaluation. Washington, DC: US Department of Health and Human Services.

Matthews, J. A. K. (2018). *Previously adopted children in care: Maltreatment and the system* (Doctoral dissertation). Tufts University, Medford, MA.

McFadden, E., & Ryan, P. (1986). *Abuse in family foster homes: Characteristics of the vulnerable child*. Retrieved from http://files.eric.ed.gov/fulltext/ED277460.pdf

McGlone, K., Santos, L., Kazama, L., Fong, R., & Mueller, C. (2002). Psychological stress in adoptive parents of special-needs children. *Child Welfare, 81*(2), 151–171.

Miller, A. (2018). IBISWorld industry report 62411: Adoption & child welfare services in the US. *IBISWorld*. Retrieved from https://clients1.ibisworld.com/reports/us/industry/keystatistics.aspx?entid=1606

Miller, L. C., Chan, W., Tirella, L., Reece, R. A., & Pertman, A. (2007). Family and research context of internationally adopted abuse fatalities. *Child Maltreatment, 12*, 385–386.

Milner, J. S., & Chilamkurti, C. (1991). Physical child abuse perpetrator characteristics: A review of the literature. *Journal of Interpersonal Violence, 6*, 346–367.

Milner, J. S., & Robertson, K. R. (1990). Comparison of physical child abusers, intrafamilial sexual child abusers, and child neglecters. *Journal of Interpersonal Violence, 5*, 37–48.

Mohanty, J., Chokkanathan, S., & Park, W. (2019). Rish and protective factors among Korean adult international adoptees: A latent class analysis. *Children and Youth Services Review, 101*, 142–150.

Murphy, J. M., Jellinek, M., Quinn, D., Smith, G., Poitrast, F. G., & Goshko, M. (1991). Substance abuse and serious child mistreatment: Prevalence, risk, and outcome in a court sample. *Child Abuse & Neglect, 15*, 197–211.

Oliver, J., & Washington, K. T. (2009). Treating perpetrators of child physical abuse: A review of interventions. *Trauma, Violence, & Abuse, 10*(2), 115–124.

Orsi, R. (2015). Predicting re-involvement for children adopted out of a public child welfare system. *Child Abuse & Neglect, 39*, 175–194.

Palacios, J., & Sánchez-Sandoval, Y. (2006). Stress in parents of adopted children. *International Journal of Behavioral Development, 30*(6), 481–487.

Pianta, B. (1984). Antecedents of child abuse. *School Psychology International, 5*, 151–160.

Pianta, R., Egeland, B., & Erickson, M. F. (1989). The antecedents of maltreatment: Results of the mother-child interaction research project. In D. Cicchetti & V. Carlson (Eds.), *Child maltreatment: Theory and research on the causes and consequences of child abuse and neglect* (pp. 203–253). New York: Cambridge University Press.

Pinderhughes, E., Matthews, J. A. K., Deoudes, G., & Pertman, A. (2013). *A changing world: Shaping best practices through understanding of the new realities of intercountry adoption*. New York, NY: Evan B. Donaldson Adoption Institute.

Poertner, J., Bussey, M., & Fluke, J. (1999). How safe are out-of-home placements?. *Children and Youth Services Review, 21*(7), 549–563.

Povich, D., Roberts, B., & Mather, M. (2014–2015). *Low-income working families: The racial/ethnic divide*. Policy Brief. Washington, DC: The Working Poor Families Project.

Sedlak, A. J., & Broadhurst, D. D. (1996). *Third national incidence study of child abuse and neglect: Final report*. Washington, DC: US Department of Health and Human Services, Administration for Children and Families, National Center on Child Abuse and Neglect.

Sedlak, A. J., Mettenburg, J., Basena, M., Petta, I., McPherson, K., Greene, A., & Li, S. (2010). *Fourth national incidence study of child abuse and neglect (NIS-4): Report to Congress*. Washington, DC: US

Department of Health and Human Services, Administration for Children and Families. Retrieved from www.childwelfare.gov/pubs/issue_briefs/cm_prevention.pdf

Stith, S. M., Liu, T., Davies, L. C., Boykin, E. L., Alder, M. C., Harris, J. M., & Dees, J. E. M. E. G. (2009). Risk factors in child maltreatment: A meta-analytic review of the literature. *Aggression and Violent Behavior, 14*(1), 13–29.

Tittle, G., Poertner, J., & Garnier, P. (2001). *Child maltreatment in out of home care: What do we know now?*. Urbana-Champaign, IL: Children and Family Research Center.

van IJzendoorn, M. H., Euser, E. M., Prinzie, P., Juffer, F., & Bakermans-Kranenburg, M. J. (2009). Elevated risk of child maltreatment in families with stepparents but not with adoptive parents. *Child Maltreatment, 14*(4), 369–375.

Walsh, C., MacMillan, H. L., & Jamieson, E. (2003). The relationship between parental substance abuse and child maltreatment: Findings from the Ontario health supplement. *Child Abuse & Neglect, 27*(12), 1409–1425.

Whipple, E. E., & Webster-Stratton, C. (1991). The role of parental stress in physically abusive families. *Child Abuse & Neglect, 15*(3), 279–291.

Zuravin, S., Benedict, M., & Somerfield, M. (1993). Child maltreatment in family foster care. *American Journal of Orthopsychiatry, 63*(4), 589–596.

PART IV

Outcomes

24
SPEECH AND LANGUAGE DEVELOPMENT IN ADOPTED CHILDREN

Sharon L. Glennen

Language learning, like many other cognitive abilities, is a combination of a child's inherited genetics and environment. This is true for all children, including children who are adopted. Language learning happens best in quality caregiving environments. When children are raised in stressful environments, neurobiological changes decrease the child's language learning potential. This chapter starts by reviewing these topics and then explores the unique language learning situation of internationally adopted children who have to learn a new language after adoption. Neurobiological information about second language learning in internationally adopted children, developmental milestones, and expected language outcomes are reviewed along with a discussion of language and learning issues in school-age children.

Genetic and environmental influences on language

Genetics and the environment both play a role in language learning, however the influence of these two factors changes over time. Studies of biological twins have found that during the early infant and preschool years the environment plays a larger role in language development (Hayiou-Thomas et al., 2006). At 4 years of age approximately 50 percent of a child's language abilities are related to shared environments, with only 34 percent attributed to genetic influences, and 16 percent to non-shared environments (Hayiou-Thomas, 2008). As children grow older, genetic influences on language increase. By age 12, inherited factors account for 60 percent of language variability seen in children (Hayiou-Thomas, Dale, & Plomin, 2012). Speech abilities, or the child's ability to articulate sounds, are strongly related to genetic influences across all ages. Approximately 56 percent of the variability in speech production is due to inherited factors and only 15 percent is due to the child's shared environment (Hayiou-Thomas, 2008). Reading abilities are even more influenced by genetics with 70 percent of early decoding and reading fluency, and 50–60 percent of reading comprehension attributed to inherited factors (Harlaar et al., 2010).

How does this relationship between genetics and environment impact speech and language abilities in adopted children? In terms of genetics, studies of adopted children have consistently found that verbal ability and educational achievement correlate more strongly to biological parents than adopted parents (Hardy-Brown & Plomin, 1985; Vinnerljung &

Hjern, 2011). However, adoption into a stable nurturing home provides an environmental boost, especially during the early years. Children domestically adopted from foster care in the US made significant improvement in cognitive and language development, primarily in the first year, with continued improvement up to 60 months post-placement (Waterman et al., 2010). Yet, when language abilities of adopted children are compared to non-adopted siblings in the same adoptive family, adopted children score significantly lower (Cohen, Lojkasek, Yaghoub Zadeh, Pugliese, & Kiefer, 2008; Gauthier & Genesee, 2011; Vinnerljung & Hjern, 2011; Vinnerljung, Lindblad, Hjern, Rasmussen, & Dalen, 2010). These differences were noted for children who were adopted both domestically and internationally and were also noted when language outcomes of adopted children were compared to neighborhood and school peers.

As children grow into adolescence, cognitive and language outcomes are affected by early environments. In Greece, 13-year-olds who were adopted domestically from institutions at young ages had better cognitive and language outcomes than same-age teens who remained behind (Vorria, Ntouma, & Rutter, 2015). Similarly, Romanian children who moved into foster care between the ages of 6 and 30 months had better verbal IQ scores at age 12 than children who remained behind in institutions (Almas, Degnan, Nelson, Zeanah, & Fox, 2016); however, Romanian children in foster care still scored lower than children who were never institutionalized.

Length of institutionalization also correlates with lower verbal IQ scores. Beckett et al. (2006) found that 11-year-old children adopted internationally from Romanian institutions to Great Britain before 6 months of age had verbal IQ and language abilities that matched non-adopted peers; children adopted after 6 months of age had lower language abilities. These findings also hold true for domestically adopted children who were never institutionalized. Vinnerljung and Hjern (2011) used a national database to compare Swedish adults who were adopted out of foster care before age 7 to adults who remained in foster care until age 18. They found that adoptees had better cognitive and educational outcomes than those who stayed in foster care. One possible factor for these differences was that the Swedish adoptees had fewer birth family risk factors and entered foster care at younger ages. Yet, when the Swedish adoptees were compared to non-adopted peers, they still scored approximately 5 points lower on standardized cognitive assessments. When cognitive potential was measured against educational outcomes, adopted and non-adopted adults tended to live up to their potential, whereas adults raised in foster care did not.

Neurobiological effect of poor caregiving on language development

Whether a child is domestically or internationally adopted, the quality of early childcare is important to later language outcomes. Unless the adoption occurs at birth, children who are domestically adopted in Western countries typically spend their pre-adoption years with birth families or in foster care. Those environments are sometimes chaotic and filled with risk factors that increase the child's stress. DeBellis, Hooper, Spratt, and Woolley (2009) measured cognitive and language outcomes in children removed from homes due to parent neglect and found they had poorer language and cognitive outcomes than matched healthy peers. Quality caregiving even outweighed other risk factors such as a parent history of substance and alcohol abuse (Motz et al., 2011).

Children who are adopted from Eastern Europe, China, India, and many other countries are frequently raised in institutional settings before adoption. Institutional care is a well-documented risk factor linked to poor developmental and language outcomes (Almas et al., 2016; Rakhlin et al., 2015). Although institutions vary in quality across countries and regions, many have a rotating staff of too few caretakers for the number of resident children. Social neglect and environmental deprivation lead to stress, which causes changes in early brain development with life-long implications for language learning (Almas et al., 2016). These neurobiological changes lead to a state of hypoactivation characterized by inattentiveness, poor sustained attention, and slow processing speeds (Tarullo, Garvin, & Gunnar, 2011). When children move into enriched environments with quality caretaking, improvements are noted in alertness, attention, and processing, which leads to long-term gains in language and cognitive performance even 10–12 years post-adoption (Almas et al., 2016; Beckett et al., 2006). Readers are referred to Chapter 26 for further information about the neurobiological outcomes of poor caregiving.

Implications for policy and practice

Language and cognitive abilities are the product of the child's inherited traits and environment. Children raised in environments that provide quality caregiving are more likely to reach their full potential in these areas, especially if they move into those homes at young ages. As a group, domestically and internationally adopted children do not reach the same language and cognitive levels as their non-adopted peers. However, factors such as prenatal care, the child's age of adoption, early caregiving experiences, and history of other risk factors play a role in determining eventual language outcomes. Research consistently shows that institutional care is a poor substitute for home care and some countries are working to close their institutions and move children into foster care. However, it is concerning that children raised in foster care also have lower language and cognitive outcomes when compared to adopted children. Additional support and training for foster parents is needed to ensure that all children are raised in quality caregiving homes.

Neurobiological effect of changing languages

Internationally adopted children often initially experience poor caregiving and then have the added factor of language change. Following adoption, the children lose exposure to their birth language, or L1, and then start learning a new adopted language. This situation is sometimes labeled "second first language learning" (Glennen, 2002; Roberts, Pollock, & Krakow, 2005), but more recently has been likened to bilingual language learning where children are learning a true second language or L2 (Norrman, Hyltenstam, & Bylund, 2016). However, internationally adopted children are not really bilingual. The reality is that most lose functional use of their L1 before they fully learn their adopted L2 (Nicoladis & Grabois, 2002). Snedecker, Geren, and Shafto (2012) tracked language development in children who were adopted internationally when they were between the ages of 2 and 5 years. Two months after adoption they rarely used their birth language. In other words, soon after adoption, internationally adopted children are functionally monolingual in L2, but neurologically are learning L2 similar to other bilingual children.

There are two types of bilingualism, simultaneous and sequential. Simultaneous bilingualism occurs when children learn two or more languages from birth, for example when each parent speaks a different language. The more typical form is sequential bilingualism, where children learn L1 from birth, then learn L2 later in life. Children who learn L2 as sequential bilinguals can acquire "native like" proficiency in the language. However, when language abilities are assessed in depth, subtle differences in L2 proficiency emerge (Abrahamsson & Hyltenstam, 2009; Norrman et al., 2016). Recent research indicates that internationally adopted children have similar L2 proficiency differences (Pierce, Genesee, & Klein, 2016).

There are critical periods of neurological growth that play a role in language learning. During the first year of life, children go through a process of attunement, where the auditory perceptual system becomes highly specialized to detect speech sounds specific to the language heard by the child (Kuhl, 2010; Maurer & Werker, 2013). During the first few months of life, children learn to recognize patterns associated with frequently heard sounds and fine tune their auditory processing system to rapidly identify them. At the same time, by 8 to 10 months of age children stop attending to sounds and patterns that occur infrequently and lose the ability to easily discriminate between them (Kuhl, 2010; Werker & Tees, 1984). For example, Japanese includes the sound /r/ but not /l/. Japanese infants easily perceive that /r/ and /l/ are different sounds, however by 8 months the same children respond to both sounds as if they are the same (Kuhl, 2010). This process of language attunement is an innate neurobiological mechanism that occurs at the same age in infants around the world. After the critical period ends, it is theorized that the neurological system engages "molecular brakes" to prevent further changes to the auditory perceptual system, thus keeping it specialized for listening to L1 (Pierce et al., 2016; Werker & Hensch, 2015). Children and adults who learn L2 after the critical period has ended have difficulty learning to perceive and produce sound differences that are not part of their L1. Young children can eventually learn to perceive and produce new L2 sounds but use different neurological processes to do so. Adults have more difficulty and are sometimes unable to learn new sounds even after intense training (Werker & Hensch, 2015).

Internationally adopted children are similar to sequential bilingual children because they start learning their adopted L2 after starting to learn L1. Some theorized that children could potentially "rewire" their neurological system toward L2 (Flege, Yeni-Komshian, & Liu, 1999). However, more recent research indicates that internationally adopted children cannot simply replace L1 with L2. Adults who were internationally adopted as young children perceive sound contrasts from their birth language (L1) better than adults who were never exposed to the language (Oh, Au, & Jun, 2010; Park, 2014; Singh, Liederman, Mierzejewski, & Barnes, 2011). Tonal languages such as Mandarin are exceptionally difficult for Westerners to learn because tone differences are not easily perceived. When fMRI was used to measure neural activation, children adopted from China responded to lexical tones by activating the left superior temporal gyrus, or planum temporale, just like sequential bilingual children whose L1 was Mandarin (Pierce, Klein, Chen, Delcenserie, & Genesee, 2014). There was an age-of-adoption effect with children adopted at older ages having greater activation in this region and children adopted at younger ages having less. Because the critical period for L1 attunement ends before most children leave their birth countries, it should not be surprising that early phonological aspects of L1 are retained rather than being replaced by L2 (Pierce et al., 2016).

Evidence indicates that internationally adopted children process and produce their new language differently from monolingual peers. fMRI was used to measure neural activation during an English language verb generation task in children adopted from China and matched monolingual peers (Rajagopal et al., 2013). Internationally adopted children used more bilateral regions of the brain to produce words than their monolingual peers. Similarly, on a non-word repetition task with French pseudo-words, French-Canadian children adopted from China had fMRI results similar to Chinese bilingual children, and both groups responded differently from French-Canadian monolingual children (Pierce et al., 2014). These results suggest that internationally adopted children, even those adopted at young ages, learn their new adopted language similar to bilingual L2 learners. Bilingual children who learn their second language sequentially use additional cognitive resources to process and produce L2. This requires recruiting more and different areas of the brain for listening and speaking tasks, but is less efficient for optimal language proficiency (Pierce et al., 2016). For example, sequential bilingual children who are proficient in two languages have better verbal working memory abilities in L1 than L2 (Archibald, 2018; Thorn & Gathercole, 1999). Similarly, internationally adopted children do not score as well as monolingual peers on measures that require strong verbal working memory such as sentence recall and non-word repetition tasks (Delcenserie & Genesee, 2014a; Scott, Pollock, Roberts, & Krakow, 2013). In summary, neurological remnants of L1, combined with the process of learning L2 after critical periods have closed, appear to affect the language learning process for internationally adopted children.

Language outcomes in internationally adopted children

The previous sections of this chapter explained the environmental and neurological risk factors faced by internationally adopted children. Most of these children are adopted from stress-filled caregiving environments which lead to neurological differences. They learn their new language after critical periods for language learning have closed and their brains process the new language like a second language. With all of these risk factors, internationally adopted children should experience significant language learning difficulties; however, the reality is that most eventually develop language abilities that fall within normal expectations for their age. The next sections will review how internationally adopted children learn L2, and documented patterns of language strength or weakness.

Children adopted internationally between 0 and 2 years

When children are adopted from other countries at young ages, they typically arrive in their adoptive homes and quickly "catch up" in language development. Children adopted before 6 months of age arrive in their adoptive countries before the critical period for phonological language learning has closed and rapidly develop language abilities well within the average range soon after adoption. Indeed, Romanian children adopted before 6 months of age were the one group that by 12 years of age had language and cognitive abilities equal to non-adopted peers. In contrast, children adopted after that age scored lower than non-adopted peers on tests of language and cognition (Beckett et al., 2006). Although long-term outcomes vary, during the first year after adoption, most children adopted before 12 months of age rapidly reach expected early milestones in their new language. Pragmatic communication abilities that are not language specific, such as use of gestures, eye contact, vocalizations, social interaction, and developmental play, can be assessed soon after adoption and should range from low-average to average for the child's age (Glennen, 2007). Joint attention skills should also develop typically (Pierce, Genesee, Gauthier, & Dubois, 2015). Children with delays in these areas were more likely to have delayed language when assessed one year later (Glennen, 2007). More importantly, newly adopted children with poor social interaction abilities, such as lack of eye contact or infrequent communication attempts, had significant language delays when assessed at older ages, including diagnoses of autism. These pragmatic communication abilities develop continuously from pre- to post-adoption and provide a non-biased way to detect early language or cognitive delays. For children adopted before 12 months of age, spoken language also catches up quickly. Most children adopted before 12 months can follow simple commands and produce first words by age-expected milestones (Glennen, 2007; Glennen & Masters, 2002; Tan, Loker, Dedrick, & Marfo, 2012).

Children adopted from abroad at slightly older ages, between 12 and 24 months, also learn their new language quickly. Soon after adoption, their pragmatic social interaction, joint attention, play, and gestural abilities should fall in the average to low-average range (Glennen, 2007; Pierce et al., 2015). Children with delays in these areas are at high risk for language or cognitive delay and should be referred for early intervention. Spoken language also develops rapidly; most children adopted before the age of 2 years quickly learn their new language. They initially make rapid progress in receptive language, and later meet expected expressive language milestones. Although the development of spoken words is slightly delayed, the children should be using vocalizations to communicate. Children who infrequently vocalize or use less variety in sounds are at higher risk of having true communication delays (Glennen, 2007). Within one year of adoption, receptive abilities in the new language should fall within the average range and expressive language in the low-average range (Cohen et al., 2008; Glennen, 2007; Hwa-Froelich & Matsuo, 2010; Tan & Yang, 2005). Articulation of speech sounds in the new language also emerges rapidly with sounds developing in a typical sequence (Pollock & Price, 2005).

One year after adoption, most children adopted between 12 and 24 months had age-appropriate L2 language abilities, and only 22 percent were classified as language delayed (Glennen, 2007). These children then continue to improve their language abilities through age 4 years and beyond (Gauthier & Genesee, 2011; Glennen, 2014, 2015; Jacobs, Miller, & Tirella, 2010; Roberts et al., 2005; Welsh & Viana, 2012). Despite the positive outlook for language development in children adopted between 0 and 2 years of age, many of them receive speech and language services during the first year in their adoptive countries (Glennen & Masters, 2002; Mason & Narad, 2005). Parents in the US reported that 62 percent of internationally adopted children were referred for speech and language evaluations during the first year after adoption, and 48 percent received early intervention services (Glennen, 2007). Follow-up evaluations showed that some children were over-referred for early intervention services, but others in need of services were not always identified (Glennen, 2014).

Although internationally adopted children do well overall, when language development is divided into components some areas take more time to develop than others. Morphosyntax, or the ability to sequence words into sentences and add grammatical markers, is relatively difficult for internationally adopted children to learn. Parent reports on the use of English grammatical forms showed that use of plurals, past tense, and others developed more slowly than expected in a group of young children adopted from Eastern Europe (Glennen & Masters, 2002). Mean length of utterance (MLU), a standard measure of sentence length, is also slow to develop to age-level expectations. Three years after adoption, children adopted from Eastern European countries had MLU scores that fell within normal limits, but on the low side of average (Glennen, 2014). Although morphosyntax develops more slowly than other language areas, the early sequence of learning grammatical forms appears to be the same as monolingual children. Young children adopted from Russian- into English-speaking homes were studied to determine whether the emergence of early English grammar would be influenced by the grammatical and phonological structure of Russian, with various grammatical forms predicted as being more or less similar across the two languages (Glennen, Rozinsky-Grunhut, & Tracy, 2005). The children's Russian did not interfere with English language grammatical development. They followed the same developmental sequence as monolingual children, but the rate of development was slightly delayed.

Implications for policy and practice

Parents and professionals need to understand the typical language learning milestones and expectations for internationally adopted children. Table 24.1 provides this information based

Table 24.1 Language and speech development of children adopted from Eastern Europe over time

Post-adoption time home		*Receptive language*		*Expressive language*		*Mean length of utterance SSE*		*Articulation*	
	N	*M*	*SD*	*M*	*SD*	*M*	*SD*	*M*	*SD*
				Age of adoption 12–17 months					
2.5 mos post-adoption	17	88.24	(7.76)	93.00	(6.49)	72.61	(23.47)		
9 mos post-adoption		97.07	(14.27)	96.20	(10.61)	78.92	(8.63)		
1 yr 3 mos post-adoption		105.00	(14.02)	94.73	(16.53)	84.86	(17.53)	99.12	(12.34)
2 yrs 3 mos post-adoption		102.53	(13.73)	100.20	(10.40)	101.10	(8.70)	106.46	(8.25)
3 yrs 4 mos post-adoption		104.13	(12.37)	100.27	(10.82)	94.66	(10.97)	105.73	(10.87)
				Age of adoption 18–23 months					
2.5 mos post-adoption	8	96.25	(21.23)	92.14	(13.49)	60.18	(18.27)		
9 mos post-adoption		94.14	(15.13)	83.71	(5.90)	71.01	(11.69)		
1 yr 3 mos post-adoption		104.14	(12.02)	97.14	(9.78)	100.26	(26.28)	99.46	(7.15)
2 yrs 3 mos post-adoption		108.43	(9.18)	101.01	(10.71)	101.24	(10.65)	101.35	(7.87)
3 yrs 4 mos post-adoption		105.29	(9.89)	102.23	(9.32)	90.03	(5.91)	95.35	(12.65)
				Age of adoption 2 years					
2.5 mos post-adoption	13	78.75	(14.17)	76.92	(8.05)	60.12	(7.74)		
9 mos post-adoption		94.31	(14.96)	88.46	(11.74)	72.07	(23.44)	91.64	(9.61)
1 yr 3 mos post-adoption		100.75	(13.85)	97.45	(16.77)	101.05	(24.43)	92.09	(11.75)
2 yrs 3 mos post-adoption		104.63	(10.22)	103.50	(12.55)	108.91	(17.58)	102.64	(13.38)
3 yrs 4 mos post-adoption		108.75	(6.38)	105.00	(15.20)	99.88	(9.69)	102.33	(10.43)
				Age of adoption 3 years					
2.5 mos post-adoption	12	67.57	(6.72)	71.29	(3.09)	65.16	(5.86)		
9 mos post-adoption		89.58	(10.95)	78.07	(10.47)	87.76	(12.36)	97.82	(12.49)
1 yr 3 mos post-adoption		91.73	(9.35)	84.27	(11.29)	92.24	(14.37)	99.82	(14.53)
2 yrs 3 mos post-adoption		96.16	(16.46)	97.10	(13.73)	86.79	(13.87)	104.22	(12.42)
3 yrs 4 mos post-adoption		100.02	(14.82)	98.78	(16.58)	93.60	(9.69)		
				Age of adoption 4 years					
2.5 mos post-adoption	6	67.67	(15.87)	62.67	(16.94)	62.73	(9.10)		
9 mos post-adoption		79.24	(9.96)	68.45	(15.09)	82.05	(16.65)	93.88	(11.19)
1 yr 3 mos post-adoption		87.75	(2.31)	83.21	(9.21)	91.42	(15.83)	98.40	(8.67)
2 yrs 3 mos post-adoption		100.13	(14.07)	93.27	(16.36)	91.13	(5.34)	103.54	(3.16)
3 yrs 4 mos post-adoption		104.23	(6.08)	97.38	(7.48)	93.03	(6.17)		
				Chronological age results					
Age 5 years*	41	102.74	(10.76)	100.58	(12.71)	95.02	(10.78)		
Age 6–7 years	44	103.86	(14.37)	98.42	(13.18)	95.37	(14.03)		

Notes: Data are from Glennen (2014, 2015). Means and standard deviations are from standardized tests of English speech and language. MLU SSE = mean length of utterance standard score equivalent = [((Child's MLU – Predicted MLU)/Predicted MLU standard deviation) * 15] + 100. Data are organized according to the child's age of adoption and length of time post-adoption. Chronological age 5 and 6–7 year data include all age-of-adoption groups.

* Chronological age data at age 5 years excludes children adopted as 4-year-olds.

on data from a cohort of children adopted from Eastern Europe (Glennen, 2014, 2015). The children were initially divided into age-of-adoption groups and followed for three years post-adoption. Additional data from the same children at age 5 years and 6–7 years is also included. Means and standard deviations from standardized assessments of language and speech are provided along with MLU standard score equivalents (SSE). For each measure, 100 is the expected mean score for monolingual children speaking English and 85 is one standard deviation below the mean. This information can be used by professionals to determine whether a particular child is developing typically when compared to internationally adopted peers. Children adopted from different regions or situations with better caregiving and health might fare slightly better than these results; children adopted from extreme conditions would be expected to initially fare worse.

Children adopted internationally between 3 and 4 years

Children adopted from other countries between 3 and 4 years of age follow a language development trajectory that is similar to children adopted at younger ages; however, the learning curve is steeper and takes longer. A child adopted internationally at 18 months of age arrives in their adoptive country and quickly catches up to developmental expectations in L2. In contrast, a newly arrived 4-year-old needs to produce 1,500 words, comprehend 4,000 to 6,000 words, and produce four- to five-word sentences in order to be considered developmentally "caught up" in their new adopted language (Shipley & McAfee, 2015). Therefore, it should not be surprising that it takes longer for older adoptees to meet age-level expectations in L2. One issue for children adopted at older ages is the rapid attrition of the birth language. Within a few months of adoption, most expressive use of L1 is gone and comprehension disappears shortly thereafter (Gindis, 1999; Snedecker, Geren, & Shafto, 2007). Until L2 develops, these children have no language that lets them function at a level that matches their communication potential. They are different from bilingual children who can fall back on L1 when having difficulty comprehending or expressing themselves in L2. Children adopted at age 3 years and older typically begin school before attaining full proficiency in L2. This can set them up for academic failure, especially if they have true language learning delays (Glennen, 2009).

Despite all of these issues, most children who are adopted internationally at preschool ages rapidly learn their new language. Their prior language experience and cognitive maturity give them a boost in learning some aspects of L2, especially vocabulary. Children adopted at 2 years of age acquired 59 words within three months of adoption; children adopted at ages 3 and 4 acquired 175 words in the same time period (Glennen, 2009). This rapid rate continues over time with children adopted before 24 months of age learning at a rate of approximately 200 words per year, while children adopted at ages 2–3 years were able to learn 400 words in six months (Pollock, 2005). Internationally adopted children who were adopted between ages 2 and 5 years actually learned new vocabulary words at a faster rate than same-age monolingual peers (Snedecker et al., 2007). The developmental sequence of learning new vocabulary is similar to monolingual peers learning English; however, because the children already understand higher level concepts such as time or direction, they acquire words to express these concepts at earlier than expected developmental stages (Snedecker et al., 2007).

Standardized measures of expressive and receptive language indicate that children adopted internationally between the ages of 3 and 4 years learn their new language quickly (See Table 24.1). Similar to younger adoptees, language comprehension emerges before language expression. One year after adoption, children from Eastern Europe at 3 and 4 years of age had low-average language comprehension abilities (Glennen, 2014). They reached age-level expectations two years post-adoption and continued to improve through the third year post-adoption. Expressive language followed a similar pattern, but scores were consistently lower than receptive language. Phonological abilities developed even more rapidly in these older international adoptees. One year after adoption they achieved average scores on a standardized test of articulation (Glennen, 2014); however, it was anecdotally noted that some of the children's sound errors showed L1 interference. This was especially true for children adopted as 4-year-olds. They sometimes made errors by substituting sounds from L1 into L2. For example, the Russian alveolar affricates /ts/ and /dz/ were substituted for the English palatal affricates /ʧ/ and /ʤ/. These types of errors are frequently seen in bilingual children when L2 has sounds that do not exist in L1. Children adopted at older ages with more L1 experience appear to retain more remnants of their first language, especially phonological remnants. Finally, just like their younger adopted peers, children adopted at 3 and 4 years of age had difficulty learning morphosyntax when compared to other language areas. Three years after adoption, when all other language areas had effectively "caught up," MLU measures were still low-average (Glennen, 2014) (See Table 24.1).

Children adopted internationally at 5 years and older

There is little information about language development in internationally adopted children who arrive in their adoptive countries at 5 years of age and older, partly because there are fewer of them. Children adopted at older ages are often grouped into studies with children adopted at younger ages, which makes it difficult to extrapolate information specific to them. It would be expected that older adoptees would need more time to reach age-level expectations in L2. In addition, older adoptees arrive with more language abilities in L1, but if the family and community do not speak the language, L1 attrition still occurs. Case studies provide some information about L1 attrition in older internationally adopted children. Isurin (2000) assessed language in a 9-year-old adopted from Russia to the US. One year post-adoption the child could label approximately 80 percent of Russian and English words on a naming task, but recall times were faster in English. Two years later the child could only name 40 percent of the Russian words, with delayed recall of 10 to 15 seconds per word. The child's conversational Russian was described as "significantly deteriorated." Similarly, two months after arrival to the US, a 6-year-old Korean child used English and Korean equally on a naming task (O'Grady & Hattori, 2016). By the fifth month English was dominant, and by the ninth month Korean vocabulary declined to less than 20 percent of responses. Lyon (2009) described two 13-year-old adoptees who attended a summer Russian language camp in the US. One was adopted at age 8 and the other at age 10. Both were judged to have weak English language skills. The child who was adopted at 10 had better oral and written Russian compared to the child adopted at age 8. However, both children had significant vocabulary gaps and grammatical errors in Russian.

Children adopted after age 5 will show signs of interference between L1 and L2. Glennen (2016) provided anecdotal information on a small number of children who were adopted at school age. The children acquired English at a rapid rate and were able to engage in conversation within a few months of adoption. Within a year, most developed what would be described as BICS proficiency in L2 (Basic Interpersonal Communication Skills) (Cummins, 1991), which sometimes masked the fact that they had significant gaps in their L2 learning. A year after adoption they were still substituting L1 sounds into L2.

Distorted vowels and stress errors that are typical of bilingual children learning English were also observed. Three years after adoption grammatical errors were still noticeable, however the frequency of errors decreased steadily over time.

Implications for policy and practice

Children adopted at ages 5 and older will learn their new language over a lengthy period of time in a process similar to other bilingual children. However, the rate of learning L2 and losing L1 may be accelerated. Unlike bilingual children who retain proficiency in L1 while learning L2, internationally adopted children lose their abilities in L1 long before L2 reaches age-expected levels of proficiency. They typically start school shortly after arriving in their new adoptive home, however without a proficient language to use for learning, they are at academic risk and might require additional tutoring or educational support to succeed in school (Glennen, 2016). Unfortunately, in most US public schools, it is difficult to qualify for special education and bilingual language services at the same time. Children have to demonstrate deficiencies in their dominant language, which is difficult to do when L1 is undergoing attrition and L2 is still in the process of being learned. When possible, at the time of adoption or shortly afterwards, parents should document the child's L1 language abilities before they undergo attrition. If needed, parents can then use evidence of a language delay in L1 to help qualify the child for additional speech and language support or other services (Glennen, 2009).

Language abilities in school-age internationally adopted children

The prior sections of this chapter reviewed language development in internationally adopted children during the first few years after adoption. As these children grow into the school years, they generally continue to score within the average range on tests of language and speech (see Table 24.1; Dalen & Rygvold, 2006; Glennen, 2015; Scott et al., 2013; Scott, Roberts, & Krakow, 2008). There is, however, a growing body of evidence that subtle language learning differences emerge with the complex language demands of school. A meta-analysis determined that school-age internationally adopted children slightly underperformed on norm-referenced language tests, a difference that was not observed in younger children (Scott, Roberts, & Glennen, 2011). One reason for the late appearance of language concerns is the fact that older children can be assessed using complex evaluation tools. Subtle language weaknesses that are not detected at young ages are visible when task complexity increases. This information adds to our knowledge of language strengths and weaknesses in internationally adopted children when they reach school age.

Vocabulary is an area of strength for most internationally adopted children after they have sufficient time to fully learn L2. Delcenserie (2016) provided vocabulary data for children adopted from China to the Montreal region of Canada. At ages 9 to 12, the children averaged 120 on French receptive vocabulary tests and 100 on expressive naming tests (test average = 100). Glennen (2015) similarly assessed English expressive vocabulary in children adopted from Eastern Europe. Children who were aged 6–7 years had average scores, and only 4.5 percent fell >1 standard deviation below the mean. Expressive vocabulary was the only language measure that correlated with age of adoption in 6–7-year-old children.

Many internationally adopted children have difficulty with complex syntactic and grammatical forms (Delcenserie, Genesee, & Gauthier, 2013; Gauthier, Genesee, & Kasparian, 2012). These weaknesses were seen during the early years when measures of

MLU lagged behind developmental expectations (Glennen, 2014). When children reached school age, L2 grammar weaknesses continued. Delcenserie et al. (2013) gave a French grammar comprehension test to 7–8-year-old children adopted from China to Canada and re-assessed the children when they were 9–12 years of age (Delcenserie & Genesee, 2014a). At age 7–8 years, the children had average scores but did not score as well as monolingual peers. At ages 9–12 years the children scored significantly below average. Glennen (2015) also noted decreases in morphosyntax when children adopted from Eastern Europe were assessed at age 5 years and again at ages 6–7 years. The group average decreased significantly with 31 percent of the 6–7-year-old children scoring >1 standard deviation below the mean. The children made irregular noun and verb errors such as "mices" and "drawed." They produced sentences such as "She was luckest" and "He's will eating next." Delcenserie and Genesee (2014b) found similar grammatical errors on a French expressive language task.

Language tasks that involve verbal memory and executive functions, such as following complex directions, are another area of relative weakness for some internationally adopted children whose language performance in all other areas is average (Desmarais, Roeber, Smith, & Pollak, 2012). Verbal memory involves short-term immediate memory, such as repeating nonsense words, word lists, sentences, or numbers. Verbal working memory involves manipulating information held in short-term storage (Adams, Nguyen, & Cowan, 2018), such as remembering a list of words and repeating them in reverse order. Internationally adopted children have difficulty with both immediate and working verbal memory, but results vary depending on the task. Glennen (2015) assessed immediate verbal memory in 7-year-olds adopted from Eastern Europe using a sentence repetition task. As a group, the overall score was average. However, 34 percent of the children scored >1 standard deviation below the test mean, which was a significant difference from expected outcomes. Similar results were found in regard to a number repetition task given to the same children. Children adopted from China also scored below non-adopted peers on French sentence repetition tasks at ages 7 and 10 years but scored as well as monolingual peers on non-verbal memory tasks (Delcenserie et al., 2013; Gauthier & Genesee, 2011). Finally, Glennen (2015) looked at verbal working memory using a task that required school-age children to re-sequence known information, for example saying the days of the week backwards. Test scores were significantly below average, with more than a third of the children scoring ≥ 1 standard deviation below the mean at both ages. In summary, as a group, internationally adopted children have relatively weak verbal memory abilities when compared to monolingual peers.

Verbal memory is important to the development of language and literacy skills (Archibald, 2018). Relative weaknesses in this area can lead to further difficulties in learning to read and write. Most studies of academic achievement and literacy abilities in internationally adopted children used indirect measures such as teacher or parent reports. Direct measures of literacy are limited. In one of the few studies, Scott et al. (2008) directly measured the reading and writing abilities of girls adopted from China using a wide battery of assessments. The girls scored the same as, or better than, age-level expectations on most measures. This was surprising given the known relationship between verbal memory and reading abilities (Dehn, 2008). Phonological processing was assessed but reported as a composite of multiple subtests including non-word repetition, rapid naming, digit repetition, and phonological awareness skills such as blending and segmenting sounds. Phonological processing test results were average but lower than scores obtained on other literacy measures. A follow-up project with additional children adopted from China examined phonological processing more thoroughly (Scott et al., 2013). The children scored well on measures of passage comprehension, rapid naming, blending, and segmenting sounds. The only area of relative weakness occurred on measures of short-term verbal memory. Glennen (unpublished data) assessed reading fluency and comprehension in 8-year-olds adopted from Eastern Europe. Overall scores for the group were average, but 30 percent of the children had reading fluency scores that fell >1 standard deviation below the mean, primarily due to slow reading rate. The children's reading comprehension was better and matched expected outcomes.

Implications for policy and practice

When internationally adopted children reach school age, their overall language abilities are typically within the average range, but they often have specific areas of relative weakness in grammar and verbal memory that can impact school performance. These concerns are shared by parents who reported that 59 percent to 64 percent of school-age internationally adopted children needed educational support to succeed in school (Glennen & Bright, 2005; Scott et al., 2008). "Support" ranged from after-school tutors all the way to self-contained special education classrooms. Speech language therapy was the most common support service (27 percent), followed by reading (16 percent) and general tutoring (13 percent). Parents and professionals need to be aware of these issues and intervene quickly if an internationally adopted child starts to struggle academically in school. Because most of these children have overall language and reading abilities within the average range, qualifying for additional services in the school system is sometimes difficult (Glennen, 2016). Parents might need to use private tutors or specialists to provide additional support.

Conclusion

Growing up in a quality caregiving environment is one of the best ways to provide children with an opportunity to boost language development. Children raised in homes with neglectful parents, poor foster care, or institutional care experience long-term stress that impacts neurobiology and language learning. Children adopted into better environments at early ages have better language outcomes than children who are adopted at older ages. Internationally adopted children face additional hurdles when their language changes. Although most catch up and do well, as a group they have observed weaknesses in verbal memory and grammar that are likely caused by a combination of neurological factors related to their early environment and second language learning.

References

Abrahamsson, N., & Hyltenstam, K. (2009). Age of onset and nativelikeness in a second language: Listener perception versus linguistic scrutiny. *Language Learning, 59*, 249–306. doi:10.1111/j.1467-9922.2009.00507.x

Adams, E., Nguyen, A., & Cowan, N. (2018). Theories of working memory: Differences in definition, degree of modularity role of attention, and purpose. *Language Speech and Hearing Services in Schools, 49*, 340–355. doi:10.1044/2018_LSHSS-17-0114

Almas, A., Degnan, K., Nelson, C., Zeanah, N., & Fox, N. (2016). IQ at age 12 following a history of institutional care: Findings from the Bucharest early intervention project. *Developmental Psychology, 52*, 1858–1866. doi:10.1037/dev0000167

Archibald, L. (2018). The reciprocal influences of working memory and linguistic knowledge on language performance: Considerations for the assessment of children with developmental language disorder. *Language Speech and Hearing Services in Schools, 49*, 424–433. doi:10.1044/2018_LSHSS-17-0094

Beckett, C., Maughan, B., Rutter, M., Castle, J., Colvert, E., Groothues, C., ... Sonuga-Barke, E. J. (2006). Do the effects of early severe deprivation on cognition persist into early adolescence? Findings from the English and Romanian adoptees study. *Child Development, 77*, 696–711. doi:10.1111/j.1467-8624.2006.00898.x

Cohen, N., Lojkasek, M., Yaghoub Zadeh, Z., Pugliese, M., & Kiefer, H. (2008). Children adopted from China: A prospective study of their growth and development. *Journal of Child Psychology and Psychiatry, 49*, 458–468. doi:10.1111/j.1469-7610.2007.01853.x

Cummins, J. (1991). Interdependence of first- and second-language proficiency in bilingual children. In E. Bialystok (Ed.), *Language processing in bilingual children* (pp. 70–89). Cambridge, England: Cambridge University Press.

Dalen, M., & Rygvold, A. (2006). Educational achievement in adopted children from China. *Adoption Quarterly, 9*, 45–58. doi:10.1300/J145v09n04_03

DeBellis, M., Hooper, S., Spratt, E., & Woolley, D. (2009). Neuropsychological findings in childhood neglect and their relationships to pediatric PTSD. *Journal of International Neuropsychology Society, 15*, 868–878. doi:10.1177/1077559513497420

Dehn, M. (2008). *Working memory and academic learning: Assessment and intervention.* Hoboken, NJ: John Wiley & Sons.

Delcenserie, A. (2016). Language, cognitive, and academic abilities of school-age internationally adopted children. In F. Genesee & A. Delcenserie (Eds.), *Starting over: The language development in internationally adopted children* (pp. 95–124). Philadelphia, PA: John Benjamins.

Delcenserie, A., & Genesee, F. (2014a). Language and memory abilities of internationally adopted children from China: Evidence for early age effects. *Journal of Child Language, 41*, 1195–1223. doi:10.1017/S030500091300041X

Delcenserie, A., & Genesee, F. (2014b). The acquisition of accusative object clitics by IA children from China: Do they still experience difficulties during school-age? *Journal of Child Language, 42*, 196–209. doi:10.1017/S0305000913000500

Delcenserie, A., Genesee, F., & Gauthier, K. (2013). Language abilities of internationally adopted children from China during the early school years: Evidence for early age effects? *Applied Psycholinguistics, 34*, 541–568. doi:10.1017/S0142716411000865

Desmarais, C., Roeber, B., Smith, M., & Pollak, S. (2012). Sentence comprehension in post-institutionalized school-age children. *Journal of Speech, Language, and Hearing Research, 55*, 45–54. doi:10.1044/1092-4388(2011/10-0246)

Flege, J., Yeni-Komshian, G., & Liu, S. (1999). Age constraints on second-language acquisition. *Journal of Memory and Language, 41*, 78–104. doi:10.1006/jmla.1999.2638

Gauthier, K., & Genesee, F. (2011). Language development in internationally adopted children: A special case of early second language learning. *Child Development, 82*, 887–901. doi:10.1111/j.1467-8624.2011.01578.x

Gauthier, K., Genesee, F., & Kasparian, K. (2012). Acquisition of complement clitics and tense morphology in internationally adopted children acquiring French. *Bilingualism: Language and Cognition, 15*, 304–319. doi:10.1017/S1366728910000635

Gindis, B. (1999). Language-related issues for international adoptees and adoptive families. In T. Tepper, L. Hannon, & D. Sandstrom (Eds.), *International adoption: Challenges and opportunities* (pp. 98–107). Meadowlands, PA: Parent Network for the Post-Institutionalized Child.

Glennen, S. (2002). Language development and delay in internationally adopted infants and toddlers: A review. *American Journal of Speech Language Pathology, 11*, 333–339. doi:10.1044/1058-0360(2002/038)

Glennen, S. (2007). Predicting language outcomes for internationally adopted children. *Journal of Speech, Language, and Hearing Research, 50*, 529–548. doi:10.1044/1092-4388(2007/036)

Glennen, S. (2009). Speech and language guidelines for children adopted from abroad at older ages. *Topics in Language Disorders, 29*(1), 50–64. doi:10.1097/TLD.0b013e3181976df4

Glennen, S. (2014). A longitudinal study of language and speech in children who were internationally adopted at different ages: Outcomes and assessment guidelines. *Language, Speech, and Hearing Services in Schools, 45*, 185–203. doi:10.1044/2014_LSHSS-13-0035

Glennen, S. (2015). Internationally adopted children in the early school years: Relative strengths and weaknesses in language abilities. *Language, Speech, and Hearing Services in Schools, 46*, 1–13. doi:10.1044/2014_LSHSS-13-0042

Glennen, S. (2016). Speech and language clinical issues in internationally adopted children. In F. Genesee & A. Delcenserie (Eds.), *Starting over: The language development in internationally adopted children* (pp. 147–177). Philadelphia, PA: John Benjamins.

Glennen, S., & Bright, B. (2005). Five years later: Language in school age internationally adopted children. *Seminars in Speech and Language, 26*, 86–101. doi:10.1055/s-2005-864219

Glennen, S., & Masters, G. (2002). Typical and atypical language development in infants and toddlers adopted from Eastern Europe. *American Journal of Speech-Language Pathology, 11*, 417–433. doi:10.1044/1058-0360(2002/045)

Glennen, S., Rozinsky-Grunhut, A., & Tracy, R. (2005). Linguistic interference between L1 and L2 in internationally adopted children. *Seminars in Speech and Language, 26*, 64–75. doi:10.1055/s-2005-864217

Hardy-Brown, K., & Plomin, R. (1985). Infant communicative development: Evidence from adoptive and biological families for genetic and environmental influences on rate differences. *Developmental Psychology, 22*, 378–385. doi:10.1037/0012-1649.21.2.378

Harlaar, N., Cutting, L., Deater-Deckard, K., Dethorne, L. S., Justice, L. M., Schatschneider, C., ... Petrill, S. A. (2010). Predicting individual differences in reading comprehension: A twin study. *Annals of Dyslexia, 60*, 265–288. doi:10.1007/s11881-010-0044-7

Hayiou-Thomas, M. (2008). Genetic and environmental influences on early speech, language and literacy development. *Journal of Communication Disorders, 41*, 397–408. doi:10.1016/j.jcomdis.2008.03.002

Hayiou-Thomas, M., Dale, P., & Plomin, R. (2012). The etiology of variation in language skills changes with development: A longitudinal twin study of language from 2 to 12 years. *Developmental Science, 15*, 233–249. doi:10.1111/j.1467-7687.2011.01119.x

Hayiou-Thomas, M., Kovas, Y., Harlaar, N., Bishop, D., Dale, D., & Plomin, R. (2006). Common genetic aetiology for diverse language skills in 4½ year old twins. *Journal of Child Language, 33*, 339–368. doi:10.1017/S0305000906007331

Hwa-Froelich, D., & Matsuo, H. (2010). Communication development and differences in children adopted from China and Eastern Europe. *Language Speech and Hearing Services in Schools, 41*, 349–366. doi:10.1044/0161-1461%282009/08-0085%29

Isurin, L. (2000). Deserted island or a child's first language forgetting. *Bilingualism: Language and Cognition, 3*, 151–166. doi:10.1017/S1366728900000237

Jacobs, E., Miller, L., & Tirella, L. (2010). Developmental and behavioral performance of internationally adopted preschoolers: A pilot study. *Child Psychiatry and Human Development, 41*, 15–29. doi:10.1007/s10578-009-0149-6

Kuhl, P. (2010). Brain mechanisms in early language acquisition. *Neuron, 67*, 713–727.

Lyon, A. (2009). Birth language attrition and reacquisition in Russian adoptees. *Russian Language Journal, 59*, 121–134.

Mason, P., & Narad, C. (2005). International adoption: A health and developmental prospective. *Seminars in Speech and Language, 26*, 1–9. doi:10.1055/s-2005-864211

Maurer, D., & Werker, J. (2013). Perceptual narrowing during infancy: A comparison of language and faces. *Developmental Psychology, 56*, 154–178. doi:10.1002/dev.21177

Motz, M., Espinet, S. D., Jeong, J. J., Major, D., Racine, N., Chamberlin, J., & Pepler, D. J. (2011). The role of the mother-child relationship in developmental outcomes of infants and young children with and without prenatal alcohol exposure. *Journal of Population Therapeutics and Clinical Pharmacology, 18*, e544-e563.

Nicoladis, E., & Grabois, H. (2002). Learning English and losing Chinese: A case study of a child adopted from China. *International Journal of Bilingualism, 6*, 441–454. doi:10.1177/13670069020060040401

Norrman, G., Hyltenstam, K., & Bylund, E. (2016). Long-term language development in international adoptees. In F. Genesee & A. Delcenserie (Eds.), *Starting over: The language development in internationally adopted children* (pp. 179–201). Philadelphia, PA: John Benjamins.

O'Grady, W., & Hattori, R. (2016). Language acquisition and language revitalization. *Language Documentation and Conservation, 10*, 46–58.

Oh, J., Au, T., & Jun, S. (2010). Early childhood language memory in the speech perception of international adoptees. *Journal of Child Language, 37*, 1123–1132. doi:10.1017/S0305000909990286

Park, H. (2014). Korean adoptees in Sweden: Have they lost their first language completely? *Applied Psycholinguistics*, *35*, 1–25. doi:10.1017/S0142716413000507

Pierce, L., Genesee, F., Gauthier, K., & Dubois, M. (2015). Communication patterns between parents and children: Comparing mothers and fathers in different learner contexts. *Applied Psycholinguistics*, *36*, 1223–1246. doi:10.1017/S0142716414000125

Pierce, L., Genesee, F., & Klein, D. (2016). Language loss or retention in internationally adopted children. In F. Genesee & A. Delcenserie (Eds.), *Starting over: The language development in internationally adopted children* (pp. 179–201). Philadelphia, PA: John Benjamins.

Pierce, L., Klein, D., Chen, J., Delcenserie, A., & Genesee, F. (2014). Mapping the unconscious maintenance of a lost first language. *Proceedings of the National Academy of Sciences*, *111*, 17314–17319. doi:10.1073/pnas.1409411111

Pollock, K. (2005). Early language growth in children adopted from China: Preliminary normative data. *Seminars in Speech and Language*, *26*, 22–32. doi:10/0155/S-2005-864213

Pollock, K., & Price, J. (2005). Phonological skills of children adopted from China: Implications for assessment. *Seminars in Speech and Language*, *26*, 54–63. doi:10.1055/s-2005-864216

Rajagopal, A., Holland, S., Walz, N., Staat, M., Altaye, M., & Wade, S. (2013). A functional magnetic resonance imaging study of language function in international adoptees. *The Journal of Pediatrics*, *163*, 1458–1464. doi:10.1016/j.jpeds.2013.06.026

Rakhlin, N., Hein, S., Doyle, N., Hart, L., Macomber, D., Ruchkin, V., ... Grigorenko, E. (2015). Language development of internationally adopted children: Adverse early experiences outweigh the age of acquisition. *Journal of Communication Disorders*, *57*, 66–80. doi:10.1016/j.jcomdis.2015.08.003

Roberts, J., Pollock, K., & Krakow, R. (2005). Continued catch-up and language delay in children adopted from China. *Seminars in Speech and Language*, *26*, 76–85. doi:10.1055/s-2005-864218

Roberts, J., Pollock, K., Krakow, R., Price, J., Fulmer, K., & Wang, P. (2005). Language development in preschool-aged children adopted from China. *Journal of Speech Language & Hearing Research*, *48*, 93–107. doi:10.1044/1092-4388(2005/008)

Scott, K., Pollock, K., Roberts, J., & Krakow, R. (2013). Phonological processing skills of children adopted internationally. *American Journal of Speech-Language Pathology*, *22*, 673–683. doi:10.1044/1058-0360%282013/12-0133%29

Scott, K., Roberts, J., & Glennen, S. (2011). How well do children who are internationally adopted acquire language? A meta-analysis. *Journal of Speech, Language, and Hearing Research*, *54*, 1153–1169. doi:10.1044/1092-4388(2010/10-0075)

Scott, K., Roberts, J., & Krakow, R. (2008). Oral and written language development of children adopted from China. *American Journal of Speech Language Pathology*, *17*, 150–160. doi:10.1044/1058-0360%282008/015%29

Shipley, K., & McAfee, J. (2015). *Assessment in speech-language pathology: A resource manual* (5th ed.). Boston: Cengage Learning.

Singh, L., Liederman, J., Mierzejewski, R., & Barnes, J. (2011). Rapid reacquisition of native phoneme contrasts after disuse: You do not always lose what you do not use. *Developmental Science*, *14*, 949–959. doi:10.1111/j.1467-7687.2011.01044.x

Snedecker, J., Geren, J., & Shafto, C. (2007). Starting over: International adoption as a natural experiment in language development. *Psychological Science*, *18*, 79–87. doi:10.1111/j.1467-9280.2007.01852.x

Snedecker, J., Geren, J., & Shafto, C. (2012). Disentangling the effects of cognitive development and linguistic expertise: A longitudinal study of the acquisition of English in internationally adopted children. *Cognitive Psychology*, *65*, 39–76. doi:10.1016/j.cogpsych.2012.01.004

Tan, T., Loker, T., Dedrick, R., & Marfo, K. (2012). Second-first language acquisition: Analysis of expressive language in a sample of girls adopted from China. *Journal of Child Language*, *39*, 365–382. doi:10.1017/S0305000911000109

Tan, T., & Yang, Y. (2005). Language development of Chinese adoptees 18–35 months old. *Early Childhood Research Quarterly*, *20*, 57–68. doi:10.1016/j.ecresq.2005.01.004

Tarullo, A., Garvin, M., & Gunnar, M. (2011). Atypical EEG power correlates with indiscriminately friendly behavior in internationally adopted children. *Developmental Psychology*, *47*, 417–431. doi:10.1037/a0021363

Thorn, A., & Gathercole, S. (1999). Language-specific knowledge and short-term memory in bilingual and non-bilingual children. *The Quarterly Journal of Experimental Psychology Human Experimental Psychology*, *52*, 303–324. doi:10.1080/713755823

Vinnerljung, B., & Hjern, A. (2011). Cognitive, educational and self-support outcomes of long-term foster care versus adoption. *Children and Youth Services Review, 33*, 1902–1910. doi:10.1016/j.childyouth.2011.05.016

Vinnerljung, B., Lindblad, F., Hjern, A., Rasmussen, F., & Dalen, M. (2010). School performance at age 16 among international adoptees: A Swedish national cohort study. *International Social Work, 53*, 510–527. doi:10.1177/0020872809360037

Vorria, P., Ntouma, M., & Rutter, M. (2015). The cognitive development and school achievement of adopted adolescents: The Greek "Metera" study. *European Journal of Developmental Psychology, 12*, 1–14. doi:10.1080/17405629.2014.933703

Waterman, J., Nadeem, E., Paczkowski, E., Foster, J., Lavner, J., Belin, T., & Miranda, J. (2010). Pre-placement risk and longitudinal cognitive development for children adopted from foster care. *Child Development, 92*, 9–30.

Welsh, J., & Viana, A. (2012). Developmental outcomes of internationally adopted children. *Adoption Quarterly, 15*, 241–264. doi:10.1080/10926755.2012.731029

Werker, J., & Hensch, T. (2015). Critical periods in speech perception: New directions. *Annual Review of Psychology, 66*, 173–196. doi:10.1146/annurev-psych-010814-015104

Werker, J., & Tees, R. (1984). Cross-language speech perception: Evidence for perceptual reorganization during the first year of life. *Infant Behavior and Development*, 7, 49–63. doi:10.1016/S0163-6383(84)80022-3

25

BEHAVIORAL AND EMOTIONAL ADJUSTMENT IN ADOPTEES

Eveliina Holmgren, Hanna Raaska, Marko Elovainio, and Helena Lapinleimu

Research on adopted children suggests that adoption has positive effects on adopted children's later development and adjustment in comparison with their non-adopted age-peers who remain in institutional care (Nickman et al., 2005; van IJzendoorn & Juffer, 2006). However, there are some identified risk factors for their socioemotional and neurocognitive development that might affect an adopted child's later adaptation. Children are typically adopted from poor conditions to ones with higher resources (Selman, 2012). Poverty, prenatal malnutrition, poor maternal health, maternal stress, and birth complications also increase risk for future developmental problems (Graf, Kekatpure, & Kosofsky, 2013; LaPrairie, Schechter, Robinson, & Brennan, 2011; Lawn, Kerber, Enweronu-Laryea, & Massee Bateman, 2009).

Many internationally adopted children have lived their first years of life in institutions, which is recognized as an independent risk factor for developmental and socioemotional problems, such as difficulties in intimate social interaction, emotion regulation, and cognitive development (Hodges & Tizard, 1989; Rutter et al., 2007; Tottenham et al., 2010). Most institutions offer a physically safe environment with medical care, nutrition, sanitation, and even toys. Staff's opportunities for primary caregiving, however, are often limited and the interaction with, and sensitivity to, the child might be low (Tirella et al., 2008).

It is not surprising that recent research on developmental outcomes of adopted children reveals that adopted children often demonstrate global delays in physical and cognitive development at the time of their arrival in their adoptive families, but experience a period of rapid catch-up following adoption (Palacios, Román, & Comacho, 2011). The catch-up might be true, especially, concerning the developmental problems caused by institutionalization (Fox, Almas, Degnan, Nelson, & Zeanah, 2011; Tottenham, 2012). In multiple domains of development, recovery seems to be associated with degree of initial impairment, and the length and severity of deprivation centrally affects the developmental outcome (Merz & McCall, 2010). See also Chapters 13 and 26 in this volume for additional information on this topic.

The role of attachment

A child's former experiences affect their adaptation, especially shortly after adoption. In settings with compromised caregiving, a child might have had no chance to form a consistent relationship (e.g., secure attachment to a primary caregiver). In need of comfort, support, nurturing, or protection, an infant has a strong tendency to seek proximity and contact with a specific primary caregiver. As a result of repetition, the child's experiences become mentally internalized as internal working models of human relationships during the first years of life (Zeanah, Berlin, & Boris, 2011). These attachment models are activated especially during stress, and they guide behavior to ensure the child's essential need for intimacy and comfort is met (Bowlby, 1973). If a child has no recognizable attachment pattern, they lack a strategy for obtaining proximity to increase feelings of security (so-called disorganized attachment pattern). The child's reactions to the caregiver might include mixtures of rapid, incoherent sequences of proximity-seeking, avoidance, or resistance. The child might be fearful of the parent or show other behaviors indicating failure to use the caregiver as an attachment figure. At the preschool age, disorganization might be transformed into controlling, punitive, or solicitous caregiving behaviors directed toward the parent (Zeanah et al., 2011). These disorganized attachment patterns are over-represented among internationally adopted children who might not have had the chance to form a secure attachment strategy (van IJzendoorn & Juffer, 2006). Although these behavioral and emotional patterns are common after adoption and can harm the child's emotional and behavioral adjustment, a number of studies have shown that these disorganized attachment patterns diminish after placement into adoptive homes (Barone, Lionetti, & Green, 2017; van den Dries, Juffer, van IJzendoorn, & Bakermans-Kranenburg, 2009). In our own study, we evaluated adopted children's attachment-related behavior among Finnish internationally adopted children (n=212) by using a parental questionnaire (Kinship Center Attachment Questionnaire; Kappenberg & Halpern, 2006). The questionnaire was sent to parents twice: two and four years after adoption. In comparisons with non-adopted children, adopted children had more attachment-related behavioral problems than their age-mates two years after adoption, but the difference was no longer statistically significant four years after adoption (Raaska, Elovainio, Lapinleimu, Matomäki, & Sinkkonen, 2015).

Some internationally adopted children might not have had a chance to form any consistent relationship with a caregiver. Among neglected or maltreated children, a subset display a specific social behavior pattern classified as Reactive Attachment Disorder (RAD), and its diagnostic criteria were first defined in the third edition of the Diagnostic and Statistical Manual of Mental Disorders (DSM-III, American Psychiatric Association, 1980). Later, both the DSM and the International Classification of Diseases (ICD; World Health Organization, 1992) defined two clinical disorders of aberrant attachment behaviors and other behavioral social abnormalities that can result from social neglect and deprivation: aforementioned RAD and Disinhibited Social Engagement Disorder (DSED).

Children with DSED are characterized by overly familiar verbal or physical behavior, a willingness to go off with an unfamiliar adult without hesitation, and a tendency not to check back with a caregiver. Of note, children with DSED might have a secure attachment with their parents despite their aberrant social behavior (Zeanah, Chesher, Boris, & American Academy of Child and Adolescent Psychiatry Committee on Quality Issues, 2016). Symptoms of DSED can be persistent across childhood and even into adulthood (Guyon-Harris, Humphreys, Fox, Nelson, & Zeanah, 2018). In contrast, children with RAD show little interaction with their caregivers, and their overall social reciprocity is minimal. They lack positive affect and can appear unresponsive. Their attachment behaviors, such as seeking proximity to specific adults and seeking comfort from caregivers, are not consistent or might be absent. They might have problems with emotional regulation: unexplained irritability, sadness, or fearfulness with caregivers. In follow-up studies, signs of RAD have shown a marked decrease after child's placement into home environments (Zeanah, Chesher, Boris, & American Academy of Child and Adolescent Psychiatry [AACAP] Committee on Quality Issues [CQI], 2016).

Emotional and behavioral adjustment

In child psychiatry, a distinction is often made between "externalizing" and "internalizing" symptoms, with externalizing symptoms referring to problems manifested in an individual's outward behavior and reflecting negative acts on the external environment (e.g., aggression and anti-social behaviors), and internalizing symptoms referring to inward-directed problems that affect an individual's internal psychological environment (e.g., anxiety and depression) (Campbell, Shaw, & Gilliom, 2000). In real life, however, the manifestations of externalizing and internalizing problems inevitably intertwine.

Concerning later behavioral and emotional adjustment in adoptees, studies have yielded mixed findings. Research has identified a trend in which, compared to their non-adopted peers, adoptees exhibit somewhat more psychological difficulties and are over-represented in mental health services (Brand & Brinich, 1999; Juffer & van IJzendoorn, 2005). However, the use of mental health services might be largely explained by the adoptive parents' lower threshold for seeking services for their children, sociodemographic characteristics of adoptive parents (Hellerstedt et al., 2008), or parents' tendency to more sensitively observe and report changes in behavior (Stams, Juffer, Rispens, & Hoksbergen, 2000). The meta-analysis performed by Juffer and van IJzendoorn (2005) showed that, compared with non-adopted controls, international adoptees showed only slightly higher rates of both emotional and behavioral disturbance. A longitudinal study on US adolescents adopted in infancy (see Keyes, Sharma, Elkins, Iacono, & McGue, 2008) as well as several single studies (e.g., Gagnon-Oosterwaal et al., 2012; Nickman et al., 2005; Stams et al., 2000; Tan & Marfo, 2006) corroborate these findings: most adoptees seem to be behaviorally and emotionally well-adjusted.

However, many studies, especially those including children with longer histories of institutional rearing, have indicated these individuals are at higher risk of developing difficulties in behavioral and emotional adjustment, among which are mental health and emotional psychological adjustment problems (Fisher, 2014). Difficulties related to emotional issues are reported to be quite persistent even after placement in an adoptive or foster home (Colvert et al., 2008). The early adverse exposures can potentially cause negative changes in both brain structure and function, leading to problems in physiological and behavioral regulation and attachment, which exacerbate risk for mental and physical problems across the lifespan (Dozier & Bernard, 2017). However, identifying the pathways between adverse early experiences and certain outcomes in emotional or behavioral adjustment is far from simple and, thus, caution is warranted when applying the findings to an individual adopted child and their future development. Research with children who have experienced multiple and/or chronic adversities early in life (e.g., maltreatment, deprivation, and institutionalization) has shown these children to be at risk for poor developmental outcomes, including behavioral problems that can persist or get worse over time (Becker-Weidman, 2009); many of these conditions apply to adopted children.

Research has indicated that despite the rapid recovery in multiple developmental domains, problems in behavioral and emotional adjustment are one of the most salient challenges in caring for children with histories of early adversities. Extensive evidence confirms that foster and adopted children may manifest the long-term effects of exposure to early life stress (Gunnar, Fisher, & the Early Experience, Stress, and Prevention Network, 2006; Rushton, Mayes, Dance, & Quinton, 2003), and rates of psychopathology and maladjustment among this group of children were noted to be considerably higher than rates among the general population (Burns et al., 2004).

On the other hand, resilience after adoptive placement can also be present in behavioral and emotional dimensions (Canzi, Rosnati, Palacios, & Román, 2018). As stated by Barone and Lionetti (2011) and van IJzendoorn and Juffer (2006), adoption appears to be an intervention that assures the adopted child an opportunity to catch up on emotional development and to (at least partially) resolve prior experiences with the support of their adoptive parents. Key factors affecting the developmental outcome in various developmental domains seem to be the degree of initial impairment and the length and severity of experienced deprivation (Merz & McCall, 2010).

Mediating mechanisms related to behavioral and emotional adjustment

Problems in behavioral and emotional adjustment among adopted children have been explained by multiple mechanisms: poor prenatal or birth circumstances (including exposure to substances); a child's genetic disposition; various developmental problems; lack of early experiences that contribute to development in multiple ways; experiences of abuse or neglect; institutional care with insensitive, unresponsive, and non-individual care; several possible traumatic breakings of attachment bonds; and problems in later attachment (see e.g., Rutter et al., 2007; Stams et al., 2000). Additional contributions to adoptees' later adjustment include parenting style (Tan, Camras, Deng, Zhang, & Lu, 2012); relations, interaction, and novel attachment patterns within families with adopted children (see Palacios & Brodzinsky, 2010); children's understanding of the adoption and adoption communication (Brodzinsky, 2006); as well as interaction between genes and environmental factors and their effect on various neurobiological and neurochemical structures and processes in adopted children (e.g., Colvert et al., 2008; Tienari et al., 2004). In fact, a topic of contemporary interest among adoption researchers is the identification of the factors and processes related to the variability of adjustment in adoptees (cf. Palacios & Brodzinsky, 2010). Among the suggested possible mediating mechanisms between early adversity and later problems in emotional and behavioral adjustment are executive functions, emotion regulation, and emotion understanding and attachment.

Executive functions

Executive function abilities refer to a set of higher order cognitive processes that allow individuals to engage in planning and conscious goal-directed problem solving (Zelazo, Carlson, & Kesek, 2008). This is increasingly recognized as an important protective factor for children experiencing adversity. Good executive skills are known to promote better stress and emotion regulation as well as social and academic adjustment, and thus they are important in an individual's emotional and behavioral adjustment (Kochanska, Murray, & Harlan, 2000).

A substantial body of research has shown that stable and responsive caregiving serves as a key environmental aspect that drives normative brain and behavioral development early in life (Bick & Nelson, 2016; Tottenham et al., 2010). There is mounting evidence showing that early adversities, such as maltreatment and institutional rearing with compromised developmental environmental characteristics, are connected to various alterations in children's neurodevelopment. The observed changes in brain structure and functions, especially in prefrontal cortex and limbic system, point to potential pathways in stress, emotional, and behavioral dysregulation, which increase the risk for internalizing and externalizing difficulties during later development (Bick & Nelson, 2016).

Research suggests that children with experiences of early psychosocial deprivation might have reduced performance in a variety of self-regulatory and executive function domains, such as inhibitory control (Pollak et al., 2009), which might increase their risk for attention, hyperactivity, and impulsivity problems (McLaughlin et al., 2014). Also, among international adoptees, early life adversity has been associated with significant reductions in executive function performance on tasks that measured cognitive flexibility, working memory, and inhibitory control (Hostinar, Stellern, Schaefer, Carlson, & Gunnar, 2012). It has also been suggested that for institutionalized children, ADHD symptoms might constitute a specific response to early institutional deprivation (MacLean, 2003; Rutter et al., 2007). Studies have shown that Romanian adoptees who had spent more time in severely depriving institutions showed more ADHD symptoms (Rutter et al., 2007), supporting the idea that these symptoms might be partially caused by institutional deprivation.

In the etiology of ADHD, in addition to genetic risk, studies support the notion of gene-by-environment interaction, referring to interaction between genetic risk and environmental factors. Adopted children might be exposed to various genetic as well as pre- and perinatal risk factors, toxins, and poor nutrition, but also to unfavorable psychosocial environmental conditions (Gunnar, van Dulmen, & the International Adoption Project Team, 2007). As elevated levels of inattention and hyperactivity/impulsivity have been reported in different institutionalized populations (McLaughlin et al., 2014; Wiik et al., 2011), with the duration and severity of deprivation increasing the effects (Merz & McCall, 2010), researchers have suggested one pathway to ADHD being predominantly social or environmental among these children with a history of deprivation. Researchers propose that the lack of response-contingent stimulation during the first few years of life (for example, in institutional settings) might hinder the development of brain regions that are important for attention (Kennedy et al., 2016). This deprivation-specific profile of ADHD has appeared distinctive in terms of its inattentive presentation, high proportion of females, co-occurrence with disinhibited social engagement, and autism symptoms. In addition, this variant of ADHD has been suggested to strongly persist into adulthood, which might refer to alterations in brain structure and function (McLaughlin et al., 2014). The rapidly developing neural and endocrine systems are sensitive to experiences of stress, and thus, lack of individualized care, exposure to pathogens, malnutrition, and abuse or neglect can also contribute to the atypical neural development. As the neural systems involved in attention are complex, more research in developmental cognitive neuroscience is needed in order to better understand the specific neural circuits contributing to attention problems in children with adverse early care histories (Gunnar & van Dulmen, 2007; Kennedy et al., 2016).

Emotion regulation

Emotion regulation generally refers to the ability to manage, control, and adjust emotional reactions in productive ways so that emotions facilitate, rather than constrain, coping in a given situation (e.g., Denham, 2006). Emotion regulation seems to be fundamental in an individual's overall adjustment and mental health (Morris, Silk, Steinberg, Myers, & Robinson, 2007). Challenges in self-regulation are related to at least some types of externalizing problems, but also to internalizing problems (Eisenberg, Spinrad, & Eggum, 2010). It is known that individual differences in children's self-regulation are fairly stable after the first year or two of life and are largely temperament-based. However, environmental factors and gene–environment interaction affect self-regulation skills, which makes this issue an interesting subject to study among adopted children.

In fact, it has been claimed that self-regulation is a core construct underlying the dysfunctional behaviors commonly seen among foster children (Racusin, Maerlender, Sengupta, Isquith, & Straus, 2005). Poor emotion regulation has also been associated with higher rates of externalizing symptomology among children with adverse early histories (Kim & Cicchetti, 2010). However, in their study on adopted children, Soares and colleagues (2017) found no difference in general emotion regulation or emotional lability/ negativity compared to non-adopted children. Their study indicated the important role played by adoptive parents in supporting the emotion regulation skills in adopted children. Other studies (Barone et al., 2017; Tan et al., 2012) have found similar results, stating that parents' organized, coherent, and flexible style in recognizing and regulating their own emotions benefited their adopted children, regardless of previous experiences of neglect.

Emotion understanding

Emotion understanding can be seen as one of the basic emotional competences, important in later emotional adjustment. Research has indicated that children who are adept at processing emotional stimuli and understanding the causes of emotions are also better at regulating their own emotional arousal (Schultz, Izard, Ackerman, & Youngstrom, 2001).

Research indicates that compared to their non-adopted peers, adopted children's skills in emotion understanding might lag behind (Vorria et al., 2006; Wismer Fries & Pollak, 2004). However, adopted children might not demonstrate fundamental differences in the processes they use to identify facial expressions, especially in simple emotion understanding tasks such as identifying basic emotional expressions and matching emotional expressions with appropriate social contexts (Barone & Lionetti, 2011; Wismer Fries & Pollak, 2004). However, in several studies, differences between adopted and non-adopted children have been observed to be more remarkable in tasks demanding more advanced emotional processing skills (Nelson, Westerlund, McDermott, Zeanah, & Fox, 2013; Tarullo et al., 2016). Thus, adopted children might have increasing difficulty with emotion understanding as they enter school age when expectations for emotional perception become increasingly sophisticated. It is possible that difficulty in reading subtle emotional cues from others could contribute to the impaired socioemotional functioning and increased behavioral problems observed in some adopted children (see Tarullo et al., 2016).

It has been speculated that one explanatory factor behind problems in emotional understanding might be that orphanage settings provide impoverished emotional learning environments, lacking the socioemotional contingencies needed for acquiring expertise in emotional processing (Wismer Fries & Pollak, 2004). Another explaining factor might be the adoptees' attachment pattern. Many adopted children experience maltreatment, abuse, neglect, various types of deprivation, and the breakdown of at least one primary relationship before coming to an adoptive family (Dozier & Rutter, 2008). Recent research suggests that children exposed to traumatic forms of maltreatment or neglect are more likely to fail to develop adequate self-regulatory functions, and they are more likely to develop disorganized rather than organized attachments (Dozier & Bernard, 2017), rendering them to be at increased risk of poor emotional adjustment in their later development (e.g., Croft et al., 2018). Studies involving adopted children and their parents have shown that secure attachment fosters current and subsequent social-emotional development (Barone et al., 2017). For example, security of attachment has been found to promote social competences, effortful control, and sharing behaviors.

Meta-analytical studies confirm the association between insecure attachment patterns and both internalizing and externalizing behavioral problems (Barone et al., 2017; Groh, Roisman, van IJzendoorn, Bakermans-Kranenburg, & Fearon, 2012). In their study on adopted children, Barone and Lionetti (2011) found that those adoptees who were disorganized in their mental representations of attachment performed worse on emotional understanding. Many scholars agree that attachment is a key variable in emotional competence and see emotional competence, emotional understanding, and attachment being tightly associated (cf., Calkins & Hill, 2007). Thus, the infant–parent relationship can be seen as the way in which the caregiver and the quality of care affect the development of emotional regulation and emotion understanding.

How to foster emotional and behavioral adjustment

How, then, can adopted children's emotional and behavioral adjustment be fostered? Among the suggested foci are adoptive parents' and children's attachment and interaction patterns, parenting behaviors and self-regulation, and communication about adoption.

Secure attachment in both adoptive parents and adopted children has been shown to substantially foster social-emotional adjustment of adopted children, who often are biologically and behaviorally dysregulated due to their early adversities (Barone et al., 2017; Yarger, Bernard, Caron, Wallin, & Dozier, 2019). Mounting evidence supports the theory of intergenerational transmission of attachment in adoptive families. Adoptive parents' general representations of attachment (also referred to as attachment states of mind) have been found to be associated with their adopted children's attachment behaviors and representations (Raby & Dozier, 2019). As children's attachment systems are known to be capable of flexible reorganization, despite the lack of genetic relatedness, adoptive parents' attachment representations may shape and support recovery in attachment quality for children with histories of early adversity (see van den Dries et al., 2009). Most internationally adoptive parents have been classified as having autonomous attachment states of mind – referring to an organized, coherent, and flexible way of recognizing and regulating their own emotions – which is associated with a sensitive manner of interacting with their children (Raby et al., 2017; Verhage et al., 2016). Thus, internationally adoptive parents seem to have a high potential to promote secure attachment in their children. A study on foster families showed that, in addition to sensitive responding, secure attachment in children who have alienating attachment behaviors is promoted by parents' therapeutic caregiving, which are behaviors that challenge the child's usual patterns of behavior and reflect nurturance (Stovall & Dozier, 2000). However, work is still needed for identifying the specific variables related to caregiving that can help promote formation of secure attachment in adopted children.

Intervention programs that enhance sensitive parenting and target children's attachment behaviors and biobehavioral stress regulation have been found to improve parenting abilities in adoptive families (e.g., Yarger et al., 2019). Among these are the Attachment and Biobehavioral Catch-up for Toddlers (ABC-T) intervention, where the focus is to help parents nurture children in times of distress, follow children's lead, and avoid behaving in frightening ways (Yarger et al., 2019). Another is the Video-enhanced Positive Parenting Intervention Directed to Foster Care and Adoptive Families (VIPP-FC/A), where the focus is on enhancing parents' emotional availability (Barone, Barone, Dellagiulia, & Lionetti, 2018), which has been found to enhance sensitive and emotionally available interactions in adoptive families. Continuing research on behavioral and neurobiological mechanisms, attachment behaviors, and the later outcomes in emotional and behavioral adjustment will shed more light on these issues in future.

Adoptive parents' role in their children's later behavioral and emotional adjustment seems crucial in a variety of adoptive families, especially in terms of parenting practices rather than the specific type (e.g., two parent, single parent, LGBT parent) of the adoptive family (cf. Grotevant & Lo, 2017). Good parental resources are also needed in managing parents' own stress in response to a child's various negative behaviors, regulating environmental stress in a child's home environment (Santos-Nunes, Narciso, Vieira-Santos, & Roberto, 2018), paying attention to parental alliance (Lionetti, Pastore, & Barone, 2015), and considering parenting styles (Tan et al., 2012).

Concerning emotional regulation, it has been suggested that the adoptive parents' use of language to describe their own feelings and mental states helps to direct adopted children's attention to mental states in themselves and others. It helps to give them the tools needed to recognize, think, and talk about their mental states, which may enhance the development of emotion understanding and regulation (Tarullo et al., 2016).

Concerning communication about adoption, it has been found that adopted children's ability to express their feelings about being adopted, and their parents' empathic sensitivity to those feelings, has been viewed as a critical process in healthy adoption adaptation. Those adopted children who experience more open, direct, and non-defensive communication about adoption with their parents show more positive adjustment, not just in the childhood years, but even into adulthood (Brodzinsky, 2006).

Summary and implications for policy and practice

There is a considerable amount of research claiming that compared to their non-adopted peers, adoptees are at risk for emotional and behavioral difficulties. However, equal amounts of research state that the risk is neither high nor widespread. Mixed results are explained, at least partly, by the variety of study settings, choices made in the samples of adoptees and comparison groups, measures used, and the time frame of studies.

Research has shown adoption to be an intervention that can shift the early adverse developmental trajectories in multiple domains of development (including socioemotional domain and attachment) and foster resilience in the face of risk and adversity. Many studies agree that, in general, adopted children are well-adjusted. However, among them there seems to be a small subset of children for whom adjustment might be more problematic, especially those spending longer periods of time in institutional settings and those who are older at adoption. In addition, some behavioral or emotional problems are more likely to manifest in adolescence rather than earlier in childhood, suggesting that the effects of depriving environments early in children's lives can impact basic processes that have far-reaching consequences as children encounter more complex social and cognitive environments. Some studies suggest that a certain length of adverse-enough experiences is sufficient to produce later problems, regardless of the exact age of exposure within the earliest years. Thus, for example, 6–18 months of exposure to a depriving institution within the first two to three years of life might be associated with later problems in emotional and behavioral adjustment (see Gunnar & van Dulmen, 2007; Hawk & McCall, 2010). It is likely that the effects of early adversities on children's neurodevelopment are due to interactions between the timing, severity, and chronicity of the exposure and the possible sensitive periods in development. The same is true for interventions: the degree to which children show recovery in neural processes and associated functioning might depend on the timing and the length of the intervention and their relations to the child's sensitive periods in development (Bick & Nelson, 2016).

We recommend that every adopted child go through a medical examination with essential laboratory tests and growth assessment soon after adoption. In addition to recognizing life-threatening conditions, any untreated medical condition could complicate a child's adjustment and well-being. In addition, we recommend psychosocial support offered for all adoptive families with low thresholds for making referrals. Adoptive parents would benefit from easy-access support given by social and health care professionals, for example to discuss their parental experiences, concerns, and emotions. As we have discussed earlier in this chapter, research indicates this kind of parental support enhances sensitive parenting and secure attachment with high-risk children. In addition, secure child-care services should be offered for adoptive parents as a concrete parental support.

If an adopted child's adjustment is an issue of concern six to nine months after adoption, we recommend that the child and adoptive family would need to be referred to a specialist who is familiar with adoption issues, attachment, and neurodevelopmental problems. When needed, a multidisciplinary diagnostic process should be available so that a child's neurodevelopmental and neurocognitive problems, in addition to potential attachment or post-traumatic symptoms, can be recognized. The early recognition of neurodevelopmental problems and symptoms of severe disorders might help adoptive parents better understand their child and his/her reactions and behaviors. In addition, it could help professionals to make an efficient treatment plan. Information concerning a child's neurocognitive profile, or his/her special needs might help professionals to find applicable methods in interventions. For instance, poor language skills or communication deficits typically cause frustrations leading to temper tantrums or anxiety/mood problems. Use of visual aid or elements of sign language could help a child to communicate his/her needs, and also offer adults a way to communicate their intentions to the child. Enhanced communication might help in reducing tantrums but also support the formation of an emotional relationship with the child by reducing misunderstandings and emotional meltdowns. What is more, a child's global cognitive level should be taken into account at school and at home; the child should not be constantly facing unachievable demands. Attention deficits, for their part, can weaken a child's ability to pay attention to important issues, including behaviors in social relationships. A child's ability to focus might be helped, for example, by structuring the situation, using visual aids, and giving clear and short enough instructions. Adults' help is also needed in social situations if a child has problems in social skills. These children might repeatedly need an adult to explain what is happening in social situations, sometimes with the help of simple drawings to make it clearer. The demands in social situations should also reflect the child's current level of skills. For example, if a child can play only with one child at a time without getting into conflict, it is unhelpful to take them into a big group without adults' support. Instead, the child should be introduced by adults into a bigger group incrementally.

When an intervention is needed, research shows that interventions that focus on positive and sensitive parenting, both children's and parents' attachment behaviors, and their stress regulation (e.g., Attachment and Biobehavioral Catch-up intervention, Video-enhanced Positive Parenting Intervention) offer effective tools for fostering adopted children's behavioral and emotional adjustment. Active collaboration via negotiations and meetings between parents, daycare/school personnel, and various intervention providers is recommended in order to strengthen the collaborative effort to enhance children's adjustment and give coherent guidance in the many contexts in which they live.

As adoption or its outcomes never occur in a vacuum, the interplay of many factors (such as pre-adoption information; support and interventions available; attachment, interaction, stress, and conflict within adoptive family; adoptive parents' expectations and satisfaction; individual characteristics of the adopted child; school; peers; cultural and societal factors) can affect post-adoption emotional and behavioral adjustment. What research quite unanimously indicates is the adoptive parents' crucial role in fostering the emotional and behavioral adjustment of their adopted child. Specifically, the security of the attachment and parents' sensitivity seem to predict adopted children's later socioemotional and behavioral development.

References

American Psychiatric Association. (1980). *Diagnostic and statistical manual of mental disorders* (3rd ed.). Washington, DC: Author.

Barone, L., Barone, V., Dellagiulia, A., & Lionetti, F. (2018). Testing an attachment-based parenting intervention-VIPP-FC/A in adoptive families with post-institutionalized children: Do maternal sensitivity and genetic markers count?. *Frontiers in Psychology* Article ID 156, *9*. doi:10.3389/fpsyg.2018.00156

Barone, L., & Lionetti, F. (2011). Attachment and emotional understanding: A study on late-adopted pre-schoolers and their parents. *Child: Care, Health and Development*, *38*, 690–696. doi:10.1111/j.1365-2214.2011.01296.x

Barone, L., Lionetti, F., & Green, J. (2017). A matter of attachment? How adoptive parents foster post-institutionalized children's social and emotional adjustment. *Attachment and Human Development*, *19*, 323–339. doi:10.1080/14616734.2017.1306714

Becker-Weidman, A. (2009). Effects of early maltreatment on development: A descriptive study using the Vineland adaptive behavior scales-II. *Child Welfare: Journal of Policy, Practice, and Program*, *88*(2), 137–161.

Bick, J., & Nelson, C. A. (2016). Early adverse experiences and the developing brain. *Neuropsychopharmacology*, *41*(1), 177–196. doi:10.1038/np.2015.252

Bowlby, J. (1973). *Attachment and loss: Separation, anxiety and anger* US: Basic Books.

Brand, A. E., & Brinich, P. M. (1999). Behavior problems and mental health contacts in adopted, foster, and nonadopted children. *Journal of Child Psychology and Psychiatry*, *40*(8), 1221–1229. doi:10.1111/1469-7610.00538

Brodzinsky, D. (2006). Family structural openness and communication openness as predictors in the adjustment of adopted children. *Adoption Quarterly*, *9*, 1–18. doi:10.1300/J145v09n04_01

Burns, B., Phillips, S., Wagner, H., Barth, R., Kolko, D., Campbell, Y., & Landsverk, J. (2004). Mental health need and access to mental health services by youths involved with child welfare: A national survey. *Journal of the American Academy of Child & Adolescent Psychiatry*, *43*, 960–970.

Calkins, S. D., & Hill, A. (2007). Caregiver influences on emerging emotion regulation: Biological and environmental transactions in early development. In J. J. Gross (Ed.), *Handbook of emotion regulation* (pp. 229–248). New York, NY: Guilford Press.

Campbell, S., Shaw, D., & Gilliom, M. (2000). Early externalizing behavior problems: Toddlers and preschoolers at risk for later maladjustment. *Development and Psychopathology, 12*, 467–488. doi:10.1017/S0954579400003114

Canzi, E., Rosnati, R., Palacios, J., & Román, M. (2018). Internationally adopted children's cognitive and social-emotional development during the first post-adoption year: A longitudinal study. *European Journal of Developmental Psychology, 15*(5), 517–530. doi:10.1080/17405629.2017.1316257

Colvert, E., Rutter, M., Beckett, C., Castle, J., Groothues, C., Hawkins, A., & Sonuga-Barke, E. (2008). Emotional difficulties in early adolescence following severe early deprivation: Findings from the English and Romanian Adoptees study. *Development and Psychopathology, 20*(2), 547–567. doi:10.1017/S0954579408000278

Croft, J., Heron, J., Teufel, C., Cannon, M., Wolke, D., Thompson, A., & Zammit, S. (2018). Association of trauma type, age of exposure, and frequency in childhood and adolescence with psychotic experiences in early adulthood. *JAMA Psychiatry, 76*(1), 79–80. doi:10.1001/jamapsychiatry.2018.3155

Denham, S. A. (2006). Social-emotional competence as support for school readiness: What is it and how do we assess it?. *Early Education and Development, 17*, 57–89. doi:10.1207/s15566935eed1701_4

Dozier, M., & Bernard, K. (2017). Attachment and biobehavioral catch-up: Addressing the needs of infants and toddlers exposed to inadequate or problematic caregiving. *Current Opinion in Psychology, 15*, 111–117. doi:10.1016/j.copsyc.2017.03.003

Dozier, M., & Rutter, M. (2008). Challenges to the development of attachment relationships faced by young children in foster and adoptive care. In J. Cassidy & P. R. Shaver (Eds.), *Handbook of attachment: Theory, research, and clinical applications* (pp. 698–717). New York, NY: Guilford Press.

Eisenberg, N., Spinrad, T., & Eggum, N. (2010). Emotion-related self-regulation and its relation to children's maladjustment. *Annual Review of Clinical Psychology, 6*, 495–525. doi:10.1146/annurev.clinpsy.121208.131208

Fisher, P. A. (2014). Review: Adoption, fostering, and the needs of looked-after and adopted children. *Child and Adolescent Mental Health, 20*(1), 5–12. doi:10.1111/camh.12084

Fox, N. A., Almas, A. N., Degnan, K. A., Nelson, C. A., & Zeanah, C. H. (2011). The effects of severe psychosocial deprivation and foster care intervention on cognitive development at 8 years of age: Findings from the Bucharest Early Intervention Project. *Journal of Child Psychology and Psychiatry, 52*(9), 919–928. doi:10.1111/j.1469-7610.2010.02355.x

Gagnon-Oosterwaal, N., Cossette, L., Smolla, N., Pomerleau, A., Malcuit, G., Chicoine, J., & Berthiaume, C. (2012). Pre-adoption adversity and self-reported behavior problems in 7-year-old international adoptees. *Child Psychiatry & Human Development, 43*(4), 648–660. doi:10.1007/s10578-011-0279-5

Graf, W., Kekatpure, M., & Kosofsky, B. (2013). Prenatal-onset neurodevelopmental disorders secondary to toxins, nutritional deficiencies, and maternal illness. *Handbook of Clinical Neurology, 111*, 143–159. doi:10.1016/B978-0-444-52891-9.00014-2

Groh, A. M., Roisman, G. I., van IJzendoorn, M. H., Bakermans-Kranenburg, M. J., & Fearon, R. (2012). The significance of insecure and disorganized attachment for children's internalizing symptoms: A meta analytic study. *Child Development, 83*, 591–610. doi:10.1111/j.1467-8624.2011.01711.x

Grotevant, H., & Lo, A. (2017). Adoptive parenting. *Current Opinion in Psychology, 15*, 71–75. doi:10.1016/j.copsyc.2017.02.020

Gunnar, M. R., Fisher, P. A., & the Early Experience Stress Prevention Network. (2006). Bringing basic research on early experience and stress neurobiology to bear on preventive interventions for neglected and maltreated children. *Development and Psychopathology, 18*, 651–677. doi:10.1017/S0954579406060330

Gunnar, M. R., van Dulmen, M., & the International Adoption Project Team. (2007). Behavior problems in post-institutionalized internationally-adopted children. *Development & Psychopathology, 19*, 129–148. doi:10.1017/S0954579407070071

Guyon-Harris, K., Humphreys, K., Fox, N. A., Nelson, C. A., & Zeanah, C. H. (2018). Course of disinhibited social engagement disorder from early childhood to early adolescence. *Journal of the American Academy of Child and Adolescent Psychiatry, 57*(5), 329–335. doi:10.1016/j.jaac.2018.02.009

Hawk, B., & McCall, R. (2010). CBCL behavior problems of post-institutionalized international adoptees. *Clinical Child and Family Psychology Review, 13*, 199–211. doi:10.1007/s10567-010-0068-x.

Hellerstedt, W., Madsen, N., Gunnar, M. R., Grotevant, H. D., Lee, R., & Johnson, D. (2008). The International Adoption Project: Population-based surveillance of Minnesota parents who adopted children internationally. *Maternal and Child Health Journal, 12*(2), 162–171. doi:10.1007/s10995-007-0237-9

Hodges, J., & Tizard, B. (1989). Social and family relationships of ex-institutional adolescents. *Journal of Child Psychology and Psychiatry, 30*(1), 77–97. doi:10.1111/j.1469-7610.1989.tb00770.x

Hostinar, C., Stellern, S., Schaefer, C., Carlson, S. M., & Gunnar, M. R. (2012). Associations between early life adversity and executive function in children adopted internationally from orphanages. *Proceedings of the National Academy of Sciences of the USA, 109*, 17208–17212. doi:10.1073/pnas.1121246109

Juffer, F., & van IJzendoorn, M. (2005). Behavior problems and mental health referrals of international adoptees. A meta-analysis. *Journal of the American Medical Association, 293*(20), 2501–2515. doi:10.1001/jama.293.20.2501

Kappenberg, E. S., & Halpern, D. F. (2006). Kinship center attachment questionnaire: Development of a caregiver-completed attachment measure for children younger than 6 years. *Educational and Psychological Measurement, 66*, 852–873. doi:10.1177/0013164405285545

Kennedy, M., Kreppner, J., Knights, N., Kumsta, R., Maughan, B., Golm, D., & Sonuga-Barke, E. (2016). Early severe institutional deprivation is associated with a persistent variant of adult attention-deficit/hyperactivity disorder: Clinical presentation, developmental continuities and life circumstances in the English and Romanian Adoptees study. *Journal of Child Psychology and Psychiatry, 57*(10), 1113–1125. doi:10.1111/jcp.12576

Keyes, M., Sharma, A., Elkins, I., Iacono, W., & McGue, M. (2008). The mental health of US adolescents adopted in infancy. *Archives of Pediatrics & Adolescent Medicine, 162*(5), 419–425. doi:10.1001/archpedi.162.5.419

Kim, J., & Cicchetti, D. (2010). Longitudinal pathways linking child maltreatment, emotion regulation, peer relations, and psychopathology. *Journal of Child Psychology and Psychiatry, 51*(6), 706–716. doi:10.1111/j.1469-7610.2009.02202.x

Kochanska, G., Murray, K. T., & Harlan, E. (2000). Effortful control in early childhood: Continuity and change, antecedents, and implications for social development. *Developmental Psychology, 36*, 220–232. doi:10.1037/0012-1649.36.2.220

LaPrairie, J., Schechter, J., Robinson, B., & Brennan, P. (2011). Perinatal risk factors in the development of aggression and violence. *Advances in Genetics, 75*, 215–253. doi:10.1016/B978-0-12-380858-5.00004-6

Lawn, J., Kerber, K., Enweronu-Laryea, C., & Massee Bateman, O. (2009). Newborn survival in low resource settings – Are we delivering?. *BJOG, 116*(Suppl. 1), 49–59. doi:10.1111/j.1471-0528.2009.02328.x

Lionetti, F., Pastore, M., & Barone, L. (2015). Parenting stress: The roles of attachment states of mind and parenting alliance in the context of adoption. *Parenting: Science and Practice, 15*(2), 75–91. doi:10.1080/15295192.2015.1020142

MacLean, K. (2003). The impact of institutionalization on child development. *Development and Psychopathology, 15*, 853–884. doi:10.1017/S0954579403000415

McLaughlin, K. A., Sheridan, M., Winter, W., Fox, N. A., Zeanah, C. H., & Nelson, C. A. (2014). Widespread reductions in cortical thickness following severe early-life deprivation: A neurodevelopmental pathway to attention-deficit/hyperactivity disorder. *Biological Psychiatry, 76*(8), 629–638. doi:10.1016/j.biopsych.2013.08.016

Merz, E. C., & McCall, R. B. (2010). Behavior problems in children adopted from psychosocially depriving institutions. *Journal of Abnormal Child Psychology, 38*, 459–470. doi:10.1007/s10802-009-9383-4

Morris, A., Silk, J., Steinberg, L., Myers, S. S., & Robinson, L. R. (2007). The role of the family context in the development of emotion regulation. *Social Development, 16*, 361–388. doi:10.1111/j.1467-9507.2007.00389.x

Nelson, C. A., Westerlund, A., McDermott, J. M., Zeanah, C. H., & Fox, N. A. (2013). Emotion recognition following early psychosocial deprivation. *Development and Psychopathology, 25*, 517–525. doi:10.1017/S0954579412001216

Nickman, S. L., Rosenfeld, A. A., Fine, P., MacIntyre, J. C., Pilowsky, D. J., Howe, R., & Sveda, S. A. (2005). Children in adoptive families: Overview and update. *Journal of the American Academy of Child and Adolescent Psychiatry, 44*, 987–995. doi:10.1097/01.chi.0000174463.60987.69

Palacios, J., & Brodzinsky, D. (2010). Adoption research: Trends, topics, and outcomes. *International Journal of Behavioral Development, 34,* 270–284. doi:10.1177/0165025410362837

Palacios, J., Román, M., & Comacho, C. (2011). Growth and development in internationally adopted children: Extent and timing of recovery after early adversity. *Child: Care, Health and Development, 37,* 282–288. doi:10.1111/j.1365-2214.2010.01142.x

Pollak, S., Nelson, C. A., Schlaak, M., Roeber, B., Wewerka, S., Wiik, K., & Gunnar, M. (2009). Neurodevelopmental effects of early deprivation in post-institutionalized children. *Child Development, 81*(1), 224–236. doi:10.1111/j.1467-8624.2009.01391.x

Raaska, H., Elovainio, M., Lapinleimu, H., Matomäki, J., & Sinkkonen, J. (2015). Changes in attachment-related behavioural problems of internationally adopted toddlers in Finland: Results from the FinAdo study. *Infant and Child Development, 24*(1), 79–83. doi:10.1002/icd.1876

Raby, K. L., & Dozier, M. (2019). Attachment across the lifespan: Insights from adoptive families. *Current Opinion in Psychology, 25,* 81–85. doi:10.1016/j.copsyc.2018.03.011

Raby, K. L., Yarger, H. A., Lind, T., Fraley, R., Leerkes, E., & Dozier, M. (2017). Attachment states of mind among internationally adoptive and foster parents. *Development and Psychopathology, 29,* 365–378. doi:10.1017/S0954579417000049

Racusin, R., Maerlender, A., Jr., Sengupta, A., Isquith, P., & Straus, M. (2005). Psychosocial treatment of children in foster care: A review. *Community Mental Health Journal, 41*(2), 199–221. doi:10.1007/s10597-005-2656-7

Rushton, A., Mayes, D., Dance, C., & Quinton, D. (2003). Parenting late-placed children: The development of new relationships and the challenge of behavioural problems. *Clinical Child Psychology and Psychiatry, 8,* 389–400. doi:10.1037/0893-3200.22.3.541

Rutter, M., Beckett, C., Castle, J., Colvert, E., Kreppner, J., Mehta, M., & Sonuga-Barke, E. (2007). Effects of profound early institutional deprivation: An overview of findings from a UK longitudinal study of Romanian adoptees. *European Journal of Developmental Psychology, 4,* 332–350. doi:10.1080/17405620701401846

Santos-Nunes, M., Narciso, I., Vieira-Santos, S., & Roberto, M. (2018). Adoptive versus mixed families: Child adjustment, parenting stress and family environment. *Journal of Child and Family Studies, 27*(6), 1858–1869. doi:10.1007/s10826-018-1019-2

Schultz, D., Izard, C., Ackerman, B., & Youngstrom, E. (2001). Emotion knowledge in economically disadvantaged children: Self-regulatory antecedents and relations to social difficulties and withdrawal. *Development and Psychopathology, 13*(1), 53–67. doi:10.1177/0734282912449441

Selman, P. (2012). Global trends in intercountry adoption 2001–2010. *Adoption Advocate, 44,* 1–17.

Soares, J., Barbosa-Ducharne, M., Palacios, J., & Pacheco, A. (2017). Adopted children's emotion regulation: The role of parental attitudes and communication about adoption. *Psicothema, 29*(1), 49–54. doi:10.7334/psicothema2016.71

Stams, G., Juffer, F., Rispens, J., & Hoksbergen, R. (2000). The development and adjustment of 7-year-old children adopted in infancy. *Journal of Child Psychology and Psychiatry, 41,* 1025–1037. doi:10.1111/1469-7610.00690

Stovall, K. C., & Dozier, M. (2000). The development of attachment in new relationships: Single subject analyses for 10 foster infants. *Development and Psychopathology, 12*(2), 133–156. doi:10.1017/S0954579400002029

Tan, T. X., Camras, L., Deng, H., Zhang, M., & Lu, Z. (2012). Family stress, parenting styles, and behavioral adjustment in preschool-age adopted Chinese girls. *Early Childhood Research Quarterly, 27*(1), 128–136. doi:10.1016/j.ecresq.2011.04.002

Tan, T. X., & Marfo, K. (2006). Parental ratings of behavioral adjustment in two samples of adopted Chinese girls: Age-related versus socio-emotional correlates and predictors. *Journal of Applied Developmental Psychology, 27*(11), 14–30. doi:10.1037/a0015682

Tarullo, A., Youssef, A., Frenn, K. A., Wiik, K., Garvin, M., & Gunnar, M. (2016). Emotion understanding, parent mental state language, and behavior problems in internationally adopted children. *Development and Psychopathology, 28*(2), 371–383. doi:10.1017/S095457941500111X

Tienari, P., Wynne, L. C., Sorri, A., Lahti, I., Laksy, K., Moring, J., ... Wahlberg, K-E. (2004). Genotype-environment interaction in schizophreniaspectrum disorder. Long-term follow-up study of Finnish adoptees. *British Journal of Psychiatry, 184,* 216–222. doi:10.1192/bjp.184.3.216

Tirella, L., Chan, W., Cermak, S., Litvinova, A., Salas, K., & Miller, L. (2008). Time use in Russian baby homes. *Child: Care, Health and Development, 34*(1), 77–86. doi:10.1111/j.1365-2214.2007.00766.x

Tottenham, N. (2012). Risk and developmental heterogeneity in previously institutionalized children. *Journal of Adolescent Health, 51*(2 Suppl), S29-233. doi:10.1016/j.jadohealth.2012.04.004

Tottenham, N., Hare, T., Quinn, B., McCarry, T., Nurse, M., Gilhooly, T., & Casey, B. (2010). Prolonged institutional rearing is associated with atypically large amygdala volume and difficulties in emotion regulation. *Developmental Science, 13*(1), 46–61. doi:10.1111/j.1467-7687.2009.00852.x

van den Dries, L., Juffer, F., van IJzendoorn, M. H., & Bakermans-Kranenburg, M. J. (2009). Fostering security? A meta-analysis of attachment in adopted children. *Children and Youth Services Review, 31*(3), 410–421. doi:10.1016/j.childyouth.2008.09.008

van IJzendoorn, M. H., & Juffer, F. (2006). Emanuel Miller Lecture, 2006. Adoption as intervention: Meta-analytic evidence for massive catch-up and plasticity in physical, socio-emotional and cognitive development. *Journal of Child Psychology and Psychiatry, 47*, 1228–1245. doi:10.1111/j.1469-7610.2006.01675.x

Verhage, M. L., Schuengel, C., Madigan, S., Fearon, R. M. P., Oosterman, M., Cassibba, R., & van IJzendoorn, M. H. (2016). Narrowing the transmission gap: A synthesis of three decades of research on intergenerational transmission of attachment. *Psychological Bulletin, 142*(4), 337–366. doi:10.1037/bul0000038

Vorria, P., Papaligoura, Z., Sarafidou, J., Kopakaki, M., Dunn, J., van IJzendoorn, M. H., & Kontopoulou, A. (2006). The development of adopted children after institutional care: A follow-up study. *Journal of Child Psychology and Psychiatry, 47*, 1246–1253. doi:10.1111/j.1469-7610.2006.01666.x

Wiik, K., Loman, M., van Ryzin, M., Armstrong, J., Essex, M., Pollak, S., & Gunnar, M. R. (2011). Behavioral and emotional symptoms of post-institutionalized children in middle childhood. *Journal of Child Psychology and Psychiatry, 52*(1), 56–63. doi:10.1111/j.1469-7610.2010.02294.x

Wismer Fries, B., & Pollak, S. (2004). Emotion understanding in post-institutionalized Eastern European children. *Development and Psychopathology, 16*, 355–369. doi:10.1017/S0954579404044554

World Health Organization. (1992). *The ICD-10 classification of mental and behavioral disorders: Clinical descriptions and diagnostic guidelines.* Geneva: Author.

Yarger, H., Bernard, K., Caron, E., Wallin, A., & Dozier, M. (2019). Enhancing parenting quality for young children adopted internationally: Results of a randomized controlled trial. *Journal of Clinical Child & Adolescent Psychology, 16*, 1–13. doi:10.1080/15374416.2018.1547972

Zeanah, C. H., Berlin, L., & Boris, N. (2011). Practitioner review: Clinical applications of attachment theory and research for infants and young children. *Journal of Child Psychology and Psychiatry, 52*(8), 619–633. doi:10.1111/j.1469-7610.2011.02399.x

Zeanah, C. H., Chesher, T., Boris, N., & American Academy of Child and Adolescent Psychiatry Committee on Quality Issues. (2016). Practice parameter for the assessment and treatment of children and adolescents with reactive attachment disorder and disinhibited social engagement disorder. *Journal of the American Academy of Child and Adolescent Psychiatry, 55*(11), 990–1003.

Zelazo, P., Carlson, S., & Kesek, A. (2008). Development of executive function in childhood. In C. Nelson & M. Luciana (Eds.), *Handbook of developmental cognitive neuroscience* (pp. 553–574). Cambridge, MA: MIT Press.

26

THE NEUROBIOLOGICAL EMBEDDING OF EARLY SOCIAL DEPRIVATION IN CHILDREN EXPOSED TO INSTITUTIONAL REARING

Rebecca Lipschutz and Johanna Bick

As altricial beings, human infants are biologically programmed to form selective attachments to primary caregivers. In cases of institutional rearing, children are reared in under-stimulating circumstances, and due to high child to caregiver ratios and frequent caregiving turnover, typically lack opportunities to develop selective attachments. Growing evidence indicates that exposure to these early forms of social deprivation has lasting developmental consequences. Recent work points to alterations in key neurobiological systems as mechanisms for explaining ongoing risk. In this chapter, we review evidence supporting the "neurobiological embedding" of early social deprivation on systems that contribute to cognitive and emotional development. We first discuss how these experiences influence the basic structural wiring, activation, and connectivity patterns of the brain in key regions that subserve emotion and cognitive functioning. We also review mounting evidence indicating altered function in key autonomic and stress regulatory functions in children exposed to severe early life deprivation. For each topic, we draw connections between these underlying neurobiological alterations and higher order emotional, behavioral, and social functioning. A second aim of our chapter is to emphasize how adoption into responsive family settings can support more normative trajectories neurobiologically and behaviorally. Importantly, we point out critical variability in recovery that often depends on timing of entry and quality of responsive family care. Finally, we discuss implications of this growing line of research for policy and practice, geared not only to reducing the prevalence of adverse rearing exposures, but for providing maximally effective services for children living in, and adopted out of, adverse conditions.

Brain development in the context of adverse rearing

The human brain begins to develop approximately two weeks post-conception and continues rapidly throughout the first years of life. By the age of 6 years the brain has increased to approximately 90 percent of its adult volume (Lenroot & Giedd, 2006; Reiss,

Abrams, Singer, Ross, & Denckla, 1996). This points to the remarkable amount of growth and development that takes place in just the first years of life. Brain regions, pathways, and tissue types all have unique developmental trajectories and vary in the timing in which they are maximally sensitive to environmental input. "Gray matter" refers to cell bodies and dendrites of neurons and includes the neocortex and subcortical structures. Gray matter develops in a non-linear fashion, peaking in middle childhood, and following an inverted U shape across the lifespan, with key regions in the prefrontal cortex among the last to reach full maturity (Sowell et al., 2003). "White matter" refers to the progressive increases in myelination of axons which connect circuitries, hemispheres, and lobes. White matter development takes on a more linear pattern. While some occurs prenatally, there are steady increases throughout childhood and adolescence (Stiles & Jernigan, 2010).

Departures from these normative trajectories of neurodevelopmental maturation have been repeatedly documented in children exposed to institutional rearing. In this chapter, we review evidence supporting alterations in global properties of brain structure, function, and connectivity, and also in specific regions and circuitries. Converging evidence on altered neural structure and function has provided insight into factors that precede or maintain behaviorally observed cognitive, social, and emotional problems in institutionally reared children. Further, work in this area has led to new targets for early detection of later risk and intervention, which may increase abilities to normalize development in children exposed to early social deprivation.

Early adverse experiences and global brain development

Youth that experienced severe early institutional deprivation showed smaller head sizes, reduced brain volumes, decreased total gray and white matter volume, and reductions in cortical thickness across prefrontal, parietal, and temporal regions when compared to non-institutionalized youth (Eluvathingal et al., 2006; Hanson et al., 2014; McLaughlin et al., 2015; Mehta et al., 2009; Sheridan, Fox, Zeanah, McLaughlin, & Nelson, 2012).

In terms of global functioning of the brain, patterns of hypo-activation and underarousal are also observed. Specifically, institutionally reared children showed reductions in both metabolic (Chugani et al., 2001) and electrophysiological (Marshall, Fox, & the Bucharest Early Intervention Project Core Group, 2004; McLaughlin et al., 2010; Tarullo, Garvin, & Gunnar, 2011) activation patterns, relative to controls. Data suggest that patterns of reduced activity contribute to broad patterns of more behaviorally observed cognitive delays, involving memory and executive functioning (Wade, Fox, Zeanah, & Nelson, 2019), hyperactivity, and inattention (McLaughlin et al., 2010).

Frontal cortex activation differences were also observed in institutionally reared children, when compared with children reared in family settings. Greater right versus left frontal electrophysiological activation has generally been associated with greater tendencies to show more negative affect, avoidance, and inhibition (Fox, 1991; Sutton & Davidson, 1997). Although inconsistent with findings from samples with other forms of early adversity, children that were adopted internationally from institutional care exhibited greater *left* frontal activation in contrast to controls (Frenkel et al., 2017). This inconsistency could be due to differences in the developmental trajectory of frontal electroencephalogram asymmetry (FEA); children exposed to institutional rearing exhibited greater left activation in infancy and toddlerhood (6–30 months old), then a prolonged period of right FEA across early childhood and slower return to left activity by middle childhood (McLaughlin, Fox, Zeanah, & Nelson, 2011). Numerous studies have drawn links between frontal asymmetry patterns in institutional rearing children and risk for cognitive and emotional problems, including increased inattention and internalizing symptoms (Frenkel et al., 2017; McLaughlin et al., 2011).

There is also evidence that adoption into responsive and supportive families promotes normalization of electrophysiological activity patterns over time. Specifically, intervention effects were strongest for children adopted before 24 months of age, indicating a potential sensitive period for development, and were long-lasting across childhood (Frenkel et al., 2017; Vanderwert, Marshall, Nelson, Zeanah, & Fox, 2010; Vanderwert, Zeanah, Fox, & Nelson, 2016). There also appear to be other timing effects such that improvements in brain functioning were not apparent until 8 years old (McLaughlin et al., 2011).

In addition to global function, attempts to understand differences in the "wiring" of the brain that results from institutional rearing have accumulated. Recent data support alterations in pathways critical for speech and language (Kumar et al., 2014) and basic sensory-motor pathways (Bick et al., 2015; Hanson et al., 2013). Key alterations were documented in structural white matter pathways that connect the frontal cortex with limbic regions and the striatum (Behen et al., 2009; Bick et al., 2015; Eluvathingal et al., 2006; Govindan, Behen, Helder, Makki, & Chugani, 2010; Hanson et al., 2013; Kumar et al., 2014), which contribute to cognitive control, emotional regulation, and impulse control. Such alterations were associated with increased risk for externalizing symptoms (Kumar et al., 2014), decreased executive functioning (Hanson et al., 2013), and elevated anxiety and depression symptoms (Bick, Fox, Zeanah, & Nelson, 2017), offering a mechanism by which early social deprivation increases risk for psychopathology. Promisingly, there is some evidence that early intervention, in the form of placement into responsive foster care, supports more normative white matter integrity throughout the brain (Bick et al., 2015), yet the extent of remediation shows variability across circuitries.

Prefrontal cortex structure and functioning

The prefrontal cortex (PFC), or the "executive command center" of the brain, has extensive reciprocal connections with other parts of the brain, supporting top-down regulation of emotions, impulses, attention, and cognition. The development of the prefrontal cortex occurs over a protracted period, finally reaching full maturity around the third decade of life. As the PFC matures, the cortical thickness typically decreases (Sowell et al., 2003). For this reason, the PFC remains highly influenced by environmental experiences encountered early in life and in subsequent developmental periods.

Prefrontal cortex structure and functioning in adopted youth

Compared to children reared in normative family settings, institutionally reared children showed decreased cortical volume, surface area (Herzberg et al., 2018; Hodel et al., 2015), and thickness (McLaughlin et al., 2015) in the PFC. Compared to children adopted earlier, children adopted later (i.e. longer than one year of institutional care; Herzberg et al., 2018), showed greater decreases in PFC volume, suggesting that timing and duration of institutional care play a key role in contributing to biological and cognitive outcomes. Decreases in cortical thickness and volume of the PFC were associated with increased attention and impulsivity problems (McLaughlin et al., 2015) and executive function problems such as risky decision-making, especially among institutionally reared children adopted at later ages (Herzberg et al., 2018).

In addition to size and thickness of the PFC, recent data point to altered functional activation patterns among institutionally reared children relative to controls. One study examined variability of the PFC while children participated in an inhibitory control task, which tests the ability to withhold a prepotent response while prioritizing one that requires more cognitive control. On this task, adolescents with early deprivation experiences took longer to switch from the prepotent to alternative non-prepotent response and displayed higher activation in the inferior prefrontal cortex and striatum, critically involved in these executive processes (Mueller et al., 2010).

The medial prefrontal cortex has important connections to the ventral striatum, a subcortical region that subserves motivation and rewards sensitivity (for review, see Fareri & Delgado, 2014). Early institutional care was associated with stronger functional connectivity in these regions, which was implicated in disruptions in social functioning as children grew older (Fareri et al., 2017).

Limbic circuitry structure and functioning

The limbic region of the brain consists of several inter-connected subcortical structures that support stress activation, emotional processing and learning, and memory. Studies involving institutional rearing have generally focused on functional and structural variability in two specific regions, the amygdala and the hippocampus. The amygdala is essential for perceiving and responding to emotional stimuli, assessing threats, and regulating emotional responses. The hippocampus is involved in forming new memories and connecting emotions to memories. Both of these structures also play pivotal roles in regulating the primary stress response systems (hypothalamic-pituitary-adrenal axis (HPA axis) and autonomic nervous system) repeatedly shown to be altered in institutionally reared children.

Amygdala structure

A growing body of work points to alterations in amygdala volume in children exposed to institutional rearing. Even years after adoption from institutional care, youth showed increased amygdala volume, with longer duration of time in institutions associated with larger amygdala volumes, increased anxiety, and emotional dysregulation (Tottenham et al., 2010). Mehta and colleagues (2009) also found increased amygdala volume in previously institutionalized youth and demonstrated that the length of deprivation accounted for the extent of morphological change.

However, decreased amygdala volume has also been documented in association with early life neglect. Smaller amygdala volume was associated with previous institutionalization, and other forms of maltreatment, such as neglect and physical abuse (Hanson et al., 2014), although results are inconsistent (Edmiston et al., 2011). Factors that contribute to variability in findings are not completely understood, but severity, duration, and timing of adoption all appear to play a role (Tottenham et al., 2010). Taking repeated assessments in the contexts of longitudinal designs will likely help to contribute to the understanding of how these key brain circuitries are affected, offering more precise implications for risk and resiliency in the long term.

Hippocampus structure

In general, differences in hippocampus volume have not been typically observed in children adopted from institutions relative to controls (Hanson et al., 2014; Mehta et al., 2009; Sheridan et al., 2012; Tottenham et al., 2010). However, in an internationally adopted sample, Hodel and colleagues (2015) found decreased hippocampal volume in previously institutionalized children compared to non-adopted controls, with increased duration of institutionalization associated with greater reductions in hippocampal volume.

Limbic functioning

Functional differences related to limbic regions and associated affective processes have also been observed. For example, youth adopted from Eastern European and Asian institutions exhibited increased amygdala responses after viewing images of a stranger compared to typically developing children. Both groups of children exhibited similar amygdala activation to images of caregivers. This suggests that institutionally reared children might have had difficulty differentiating between caregivers and strangers (Olsavsky et al., 2013), pointing to a potential neural substrate of ongoing attachment-related difficulties. Further, previously institutionalized children were less likely to show decreased amygdala responses to images of their adoptive parent, unlike comparison children, and their amygdala reactivity was associated with the extent to which they showed secure attachment behavior (Callaghan et al., 2019). Similarly, non-institutionalized youth showed differential amygdala reactivity to trustworthy and untrustworthy faces, whereas previously institutionalized children showed similar amygdala responses to both faces (Green et al., 2016). This diminished amygdala discrimination was also associated with older age of adoption. In addition, heightened amygdala activation to fearful faces compared to neutral faces was observed in previously institutionalized children and mediated the association between institutional rearing and decreased eye contact during a dyadic interaction. Together, these findings might point to mechanisms underlying attachment and social difficulties often observed in this population (Tottenham et al., 2011). Children with histories of caregiver deprivation or neglect (adopted from foster care and international orphanages) showed heightened left amygdala responses to fearful and angry faces versus neutral faces. Longer durations of foster care or institutional rearing and less time spent with adoptive families predicted higher levels of activation (Maheu et al., 2010), again pointing to the role of timing and duration in explaining effects. Additionally, enhanced left anterior hippocampus activation to fearful faces in youth with history of deprivation and/or neglect was observed (Maheu et al., 2010).

Given that the amygdala plays a central role in emotion detection and processing, there is growing interest in whether altered amygdala activation helps explain risk for mood and anxiety symptoms common in institutionally reared children. Associations between anxiety and amygdala reactivity to threatening stimuli was observed in previously institutionalized youth and not comparison youth (Silvers et al., 2017). Diminished amygdala discrimination between trustworthy and untrustworthy faces was also associated with increased social anxiety two years later (Green et al., 2016). Decreased amygdala responses to images of their parents predicted decreased anxiety symptoms over time and could be a protective mechanism within children and adolescents exposed to early caregiving deprivation (Callaghan et al., 2019).

Growing work has examined developmental patterns of increased connectivity between the PFC and amygdala. These connections typically increase in strength, especially during the period of adolescence. Recent work suggests that early maternal deprivation might accelerate this developmental process. Previously institutionalized children exhibited more mature amygdala–prefrontal connectivity (Gee et al., 2013) and hippocampal–prefrontal connectivity, resembling patterns that are more typical of more mature connectivity patterns in adults (Silvers et al., 2016). These age-atypical patterns of connectivity were also associated with decreased anxiety, indicating potentially protective neural adaptations after adversity (Gee et al., 2013; Silvers et al., 2016).

HPA axis

The HPA axis, part of the neuroendocrine system, is one of two major stress systems intricately connected to and regulated by limbic circuitry. Cortisol, the end product of this system, plays an important regulatory role, in that it acts as a negative feedback signal at multiple levels of the limbic-HPA axis. Under typical conditions, cortisol effectively dampens the activity of the hypothalamus and pituitary glands, reducing activation of the HPA system. However, in atypical circumstances, such as in cases of adverse rearing, the normative regulatory patterns can become disrupted. Long-term disruptions are theorized to have negative consequences for both physical and emotional health (Sapolsky, 2000). Deprivation-induced alterations of HPA activity, especially when experienced during sensitive periods of neurophysiological development, have a lasting impact on the HPA axis and associated brain regions that support cognitive and emotional functioning. Chronic alterations may increase risk for a multitude of mental health and cognitive problems in the long term (Heim & Nemeroff, 2001).

HPA axis activation supports two relatively orthogonal physiological processes, one that supports the adaptive mounting of a stress response and the other that supports basic diurnal and homeostatic processes. Both of these functions have been investigated in the context of institutional rearing exposure. Findings point to the various ways in which early experiences shape basic neuroendocrine system regulation, stress physiology, and developmental outcomes.

HPA axis alterations

Cortisol reactivity

Developmental studies indicate that humans show immediate cortisol increases to stress at birth, which is followed by a hyporesponsive period in later infancy, during which HPA activation to stress is typically not observed (Gunnar & Donzella, 2002). Similar patterns are observed in non-human mammals, and it is theorized that this hyporesponsive period might be protective, in that it prevents the immature brain from being exposed to potentially harmful glucocorticoids during its most malleable phases. Another important sensitive period of development for the HPA axis emerges in adolescence, and evidence suggests that the HPA axis might develop more adultlike patterns of reactivity (i.e. increases in cortisol to stressors) over the transition to puberty (Gunnar, Wewerka, Frenn, Long, & Griggs, 2009).

Children with early deprivation experiences, including institutionalization or maltreatment, show dysregulated HPA axis functioning that can persist into adulthood. An initial preliminary study with a smaller sample size (n=18) found severe neglect experienced by post-institutionalized children was associated with impaired cortisol regulation. Specifically, severely neglected children showed increased cortisol levels in response to interactions with their adoptive mothers compared to children with none to less severe neglect (Gunnar, Morison, Chisholm, & Schuder, 2001).

A more common pattern in the literature provides evidence for more blunted cortisol reactivity in adopted children exposed to early deprivation than in non-adopted children. In studies of children adopted internationally from both foster care and institutional care, both groups of children exhibited blunted cortisol responses to a stressor (Koss, Mliner, Donzella, & Gunnar, 2016; McLaughlin et al., 2015). The patterns of blunted cortisol reactivity persisted in adulthood for individuals who were adopted post-institutionalization (Hengesch et al., 2018). There is evidence that blunted cortisol reactivity is associated with externalizing problems in youth with early adversity (Koss et al., 2016; Ouellet-Morin et al., 2011). Recent work has begun to examine how emotion regulation capacities relate to cortisol relativity in previously institutionalized youth; lower emotion regulation was associated with lower cortisol baselines, increased reactivity, and slower recovery, and worse emotion regulation predicted greater internalizing problems (Perry, Donzella, Parenteau, Desjardins, & Gunnar, 2019). Further supporting the idea that early positive caregiving experiences can help ameliorate HPA dysfunction, DePasquale and colleagues (2018) found that among post-institutionalized youth, increased sensitive caregiving post-adoption was associated with increased cortisol responses.

Diurnal rhythms

In terms of the typical diurnal rhythm, cortisol levels rise in the morning when an individual awakens, with peak cortisol levels approximately 30–45 minutes after awakening. This is referred to as the cortisol awakening response (CAR). Following this peak, cortisol values gradually decrease across the day. The diurnal rhythm of cortisol maintains regulatory functioning, including maintaining circadian sleep/wake patterns, metabolism, and temperature regulation (Contrada & Baum, 2011). Therefore, disruptions in diurnal patterns might signify altered functioning in basic homeostatic functions.

In terms of disruptions in diurnal rhythms, children adopted from adverse early caregiving environments typically show patterns of hypocortisolism, evidenced as low morning cortisol and flatter diurnal slope of cortisol across the day (Carlson & Earls, 1997; Flannery et al., 2017; Gunnar & Vazquez, 2001; Koss et al., 2016). Patterns of blunted CAR have also been observed in adults who were adopted from institutions or maltreated as young children (Kumsta et al., 2017; van der Vegt, van der Ende, Kirschbaum, Verhulst, & Tiemeier, 2009). These effects for diurnal cortisol and CAR also appear to be sensitive to developmental timing of adoption and puberty. Pubertal development and earlier adoption contributed to steeper diurnal cortisol slopes in adolescents (Flannery et al., 2017). Leneman and colleagues (2018) found blunted CAR for children adopted at 16 months or later, but not for children adopted earlier. Blunted CAR was also observed only for adopted youth who are in earlier stages of puberty compared to those later in puberty, suggesting regulation of the hormone cortisol could change across these developmental stages depending on timing of early deprivation experiences (Quevedo, Johnson, Loman, LaFavor, & Gunnar, 2012).

There is growing evidence that severity of early neglect or abuse can differentially influence patterns of HPA axis development. In a sample of youth followed from childhood to adulthood, adoptive parents reported on varying levels of pre-adoption abuse and neglect, and diurnal cortisol was measured in adulthood. Severe neglect was associated with flatter diurnal cortisol rhythm, whereas moderate to severe abuse was associated with steeper increases in cortisol across the day (van der Vegt et al., 2009). Within adopted children, dysregulated HPA axis functioning has significant implications for increased risk of psychopathology, as flatter diurnal cortisol rhythms have been associated with increased behavioral and emotional problems (Kroupina et al., 2012) and attention and externalizing problems (Koss et al., 2016). However, research supports that the hypocortisolism patterns observed might improve once children are removed from institutions and adopted into supportive caregiving environments (Fries, Shirtcliff, & Pollak, 2008; Gunnar et al., 2001; Kertes, Gunnar, Madsen, & Long, 2008; Kroupina et al., 2012).

Autonomic nervous system

Typical autonomic nervous system functioning

There is substantially less work on how institutional rearing shapes the autonomic nervous system (ANS), another central biological stress response system. When a stress response is triggered by the amygdala to the hypothalamus, a signal is then sent to both the pituitary gland to activate the HPA axis, and to the adrenal medulla region of the brain to activate the ANS. In contrast to the relatively slow acting HPA axis (in which peak activation occurs around 20 minutes following the peak stressor), the ANS activates a quick-acting response, helping the body mount a response to protect against imminent threat.

The ANS includes two opposing branches, the parasympathetic nervous system (PNS), which is responsible for maintaining homeostasis at rest and calming the body down ("rest and digest"), and sympathetic nervous system (SNS), which activates physiological arousal in response to a stressor ("fight or flight response"). At rest, the PNS acts as a "brake" by maintaining inhibitory control over heart rate (HR), slowing it down. In response to stress, the PNS disengages, thus leading to an increase in HR. Parasympathetic regulation of HR is often measured through respiratory sinus arrhythmia (RSA), a measure of high frequency heart rate variability during the respiratory cycle.

In contrast to the PNS, the SNS is like the "gas pedal" and increases cardiac output and increases HR in response to stress. SNS activity can be measured through the pre-ejection period (PEP), which reflects the time elapsed from the start of the heartbeat until the ejection of blood into the aorta. Greater SNS input is observed as shorter PEP (Berntson et al., 1994).

ANS functioning in adopted youth

Few studies have examined the effect of early caregiving deprivation on ANS functioning. Two studies examined ANS in adopted youth approximately 10 years post-institutionalization in response to a standardized stressor task. They found previously institutionalized children exhibited greater sympathetic baseline activity (Gunnar et al., 2009; McLaughlin et al., 2015) and blunted SNS reactivity (McLaughlin et al., 2015). Increased SNS activity at baseline suggests that children who have experienced early deprivation might be in a hyperactive state of arousal at rest, making it more difficult to mount an additional response when a stressor is present, observed as blunted reactivity to stressors. In a third study that examined ANS within the first 16 months post-adoption (Esposito, Koss, Donzella, & Gunnar, 2016), previously institutionalized children similarly displayed higher sympathetic activity at baseline compared to non-adopted youth, and no differences in PNS activity were observed. Enhanced sympathetic activity soon after adoption was also associated with greater behavioral problems two years post-adoption (Esposito et al., 2016). Earlier adoption into a foster care intervention (before 18 months) is associated with enhanced vagal regulation during social tasks (McLaughlin et al., 2015), providing evidence of a sensitive period of development for the ANS stress response system. Studies of ANS in other high-risk populations have examined how ANS functioning interacts with environmental risk to predict behavioral outcomes and child psychopathology (Gray, Theall, Lipschutz, & Drury, 2017). Considering children with experiences of institutionalization or maltreatment might then be adopted into families with supportive caregiving, future research should continue to examine patterns of biological sensitivity to these differential contexts and how they might confer risk or buffer developmental outcomes.

Interventions that influence neurobiology in adopted youth

The Bucharest Early Intervention Program (BEIP) is the only randomized clinical trial of an intervention designed to remove children from institutions and place them into high-quality responsive family settings. Evidence from the BEIP has shown myriad neurobiological improvements for previously institutionalized children placed in foster care. For example, intervention effects have been observed for differences in total white matter volume (Sheridan et al., 2012), neural responses during an error-processing cognitive task (McDermott, Westerlund, Zeanah, Nelson, & Fox, 2012), neural responses to emotional stimuli at 8 years old (Nelson, Westerlund, McDermott, Zeanah, & Fox, 2013), EEG activity patterns (Vanderwert, 2010, 2016), structural connectivity (Bick et al., 2015, 2017), and ANS reactivity (McLaughlin et al., 2015). These interventions provide evidence for the developmental sensitivity of these neurobiological systems; they are both susceptible to detrimental effects of deprivation and stress, and also responsive to positive, supportive caregiving environments.

Other interventions have been developed to support children exposed to neglect experiences in contexts outside of institutional rearing. The Multidimensional Treatment Foster Care for Preschoolers (MTFC-P; Fisher, Stoolmiller, Gunnar, & Burraston, 2007) involves intensive caregiver training to promote warm, responsive, and consistent caregiving environments, and behavioral treatment for children to enhance pro-social skills. MTFC-P has been shown to normalize dysfunctional diurnal cortisol patterns (Fisher et al., 2007) and neural responses to positive and negative feedback conditions (Bruce, McDermott, Fisher, & Fox, 2009) in children randomized to MTFC-P compared to regular foster care and a community control group. Another example includes the Attachment and Biobehavioral Catch-up (ABC; Dozier et al., 2006), developed for families at high risk for maltreatment or involved with foster care. The goals of this program are to enhance parent–child synchrony, nurturing, and non-frightening behaviors, which is theorized to promote greater behavioral, emotional, and physiological regulation in children exposed to early adversity. A randomized control trial found that children receiving the ABC intervention showed more typical cortisol patterns (Bernard, Dozier, Bick, & Gordon, 2015a; Bernard, Hostinar, & Dozier, 2015b), normalized neural function (Bick, Palmwood, Zajac, Simons, & Dozier, 2019), and improved resting autonomic functioning (Tabachnick, Raby, Goldstein, Zajac, & Dozier, 2019) compared to children in the control group. Results from these studies suggest that MTFC-P and ABC interventions could also be promising for children who have experienced early institutional rearing.

Policy and practice implications

Evidence reviewed here shows that early caregiving deprivation experiences, including institutionalization and maltreatment, can have long-lasting negative impacts on children's neurobiological development and functioning. Fortunately, research also suggests that early adoption into supportive caregiving environments, through foster care or permanent placements, can ameliorate some of these consequences and promote more adaptive neurobiological outcomes.

As described above, neurobiological alterations have important implications for cognitive, social, and emotional development and functioning in adopted youth. Adopted children might be at increased biological vulnerability for development of behavioral problems and psychopathology that require therapeutic intervention. Caregivers and other individuals who support adopted children should aim to understand how these neurobiological risks might manifest behaviorally to best provide care and resources to meet their needs.

In terms of policies, this line of research highlights the potential long-term detrimental effects of institutional care that is typical in some countries. Countries that implement and utilize policies that allow institutionalization and systematic deprivation of caregiving should consider the negative outcomes for children and reconsider best practices for providing caregiving environments for children. Research also highlights the importance of earlier adoption for more optimal outcomes.

Conclusions

Early deprivation such as institutionalization or maltreatment can disrupt typical development of socioemotional, behavioral, and physiological systems in adopted youth. Understanding how these early adverse caregiving experiences might alter neurobiological functioning can elucidate trajectories of risk for psychopathology and other behavioral outcomes. Adaptations to the affective and cognitive brain structures and functioning, and stress response systems (HPA axis and ANS) in adopted youth might confer risk for negative developmental outcomes and also provide therapeutic targets by which to intervene. Additional research is needed to understand how early life experiences of adopted youth affect neurobiological development and environment or individual factors that might moderate these effects.

References

Behen, M. E., Muzik, O., Saporta, A. S. D., Wilson, B. J., Pai, D., Hua, J., & Chugani, H. T. (2009). Abnormal fronto-striatal connectivity in children with histories of early deprivation: A diffusion tensor imaging study. *Brain Imaging and Behavior, 3*(3), 292–297. doi:10.1007/s11682-009-9071-6

Bernard, K., Dozier, M., Bick, J., & Gordon, M. K. (2015a). Intervening to enhance cortisol regulation among children at risk for neglect: Results of a randomized clinical trial. *Development and Psychopathology, 27*(3), 829–841. doi:10.1017/S095457941400073X

Bernard, K., Hostinar, C. E., & Dozier, M. (2015b). Intervention effects on diurnal cortisol rhythms of Child Protective Services-referred infants in early childhood: Preschool follow-up results of a randomized clinical trial. *JAMA Pediatrics, 169*(2), 112–119. doi:10.1001/jamapediatrics.2014.2369

Berntson, G. G., Cacioppo, J. T., Binkley, P. F., Uchino, B. N., Quigley, K. S., & Fieldstone, A. (1994). Autonomic cardiac control. III. Psychological stress and cardiac response in autonomic space as revealed by pharmacological blockades. *Psychophysiology, 31*(6), 599–608. Retrieved from www.ncbi.nlm.nih.gov/pubmed/7846220

Bick, J., Fox, N., Zeanah, C., & Nelson, C. A. (2017). Early deprivation, atypical brain development, and internalizing symptoms in late childhood. *Neuroscience, 342*, 140–153. doi:10.1016/j.neuroscience.2015.09.026

Bick, J., Palmwood, E. N., Zajac, L., Simons, R., & Dozier, M. (2019). Early parenting intervention and adverse family environments affect neural function in middle childhood. *Biological Psychiatry, 85*(4), 326–335. doi:10.1016/j.biopsych.2018.09.020

Bick, J., Zhu, T., Stamoulis, C., Fox, N. A., Zeanah, C. H., & Nelson, C. A. (2015). A randomized clinical trial of foster care as an intervention for early institutionalization: Long term improvements in white matter microstructure. *JAMA Pediatrics, 169*(3), 211–219. doi:10.1001/jamapediatrics.2014.3212.A

Bruce, J., McDermott, J. M., Fisher, P. A., & Fox, N. A. (2009). Using behavioral and electrophysiological measures to assess the effects of a preventive intervention: A preliminary study with preschool-aged foster children. *Prevention Science: The Official Journal of the Society for Prevention Research, 10*(2), 129–140. doi:10.1007/s11121-008-0115-8

Callaghan, B., Gee, D. G., Gabard-Durnam, L., Telzer, E. H., Humphreys, K. L., Goff, B., ... Tottenham, N. (2019, in press). Decreased amygdala reactivity to parent cues protects against anxiety following early adversity: An examination across 3-years. *Biological Psychiatry: Cognitive Neuroscience and Neuroimaging.* doi:10.1016/J.BPSC.2019.02.001.

Carlson, M., & Earls, F. (1997). Psychological and neuroendocrinological sequelae of early social deprivation in institutionalized children in Romania. *Annals of the New York Academy of Sciences, 807*, 419–428. Retrieved from www.ncbi.nlm.nih.gov/pubmed/9071367

Chugani, H. T., Behen, M. E., Muzik, O., Juhász, C., Nagy, F., & Chugani, D. C. (2001). Local brain functional activity following early deprivation: A study of postinstitutionalized Romanian orphans. *NeuroImage, 14*(6), 1290–1301. doi:10.1006/nimg.2001.0917

Contrada, R. J., & Baum, A. (2011). *The handbook of stress science: Biology, psychology, and health. - PsycNET.* New York: Springer Publishing Company. Retrieved from https://psycnet.apa.org/record/2010-21826-000

DePasquale, C. E., Raby, K. L., Hoye, J., & Dozier, M. (2018). Parenting predicts strange situation cortisol reactivity among children adopted internationally. *Psychoneuroendocrinology, 89*, 86–91. doi:10.1016/j.psyneuen.2018.01.003

Dozier, M., Peloso, E., Lindhiem, O., Gordon, M. K., Manni, M., Sepulveda, S., ... Levine, S. (2006). Developing evidence-based interventions for foster children: An example of a randomized clinical trial with infants and toddlers. *Journal of Social Issues, 62*(4), 767–785. doi:10.1111/j.1540-4560.2006.00486.x

Edmiston, E. E., Wang, F., Mazure, C. M., Guiney, J., Sinha, R., Mayes, L. C., & Blumberg, H. P. (2011). Corticostriatal-limbic gray matter morphology in adolescents with self-reported exposure to childhood maltreatment. *Archives of Pediatrics & Adolescent Medicine, 165*(12), 1069–1077. doi:10.1001/archpediatrics.2011.565

Eluvathingal, T. J., Chugani, H. T., Behen, M. E., Juhász, C., Muzik, O., Maqbool, M., ... Makki, M. I. (2006). Abnormal brain connectivity in children after early severe socioemotional deprivation: A diffusion tensor imaging study. *Pediatrics, 117*(6), 2093–2100. doi:10.1542/peds.2005-1727

Esposito, E. A., Koss, K. J., Donzella, B., & Gunnar, M. R. (2016). Early deprivation and autonomic nervous system functioning in post-institutionalized children. *Developmental Psychobiology, 58*(3), 328–340. doi:10.1002/dev.21373

Fareri, D. S., & Delgado, M. R. (2014). Social rewards and social networks in the human brain. *Neuroscientist, 20*(4), 387–402. doi:10.1177/1073858414521869

Fareri, D. S., Gabard-Durnam, L., Goff, B., Flannery, J., Gee, D. G., Lumian, D. S., ... Tottenham, N. (2017). Altered ventral striatal-medial prefrontal cortex resting-state connectivity mediates adolescent social problems after early institutional care. *Development and Psychopathology, 29*(5), 1865–1876. doi:10.1017/S0954579417001456

Fisher, P. A., Stoolmiller, M., Gunnar, M. R., & Burraston, B. O. (2007). Effects of a therapeutic intervention for foster preschoolers on diurnal cortisol activity. *Psychoneuroendocrinology, 32*(8–10), 892–905. doi:10.1016/j.psyneuen.2007.06.008

Flannery, J. E., Gabard-Durnam, L. J., Shapiro, M., Goff, B., Caldera, C., Louie, J., ... Tottenham, N. (2017). Diurnal cortisol after early institutional care – Age matters. *Developmental Cognitive Neuroscience, 25*(1), 160–166. doi:10.1016/j.dcn.2017.03.006

Fox, N. A. (1991). If it's not left, it's right. Electroencephalograph asymmetry and the development of emotion. *The American Psychologist, 46*(8), 863–872. Retrieved from www.ncbi.nlm.nih.gov/pubmed/1928939

Frenkel, T. I., Koss, K. J., Donzella, B., Frenn, K. A., Lamm, C., Fox, N. A., & Gunnar, M. R. (2017). ADHD symptoms in post-institutionalized children are partially mediated by altered frontal EEG asymmetry. *Journal of Abnormal Child Psychology, 45*(5), 857–869. doi:10.1007/s10802-016-0208-y

Fries, A. B. W., Shirtcliff, E. A., & Pollak, S. D. (2008). Neuroendocrine dysregulation following early social deprivation in children. *Developmental Psychobiology, 50*(6), 588–599. doi:10.1002/dev.20319

Gee, D. G., Gabard-Durnam, L. J., Flannery, J., Goff, B., Humphreys, K. L., Telzer, E. H., ... Tottenham, N. (2013). Early developmental emergence of human amygdala-prefrontal connectivity after maternal deprivation. *Proceedings of the National Academy of Sciences, 110*(39), 15638–15643. doi:10.1073/pnas.1307893110

Govindan, R. M., Behen, M. E., Helder, E., Makki, M. I., & Chugani, H. T. (2010). Altered water diffusivity in cortical association tracts in children with early deprivation identified with Tract-Based Spatial Statistics (TBSS). *Cerebral Cortex*, *20*(3), 561–569. doi:10.1093/cercor/bhp122

Gray, S. A., Theall, K., Lipschutz, R., & Drury, S. (2017). Sex differences in the contribution of respiratory sinus arrhythmia and trauma to children's psychopathology. *Journal of Psychopathology and Behavioral Assessment*, *39*(1), 67–78. doi:10.1007/s10862-016-9568-4

Green, S. A., Goff, B., Gee, D. G., Gabard-Durnam, L., Flannery, J., Telzer, E. H., … Tottenham, N. (2016). Discrimination of amygdala response predicts future separation anxiety in youth with early deprivation. *Journal of Child Psychology and Psychiatry and Allied Disciplines*, *57*(10), 1135–1144. doi:10.1111/jcp.12578

Gunnar, M. R., & Donzella, B. (2002). Social regulation of the cortisol levels in early human development. *Psychoneuroendocrinology*, *27*(1–2), 199–220. doi:10.1016/S0306-4530(01)00045-2

Gunnar, M. R., Morison, S. J., Chisholm, K., & Schuder, M. (2001). Salivary cortisol levels in children adopted from Romanian orphanages. *Development and Psychopathology*, *13*(3), 611–628. Retrieved from www.ncbi.nlm.nih.gov/pubmed/11523851

Gunnar, M. R., & Vazquez, D. M. (2001). Low cortisol and a flattening of expected daytime rhythm: Potential indices of risk in human development. *Development and Psychopathology*, *13*(3), 515–538. Retrieved from www.ncbi.nlm.nih.gov/pubmed/11523846

Gunnar, M. R., Wewerka, S., Frenn, K., Long, J. D., & Griggs, C. (2009). Developmental changes in hypothalamus–pituitary–adrenal activity over the transition to adolescence: Normative changes and associations with puberty. *Development and Psychopathology*, *21*(1), 69–85. doi:10.1017/S0954579409000054

Hanson, J. L., Adluru, N., Chung, M. K., Alexander, A. L., Davidson, R. J., & Pollak, S. D. (2013). Early neglect is associated with alterations in white matter integrity and cognitive functioning. *Child Development*, *84*(5), 1566–1578.

Hanson, J. L., Nacewicz, B. M., Sutterer, M. J., Cayo, A. A., Schaefer, S. M., Rudolph, K. D., … Davidson, R. J. (2014). Behavioral problems after early life stress: Contributions of the hippocampus and amygdala. *Biological Psychiatry*, 77(4), 314–323. doi:10.1016/j.biopsych.2014.04.020

Heim, C., & Nemeroff, C. B. (2001). The role of childhood trauma in the neurobiology of mood and anxiety disorders: Preclinical and clinical studies. *Biological Psychiatry*, *49*(12), 1023–1039. Retrieved from www.ncbi.nlm.nih.gov/pubmed/11430844

Hengesch, X., Elwenspoek, M. M. C., Schaan, V. K., Larra, M. F., Finke, J. B., Zhang, X., … Schächinger, H. (2018). Blunted endocrine response to a combined physical-cognitive stressor in adults with early life adversity. *Child Abuse & Neglect*, *85*, 137–144. doi:10.1016/j.chiabu.2018.04.002

Herzberg, M. P., Hodel, A. S., Cowell, R. A., Hunt, R. H., Gunnar, M. R., & Thomas, K. M. (2018). Risk taking, decision-making, and brain volume in youth adopted internationally from institutional care. *Neuropsychologia*, *119*, 262–270. doi:10.1016/j.neuropsychologia.2018.08.022

Hodel, A. S., Hunt, R. H., Cowell, R. A., Van Den Heuvel, S. E., Gunnar, M. R., & Thomas, K. M. (2015). Duration of early adversity and structural brain development in post-institutionalized adolescents. *NeuroImage*, *105*, 112–119. doi:10.1016/j.neuroimage.2014.10.020

Kertes, D. A., Gunnar, M. R., Madsen, N. J., & Long, J. D. (2008). Early deprivation and home basal cortisol levels: A study of internationally adopted children. *Development and Psychopathology*, *20*(2), 473–491. doi:10.1017/S0954579408000230

Koss, K. J., Mliner, S. B., Donzella, B., & Gunnar, M. R. (2016). Early adversity, hypocortisolism, and behavior problems at school entry: A study of internationally adopted children. *Psychoneuroendocrinology*, *66*, 31–38. doi:10.1016/j.psyneuen.2015.12.018

Kroupina, M. G., Fuglestad, A. J., Iverson, S. L., Himes, J. H., Mason, P. W., Gunnar, M. R., … Johnson, D. E. (2012). Adoption as an intervention for institutionally reared children: HPA functioning and developmental status. *Infant Behavior and Development*, *35*(4), 829–837. doi:10.1016/j.infbeh.2012.07.011

Kumar, A., Behen, M. E., Singsoonsud, P., Veenstra, A. L., Wolfe-Christensen, C., Helder, E., & Chugani, H. T. (2014). Microstructural abnormalities in language and limbic pathways in orphanage-reared children: A diffusion tensor imaging study. *Journal of Child Neurology*, *29*(3), 318–325. doi:10.1177/0883073812474098

Kumsta, R., Schlotz, W., Golm, D., Moser, D., Kennedy, M., Knights, N., … Sonuga-Barke, E. (2017). HPA axis dysregulation in adult adoptees twenty years after severe institutional deprivation in childhood. *Psychoneuroendocrinology*, *86*(July), 196–202. doi:10.1016/j.psyneuen.2017.09.021

Leneman, K. B., Donzella, B., Desjardins, C. D., Miller, B. S., & Gunnar, M. R. (2018). The slope of cortisol from awakening to 30 min post-wake in post-institutionalized children and early adolescents. *Psychoneuroendocrinology, 96,* 93–99. doi:10.1016/j.psyneuen.2018.06.011

Lenroot, R. K., & Giedd, J. N. (2006). Brain development in children and adolescents: Insights from anatomical magnetic resonance imaging. *Neuroscience & Biobehavioral Reviews, 30*(6), 718–729. doi:10.1016/j.neubiorev.2006.06.001

Maheu, F. S., Dozier, M., Guyer, A. E., Mandell, D., Peloso, E., Poeth, K., … Ernst, M. (2010). A preliminary study of medial temporal lobe function in youths with a history of caregiver deprivation and emotional neglect. *Cognitive, Affective, & Behavioral Neuroscience, 10*(1), 34–49. doi:10.3758/CABN.10.1.34

Marshall, P. J., Fox, N. A., & the Bucharest Early Intervention Project Core Group. (2004). A comparison of the electroencephalogram between institutionalized and community children in Romania. *Journal of Cognitive Neuroscience, 16*(8), 1327–1338. Retrieved from www.ncbi.nlm.nih.gov/pubmed/15532128

McDermott, J. M., Westerlund, A., Zeanah, C. H., Nelson, C. A., & Fox, N. A. (2012). Early adversity and neural correlates of executive function: Implications for academic adjustment. *Developmental Cognitive Neuroscience, 2,* S59–S66. doi:10.1016/j.dcn.2011.09.008

McLaughlin, K. A., Fox, N. A., Zeanah, C. H., & Nelson, C. A. (2011). Adverse rearing environments and neural development in children: The development of frontal electroencephalogram asymmetry. *Biological Psychiatry, 70*(11), 1008–1015. doi:10.1016/j.biopsych.2011.08.006

McLaughlin, K. A., Fox, N. A., Zeanah, C. H., Sheridan, M. A., Marshall, P., & Nelson, C. A. (2010). Delayed maturation in brain electrical activity partially explains the association between early environmental deprivation and symptoms of attention-deficit/hyperactivity disorder. *Biological Psychiatry, 68*(4), 329–336. doi:10.1016/j.biopsych.2010.04.005

McLaughlin, K. A., Sheridan, M. A., Tibu, F., Fox, N. A., Zeanah, C. H., & Nelson, C. A. (2015). Causal effects of the early caregiving environment on development of stress response systems in children. *Proceedings of the National Academy of Sciences, 112*(18), 5637–5642. doi:10.1073/pnas.1423363112

Mehta, M. A., Golembo, N. I., Nosarti, C., Colvert, E., Mota, A., Williams, S. C., Rutter, M., & Sonuga-Barke, E. J. S. (2009). Amygdala, hippocampal and corpus callosum size following severe early institutional deprivation: The English and Romanian Adoptees study pilot. *Journal of Child Psychology and Psychiatry, and Allied Disciplines, 50*(8), 943–951. doi:10.1111/j.1469-7610.2009.02084.x

Mueller, S. C., Maheu, F. S., Dozier, M., Peloso, E., Mandell, D., Leibenluft, E., … Ernst, M. (2010). Early-life stress is associated with impairment in cognitive control in adolescence: An fMRI study. *Neuropsychologia, 48*(10), 3037–3044. doi:10.1016/J.NEUROPSYCHOLOGIA.2010.06.013

Nelson, C. A., Westerlund, A., McDermott, J. M., Zeanah, C. H., & Fox, N. A. (2013). Emotion recognition following early psychosocial deprivation. *Development and Psychopathology, 25*(2), 517–525. doi:10.1017/S0954579412001216

Olsavsky, A. K., Telzer, E. H., Shapiro, M., Humphreys, K. L., Flannery, J., Goff, B., & Tottenham, N. (2013). Indiscriminate amygdala response to mothers and strangers after early maternal deprivation. *Biological Psychiatry, 74*(11), 853–860. doi:10.1016/j.biopsych.2013.05.025

Ouellet-Morin, I., Odgers, C. L., Danese, A., Bowes, L., Shakoor, S., Papadopoulos, A. S., … Arseneault, L. (2011). Blunted cortisol responses to stress signal social and behavioral problems among maltreated/bullied 12-year-old children. *Biological Psychiatry, 70*(11), 1016–1023. doi:10.1016/j.biopsych.2011.06.017

Perry, N. B., Donzella, B., Parenteau, A. M., Desjardins, C., & Gunnar, M. R. (2019). Emotion regulation and cortisol reactivity during a social evaluative stressor: A study of post-institutionalized youth. *Developmental Psychobiology.* doi:10.1002/dev.21828

Quevedo, K., Johnson, A. E., Loman, M. L., LaFavor, T. L., & Gunnar, M. (2012). The confluence of adverse early experience and puberty on the cortisol awakening response. *International Journal of Behavioral Development, 36*(1), 19–28. doi:10.1177/0165025411406860

Reiss, A. L., Abrams, M. T., Singer, H. S., Ross, J. L., & Denckla, M. B. (1996). Brain development, gender and IQ in children. A volumetric imaging study. *Brain: A Journal of Neurology, 119,* 1763–1774. Retrieved from www.ncbi.nlm.nih.gov/pubmed/8931596

Sapolsky, R. M. (2000). Stress hormones: Good and bad. *Neurobiology of Disease,* 7(5), 540–542. doi:10.1006/nbdi.2000.0350

Sheridan, M. A., Fox, N. A., Zeanah, C. H., McLaughlin, K. A., & Nelson, C. A. (2012). Variation in neural development as a result of exposure to institutionalization early in childhood. *Proceedings of the National Academy of Sciences, 109*(32), 12927–12932. doi:10.1073/pnas.1200041109

Silvers, J. A., Goff, B., Gabard-Durnam, L. J., Gee, D. G., Fareri, D. S., Caldera, C., & Tottenham, N. (2017). Vigilance, the amygdala, and anxiety in youths with a history of institutional care. *Biological Psychiatry: Cognitive Neuroscience and Neuroimaging, 2*(6), 493–501. doi:10.1016/j.bpsc.2017.03.016

Silvers, J. A., Lumian, D. S., Gabard-Durnam, L., Gee, D. G., Goff, B., Fareri, D. S., … Tottenham, N. (2016). Previous institutionalization is followed by broader amygdala–hippocampal–PFC network connectivity during aversive learning in human development. *The Journal of Neuroscience, 36*(24), 6420–6430. doi:10.1523/JNEUROSCI.0038-16.2016

Sowell, E. R., Peterson, B. S., Thompson, P. M., Welcome, S. E., Henkenius, A. L., & Toga, A. W. (2003). Mapping cortical change across the human life span. *Nature Neuroscience, 6*(3), 309–315. doi:10.1038/nn1008

Stiles, J., & Jernigan, T. L. (2010). The basics of brain development. *Neuropsychology Review, 20*(4), 327–348. doi:10.1007/s11065-010-9148-4

Sutton, S. K., & Davidson, R. J. (1997). Prefrontal brain asymmetry: A biological substrate of the behavioral approach and inhibition systems. *Psychological Science, 8*(3), 204–210. doi:10.1111/j.1467-9280.1997.tb00413.x

Tabachnick, A. R., Raby, K. L., Goldstein, A., Zajac, L., & Dozier, M. (2019). Effects of an attachment-based intervention in infancy on children's autonomic regulation during middle childhood. *Biological Psychology, 143*, 22–31. doi:10.1016/j.biopsycho.2019.01.006

Tarullo, A. R., Garvin, M. C., & Gunnar, M. R. (2011). Atypical EEG power correlates with indiscriminately friendly behavior in internationally adopted children. *Developmental Psychology, 47*(2), 417–431. doi:10.1037/a0021363

Tottenham, N., Hare, T. A., Millner, A., Gilhooly, T., Zevin, J. D., & Casey, B. J. (2011). Elevated amygdala response to faces following early deprivation. *Developmental Science, 14*(2), 190–204. doi:10.1111/j.1467-7687.2010.00971.x

Tottenham, N., Hare, T. A., Quinn, B. T., McCarry, T. W., Nurse, M., Gilhooly, T., … Casey, B. J. (2010). Prolonged institutional rearing is associated with atypically large amygdala volume and difficulties in emotion regulation. *Developmental Science, 13*(1), 46–61. doi:10.1111/j.1467-7687.2009.00852.x

van der Vegt, E. J. M., van der Ende, J., Kirschbaum, C., Verhulst, F. C., & Tiemeier, H. (2009). Early neglect and abuse predict diurnal cortisol patterns in adults. A study of international adoptees. *Psychoneuroendocrinology, 34*(5), 660–669. doi:10.1016/j.psyneuen.2008.11.004

Vanderwert, R. E., Marshall, P. J., Nelson, C. A., Zeanah, C. H., & Fox, N. A. (2010). Timing of intervention affects brain electrical activity in children exposed to severe psychosocial neglect. *PLoS ONE, 5*(7), e11415. doi:10.1371/journal.pone.0011415

Vanderwert, R. E., Zeanah, C. H., Fox, N. A., & Nelson, C. A. (2016). Normalization of EEG activity among previously institutionalized children placed into foster care: A 12-year follow-up of the Bucharest Early Intervention Project. *Developmental Cognitive Neuroscience, 17*, 68–75. doi:10.1016/j.dcn.2015.12.004

Wade, M., Fox, N. A., Zeanah, C. H., & Nelson, C. A. (2019). Long-term effects of institutional rearing, foster care, and brain activity on memory and executive functioning. *Proceedings of the National Academy of Sciences, 116*(5), 1808–1813. doi:10.1073/pnas.1809145116

27

POST-ADOPTION SHORT- AND LONG-TERM SOCIAL ADAPTATION AND COMPETENCE OF INTERNATIONALLY ADOPTED CHILDREN

Tony Xing Tan, Yanhong Liu, and Cherry Smith

From 2000 to 2017, families in fewer than 30 countries adopted over half a million children from nearly 100 sending countries (Selman, 2017). While most of the children were born to parents living in developing countries (Briggs, 2012), across different sending countries, the primary reasons for children to become available for adoption varied, resulting in distinctive characteristics in children adopted from different countries. Poverty, social stigma, and government policies appeared to play a role in fueling the availability of children for international adoption (Tan, Major, Marn, Na, & Jackson, 2015). The vast majority of these children were adopted by families in Canada, France, Italy, Spain, and the United States (Selman, 2017). The United States is the largest adopting country, receiving about half of all internationally adopted (IA) children. Over the same period, about 90 percent of IA children in the United States came from four countries: China, Guatemala, Russia, and South Korea (US Department of State, 2018). Like their non-adopted peers, IA children need to acquire age-appropriate social skills and competence in order to meet the social demands of their post-adoptive environment. The skills and competence usually include situation-specific abilities that children need in order to respond to various social demands (Dirks, Treat, & Weersing, 2007), and they vary with the age of children (Bierman & Montminy, 1993). Social skills (e.g., the ability to relate to others) constitute the most basic construct of children's social competence (Cavell, Meehan, & Fiala, 2003), and social interaction is a key process through which children acquire and apply these skills (Mueller & Brenner, 1977).

Early parent–child interaction and peer interaction play a foundational role in children's short- and long-term social development (Symons & Clark, 2000). Along with parent–child interaction, age-appropriate developmental maturation is also critical, since it heavily influences children's cognitive abilities to appropriately respond to social demands, such as recognizing others' feelings and facial expressions and following social norms (Dodge, Pettit, McClaskey, & Brown, 1986; Semrud-Clikeman, 2007). The absence or severe compromise of these important experiences can be a source of problematic social development in children. Because of separation from birth parents and institutional rearing, IA children often experienced minimal meaningful social interactions and varying degrees of developmental delays before adoption, both of which can significantly challenge their post-adoption social development. The adoptive environment is thus tasked with neutralizing these risks through facilitating IA children's developmental catch-up during the early periods of adoption, fostering their recovery from earlier social and relational deprivation, and promoting long-term social development (Stams, Juffer, & van IJzendoorn, 2002).

Research on IA children's social development outcomes has demonstrated that, similar to the non-adopted population, there are general adjustment profiles, as well as individual and group differences, within the population of IA children. Understanding these similarities and differences is a first step toward developing policies and services that meet the best interests of IA children. In this chapter, we focus on how international adoptees develop attachment to the adoptive parents, form relationships with others, explore adoptive and ethnic identity, and find their places within the broader adoptive society as adopted individuals.

Child–parent attachment

Child–parent attachment has become a burgeoning area in the adoption literature due to its crucial role in children's social development, and has been consistently investigated in IA children since the 1990s (e.g., Chisholm, Carter, Ames, & Morison, 1995; O'Connor, Marvin, Rutter, Olrick, & Britner, 2003; Román, Palacios, Moreno, & Lopez, 2012; Stams et al., 2002). According to attachment theory (Bowlby, 1973), timing (i.e., the initial period after a child's birth), stability, and continuity of maternal care are critical factors for children to develop strong and favorable internal working models that function as the core of attachment (Bretherton, 1996). Children receiving consistent and sensitive care likely will develop secure attachment; in contrast, those who experience inconsistent and insufficient care are at a higher risk of forming insecure attachment (Bretherton, 1996). Due to prolonged separation from their birth families during institutionalization and discontinuation of care, adopted children can experience challenges in forming attachment to the adoptive parents (Juffer et al., 2011). As a result, despite that IA children were found to experience rapid catch-up in attachment development, IA children demonstrated more challenges in forming attachment with their adoptive parents compared to their non-adopted peers in the countries into which they were adopted (van den Dries, Juffer, van IJzendoorn, & Bakermans-Kranenburg, 2009).

Furthermore, variability exists in their attachment outcomes depending on a spectrum of factors such as age at adoption (van den Dries et al., 2009), pre-adoption adversity (Román et al., 2012), institutionalization experiences (Gunnar, Bruce, & Grotevant, 2000), self-report versus observational measure variation (van den Dries et al., 2009), and adoptive parents' caregiving quality (Stams et al., 2002; van den Dries, Juffer, van IJzendoorn, Bakermans-Kranenburg, & Alink, 2012) or parenting styles (Liu & Hazler, 2017a). Despite some level of discrepancy, more optimal attachment outcomes were reported to be associated with a younger age at the time of adoption, typically before 12 months old (Juffer, Bakermans-Kranenburg, & van IJzendoorn, 2008; van den Dries et al., 2009), increases in adoptive parental sensitivity (e.g., Bakermans-Kranenburg, van IJzendoorn, & Juffer, 2003), authoritative parenting (Liu & Hazler, 2017a), and when assessed using self-report attachment measure (van den Dries et al., 2009). Conversely, while some studies have suggested that age at adoption is an important determinant of secure attachment (Portello, 1993), other recent studies have found age at adoption to be a non-significant predictor of adoptees' secure attachment (e.g., Barone, Lionetti, & Green, 2017; Liu & Hazler, 2017a). With data collected at three points of time (i.e., at adoption; at one year after adoption; and at two years after adoption) on 48 post-institutionalized children and their adoptive parents, Barone et al. (2017) found that age at adoption was a non-significant predictor of children's secure attachment one year after adoption, nor did it significantly predict their social-emotional adjustment two years after adoption. Another study (Liu & Hazler, 2017a) on 92 Chinese adoptees in the US yielded a similar result that age at adoption was not significantly associated with adoptees' attachment outcomes. Furthermore, between-group differences were identified in IA children's attachment outcomes. For example, positive attachment was reported in Chinese adoptees (e.g., Cohen & Farnia, 2011; Liu & Hazler, 2017a; Pugliese, Cohen, Farnia, & Lojkasek, 2010), whereas among Romanian adoptees, post-adoption attachment issues appear to be prevalent, presumably due to severe pre-adoption deprivation (Chisholm, 1998; Marcovitch et al., 1997; O'Connor, Rutter, & the English and Romanian Adoptees Study Team, 2000; Rutter et al., 2007).

In spite of significant resilience observed in most IA children (Welsh, Viana, Petrill, & Mathias, 2007), they were still identified to be at a higher risk of developing insecure and disorganized attachment compared to their non-adopted peers (Barone et al., 2017; van Londen, Juffer, & van IJzendoorn, 2007). For instance, in the UK, IA children adopted from Romania were found to exhibit significantly more disinhibited attachment compared to their within-UK adopted counterparts (Rutter et al., 2007). Furthermore, about half of the 83 children with mild to marked disinhibited attachment at 6 years of age continued to show the pattern at 11 years (Rutter et al., 2007). Related to disinhibited attachment, an absence or lack of attachment is also common among IA children. According to Zeanah and Gleason (2015), emotional withdrawal and lack of seeking comfort from parents form "the core deficit" in children with *Reactive Attachment Disorder* (RAD; p. 209). Although the prevalence of RAD has not been thoroughly examined, it is a common concern in the adoption community (Bruce et al., 2019) and among pediatric care professionals (Follan & McNamara, 2014).

Indiscriminate social behavior

What has often been discussed along with child–parent attachment is IA children's *indiscriminate social behavior*, which was initially studied through the construct of *indiscriminate friendliness* (Chisholm, 1998; Chisholm et al., 1995). Indiscriminate friendliness is defined as children's unreserved affection directed toward all adults, including strangers (Tizard, 1977). It has been consistently investigated in the context of early institutionalization experiences (Bruce, Tarullo, & Gunnar, 2009; Liu & Hazler, 2017b; Love, Minnis, & O'Connor, 2015; Smyke, Dumitrescu, & Zeanah, 2002), with evidence supporting that approximately 20 percent of post-institutionalized children exhibit some indiscriminate social behaviors (Lawler, Koss, Doyle, & Gunnar, 2016). As most IA children experienced institutionalization prior to adoption, indiscriminate social behavior has been commonly examined in the IA population (e.g., Chisholm, 1998; Liu & Hazler, 2017b; van den Dries et al., 2012). IA children's indiscriminate social behavior is characterized as lacking social boundaries when interacting with strangers and with a tendency to wander off with strangers without checking back with their caregivers (Zeanah & Gleason, 2015). Bruce et al. (2009) compared indiscriminate social behavior in IA children from institutional care or foster care with a group of non-adopted peers and found that 65 percent of the IA sample presented indiscriminate social behaviors, such as making personal comments and initiating intimate physical contact with strangers.

While IA children's indiscriminate social behavior is frequently investigated with attachment, findings and discussions from recent studies have shed light onto the unique features, as well as phenotypes, that differentiate the two constructs (e.g., Lehmann et al., 2018; Zeanah & Gleason, 2015). Accordingly, IA children's indiscriminate social behavior toward unfamiliar adults is considered a primary representation of *Disinhibited Social Engagement Disorder* (DSED) within the most recent *Diagnostic and Statistical Manual of Mental Disorders* (DSM-5; American Psychiatric Association, 2013), because children's indiscriminate social pattern can coexist with, but might not necessarily correlate with, their attachment with caregivers (Bruce et al., 2009; Liu, Li, & Xu, 2017). In the review by Zeanah and Gleason (2015), DSED is often detected with impulsivity patterns speculated to be associated with earlier pathogenic care that children received, and such patterns may persist despite children's access to a stable and selective attachment figure. Research tends to ascribe disinhibited social behavior to children's inhibitory control (i.e., inability to regulate interactions with unfamiliar adults) distinct from attachment to primary caregivers (Bruce et al., 2009; Pears, Bruce, Fisher, & Kim, 2010). For instance, an IA child might successfully form attachment to the adoptive parents, yet still show indiscriminate social behaviors toward unfamiliar adults. More research on the nature of this unique type of co-existence can provide valuable insights into how early social deprivation can shape children's perception of their relationships with primary caregivers and with strangers.

Social competence and identity development

As IA children get older, other social competencies are needed in order for them to function properly within the broader post-adoptive environment (e.g., in school settings). Existing studies have demonstrated both challenges and resilience that adoptees experience in many aspects of their social development, including relationship qualities, social and academic competence, and identity development (e.g., Caprin, Benedan, Ballarin, & Gallace, 2017; Fensbo, 2004; Mohanty & Newhill, 2006).

Relationship qualities

Adoptees' relationship quality with adoptive parents can be seen as an extension of early child–parent attachment, which is more often investigated as children mature from childhood to adolescence, and then into young adulthood. Research in this area is rather limited, but findings suggest that adoptees' relationship quality with their adoptive parents is usually favorable (e.g., Groza & Muntean, 2016). However, some research suggests that challenging relationships with adoptive parents might be one of the contributing factors to adoption disruption and dissolution (Palacios, Rolock, Selwyn, & Barbosa-Ducharne, 2019; Verbovaya, 2016). Heterogeneity in parent–child relationship quality is related to adoptees' demographic backgrounds (e.g., special needs status) and country of origin (Tan et al., 2015). For instance, the US national survey of adoptive parents revealed that adoptive parents of children from China, Russia, and South Korea reported higher parent–child relationship quality than those whose children were from Guatemala, or those who adopted from the US foster care system (Tan et al., 2015). Chinese adoptees' favorable relationship quality with their parents was later replicated with self-report data comparing Chinese adoptees with non-adopted American peers (Tan, 2018). Overall, adoptees' relationship quality with adoptive parents might be an indicator and predictor of adoptees' mental and behavioral health (Tan & Marn, 2014), their post-adoption adjustment outcomes such as academic competence (Tan, Rice, & Mahoney, 2015), and future relationship qualities with others (Grant, Grotevant, & Sayer, 2015; Hawk & McCall, 2014).

Peer relation is another domain that is important in adoptees' social development. A recent meta-analysis by DeLuca, Claxton, and van Dulmen (2018) concludes that adoptees have more difficulties forming close peer relationships than non-adoptees, although they do not differ from each other in the quality of peer relations. Difficult peer relations in the form of peer victimization (e.g., Pitula et al., 2014), peer rejection (Palacios, Moreno, & Román, 2013), and peer relationship problems (Borders, Penny, & Portnoy, 2000; Westhues & Cohen, 1997) have all been reported among IA children. As with parent–child relationship quality, the adoptees' country of origin again seems to be related to their peer relation outcomes. For instance, UK adoptees from Romania have been reported to develop poorer peer relationships than domestic UK adoptees (Sonuga-Barke, Schlotz, & Kreppner, 2010). Some research has shown that some IA children had more favorable peer relations than non-adoptees, but they did not fare as well as their siblings who were the biological children of the adoptive parents (Cohen & Westhues, 1995). Recent research has also documented favorable peer relations in adoptees, particularly those who were adopted out of Asian countries. For instance, Tan (2018) found that teen Chinese adoptees outperformed their non-adopted American peers on 14 of the 16 domains of social-behavioral and personal adjustment measured with the *Behavioral Assessment System for Children* (BASC), including peer relations. The discrepancy among research findings, again, reveals within-group differences in IA children, and the causes for such differences remains inconclusive.

Social and academic competence

Adoptees' social adaptation in meeting the cultures of their school and community is highlighted as an under-conceptualized area that warrants further investigation (Palacios & Brodzinsky, 2010, p. 279). Nevertheless, their post-adoption social competence outcomes have gained considerable interest demonstrated through mixed findings. Some studies have reported that adopted children show poorer social competence (e.g., interpersonal relations) than non-adopted peers (e.g., Barcons et al., 2012; Palacios et al., 2013). Specifically, one longitudinal investigation conducted in the Netherlands with 2,148 IA children showed that they scored significantly lower in social competence than their non-adopted Dutch peers measured with the *Child Behavior Checklist* (CBCL; Verhulst, Althaus, & Versluis-den Bieman, 1992). Similarly, a follow-up study by the same authors (Versluis-den Bieman & Verhulst, 1995) followed 1,538 IA children for three years and noted a significant decrease in social competencies in the IA children over time. In terms of academic competence, although adoptive families often have high SES and invest more resources in raising their children (Hamilton, Cheng, & Powell, 2007), adoptees have been shown to have lower academic competence, according to self-, parent-, or teacher-report, than their non-adopted environmental peers (van IJzendoorn, Juffer, & Klein Poelhuis, 2005), with international adoptees outperforming domestic adoptees (Harwood, Feng, & Yu, 2013).

Similar to IA children's attachment and peer relation outcomes, heterogeneity is widely documented in their social and academic competence. Children adopted from Asia (e.g., Korea and China) have been consistently reported to demonstrate optimal social and academic outcomes, more favorable than those from other regions and equivalent to their non-adopted normative peers (e.g., Clark & Hanisee, 1982; Dalen, 2001; Dalen & Rygvold, 2006; Jaffari-Bimmel, Juffer, van IJzendoorn, Bakermans-Kranenburg, & Mooijaart, 2006; Juffer & van IJzendoorn, 2007; Stams, Juffer, Rispens, & Hoksbergen, 2000; Tan, 2009, 2018; Tan & Camras, 2011; Vinnerljung, Lindblad, Hjern, Rasmussen, & Dalen, 2010). For example, the Swedish national study of 6,448 IA children (Vinnerljung et al., 2010) showed that adolescent Korean adoptees were similar in school performance to their non-adopted peers, whereas adoptees from other countries performed more poorly. Likewise, Tan and Camras (2011) found that both parents and teachers reported that the adopted Chinese girls scored similarly to or higher than same-age girls from the US normative sample on social and academic competence. In addition, through four studies using varied measures (e.g., self-report; parent-report; teacher-report), Tan (2018) echoed the similar pattern of Chinese adoptees' optimal academic and social competence, in comparison with their US non-adopted peers and biological children born in their adoptive families.

Adoptive identity and ethnic identity

Identity formation is a dynamic process and a major developmental task in adolescence (Jackson, 1995). In line with IA children's social adaptation, adoptive identity development comprises a key task of their post-adoption experience (Kohler, Grotevant, & McRoy, 2002). Adoptive identity is defined as "how the individual constructs meaning about his/her adoption" (Grotevant, Dunbar, Kohler, & Esau, 2000, p. 381). Adoptive identity development and adoptees' consolidation of ethnicity is stressed as another underexplored area in the adoption literature (Palacios & Brodzinsky, 2010). Relatedly, the task of adoptive identity development becomes particularly salient when adoptees reach adolescence. During this period, adoptees tend to incorporate their adoption status in the formation and exploration of their self-concept (Grotevant, 1997; Grotevant et al., 2000; Smith & Brodzinsky, 2002; Tan & Jordan-Arthur, 2012). Thus, their feelings about their adoption are likely an important aspect of their self-evaluations. According to Benson, Sharma, and Roehlkepartain (1994), adopted youth's feelings toward their adoption encompass three dimensions: positive affect toward adoption, negative affect toward adoption, and preoccupation with adoption. The "bittersweet" emotion represents a common experience of adoptees during adolescence. Similarly, research on adolescent Chinese adoptees revealed that thinking about their adoption evoked a combination of positive, negative, and inquisitive/curious feelings, with fewer positive feelings among older adoptees (Tan & Jordan-Arthur, 2012).

Ethnicity has been examined as the core of one's adoptive identity and naturally becomes a focus of self-concept and identity work for members of a minority group (McGuire, McGuire, Child, & Fujioka, 1978; Phinney, 1991). Without exception, IA children were placed at a unique intersection of race and ethnicity given the "visible" nature of their adoption; consequently, their ethnic or racial self-identification might be different from how others might perceive them (Wilkinson, 1995). IA children inevitably have to cope with issues stemming from physical differences between themselves and their parents as well as between themselves and the larger society (Brodzinsky, Schechter, & Henig, 1992; Hollingsworth, 1997; Tigervall & Hübinette, 2010). Their ethnic identity thus is constructed within the context of both belonging and exclusion in regard to their birth cultural membership and the adoptive cultural membership (Godon-Decoteau, Ramsey, & Suyemoto, 2018; Shiao & Tuan, 2008). The ways adoptees negotiate their birth culture and adoptive culture undoubtedly play an important role in their ethnic identity development (Huh & Reid, 2000).

In existing studies, the construct of ethnicity among adoptees has usually been operationalized as ethnic self-identification (e.g., McRoy, Zurcher, Lauderdale, & Anderson, 1982; Vroegh, 1997) or a socialization process (e.g., Hollingsworth, 1997; Mohanty, Keokse, & Sales, 2006) including ethnic identity search and ethnic identity affirmation (Phinney, 1992; Ponterotto, Gretchen, Utsey, Stracuzzi, & Saya, 2003). Tan and Jordan-Arthur (2012) found that a majority of adopted Chinese teen girls use "Chinese," "Chinese-American," "Asian-American," "Asian," and "White" to describe their ethnic identity, whereas about 15 percent of the adoptees chose not to use any label to describe themselves. In another study on Korean adoptees (Huh & Reid, 2000), "Korean-American" appeared to be the most commonly used label. The labels (or lack of) confirm heterogeneity in how/whether adoptees acknowledge their birth heritage and adoptive heritage. The heterogeneity in IA children's ethnic resonance is coupled with uncertainty about how to construct their ethnic identity (e.g., Hu, Zhou, & Lee, 2017; Lee, 2003; McRoy et al., 1982). Unlike immigrant children or children with same-race adoptive parents, transracial adoptive parents are outsiders to their children's birth cultures (Tan & Nakkula, 2004). As a result, the adoptive environment is usually not adequately equipped to allow the adoptees to explore their birth heritage in daily life. These challenges might negatively influence the adoptees' engagement in ethnic identity search. Consequently, adoptees might feel that they do not fully belong to either culture, and thus experience feelings of ethnic marginality (Kim, Suyemoto, & Turner, 2010).

Self-esteem

Self-esteem can be seen as an accumulation of different areas of competence. That is, self-esteem may result from adoptees' academic competence, social competence, and identity search and formation experiences (Mohanty, 2013; Tan & Jordan-Arthur, 2012). Although a meta-analysis has concluded that adoptees are not different from non-adoptees on self-esteem (Juffer & van IJzendoorn, 2007), heterogeneity again remains an important pattern. Earlier, Westhues and Cohen (1997) found that adoptees had lower self-esteem than their non-adopted siblings. In contrast, a recent comparison of adopted Chinese youth with non-adopted American peers demonstrated that the adopted youth scored higher on self-esteem (Tan, 2018).

Predictors of self-esteem in IA children have also been investigated. In an earlier study, Westhues and Cohen (1997) found that teen and young adult international adoptees had favorable self-esteem, but they scored lower than the adoptive parents' biological children. Cederblad, Höök, Irhammar, and Mercke (1999) investigated the adjustment of 211 IA children aged 13 years or older in Sweden, with results supporting that adoptees who often thought about birth parents, or who felt uncomfortable with their adoption status, scored lower on self-esteem. The study further suggests that IA children who described themselves as Swedish scored higher on self-esteem than their peers who described themselves as non-Swedish. However, some other research (McRoy et al., 1982; Vroegh, 1997) suggests that the ethnic labels that transracial adoptees used to describe their ethnicity were not indicative of their self-esteem. For international adoptees from China, Tan and Jordan-Arthur (2012) showed that higher global self-esteem was significantly predicted by adopted youth's positive affect toward adoption, ethnic identity affirmation, lower ethnic marginality, higher academic functioning, and the interaction between positive affect toward adoption and ethnic marginality.

Summary and policy implications

Studies that have investigated IA children's social development have yielded mixed results, likely due to differences within the population of adopted children (e.g., country of origin, age at assessment, age at adoption, pre-adoption living situations), variations of assessment instruments, and/or utilization of different types of comparison groups (e.g., non-adopted peers, normative samples, non-adopted children in the family). Areas comprising adoptees' social development range from early child–parent attachment to later negotiation of adoptive identity, and heterogeneity seems to be the norm, not the exception, when it comes to social competence outcomes. The heterogeneity is reflected in the children's country of origin, age at adoption, current age, and pre-adoption as well as post-adoption experiences. Given the different levels (e.g., individual, familial, social, and systemic) of influential factors and the multi-party involvement in adoption (i.e., adoptees, birth parents, adoptive parents), policy considerations can be conceptualized from an ecological lens encompassing potential changes at individual, micro-, and macro- levels (Bronfenbrenner, 1979).

Several policy implications can be drawn from IA children's general social development outcomes and between-group heterogeneity. First, since country of origin has been consistently highlighted to be significantly related to IA children's adjustment, with particularly positive outcomes in Asian (e.g., Chinese; Korean) adoptees, further investigation into potential factors that might have contributed to such favorable outcomes would be valuable. At the macrosystemic level, adoption stakeholders could consider advocacy in social policies to foster adoptees' social development. For example, for adoptive identity development, latent factors such as poverty and gender inequality in birth and adoptive countries could be evaluated (Lewis & Brady, 2018). As effects of such social realities might not become detectable until post-adoption when adoptees reach late childhood or adolescence, IA children's background, including their birth cultural characteristics, could be considered in conceptualizing different presenting issues such as atypical social behaviors or emotions.

Alongside the significant differences in social-cultural practices, economic conditions, and political climate across the sending countries, it is common for many IA children to have experienced deprivation-related delays and adversities prior to adoption at the microsystemic level (e.g., Smyke et al., 2007). Most existing studies have shown that pre-adoption adversity increases later risk for poorer social development (e.g., McGuinness, Ryan, & Robinson, 2005; Pearlmutter, Ryan, Johnson, & Groza, 2008; Tan, 2006; Verhulst et al., 1992; Versluis-den Bieman & Verhulst, 1995). As such, policies that reduce adversity and promote recovery from early deprivation could be deliberated at the microsystem level, as catching up in development appears to be the key issue facing IA children after their arrival to their adoptive homes. Specifically, significant risk and protective factors such as institutional care quality and post-adoption caregiving might become an area of focus. Intervention programs that target reducing developmental delays could be initiated prior to children's arrival in their adoptive families. Likewise, post-adoption trust-based or trauma-informed interventions (Purvis et al., 2015) can be implemented, at individual and microsystemic levels, in tackling social adjustment issues associated with pre-adoption adversities that IA children had experienced.

In addition, given the heterogeneity in IA children's social development outcomes in the extant literature, adoption practitioners and prospective parents can easily be overwhelmed by myriad findings. One challenge associated with the literature is the disconnection between child welfare and mental health professions, with the former focusing on adoption practices (e.g., adoptees' conditions; adoptive family satisfaction) and the latter attending to adoptees' mental health struggles (e.g., development catch-up; psychological issues; attachment) (Palacios & Brodzinsky, 2010). Consequently, adoptees' and adoptive families' needs cannot be fully met. Aligning with the microsystemic interventions, collaboration between child welfare and mental health professionals is thus desirable (Palacios & Brodzinsky, 2010), through which knowledge can be shared and tailored services can be planned conjointly. Transferrable to policy-making, interdisciplinary collaborations in both scholarly and clinical domains can be fostered in meeting the holistic needs of adoptees and their families. Relatedly, psychoeducation programs are recommended to train prospective parents to prepare for the arrival of their adopted children and potential issues they are likely to encounter post-adoption.

References

American Psychiatric Association. (2013). *Diagnostic and statistical manual of mental disorders* (5th ed.). Arlington, VA: Author.

Bakermans-Kranenburg, M. J., van IJzendoorn, M. H., & Juffer, F. (2003). Less is more: Meta-analyses of sensitivity and attachment interventions in early childhood. *Psychological Bulletin, 129*, 195–215. doi:10.1037/0033-2909.129.2.195

Barcons, N., Abrines, N., Brun, C., Sartini, C., Fumadó, V., & Marre, D. (2012). Social relationships in children from intercountry adoption. *Children and Youth Services Review, 34*(5), 955–961. doi:10.1016/j.childyouth.2012.01.028

Barone, L., Lionetti, F., & Green, J. (2017). A matter of attachment? How adoptive parents foster post-institutionalized children's social and emotional adjustment. *Attachment & Human Development, 19*, 323–339. doi:10.1080/14616734.2017.1306714

Benson, P. L., Sharma, A. R., & Roehlkepartain, E. C. (1994). *Growing up adopted*. Minneapolis, MN: Search Institute.

Bierman, K. L., & Montminy, H. P. (1993). Developmental issues in social skills assessment and intervention with children and adolescents. *Behavior Modification, 17*(3), 229–254. doi:10.1177/01454455930173002

Borders, L. D., Penny, J. M., & Portnoy, F. (2000). Adult adoptees and their friends: Current functioning and psychosocial well-being. *Family Relations, 49*, 407–418. doi:10.1111/j.1741-3729.2000.00407.x

Bowlby, J. (1973). *Attachment and loss: Separation* (Vol. II). New York, NY: Basic Books.

Bretherton, I. (1996). Internal working models of attachment relationships as related to resilient coping. In G. G. Noam & K. W. Fischer (Eds.), *Development and vulnerability in close relationships* (pp. 3–27). Mahwah, NJ: Erlbaum.

Briggs, L. (2012). Feminism and transnational adoption: Poverty, precarity, and the politics of raising (other people's?) children. *Feminist Theory, 13*, 81–100. doi:10.1177/1464700111430177

Brodzinsky, D. M., Schechter, M. D., & Henig, R. M. (1992). *Being adopted: The lifelong search for self.* New York: Anchor Books.

Bronfenbrenner, U. (1979). *The ecology of human development: Experiments by nature and design.* Cambridge, MA: Harvard University Press.

Bruce, J., Tarullo, A. R., & Gunnar, M. R. (2009). Disinhibited social behavior among internationally adopted children. *Development and Psychopathology, 21*, 157–171. doi:10.1017/S0954579409000108

Bruce, M., Young, D., Turnbull, S., Rooksby, M., Chadwick, G., Oates, C., … Syoung-Southward, G. (2019). Reactive Attachment Disorder in maltreated young children in foster care. *Attachment & Human Development, 21*(2), 152–169. doi:10.1080/14616734.2018.1499211

Caprin, C., Benedan, L., Ballarin, L., & Gallace, A. (2017). Social competence in Russian post-institutionalized children: A comparison of adopted and non-adopted children. *Children and Youth Services Review, 75*, 61–68. doi:10.1016/j.childyouth.2017.02.0200190-7409

Cavell, T., Meehan, B., & Fiala, S. (2003). Assessing social competence in children and adolescents. In C. R. Reynolds & R. W. Kamphaus (Eds.), *Handbook of psychological and educational assessment of children: Personality, behavior, and context* (2nd ed., pp. 433–454). NY: Guilford Press.

Cederblad, M., Höök, B., Irhammar, M., & Mercke, A. (1999). Mental health in international adoptees as teenagers and young adults: An epidemiological study. *Journal of Child Psychology and Psychiatry, 40*(8), 1239–1248. doi:10.1111/1469-7610.00540

Chisholm, K. (1998). A three year follow-up of attachment and indiscriminate friendliness in children adopted from Romanian orphanages. *Child Development, 69*, 1092–1106. doi:10.2307/1132364

Chisholm, K., Carter, M. C., Ames, E. W., & Morison, S. J. (1995). Attachment security and indiscriminate friendliness in children adopted from Romanian orphanages. *Child Development*, 7, 283–294. doi:10.1111/j.1467-8624.1998.tb06162.x

Clark, E. A., & Hanisee, J. (1982). Intellectual and adaptive performance of Asian children in adoptive American settings. *Developmental Psychology, 18*, 595–599. doi:10.1037/0012-1649.18.4.595

Cohen, J. S., & Westhues, A. (1995). A comparison of self-esteem, school achievement and friends between intercountry adoptees and their siblings. *Early Child Development and Care, 1*, 205–224. doi:10.1080/016502597385432

Cohen, N. J., & Farnia, F. (2011). Children adopted from China: Attachment security two years later. *Children and Youth Services Review, 33*, 2342–2346. doi:10.1016/j.childyouth.2011.08.006

Dalen, M. (2001). School performances among internationally adopted children in Norway. *Adoption Quarterly, 5*(2), 39–58. doi:10.1300/J145v05n02_03

Dalen, M., & Rygvold, A. L. (2006). Educational achievement in adopted children from China. *Adoption Quarterly, 9*(4), 45–58. doi:10.1300/J145v09n04_03

DeLuca, H. K., Claxton, S. E., & van Dulmen, M. H. M. (2018). The peer relationships of those who have experienced adoption or foster care: A meta-analysis. *Journal of Research on Adolescence*, doi:10.1111/jora.12421

Dirks, M. A., Treat, T. A., & Weersing, V. R. (2007). Integrating theoretical, measurement, and intervention models of youth social competence. *Clinical Psychology Review, 27*(3), 327–347. doi:10.1016/j.cpr.2006.11.002

Dodge, K. A., Pettit, G. S., McClaskey, C. L., & Brown, M. M. (1986). Social competence in children. *Monographs of the Society for Research in Child Development, 51*(2), Serial No. 213.

Fensbo, C. (2004). Mental and behavioural outcome of inter-ethnic adoptees: A review of the literature. *European Child & Adolescent Psychiatry, 13*, 55–63. doi:10.1007/s00787-004-0358-2

Follan, M., & McNamara, M. (2014). A fragile bond: Adoptive parents' experiences of caring for children with a diagnosis of reactive attachment disorder. *Journal of Clinical Nursing, 23*(7–8), 1076–1085. doi:10.1111/jocn.12341

Godon-Decoteau, D., Ramsey, P. G., & Suyemoto, K. L. (2018). Korean transracial and international adoptees: Ethnic identity and sense of belonging and exclusion in relation to birth and adoptive groups. *Identity: an International Journal of Theory and Research, 18*(3), 178–194. doi:10.1080/15283488.2018.1487299

Grant, M. H. A., Grotevant, H. D., & Sayer, A. G. (2015). Links between adolescents' closeness to adoptive parents and attachment style in young adulthood. *Family Relations, 64*(2), 221–232. doi:10.1111/fare.12113

Grotevant, H. D. (1997). Coming to terms with adoption: The construction of identity from adolescence into adulthood. *Adoption Quarterly, 1*, 3–27. doi:10.1300/J145v01n01_02

Grotevant, H. D., Dunbar, N., Kohler, J., & Esau, A. M. L. (2000). Adoptive identity: How contexts within and beyond the family shape developmental pathways. *Family Relations, 49*, 379–387. doi:10.1111/j.1741-3729.2000.00379.x

Groza, V., & Muntean, A. (2016). A description of attachment in adoptive parents and adoptees in Romania during early adolescence. *Child & Adolescent Social Work Journal, 33*(2), 163–174. doi:10.1007/s10560-015-0408-2

Gunnar, M. R., Bruce, J., & Grotevant, H. D. (2000). International adoption of institutionally reared children: Research and policy. *Development and Psychopathology, 12*, 677–693. doi:10.1017/S095457940000407

Hamilton, L., Cheng, S., & Powell, B. (2007). Adoptive parents, adaptive parents: Evaluating the importance of biological ties for parental investment. *American Sociology Review, 72*, 95–116. doi:10.1177/000312240707200105

Harwood, R., Feng, X., & Yu, S. (2013). Preadoption adversities and postadoption mediators of mental health and school outcomes among international, foster, and private adoptees in the United States. *Journal of Family Psychology, 27*(3), 409–420. doi:10.1037/a0032908

Hawk, B., & McCall, R. B. (2014). Perceived relationship quality in adolescents following early social-emotional deprivation. *Clinical Child Psychology & Psychiatry*, *19*(3), 439–459. doi:10.1177/1359104513489978

Hollingsworth, L. D. (1997). Effect of transracial/transethnic adoption on children's racial and ethnic identity and self-esteem. *Marriage & Family Review*, *25*(1–2), 99–130.

Hu, A. W., Zhou, X., & Lee, R. M. (2017). Ethnic socialization and ethnic identity development among internationally adopted Korean American adolescents: A seven-year follow-up. *Developmental Psychology*, *53*(11), 2066–2077. doi:10.1037/dev0000421

Huh, N. S., & Reid, W. J. (2000). Intercountry, transracial adoption and ethnic identity: A Korean example. *International Social Work*, *43*(1), 75–87. doi:10.1177/a010522

Jackson, S. (1995). Adolescent identity development and social context: Towards an integrative perspective. In A. Oosterwegel & R. A. Wicklund Eds., NATO ASI Series (Series D: Behavioural and Social Sciences). *The self in European and North American culture: Development and processes* (Vol. 84, pp. 33–44). Dordrecht: Springer.

Jaffari-Bimmel, N., Juffer, F., van IJzendoorn, M. H., Bakermans-Kranenburg, M. J., & Mooijaart, A. (2006). Social development from infancy to adolescence: Longitudinal and concurrent factors in an adoption sample. *Developmental Psychology*, *42*, 1143–1153. doi:10.1037/0012-1649.42.6.1143

Juffer, F., Bakermans-Kranenburg, M. J., & van IJzendoorn, M. H. (Eds.). (2008). *Monographs in parenting series. Promoting positive parenting: An attachment-based intervention*. New York, NY: Taylor & Francis Group/Lawrence Erlbaum Associates.

Juffer, F., Palacios, J., Le Mare, L., Sonuga-Barke, E. J. S., Tiemann, W., Bakermans-Kranenburg, M., & Verhulst, F. C. (2011). Development of adopted children with histories of early adversity. *Monographs of the Society for Research in Child Development*, *76*, 31–61. doi:10.1111/j.1540-5834.2011.00627.x

Juffer, F., & van IJzendoorn, M. H. (2007). Adoptees do not lack self-esteem: A meta-analysis of studies on self-esteem of transracial, international, and domestic adoptees. *Psychological Bulletin*, *133*(6), 1067–1083. doi:10.1037/0033-2909.133.6.1067

Kim, G. S., Suyemoto, K. L., & Turner, C. B. (2010). Sense of belonging, sense of exclusion, and racial and ethnic identities in Korean transracial adoptees. *Cultural Diversity and Ethnic Minority Psychology*, *16*, 179–190. doi:10.1037/a0015727

Kohler, J. K., Grotevant, H. D., & McRoy, R. G. (2002). Adopted adolescents' preoccupation with adoption: The impact on adoptive family relationships. *Journal of Marriage and Family*, *64*(1), 93–104. doi:10.1111/j.1741-3737.2002.00093.x

Lawler, J. M., Koss, K. J., Doyle, G. M., & Gunnar, M. R. (2016). The course of early disinhibited social engagement among post-institutionalized adopted children. *Journal of Child Psychology and Psychiatry*, *57*, 1126–1134. doi:10.1111/jcp.12606.s

Lee, R. M. (2003). The transracial adoption paradox history, research, and counseling implications of cultural socialization. *The Counseling Psychologist*, *31*(6), 711–744. doi:10.1177/0011000003258087

Lehmann, S., Monette, S., Egger, H., Breivik, K., Young, D., Davidson, C., & Minnis, H. (2018). Development and examination of the reactive attachment disorder and disinhibited social engagement disorder assessment interview. *Assessment*. doi:10.1177/1073191118797422

Lewis, S., & Brady, G. (2018). Parenting under adversity: Birth parents' accounts of inequality and adoption. *Social Science*, 7, 257–271. doi:10.3390/socsci7120257

Liu, Y., & Hazler, R. J. (2017a). Predictors of attachment security in children adopted from China by US families: Implication for professional counsellors. *Asia Pacific Journal of Counselling and Psychotherapy*, *8*, 115–130. doi:10.1080/21507686.2017.1342675

Liu, Y., & Hazler, R. J. (2017b). Variables associated with indiscriminate friendliness displayed by Chinese adoptees in US Families. *The Family Journal*, *25*, 414–422. doi:10.1177/1066480717731345

Liu, Y., Li, D., & Xu, Y. (2017). Indiscriminate friendliness in children adopted from China to the US: A mixed methods study. *The Professional Counselor*, 7, 208–222. doi:10.15241/yl.7.3.208

Love, L., Minnis, H., & O'Connor, S. (2015). Factors associated with indiscriminate friendliness in high-risk children. *Infant Mental Health Journal*, *36*, 427–445. doi:10.1002/imhj.21520.

Marcovitch, S., Goldberg, S., Gold, A., Washington, J., Wasson, C., Krekewich, K., & Handley-Derry, M. (1997). Determinants of behavioural problems in Romanian children adopted in Ontario. *International Journal of Behavioral Development*, *20*, 17–31. doi:10.1080/016502597385414

McGuinness, T. M., Ryan, R., & Robinson, C. B. (2005). Protective influences of families for children adopted from the former Soviet Union. *Journal of Nursing Scholarship*, *37*(3), 216–221. doi:10.1111/j.1547-5069.2005.00038.x

McGuire, W. J., McGuire, C. V., Child, P., & Fujioka, T. (1978). Salience of ethnicity in the spontaneous self-concept as a function of one's ethnic distinctiveness in the social environment. *Journal of Personality and Social Psychology, 36*(5), 511–520. doi:10.1037/0022-3514.36.5.511

McRoy, R., Zurcher, L. A., Lauderdale, M. L., & Anderson, R. A. (1982). Self esteem and racial identity in transracial and inracial adoptees. *Social Work, 27*, 522–526. doi:10.1093/sw/27.6.522

Mohanty, J. (2013). Ethnic and racial socialization and self-esteem of Asian adoptees: The mediating role of multiple identities. *Journal of Adolescence, 36*, 161–170. doi:10.1016/j.adolescence.2012.10.003

Mohanty, J., Keokse, G., & Sales, E. (2006). Family cultural socialization, ethnic identity, and self-esteem: Web-based survey of international adult adoptees. *Journal of Ethnic & Cultural Diversity in Social Work: Innovation in Theory, Research & Practice, 15*(3–4), 153–172. doi:10.1300/J051v15n03_07

Mohanty, J., & Newhill, C. (2006). Adjustment of international adoptees: Implications for practice and a future research agenda. *Children and Youth Services Review, 28*, 384–395. doi:10.1016/j.childyouth.2005.04.013

Mueller, E., & Brenner, J. (1977). Origins of social skills and interaction among playgroup toddlers. *Child Development, 48*, 854–861. doi:10.2307/1128334

O'Connor, T. G., Rutter, M. & the English and Romanian Adoptees Study Team. (2000). Attachment disorder behavior following early severe deprivation: Extension and longitudinal follow-up. *Journal of the American Academy of Child & Adolescent Psychiatry, 39*(6), 703–712.

O'Connor, T. G., Marvin, R. S., Rutter, M., Olrick, J. T., Britner, P. A. &; English and Romanian Adoptees Study Team. (2003). Child-parent attachment following early institutional deprivation. *Developmental Psychopathology, 15*(1), 19–38.

Palacios, J., & Brodzinsky, D. (2010). Adoption research: Trends, topics, outcomes. *International Journal of Behavioral Development, 34*, 270–284. doi:10.1177/0165025410362837

Palacios, J., Moreno, C., & Román, M. (2013). Social competence in internationally adopted and institutionalized children. *Early Childhood Research Quarterly, 28*(2), 357–365. doi:10.1016/j.ecresq.2012.08.003

Palacios, J., Rolock, N., Selwyn, J., & Barbosa-Ducharne, M. (2019). Adoption breakdown: Concept, research, and implications. *Research on Social Work Practice, 29*(2), 130–142. doi:10.1177/1049731518783852

Pearlmutter, S., Ryan, S. D., Johnson, L. B., & Groza, V. (2008). Romanian adoptees and pre-adoptive care: A strengths perspective. *Child & Adolescent Social Work Journal, 25*(2), 139–156. doi:10.1007/s10560-008-0117-1

Pears, K. C., Bruce, J., Fisher, P. A., & Kim, H. K. (2010). Indiscriminate friendliness in maltreated foster children. *Child Maltreatment, 15*, 64–75. doi:10.1177/1077559509337891

Phinney, J. (1991). Ethnic identity and self-esteem: A review and integration. *Hispanic Journal of Behavioral Sciences, 13*(2), 193–208. doi:10.1177/07399863910132005

Phinney, J. (1992). The Multigroup Ethnic Identity Measure: A new scale for use with adolescents and young adults from diverse groups. *Journal of Adolescent Research*, 7, 156–176. doi:10.1177/074355489272003

Pitula, C., Thomas, K., Armstrong, J., Essex, M., Crick, N., & Gunnar, M. (2014). Peer victimization and internalizing symptoms among post-institutionalized, internationally adopted youth. *Journal of Abnormal Child Psychology, 42*, 1069–1076. doi:10.1007/s10802-014-9855-z

Ponterotto, J. G., Gretchen, D., Utsey, S. O., Stracuzzi, T., & Saya, R., Jr. (2003). The Multigroup Ethnic Identity Measure (MEIM): Psychometric review and further validity testing. *Educational and Psychological Measurement, 63*(3), 502–515. doi:10.1177/0013164403063003010

Portello, J. Y. (1993). The mother-infant attachment process in adoptive families. *Canadian Journal of Counselling, 27*(3), 177–190.

Pugliese, M., Cohen, N. J., Farnia, F., & Lojkasek, M. (2010). The emerging attachment relationship between adopted Chinese infants and their mothers. *Children and Youth Services Review, 32*, 1719–1728. doi:10.1016/j.childyouth.2010.07.015

Purvis, K. B., Razuri, E. B., Hiles Howard, A. R. H., Call, C. D., Deluna, J. H., Hall, J. S., & Cross, D. R. (2015). Decrease in behavioral problems and trauma symptoms among at-risk adopted children following trauma-informed parent training intervention. *Journal of Child & Adolescent Trauma, 8*, 201–210. doi:10.1007/s40653-015-0055-y

Román, M., Palacios, J., Moreno, C., & Lopez, A. (2012). Attachment representations in internationally adopted children. *Attachment & Human Development, 14*, 585–600. doi:10.1080/14616734.2012.727257

Rutter, M., Beckett, C., Castle, J., Colvert, E., Kreppner, J., Mehta, M., & Sonuga-Barke, E. (2007). Effects of profound early institutional deprivation: An overview of findings from a UK longitudinal study of Romanian adoptees. *European Journal of Developmental Psychology, 4*(3), 332–350. doi:10.1080/17405620701401846

Selman, P. (2017). "A million children moving: Intercountry adoption 1946–2017," paper presented at a conference at the University of Kassel, Germany on the History and Practices of International Adoptions, under the title Designing Modern Families; International Perspectives on, Intercountry and Transracial Adoptions.

Semrud-Clikeman, M. (2007). *Social competence in children*. New York, NY: Springer.

Shiao, J. L., & Tuan, M. H. (2008). Korean adoptees and the social context of ethnic exploration. *American Journal of Sociology, 113*, 1023–1066. doi:10.1086/522807

Smith, D. W., & Brodzinsky, D. M. (2002). Coping with birthparent loss in adopted children. *Journal of Child Psychology and Psychiatry, 4*(2), 213–223. doi:10.1111/1469-7610.00014

Smyke, A. T., Dumitrescu, A., & Zeanah, C. H. (2002). Attachment disturbances in young children. I: The continuum of caretaking casualty. *Journal of the American Academy of Child and Adolescent Psychiatry, 41*, 972–982. doi:10.1111/j.1467-8624.2009.01390.x

Smyke, A. T., Koga, S. F., Johnson, D. E., Fox, N. A., Marshall, P. J., Nelson, C. A., & Zeanah, C. H. (2007). The caregiving context in institution-reared and family-reared infants and toddlers in Romania. *Journal of Child Psychology and Psychiatry, 48*(2) the BEIP Core Group, 210–218. doi:10.1111/j.1469-7610.2006.01694.x.

Sonuga-Barke, E. J., Schlotz, W., & Kreppner, J. (2010). Differentiating developmental trajectories for conduct, emotion, and peer problems following early deprivation. *Monographs of the Society for Research in Child Development, 75*(1), 102–124. doi:10.1111/j.1540-5834.2010.00552.x

Stams, G. J. M., Juffer, F., Rispens, J., & Hoksbergen, R. C. (2000). The development and adjustment of 7-year-old children adopted in infancy. *Journal of Child Psychology and Psychiatry, 41*(8), 1025–1037. doi:10.1111/1469-7610.00690

Stams, G. J. M., Juffer, F., & van IJzendoorn, M. H. (2002). Maternal sensitivity, infant attachment, and temperament in early childhood predict adjustment in middle childhood: The case of adopted children and their biologically unrelated parents. *Developmental Psychology, 38*, 806–821. doi:10.1037/0012-1649.38.5.806

Symons, D. K., & Clark, S. E. (2000). A longitudinal study of mother-child relationships and theory of mind in the preschool period. *Social Development, 9*, 3–23. doi:10.1111/1467-9507.00108

Tan, T. X. (2006). History of early neglect and middle childhood social competence: An adoption study. *Adoption Quarterly, 9*(4), 59–72. doi:10.1300/J145v09n04_04

Tan, T. X. (2009). School-age adopted Chinese girls' behavioral adjustment, academic performance, and social skills: Longitudinal results. *American Journal of Orthopsychiatry, 79*(2), 244–251. doi:10.1037/a0015682

Tan, T. X. (2018). Model minority of a different kind? Academic competence and behavioral health of Chinese children adopted by White parents. *Asian American Journal of Psychology, 9*(3), 169–178. doi:10.1037/aap0000106

Tan, T. X., & Camras, L. A. (2011). Social skills of adopted Chinese girls at home and in school: Parent and teacher ratings. *Children and Youth Services Review, 33*(10), 1813–1821. doi:10.1016/j.childyouth.2011.05.006

Tan, T. X., & Jordan-Arthur, B. (2012). Adopted Chinese girls come of age: Feelings about adoption, ethnic identity, academic functioning, and global self-esteem. *Children and Youth Services Review, 34*(8), 1500–1508. doi:10.1016/j.childyouth.2012.04.001

Tan, T. X., Major, D., Marn, T., Na, E., & Jackson, A. L. (2015). Adopted children's country of origin and post-adoption parent-child relationship quality: Findings from the United States National Survey of Adoption Parents (NSAP). *Children and Youth Services Review, 48*, 117–125. doi:10.1016/j.childyouth.2014.12.001

Tan, T. X., & Marn, T. (2014). Mother-daughter agreement on adolescent adopted Chinese girls' academic performance and internalizing symptoms. *School Psychology Forum, 8*(2), 103–112.

Tan, T. X., & Nakkula, M. J. (2004). A case study of White American parents' attitudes toward their adopted Chinese daughters' ethnic identity. *Adoption Quarterly*, 7(4), 57–76. doi:10.1300/J145v07n04_03

Tan, T. X., Rice, J. L., & Mahoney, E. E. (2015). Developmental delays at arrival and post-menarcheal Chinese adolescents' adjustment. *American Journal of Orthopsychiatry, 85*(1), 93–100. doi:10.1037/ort0000045

Tigervall, C., & Hübinette, T. (2010). Adoption with complications: Conversations with adoptees and adoptive parents on everyday racism and ethnic identity. *International Social Work, 53*(4), 489–509. doi:10.1177/0020872809359272

Tizard, B. (1977). *Adoption: A second chance*. London, England: Open Books.

US Department of State. (2018, March 31). Annual report on intercountry adoption in Fiscal Year 2017. Retrieved from http://adoption.state.gov/about_us/statistics.php

van den Dries, L., Juffer, F., van IJzendoorn, M. H., & Bakermans-Kranenburg, M. J. (2009). Fostering security? A meta-analysis of attachment in adopted children. *Children and Youth Services Review, 31*(3), 410–421. doi:10.1016/j.childyouth.2008.09.008

van den Dries, L., Juffer, F., van IJzendoorn, M. H., Bakermans-Kranenburg, M. J., & Alink, L. R. A. (2012). Infants' responsiveness, attachment, and indiscriminate friendliness after international adoption from institutions or foster care in China: Application of emotional availability scales to adoptive families. *Development and Psychopathology, 24*, 49–64. doi:10.1017/S0954579411000654

van IJzendoorn, M. H., Juffer, F., & Klein Poelhuis, C. W. (2005). Adoption and cognitive development: A meta-analytic comparison of adopted and nonadopted children's IQ and school performance. *Psychological Bulletin, 131*(2), 301–316. doi:10.1037/0033-2909.131.2.301

van Londen, W. M., Juffer, F., & van IJzendoorn, M. H. (2007). Attachment, cognitive, and motor development in adopted children: Short-term outcomes after international adoption. *Journal of Pediatric Psychology, 32*(10), 1249–1258. doi:10.1093/jpepsy/jsm062

Verbovaya, O. (2016). Theoretical explanatory model of international adoption failure: Attachment and ecological systems perspectives. *Adoption Quarterly, 19*(3), 188–209. doi:10.1080/10926755.2015.1113219

Verhulst, F. C., Althaus, M., & Versluis-den Bieman, H. J. (1992). Damaging backgrounds: Later adjustment of international adoptees. *Journal of the American Academy of Child & Adolescent Psychiatry, 31*(3), 518–524. doi:10.1097/00004583-199205000-00020

Versluis-den Bieman, H. J. M., & Verhulst, F. C. (1995). Self-reported and parent reported problems in adolescent international adoptees. *Journal of Child Psychology and Psychiatry, 36*, 1411–1428. doi:10.1111/j.1469-7610.1995.tb01672.x

Vinnerljung, B., Lindblad, F., Hjern, A., Rasmussen, F., & Dalen, M. (2010). School performance at age 16 among international adoptees: A Swedish national cohort study. *International Social Work, 53*(4), 510–527. doi:10.1177/0020872809360037

Vroegh, K. S. (1997). Transracial adoptees: Developmental status after 17 years. *American Journal of Orthopsychiatry, 67*(4), 568–575. doi:10.1037/h0080254

Welsh, J. A., Viana, A. G., Petrill, S. A., & Mathias, M. D. (2007). Interventions for internationally adopted children and families: A review of the literature. *Child and Adolescent Social Work Journal, 24*, 285–311. doi:10.1007/s10560-007-0085-x

Westhues, A., & Cohen, J. (1997). A comparison of the adjustment of adolescent and young inter-country adoptees and their siblings. *International Journal of Behavioral Development, 20*, 47–65. doi:10.1080/016502597385432

Wilkinson, H. S. (1995). Psychological process and issues in international adoption. *American Journal of Family Therapy, 23*, 173–183. doi:10.1080/01926189508251347

Zeanah, C. H., & Gleason, M. M. (2015). Annual research review: Attachment disorders in early childhood-clinical presentation, causes, correlates, and treatment. *Journal of Child Psychology and Psychiatry, 56*, 207–222. doi:10.1111/jcp.12347

28

ACADEMIC PERFORMANCE AND SCHOOL ADJUSTMENT OF INTERNATIONALLY ADOPTED CHILDREN IN NORWAY

Monica Dalen and Steinar Theie

Norwegian adoption of children from abroad started at the end of the 1990s. Today there are around 20,000 international adoptees in Norway (Dalen & Theie, 2015). The children are mainly adopted from South Korea, Colombia, China, and South Africa (Selman, 2012). The adoption rate has steadily decreased since 2006, having peaked in 1998 with 800 international adoptions, compared to only 130 such adoptions in 2018 (Statistics Norway, 2018).

Research on outcomes among international adoptees has often paid attention to behavioral and emotional adjustment (Hjern, Lindblad, & Vinnerljung, 2002; Juffer & van IJzendoorn, 2005). In contrast, Norway started quite early to focus on academic performance relative to research conducted in other regions (Dalen, 1995, 2001; Dalen & Rygvold, 2006; Kvifte-Andresen, 1992). In the last ten years, researchers have shown greater interest in academic achievement as an important factor for psychological wellbeing, academic competence, and socioeconomic attainment (Dalen et al., 2008; Lindblad, Hjern, & Vinnerljung, 2003; Odenstad, Hjern, Lindblad, Vinnerljung, & Dalen, 2008; Raaska, Elovainio, Sinkkonen, Matomäki, & Lapinleimu, 2011; Raleigh & Kao, 2013; Vinnerljung, Lindblad, Rasmussen, & Dalen, 2010).

Internationally adopted children represent a highly heterogeneous group. Children vary in age at placement and quality of pre-adoptive experience. This heterogeneity is important to keep in mind both when describing them as a group and in drawing conclusions from research and observations. These children are adopted from countries with important differences regarding pre-adoption conditions, which include the level of caregiving and health care for infants and young children. A high percentage of internationally adopted children have spent their first months of life in institutions and orphanages (Gunnar, van Dulmen, & the International Adoption Project Team, 2007; Vorria, Papaligoura, Kopakaki, Dunn, & van IJzendoorn, 2006), which research has documented is associated with a risk for higher levels of developmental delay and behavior problems (Bakermans-Kranenburg, van IJzendoorn, & Juffer, 2008; Rutter et al., 2009; Zeanah, Smyke, Koga, & Carlson, 2005).

Children adopted from South Korea and China seem to have had more favorable developmental outcomes than children adopted from countries in Eastern Europe and Russia (Cohen, Lojkasek, Zadeh, Pugliese, & Kiefer, 2008; McGuinness & Pallansch, 2000; Vinnerljung et al., 2010). One reason for this could be that the quality of pre-adoption conditions is better in these countries. Additionally, children adopted from Eastern Europe and Russia have more often experienced adverse pre-adoption conditions, such as alcohol exposure during pregnancy, placement in institutions of very poor quality where there is both lack of stimulating contact with caregivers and other children, and lack of a rich learning environment (Kreppner et al., 2010; Raleigh & Kao, 2013).

Academic achievement of international adoptees

Outcomes from studies of internationally adopted children provide a mixed picture of adoptees' academic achievement (van IJzendoorn, Juffer, & Klein Poelhuis, 2005). Studies carried out both in the Netherlands and in Norway documented lower academic performance among internationally adopted children compared to their environmental peers (Dalen, 1995; Kvifte-Andresen, 1992; Dalen & Rygvold, 2006; Verhulst, Althaus, & Verluis-den Bierman, 1990). Other studies carried out in Sweden reported great heterogeneity within the group of international adoptees (Dalen et al., 2008; Lindblad, Dalen, Rasmussen, Vinnerljung, & Hjern, 2009; Vinnerljung et al., 2010). Children adopted from Asia seem to perform much better compared to adoptees from other continents. The meta-analysis of van IJzendoorn, Juffer, and Klein Poelhuis from 2005 points to an adoption décalage describing a gap between cognitive competence and actual school performance of adoptees. This gap was largest for those children who came from extremely deprived pre-adoption backgrounds. It is important to be aware of the fact that academic outcomes often are related to age at adoption and country of origin (Helder, Mulder, & Gunnoe, 2014; Raleigh & Kao, 2013; Tirella, Chan, & Miller, 2006). Age at adoption is a classic variable in adoption literature, but it is difficult to determine its effect on developmental outcomes on cognitive and academic competence. Some studies show that age of adoption has no effect (Dalen, 2001; Kvifte-Andresen, 1992) while others give a quite different picture (Rutter et al., 2010; Verhulst et al., 1990). Studies also differ in their cut-off points for an early or late adoption (van IJzendoorn et al., 2005). It is important to discuss to what extent age of adoption is the crucial factor when it comes to a child's development and achievement, as the environmental conditions experienced by the adopted child in the first months or year of life might be an equal or even far more important variable. However, there is often very limited valid information about an internationally adopted child's concrete life conditions during the first months or years of life.

Adverse pre-adoption conditions have been well documented to have a negative effect on later cognitive development (Harwood, Feng, & Yu, 2013). These conditions often include preplacement experiences, prior maltreatment, and prenatal substance exposure (van IJzendoorn & Juffer, 2006). Raaska et al. (2011) studied the effect of reactive attachment disorder and learning difficulties among international adoptees in Finland. A total of 395 internationally adopted children (aged 9–15) participated in this study consisting of 51.6 percent girls and 48.4 percent boys. They found that children with symptoms of reactive attachment disorders, stated at time of adoption, were associated with higher frequency of learning difficulties at school age.

Factors mediating relationship between adversity and academic outcomes

In addition to a direct influence of adverse pre-adoption conditions on academic achievement, many other factors might serve as mediating factors that influence a child's academic performance. For example, mastering of social skills has been discussed as a protective factor in children's development (Gresham & Elliot, 1990, 2008). Due to their pre-adoption adversity, many internationally adopted children are vulnerable to delays in their social development. Studies have documented that internationally adopted children have poorer social competence compared to environmental peers (Hjern et al., 2002; Tan, 2009). Social issues and peer relationship are of concern to many families who have adopted internationally (Tirella et al., 2006). Adoptive families provide a safe and secure environment which again stimulates their adopted children's development of social skills. Studies have documented that social skills can be a mediator for better academic achievement (Jaffari-Bimmel, Juffer, van IJzendoorn, Bakermans-Kranenburg, & Mooijaart, 2006; Tan & Marfo, 2006; Tan et al., 2017).

Behavior problems also seem to interfere negatively with academic performance in school, and there is an overrepresentation of behavior problems among internationally adopted children (Juffer & van IJzendoorn, 2005). Children adopted at later ages (often defined as older than three years) and from countries with poor pre-adoption conditions have the highest prevalence of behavior problems (McGuinness & Pallansch, 2000; Rosnati, Montirosso, & Barni, 2008). Behavior problems are often divided into three categories: internalizing, externalizing, and hyperactive behavior (Achenbach, 1991; Gresham & Elliot, 2008). Several studies have documented a higher prevalence in all three categories, with hyperactive behavior especially prevalent among internationally adopted children (Dalen, 1995, 2001; Kvifte-Andresen, 1992; Lindblad et al., 2009; Rutter et al., 2009). Hyperactive behavior is often described as attention-deficit/hyperactivity disorder characterized by inattention, impulsiveness, and hyperactivity in different combinations. Both genetic and prenatal factors (such as undernourishment, neurological deficiency, and alcohol exposure under pregnancy), and environmental factors (such as little social contact and lack of stimulation), might explain the adopted children's hyperactive behavior. Environmental factors are often related to the duration of institutional deprivation (Julian, 2013; Rutter et al., 2009). Studies have documented that hyperactive behavior interferes negatively with academic achievement (Dalen, 2012; McGuinness & Pallansch, 2000; Merz, McCall, & Wright, 2013).

Scandinavian researchers were among the first to highlight language development as a risk factor for further delays in cognitive development among internationally adopted children (Dalen, 2012; Dalen & Rygvold, 2006; Rygvold, 1999). The language acquisition of internationally adopted children is unique as they are neither bilingual nor monolingual (Rygvold & Theie, 2016). Internationally adopted children have to switch their first language and start to learn their adoptive parents' language as their new first language. This is the case even if the child is very young and has limited skills in using language (e.g. under one year), as all children are exposed to language from birth. Exposure to language is crucial for development, so a shift in exposure of first language represents a risk factor. As such, internationally adopted children are more vulnerable for developing language problems, both due to their pre-adoption conditions and to the change of language (Cohen et al., 2008; Jacobs, Miller, & Tirella, 2010; Loman, Wiik, Frenn, Pollak, & Gunnar, 2009; van London, Juffer, & van IJzendoorn, 2007). Rygvold and Theie (2016) followed 38 internationally adopted and a control group of 79 Norwegian-born children from age 4 years to age 11. The adopted group consisted of 27 girls and 11 boys, and the adoption age varied from 3 to 48 months with a mean age of 5.1 months (SD=9.6). The two groups were tested at age 4 (T1) and then again at second grade in primary school. Rygvold and Theie reported that most of the adopted children had similar language development to the Norwegian-born control group. However, some of the adopted children lagged behind in the area of language comprehension at age 4 (T1) and in reading comprehension in second grade (T2). This result might indicate that comprehension of oral and written language is particularly challenging for internationally adopted children. Other studies have documented those children with oral language problems are at risk for developing reading problems (Hulme & Snowling, 2009; Bishop & Snowling, 2004). Having a good command of language becomes more and more important for keeping up in school, especially at higher grade levels. Studies have documented that a higher percentage of internationally adopted children have problems with language comprehension, which is needed to engage in more abstract and decontextualized educational settings (Dalen & Rygvold, 2006; Glennen & Masters, 2002; Roberts et al., 2005). See Chapter 24 in this volume for more detail on speech and language development among international adoptees.

Studies also document some protective factors related to academic performance among internationally adopted children. Adoptive parents often have a higher level of education and represent a higher socioeconomic level than biological parents (Dalen, 2001; Raleigh & Kao, 2013). Adoptive families are more often concerned than biological families about their children's cognitive and academic development (Dalen, 2012). They are highly supportive and are strongly engaged in helping their children with homework (Dalen & Rygvold, 2006).

Academic performance and school adjustment of international adoptees in Norway

In order to examine academic performance and school adjustment among international adoptees within Norway, the latest results from a longitudinal project directed by Dalen and Theie will be presented. The project began in 2008 and was finalized in 2018. Data from early school years will be presented with a special focus on academic performance and school adjustment based on teachers' assessments. The aim of the school study was to compare academic achievement and school adjustment among internationally adopted children to that of non-adopted children and, in addition, examine to what extent language skills, social skills, and behavior problems interfered with academic achievement among the adopted children.

Participants and procedure

All families living in the eastern part of Norway who had adopted internationally a child below the age of 2 years between 2007 and 2009 were contacted. Of the families fulfilling these criteria, 119 were included in the study (the response rate was 67 percent). All the children were adopted before the age of 2 (most of them around 1 year), and they came from China (n=42), South Korea (n=23), South Africa (n=17), Colombia (n=14), Ethiopia (n=13), the Philippines (n=6), and a small number from other countries (n=4).

Information about the children was collected in six waves: when they arrived, and at the ages of 2, 3, 4, 6, and 11 years. Through 4 years of age, parents were interviewed in their homes using computer-based interviews. At first and third grade in elementary school, the data collection was based on surveys to parents and teachers (Dalen & Theie, 2012, 2014, 2015).

The majority of children in Norway are enrolled in public, local schools from first through tenth grade (age 6–16), and the local authorities decide which school a child will attend. The 119 adopted children in the present study were scattered throughout different schools all over eastern Norway. A control group consisted of a matched non-adopted classmate for each adopted child. The matching criteria for the control group were two-fold: the child must be the same gender and have been born in the same month and year as the adopted target child.

Table 28.1 The sample of internationally adopted and non-adopted children at Wave 5 and Wave 6

First grade – Wave 5						*Third grade – Wave 6*					
Adopted			*Non-adopted*			*Adopted*			*Non-adopted*		
	Girls	*Boys*		*Girls*	*Boys*		*Girls*	*Boys*		*Girls*	*Boys*
95	55%	45%	90	55%	45%	98	43%	57%	92	43%	57%

The results that are presented here are based on data from questionnaires sent to each adopted child's teacher in the last semester of first and third grade, one for the adopted child and one for a non-adopted classmate. The samples included in the study in first and third grade are presented in Table 28.1.

Academic achievement, social competence, language skills, and behavior problems (hyperactive behavior) were measured with standardized scales (Gresham & Elliott, 1990; Ottem, 2009). The teachers were also asked to rate the children's school adjustment measured by two scales: school motivation and relationships in school. School motivation was measured by items such as: the child is doing academically well, likes to do homework, and is motivated to do well in school. Relationships in school were measured by items such as: the child has good relationship with classmates, main teacher, and teachers in general.

Main results from the Norwegian study

The results from the study are presented in Table 28.2. First, no significant differences in teacher-rated academic achievement between adopted and non-adopted children were found either in first or in third grade. This is to some extent surprising and not in line with many other important studies, especially studies that involved a high-risk group of internationally adopted children (Pomerleau et al., 2005; Raleigh & Kao, 2013; Rutter et al., 2010; Tirella et al., 2006) characterized by older age of adoption (older than 3 years) and adopted from countries with low-quality pre-adoption conditions (such as Colombia, Russia, and countries in Eastern Europe). The results are more similar to research based on children adopted from China and South Korea (Dalen & Rygvold, 2006; Vinnerljung et al., 2010). However, the adopted Norwegian children did not increase their academic achievement in third grade when compared to first grade based on teachers' evaluation (see Table 28.2), but the variation (SD) in the children's achievement between first and third grade increased. This might indicate that academic challenges can be more problematic for a subset of adoptees at the third grade level (Dalen, 2012).

With regard to school adjustment (school motivation and relationship in school), no significant differences between adopted and non-adopted children either in first or third grade were documented. However, the differences between the two groups were larger in third grade. Also, the adopted children had a significantly lower mean score both on school adjustment and motivation in third grade compared to their mean score in first grade. This confirms that the heterogeneity in the internationally adopted group had increased from first to third grade.

Again, no significant differences were found between adopted and non-adopted children in social skills either in first or in third grade. This is not what would be expected, taking theories on attachment and early deprivation into consideration (van der Voort et al., 2014; Vorria et al., 2006). Some adopted children are vulnerable to delays in their social development due to lack of interpersonal contact with caregivers in the early months of their lives (Gunnar & van

Table 28.2 Comparisons between adopted and non-adopted in first and third grade as rated by teachers at Wave 5 and Wave 6

	Range of scores for measure	*Adopted*			*Non-adopted*			*t-value*	*sig.*
		N	*Mean*	*SD*	*N*	*Mean*	*SD*		
First grade – Wave 5									
Academic achievement[2]	9–45	92	34.40	7.55	90	34.69	7.19	.262	.793
Language skills[1]	20–100	95	29.73	14.73	85	26.02	8.15	−2.125	.035
Hyperactive behavior[3]	6–24	94	9.83	3.39	90	9.62	3.51	−.408	.684
Social skills[2]	30–120	81	86.27	14.43	77	89.27	13.06	−1.371	.172
School motivation[2]	3–12	92	9.26	2.28	88	9.35	2.10	.280	.780
Relationships in school[2]	3–12	93	9.81	1.38	89	9.92	1.63	.519	.608
Third grade – Wave 6									
Academic Achievement[2]	9–45	97	33.41	8.68	91	34.15	6.96	.648	.518
Language skills[1]	20–100	97	35.72	6.45	91	34.34	5.00	−1.630	.105
Hyperactive behavior[3]	6–24	96	9.71	4.08	92	8.43	2.66	−2.547	.012
Social skills[1]	30–120	87	88.68	13.92	84	91.24	11.08	−1.333	.184
School Motivation[2]	3–12	94	8.49	2.25	92	9.03	1.97	1.755	.081
Relationships in School[2]	3–12	98	9.83	1.80	91	10.13	1.53	1.260	.209

1 Low score indicates better performance
2 High score indicates better performance
3 High score indicates higher frequency

Dulmen, 2007). In this light, the results from the present study are quite encouraging. One has to keep in mind that the children in the present study were all adopted before the age of 2 (most of them around 1 year). They showed some, but few, problems compared with the non-adopted group and to other studies including children adopted at later ages (McGuinness & Pallansch, 2000; Rosnati et al., 2008; Raaska et al., 2012).

Despite the similarity between adopted and non-adopted children in the study, important differences were found. First, there were some differences in behavior problems among adopted and non-adopted children. Adopted children displayed significantly more hyperactivity in third grade compared to non-adopted children. This is in line with other studies (Cohen & Farnia, 2011; Pugliese, Cohen, Farnia, & Lojkasek, 2010; Zeanah et al., 2005). Hyperactive behavior has often been pointed to in explaining learning difficulties among internationally adopted children (Juffer & van IJzendoorn, 2005; Rosnati et al., 2008). There was also a significant difference between adopted and non-adopted children in language skills in first grade. Adopted children had lower skills than their non-adopted classmates. This is in line with other studies focusing on language (Merz et al., 2013; Rygvold & Theie, 2016; van IJzendoorn et al., 2005). We did not find the same significant differences in third grade. This is encouraging, as the adoptees seem to catch up concerning language difficulties.

There was also a significant difference in the percentage of adopted children needing special education support in third grade compared to non-adopted children (adopted: 15.3 percent, non-adopted: 5.8 percent). The number of adopted children that needed special education increased from first (n=14) to third grade (n=29). Since there were no differences in academic achievement between adopted and non-adopted children either in first or third grade, this could be explained by the fact that adopted children received more help and support from their parents with homework compared to their non-adopted classmates. The percentage of adopted children receiving a lot of help from their parents in third grade was 51.0 percent compared to 25.8 percent among non-adopted children. This has also been documented in other studies (Dalen, 2012; Raleigh & Kao, 2013).

The Norwegian study also examined to what extent language skills, social skills, and hyperactive behavior interfered with academic achievement among the internationally adopted children. A regression model with academic achievement as dependent variable and language skills, social skills, and hyperactivity as independent variables was applied for the adopted group in first and third grade. The results are presented in Table 28.3.

Language skills made a meaningful, significant contribution in explaining the variance in academic performance both in first and third grade. Children with a good command of language showed better school performance both in first and third grade. This is confirmed in several other studies (e.g. Simonsen, Kristoffersen, Bleses, Wehberg, & Jørgensen, 2014; Tomblin, Zhang, Buckwalter, & Catts, 2000). A relatively high percentage of internationally adopted children lag behind in the area of language and reading comprehension (Rygvold & Theie, 2016). This is critical because language and reading comprehension are important skills and are strongly connected to high academic performance in school (Dalen, 2012; Glennen & Masters, 2002).

Hyperactive behavior also contributed significantly in explaining variance in academic performance among the adopted Norwegian children, both in first and third grade. It is confirmed in many studies that hyperactive behavior interferes negatively with academic performance (Dalen, 2012; Merz et al., 2013). Both language skills and ability to concentrate are important for doing well in school. Teachers should therefore be aware of the fact that internationally adopted children seem vulnerable for developing learning problems, which again might qualify them for special education.

Social skills also made a significant contribution in explaining the variance in adopted children's academic performance in first grade. Social skills contributed to higher academic achievement. In third grade this contribution is no longer significant. Internationally

Table 28.3 Regression: academic achievement as dependent variable; language skills,[1] hyperactivity,[2] and social skills[3] as independent variables in first and third grade

	First grade β	*Third grade β*
Language skills[1]	–.313**	–.424***
Hyperactivity[2]	–.337***	–.328**
Social skills[3]	.251*	.140 n.s.
	R^2=.542	R^2=.536
	F(3,76)=29.932***	F(3,82)=31.534***

*p< .05, **p < .01, ***p < .001, n.s. not significant

1 Low score indicates better performance

2 Higher score indicates higher frequency

3 Higher score indicates better performance

adopted children are especially vulnerable to delays in their social development due to early institutionalization (Gunnar, van Dulmen, & the International Project Team, 2007; Vorria et al., 2006). The Norwegian results could indicate that adoptive families seem to have a positive influence on their children's social development, especially soon after the children arrive in their new family.

Conclusion and implications for policy and practice

The research outcomes from studies on academic performance among internationally adopted children provide a rather mixed picture. Some of the outcomes are based on high-risk samples and suggest that internationally adopted children experience more difficulties with academic achievement than their peers (McGuinness & Pallansch, 2000; Rosnati et al., 2008). Others find no areas of concern regarding academic achievement and are based on low-risk samples, which are characterized by children who are adopted at a young age (below 6 months) and come from countries with better pre-adoption conditions (Cohen et al., 2008; Vinnerljung et al., 2010). The sample of children in the Norwegian study conducted by Dalen and Theie represent a low-risk group of internationally adopted children. None of the children had an age of adoption above 2 years and none were adopted from countries in Eastern Europe or Russia. Research outcomes have documented that these factors are strong predictors for developmental delays and behavior problems among internationally adopted children (McGuinness & Pallansch, 2000; Raleigh & Kao, 2013). It is also important to emphasize that no child in the sample had any defined special need when they were adopted.

Academic performance will always depend on a child's cognitive ability, which is always a result of interaction between genes and environmental conditions. There is often no information about an internationally adopted child's background, making it difficult to really know the child's developmental cognitive potentials. Due to the fact that we often have limited information about both genetic status and the environmental conditions before adoption, it is often a frustrating discussion when focusing on the impact this interaction has on internationally adopted children's development. It is a kind of "black box" where one can only infer the impact of pre-adoption conditions. However, it is generally accepted that the development of a child's cognitive potential has to be stimulated to achieve competence.

Many studies have documented a great heterogeneity among internationally adopted children's academic performance, as well as in other areas of competence and skill, such as language and social skills as well as behavior problems. This heterogeneity has to be taken into consideration when one compares adopted and non-adopted children's performance. In a sample of adoptees, one will find children who perform very well and children with extremely low performance. The great disparity in performance can be disguised when only mean values are being compared. We have to go beyond mean values and pay more attention to the individual differences that better reveal this variation in outcomes.

In Norway, all children are afforded an education that is adapted to their capabilities. Children have the right to receive accommodations and special education services when they have documented learning disabilities or other disabilities. Many more internationally adopted children receive special education compared to non-adopted children. This could be due to the fact that a higher percentage of these children have stated special needs at placement (Juffer & van IJzendoorn, 2005; Raaska et al., 2011; Tirella et al., 2006). However, it could also be a result of adoptive parents' supportive behavior and their eagerness to proactively work with the school early in the process of diagnosing learning problems.

There is limited research in Norway and elsewhere about how internationally adopted individuals manage schooling in higher grades and universities. In the future, more studies should focus on internationally adopted individuals' academic performance at later age stages, paying particular attention to how they manage more demanding academic challenges. The outcomes from the Norwegian study give some indications that ought to be considered when focusing on later academically challenging school environments. Both language and hyperactivity make internationally adopted children vulnerable for developing learning problems later on. The Norwegian adopted children's academic performance as well as their school motivation had decreased from first to third grade. It might be that the academic demands of third grade challenged some of the adopted children's school motivation to a larger degree than for non-adoptees. Social skills seem to be one important protective factor for doing well in school. Internationally adopted children generally come from very supportive homes and receive a lot of stimulation supporting their cognitive and social development. These areas are important for doing academically well in school. It is important to continue to pay attention to the supports and challenges adopted children experience during their early school years as they age and meet greater academic rigor. Continued attention to factors influencing academic development across time will provide the long-term support needed for internationally adopted children to adjust to the increasing demands of continued schooling.

Overall, one might conclude that international adoption is a successful intervention for children at risk. However, one should always be aware of the heterogeneity within this group of adoptees. To treat international adoptees as a homogeneous group, to talk about them in general terms, can easily hide problems and needs for support and help as well as potential for good adjustment.

References

Achenbach, T. M. (1991). *Manual for the child behavior checklist 4/18 and 1991 profile*. Burlington: University of Vermont, Department of Psychiatry.

Bakermans-Kranenburg, M. J., van IJzendoorn, M. H., & Juffer, F. (2008). Earlier is better. A meta-analysis of 70 years of intervention improving cognitive development in institutionalized children. *Monographs of the Society for Research in Child Development*, *73*, 279–293. doi:10.1111/j.1540-5834.2008.00498.x

Bishop, D. V. M., & Snowling, M. (2004). Developmental dyslexia and specific language impairment: Same or different? *Psychological Bulletin*, *130*(69), 858–886.

Cohen, N. J., & Farnia, F. (2011). Social-emotional adjustment and attachment in children adopted from China: Processes and predictors of change. *International Journal of Behavioral Development*, *35*, 67–77. doi:10.1177/0165025410371602

Cohen, N. J., Lojkasek, M., Zadeh, Z. Y., Pugliese, M., & Kiefer, H. (2008). Children adopted from China: A prospective study of their growth and development. *Journal of Child Psychology and Psychiatry*, *49*, 458–468. doi:10.1111/j.1469-7610.2007.01853.x

Dalen, M. (1995). Learning difficulties among inter-country adopted children. *Nordisk Pedagogik*, *1*(4), 195–208.

Dalen, M. (2001). School performances among internationally adopted children in Norway. *Adoption Quarterly*, *5*(2), 39–58. doi:10.1300/J145v05n02_03

Dalen, M. (2012). Cognitive competence, academic achievement, and educational attainment among intercountry adoptees: Research outcomes from the Nordic countries. In J. L. Gibbons & K. S. Rotabi (Eds.), *Intercountry adoption. Policies, practices, and outcomes* (pp. 187–199). New York: Ashgate.

Dalen, M., Lindblad, F., Odenstad, A., Rasmussen, F., Vinnerljung, B., & Hjern, A. (2008). Educational attainment and cognitive competence in adopted men – A study of international and national adoptees, siblings and a general Swedish population. *Children and Youth Services Review, 30*, 1211–1219. doi:10.1016/j.childyouth.2008.03.006

Dalen, M., & Rygvold, A. L. (2006). Educational achievement in adopted children from China. *Adoption Quarterly, 9*(4), 45–58. doi:10.1300/J145v09n04_03

Dalen, M., & Theie, S. (2012). Internationally adopted children from non-European countries: General development during the first two years in the adoptive family. *Scientific World Journal, 2012*, 1–9. doi:10.1100/2012/375436

Dalen, M., & Theie, S. (2014). Similarities and differences between internationally adopted and non-adopted children in their toddler years: Outcomes from a longitudinal study. *American Journal of Orthopsychiatry, 84*(4), 397–408. doi:10.1037/ort0000010

Dalen, M., & Theie, S. (2015). Temperament, social competence and behavior problems among internationally adopted children at age four. *Journal of Basic and Applied Research International, 5*(2), 61–72.

Glennen, S., & Masters, M. G. (2002). Typical and atypical language development in infants and toddlers adopted from Eastern Europe. *American Journal of Speech and Language Therapy, 11*, 417–433. doi:10.1044/1058-0360(2002/045)

Gresham, R. M., & Elliot, S. N. (2008). *Social skills improvement system*. Minneapolis, MN: NCS Pearson, Inc.

Gresham, R. M., & Elliott, S. N. (1990). *Social skills rating system*. Minneapolis, MN: NCS, Pearson, Inc.

Gunnar, M. R., & van Dulmen, M. H.; the International Adoption Project Team (IAP). (2007). Behavior problems in post institutionalized internationally adopted children. *Development and Psychopathology, 19*, 129–148.

Harwood, R., Feng, X., & Yu, S. (2013). Preadoption adversities and post adoption mediators of mental health and school outcomes among international, foster, and private adoptees in the United States. *Journal of Family Psychology, 27*(3), 409–420. doi:10.1037/a0032908

Helder, E. J., Mulder, E., & Gunnoe, M. L. (2014). A longitudinal investigation of children internationally adopted at school age. *Child Neuropsychology, 22*(1), 39–64. doi:10.1080/09297049.2014.967669

Hjern, A., Lindblad, F., & Vinnerljung, B. (2002). Suicide, psychiatric illness, and social maladjustment in intercountry adoptees in Sweden: A cohort study. *The Lancet, 360*, 443–448. doi:10.1016/S0140-6736(02)09674-5

Hulme, C., & Snowling, M. (2009). *Developmental disorders of language, learning and cognition*. Sussex: Wiley-Blackwell.

Jacobs, E., Miller, L. C., & Tirella, L. G. (2010). Developmental and behavioral performance of internationally adopted preschoolers: A pilot study. *Child Psychiatry and Human Development, 41*, 15–29. doi:10.1007/s10578-009-0149-6

Jaffari-Bimmel, N., Juffer, F., van IJzendoorn, M. H., Bakermans-Kranenburg, M. J., & Mooijaart, A. (2006). Social development from infancy to adolescence: Longitudinal and concurrent factors in an adoption sample. *Developmental Psychology, 42*, 1143–1153. doi:10.1037/0012-1649.42.6.1143

Juffer, F., & van IJzendoorn, H. M. (2005). Behavior problems and mental health referrals of international adoptees. A meta-analysis. *The Journal of the American Medical Association, 293*, 2501–2515. doi:10.1001/jama.293.20.2501

Julian, M. M. (2013). Age at adoption from institutional care as a window into the lasting effects of early experiences. *Clinical Child and Family Psychology Review, 16*, 101–145. doi:10.1007/s10567-013-0130-6

Kreppner, J., Kumsta, R., Rutter, M., Beckett, C., Castle, J., Stevens, S., & Sonuga-Barke, E. J. (2010). Developmental course of deprivation-specific psychological patterns: Early manifestations, persistence to age 15, and clinical features. *Monographs of the Society for Research in Child Development, 75*, 79–101. doi:10.1111/j.1540-5834.2010.00551.x

Kvifte-Andresen, I. L. (1992). Behavioral and school adjustment of 12–13 year old internationally adopted children in Norway. *Journal of Child Psychology and Psychiatry, 33*, 427–439. doi:10.1111/j.1469-7610.1992.tb00877.x

Lindblad, F., Dalen, M., Rasmussen, F., Vinnerljung, B., & Hjern, A. (2009). School performance of international adoptees better than expected from cognitive test results. *European Child & Adolescent Psychiatry, 18*, 301–308. doi:10.1007/s00787-008-0731-7

Lindblad, F., Hjern, A., & Vinnerljung, B. (2003). Intercountry adopted children as young adults – A Swedish cohort study. *American Journal of Occupational Therapy, 73*(2), 190–202. doi:10.1037/0002-9432.73.2.190

Loman, M. M., Wiik, K. L., Frenn, K. A., Pollak, S. D., & Gunnar, M. R. (2009). Postinstitutionalized children's development: Growth, cognitive, and language outcomes. *Journal of Developmental & Behavioral Pediatrics, 30*(5), 426–434. doi:10.1097/DBP.0b013e3181b1fd08

McGuinness, T. M., & Pallansch, L. (2000). Competence of children adopted from the former Soviet Union. *Family Relations, 49*, 457–464. doi:10.1111/j.1741-3729.2000.00457.x

Merz, E. C., McCall, R. B., & Wright, A. J. (2013). Attention and language as mediators of academic outcomes following early psychosocial deprivation. *International Journal ofBehavioral Development, 37*(5), 451–459. doi:10.1177/0165025413490867

Odenstad, A., Hjern, A., Lindblad, F., Vinnerljung, B., & Dalen, M. (2008). Does age at adoption and geographic origin matter? A national cohort study of cognitive test performance in adult intercountry adoptees. *Psychological Medicine, 38*, 1803–1814. doi:10.1017/S0033291708002766

Ottem, E. (2009). *20 questions about language skills.* Oslo: Statped.

Pomerleau, A., Malcuit, G., Chicoine, J. F., Seguin, R., Belhumeur, C., Germain, P., & Jeliu, G. (2005). Health status, cognitive and motor development of young children adopted from China, East Asia, and Russia across the first 6 months after adoption. *International Journal of Behavioral Development, 29*, 445–457. doi:10.1080/01650250500206257

Pugliese, M., Cohen, N., Farnia, F., & Lojkasek, M. (2010). The emerging attachment relationship between adopted Chinese infants and their mothers. *Children and Youth Services Review, 32*, 1719–1728. doi:10.1016/j.childyouth.2010.07.015

Raaska, H., Elovainio, M., Sinkkonen, J., Matomäki, S., & Lapinleimu, H. (2011). Internationally adopted children in Finland: Parental evaluations of symptoms of reactive attachment disorder and learning difficulties – FINADO study. *Child: Care, Health and Development, 34*, 152–160. doi:10.1111/j.1365-2214.2011.01289.x

Raaska, H., Elovainio, M., Sinnonen, J., Matomäki, J., Mäkipää, S., & Lapinleimu, H. (2012). Internationally adopted children in Finland: Parental evaluations of symptoms of reactive attachment disorder and learning difficulties – FINADO study. *Child: Care, Health and Development, 38*(5), 697–705.

Raleigh, E., & Kao, G. (2013). Is there a (transracial) adoption achievement gap? A national longitudinal analysis of adopted children's educational performance. *Children and Youth Services Review, 35*, 142–150. All rights reserved. doi:10.1016/j.childyouth.2012.09.019

Roberts, J. A., Pollock, K. E., Krakow, R., Price, J., Fulmer, K. C., & Wang, P. (2005). Language development in preschool-age children adopted from China. *Journal of Speech, Language, and Hearing Research, 48*, 93–107. doi:10.1044/1092-4388(2005/008)

Rosnati, R., Montirosso, R., & Barni, D. (2008). Behavioral and emotional problems among Italian international adoptees and non-adopted children: Father's and mother's reports. *Journal of Family Psychology, 22*(3), 541–549. doi:10.1037/0893-3200.22.3.541

Rutter, M., Beckett, C., Castle, J., Colvert, E., Kreppner, J., Metha, M., & Sonuga-Barke, E. (2009). Effects of profound early institutional deprivation: An overview of findings from a UK longitudinal study of Romanian adoptees. In G. M. Wrobel & B. Neil (Eds.), *International advances in adoption research for practice* (pp. 147–167). Oxford, UK: Wiley-Blackwell.

Rutter, M., Sonuga-Barke, E. J., Beckett, C., Castle, J., Kreppner, J., Kumsta, R., ... Bell, C. A. (2010). Deprivation-specific psychological patterns: Effects of institutional deprivation. *Monographs of the Society for Research in Child Development, 95*(75), 1–252.

Rygvold, A. L. (1999). Better or worse? Intercountry adopted children's language. In A. L. Rygvold, M. Dalen, & B. Sætersdal (Eds.), *Mine – yours – ours and theirs. Adoption, changing kinship and family patterns* (pp. 221–229). Oslo: Department of Special Needs Education, University of Oslo.

Rygvold, A. L., & Theie, S. (2016). Internationally adopted children's reading comprehension in second grade. *Adoption Quarterly, 19*(3), 166–187. doi:10.1080/10926755.2016.1182954

Selman, P. (2012). The rise and fall of intercountry adoption in the 21st century: Global trends from 2001 to 2010. In J. L. Gibbons & K. S. Rotabi (Eds.), *Intercountry adoption. Policies, practices, and outcomes* (pp. 187–199). New York: Ashgate.

Simonsen, H. G., Kristoffersen, K. E., Bleses, D., Wehberg, S., & Jørgensen, R. N. (2014). The Norwegian communicative development inventories; Reliability, main developmental trends and gender differences. *First Language, 34*(1), 3–23. doi:10.1177/0142723713510997

Statistics Norway (2018, June 1). Adoptions. Downloaded October 25 from https://www.ssb.no/befolkning/statistikker/adopsjon/.

Tan, T. (2009). School-age adopted Chinese girls' behavioral adjustment, academic performance, and social skills: Longitudinal results. *American Journal of Orthopsychiatry, 79*(2), 244–251.

Tan, T., & Marfo, K. (2006). Parental ratings of behavioral adjustment in two samples of adopted Chinese girls: Age-related versus socio-emotional correlates and predictors. *Journal of Applied Developmental Psychology, 27*, 14–30. doi:10.1016/j.appdev.2005.12.004

Tan, T., Wang, Y., & Ruggerio, A. (2017). Childhood adversity and children's academic functioning: Roles of parenting stress and neighborhood support. *Journal of Child and Family Studies, 27*(10), 2742–2752.

Tirella, L. G., Chan, W., & Miller, L. C. (2006). Educational outcomes of children adopted from Eastern Europe, now ages 8–12. *Journal of Research in Childhood Education, 20*(4), 245–254. doi:10.1080/02568540609594565

Tomblin, B. J., Zhang, X., Buckwalter, P., & Catts, H. (2000). The association of reading disability, behavioral disorders, and language impairment among second-grade children. *Journal of Child Psychology and Psychiatry*, 473–482. doi:10.1111/1469-7610.00632

van der Voort, A., Linting, M., Juffer, F., Schoenmaker, C., Bakermans-Kranenburg, M., & van IJzendoorn, H. M. H. (2014). More than two decades after adoption: Associations between infant attachment, early maternal, sensitivity and the diurnal cortisol curve of adopted young adults. *Children and Youth Services Review, 46*, 186–194. doi:10.1016/j.childyouth.2014.08.022

van IJzendoorn, M. H., & Juffer, F. (2006). The Emanuel Miller Memorial Lecture 2006: Adoption as intervention. Meta-analytic evidence for massive catch-up and plasticity in physical, socio-emotional, and cognitive development. *Journal of Child Psychology and Psychiatry, 47*(12), 1228–1245.

van IJzendoorn, M., Juffer, F., & Klein Poelhuis, C. (2005). Adoption and cognitive development: A meta-analytic comparison of adopted and nonadopted children's IQ and school performance. *Psychological Bulletin, 131*(2), 301–316. doi:10.1037/0033-2909.131.2.301

van London, M. W., Juffer, F., & van IJzendoorn, H. M. H. (2007). Attachment, cognitive, and motor development in adopted children: Short-term outcomes after international adoption. *Journal of Pediatric Psychology, 32*, 1249–1258. doi:10.1093/jpepsy/jsm062

Verhulst, F. C., Althaus, M., & Verluis-den Bierman, H. (1990). Problem behaviour in international adoptees. *Journal of American Academy of Child and Adolescent Psychiatry, 29*, 94–103.

Vinnerljung, B., Lindblad, F., Rasmussen, F., & Dalen, M. (2010). School performance at age 16 among international adoptees: A Swedish national cohort study. *International Social Work, 53*, 443–456.

Vorria, P., Papaligoura, Z., Kopakaki, M., Dunn, J., & van IJzendoorn, M. H. (2006). The development of adopted children after institutional care: A follow-up study. *Journal of Child Psychiatry and Psychology and Psychiatry, 47*, 1246–1253. doi:10.1111/j.1469-7610.2006.01666.x

Zeanah, C. H., Smyke, A. T., Koga, S. F., & Carlson, E.; the Bucharest Early Intervention Project Core Group. (2005). Attachment in institutionalized and community children in Romania. *Child Development, 76*, 1015–1028. doi:10.1111/j.1467-8624.2005.00894.x

29
PARENTING STRESS IN ADOPTIVE FAMILIES

Marta Santos-Nunes, Isabel Narciso, and Salomé Vieira-Santos

The upbringing of children is of the utmost importance for their physical, psychological, and social wellbeing. Parents continuously face enormous responsibility which can involve not only joy and fulfillment, but also fatigue, frustration, and stress. Adoptive parents, in particular, can experience stress, as their adoptive children often present unique emotional and social difficulties, challenging behaviors, insecure attachment patterns, and health problems. Thus, parenting stress is an important topic in the field of adoption research and practice.

Parenting stress, one of the most researched dimensions of parenting (Barroso, Mendez, Graziano, & Bagner, 2018), is widely considered as the stress experienced in the exercise of a parental role (Abidin, 1992). As introduced by Abidin (1992), it was conceptualized as a motivating variable that activates the search for, and use of, available resources. Abidin emphasized its relevance as a determinant of the quality of parenting and also for children's consequent adjustment.

Parenting stress has multiple determinants (Abidin, 1995; Crnic & Low, 2002; Deater-Deckard, 2004) including child characteristics, parent characteristics, and the parent–child relationship (e.g., Abidin, 1995; Deater-Deckard, 2004). These determinants of parenting stress, as well as the contextual factors, constitute relevant factors affecting the parental role. This role is derived from the internal model of a parental figure that one holds, based on one's own definition of parental goals, and from the social expectations one has internalized (Abidin, 1992). Although parenting stress is considered a normative part of the parenting role (Crnic & Greenberg, 1990), it negatively affects both parents' and children's wellbeing (Deater-Deckard, 1998; Goldberg & Smith, 2014; Harris-Waller, Granger, & Gurney-Smith, 2016; Judge, 2003; Santos-Nunes, Narciso, Vieira-Santos, & Roberto, 2017).

Different outcomes have been reported in the literature concerning the association of parenting stress with children's behavior and with other parenting-related variables. For instance, Garcia, Ren, Esteraich, and Raikes (2017) recently found that higher levels of parenting stress are associated with greater parent–child conflict. In fact, Elder, Eccles, Ardelt, and Lord (1995) assert that it is hard to maintain a positive relationship with the child if parents lack emotional resources to deal with the demands inherent to parenthood. Additionally, some of the outcomes associated with high levels of parenting stress, substantiated in the interactions between parent and child, are low levels of family functioning quality, less positive parenting styles (e.g., more authoritarian style, less responsiveness), perception of a higher level of children's behavioral problems, lower development competence, higher levels of negative affectivity, and attachment disorders (Crnic & Greenberg, 1990; Grolnick, 2003; Pesonen et al., 2008; Tharner et al., 2012). Furthermore, a bidirectional relationship has been observed between parenting stress and children's behavior problems, meaning that parenting stress is both an antecedent and a consequence of child behavioral outcomes; however, this seems to vary according to the type of behavior problems and the family life stage (Neece, Green, & Baker, 2012; Woodman, Mawdsley, & Hauser-Cram, 2015).

This chapter begins with a review of the literature on parenting stress comparing non-adoptive and adoptive families. It then explores what has been learned about the relationship between parenting stress and characteristics of children and between parenting stress and characteristics of parenting. It concludes with a consideration of the implications of these findings for adoption practice and recommendations.

Non-adoptive and adoptive families

In the case of adoptive parenthood, parenting stress assumes particular relevance as adoption refers to a non-normative situation (McGoldrick & Carter, 2003). Some of the factors unique to adoptive families that adoptive parents may have to face are children's age at arrival, background of the biological family, institutional care trajectory, adoptive parents' infertility, and the need for a (re)construction of the identity of the family that arises from different "subcultures" (Bejenaru & Roth, 2012; Judge, 2003, 2004; Juffer & van IJzendoorn, 2005; Tan & Marfo, 2016). Additionally, the different stages of the life cycle of an adoptive family are characterized by multiple challenges and strains, such as the agencies' evaluation process, taking on an instant parenthood role, and the time after the "honeymoon" period (i.e., the initial period of mutual "enchantment" and discovery in the parent–child interactions) has ended (Bird, Peterson, & Miller, 2002; Goldberg, 2010). These have to be added to the typical experiences of non-adoptive parents, such as establishment of rules and limits and development of family rituals (Crnic & Low, 2002). Moreover, some challenges (e.g., revelation to the child of their unknown adoptive status, communication regarding adoption, [re]construction of self and family identity) are revisited in different stages of the family life cycle, despite how well they have been dealt with previously. The use of positive coping strategies facilitates the adaptation process and allows adoptive parents to deal with the diversity of challenges in constructive ways.

The literature comparing parenting stress levels in adoptive and non-adoptive families reveals contradictory results. While some studies reported lower levels of parenting stress in adoptive families when compared to non-adoptive families (Rosnati, Ranieri, & Barni, 2013; Sánchez-Sandoval & Palacios, 2012), others have found higher levels in the former (Harris-Waller et al., 2016; McGlone, Santos, Kazama, Fong, & Mueller, 2002; Santos-Nunes, Narciso, Vieira-Santos, & Roberto, 2018b; Santos-Nunes et al., 2017). Furthermore, some other studies found no significant differences between adoptive and non-adoptive families (e.g., Judge, 2003; León, Palacios, Román, Moreno, & Peñarrubia, 2015). The discrepancies in these findings might be explained by the use of samples with different features such as children's characteristics and adoption-related variables. For instance, some researchers have shown that certain age levels of adoptive children are a factor contributing to the increase of parenting stress in adoptive parents, particularly the school-aged period, from six to 12 years (Brodzinsky, Smith, & Brodzinsky, 1998). During this period, children's sensitivity to the adoption issue is heightened and they become more aware of adoption implications, namely in terms of relinquishment (Palacios & Sánchez-Sandoval, 2005). This new awareness can be painful and has been found to contribute to maladaptation in children, which affects the levels of parenting stress (Neece et al., 2012; Woodman et al., 2015). Furthermore, a recent study used a sample consisting of families with only biological children, families with only adoptive children, and families with both biological and adoptive children, to analyze whether these groups differed in terms of the perception held by the parents of their children's behavior problems, their own levels of parenting stress, and the levels of family cohesion and conflict (Santos-Nunes et al., 2018b). In regard to parenting stress, both types of adoptive families (with only adoptive children and with both adoptive and biological children) evidenced higher levels of parenting stress compared to families with only biological children (Santos-Nunes et al., 2018b). In sum, the different methodological characteristics of the studies that compare adoptive and non-adoptive parents regarding parenting stress might explain the inconsistency of results in the literature, namely the different sample characteristics (e.g., age of adoptees, harshness of their previous life history, institutional care trajectories, and structure of adoptive families).

Child characteristics and parenting stress

Child-related stress (i.e., parenting stress due to parents' perceptions of their children's characteristics) and parent–child dysfunctional interactions have been consistently reported as the most significant components of parenting stress in adoptive samples (Judge, 2003; León et al., 2015; Mainemer, Gilman, & Ames, 1998; McGlone et al., 2002; Santos-Nunes et al., 2018b). For instance, Santos-Nunes et al. (2018b) recently demonstrated that adoptive parents tend to attribute more stress to their interactions with the children and to the perception of the children's characteristics, rather than to the perception of their own characteristics. This is in line with the previous proposal of Sánchez-Sandoval and Palacios (2012) that adoptive parents might hold a positive perspective of their own parental resources and avoid internal attributions for their children's behavioral outcomes. Moreover, the fact that adoptive children have been reported to be more challenging and present more difficulties than their biological peers (Grotevant & McDermott, 2014; Harris-Waller et al., 2016; Juffer & van IJzendoorn, 2005) might support the adoptive parents' belief that parenting stress is mainly due to their child's characteristics. The study developed by Judge (2003), with a sample of mother–father dyads who had adopted children from Eastern Europe, also illustrates that adoptive parents are more likely to attribute parenting stress to child factors rather than parental factors. Judge found that reports of more behavioral problems among the adoptees were associated with an increase in the stress of both the mother and the father.

It should be noted that, in the context of adoption, many children have negative pre-adoptive experiences, including negligence, abuse, lack of stimulation, intermittent care, and other adverse experiences. Therefore, these children have been described as prone to display high levels of cognitive, behavioral, and socio-emotional problems (Grotevant & McDermott, 2014). These problems, along with specific stressors, such as children who are older at the time of adoption, sibling groups, and children with medical conditions, have contributed to their classification as "children with special needs" (Brodzinsky et al., 1998; Palacios & Sánchez-Sandoval, 2006). All of these factors increase the difficulty of their placement in a family (O'Dell, McCall, & Groark, 2015) and represent a set of challenges that impact the levels of parenting stress of their adoptive parents (Santos-Nunes et al., 2017, 2018b).

Parenting stress contributes both directly and indirectly to children's adjustment to adoption (e.g., Harris-Waller et al., 2016; Judge, 2003; Rosnati, Montirosso, & Barni, 2008). A recent study (Santos-Nunes et al., 2017) analyzed the association among parenting stress, children's attachment (i.e., a pattern that supposes an internal model of the caregiver as a secure base and as a refuge in times of need and stress; Ainsworth, Blehar, Waters, & Wall, 1978), and emotional wellbeing (measured as positive and negative affect). It revealed that high levels of parenting stress were associated with low levels of secure attachment, which were associated with low levels of positive affect (i.e., emotions such as pleasure, engagement, and enthusiasm; Watson & Tellegen, 1985) and with high levels of negative affect (i.e., emotions such as being upset, sad, or unpleasant; Watson & Tellegen, 1985). Additionally, parenting stress was found to be associated with an anxious/ambivalent attachment pattern; a pattern characterized by the ambivalence of behaviors, which alternate between the search for contact with the attachment figure and active resistance to this contact (Ainsworth et al., 1978), which, in turn, was related to negative affect.

These were important findings, as attachment has been referred to as the cornerstone of a healthy psychological adjustment (Brodzinsky et al., 1998) and the basis for all future close relationships once it provides an internal working model from which the child understands the social world (Bowlby, 1969). The internal working models of attachment developed by many adoptive children prior to adoption are characterized by negative perceptions and expectations about others (adults) and themselves (Román & Palacios, 2011). Therefore, parenthood characterized by negativity (e.g., parenting stress) might reinforce the insecure patterns of attachment and/or reduce the secure pattern. Furthermore, research has demonstrated that the change of the internal working models of attachment is a difficult and slow process (Hodges, Steele, Hillman, Henderson, & Kaniuk, 2005). Notwithstanding the opportunity that adoption constitutes for the development of a secure pattern, insecure attachment representations seem to persevere, competing with the secure ones. Therefore, it is understandable that negative parenting factors, such as parenting stress, significantly contribute to the (re)activation of insecure attachment and the reduction of secure attachment behavior, which then leads to less positive and more negative emotionality (Carvalho, 2007; Kochanska, 2001).

The relationship that parents establish with an adoptive child is of utmost importance for the repairing of these insecure patterns of attachment that can characterize adoptees prior to adoption (Dozier et al., 2009) and for the development of their emotional wellbeing (Crnic & Greenberg, 1990; Grolnick, 2003; Pesonen et al., 2008; Tharner et al., 2012). We might, then, conclude that parents with lower levels of parenting stress can more easily engage in positive parenting, and might be more available to strengthen the relationship with their children. This would allow the adoptive children to feel secure enough to explore the world and to develop a sense of greater wellbeing.

Parent(ing) characteristics and parenting stress

The stress that parents in general experience in the fulfillment of their role impacts and is impacted by parents' individual characteristics, which, in turn, affect their wellbeing and children's outcomes. For example, Deater-Deckard's (1998) literature review showed that parenting stress contributes to poorer parenting quality – highly stressed parents are more authoritarian and less responsive – which, in turn, has a negative impact on children's wellbeing.

As far as adoptive families are concerned, most of the studies have related parenting stress to children's outcomes, while the relationship with parent(ing) variables has received little attention. Nevertheless, some studies have highlighted this relationship. In line with Deater-Deckard (1998), in adoptive families parenting stress and negative parenting styles taken together were found to contribute to children's behavioral problems and emotional negativity (Lipscomb et al., 2011; Tan, Camras, Deng, Zhang, & Lu, 2012). In fact, these two dimensions have been used to define the quality of parenting. For instance, Santos-Nunes et al. (2017) found that a high level of parenting stress in adoptive families is associated with a low level of positive parenting (characterized by emotional warmth) and also with a high level of negative parenting (characterized by rejection behaviors among the parents).

Parents' expectations prior to adoption is another parenting dimension associated with parenting stress, particularly considering the mismatch between those expectations and parents' current experiences (Chesney, 2008; Moyer & Goldberg, 2015; Santos-Nunes, Narciso, Vieira-Santos, & Roberto, 2018a). Research has revealed that adoptive parents hold very positive expectations concerning their children's future (Ward, 1997; Welsh, Viana, Petrill, & Mathias, 2008). However, when these expectations do not match the reality, or if this mismatch is perceived as a negative experience, it might lead parents to feel guilty, unsatisfied, and distressed. Ultimately, this dynamic might interfere with their capacity to face and cope with that reality. Santos-Nunes et al. (2018a) showed that when parents' evaluation of expectations (i.e., the evaluation that parents make of the confrontation between their previous expectations with their current experience) is more positive, their parenting stress levels are lower, which is associated with lower perceptions of problems in their children's behavior. The same study also showed that this negative association between parents' evaluation of expectations and parenting stress leads to higher levels of parents' satisfaction, which is associated with lower perceptions of problems in their children's behavior. Cognitive flexibility, formal and/or informal support, and pre-adoption preparation were also found to be important to avoiding high levels of parenting stress in the face of unmet expectations (Chesney, 2008; Moyer & Goldberg, 2015).

Parental satisfaction is another parenting-related variable that has been associated with parenting stress. In a study focusing on the stress experienced by parents of children with a deprived early childhood, the researchers found that a higher level of parenting stress was associated with less parental satisfaction (Rijk, Hoksbergen, Ter Laak, van Dijkum, & Robbroeckx, 2006). Parental satisfaction has been associated with a higher quality of parent–child relationships (Reilly & Platz, 2003) which, as previously mentioned, has proven to be one of the most prominent dimensions of parenting stress in adoptive families (e.g., Judge, 2003; León et al., 2015; Mainemer et al., 1998; McGlone et al., 2002; Santos-Nunes et al., 2018b).

Parents' individual characteristics, such as mental health and attachment patterns, have also been associated with levels of parenting stress (Goldberg & Smith, 2014; Salcuni, Miconi, Altoè, & Moscardino, 2015). In a longitudinal study, Goldberg and Smith (2014) found that parents' mental health, namely depressive symptoms, were associated with high levels of parenting stress in the post-adoption period. Viana and Welsh (2010) have also demonstrated that mothers with depression in the pre-adoption period experienced higher levels of parenting stress later in the post-adoption period. Salcuni et al. (2015) studied the relationship among dyadic adjustment (i.e., quality of couples' dyadic functioning), parents' insecure patterns of attachment (anxious and avoidant), and parenting stress in international adoption. For both mothers and fathers, the attachment patterns (anxious and avoidant) contributed to an increase of parenting stress levels. Furthermore, insecure attachment patterns, for both parents, mediated the relationship between dyadic adjustment and parenting stress. Yet, there were differences in the type of attachment pattern as a function of being a mother or a father: a better dyadic adjustment was associated with lower levels of insecure patterns of attachment, which in the case of mothers was anxious and in the case of fathers, avoidant. Both were related to lower levels of parenting stress.

Salcuni et al. (2015) also emphasized the importance of family-related variables for the emergence and expression of parenting stress, as dyadic adjustment was found to have such a significant association with this variable. In fact, a positive marital relationship represents a strength and a resource for families in general, and particularly for adoptive families, as has been demonstrated by different studies (Goldberg & Smith, 2014; Goldberg, Smith, & Kashy, 2010; Lionetti, Pastore, & Barone, 2015).

Implications for intervention with adoptive families

Adoption is an intervention that has been found to have a recovery effect in children (Juffer & van IJzendoorn, 2005). However, it is not a miracle that heals all the wounds caused by the difficulties previously experienced by the adoptive children. Furthermore, adoption has its own unique challenges that reinforce the need to support adoptive parents (Juffer et al., 2011). Literature on adoption highlights the presence of more difficulties in the adaptation processes and wellbeing of adoptive families when compared to non-adoptive families (e.g., Brodzinsky, 2013; Grotevant & McDermott, 2014; Santos-Nunes et al., 2017, 2018b). Furthermore, it identifies a need for intervention in different stages of the process of adoption.

Interventions before and after the adoption process are crucial to support adoptive families (Gunnar & Pollak, 2007; Juffer et al., 2011). A literature review on training and interventions available for adoptive parents pointed to the positive impact of post-adoption services on caregivers and the need for more studies on pre-adoption services (Drozd, Bergsund, Hammerstrøm, Hansen, & Jacobsen, 2018). It is known that families apply to such services requesting different types of help related to difficulties such as child emotional-behavioral problems, caregiver strain, school challenges, and assistance needs (Waid & Alewine, 2018); however, more studies are required to understand the particulars of the effectiveness of these services that support the adoption process.

Unfortunately, there is a diversity of countries in which post-adoption services are scarce (Gunnar & Pollak, 2007) or even nonexistent. Consequently, parents must turn to psychologists and other professionals who might not be familiar with the specific features of adoption and are thus not equipped with the tools to develop more effective interventions (Brodzinsky, 2013; Stokes & Poulsen, 2014).

Therefore, we suggest that the preparation of future adoptive parents and children should include a preventive and follow-up intervention plan to be implemented during the initial stage of the process. As this tends to be a smoother period in the adoption process, primarily characterized by adoptive parents' and children's mutual exploration and discoveries, this plan could focus on topics associated with potential parental difficulties (e.g., management of expectations, establishment of the relationship, attachment, emotional and behavioral problems, communication regarding the adoption, and stress related to the parental role) and address the development of individual and parenting skills.

Specifically, we suggest the narrative approach (e.g., White & Epston, 1990) as a theoretical framework for both preventive and therapeutic intervention. Adoptive families are characterized in their genesis and in their identity by two different stories – the parents' and children's. Therefore, narrative intervention, through the utilization of stories, could be helpful in different ways. For instance, it can lead children to make sense of, and recover from the loss of their biological family, as well as to contribute to the understanding of the adoption experience from the intrapsychic, relational, family, and social perspectives (Stokes & Poulsen, 2014). Schank and Berman's (2002) five types of stories (official, invented, first-hand, second-hand, and culturally shared) might work well for the preventive and therapeutic interventions. For instance, *official stories*, referred to as such since they tell an innocuous version of the facts, could be used to work with older children, adolescents, and adults, namely in their search for origins. The *invented stories*, consisting of fictional reports, could support comprehension of real facts, mostly in younger children, or they could serve as symbolic narratives of a story co-constructed by the family members. The *first-hand stories*, namely personal testimonies of meanings, beliefs, expectations, interpretations, and feelings, might possibly be useful to work with groups of parents or groups of children. The *second-hand stories* could serve to support parents who seek close examples of the reality experienced by other parents. The *stories culturally shared* that frame the phenomena and events could support deconstruction, seeking to expand on an understanding of the truths and myths they encompass. The construction of narrative genograms with symbols that identify the family's characteristics, in addition to the identification and prescription of familiar rituals could also be useful in terms of prevention and therapeutic intervention.

Great demands in life can bring tiring days, overwhelming doubts, and desperate feelings. In regard to adoptive parenthood, all of these issues might be intensified by the experience of having a child that has already experienced disappointment and hurt, thus requiring parents to develop a (re)construction approach. Thus, the challenge for these parents is also the opportunity to develop in-depth learning, growth, and role fulfillment, and consequently, to attain the much-desired state of happiness. All this could be facilitated by simply "being there"

> The children came downstairs to meet us where we were … my son ran into my husband's arms and my daughter ran to me, and held me tightly by my neck with such force … and at that moment she said something to me that I will hold with me for life: "Why did you take so long?" I was absorbing that sentence and holding my tears, my urge to cry, because at that moment I couldn't show any weaknesses. I told her, "I'm here now, I took a long time, but I'm here."
>
> *(excerpt from an interview with an adoptive mother)*

References

Abidin, R. R. (1992). The determinants of parenting behavior. *Journal of Clinical Child Psychology, 21*(4), 407–412. doi:10.1207/s15374424jccp2104_12

Abidin, R. R. (1995). *Parenting stress index – Professional manual.* Odessa, FL: Psychological Assessment Resources.

Ainsworth, M. D. S., Blehar, M. C., Waters, W., & Wall, S. (1978). *Patterns of attachment: A psychological study of the Strange Situation.* Hillsdale, NJ: Erlbaum.

Barroso, N. E., Mendez, L., Graziano, P. A., & Bagner, D. M. (2018). Parenting stress through the lens of different clinical groups: A systematic review & meta-analysis. *Journal of Abnormal Child Psychology, 46*(3), 449–461. doi:10.1007/s10802-017-0313-6

Bejenaru, A. A., & Roth, M. M. (2012). Romanian adoptive families: Stressors, coping strategies and resources. *Children & Youth Services Review, 34*(7), 1317–1324. doi:10.1016/j.childyouth.2012.03.011

Bird, G., Peterson, R., & Miller, S. H. (2002). Factors associated with distress among support-seeking adoptive parents. *Family Relations, 51*, 215–220. doi:10.1111/j.1741-3729.2002.00215.x

Bowlby, J. (1969). *Attachment and loss: Attachment.* New York: Basic Books.

Brodzinsky, D. M. (2013). *A need to know: Enhancing adoption competence among mental health professionals.* New York: Donaldson Adoption Institute.

Brodzinsky, D. M., Smith, D. W., & Brodzinsky, A. B. (1998). *Children's adjustment to adoption. Developmental and clinical issues.* London: Sage.

Carvalho, M. (2007). Vinculação, temperamento e processamento da informação: Implicações nas perturbações emocionais e comportamentais no início da adolescência [Attachment, temperament, and information processing: Effects on emotional and behavioral disorders in early adolescence]. Doctoral dissertation. Portugal: University of Minho. Retrieved from http://repositorium.sdum.uminho.pt/handle/1822/8410

Chesney, M. L. (2008). Discrepancies between pre-adoption expectations and post-adoption experiences for parents of children adopted from institutional care. (Doctoral dissertation). Retrieved from ProQuest LLC. (UMI Microform 3328301).

Crnic, K., & Greenberg, M. (1990). Minor parenting stresses with young children. *Child Development, 61*(5), 1628–1637.

Crnic, K., & Low, C. (2002). Everyday stresses and parenting. In M. Bornstein (Ed.), *Handbook of parenting: Vol. 5. Practical issues in parenting* (2nd ed., pp. 243–267). Mahwah, NJ: Lawrence Erlbaum Associates.

Deater-Deckard, K. (1998). Parenting stress and child adjustment: Some old hypotheses and new questions. *Clinical Psychology: Science and Practice, 5*(3), 314–332. doi:10.1111/j.1468-2850.1998.tb00152.x

Deater-Deckard, K. (2004). *Parenting stress.* New Haven, CT: Yale University Press.

Dozier, M., Lindhiem, O., Lewis, E., Bick, J., Bernard, K., & Peloso, E. (2009). Effects of a foster parent training program on young children's attachment behaviors: Preliminary evidence from a randomized clinical trial. *Child & Adolescent Social Work Journal, 26*(4), 321–332. doi:10.1007/s10560-009-0165-1

Drozd, F., Bergsund, H. B., Hammerstrøm, K. T., Hansen, M. B., & Jacobsen, H. (2018). A systematic review of courses, training, and interventions for adoptive parents. *Journal of Child & Family Studies, 27*(2), 339–354. doi:10.1007/s10826-017-0901-7

Elder, G. H., Eccles, J. S., Ardelt, M., & Lord, S. (1995). Inner-city parents under economic pressure: Perspectives on the strategies of parenting. *Journal of Marriage and Family, 57*(3), 771–784. doi:10.2307/353931

Garcia, A. S., Ren, L., Esteraich, J. M., & Raikes, H. H. (2017). Influence of child behavioral problems and parenting stress on parent-child conflict among low-income families: The moderating role of maternal nativity. *Journal of Developmental Psychology, 63*(3), 311–339. doi:10.13110/merrpalmquar1982.63.3.0311

Goldberg, A. A., & Smith, J. Z. (2014). Predictors of parenting stress in lesbian, gay, and heterosexual adoptive parents during early parenthood. *Journal of Family Psychology, 28*(2), 125–137. doi:10.1037/a0036007

Goldberg, A. E. (2010). The transition to adoptive parenthood. In T. W. Miller (Ed.), *Handbook of stressful transitions across the lifespan* (pp. 165–184). New York: Springer.

Goldberg, A. E., Smith, J. Z., & Kashy, D. A. (2010). Preadoptive factors predicting lesbian, gay, and heterosexual couples' relationship quality across the transition to adoptive parenthood. *Journal of Family Psychology, 24*, 221–232. doi:10.1037/a0019615

Grolnick, W. S. (2003). *The psychology of parental control: How well-meant parenting backfires.* Mahwah, NJ: Erlbaum.

Grotevant, H. D., & McDermott, J. M. (2014). Adoption: Biological and social processes linked to adaptation. *Annual Review of Psychology, 65*(1), 235–265. doi:10.1146/annurev-psych-010213-115020

Gunnar, M., & Pollak, S. D. (2007). Supporting parents so that they can support their internationally adopted children: The larger challenge lurking behind the fatality statistics. *Child Maltreatment, 12*, 381–382. doi:10.1177/1077559507306719

Harris-Waller, J., Granger, C., & Gurney-Smith, B. (2016). A comparison of parenting stress and children's internalising, externalising and attachment-related behavior difficulties in UK adoptive and non-adoptive families. *Adoption & Fostering, 40*(4), 340–351. doi:10.1177/0308575916667911

Hodges, J., Steele, M., Hillman, S., Henderson, K., & Kaniuk, J. (2005). Change and continuity in mental representations of attachment after adoption. In D. M. Brodzinsky & J. Palacios (Eds.), *Psychological issues in adoption: Research and practice* (pp. 93–116). Westport, CT: Praeger.

Judge, S. (2003). Determinants of parental stress in families adopting children from Eastern Europe. *Family Relations, 52*, 241–248. doi:10.1111/j.1741-3729.2003.00241.x

Judge, S. (2004). The impact of early institutionalization on child and family outcomes. *Adoption Quarterly*, 7(3), 31–48. doi:10.1300/J145v07n03_02

Juffer, F., Palacios, J., LeMare, L., Sonuga-Barke, E. J. S., Tiemann, W., Bakermans-Kranenburg, M., … Verhulst, F. C. (2011). Development of adopted children with histories of early adversity. *Monographs of the Society for Research in Child Development*, *76*(4), 31–61. doi:10.1111/j.1540-5834.2011.00627.x

Juffer, F., & van IJzendoorn, M. H. (2005). Behavior problems and mental health referrals of international adoptees. *Journal of the American Medical Association*, *293*, 2501–2515. doi:10.1111/j.1741-3729.2003.00241.x

Kochanska, G. (2001). Emotional development in children with different attachment histories: The first three years. *Child Development*, *72*(2), 474–490. doi:10.1111/1467-8624.00291

León, E., Palacios, J., Román, M., Moreno, C., & Peñarrubia, M. G. (2015). Parental stress, family functioning and children's psychological adjustment in adoptive families: A comparative and longitudinal study. *Family Science*, *6*, 50–57. doi:10.1080/19424620.2015.1080991

Lionetti, F., Pastore, M., & Barone, L. (2015). Parenting stress: The roles of attachment states of mind and parenting alliance in the context of adoption. *Parenting: Science and Practice*, *15*(2), 75–91. doi:10.1080/15295192.2015.1020142

Lipscomb, S. T., Leve, L. D., Harold, G. T., Neiderhiser, J. M., Shaw, D. S., Ge, X., & Reiss, D. (2011). Trajectories of parenting and child negative emotionality during infancy and toddlerhood: A longitudinal analysis. *Child Development*, *82*, 1661–1675. doi:10.1111/j.1467-8624.2011.01639.x

Mainemer, H., Gilman, L. C., & Ames, E. W. (1998). Parenting stress in families adopting children from Romanian orphanages. *Journal of Family Issues*, *19*(2), 164–180. doi:10.1177/019251398019002003

McGlone, K., Santos, L., Kazama, L., Fong, R., & Mueller, C. (2002). Psychological stress in adoptive parents of special-needs children. *Child Welfare*, *81*, 151–171.

McGoldrick, M., & Carter, B. (2003). The family life cycle. In F. Walsh (Ed.), *Normal family processes: Growing diversity and complexity* (3rd ed., pp. 375–398). New York: Guilford Press.

Moyer, A. M., & Goldberg, A. (2015). "We were not planning on this, but …": Adoptive parents' reactions and adaptations to unmet expectations. *Child Family Social Work*, *2*, 1–10. doi:10.1111/cfs.12219

Neece, C. L., Green, S. A., & Baker, B. L. (2012). Parenting stress and child behavior problems: A transactional relationship across time. *American Journal on Intellectual and Developmental Disabilities*, *117*, 48–66. doi:10.1352/1944-7558-117.1.48

O'Dell, K. E., McCall, R. B., & Groark, C. J. (2015). Supporting families throughout the international special needs adoption process. *Children and Youth Services Review*, *59*, 161–170. doi:10.1016/j.childyouth.2015.11.008

Palacios, J., & Sánchez-Sandoval, Y. (2005). Beyond adopted/non-adopted comparisons. In D. M. Brodzinsky & J. Palacios (Eds.), *Psychological issues in adoption: Research and practice* (pp. 117–144). Westport, CT: Greenwood.

Palacios, J., & Sánchez-Sandoval, Y. (2006). Stress in parents of adopted children. *International Journal of Behavioral Development*, *30*, 481–487. doi:10.1177/0165025406071492

Pesonen, A., Räikkönen, K., Heinonen, K., Komsi, N., Järvenpää, A., & Strandberg, T. (2008). A transactional model of temperamental development: Evidence of a relationship between child temperament and maternal stress over five years. *Social Development*, *17*(2), 326–340. doi:10.1111/j.1467-9507.2007.00427.x

Reilly, T., & Platz, L. (2003). Characteristics and challenges of families who adopt children with special needs: An empirical study. *Children and Youth Services Review*, *25*, 781–803. doi:10.1016/S0190-7409(03)00079-3

Rijk, C. M., Hoksbergen, R. C., Ter Laak, J. F., van Dijkum, C., & Robbroeckx, L. M. (2006). Parents who adopt deprived children have a difficult task. *Adoption Quarterly*, *9*(2–3), 37–61. doi:10.1300/J145v09n02_03

Román, M., & Palacios, J. (2011). Separación, pérdida y nuevas vinculaciones: El apego en la adopción. *Acción Psicológica*, *8*(2), 99–111. doi:10.5944/ap.8.2.446

Rosnati, R., Montirosso, R., & Barni, D. (2008). Behavioral and emotional problems among Italian international adoptees and non-adopted children: Father's and mother's reports. *Journal of Family Psychology*, *22*(4), 541–549. doi:10.1037/0893-3200.22.3.541

Rosnati, R., Ranieri, S., & Barni, D. (2013). Family and social relationships and psychosocial well-being in Italian families with internationally adopted and non-adopted children. *Adoption Quarterly*, *16*, 1–16. doi:10.1080/10926755.2012.731030

Salcuni, S., Miconi, D., Altoè, G., & Moscardino, U. (2015). Dyadic adjustment and parenting stress in internationally adoptive mothers and fathers: The mediating role of adult attachment dimensions. *Frontiers in Psychology*, *6*(1279), 1–10. doi:10.3389/fpsyg.2015.01279

Sánchez-Sandoval, Y., & Palacios, J. (2012). Stress in adoptive parents of adolescents. *Children and Youth Services Review*, *34*, 1283–1289. doi:10.1016/j.childyouth.2012.03.002

Santos-Nunes, M., Narciso, I., Vieira-Santos, S., & Roberto, M. S. (2017). Parenting and emotional well-being of adoptive school-aged children: The mediating role of attachment. *Children & Youth Services Review*, *81*, 390–399. doi:10.1016/j.childyouth.2017.08.026

Santos-Nunes, M., Narciso, I., Vieira-Santos, S., & Roberto, M. S. (2018a). Adoptive parents' evaluation of expectations and children's behavior problems: The mediational role of parenting stress and parental satisfaction. *Children & Youth Services Review*, *88*, 11–17. doi:10.1016/j.childyouth.2018.02.044

Santos-Nunes, M., Narciso, I., Vieira-Santos, S., & Roberto, M. S. (2018b). Adoptive versus mixed families: Child adjustment, parenting stress and family environment. *Journal of Child & Family Studies*, *27*(6), 1858–1869. doi:10.1007/s10826-018-1019-2

Schank, R. C., & Berman, T. R. (2002). The pervasive role of stories in knowledge and action. In M. C. Green, J. J. Strange, & T. C. Brock (Eds.), *Narrative impact: Social and cognitive foundations* (pp. 287–313). Mahwah, NJ: Lawrence Erlbaum.

Stokes, L. D., & Poulsen, S. S. (2014). Narrative therapy for adoption issues in families, couples, and individuals: Rationale and approach. *Journal of Family Psychotherapy*, *25*(4), 330–347. doi:10.1080/08975353.2014.977681

Tan, T. X., Camras, L. A., Deng, H., Zhang, M., & Lu, Z. (2012). Family stress, parenting styles, and behavioral adjustment in preschool-age adopted Chinese girls. *Early Childhood Research Quarterly*, *27*(1), 128–136. doi:10.1016/j.ecresq.2011.04.002

Tan, T. X., & Marfo, K. (2016). Pre-adoption adversity and behavior problems in adopted Chinese children: A longitudinal study. *Journal of Applied Developmental Psychology*, *42*, 49–57. doi:10.1016/j.appdev.2015.11.006

Tharner, A., Luijk, M. M., van IJzendoorn, M. H., Bakermans-Kranenburg, M. J., Jaddoe, V. V., Hofman, A., … Tiemeier, H. (2012). Infant attachment, parenting stress, and child emotional and behavioral problems at age 3 years. *Parenting: Science and Practice*, *12*(4), 261–281. doi:10.1080/15295192.2012.709150

Viana, A. G., & Welsh, J. A. (2010). Correlates and predictors of parenting stress among internationally adopting mothers: A longitudinal investigation. *International Journal of Behavioral Development*, *34*, 363–373. doi:10.1177/0165025409339403

Waid, J., & Alewine, E. (2018). An exploration of family challenges and service needs during the post-adoption period. *Children & Youth Services Review*, *91*, 213–220. doi:10.1016/j.childyouth.2018.06.017

Ward, M. (1997). Family paradigms and older-child adoption: A proposal for matching parents' strengths to children's needs. *Family Relations*, *46*(3), 257–262. doi:10.2307/585123

Watson, D., & Tellegen, A. (1985). Toward a consensual structure of mood. *Psychological Bulletin*, *98*, 219–235. doi:10.1037/0033-2909.98.2.219

Welsh, J. A., Viana, A. G., Petrill, S. A., & Mathias, M. D. (2008). Ready to adopt: Characteristics and expectations of preadoptive families pursuing international adoptions. *Adoption Quarterly*, *11*(3), 176–203. doi:10.1080/10926750802421

White, M., & Epston, D. (1990). *Narrative means to therapeutic ends*. New York: W.W. Norton & Company.

Woodman, A. C., Mawdsley, H. P., & Hauser-Cram, P. (2015). Parenting stress and child behavior problems within families of children with developmental disabilities: Transactional relations across 15 years. *Research in Developmental Disabilities*, *36*, 264–276. doi:10.1016/j.ridd.2014.10.011

30
ADOPTION INSTABILITY, ADOPTION BREAKDOWN

Jesús Palacios

Compared to other child protection alternatives, permanence is the feature that characterizes adoption. Adoption involves a permanent change for the adopters, who forever become the new parents of a child; and the child, through adoption and for the rest of his or her life, acquires a new permanent filiation. According to Brodzinsky and Smith (2019), adoption permanence encompasses legal permanence (adoptive parents have full authority and responsibility for their adopted children), residential permanence (stability in the adoptive placement), and relational permanence (feelings of attachment, commitment, and belonging). In fact, most adoptions are characterized by these permanent links between the adoptive parents and the child. While adoption can refer to different family configurations (e.g., single or dual parents, one or more children), permanence is always at its very heart.

This chapter refers to those cases in which adoption fails to achieve full permanence and the connection between adopters and adoptees becomes unstable, at times ending in permanent breakdown. First, different levels of adoption instability and different types of breakdown are considered. Research difficulties in the identification and analysis of cases of instability and breakdown will be analyzed. Although not always fully consistent, the accumulated research on the topic has provided a good amount of information regarding the incidence and causes of adoption breakdown, while less research has been devoted to adoption instability. The chapter will conclude with a reference to policy and practice implications derived from the existing knowledge on the topic.

Permanence, instability, breakdown

The pathway leading to legal, residential, and relational adoption permanence as described by Brodzinsky and Smith (2019) is shown on the left side of Figure 30.1. Some of the children in need of out-of-home care are legally declared to be adoptable, which implies termination of parental rights and the possibility of acquiring new legal parents. Once suitable parents have been identified and matched with the child, life together starts, typically in a pre-adoption arrangement. In most cases, the relationships between the parents and the child are considered satisfactory, and the case is taken to court for completion of procedures declaring the permanent legal binding between them. The adoption is then legally finalized. Family life continues thereafter as in any other family, with some days better than others, but with an unquestioned permanence of the links and relationships.

This chapter refers to the right side of Figure 30.1, those cases where the relationships unfold more negatively, and permanence is difficult or not achieved. Conflicts and difficulties could manifest once life together starts, but before finalization of the legal procedures. In those cases, the child leaves the home and re-enters the care system with the expectation of a new family providing a better and more satisfactory fit. These are cases known as adoption disruption (USA terminology) or pre-order disruption (UK terminology).

In other cases, problems and dissatisfaction manifest or exacerbate after the case is legally finalized. In some instances, relationships in the adoptive family are difficult or very difficult, but residential permanence is not at risk, and the legal permanence is unquestioned. The level of instability within the family could be more or less intense and chronic, but the child remains in the family. In other cases, when the conflicts reach an undesirable level, the child could eventually leave the adoptive home with at least three possibilities depicted in the lower right section of Figure 30.1:

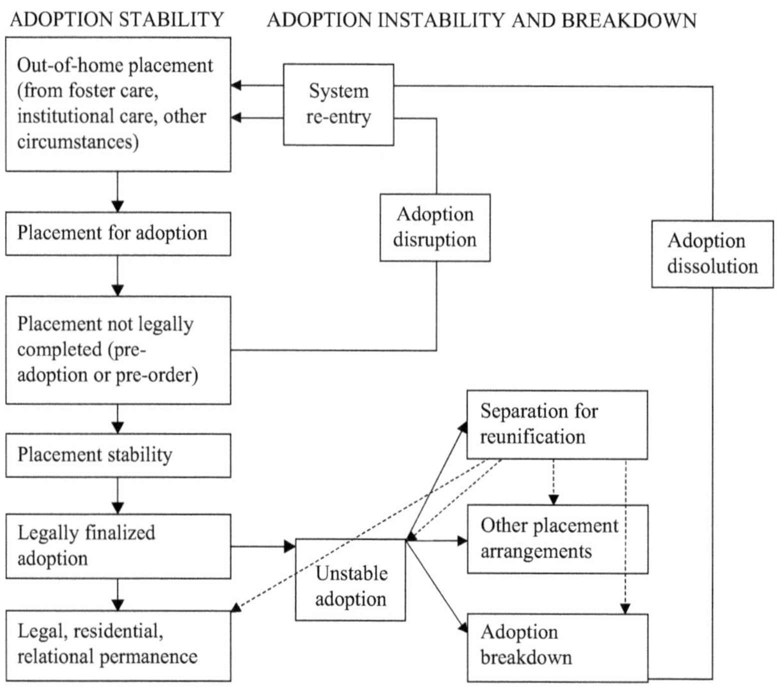

Figure 30.1 Adoption permanence, instability, and breakdown

- *Separation for reunification.* The separation could be temporary while intervention takes place to improve the relationships and make the child's return home possible. In these cases, relational permanence is questioned and residential permanence is interrupted, while legal permanence remains untouched. If the relationships improve, the child may eventually return home permanently.
- *Other placement arrangements.* In other cases, as well as in some cases of separation not ending in reunification, the child could be placed elsewhere as a long-term option, perhaps with a neighbor or relative, perhaps with strangers or in a boarding school. In these cases, parent–child relationships are very problematic or broken. There is a change of residence and reunification is not pursued, but the legal status of the child as being adopted does not change, perhaps because all the new arrangements were made privately, without involvement of child protection services.
- *Adoption breakdown.* Finally, there are cases – which could include the previous categories when known by protective services – where the legal adoption binding is finally cancelled and the child re-enters the system, with the possibility of a new adoption. These are adoption dissolutions (USA terminology) or post-order disruptions (UK terminology).

All the previous distinctions help us understand that adoption permanence is not a yes-or-no matter. Some adoption placements function successfully; others need to be interrupted due to a critical accumulation of problems and difficulties. The space between these two extremes is wide and full of nuance, including cases where the relationships are very problematic, but the residential and legal permanence are not questioned, and others in which the residential and legal permanence have come to an end, but where some level of positive relationships are maintained. So far, the research literature on adoption breakdown has focused almost exclusively on those cases where all levels of permanence have ended, with less attention paid to those where the relationships are at risk but maintained at certain levels.

The proliferation of publications reviewing the existing literature on adoption breakdown (Faulkner, Adkins, Fong, & Rolock, 2017; Festinger, 2014; Palacios, Rolock, Selwyn, & Barbosa-Ducharne, 2019; Rosnati, Ranieri, & Ferrari, 2017; White, 2016) indicates the importance of the problem and the existence of a significant number of empirical studies. In comparison, studies with the broader view of adoption instability have been far scarcer (Smith, 2014). There is agreement that the scarcity is related to the difficulty of researching adoption instability and breakdown.

Conceptual and methodological difficulties

As reviewed by Palacios, Rolock et al. (2019), a rich variety of terms has been proposed to refer to adoptions with permanence problems. The older terms (e.g., "failed adoptions") reflected a "forbidding sense of finality and doom" (Donley, 1978, p. 34), while other more recent terms emphasize the instability or discontinuity of post-adoption relationships (Rolock, 2015; Smith, 2014). While older approaches depicted a yes/no picture of success versus failure, more recent terms lend themselves to the continuum of adoption permanence. The term adoption breakdown is often chosen to reflect the fact that most empirical studies refer to cases in which adopted children re-enter the child protective system and could eventually be adopted by another family. The choice of one term over another is not mainly a matter of the researchers' personal preference, but refers to different realities and experiences, as reflected in the following section.

In terms of empirical research, the two main obstacles to studying unstable adoptions are case identification and access to relevant information of the identified cases. Obviously, only cases that have been identified can be counted and analyzed. However, the cases known to the researchers are typically those that have come to the knowledge of the agencies or systems involved. More likely, these will be instances of system re-entry either at the pre-adoption or the post-adoption stage as depicted in Figure 30.1. Cases where the family is struggling with serious difficulty in the relationships without seeking help, as well as those where help is sought from private providers, probably remain unknown. Similarly, those with private arrangements (from informally placing the child in another family to sending her or him to a boarding school or any similar arrangement, often with little or no contact between adopters and adoptee) will probably not come to agency or children's protective system's attention. An obvious implication is that the reported incidence of problematic adoptions typically reflects only the most extreme cases and, of those, only the ones known by the agencies or the child protective system.

Once a case has been identified, accessing the relevant information is also a complicated task. For instance, administrative data sets typically allow only for what Brodzinsky and Smith (2019) describe as a "broad stroke" perspective, reflecting at times little more than changes of placement and dates. Qualitative case analysis is compromised by the difficulty gaining access to the files, as well as by the quality of the recorded information. Whereas some information is usually available (e.g., the child's age at placement), other relevant circumstances (e.g., adopters' expectations at the time of adoption application or quality of attachment relationships) tend not to be recorded. Although some researchers are now beginning to interview those unstable adoptive families involved in serious difficulties (e.g., Selwyn, 2019), their subjective perspectives are usually not included.

Finally, research designs are very diverse and provide avenues for different types of conclusions. Prospective studies of children in care, such as the Longitudinal Studies on Child Abuse and Neglect (LONGSCAN) are unusual, but very informative (see below). Studying adopted youngsters in group treatment informs about a selected group of those for whom family reunification is perhaps being pursued (Brodzinsky, Santa, & Smith, 2016). For adoption breakdown, some studies consider only disruptions during the pre-adoption placement, others only legally finalized cases, while others consider both. Some studies refer only to domestic or to intercountry adoptions, as well as some that study only specific types of adoption (e.g., special needs), and more that consider any type of adoption. Matched designs comparing intact and disrupted cases (Barbosa-Ducharne & Marinho, 2019) convey information very differently than studies derived from agency surveys (Donaldson Adoption Institute, 2004), to mention just two possibilities. Palacios, Rolock et al. (2019) have analyzed the diversity of research designs and the implications for the reported incidence and causes of adoption instability discussed in the two following sections.

How many cases of adoption instability or breakdown?

Given the identification of cases is problematic, reported incidence rates must be taken as an approximation of a more complex reality. To illustrate this, the adoption instability survey of 15 child welfare systems in the United States by the Donaldson Adoption Institute (2004) found a lack of common definitions of disruption and dissolution, inadequate management of information systems, and failure of overworked staff to collect and/or enter the data. The reported incidence typically reflects the source of information, the composition of the sample, and the duration of the study. As indicated by Festinger (2014), global incidence rates are misleading, as they represent a composite of many rates that differ from one study to another depending on each study's characteristics. For all the reasons discussed, instability and breakdown rates underestimate the magnitude of the problem.

Adoption instability

Reporting the incidence of adoption instability is even more difficult than reporting the incidence of adoption breakdown, as the latter group – even in its heterogeneity – is more homogeneous than the former. As explained before, adoption instability could refer to children who remain in the adoptive home amid very significant relational problems, or to those who are temporarily living outside the adoptive home perhaps with a reunification plan, or to those for whom only legal permanence remains, in the absence of residential and relational permanence. Reporting a global incidence rate is even more misleading here than in the case of adoption breakdown.

According to Maza's (2014) national study, in the US around 20–30 percent of youth adopted from foster care face significant challenges, some of which could require therapeutic intervention. From the available information, it is not possible to determine the proportion of cases where the placement is at risk due to such challenges. In Maza's (2014) data, approximately 10 percent of additional cases re-enter care at some point through the child protective system, with one-quarter to one-third of them ending in adoption dissolution. This indicates that the percentage of adoption dissolution is only a small portion of the cases experiencing some level of instability. Moreover, another 10 percent of cases experiencing difficulty might leave the adoptive home for either short- or long-term periods other than through the welfare system.

The use of mental health services by adopted children and youth cannot be assumed to involve family instability. However, it is worth remembering that the use of mental health services by children adopted out of the foster care system is much higher than in the general population of children: 37 percent versus less than 10 percent, according to Zill and Bramlet (2014). It is also worth remembering that, although most adopted adolescents are psychologically healthy, they might be at elevated risk for some externalizing disorders. According to Keyes, Sharma, Elkins, Iacono, and McGue (2008), being adopted approximately doubled the odds of having contact with a mental health professional, mainly in connection with disruptive behavior, especially among domestic adoptees. It is probably in these circumstances that some adoptive families might consider the possibility of out-of-home placement. Research has shown that adopted children are over-represented in residential care. For the US, clinical program directors from 59 residential treatment facilities surveyed by Brodzinsky et al. (2016) reported adopted youth to be over-represented in these programs: although they only represent 2–3 percent of the US general child population, 25–30 percent of the enrolled youngsters were adopted.

As shown in the right lower section of Figure 30.1, the use of out-of-home placement can have different outcomes. Some children might return home permanently, while others might return home just to confirm the persistence of the relational difficulties, and still others might simply not return home, with different alternatives explored, including reunification with birth parents, once residential placement ends (Maza, 2014).

Different sources of information indicate that adoption instability increases with time. According to Rolock and Testa (2008), at two years post-finalization about 2 percent of adoptions had experienced discontinuity, 4 percent at five years, and 9 percent at ten years. Research has also shown that the probability of instability for adopted children increases after age 11 (Maza, 2014). This increase of instability is clearly illustrated by the information from LONGSCAN, a multi-site longitudinal study analyzing the antecedents and consequences of child maltreatment in five US sites representing varying levels and types of risk and exposure to maltreatment. The LONGSCAN samples were recruited at ages 4 and 6 years and followed at regularly scheduled intervals (ages 6, 8, 12, 14, 16, and 18). Evidence about adoption instability (defined as change of primary caregiver) has been reported for the San Diego site, which, according to the researchers (Litrownik, Proctor, & Yeh, 2018) represents the most extreme level of risk. At ages 6 and 8, the adopted group had a very low rate of instability at 2.3 percent (Proctor et al., 2011). However, at age 14 the rate increased to 11.4 percent, as only 88.6 percent of the adoptees were living with the same primary caregiver (Villodas, Litrownik, Newton, & Davis, 2016). This increased to almost 30 percent at age 16 and to almost 50 percent at age 18 (Litrownik et al., 2018). The authors are quite cautious regarding the generalization of the San Diego findings, which might not be valid for the other sites in the LONGSCAN study. In addition, they are prudent with the interpretation of the 50 percent instability at age 18, since living independently at this age is relatively frequent in the US (Litrownik & Villodas, personal communication, January 17, 2019).

Adoption breakdown

As analyzed by Palacios, Rolock et al. (2019), reviews of incidence rates for adoption breakdown offer a wide range of estimates: 10 to 50 percent (Rushton, 2004); 10 to 25 percent (Child Welfare Information Gateway, 2012); 10 to 27 percent (Donaldson Adoption Institute, 2004); and 10 to 20 percent (Berry, 1997). Each reported rate reflects a part of the heterogeneous reality of adoption breakdown, as illustrated with the following two examples. A study of US cases where breakdown occurred during the process of leaving the country of origin to being administratively settled in the US reported an incidence of 1 percent for disruptions and dissolutions (US Government Accountability Office [GAO], 2015). Obviously, this small percentage only reflects what happened while the paperwork was being processed, telling nothing about what happens thereafter. On the other extreme, Rushton and Dance (2006) report a 23 percent disruption rate in a group of children placed for adoption at an average age of 8.8 years, after a very troubled care trajectory and with a high level of behavioral disturbances. In this case, generalizations from the sample to the majority of adoption placements would be problematic.

Research reviews and studies looking into wider samples can provide a better estimate of adoption breakdown incidence than more specific individual studies. This is more feasible for the US than for other parts of the world, since more research has been devoted to the problem. Summarizing studies published since the early 1990s, Coakley and Berrick (2008) estimated a breakdown incidence of 6 to 11 percent before legal finalization. A study cited by the Donaldson Adoption Institute (2004), with information from 21 states, reported a breakdown rate of 5 percent before legal finalization (disruption) and 1 percent after legal finalization (dissolution). The data reported in Smith (2014) summarize the overall picture for the United States in recent years: 9.5 percent adoption disruptions and 2.2 percent adoption dissolutions.

Information from other parts of the world is less abundant, apart from the UK. In their review of studies, Selwyn, Meakings, and Wijedasa (2015) report a 3–10 percent pre-order (disruptions, in the US terminology) and 4–6 percent post-order disruptions (US dissolutions) for the UK. In their own study of post-order breakdown in the UK, the incidence was similarly 3.2 percent. Information from other European countries is more limited. For pre-legalized adoptions, data from Portugal indicate a breakdown rate of 5.8 percent (Barbosa-Ducharne & Marinho, 2019). In Holland, Hoksbergen (1991) identified 5.7 percent of all intercountry adoptees (i.e., already finalized adoptions) were placed in residential care, but indicated that around 50 percent might eventually return to the adoptive family. The Swedish study by Elmund, Lindblad, Vinnerljung, and Hjern (2007) also referred to placement in residential or family care for 4 percent of intercountry adoptees, some of which might eventually return to the care of their adoptive parents. In Spain, Palacios, Jiménez-Morago, and Paniagua (2015) identified a 2 percent breakdown incidence for domestic adoptions (including both pre- and post-finalized placements) and 0.3 percent for intercountry adoptions.

In summary, the information obtained from different European countries suggests an incidence of adoption breakdown that in some cases is similar to the US data, and in other cases is lower. It is not possible to discern if the reported percentages are lower because the real incidence of the problem is lower in some countries, or because the ability to keep track of the breakdown cases is poorer.

Although the available information is limited, data reported by some researchers indicate that a certain percentage of the children whose adoptions broke down were successfully adopted into another family. In her review of studies during the 1970s and 1980s, Festinger (2014) refers to percentages of new adoptions ranging from 40 to 90 percent of the cases. In her national study of post-adoption instability, Maza (2014) reports that the majority (60.5 percent) of children with dissolved adoptions were adopted again. Even if some of these new placements are not successful, as research cited by Festinger (2014) suggests, most seem stable.

Three observations can be offered to conclude this section on incidence rates. First, even if we know that the rates reported for adoption instability and breakdown underestimate the real incidence of the problem, it still seems safe to conclude that the great majority of adoption placements achieve the goal of legal, residential, and relational permanence as characterized by Brodzinsky and Smith (2019). Second, it seems equally important not to underestimate the importance of the problem. The fact that almost one in every ten adoption placements disrupts (Smith, 2014) indicates that the known cases involved are not exceptional. Finally, the fact that a significant proportion of the children with a breakdown experience are later adopted successfully in another family tells that they were not "impossible" cases and that perhaps the previous failure could have been avoided.

Causes of adoption instability and breakdown

In the previous sections a distinction has been made between instability (i.e., adoption placements at different levels of risk for maintaining permanence) and breakdown (i.e., when the adoption has ended) for definitions and incidence. Research exploring the causes of adoption instability and adoption breakdown tends to report similar findings for all cases, irrespective of the final outcome, and this section will make no distinction. Why some placements end before and others after legal finalization of the adoption might be a matter of when the problems manifest, or their intensity, to what extent attempts are made to avoid the separation, differing thresholds of parental commitment, or other causes, but the main factors associated with significant difficulties in the adoptive families seem to be the same.

Research consistently indicates that rather than being a consequence of a particular problem, adoption instability and breakdown are the results of a critical accumulation of risk factors. More specifically, all research reviews agree that these risk factors reside in three different domains: the child, the adopters and family life, and the support and services involved (Faulkner et al., 2017; Festinger, 2014; Palacios, Rolock et al., 2019; Rosnati et al., 2017; Smith, 2014). The highest level of consensus refers to children's characteristics, but this is probably the consequence of a methodological problem. Each empirical study involving adopted children is different and covers different variables, particularly in the case of parents and support and service variables. For example, some researchers consider parental expectations regarding their adoption (e.g., Randall, 2013), while others focus on parents' commitment to the child (e.g., Dance & Rushton, 2005). However, all the studies take account of some basic characteristics of the children involved, such as age at placement. It is then inevitable that the highest level of consensus is with the child characteristics which are covered in most studies, but this should not be taken to necessarily mean that the other factors are less relevant.

Child characteristics

Since the beginning of adoption breakdown research to the present, all studies and research reviews mention an older age at placement as the most salient characteristic of the children involved in adoption instability and breakdown (e.g., Child Welfare Information Gateway, 2012; Coakley & Berrick, 2008; Donaldson Adoption Institute, 2004; Faulkner et al., 2017; Festinger, 2014; Rushton, 2004; Smith, 2014). As summarized by Palacios, Rolock et al. (2019) this is true for any type of adoption, domestic or intercountry, special or non-special needs. A later age at adoption is typically associated with a longer exposure to previous adversities, to more separations and distrust, as well as to more emotional and behavioral dysregulation, and it is not age per se but these enhanced difficulties that interfere with the stability of the placement. Although it is critically important to highlight the fact that most late adoptions are stable (e.g., Rushton & Dance, 2006), the association between older age at placement and a higher probability of breakdown cannot be ignored.

Regarding the child's age, research also consistently indicates that adolescence seems to be a critical time for the stability of adoption placements, as shown in the LONGSCAN data mentioned before (Litrownik et al., 2018). In fact, several studies report ages 13–14 years as the average age when adoptees leave their families (Maza, 2014; Palacios et al., 2015; Rolock & White, 2016; Selwyn et al., 2015). Since research also indicates that children leave the family after an average of five or six years together (Palacios et al., 2015; Selwyn et al., 2015), the implication is that the problems leading to breakdown were there before adolescence and exacerbated in this complicated developmental transition.

A second child-related characteristic systematically associated with instability and breakdown is the presence of behavioral and emotional problems. The research by Selwyn et al. (2015) nicely shows that some of these difficulties are more likely to start in the initial stages of the placement, while others are more often associated with the transition into adolescence. In this particular study, problems with early onset included difficulties with forming close attachments, manipulation and control, anger and aggression, mood and self-esteem problems, inappropriate sexual behaviors, and thinking and learning problems. The difficulties starting or escalating during adolescence included anger, aggression, violence within the adoptive home, oppositional behavior, running away, criminal offences, and sexualized behaviors. Significant levels of family violence were also described in Palacios et al. (2015), more often from children to parents, but also from parents to children or between children in the family.

Among emotional problems, difficulties in forming attachment relationships have been mentioned by different researchers (e.g., Paniagua, Palacios, Jiménez-Morago, & Rivera, 2019; Selwyn et al., 2015). These difficulties can be associated with problematic initial attachment experiences, but also with an accumulation of previous separations and relational disruptions. Previous instability increases the risk of new instability, probably in connection with learned distrust of adults and fear of new emotional commitments (Palacios, Rolock et al., 2019). Although all these experiences are of clear relevance, it is always important to remember that attachment is a relational construction and that the parents' capacity for attachment relationships need also to be taken into account, as discussed below.

Finally, although research consistently indicates that domestic adoptions are less stable than international adoptions, there is also evidence indicating that international adoptions break down more rapidly than domestic adoptions (Paniagua et al., 2019). The latter might be in part due to the fact that some domestic adoptions were initially foster care placements later converted into adoptions, which inevitably means longer time in the family.

Research findings have been more mixed regarding other child-related factors associated with instability. This has been the case with type of maltreatment before separation from the birth family, sibling adoption, gender, and race. While some studies, for example, have reported more instability in the case of sibling adoptions (Smith, Howard, Garnier, & Ryan, 2006), others had opposite findings (Rolock & White, 2016). A way to interpret these contradictory findings is that other factors besides sibling placement per se might be involved, such as the composition of the household where the siblings are placed, the presence of biological children in the house, and the ages of the children involved (Donaldson Adoption Institute, 2004; Festinger, 2014; Selwyn, 2019).

Adoptive parents and family life

In contrast to child's age at placement – an easy and straightforward quantitative variable – adoptive parent and family life factors (e.g., prospective adopters' motivation and expectations before adoption) are more difficult to assess and less often present in the literature. It is not surprising that, in comparison with child-related factors, research into adopters' characteristics associated with adoption difficulties has provided results that are more varied and where the link with breakdown is statistically weaker. However, a few traits of the adoptive parents and adoptive family life after placement are often present in empirical studies. It is important to remember that any of the following highlighted characteristics are normally critical only in the context of other risk circumstances of the child and support services provided, and should always be interpreted within the framework of the accumulation of risk factors model. Palacios, Rolock et al. (2019) provided a detailed synthesis of the main research findings which guides the following discussion.

Prospective adopters' motivation and expectations are two parent characteristics explored by some researchers in connection with adoption placement difficulties. Motivation issues involve a predominance of adult-centered ideas ("we need to expand our family," "we need to give love") over child-centered ones (a child in need of a permanent family) (Palacios et al., 2015). Problems with expectations typically involve idealized views of parents' own abilities, family life, or the to-be-adopted child. The latter might be facilitated by lack of accurate information provided to parents about the child at the time of placement, an issue to be discussed later in this chapter (Paniagua et al., 2019; Randall, 2013; Smith, 2014).

Deficiencies in parenting ability to deal with difficult child characteristics has also been related to instability and breakdown, even if the identified specific abilities differ from one study to another. Identified parenting abilities include: parents' capacity to emotionally distance themselves from the child's problems, their ability to advocate for services for the child, their expectations, and their flexibility (Partridge, Hornby, & McDonald, 1986): flexibility toward the child's needs and self-confidence in their parenting role (Marinho, Barbosa-Ducharne, & McRoy, 2012); warmth, involvement with the child, and parental sensitivity (Dance & Rushton, 2005); and parental inability to cope with children's problematic behavior (Maza, 2014).

Parents' attachment capacity has also been identified as related to instability and breakdown. As mentioned before, the child's attachment behaviors might be more problematic due to previous experiences of disturbed emotional relationships and separations. In these circumstances, parents' emotional capacity and behavior are even more important than with less problematic children. Research has also documented the importance of the internal working models of attachment of adoptive parents – a product of their own attachment history – with a significant concordance between their own models and the adopted child's internal working models (Pace, Di Folco, Guerreiro, Santona, & Terrone, 2015).

Research has also documented connections between attachment relationships and parental commitment to the child. In a study by Rushton, Mayes, Dance, and Quinton (2003), when adoptive mothers felt that they were getting something back from their child, they were more likely to develop an attachment and remain committed despite the difficulties. Highlighting the interconnected nature of all these processes, especially the positive association between attachment and commitment to the child, Testa, Snyder, Wu, Rolock, and Liao (2014) reported that as adoptive parents' rating of difficulties increases, so do their thoughts about ending the adoptive relationship, which, mediated by the level of parental commitment, is a predictor of breakdown.

The parent's social network, as well as the availability of adoption support services (to be discussed below), has also been mentioned as part of the context where problems might not be solved. As with other families, research has identified a social support network (family, friends, resources in the community, other adoptive parents) to be associated with placement stability (Marinho et al., 2012; McRoy, 1999; Randall, 2013). Obviously, this social network is useful only if adoptive parents are willing to seek help when in trouble. Perhaps because of their fear of being blamed for the difficulties, of seeing their child removed from the family, or experiences of ineffective support when requested, very often adoptive parents contact child protection services when it is already too late: the relationship has already broken down and little can be done except for protective services to take over responsibility for the child's care.

Amid all the previous risk factors, establishing a relationship with the child before the adoption plan is implemented has frequently appeared in research as a protective factor. When parents and child have been living together for some time before considering adoption (typically, in a foster care placement converted to adoption), the emotional bond might be already there, parental expectations might be better adjusted to the child's characteristics, and the parents are committed to continue parenting the child. All these circumstances might help to explain why adoption by "known" parents seems to have more stability (e.g., McRoy, 1999). Adoptions by relatives might be more stable for the same reason (e.g., Smith et al., 2006).

Other parent variables have produced mixed findings, with some but not all indicating their relevance. Some of the characteristics with mixed evidence include parents' age, socioeconomic status, and length of marital relationships (Palacios et al., 2019).

Support and services

Research covering support and service factors associated with adoption instability and breakdown is even more scarce and heterogeneous than in the case of parent and family life characteristics. Some of these characteristics are mentioned often but explored more rarely.

Pre-placement professional activities, such as prospective adopters' preparation, suitability assessment, and matching, are now mandatory in most jurisdictions. While it seems quite reasonable to think that superficial and naive assessments, nonexistent or poor preparation, and matching errors pave the way for later problems, the research evidence is very limited. Virtually nothing is known about the characteristics of the suitability assessment of parents whose adoptions did not develop well. There is little evidence about the content and role of adoption preparation (Palacios, Sánchez-Sandoval, & León, 2005). The same is true concerning risky matches, such as misjudging the balance between the child's difficulties and the adopters' strengths, as well as lack of consideration of the ages and age-order of the children involved when adopted children are added to those already in the family (Barbosa-Ducharne & Marinho, 2019; McRoy, 1999).

Failure to share and explain information about the child has been identified as a risk factor in some studies that have emphasized the importance of honest and accurate pre-placement information about the child (Barbosa-Ducharne & Marinho, 2019; Randall, 2013). In fact, there are cases where the parents learn important information (e.g., child's sexual abuse) only when the child is placed with them (Barth & Berry, 1988). Perhaps the caseworkers ignored this information, or maybe they failed to communicate it at the right moment or in a meaningful way, or perhaps the problem was more on the side of the adopters – who did not hear what they were told – than with the adoption professionals (Barth & Berry, 1988; Selwyn et al., 2015).

Once the child has been placed, new circumstances can add risks and problems. Since, as discussed above, difficulties tend to start sooner rather than later, early detection is of critical importance. The identification of problems can be jeopardized by lack of willingness on the part of adoptive parents to engage supportive services in an attempt to avoid being identified as failure cases with possible removal of the child from the family, or to avoid being blamed for the difficulties they face, or frustrated by a lack of recognition of the importance of their problems (Rushton, 2004). In addition, professionals can misinterpret problems as "typical of the adaptation stage," expecting a "normalization" with time that does not happen (Palacios et al., 2015).

To make things less optimistic, post-adoption services are in place "rarely and irregularly" (Barth & Miller, 2000, p. 449). In fact, for those adopting children out of the foster care system, the support they receive after adoption has been described as lower than when in foster care (Festinger, 2014), while the child's problems might have increased with age rather than diminished. In fact, Berry, Propp, and Martens (2007) showed that the importance of available post-adoption support for achieving permanence increases with time after placement.

When professional support is available, staff discontinuities, as well as the existence of fragmented responsibilities and services, are of little help for troubled families (Barbosa-Ducharne & Marinho, 2019; Donaldson Adoption Institute, 2004). Also, the quality of the mental health services offered is often very problematic (Randall, 2013; Selwyn et al., 2015), and there is a clear mismatch between the problems faced and the amount and quality of the support provided, which is often limited to well-intended advice and counseling (Palacios et al., 2015). On the contrary, the use of professionals with more experience in the field of adoption is related to a lower breakdown risk (Smith et al., 2006).

To conclude this section, it is important to remember that none of the factors analyzed in this section are per se determinant for adoption instability. The placement of a 10-year-old child with disturbing behaviors with highly skilled and committed parents who are well supported by adoption caseworkers; a resilient child placed with less competent and more poorly supported parents; or poor or ineffective support services in the case of families who manage to handle the difficulties, are all examples illustrating the fact that instability and breakdown are not the consequence of any isolated characteristic, but rather of an undesirable accumulation of risk factors in the child, the parents, and the adoption services.

Policy and practice implications

The accumulated evidence about adoption instability and adoption breakdown summarized in the preceding sections has important implications for policy makers and adoption professionals. These implications are valid for both circumstances, disruptions and dissolutions, and no distinction will be made between them.

Policy implications refer to the regulation of adoption and to the principles governing its enactment. Two of the reported findings reported deserve special mention given their importance for decision-making and planning: age at placement and minimization of placement changes (Palacios, Adroher et al., 2019). Since research is consistent that a later placement age is associated with more risk of instability and breakdown, anything that can be reasonably done to make early placements more likely and more stable should be attempted. Some of the actions to consider include early identification of cases where children's security and well-being are at risk; time-limited efforts to achieve family reunification when it is the initial goal; placement in stable family alternatives rather than in short-term ones; a constant concern for the importance of the passage of time; and the avoidance of undesirable delays in decision-making when children are involved. Whatever leads to earlier and fewer time-limited placements will be in the best interest of the child and will help prevent adoption instability and breakdown.

Regarding adoption practice, some of the actions to consider are prior to the child's placement. Adoption has changed significantly in recent years. For the US, in 2013–2014, 81 percent of the adoptions nationwide involved special needs children (US Children's Bureau, 2016). Are our models of adoption preparation suited to this new reality? Similarly, our current models of adoption suitability assessment pay little attention – if any – to risk factors in the adopters (Lind & Lindgren, 2017), ignoring the fact that risk of instability and breakdown exists. The era when adoption involved young children, with little exposure to trauma, separations, and loss, is long past. Prospective adopters must be informed, prepared and assessed, taking into account the challenges of our current adoptions. They should also be properly informed about the positive and difficult characteristics of the child to be placed with them, so that their expectations are better adjusted to the child. Similarly, all children need preparation for adoption, but particularly when their previous history has involved separations and disruptions. All the lessons learned from research regarding adoption instability and breakdown should be instilled in these pre-placement professional actions (Brodzinsky & Smith, 2019).

Once children are placed in an adoptive family, their needs continue to exist and manifest. Not just the needs of the child, but also those of the whole family. When legal and residential permanence have been achieved, we still need to pay attention to relational permanence. Litrownik et al. (2018) highlight the fact that placing the child in a permanent new family does not assure her or his well-being, and we may add that the well-being of the adoptive family should not be taken for granted. Research has shown that, even if exacerbated at the entrance into adolescence, relational problems tend to start soon and do not just disappear with the passage of time. Early identification of problems is of critical importance. Close monitoring of children and families, identification of problems, and provision of effective support are essential. Not only during the initial post-placement stages, as has tended to be the case, but continuing in the years thereafter, particularly in cases where any element of risk is present.

Professional intervention with adopted children and adoptive families must be fully informed by the specific characteristics of adoption and by the needs of those involved. Brodzinsky and Smith (2019) highlight the fact that the complexities faced by many adoptive families are not understood by most mental health professionals, which translates into inadequate assessment and treatment. Adoption clinical competence (Brodzinsky, 2013) is essential to ensure an efficient response to adoption-specific needs, which typically include trauma, attachment, and behavioral issues, as well as those related to loss, grief, and identity (Brodzinsky & Smith, 2019).

When professional actions informed by all of these principles are in place, adopted children and their families will be better served and the placements will be more likely to achieve the goal of permanence and well-being. Instability and breakdown are not inevitable. The fact that a significant proportion of children with dissolved adoptions achieve stability in a later placement is the best indicator. Although we do not know the circumstances of these new adoptions, the problems the children bring to the new relationship cannot be easier or less complex. Probably, new parents more thoroughly prepared and assessed, assisted by better professional practices, are responding more effectively to their needs. The responsibility is largely on our side.

References

Barbosa-Ducharne, M., & Marinho, S. (2019). Beyond the child's age at placement: Risk and protective factors in pre-adoption breakdown in Portugal. *Research on Social Work Practice, 29*, 143–152. doi:10.1177/1049731518783855

Barth, R., & Berry, M. (1988). *Adoption & disruption: Rates, risks and responses*. Hawthorne, New York: Aldine de Gruyter.

Barth, R., & Miller, J. (2000). Building effective post-adoption services: What is the empirical foundation?. *Family Relations, 49*, 447–455. doi:10.1111/j.1741-3729.2000.00447.x

Berry, M. (1997). Adoption disruption. In R. Avery (Ed.), *Adoption policy and special needs children* (pp. 77–106). Westport, CT: Auburn House.

Berry, M., Propp, J., & Martens, P. (2007). The use of intensive family preservation services with adoptive families. *Child & Family Social Work, 12*, 43–53. doi:10.1111/j.1365-2206.2006.00426.x

Brodzinsky, D. (2013). *A need to know. Enhancing adoption competence among mental health professionals*. New York: Evan B. Donaldson Institute.

Brodzinsky, D., Santa, J., & Smith, S. L. (2016). Adopted youth in residential care: Prevalence rate and professional training needs. *Residential Treatment for Children and Youth, 33*, 118–134. doi:10.1080/0886571X.2016.1175993

Brodzinsky, D., & Smith, S. L. (2019). Commentary: Understanding research, policy and practice issues in adoption instability. *Research on Social Work Practice, 29*, 185–194. doi:10.1177/1049731518782647

Child Welfare Information Gateway. (2012). *Adoption disruption and dissolution*. Washington, DC: Children's Bureau.

Coakley, J. F., & Berrick, J. D. (2008). In a rush to permanency: Preventing adoption disruption. *Child and Family Social Work, 13*, 101–112. doi:10.1111/j.1365-2206.2006.00468.x

Dance, C., & Rushton, A. (2005). Predictors of outcome for unrelated adoptive placements made during middle childhood. *Child and Family Social Work, 10*, 269–280. doi:10.1111/j.1365-2206.2005.00357.x

Donaldson Adoption Institute. (2004). *What's working for children: A policy study of adoption stability and termination.* New York: Author.

Donley, K. (1978). The dynamics of disruption. *Adoption & Fostering, 92*, 34–39. doi:10.1177/030857597809200211

Elmund, A., Lindblad, F., Vinnerljung, B., & Hjern, A. (2007). Intercountry adoptees in out-of-home care: A national cohort study. *Acta Paediatrica, 96*, 437–442. doi:10.1111/j.1651-2227.2006.00149.x

Faulkner, M., Adkins, T., Fong, R., & Rolock, N. (2017). *Risk and protective factors for discontinuity in public adoption and guardianship: A review of the literature.* Southfield, MI: National Quality Improvement Center for Adoption and Guardianship Support and Preservation.

Festinger, T. (2014). Adoption disruption. In G. P. Mallon & P. M. Hess (Eds.), *Child welfare for the 21st century: A handbook of practices, policies, and programs* (2nd ed., pp. 437–454). New York: Columbia University Press.

Hjern, A., Vinnerljung, B., & Brännströn, L. (in press). Outcomes in adulthood after long-term foster care: A sibling study. *Developmental Child Welfare, 1*, 61–75.

Hoksbergen, R. A. C. (1991). Understanding and preventing "failing adoptions.". In E. D. Hibbs (Ed.), *Adoption: International perspectives* (pp. 265–278). Madison, CT: International University Press.

Keyes, M. A., Sharma, A., Elkins, I. J., Iacono, W. G., & McGue, M. (2008). The mental health of US adolescents adopted in infancy. *Archives of Pediatric Adolescent Medicine, 162*, 419–425. doi:10.1001/archpedi.162.5.419

Lind, J., & Lindgren, C. (2017). Displays of parent suitability in adoption assessment reports. *Child & Family Social Work, 22*, 53–63. doi:10.1111/cfs.12305

Litrownik, A. J., Proctor, L. J., & Yeh, M. (2018). Trauma and socioemotional development in foster youth: Lessons learned from LONGSCAN. In E. Trejos-Castillo & N. Trevino (Eds.), *Handbook of Foster Youth* (pp. 57–76). New York: Routledge.

Marinho, S., Barbosa-Ducharne, M., & McRoy, R. (2012). Predictors of adoption disruption and permanency. In *Proceedings of The XV European Conference on Developmental Psychology* (pp. 225–233). Roma: Medimond.

Maza, P. (2014). Post-adoption instability: A national study. In S. L. Smith, *Keeping the promise. The case for adoption support and preservation* (pp. 51–64). New York: The Donaldson Adoption Institute.

McRoy, R. G. (1999). *Special needs adoptions: Practice issues.* New York: Garland.

Pace, C. S., Di Folco, S., Guerreiro, V., Santona, A., & Terrone, G. (2015). Adoptive parenting and attachment: Association of the internal working models between adoptive mothers and their late-adopted children during adolescence. *Frontiers in Psychology, 6*, 1433. doi:10.3389/fpsyg.2015.01433

Palacios, J., Adroher, S., Brodzinsky, D. M., Grotevant, H. D., Johnson, D. E., Juffer, F., & Tarren-Sweeney, M. (2019). Adoption in the service of child protection: An international interdisciplinary perspective. *Psychology, Public Policy, and Law, 25*, 57–72. doi:10.1037/law0000192

Palacios, J., Jiménez-Morago, J. M., & Paniagua, C. (2015). *Rupturas en adopción y acogimiento familiar en Andalucía. Incidencia, factores de riesgo, procesos e implicaciones (Breakdown in adoption and foster care in Andalucia. Incidence, risk factors, processes and implications).* Sevilla: Junta de Andalucía.

Palacios, J., Rolock, N., Selwyn, J., & Barbosa-Ducharne, M. (2019). Adoption breakdown: Concept, research and implications. *Research on Social Work Practice, 29*, 130–142. doi:10.1177/1049731518783852

Palacios, J., Sánchez-Sandoval, Y., & León, E. (2005). Intercountry adoption disruption in Spain. *Adoption Quarterly, 9*, 35–55. doi:10.1300/J145v09n01_03

Paniagua, C., Palacios, J., Jiménez-Morago, J., & Rivera, F. (2019). Adoption breakdown in Spain: A survival and age-related analysis. *Research on Social Work Practice, 29*, 176–184. doi:10.1177/1049731518791037

Partridge, S., Hornby, H., & McDonald, T. (1986). *Legacies of loss – Visions of gain: An inside look at adoption disruptions.* Portland: Center for Research and Advanced Study, University of Southern Maine.

Proctor, L. J., Randazzo, K. V. D., Litrownik, A. J., Newton, R. R., Davis, I. P., & Villodas, M. (2011). Factors associated with caregiver stability in permanent placements: A Classification Tree approach. *Child Abuse & Neglect, 35*, 425–436. doi:10.1016/j.chiabu.2011.02.002

Randall, J. (2013). Failing to settle: A decade of disruptions in a voluntary adoption agency in placements made between 2001 and 2011. *Adoption & Fostering, 37*, 188–199. doi:10.1177/0308575913490493

Rolock, N. (2015). Post-permanency continuity: What happens after adoption and guardianship from foster care?. *Journal of Public Child Welfare, 9*(2), 153–173. doi:10.1080/15548732.2015.1021986

Rolock, N., & Testa, M. F. (2008). *Conditions of children in or at risk of foster care in Illinois: An assessment of their safety, stability, continuity, permanence, and well-being.* Urbana, IL: Children and Family Research Center.

Rolock, N., & White, K. R. (2016). Post-permanency discontinuity: A longitudinal examination of outcomes for foster youth after adoption or guardianship. *Children and Youth Services Review, 70,* 419–427. doi:10.1016/j.childyouth.2016.10.025

Rosnati, R., Ranieri, S., & Ferrari, L. (2017). Research on adoption breakdowns: An international outlook. In C. Jeannin (Ed.), *Towards a greater capacity. Learning from intercountry adoption breakdowns* (pp. 40–43). Geneva: International Social Service.

Rushton, A. (2004). A scoping and scanning review of research on the adoption of children placed from public care. *Clinical Child Psychology and Psychiatry, 9,* 89–106. doi:10.1177/1359104504039768

Rushton, A., & Dance, C. (2006). The adoption of children from public care: A prospective study of outcome in adolescence. *Journal of the American Academy of Child and Adolescent Psychiatry, 45,* 877–883. doi:10.1097/01.chi.0000220850.86768.e8

Rushton, A., Mayes, D., Dance, C., & Quinton, D. (2003). Parenting late-placed children: The development of new relationships and the challenge of behavioral problems. *Clinical Child Psychology and Psychiatry, 8,* 389–400. doi:10.1177/1359104503008003008

Selwyn, J. (2019). Sibling relationships in adoptive families that disrupted or were in crisis. *Research on Social Work Practice, 29,* 165–175. doi:10.1177/1049731518783859

Selwyn, J., Meakings, S., & Wijedasa, D. (2015). *Beyond the adoption order: Challenges, interventions and adoption disruption.* London: British Association for Adoption and Fostering.

Smith, S. L. (2014). *Keeping the promise. The case for adoption support and preservation.* New York: The Donaldson Adoption Institute.

Smith, S. L., Howard, J., Garnier, P., & Ryan, S. (2006). Where are we now? A post-ASFA examination of adoption disruption. *Adoption Quarterly, 9,* 19–44. doi:10.1300/J145v09n04_02

Testa, M. F., Snyder, S., Wu, Q., Rolock, N., & Liao, M. (2014). Adoption and guardianship: A moderated mediation analysis of predictors of post-permanency continuity. *American Journal of Orthopsychiatry, 85,* 107–118. doi:10.1037/ort0000019

US Children's Bureau. (2016). *Adoption data 2014.* Washington, DC: Administration for Children and Families.

US Government Accountability Office (September, 2015). Child welfare: Steps have been taken to address unregulated custody transfers of adopted children. GAO-15-733.

Villodas, M. T., Litrownik, A. J., Newton, R. R., & Davis, I. P. (2016). Long-term placement trajectories of children who were maltreated and entered the Child Welfare System at an early age: Consequences for physical and behavioral well-being. *Journal of Pediatric Psychology, 41,* 46–54. doi:10.1093/jpepsy/jsv031

White, K. R. (2016). Placement discontinuity for older children and adolescents who exit foster care through adoption or guardianship: A systematic review. *Child and Adolescent Social Work Journal, 33*(4), 377–394. doi:10.1007/s10560-015-0425-1

Zill, Z., & Bramlet, B. (2014). Health and well-being of children adopted from foster care. *Children and Youth Services Review, 40,* 29–40. doi:10.1016/j.childyouth.2014.02.008

PART V

Adoption competency

31
ADOPTION COMPETENT CLINICAL PRACTICE

Anne J. Atkinson

Adoption competent clinical practice is currently thought to involve the use of an ecological perspective and family-based, strengths-based, and evidence-based approaches; to require advanced understanding of the nature of adoption as a form of family formation and clinical issues associated with grief and loss, attachment, and adoptive identity formation; and to demonstrate particular clinical skills that facilitate healing and family well-being. Over the past decade our understanding of adoption competent clinical practice has advanced steadily and will likely continue to advance as ongoing research further informs general mental health practice, improves understanding of the needs of adoptive families, and examines outcomes of adoption competent clinical practices, particularly in comparison to outcomes from standard clinical practice. Following brief highlights of recent key developments in building consensus around therapist competencies, practice principles, and overarching approaches that distinguish adoption competent clinical practice as a specialized area of practice, the chapter focuses centrally on describing competencies and their application in primary areas of intervention. The chapter concludes with a brief discussion of implications for policy, practice, and research.

Adoption competence: toward consensus

Although adoption training programs for professionals were developed earlier by at least two organizations, the first National Conference on Post-Adoption Services organized by Casey Family Services in December 2001 and their subsequent related publication of *Promising Practices in Adoption-Competent Mental Health Services: A White Paper* (Casey Family Services, 2003) appear to have served as catalysts in prompting development over the next several years of at least ten adoption competency training programs in the United States and one in Canada. Three of the programs developed during that period and 16 other organizations have since partnered with the Center for Adoption Support and Education (CASE) to become Training for Adoption Competency (TAC) sites (see Chapter 32 for a description of TAC). The availability and accessibility of quality adoption competent mental health services for adopted children and their families emerged as a high priority at the conference, and the subsequent publication contained a review of research supporting the need for adoption competent mental health services, perspectives from adoptive families, examples of emerging promising practices, and a set of recommendations to facilitate access to adoption competent services. During this period the National Child Welfare Resource Center for Adoption published *Adoption Competence: A Guide to Developing an Adoption Certificate Program for Mental Health Practitioners* (2007) to support the development of such programs.

Despite the well-documented need for adoption competent mental health services (Brodzinsky, 2013; Casey Family Services, 2003; Freundlich, 2006; Lenerz, Gibbs, & Barth, 2006; Smith, 2014) and rather widespread use of the terms "adoption competent" and "adoption sensitive" in professional literature and research, the terms lacked standardized, well-accepted definitions, and there had been no formal specification of knowledge, skills, and values associated with adoption competency. That work was undertaken in 2008 when CASE convened a group of nationally recognized experts, including parents, who methodically defined knowledge, skills, and values that therapists needed to be adoption competent. The expert panel also developed a definition of an adoption competent mental health professional and provided advisory guidance to the creation of the TAC curriculum that was designed to develop the defined competencies.

Contributing to the validation of the expert consensus definition were findings from an online survey in which 485 members of adoption kinship networks registered strong agreement with the components of the definition. In the same survey, of the 382 respondents who reported seeing a mental health professional, only 24.87 percent reported that the mental health professionals they saw were adoption competent, while 26.18 percent reported the mental health professionals were not adoption competent and 48.95 percent reported a more mixed experience with some adoption competent and some not. Many reported they had to search carefully and for a long period of time to find a competent therapist and that some therapists had actually harmed their families (Atkinson, Gonet, Freundlich, & Riley, 2013). The nature of adoption competent practice and how it can be distinguished from standard clinical practice has been further illuminated by the ongoing TAC outcomes evaluation and, beginning in 2015, CASE's work in developing two web-based curricula designed to increase the capacity of child welfare professionals and of mental health professionals to address the mental health needs of children in foster care who are moving toward, or have achieved, permanency through adoption or guardianship. The process involved re-convening child welfare and mental health experts, including adoptive parents and youth, who produced an updated specification of core competencies and reviews of research and best practice literature that further advanced consensus around the nature of adoption competent clinical practice. Additional information about TAC and the web-based curricula are provided in Chapter 32 of this volume.

At the same time, consensus has grown about what constitutes adoption competent clinical practice, research has continued to shed light on clinical issues observed in work with adoptive families, on interventions to address the issues, and on related policy and practice implications. Palacios and Brodzinsky (2010) observe that adoption research has taken two parallel tracks: one track has been from a social work and child welfare perspective, seeking to understand best policies and practices in placement and supports to ensure adoption stability, and the other track has been from the perspective of developmental psychology, examining mental health issues, child development and adjustment, and adoptive parenthood. This research has further clarified that many of the emotional and academic problems manifested have less to do with being adopted per se than with biological and experiential risk factors pre-dating adoptive placement and the failure to prepare, educate, and support parents in managing challenges faced after adoptive placement. They assert that the two research perspectives are not incompatible, and there is benefit in bridging the gap between the two. The contributions of both these research traditions are evident in the advancing understanding of what constitutes adoption competent clinical practice.

The definition, practice principles, and elements of adoption clinical competencies described here were derived from and informed by expert panels advising CASE in development of adoption competency training curricula, from reviews of current research and practice literature, and are based on findings from the ongoing TAC outcomes evaluation that has been collected from more than 1,400 participants in 95 cohorts including nearly 10,000 narrative descriptions of ways the specialty training has modified their clinical practices (Atkinson & Riley, 2017). Data from all these sources continue to illuminate the specialty nature of adoption competent practice and further distinguish it from standard clinical practice.

Adoption competent practice defined

The current expert consensus definition of an adoption competent mental health professional states that the professional has "a family-based, strengths-based, and evidence-based approach to children and youth and their adoptive and birth families" (CASE, 2016). Exploring the rationale for these approaches and ways they are manifest in practice can help illuminate distinguishing features of adoption competent clinical practice.

Therapists employing a *family-based approach* believe that healing occurs best in the context of family, that a family-based approach is necessary in addressing the critical issues of trauma and attachment, and demonstrates a commitment to work with the family as the core client and not the child in isolation. Therapists recognize challenging behaviors as manifestations of the array of biological and experiential risk factors that pre-date adoptive placement and avoid blaming the parents. In viewing parents as primary agents of healing, therapists embrace a genuine collaboration with parents that features a great deal more psychoeducation and guidance related to therapeutic parenting than is typically seen in standard mental health practice.

Reflecting a *strengths-based approach*, therapists place less emphasis on assigning diagnostic labels to children, greater emphasis on addressing underlying issues of trauma, loss, attachment, and identity, and are careful to avoid pathologizing normal developmental processes. Work with parents focuses on empowering them to develop an in-depth understanding of their children's unique histories and related implications, to reframe behaviors based on a deeper understanding of their children's development and experiences, to establish age- and developmental stage-appropriate behavioral expectations, and, in the long run, master the art of therapeutic parenting. Work with children and youth places greater importance on their understanding and making sense of their own unique stories and processing emotions associated with their experiences so that they can begin to form new attachments, healthy relationships, and positive identity.

An *evidence-based approach* means practices are supported by research evidence and recognized best practices and are consistent with family needs and values. Within the context of adoption competent clinical practice, there is recognition of the complex mental health needs of children and the limitations of current diagnostic, treatment, and medication practices, and use of a more ecological perspective that considers biological, psychosocial, and contextual factors and processes that affect development and adjustment. A particular challenge in clinical work is that most intervention models that in recent years have been deemed evidence-based or promising have not demonstrated their effectiveness with adoptive populations. As noted by Brodzinsky (2013), there will undoubtedly continue to be advances in our understanding and changes in practices, and therapists must maintain their competence by remaining current with knowledge and interventions that can inform their work with adoptive families. Recognizing that there is currently no single model addressing the array of complex mental health issues of adoptive families, TAC is designed to introduce participants to a broad range of current evidence-based and promising practice interventions with an aim of developing an understanding of their strategic, appropriate use. The training does not seek to develop proficiency in any specific model but to develop understandings of underlying therapeutic processes that experienced practitioners, for whom TAC is designed, can incorporate into their practice. Although numerous TAC participants do report an intention to pursue available formal training in particular treatment models or to work on developing proficiency within the context of their clinical practice with appropriate consultation and/or supervision, TAC supports broader understandings and strategic use of an array of therapeutic approaches and interventions.

Adoption competent clinical practice principles

The adoption competent therapist is guided by practice principles that form a theoretical and philosophical framework, are infused in values held, and are manifest in practice. Among the most basic principles are:

1. Adoption is not an event; it is a lifelong process with intergenerational impact.
2. Forming a family through adoption is a different experience than doing so by birth, and it involves normative challenges that can influence identity, family relationships, and psychological adjustment.
3. The adoptive family is the child's permanent family.
4. The child's past and current relationships with birth parents and other birth family members, including siblings, play a critical role in the child's development and adjustment.
5. The adoption kinship network is the constellation of relationships that must be acknowledged among adoptive, birth, and sometimes foster and extended family members.
6. Adoptive parents have a critical role in facilitating the child's adjustment and healthy identity formation, establishing communicative openness related to adoption.
7. Post-adoption supports and services are important in promoting healthy development of stability for adoptive families; the need for help should be normalized and help-seeking viewed as a strength.
8. Services demonstrate sensitivity to and respect for racial, ethnic, and cultural heritage, class differences, sexual orientation and gender identity, and health and disability issues.

In clinical work:

9. Approaches used are family-based, strengths-based, and informed by evidence of effectiveness and recognized clinical best practice.

10. The therapist employs an ecological perspective that considers biological, psychosocial, and contextual factors and processes that affect development and adjustment.
11. The therapist avoids pathologizing normative developmental processes and blaming parents for challenging behaviors.
12. Services are attachment-focused, reflect the belief that healing occurs best in the context of family, and engage parents as partners in the therapeutic process and as primary agents of healing.
13. The therapist demonstrates and promotes with others a strong appreciation for and commitment to understanding the child's unique story.
14. Approaches acknowledge the child's history of relationships with their parents and the impact of the birth parents' psychological and sometimes physical presence in the child's life.
15. Core issues of adoption (i.e., loss, rejection, guilt and shame, grief, identity, intimacy, and mastery/control) are consistently assessed and addressed, as needed, with members of the adoption kinship network.

Foundational requirements

Clinical practice that is adoption competent is built upon a foundation of (a) successful completion of graduate training in a profession such as psychiatry, psychology, social work, marriage and family therapy, or counseling and (b) meeting state licensure requirements for clinical practice in the profession. Completion of such training and licensure requirements establishes a foundation of clinical knowledge, practice skills, and presumably basic ethics and cultural competence on which more specialized adoption competencies can be developed.

Complexity of mental health needs

In recent years, as increasing numbers of children are adopted at older ages and with histories of neglect, abuse, institutionalization, or other forms of trauma, parenting challenges in adoptive families have grown. Adoption competent clinical practice requires a full appreciation for the complex and often nuanced mental health needs of children experiencing adoption as well as limitations of current diagnostic, treatment, and medication practices commonly used with children with foster and/or institutional care experiences. Zilberstein and Popper (2014) note the presence of multiple overlapping risk factors, incomplete family and health history, and multiple domains of impairment that challenge standard assessment and treatment planning practice. Therapists must be skilled in addressing not only the normative issues related to adoptive family formation such as grief and loss, attachment, and identity formation, but also the effects of early trauma and other adverse childhood experiences prior to adoption that produce elevated risk for an array of mental health disorders.

Arising in large measure from the complexity of mental health needs at work within adoptive families, clinical practice requires well-developed competencies related to collaboration and advocacy with multiple systems that support adoptive families. The therapist values working collaboratively with other systems to address complex needs, has an understanding of the policies, procedures, jurisdiction, and constraints of legal, child welfare, education, and other systems, and is skilled in effective interagency collaboration toward a common goal of family preservation and well-being. There is also a well-developed understanding of the goals and therapeutic processes of adjunct therapies and skill in their strategic use within the context of a comprehensive plan of treatment.

The biological and experiential risk factors and resulting complexity of mental health needs require assessment approaches and protocols that examine not only basic child and parent behavioral, social, and emotional functioning, but include specific inquiry into trauma exposure, parent–child attachment, grief and loss experiences of child and parents, level of adoption openness, child and parent understandings and expectations about adoption and permanence, and relevant issues of race and culture. Sound guidance on assessment is offered by Murray and Sullivan (2017), who further urge therapists to share results with parents, recognizing it as a critical opportunity for psychoeducation that improves parental understandings of the child, increases treatment motivation, and contributes to parental capacity to reframe behaviors, reducing blaming of either the child or themselves for problems being experienced.

Competencies in practice

Competencies are the elements of learning (i.e., discrete knowledge, values, and skills) that, once synthesized, produce in clinicians an "adoption lens" that informs clinical practice that is consistent with adoption competent practice principles. Described here are the main distinguishing features of adoption competent clinical practice in major areas of clinical intervention regularly seen in work with adoptive children and youth and their parents. The focus on features of practice with birth parents and other birth and adoptive family members presented here is very narrow, both because of space limitations and because there is less research in the area available for discussion.

Adoption as a form of family formation

In adoption competent clinical practice, therapists recognize that adoption is a lifelong process, rather than an event, and that forming a family through adoption is different than doing so through procreation. Therapists understand the evolution of adoption practice within a historical context, are knowledgeable about the salient clinical issues associated with current pathways to adoption, and employ positive adoption language. The impact of adoption on family functioning is fully recognized and not minimized, as is often the case in standard mental health practice (Riley & Meeks, 2006). Therapists understand phases of adoptive family development and normative challenges that can influence identity, family relationships, and psychological adjustment and are skilled in helping parents promote secure attachments, healthy relationships, and positive identity. Therapists further understand sibling dynamics when both birth and adoptive children are in a family and are skilled in assisting families to address the dynamics in ways that affirm family membership and enhance cohesion.

Therapists involved with the preparation of adoptive parents are skilled in helping them to understand the implications of their children's known history, and in normalizing help-seeking as a strength rather than a sign of failure. Therapists understand the importance of communicative openness about adoption and are skilled in guiding families to engage in conversations in a developmentally appropriate manner and, more generally, fostering an honest and respectful communicative openness within the family that allows children to talk about their adoption, birth family, and early life circumstances. Therapists recognize that children's birth families are important and often psychologically present, whether there is contact or not, even in infant adoption, and are skilled in assisting adoptive parents to understand and respond appropriately to their psychological presence.

In work with birth parents, adoption competent clinical practice requires an understanding of clinical issues associated with voluntary adoption planning and with involuntary termination of parental rights, including cultural implications of relinquishment, the impact of loss on birth family members, the impact of search and reunion on birth family members, and appropriate therapeutic approaches that support birth parents in understanding the emotional aspects of separation from the child, addressing grief issues, and potentially redefining their role(s) in the child's life. Therapists appreciate the value of children retaining connections to their families of origin when it is safe to do so and the contribution that birth parents and other family members can make in the lives of adopted children. They also recognize that the birth father is as important in the child's life as the birth mother and that birth parents might need therapeutic support episodically throughout their lives.

Loss, grief, and separation

Issues of grief and loss have been identified as the most prevalent of adoption core issues for adoptive families (Timm, Mooradian, & Hock, 2011). In adoption competent clinical practice, therapists understand critical issues of loss, grief, and separation, how these are experienced by members of the adoption kinship network, therapeutic strategies to help children grieve and heal, strategies parents can use to support grieving children, and the importance of maintaining connections to past family and culture to mitigate losses. The work reflects underlying beliefs that children need to understand and grieve their losses in order to establish new meaning and form new attachments and, with rare exception, that openness and maintaining connections to the past can mitigate loss. Adoption competent clinical practice requires therapists to:

- understand children's loss within a developmental framework that informs clinical assessment of loss experiences of parents and child and have skills in recognizing behaviors associated with unresolved losses, in using a grief model to help children and youth process their grief and feelings of rejection and loss, to work with adoptive parents in understanding behaviors within the context of the child's loss history, and to help the child put voice to their losses in safe ways;
- understand the nature and therapeutic value of, and demonstrate skill in using, life books, loss boxes, journaling, bibliotherapy, and other tools that provide opportunities for children to integrate (rather than asking them to forget) people, places, and things they have lost;
- understand adoptive parents might experience grief and loss related to infertility, to unmet expectations for their adoption experience, and/or to their inability to protect their children from hurtful pre-adoption experiences, and demonstrate skill in using therapeutic strategies that help parents become aware of and grieve their own losses; and
- understand different types of grief and loss, how each affects members of the adoption kinship network, and be skilled in therapeutic strategies to address each, including
    - disenfranchised grief (Doka, 2002) and using frameworks and therapeutic strategies that acknowledge and grieve the hidden losses;

- complicated grief as an intense and long-lasting form of grief and use of therapeutic strategies such as Complicated Grief Therapy (Wetherell, 2012) to promote natural healing and the Good Grief Model (Boston Medical Center, 2018) to achieve four key psychological tasks that allow integration and resolution of losses; and
- ambiguous loss involving confusion or uncertainty about a person or relationship (Boss, 1999) and the use of therapeutic strategies that give voice to the ambiguity and permission to grieve.

A noteworthy intervention model that addresses multiple adoption core issues is the 3-5-7 Model®, a strengths-based approach that uses tools (e.g., lifebooks, loss/life lines) to support work around issues of separation and loss, identity formation, and attachment; to build relationships; and to support deeper therapeutic work around abuse, abandonment, and neglect experiences (Henry, 2005).

Trauma and brain development

Adoption competent clinical practice is deeply trauma informed. It requires an understanding of basic brain structure and functioning that provides the basis for developmental sensitivity and trauma-informed clinical assessment and intervention. Therapists understand the neurodevelopmental effects of prenatal exposure to alcohol, the roles of sensitization and tolerance in children's response to trauma, behaviors along the hyperarousal continuum and the dissociative continuum, and how early caregiving impacts templates for future relationships. There is an advanced understanding of the features of Trauma Focused Cognitive Behavioral Therapy (TF-CBT) (Cohen, Mannario, & Deblinger, 2012; Dorsey & Deblinger, 2012), its appropriate use, and practice components. Therapists appreciate ongoing advances in the body of knowledge about the neurodevelopmental impact of trauma and implications for clinical practice and demonstrate a strong commitment to remaining abreast of these developments. Therapists are skilled in appropriate assessment for not only symptoms of traumatic stress and exposure to trauma, but also the effects of complex trauma, which refers to exposure to multiple early traumatic events within the caregiving system (Schmid, Petermann, & Fegert, 2013; van der Kolk, 2005). Therapists are knowledgeable about trauma assessment practices and tools, are skilled in assessing domains of impairment, and can distinguish Post Traumatic Stress Disorder, Developmental Trauma Disorder (Schmid et al., 2013), and Attention Deficit Hyperactivity Disorder. Treatment of complexly traumatized children is informed by an understanding of and skill in core components of treatment (Cook et al., 2005). Therapists are highly skilled in using therapeutic strategies with children that help them build coping and regulatory skills, and with parents to help them provide structure and routine and experiences that nurture and heal while supporting development of coping and self-regulation skills in their children (Blaustein & Kinniburgh, 2010).

Attachment

Therapists place a high value on the power of a positive parent–child relationship to buffer the impact of pre-adoption adverse experiences and to improve outcomes (Harwood, Feng, & Yu, 2013). Adoption competent clinical practice requires a foundational understanding of attachment theory (Ainsworth & Bowlby, 1991; Bowlby, 1988), how attachments are formed, and the impact of complex trauma on the capacity of children to form attachments (Kinniburgh, Blaustein, & Spinazzola, 2005). Therapists are knowledgeable about and skilled in using appropriate protocols and tools to assess the parent–child relationships, including observations, semi-structured interviews, and self-reported measures from both parent and child perspectives. There is particular awareness of the overdiagnosis of Reactive Attachment Disorder in community mental health settings (Woolgar & Scott, 2014), the need to assess for specific symptoms for Disinhibited Social Engagement Disorder (Lehmann, Breivik, Heiervang, Havik, & Havik, 2015), and clear understanding that any diagnosis of attachment disorder should be reserved for the few cases that clearly meet diagnostic criteria. In addressing attachment, therapists understand the appropriate uses of numerous current treatment modalities, such as: Dyadic Developmental Psychotherapy (DDP) (Becker-Weidman & Hughes, 2008; Hughes, 2014) and how to apply the principles of intersubjectivity and PACE (playful, accepting, curious, and empathetic) in treatment; Circle of Security® (Woodhouse, Lauer, Beeney, & Cassidy, 2015) to strengthen parents' abilities to observe and improve their caregiving skills; the five specific tasks of Attachment Based Family Therapy (Diamond, Diamond, & Levy, 2014; Diamond, Russon, & Levy, 2016); the goals, components, and specific therapeutic techniques employed in Trust Based Relational Intervention (TBRI) (Purvis, Cross, Dansereau, & Parris, 2013) and Parent Child Interaction Therapy (Hood & Eyberg, 2003; Shuhman, Foote, Eyberg, Boggs, & Algina, 1998); and use of Attachment and Biobehavioral Catchup (Dozier et al., 2006) to teach parents to nurture and respond sensitively to their infants and toddlers to help foster their development and form strong and healthy relationships. Therapists are skilled in one or more of these therapies and/or referring families to other adoption competent therapists who specialize in the needed intervention.

Therapeutic parenting in addressing challenging behaviors

Adoptive families most frequently seek mental health services because of concerning behaviors. Consistent with the family-based and strengths-based approaches, therapists focus less on behavioral interventions and more on addressing underlying issues and building parents' capacity to create and sustain therapeutic homes. In such work, therapists initially help parents gain awareness of their own parenting values, triggers, and issues, then support them in ongoing self-reflection to strengthen their capacity to parent therapeutically. Therapists are skilled at helping parents to recognize children's behaviors as often adaptive to past negative relationships and adverse circumstances, to reframe discipline as teaching and, more generally, to apply principles of therapeutic parenting, such as establishing a calm and consistent routine, recognizing children's triggers and developing plans to manage the behaviors before they occur, and applying IDEAL responses (immediate, direct, efficient, action-based, leveled at behavior) to promote self-regulation in their children. Therapists understand and are skilled in the Secure Base Model (Schofield & Beek, 2014) and Emotionally Focused Family Therapy (Foroughe et al., 2018) that help parents to be attuned to emotions and to respond appropriately to their children's needs. Therapists also recognize that adoptive parents are at elevated risk for secondary and vicarious trauma and are skilled in helping parents recognize signs of stress, set limits, create time for rest and leisure, and effectively choose their battles (McGlone, Santos, Kazama, Fong, & Mueller, 2002).

Identity formation

Work on identity formation is informed by a strong belief that children need to know and understand their own stories, recognition that adoption is a lifelong process, commitment to an integration of birth and adoptive families in the child's identity, and commitment to a positive cultural identity. Therapists know how identity is shaped and the impact of adoption on identity, recognize adolescence as a pivotal time, and are skilled at assisting youth to explore dimensions of their identity, manage difficult information about their adoption stories, and integrate their stories into coherent adoptive identity narratives. More specifically, therapists are knowledgeable about the six stuck spots in adoptive identity formation (difference, reason, missing information, identity, loyalty, and permanence), related developmental tasks, and appropriate therapeutic strategies to resolve core issues (CASE, 2018; Riley & Meeks, 2006). In work with adoptive parents, therapists are skilled in helping them understand and support the formation process, share difficult information, and overcome their own fears about their children's individuation from them.

In transracial and transcultural adoptions, the children and youth have additional dimensions of identity to be integrated. In adoption competent clinical practice, therapists understand children's awareness of differences at various developmental stages, the process of racial identity development throughout the lifespan, the complexities of adoption in diverse families, and strategies for supporting positive racial, cultural, and ethnic identity development. Therapists are skilled in assessing racial/cultural identity in children/youth and parental capacity to parent children of different racial, cultural, or gender identities and in building their capacity to parent in such adoptions. Specifically, therapists are skilled in assisting parents to understand how racial and gender identity, bias, and discrimination impact the mental health of their children/youth and to initiate conversations about race, ethnicity, culture, sexual orientation, and gender identity/expression to support the integration of identities.

The issue of adoption openness is often raised within the context of work on positive identity formation and attachment in which children experience divided loyalties and need assistance in integrating their birth and adoptive identities. Therapists engaged in adoption competent clinical practice are knowledgeable about different levels of openness and the clinical implications of the levels, the negative impact of secrecy, and benefits of open, honest, and respectful communication about and with birth family members. Therapists are knowledgeable about search and reunion practices and the role of search and reunion in identity formation. They are skilled in exploring with parents their own expectations, fears, and fantasies, in building and managing adoptive/birth family relationships, and in assisting with issues that arise related to ongoing connections, search and reunion, and stages of adjustment following reunion.

Adoption lens

Therapists who have acquired the specialized knowledge, values, and skills to engage in adoption competent clinical practice are often said to have developed an "adoption lens." As our understanding of features of such practice has advanced and consensus around therapist competencies has grown, it is becoming clearer that an "adoption lens" is best characterized as employing an ecological perspective that considers biological, psychosocial, and contextual factors and processes that affect development and adjustment while addressing issues inherent in adoption. Work with families through an "adoption lens" is evident at the organizational level at CASE, where an array of services and supports, developed and refined over two decades, are offered and feature a central focus on adoption competent clinical assessment and intervention, including psychoeducation with adults and children, as well as multiple opportunities for peer support, trainings for parents, and trainings and consultations for professionals working with adoptive families.

Conclusion

This chapter focuses centrally on the main distinguishing features of adoption competent clinical practice in major areas of clinical intervention. Built upon a foundation of basic clinical competence demonstrated through licensure, such practice requires more advanced knowledge, values, and skills competencies developed through specialized post-graduate training paired with clinical consultation and/or supervision to support the transfer of knowledge to day-to-day practice. Adoption clinical competency enables mental health professionals to view families they treat through an "adoption lens" and to more effectively address the unique and often complex clinical needs of adoption kinship members.

Implications for policy, practice, and research

Although opportunities for specialized training in adoption clinical competencies have increased, only a small fraction of mental health professionals who work daily with adoptive families have completed such training. There remains a critical need to increase the numbers of therapists prepared to effectively address the mental health needs of adoptive family members. TAC is currently available only in approximately 20 geographic areas in the United States served by training partner organizations, and although it is expanding by one or two partners annually, the need and demand for training far exceeds existing training capacity. The remaining training programs are even more limited in their geographic reach with capacity to train a very limited number of therapists annually. The web-based training developed by CASE promises to make foundational training accessible to more therapists but will not offer opportunities for advanced application to practice or clinical consultation that enhances transfer of learning to clinical practice. Ensuring that the existing effective training is more broadly available would immediately begin to increase the number of therapists prepared to engage in adoption competent clinical practice.

In light of well-documented negative experiences of adoptive families seeing mental health professionals and evidence of effectiveness of training in strengthening adoption competent clinical practice, agencies treating adoptive families should recognize the value of the advanced specialized training in hiring and assignment practices to help ensure that their clients are provided with services that meet their needs. Additionally, entities referring adoptive families for clinical services should view therapists who have completed specialized training as preferred providers and establish referral policies that reflect this preference. The capacity to identify therapists who engage in adoption competent clinical practice can be aided by an online registry that could be accessible to adoptive families seeking services as well as referring entities.

Given the level of expert consensus that has emerged around competencies distinguishing adoption competent clinical practice as a specialty area of practice and evidence that training is effective in building the competencies, there appears to be readiness for a more formalized credentialing process. CASE, in consultation with a broad range of stakeholders and credentialing experts, has examined the feasibility of various options including practitioner certification, certificate issuance, and program accreditation processes. Credentialing of some type would not only provide greater assurance to adoptive family consumers that their therapist has competencies to provide more appropriate and effective services, but can also provide additional justification for insurance companies to recognize and value adoption competent clinical practice as a specialized practice with potentially higher reimbursement rates that would encourage additional clinicians to seek training.

One especially important area for further research is extending the TAC evaluation to examine family outcomes. Following a small-scale pilot study that found that clients of TAC-trained clinicians reported higher levels of satisfaction, therapeutic alliance, and adoption relevance of therapy, as well as problem resolution and functioning than were reported by clients of comparably qualified, non-TAC-trained clinicians, a larger scale rigorous study has been undertaken. Additional practice and family outcomes studies are needed to build a more substantial body of evidence to inform future training, practice, and policy related to adoption competent clinical practice.

References

Ainsworth, M. D. S., & Bowlby, J. (1991). An ethological approach to personality development. *American Psychologist, 46*, 331–341. doi:10.1037/0003-066X.46.4.333

Atkinson, A. J., Gonet, P. A., Freundlich, M., & Riley, D. (2013). Adoption competent clinical practice: Defining its meaning and development. *Adoption Quarterly, 16*(3–4), 156–174. doi:10.1080/10926755.2013.844215

Atkinson, A. J., & Riley, D. B. (2017). Training for adoption competency: Building a community of adoption-competent clinicians. *Families in Society: The Journal of Contemporary Social Services, 98*(3), 235–242. doi:10.1606/1044-3894.2017.98.23

Becker-Weidman, A., & Hughes, D. (2008). Dyadic developmental psychotherapy: An evidence based treatment for children with complex trauma and disorders of attachment. *Child and Family Social Work, 13*, 329–337. doi:10.1111/j.1365-2206.2008.00557.x

Blaustein, M., & Kinniburgh, K. (2010). *Treating traumatic stress in children and adolescents: How to foster resilience through attachment, self-regulation, and competency*. New York: Guilford Press.

Boss, P. (1999). *Ambiguous loss: Learning to live with unresolved grief.* Cambridge, MA: Harvard University Press.

Boston Medical Center. (2018). *The good grief program: Supporting children through grief.* Boston, MA: Author.

Bowlby, J. (1988). *A secure base: Parent-child attachment and healthy human development.* New York: Basic Books.

Brodzinsky, D. (2013). *A need to know: Enhancing adoption competence among mental health professionals.* New York: Donaldson Adoption Institute.

CASE. (October 2016). *Definition of an adoption competent mental health professional.* Burtonsville, MD: Center for Adoption Support and Education.

CASE. (2018). *Beneath the mask: For teen adoptees: Teen and young adults share their stories.* Burtonsville, MD: Center for Adoption Support and Education.

Casey Family Services. (2003). *Promising practices in adoption-competent mental health services.* Report from Casey Family Services, New Haven, CT.

Cohen, J., Mannario, A., & Deblinger, E. (Eds.). (2012). *Trauma-focused CBT for children and adolescents: Treatment applications.* New York: Guilford Press.

Cook, A., Spinazzola, J., Ford, J., Lanktree, C., Blaustein, M., Cloitre, M., & van der Kolk, B. (2005). Complex trauma in children and adolescents. *Psychiatric Annals, 35*(5), 390–398.

Diamond, G., Russon, J., & Levy, S. (2016). Attachment-based family therapy: A review of the empirical support. *Family Process, 55*(3), 595–610. doi:10.1111/famp.12241

Diamond, G. S., Diamond, G. M., & Levy, S. A. (2014). *Attachment-based family therapy for depressed adolescents.* Washington, DC: American Psychological Association.

Doka, K. J. (Ed.). (2002). *Disenfranchised grief: Recognizing hidden sorrow*. Lexington, MA: Lexington Books.

Dorsey, S., & Deblinger, E. (2012). Children in foster care. In J. Cohen, A. Mannario, & E. Deblinger (Eds.), *Trauma-focused CBT for children and adolescents: Treatment applications* (pp. 49–72). New York: Guilford Press.

Dozier, M., Peloso, E., Lindhiem, O., Gordon, M. K., Manni, M., Sepulveda, S., & Ackerman, J. (2006). Developing evidence-based interventions for foster children: An example of a randomized clinical trial with infants and toddlers. *Journal of Social Issues, 62*, 767–785. doi:10.1111/j.1540-4560.2006.00486.x

Foroughe, M., Stillar, A., Goldstein, L., Dolhanty, J., Goodcase, E. T., & Lafrance, A. (2018). Brief emotion-focused family therapy: An intervention for parents of children and adolescents with mental health issues. *Journal of Marital and Family Therapy*. doi:10.1111/jmft.12351

Freundlich, M. (2006). Research on post-adoption services: Implications for practice, program development, and policy. In M. Dore (Ed.), *The postadoption experience: Adoptive families' service needs and service outcomes* (pp. 283–298). Washington, DC: CWLA Press.

Harwood, R., Feng, X., & Yu, S. (2013). Preadoption adversities and postadoption mediators of mental health and school outcomes among international, foster, and private adoptees in the United States. *Journal of Family Psychology, 27*(3), 409–420. doi:10.1037/a0032908

Henry, D. L. (2005). The 3–5–7 model: Preparing children for permanency. *Children and Youth Services Review, 27*(2), 197–212. doi:10.1016/j.childyouth.2004.09.002

Hood, K. K., & Eyberg, S. M. (2003). Outcomes of parent-child interaction therapy: Mothers' reports on maintenance three to six years after treatment. *Journal of Clinical Child and Adolescent Psychology, 32*, 419–429. doi:10.1207/S15374424JCCP3203_10

Hughes, D. (2014). *Dyadic developmental psychotherapy: Toward a comprehensive trauma-informed treatment for developmental trauma disorder*. South Portland, ME: DDP Network.

Kinniburgh, K., Blaustein, M., & Spinazzola, J. (2005). Attachment, self-regulation, and competency: A comprehensive intervention framework for children with complex trauma. *Psychiatric Annals, 35*, 424–430.

Lehmann, S., Breivik, K., Heiervang, E. R., Havik, T., & Havik, O. E. (2015). Reactive attachment disorder and disinhibited social engagement disorder in school-aged foster children – A confirmatory approach to dimensional measures. *Journal of Abnormal Child Psychology, 44*(3), 445–457. doi:10.1007/s10802-015-0045-4

Lenerz, K., Gibbs, D., & Barth, R. (2006). Postadoption services: A study of program participants, services, and outcomes. In M. M. Dore (Ed.), *The postadoption experience. Adoptive families' service needs and service outcomes* (pp. 95–110). Washington, DC: Child Welfare League of America and Casey Family Services.

McGlone, K., Santos, L., Kazama, L., Fong, R., & Mueller, C. (2002). Psychological stress in adoptive parents of special-needs children. *Child Welfare, 81*(2), 151–171.

Murray, K. J., & Sullivan, K. M. (2017). Using clinical assessment to enhance adoption success. *Families in Society: The Journal of Contemporary Social Services, 98*(3), 217–224. doi:10.1606/1044-3894.2017.98.29

National Child Welfare Resource Center for Adoption. (2007). *Adoption competence: A guide to developing an adoption certificate program for mental health practitioners*. Southfield, MI: Spaulding for Children.

Palacios, J., & Brodzinsky, D. (2010). Adoption research: Trends, topics, outcomes. *International Journal of Behavioral Development, 34*, 270–284. doi:10.1177/0165025410362837

Purvis, K. B., Cross, D. R., Dansereau, D. F., & Parris, S. R. (2013). Trust-Based Relational Intervention (TBRI): A systemic approach to complex developmental trauma. *Child & Youth Services, 34*(4), 360–386. doi:10.1080/0145935X.2013.859906

Riley, D., & Meeks, J. (2006). *Beneath the mask: Understanding adopted teens*. Silver Spring, MD: Center for Adoption Support and Education.

Schmid, M., Petermann, F., & Fegert, J. M. (2013). Developmental trauma disorder: Pros and cons of including formal criteria in the psychiatric diagnostic systems. *BMC Psychiatry, 13*, 3. doi:10.1186/1471-244X-13-3

Schofield, G., & Beek, M. (2014). *The secure base model: Promoting attachment in foster care and adoption*. London: BAAF.

Shuhman, E. M., Foote, R. C., Eyberg, S. M., Boggs, S., & Algina, J. (1998). Efficacy of parent child interaction therapy: Interim report of a randomized trial with short term maintenance. *Journal of Clinical Child Psychology*, *27*(1), 34–45. doi:10.1207/s15374424jccp2701_4

Smith, S. L. (2014). *Keeping the promise: The case for adoption support and preservation*. New York: Evan B. Donaldson Adoption Institute.

Timm, T. M., Mooradian, J. K., & Hock, R. M. (2011). Exploring core issues in adoption: Individual and marital experience of adoptive mothers. *Adoption Quarterly*, *14*(4), 268–283. doi:10.1080/10926755.2011.628264

van der Kolk, B. A. (2005). Developmental trauma disorder. *Psychiatric Annals*, *35*(5), 401–408.

Wetherell, J. L. (2012). Complicated grief therapy as a new treatment approach. *Dialogues in Clinical Neuroscience*, *14*(2), 159–166.

Woodhouse, S. S., Lauer, M., Beeney, J. R., & Cassidy, J. (2015). Psychotherapy process and relationship in the context of a brief attachment-based mother-infant intervention. *Psychotherapy*, *52*(1), 145–150. doi:10.1037/a0037335

Woolgar, M., & Scott, S. (2014). The negative consequences of over-diagnosing attachment disorders in adopted children: The importance of comprehensive formulations. *Clinical Child Psychology and Psychiatry*, *19*(3), 355–366. doi:10.1177/1359104513478545.

Zilberstein, K., & Popper, S. (2014). Clinical competencies for the effective treatment of foster children. *Clinical Child Psychology and Psychiatry*, *21*(1), 32–47. doi:10.1177/1359104514547597

32
TRAINING FOR ADOPTION COMPETENCY CURRICULUM

Debbie Riley and Ellen Singer

Introduction

The significant mental health needs of adopted children and youth, particularly those with histories of foster or institutional care, are well documented (Juffer & van IJzendoorn, 2005; Keyes, Malone, Sharma, Iacono, & McGue, 2013; Tan & Marn, 2013). The American Academy of Pediatrics (2014) has identified mental health as the greatest unmet need of children in foster care given their exposure to childhood trauma. The development of international adoptees is greatly impacted by post-natal maltreatment related to institutional care. Children adopted from foster care and from institutional settings are at greater risk for mental health challenges, attachment disorders, and school performance issues (Harwood, Feng, & Yu, 2013). Perhaps the most important conclusion of recent research on the adjustment of adopted children is that many of the emotional and academic problems they manifest are closely associated with an array of biological and experiential risk factors that predate their adoptions and the failure of adoption professionals to adequately prepare, educate, and support parents in managing the challenges they face post-adoption (Brodzinsky, 2013).

The efforts of numerous organizations to improve access to and the quality of child and family mental health services provide strong evidence of the difficulty in accessing quality mental health services. The Child and Family Service Reviews show that child welfare systems have struggled to provide accessible and effective behavioral health services to children in foster care (US Department of Health and Human Services, 2017). A contributing factor is the shortage of specialized permanency and adoption competent mental health professionals – fully qualified, skillful clinicians who understand complex adoption/guardianship-related issues such as trauma, attachment, grief and loss, and identity formation (Brodzinsky, 2013). Equally needed are child welfare professionals who understand the mental health needs of children in foster care with permanency goals of adoption or guardianship and who have casework skills to promote healing and collaborate effectively with mental health professionals (McCrae, Barth, & Guo, 2010).

The negative experiences of adoptive families in seeking professional help underscore the reality that therapists lacking adoption competence can, at times, do more harm than good.

Adoptive parents and adoption professionals report that therapists often fail to validate or believe their experiences; blame parents for their children's problems; pathologize adoption and view the family as pathological; question the parents' motives for adoption; advise parents not to talk about adoption with children because it will "stir things up"; see children with attachment problems without parental presence or input; tell parents to give their children back to the state; and fail to gather information about the children's histories or to address the impact of previous maltreatment (Brodzinsky, 2013).

Many parents report having given up trying to locate qualified professionals, and others describe involvement with as many as ten different therapists before engaging with a mental health professional who demonstrated understanding and provided helpful assistance (Brodzinsky, 2013). Brodzinsky (2013) describes several studies that found that most mental health professionals are not prepared to address the diverse/complex clinical needs of adoptive families and that clinicians often view adoption as not clinically relevant.

Responding to the need: The Center for Adoption Support and Education

As a mother of 12 children, four by birth and eight by adoption from foster care, Kathleen Dugan and her husband Mike struggled to get the help needed for their children who, with histories of traumatic beginnings, were struggling with serious emotional and behavioral problems. The Dugans encountered professionals who told them to return their "too damaged" children to foster care. Debbie Riley, a therapist, administrator, and adoptive mother, had experience working in various mental health programs that left her acutely aware of the overrepresentation of youth from adoptive families. She understood that adoptive families were unable to access effective treatment that specialized in adoption-related issues.

In 1998, frustrated by the lack of available support and committed to ensuring that no child would return to foster care because of behavioral health needs, Kathleen invested her own financial resources and engaged the passion and expertise of Debbie to co-found and become the chief executive officer of Center for Adoption Support and Education (CASE). CASE was created as a unique, free-standing agency not connected to adoption placement whose sole mission was to provide specialized pre- and post-adoption counseling and educational services to foster and adoptive families, as well as training for child welfare staff, mental health providers, and educators in the Washington, DC Metro area.

Over the course of 20 years, CASE has become a national leader in direct clinical services for families, adding additional offices throughout Maryland, Northern Virginia, and Albany, New York. As a national resource for foster and adoptive families and the professionals who support them, CASE provides webinars, training programs, publications, and distance consultations. CASE has served over 6,000 children and adolescents and their foster and adoptive families, adult adoptees, expectant/birth parents, and over 30,000 professionals. Its clinical interventions have resulted in successful transitions from foster care/institutionalization to permanency; healing of early trauma, loss, and grief; stabilization of families in crisis; promotion of secure attachments; an increase in children's self-regulatory behaviors; improvement in children's emotional, social, academic/learning, and behavioral functioning; and most importantly, adoption preservation.

CASE's clinical treatment approach and services

CASE's clinical model was influenced by the guiding principles established by the National Consortium for Post Legal Adoption Services: Adoption Support and Education

(Arneaud et al., 1996). The CASE approach emphasizes the need for family-focused treatment and incorporates an array of services ranging from advocacy to psychosocial services. CASE's framework integrates several theoretical models around attachment, grief and mourning, and trauma-informed treatment. It incorporates knowledge of children's thoughts and feelings about adoption from a developmental lens, the impact of compromised beginnings, and the importance of birth family connections. CASE's model includes a thorough assessment involving the individual child, adolescent, or adult and their family that focuses on emotional, social, behavioral, and academic functioning; marital and family relationships; attitudes, communication about, and relationship with birth family; and the family's access to social supports.

As CASE continues its adoption competent practice development, it has incorporated best practice approaches, strategies, interventions, and evidence-informed/evidenced-based treatment modalities from an adoption lens. CASE utilizes psychoeducation for parents about the impact of compromised beginnings, including trauma, breaks in attachment, loss and grief, and neurobiology. Psychoeducation includes helping both parents and professionals understand the importance of birth family to adoptees. Assessment and treatment with transracial adoptive families focuses on the family's promotion of positive identity development and the need for racial socialization. The clinical team utilizes a range of evidence-based models. (See adoptionsupport.org/member-types/therapists.)

The CASE model includes referrals to other adoption competent professionals who provide adjunct therapies including those who specialize in occupational and speech therapy. To assist families with their children's academic, social, emotional, and behavioral needs in school, CASE therapists advocate for families in school, consulting with counselors and teachers, and attend Individual Education Program meetings. When indicated, CASE clinicians collaborate with hospitals and psychiatrists. CASE has an in-house psychiatrist who provides consultation and medication management. CASE clients also have access to non-clinical services, including bibliotherapy, adoption-related materials, webinars, workshops, and publications. CASE has created a support group curriculum for children, teens, and adoptive parents. The WISE Up! Program teaches parents and children how to respond to questions and comments about adoption. All CASE therapists have received the Training in Adoption Competency (TAC) outlined next.

Defining adoption competency and developing TAC

As CASE continued its adoption competent practice, it recognized the direct correlation between the positive outcomes it achieved and its adoption-specific clinical model. In 2008, that recognition led to CASE's implementation of a multi-year initiative, Training and National Certification for Adoption Competent Mental Health Practitioners. Funded by multiple national private foundations, the initiative's long-term goals were greater access for prospective adoptive parents, adopted individuals, adoptive families, and kinship families to adoption competent mental health professionals; provision of mental health services to adoptive families to promote their stability and health; reduction of the rates of adoption disruption and dissolution; and strengthening the post-adoption services offered by mental health and child welfare systems nationwide.

CASE convened a National Advisory Group of nationally recognized child welfare and adoption experts, including those with personal adoption experiences. The Advisory Group focused on defining "adoption competency" for mental health professionals and developing a strong statement of need for adoption competency training. The work of the group was informed by an online survey of 485 adoptive parents and other members of the adoption kinship network conducted in 2011 and early 2012 (Atkinson, Gonet, Freundlich, & Riley, 2013). Respondents provided accounts of seeing multiple incompetent therapists over the years, and nearly one-quarter found that therapists lacked knowledge about attachment, trauma, or loss, and that many did not have a basic understanding of adoption.

CASE's experience in working with families who had previous unhelpful therapeutic experiences added to the understanding of the critical need to develop and expand the availability of adoption competent mental health professionals. Families reported therapeutic interventions that had been completely ineffective, had escalated the difficulties, or were directly harmful. In therapy at CASE, one parent reported,

> We were referred to a therapist who was trained in Trauma-Focused Cognitive Behavioral Therapy (TF-CBT). When my seven-year-old son began smearing feces all over his room after visits with his birthmother, the therapist said that we needed to finish the treatment sessions first before we could address what was happening with the visits. This rigid adherence to a model of treatment without the flexibility to talk about our son's and our distress from these visits left us feeling completely helpless.
>
> *(Edna, adoptive mother, age 32; CASE, 2018)*

Many parents shared that they often were not given much time with the therapist, spending most of the time in the waiting room. Consequently, parents lacked guidance even when they reported that they could not manage their child's behavior or felt no real attachment between the child and themselves. Many families reported that the subject of adoption was either not addressed, only superficially addressed, or dismissed as unimportant. One teen told her therapist that being adopted meant "suffering the greatest loss of my life" (Center for Adoption Support and Education, 2018). The therapist responded by saying that "birth parents are only a sperm and an egg."

Other reports focused on the harm done to the adopted child or teen. One family credits CASE with saving their daughter and their family from serious destruction. The parents' six-year-old daughter, adopted from the Philippines at the age of two, was exhibiting out of control behavior. The treating psychiatrist's recommendation included removal of the child's toys and stuffed animals until she calmed down; shaving the child's head when the child engaged in hair pulling; and taking their daughter to the Emergency Room for hospitalization. Instead, the family brought their daughter to CASE, where the family found the needed healing support.

In response to these needs expressed by families and professionals, again in 2008, the National Advisory Group, under CASE's leadership, undertook the development and implementation of the TAC program, an advanced adoption competency clinical training program for licensed mental health professionals. The group produced two expert consensus foundational products: the current definition of an adoption competent mental health professional and a set of specifically defined knowledge, values, and skills – core competencies in 18 domains essential for adoption competent mental health professionals. The TAC competency-based curriculum and evaluation design were guided by expert advisers and informed by research and practice literature reviews of adoption and mental health-related best practice, adult competency-based learning, and assessment of clinical competencies. The current definition of an adoption competent mental health professional is in Table 32.1.

Table 32.1 Definition: an adoption competent mental health professional

An adoption competent mental health professional has:

- The requisite professional education and professional licensure to provide clinical interventions (services)
- A family-based, strengths-based, and evidence-based approach to working with children and youth and their adoptive and birth families
- Well-developed knowledge, skills, and values in clinically working with children and youth with a history of abuse, neglect, trauma, and other adverse early experiences
- Well-developed knowledge, skills and values in clinically working with adoptive families and birth families
- The ability to clinically work with adopted children and youth and their adoptive and birth families with sensitivity to and respect for racial, ethnic, and cultural heritage, sexual orientation and gender identity, and health and disability issues

An adoption competent mental health professional has a full understanding of the nature of adoption as a form of family formation and the different types of adoption; the clinical issues that are associated with grief, separation and loss, attachment, and adoptive identity formation; the common individual and family developmental challenges in the experience of adoption; and the characteristics and skills that make adoptive families successful.

An adoption competent mental professional is highly skilled in conducting full assessments and using a range of evidence-based and promising therapies that are trauma informed in order to:

- effectively engage adoptive families toward the mutual goal of helping the child or youth to heal
- empower parents to recognize themselves as agents of healing and the experts on their child or youth and to advocate for their child or youth
- assist adoptive families to strengthen or develop and practice parenting skills that support attachment, healthy family relationships, and long-term well-being
- engage extended families and other networks to support adopted children and youth and their adoptive and birth families.

Creating a sub-specialty in adoption clinical practice

TAC is designed to produce clinicians who provide mental health services to birth, kinship, and adoptive families consistent with the definition of an adoption competent mental health professional. Eligible students hold graduate degrees in counseling-related fields, have clinical skills reflective of a professional license, and possess a basic knowledge of mental health issues as they impact children, youth, and families. TAC differs from other existing training programs in its in-depth clinical focus, transfer of learning to practice through multiple learning opportunities, a manualized delivery, and the rigor of its evaluation. TAC is an evidence-informed, 12-session (72 hour) training with a six-month case consultation component to further aid in transferring learning to practice.

The TAC curriculum

The TAC curriculum continues to evolve to respond to emerging research, practice development, and evidence-informed and evidence-based interventions appropriate to work with members of the adoption kinship network. As of December 2018, TAC includes a 12-module curriculum culminating in a final project requiring integration of learning and application to practice; six monthly clinical case consultation sessions designed to reinforce the

Table 32.2 TAC training topics

- The principles that form the bases for adoption competent mental health practice
- Clinical skills for engaging adoptive families as healing agents
- Adoption-related grief, loss, and separation and evidence-informed clinical interventions
- The impact of traumatic experiences on children's physical, emotional, cognitive, social, and neurodevelopment and relevant clinical assessment and evidence-based interventions
- Attachment formation and disruption and elements of effective treatment including attachment-based interventions
- Adopted adolescents and identity development, including the "six stuck spots" that are key areas of vulnerability in adolescence (Riley & Meeks, 2005) and relevant clinical intervention
- Clinical issues in working with birth and adoptive families, including the transition from foster parent to adoptive parent, LGBT adoptive parents, and adoptive parenting through the life cycle and developmental tasks
- Clinical work with adoptive families around managing children's behaviors with an understanding of trauma, attachment, and therapeutic parenting
- Clinical issues involved in different levels of openness in adoption and clinical approaches to supporting and educating families on openness issues
- Race and ethnicity in adoption, including the formation of racial identity and strategies for effective racial socialization and healthy identity development
- Participants' demonstration of their application of knowledge and skills to practice

transfer of learning into clinical practice and facilitated by expert clinicians; and an ongoing multicomponent evaluation examining training delivery, effectiveness, and outcomes. The robust TAC trainer credentialing and support process, featuring selection in accordance with prescribed qualifications, includes a weeklong in-person orientation, debriefing calls after modules that are informed by participant feedback and fidelity observations, and ongoing supportive technical assistance. Table 32.2 provides the major TAC training topics.

TAC is currently being offered in 17 states in the US with 19 training partners. As of December 2018, training has been replicated with 95 cohorts, training a total of 1,448 professionals. Additional cohorts are added throughout the year. Partnerships include a diverse array of organizations including four universities, three state/county child welfare agencies, and ten private non-profit organizations. Given the impact of TAC in the United States, discussions are under way with several countries for the potential of expanding TAC internationally.

TAC participants

The nearly 1,400 participants in the first 95 cohorts report an average of 8.9 years clinical experience and an average 13.7 years professional experience. Almost 12 percent hold doctorates and 82 percent hold master's degrees. A remarkable 76 percent report a personal connection to adoption, many as adoptive parents but also as adopted persons or having family and/or close friends touched by adoption. Fifty-four percent are social workers, 23 percent are counselors, 13 percent are marriage and family therapists, and 10 percent are psychologists. Work settings of TAC participants include public and private mental health agencies (32 percent) and private practices (15 percent), adoption specialty organizations (26 percent), family services organizations (21 percent), child welfare agencies (13 percent), residential treatment facilities (8 percent), and other settings (8 percent). More than 12 percent of TAC participants reported more than one work setting, the majority reporting a part-time private practice.

Evaluation of TAC

As pointed out by Brodzinsky (2013, p. 43), "translating knowledge into practice is another area that needed empirical attention." One of the unique aspects of TAC is the inclusion of assessment and research to study how the acquisition of knowledge gained through TAC influences practice change for the individual professional and his or her organization. Fidelity observations and participant and trainer feedback are used to assess the quality and relevance of the training and fidelity of the delivery (Atkinson & Riley, 2017).

TAC has been subject to ongoing, rigorous evaluation by an independent external evaluator, Policy Works, Ltd., since its inception. Findings represent a strong body of evidence that TAC is a sound and effective training model that produces changes in clinical assessment and intervention practices that enable clinicians to apply trauma-informed, attachment-based skills to address core adoption issues such as loss, grief, control, and identity. The evaluation is designed to assess training delivery, outcomes, and effectiveness.

Training outcomes are assessed using pre- and post-training self-assessments of adoption competency and surveys reporting changes in clinical practices at the midpoint and conclusion of training. Interviews are conducted with TAC-trained clinicians six to eight months after training completion to identify and explore the longer-term impact(s) of training on clinical practices. Training effectiveness is assessed using a 34-item pre- and post-test based on curriculum content which is administered to training participants and a control group of comparably qualified clinicians. On TAC pre- and post-tests, TAC participants experienced average gain scores of 51.35 points on a 100-point scale, while those in the control groups experienced a gain of only 4.50 points. TAC participants scored an average 46.45 points higher on TAC post-tests than control group members.

TAC participants are asked at the midpoint and conclusion of training to identify and comment on the aspects of practice influenced by information or insights gained from the training. Findings to date are based on more than 1,900 responses that contain nearly 10,000 separate narrative descriptions of ways their practices have been influenced by the training and most important learning. At the end of training, all TAC participants to date report change in at least two of the six defined aspects of practice. Key findings are that 61.90 percent report change in all five aspects at the individual clinician level; and 50.86 percent report change in procedures, programming and/or services at the organizational level. The six key areas of changed practice that participants report are: information about adoption collected at intake, with the referral, or in initial phase of assessment; methods used to assess the family and the child; clinical approaches used; techniques used in work with children and youth; use of or referral to other (adjunct) resources and/or therapies; and changes at organizational level in procedures, services, and programming.

Case example: Adoption competent mental health practice

Tanya was placed in foster care at the age of two with her older sister, who was 5 years old. Prior to foster care, Tanya had been separated from her sister several times when her mother placed her with her maternal aunt. Tanya experienced repeated physical abuse at the hands of her aunt and has burn scars on her hands. While in foster care, Tanya and her sister remained together but were moved three times. Tanya was 6 years old and her sister was 9 years old when they were adopted. Beginning at placement, Tanya's adoptive parents had contacted nine different therapists, seeking help for Tanya's hiding and hoarding food, emotional overeating, stealing, lying, and raging tantrums. Tanya was constantly in conflict with her parents and her sister. At age 14, Tanya was seen by a TAC-trained CASE therapist. Her parents reported feeling overwhelmed and in despair about not being able to find anyone who could help Tanya or their family.

Changes in information collected at intake

"Following TAC, I integrate more comprehensive assessment practices, including a greater focus on prenatal development, exposure to trauma and parent-child bonding."

Tanya's new therapist delved deeply into her preplacement history, collecting significant background information pertaining to her trauma history, significant losses and separation from caregivers, as well as the bonding process between Tanya and her parents. She learned more about the adoptive parents' experience of infertility and loss and their motivation to adopt. The assessment process included individual sessions with Tanya, with her parents, and with the entire family. Tanya's parents were surprised by the inclusion of her sister in the assessment process, which no previous treatment had incorporated.

Methods used to assess child/family

"I liked using the genograms. I never had used these in assessment before and experienced how powerful it was in working with adoptive families."

The TAC therapist used a genogram to help the family visualize separations and connections that were important in Tanya's life. It was the first time that the parents were able to fully appreciate the magnitude of losses and separations inflicted upon a child so young. In the past, the parents were told not to worry so much about these transitions, being assured children are resilient and that "all they need is love."

Clinical approaches used

"I'm able to identify grief/loss issues more quickly and have a better understanding of the child's aversive behaviors."

"Since completing TAC, I've been doing more 'hands on' activities in therapy with kids I'm working with, i.e., loss boxes and masks, writing letters to biological parents."

"Firmer on need for parent to be involved in treatment."

Tanya's treatment plan included individual therapy to help her express feelings and gain insight into her struggles that were deeply embedded in trauma and loss. The therapist worked with Tanya to explore her unique and complete story and to fill in the missing pieces. In working with Tanya around her unresolved loss and grief, the TAC therapist helped her create a Lifebook, write goodbye letters, and make a loss box. Through these interventions, Tanya was able to identify her losses, develop an understanding of why these losses occurred, and experience a mourning process so that she could be emotionally available to new attachments and new relationships. Slowly, Tanya was able to say goodbye to the people, places, and things that had been a part of her life, allowing her pain to subside.

The therapist utilized therapeutic interventions to help Tanya establish feelings of safety and readiness so that she could process her emotions related to traumatic experiences. Tanya could share with her therapist,

> "I am a victim of child abuse. Every time I look at my hands, it reminds me I was victimized. I could hide the emotional scars, but the physical scars are a daily reminder – victim of abuse. I never wanted to talk about it. I would do everything I could think of to avoid the topic because of how disturbing it was to me."

Treatment also focused on helping Tanya learn coping and self-regulatory skills so that she could better control tantrums and aggressive behavior.

Treatment acknowledged the significant identity issues impacting Tanya as a Latina female raised by White adoptive parents. Tanya felt a loss of racial connections, compounded by having little knowledge about her birth father.

> "My birthmother and birthfather split when I was two years old, that is the last time I think I saw him. What does it mean I am Latina? I have been with White people most of my life. It depresses me not to know where I came from and who my birth father is."

Tanya welcomed the opportunity to talk about these issues, as none of her previous therapists had mentioned race, seemingly endorsing being color blind.

The therapist was clear with Tanya's parents that her healing would be fostered through her family's involvement and that the treatment would include them. Parental involvement was new to them, and they were relieved that the therapist saw them as part of the solution and not the problem. The treatment plan moved them away from behavior management approaches used in previous therapies to a focus on addressing the underpinnings of loss, grief, and trauma.

Given the impact of previous unsuccessful therapy, initial attempts at family sessions were not productive. Tanya and her parents were very angry and were not able to open their communication to reach a better understanding of one another or problem-solve. Tanya's parents had not previously received a framework for parenting a traumatized child and had, in fact, been blamed for Tanya's difficulties. They were initially defensive and guarded as the therapist tried to gently help them understand that they had been applying parenting strategies appropriate only for children who had not come from traumatic beginnings. The therapist employed a strength-based approach, lifting the parents from a foundation of failure to empowerment.

Providing empathy for the parents' struggles, the therapist helped them develop empathy for Tanya as she handled the impact of her trauma history. Through therapy and recommended reading and webinars, the therapist provided psychoeducation to Tanya's parents about the impact of abuse, breaks in attachment, and loss and grief on her brain and subsequent behavior. Through this new understanding, Tanya's parents learned not to take Tanya's behavior personally and became more receptive to implementing trauma- and attachment-focused parenting approaches. The therapist's attachment-based family therapy model further facilitated deeper attachment and an improved relationship between Tanya, her parents, and her sister. Tanya's parents were provided with education to help them support Tanya in her need for connections with her racial heritage as key components of racial socialization and identity development. To provide a deeper understanding to their daughter's struggles, the book *Beneath the Mask: Understanding Adopted Teens* was recommended (Riley & Meeks, 2005).

> **Therapist's awareness of the importance of birthparents**
>
> "As a result of TAC, I am more tuned in to the psychological presence of birthparents."
> "I am more comfortable in asking questions about birthparents and validating clients' experiences with them."

Tanya's sister wanted to be in touch with their birth mother, and Tanya made the decision to have contact as well. At age 12, she began having periodic visits with her birth mother. Previous therapy had not provided guidance to Tanya or her parents about managing contact with her birth family and preparing Tanya for the inevitable up and down emotions triggered by these visits. Tanya struggled with challenging feelings toward her birth mother, especially for placing her with caregivers that were anything but caring and protective. Her therapist helped her work through her painful, conflicted feelings, including loyalty issues that she did not understand. "Why should I even care about people who were responsible for my being hurt?" This work enabled Tanya to tap into feelings of empathy for her birth mother's precarious life circumstances as an undocumented immigrant in the United States.

> **Referral to adjunct resources and therapies**
>
> "I now strongly consider if a therapist is adoption competent prior to referring my families."
> "We are trying to encourage therapists in the community/regionally to participate in TAC to increase the overall adoption competency and capacity of therapists regionally."

Because so much of Tanya's trauma experiences were pre-verbal and not part of her conscious memory, non-verbal therapies to address trauma were important in addressing Tanya's triggers for both anxiety and rage. Tanya's therapist referred her to an adoption competent therapist who was skilled in the use of Eye Movement Desensitization and Reprocessing. She also arranged for Tanya to see an adoption competent psychiatrist for medication management in the form of anti-depressants and mood stabilizers. Tanya also participated in an eight-week support group for high school adoptees that had a concurrent parent group.

An adoption competent therapist understands that progress in complex treatment is not linear. Tanya and her family took one step forward, two steps back, but over time, many gains were achieved. At age 22, Tanya has successfully completed a two-year medical technician program at her local community college and wants to pursue a degree in nursing. She continues to see her therapist on an as-needed basis along with her parents and has sporadic visits with her birthmother.

Expanding the reach: National Adoption Competency Mental Health Training Initiative

In 2014, CASE was awarded the five-year National Adoption Competency Mental Health Training Initiative (NTI), a competitive cooperative agreement with the Children's Bureau (grant #90CO1121) to develop, deliver, and evaluate a free, state-of-the-art, evidence-informed, web-based training curriculum for child welfare and mental health professionals. The goal is to enhance these professionals' capacity to meet the mental health needs of children and families moving toward adoption or guardianship and adoptive and guardianship families. The initiative seeks to infuse adoption mental health competencies in professional practice to improve well-being, stability, and permanency outcomes and to improve collaboration between child welfare and mental health service systems to assure a skilled and competent workforce and readily available, appropriate, adoption competent services.

Like TAC, the NTI curriculum is competency-based, integrating the knowledge, values, and skills needed for adoption competent child welfare and mental health practice. The competencies were identified by 21 national advisers, including experts in the field and individuals with lived experience as foster and/or adoptive parents, adoptees, and former foster youth. The two state-of-the-art, web-based trainings developed through this initiative utilize adult learning principles to actively engage the web user. The trainings include links to resources, activities, and opportunities for reflection and use case scenarios and stories from adoptive and guardianship parents, children and youth, and experts in each content area.

The 20-hour NTI Training for Child Welfare Professionals focuses on casework practices for staff across the child welfare continuum to promote child well-being and family stability. Child welfare supervisors receive an additional three hours of training and a *Supervisor Coaching and Activity Guide* to support their staff to transfer learning to daily practice. The 25-hour NTI Training for Mental Health Professionals provides clinical skills and therapeutic approaches for work with adoptive and guardianship families. This training is intended for agency-based and private practice mental health professionals providing services to children, youth, and families experiencing foster care, guardianship, or adoption through public child welfare agencies, private/domestic adoption agencies, and inter-country adoption. Table 32.3 provides the competencies on which the two curricula are based.

NTI piloted both trainings in nine sites across the US: California, Illinois, Maine, Minnesota, South Carolina, Oklahoma, Tennessee, Washington, and the Cherokee Nation. The trainings were implemented first with child welfare service systems and then through collaborations between child welfare and mental health service systems in each site. Sites

Table 32.3 NTI curricula competencies

Understanding children's mental health needs
Supporting and strengthening attachment
Understanding the impact of race, culture, and diversity on adoptive and guardianship families
Supporting loss and grief
Understanding the impact of trauma on brain development and behavior
Supporting positive identity formation
Promoting family stability post-placement
Assessment and treatment planning through an adoption lens (for mental health professionals)
Therapeutic parenting strategies to address challenging behaviors (for mental health professionals)

were selected to be collectively representative of child welfare systems in terms of demographics, public/privatization, and state/county administration of child welfare services, ensuring that the range of implementation conditions experienced in the pilot could facilitate preparation for nationwide implementation.

The mental health curriculum was piloted in 2018 and had over 2,900 participants enrolled across nine pilot sites with a 51 percent completion rate for all enrollees and a 69 percent completion rate for those who started the training. Of the 2,403 enrollees who consented to the evaluation, 48 percent or 1,146 completed the training, and preliminary findings are based on this pool.

In terms of education, 89 percent of completers had a master's degree and 4 percent a bachelor's degree, with 64 percent indicating that they had licensure. Completers had an average of 10 years of experience in the mental health field and 8 years of adoption/guardianship experience. One element of the NTI pilot evaluation examined pre- and post-test performance of 1,876 participants as of December 2018. Across all ten modules, the average pre-test performance was 50 percent and 95 percent on the post-test.

Implications for research, practice, and policy

CASE's experience of ten years with the TAC and its early experience with the NTI strongly indicate that there is a critical need for adoption competent mental health training; current efforts are making a meaningful impact on the knowledge, skill, and values competencies of participating mental health professionals; more needs to be learned about training outcomes and effectiveness; and current efforts need to be enhanced with deeper clinical learning opportunities to provide clinicians with in-depth skills in working with vulnerable children, youth, and families. Specifically, the following are important next steps:

1. Incentives need to be constructed to educate a larger audience of clinicians who are working with members of the adoption kinship network without the requisite competencies to provide clients with safe and effective interventions with lasting value. In some communities, state, county, and city child welfare agencies refer children, youth and families only to mental health professionals who have completed the TAC. Another potential incentive is to require all mental health professionals who contract with child welfare systems to complete NTI training to ensure a foundational level of adoption mental health competence in their clinical practice.
2. Mental health professionals need ongoing transfer of learning and coaching activities and booster sessions to support practice change and transfer of learning skills. Research shows that during learning events, the memory strengthens, but as soon as the learning event ends, forgetting begins (Thalheimer, 2006). For mental health professionals, ongoing contact through case presentations, supervision, and coaching is important because of the length of time required to build proficiency in a new practice and the opportunity for active learning (Birman, Desimone, Porter, & Garet, 2000). Within the education literature, studies estimate that it requires 20–25 implementation attempts to achieve consistent professional behavior change (Joyce & Showers, 2002). The medical and mental health literatures also support the importance of continued contact (Bruns, Rast, Walker, Peterson, & Bosworth, 2006).
3. Networks of peer supervision groups are needed to reduce isolation and mitigate impact of secondary trauma when working with this vulnerable population. Research supports the effectiveness of peer supervision groups in promoting the professional

development of experienced clinicians (Golia & McGovern, 2015; Schreiber & Frank, 2018). Other benefits of group supervision include increased opportunity for reflection and exploration; increased accountability to professional standards and codes of ethics; a vehicle for the transmission of new ideas and current trends; opportunity to practice clinical skills in a safe, supported space; stronger professional networks; reduction of isolation; and enhancement of practitioner well-being (Bailey, Bell, Kalle, & Pawar, 2014).

4. Adoption competency training programs need to be certified. Certification of adoption competency training programs provides trainees, the organizations for which they work, and, most importantly, the clients of trained clinicians, with assurance that the program follows best practices. Key stakeholders have proof of an impartial, third-party validation that an organization's program has met recognized national and international credentialing standards for development, implementation, administration, and maintenance of education and training (Institute for Credentialing Excellence, 2019).
5. Adoption competency training needs to be offered in graduate programs and other post-graduate clinical training programs (see Chapter 35 in this volume). To date, graduate training programs have offered little relevant adoption coursework to their students (Brodzinsky, 2013). One study of clinical training programs in marriage and family therapy, social work, and counseling found that only 4.8 percent to 16.3 percent of the programs offered specific coursework in adoption and only 2.6 percent to 22.1 percent offered coursework on foster care, although other courses at times included these issues as subcomponents (Weir, Fife, Whiting, & Blazewick, 2008). A troubling finding of another study was that only 16 percent of family therapists who reviewed a simulated case study of an adoptive family with an explicit presenting problem related to adoption focused their interventions on adoption (McDaniel & Jennings, 1997).
6. Research is needed to more fully assess outcomes for members of the adoption kinship network. Important areas of inquiry are families' satisfaction with mental health treatment, the quality of the clinician–client relationship, clinicians' adoption sensitivity in treatment, and evidence of improvements in child and family well-being, stability, and permanence.
7. Research is needed to fully evaluate the effectiveness of current evidence-based/evidence-informed treatment interventions with foster and adopted children.

Conclusion

CASE is proud to have played an important role in responding to the need for building an adoption competent work force comprised of mental health professionals and other professionals who work with the adoption and foster care community. In providing leadership in the creation of two adoption competent training products, CASE has contributed to the field in ensuring adoptive families' ability to access adoption competent mental health services. Evaluations of the TAC and NTI trainings demonstrate that among mental health professionals, there are significant gaps in knowledge and understanding about adoption and the mental health challenges of adoptees and their families. High-quality training addresses those gaps, with participants showing significant knowledge gains in all modules for TAC and NTI. More importantly, the evaluation of TAC to date has demonstrated the ability of trainees to translate knowledge into clinical practice – ranging from changes in assessment practice to use of treatment modalities and clinical approaches to more systemic organizational impacts. The evaluation regarding impact on practice for NTI is incomplete at this writing, but given the improvements from pre- to post-test, it seems highly likely that, as with TAC, NTI participants will report significant changes in their practice.

References

American Academy of Pediatrics. (2014). Healthy FC America: Mental and behavioral health. Retrieved January 19, 2019, from www.aap.org/en-us/advocacy-and-policy/aap-health-initiatives/healthy-foster-care-america/Pages/Mental-and-Behavioral-Health.aspx

Arneaud, S., Hayes, K., Hoekstra, R., Jackson, R., Kerr, B., Lakin, D., & Wasserman, K. (1996). *Adoption support and preservation services*. Southfield, MI: Spaulding for Children.

Atkinson, A. J., Gonet, P. A., Freundlich, M., & Riley, D. B. (2013). Adoption competent clinical practice: Defining its meaning and development. *Adoption Quarterly*, *16*(3–4), 156–174. doi:10.1080/10926755.2013.844215

Atkinson, A. J., & Riley, D. B. (2017). Training for adoption competency: Building a community of adoption-competent clinicians. *Families in Society: the Journal of Contemporary Social Services*, *98*(3), 235–242. doi:10.1606/1044-3894.2017.98.23

Bailey, R., Bell, K., Kalle, W., & Pawar, M. (2014). Restoring meaning to supervision through a peer consultation group in rural Australia. *Journal of Social Work Practice*, *28*(4), 479–495. doi:10.1080/02650533.2014.896785

Birman, B. F., Desimone, L., Porter, A. C., & Garet, M. S. (2000). Designing professional development that works. *Educational Leadership*, *57*, 28–33. Retrieved from www.ascd.org/ASCD/pdf/journals/ed_lead/el200005_birman.pdf

Brodzinsky, D. M. (2013). *A need to know: Enhancing adoption competence among mental health professionals*. New York: Donaldson Adoption Institute. Retrieved from www.adoptioninstitute.org/wp-content/uploads/2017/03/2013_08_ANeedToKnow.pdf

Bruns, E. J., Rast, J., Walker, J. S., Peterson, C. R., & Bosworth, J. (2006). Spreadsheets, service providers, and the statehouse: Using data and the wraparound process to reform systems for children and families. *American Journal of Community Psychology*, *38*, 201–212. doi:10.1007/s10464-006-9074-z

Center for Adoption Support and Education. (2018). *Beneath the mask: For teen adoptees: Teens and young adults share their stories*. Burtonsville, MD: Author.

Golia, G. M., & McGovern, A. R. (2015). If you save me, I'll save you: The power of peer supervision in clinical training and professional development. *British Journal of Social Work*, *45*(2), 634–650. doi:10.1093/bjsw/bct138

Harwood, R., Feng, X., & Yu, S. (2013). Preadoption adversities and postadoption mediators of mental health and school outcomes among international, foster, and private adoptees in the United States. *Journal of Family Psychology*, *27*(3), 409–420. doi:10.1037/aoo32908

Institute for Credentialing Excellence. (2019) *The ABCs of Assessment-Based Certificate (ABC) program accreditation*. Retrieved January 19, 2019, from www.nxtbook.com/nxtbooks/smithbucklin/ice_digest_2016q2/index.php#/20

Joyce, B. R., & Showers, B. (2002). *Student achievement through staff development* (3rd ed.). Alexandria, VA: Association for Supervision and Curriculum Development.

Juffer, F., & van IJzendoorn, M. H. (2005). Behavior problems and mental health referrals of international adoptees: A meta-analysis. *JAMA: Journal of the American Medical Association*, *293*, 2501–2515. doi:10.1001/jama.293.20.2501

Keyes, M. A., Malone, S. M., Sharma, A., Iacono, W. G., & McGue, M. (2013). Risk of suicide attempt in adopted and nonadopted offspring. *Pediatrics*, *132*(4), 639–646. doi:10.1542/peds.2012-3251

McCrae, J. S., Barth, R. P., & Guo, S. Y. (2010). Changes in maltreated children's emotional-behavioral problems following typically provided mental health services. *American Journal of Orthopsychiatry*, *80*(3), 350–361. doi:10.1111/j.1939-0025.2010.01039.x

McDaniel, K., & Jennings, G. (1997). Therapists' choice of treatment for adoptive families. *Journal of Family Psychotherapy*, *8*, 47–68. doi:10.1300/J085V08N04_04

Riley, D. B., & Meeks, J. (2005). *Beneath the mask: Understanding adopted teens*. Burtonsville, MD: Center for Adoption Support and Education.

Schreiber, P., & Frank, E. (2018). The use of a peer supervision group by social work clinicians. *The Clinical Supervisor*, *1*(1), 29–36. doi:10.1300/J001v01n01_04

Tan, T. X., & Marn, T. (2013). Mental health service utilization in children adopted from US foster care, US private agencies and foreign countries: Data from the 2007 National Survey of Adoption Parents (NSAP). *Children and Youth Services Review, 35*(7), 1050–1054. doi:10.1016/j.childyouth.2013.04.020

Thalheimer, W. (2006). *Spacing learning events over time: What the research says.* Somerville, MA: Work-Learning Research, Inc. Retrieved January 19, 2019, from http://q-mindshare.com/assets/spacing_learning_over_time__march2009v1_.pdf

US Department of Health and Human Services. (2017). *Child and Family Services Review: Aggregate Report – Round 3 Findings 2015–2016.* Retrieved January 19, 2019, from www.acf.hhs.gov/sites/default/files/cb/cfsr_round3_findings_2015_2016.pdf

Weir, K. N., Fife, S. T., Whiting, J. B., & Blazewick, A. (2008). Clinical training of MFTs for adoption, foster care, and child development settings: A comparative survey of CACREP, COAMFTE, and CSWE accredited programs. *Journal of Family Psychotherapy, 19*, 277–290. doi:10.1080/08975350802269517

33

AWARENESS OF ADOPTION AT SCHOOL

Francine Fishman

Introduction and case example

Ms. Forte's/Ms. Peters' integrated co-taught science class

MS. FORTE: "Now that we understand what an inherited trait is, let's find out what some of our classmates have inherited from their families."

FRANK: Oh no. She's randomly picking kids. What will I say? I'll just make something up. Or maybe she does know? Ugh, I'm so nervous. If I keep my head down, she won't see me. Keep it down, keep it down, keep it down …

MS. FORTE: "How about you, Frank? What did you inherit from your family?"

FRANK: "Ummmm, ahhhh … my hair?"

Similar narratives can be told in countless classrooms across America, thus contributing to the silent culture of adoption. Adopted students may encounter similar situations numerous times throughout their educational careers. These moments can bring on a flood of emotions and more questions to process. In the example above, all learning at that moment has been derailed for Frank. Frank, a 9-year-old student in the fourth grade, remembers learning he was adopted at about age 7. During a typical school day, a friend on the playground, upset with Frank, blurted out, "I don't care if you beat me! YOU'RE ADOPTED AND ADOPTED KIDS ARE STUPID!" Other friends and classmates looked on curiously and began to question what "adopted" meant. His teacher quickly quieted the conversation. Stunned, he remembers returning home to query his mother on exactly what adopted meant, and why did his friends know while he didn't? He recalls his mother crying, which was a clear signal to him that this was a scary topic. His mother explained Frank's beginnings as best she could, however, one glaring fact stood out to him: he had another mother and father who didn't want him.

The aim of this chapter is to help teachers like Ms. Forte facilitate culturally responsive teaching practices into their classrooms and to include adopted students or students touched by adoption in the diversity mix, whether or not the school has identified them as such. When considering diversity, many schools might immediately consider race or religion; however, it is crucial to be aware of the many diverse considerations in the classroom, such as family dynamics, language, socio-economic status (SES), and student trauma. In order to facilitate learning, teachers and administrators must think critically about the ways diversity directly impacts education. While Ms. Forte was likely well-intentioned, compassionate, and caring, she was not fully aware of the diverse background of her student. Frank might have felt that if he shared his story, his teacher would not understand, or that she would see him as bad or less than. The emotions elicited from both of these scenarios overwhelmed Frank. As Frank has learned from his experience at home, compliance and acquiescence help to avoid any intense reactions.

This chapter will offer strategies for educators to deal with scenarios similar to the one discussed here. In consideration of the culture of adoption, the reader will explore what it means for a school to engage in culturally responsive teaching, with a critical lens on the traumatizing effects of loss and separation. It will also explore the special education process and suggest school partnerships that encourage whole child education. Finally, resources and assignments are made available to promote student success.

Culturally responsive teaching

Culturally responsive teaching is a student-centered approach in which teachers integrate content, pedagogy, and knowledge of students into one cohesive framework. Within this lens, content refers to traditional subject matter, pedagogy refers to teaching methods and strategies, and knowledge of students constitutes the instructor's understanding of students' cultural backgrounds, learning styles, and abilities (Horowitz, Domzalski, & Elizalde-Utnick, 2018). In her book, Gay (2010) defined culturally responsive teaching as "using the cultural knowledge, prior experiences, frames of reference, and performance styles of diverse students to make learning encounters more relevant to and effective for students" (p. 31). This chapter will further explore culturally responsive teaching practices and how they can be impactful in the classroom, especially in classrooms that contain adopted students.

All learners construct knowledge from an inner scaffolding of their individual and social experiences, emotions, will, aptitudes, beliefs, values, self-awareness, and purpose (Senge et al., 2012). When considering a student's schema, it is important to acknowledge that there might be disconnects between content being taught and previous cultural experiences and knowledge (An, 2013).

Adopted children as learners are not only learning as academic students at school; they are also learning the language and realities of adoption. In the preschool years, they often begin to learn parts of their adoption story (Brodzinsky & Roberts, 2011). In the middle years between 6 and 12 years of age, they undergo many changes in their cognitive and socio-emotional development, which have significant implications for their understanding of and adjustment to adoption (Brodzinsky & Pinderhughes, 2002). Reflecting on Frank's situation, we can infer that due to his age, his logical thought and reasoning are likely somewhat limited (Brodzinsky & Roberts, 2011). Frank's black hair represents much more to him now as he begins to develop insight into the realities and loss associated with adoption (Brodzinsky, 1990; Brodzinsky & Pinderhughes, 2002; Leon, 2002; Nickman, 1985). The recognition of these differences simply connotes the varying realities of the many types of families that make up the American landscape today (Evan B. Donaldson Adoption Institute & CASE, 2006). For adopted students, this differentness might feel isolating; however, it is likely that they are not alone in their thoughts or in their classrooms, especially if we consider that 100 million Americans have adoption in their immediate families and around 7 million Americans are adopted (Adoption, 2013).

The benefit of educating schools to be culturally responsive is two-fold. First it is with the intent that educators will seek to gain knowledge of their students, and second, that knowledge will guide their own beliefs and behaviors to best practice. When schools value culture as an important part of the educational system, the classroom becomes a safe space, and a sense of belonging for all students is cultivated. Given the number of individuals affected by adoption, it is prudent for teachers and administrators to understand the impact of the issues within the culture of adoption and how they affect students' school performance. Schools must also realize that there is no specific set of symptoms attached to the adopted student.

Variables, such as the individual's age, origin of adoption, or experiences, can further complicate the teaching and understanding of adoption. For example, according to Brodzinsky (1990), children adopted later in life come to understand the meaning of adoption during a different developmental stage than their younger counterparts. Those who have experienced trauma or neglect might remember such experiences, which further complicate their self-image. Transracial, cross-cultural, and special needs issues can also affect a child's adoption experience (Melina, 2002). These diverse circumstances illustrate the various complexities and considerations for educators and school systems to consider in the classroom.

The influence of culture on educational outcomes cannot be overestimated (Rosenberg, Westling, & McLeskey, 2011). However, schools are often laser focused on the achievement gap, which refers to how various student demographic groups differ in scores on state or national achievement tests. Educational systems are concerned about the achievement disparities across all groups, but concern does not always result in action (Anderson, Medrich, & Fowler, 2007). Once educators become aware of the culture gap that exists and see themselves as facilitators of change, they can then begin to close the achievement gaps. The culture gap embedded in adoption is sometimes muted, overlooked by educators, or riddled with misconceptions and stereotypes.

An understanding of loss and separation for educators

Trauma-informed schools

In order for schools to best support students who have been adopted, educators must have a fundamental understanding of the adoption process and its implications for the individual, the family, and the school. Additionally, it is critical for educators to recognize the symptoms of trauma and to be equipped with the tools and strategies to undertake related issues that may arise. Schools must undergo a paradigm shift in their understanding, awareness, and sensitivity to adoption-related issues. For this shift to be sustained, systemic commitment to include adoption awareness and education in the school culture, practice, and policy must exist.

Schools are encountering children adopted through foster care at an increasing rate, thus intensifying the need for a trauma-informed approach (see Chapter 14 in this volume for a more detailed discussion). Since the 1970s, the rate of planned newborn adoption has dropped steadily, while the adoption rate from foster care has surged (Gray, 2012). Children adopted from foster or institutional care might be dealing with complexities such as abuse, neglect, or frequent residential moves.

Much of the known information about the potential impact of childhood experiences on outcomes later in life stems from the Adverse Childhood Experiences (ACEs) study first issued in the mid-1990s (Centers for Disease Control and Prevention, 2019). Felitti et al.

(1998) defined ACEs as incidents of psychological, physical, or sexual abuse, and/or household dysfunction. Individual ACEs were found to be positively associated with the risk of poor health behaviors, while the total number of ACEs was positively associated with a variety of diseases and poor self-rated health in adulthood (Felitti et al., 1998).

The word trauma often takes on a negative connotation as it conjures up images of catastrophic events and/or intense, debilitating experiences. When trauma is referenced specifically in adoption, it is important for schools to put into perspective the individuals' experiences. The loss and separation inherent in adoption is considered a traumatic event. Despite the trauma, many adopted children show resilience and have very positive outcomes (Van, Juffer, van IJzendoorn, Bakermans-Kranenburg, & Alink, 2012). When neglect is coupled with separation, however, the trauma becomes more complex. Neglect and separation are reported to be two of the most ominous risk factors when examining which children will recover from traumatic stress symptoms (van der Kolk, 2002). Because a neglectful environment diverges sharply from the average expected environment, it is conceptualized as one of the most toxic and severe environmental conditions for development (Rogosch, Oshri, & Cicchetti, 2010).

Unfortunately, knowledge of complex trauma is often lacking among educators, which leads to various implications for schools, such as the misinterpretation of behaviors and disproportionate consequences. When adopted students display behaviors at school as a result of individual trauma experienced, they might be punished or ostracized because those behaviors are misunderstood by peers or school personnel. Fortunately, preliminary evidence suggests that trauma-focused training delivered to service providers builds knowledge, changes attitudes, and fosters practices favorable to trauma-informed approaches (Brown, Baker, & Wilcox; 2012; Green et al., 2015). Using evidenced-based practices and strategies in the classroom to address potential school issues will help facilitate culturally responsive teaching. See Chapters 25, 27, and 28 for in-depth discussion of the behavioral, emotional, and academic adjustment that is typical of adopted children.

Case study

The following case study examines a pattern of behavior for a student adopted from foster care.

Presenting problem

Before Ana was adopted at age 7, she had been in many foster homes. She had no ties to her biological family. Reports state that she endured abuse and neglect during the first six years of her life. Details of the abuse and neglect were not shared with the family. Ana has shared what she remembers, but struggles to recall details.

For three consecutive years, Ana has had intense meltdowns in the weeks leading up to the last day of school as the end of the school year represents the disappearance of another wave of people she cares about. While her classmates celebrated with excitement about summer, Ana experienced some of the most difficult times of the school year, especially because of her upcoming transition to middle school. Although she had a positive relationship with her teacher, she began to refuse to go to school. Ana became disruptive in class and even verbally and physically aggressive toward her teacher and friends.

Unfortunately, many imposed consequences resulted in suspension from school, which were seemingly welcomed by Ana. Subsequently, Ana missed crucial instruction, social interactions, and the opportunity for relationship building. During a meeting, her teacher commented, "perhaps Ana may be suffering from adopted child syndrome." Her mother was surprised by this comment and wondered if perhaps this was a window into an implicit bias held by the teacher. In an effort to avoid a repeat of the last three years, the family welcomed early communication with Ana's new school as a proactive measure.

Intervention

In late August, Ana's family requested a meeting at her new school, where they openly shared Ana's background and history with present administrators and teachers. While they proceeded with caution to protect their daughter's privacy, they also understood that sharing her history would allow insight into her early life experiences. To the family's surprise, a member of the administration team shared his own journey with adoption. The family felt comforted and understood, especially because his experiences strikingly resembled Ana's. In the subsequent months, Ana's family participated in numerous advocacy meetings and were asked to participate as parent members on the district's initiative to create a trauma-informed school.

Implications

The systemic shift necessary for a successful trauma-informed approach is a slow and arduous task as it involves a change in the culture, beliefs, practices, and policies in a school district. Unlike academic issues, where identification of need and provision of assistance are relatively focused and non-controversial, a host of layered complexities surround trauma-informed delivery in schools (e.g. involvement of multiple systems of care, family privacy, and school resource capacity). Thus, successful implementation of a trauma-informed approach is dependent on the identification of these complexities and alignment with careful planning and decision making (Chafouleas, Johnson, Overstreet, & Santos, 2016).

When professionals use effective approaches and understand the etiology of behavior, they can help create positive outcomes for students. At the heart of these approaches is the belief that students' actions are a direct result of their experiences. When students act out or disengage, we should not ask "What's wrong with you?" but rather "What happened to you?" (SAMHSA & NCTIC, 2015). With this better understanding of ACEs and their impact on behavior, some state legislatures and schools have banned suspending or expelling children for behavioral problems (Metzler, Merrick, Klevens, Ports, & Ford, 2017). The deleterious nature of suspension is evidenced by the fact that receiving just one out-of-school suspension can potentially alter a student's educational trajectory (Balfanz, Byrnes, & Fox, 2013). School systems need to consider other alternatives to suspending or expelling children when addressing the behavioral problems that are likely the result of ACEs (Metzler et al., 2017).

Children's reaction to trauma can disrupt learning and interfere greatly with behaviors at school. Schools are critical systems of support for children who have experienced trauma. All stakeholders have a tremendous responsibility to recognize trauma responses, accommodate, and respond to traumatized students within the classroom. It is important for educators to realize that every behavior serves a function. When using proactive strategies in the classroom, it is essential to realize not all behaviors will be overt. A child can cope with the pain of loss in a variety of ways, such as compliance/acquiescence, withdrawal, aggression, provocation, and/or acting out. In Ana's case study, her verbal aggression toward her teacher and peers resulted in suspension, which ultimately led to avoidance of emotions.

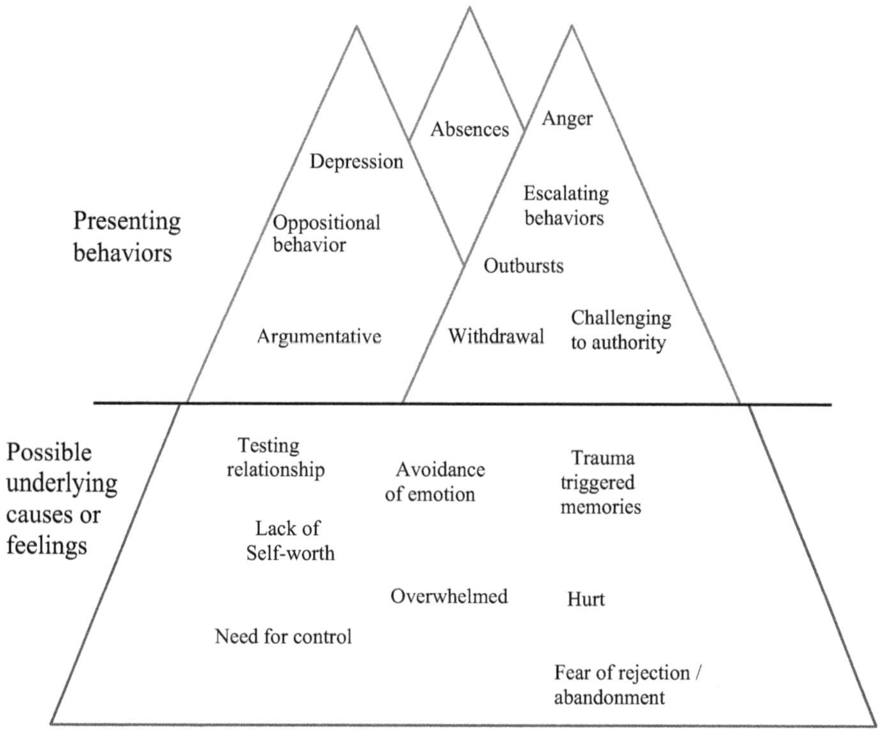

Figure 33.1 Possible causes for behaviors

Her verbal aggression suggests that the function of her behavior was to avoid a situation all too familiar and hurtful to her. By using proactive strategies, like the ones suggested within the Positive Behavioral Interventions and Supports (PBIS) framework, educators can begin to break the cycle of trauma and behavior. Perhaps if her teacher was focused on "What happened to you?" instead of "What's wrong with you?", she might have been able to see below Ana's presenting behavior (Tenner, 2017). See Figure 33.1 for examples of presenting behaviors and possible underlying causes or feelings.

Strategies for educators

Numerous opportunities exist to help students cope with unique issues of adoption and address behavioral challenges that could be related to adopted children's early experiences of abuse and/or neglect.

Positive behavioral interventions and supports (PBIS)

Preventative interventions to address behaviors in the classroom are crucial to creating a safe and nurturing environment. The increased legislative pressure on schools to prevent disruptive and violent behavior, often resulting in suspension, has likely contributed to the popularity of preventative interventions, such as PBIS (Bradshaw, Reinke, Brown, Bevans, & Leaf, 2008). According to Horner and Sugai (2015), schools that adopt a schoolwide behavior intervention, such as PBIS, report a reduction of office discipline referrals, a reduction in suspension and expulsions, and improved social emotional competence and academic outcomes.

PBIS is a continuum of increasingly intensive interventions, assessment methods, and organizational systems that support the implementation of practices and ongoing use of data (Horner & Sugai, 2015; Sugai & Horner, 2006). Much of what teachers do on a daily basis is rooted in basic and commonly understood behavioral, social, and organizational principles, and therefore can be considered Tier 1 interventions. Because not all adopted students will respond to the same curricula and teaching strategies, some students with identified needs require supplemental or targeted instruction and intervention in Tier 2. Last, in Tier 3, intensive, individualized interventions and supports are provided for the smaller percentage of students with the most severe needs. Included in Table 33.1 are Tier 1 strategies for classroom management to support students.

Using adoption-friendly language

As the fabric of adoption has changed over the decades, so has the acceptable language used when adoption is referenced. Despite progress, there is much room for improvement with respect to everyday language. Historically, the language used in the adoption process focused on finding a child for a family, rather than a family for a child, and through the present-day

Table 33.1 Potential classroom management strategies used by educators

Greeting at the door	Greeting students at the door sets a tone for the culture of the classroom. It welcomes students and provides them a feeling of security and acceptance. It helps to build relationships between students and teachers. It allows a sense of community and belonging.
Arrange orderly physical environment	Organized classrooms can provide a sense of stability and order for students. Setting up a physical environment to allow teachers to monitor all students and activities promotes feelings of safety and predictability for students.
Define, teach, and acknowledge rules and expectations	All students, and especially students impacted by trauma, thrive from established expectations. For students impacted by trauma, high expectations show the student they are capable and worthy and help to build self-confidence. Consistent classroom rules and expectations help students differentiate purposeful rules from unpredictable rules that might occur in other areas of their lives.
Define and teach classroom routines	When we provide clearly defined routines and procedures, students know what to expect. Reducing the stress of the unknown helps students to operate in a state of calm. Clearly established routines also encourage adults to identify and prompt students of changes in routine, to prevent behaviors due to unpredictability.
Employ active supervision	Maintaining active supervision provides a sense of safety for students. Active supervision creates frequent opportunities to interact with students to develop, strengthen, and maintain relationships.

Table 33.2 Words or phrases commonly associated with adoption

Instead of this …	*Message*	*Say this …*
"put up for adoption"	The history of "put up for adoption" originated from children who were forced onto trains, where they would ride across the country, stopping in city after city, and be "put up" literally on stages or tall stumps at auctions to perform for and be inspected by prospective adoptive families.	"place for adoption" "made an adoption plan"
"gave away"	Giving a child away implies not being wanted or being discarded.	"place for adoption" "made an adoption plan"
"real parent/s"	No matter by birth or by adoption, a parent is always a real parent.	first parent, birth parent
"adopted child," "is adopted"	Adoption is the process, not the identifier. If clarification is not relevant, there is no reason to use this reference.	"child who was adopted"
"She's so lucky" "It's so wonderful that you adopted"	This is a subtle message received by parents and children that glorifies the parents and sends a message of unworthiness to the child.	"What a beautiful family, so filled with love"

lens can be viewed as dehumanizing to the adoptee and the process of adoption. For example, the historical notion that the "child could be returned if found to be unsatisfactory, or if for any reason the family decided it ought not keep the child" is directly and unequivocally contrary to today's adoption ideologies. Adoption professionals have more compassionate and holistic views regarding the process and the emotional underpinnings of the process. We now know that the abuse, neglect, trauma, and loss that these children experience can have an enduring impact on their brains and on their psychological, emotional, and cognitive development. Without this knowledge, schools often view adoption only as a "new beginning" or a "happy event" or think "how lucky" the child is to have been adopted. These idealistic views tend to overlook or even refute the very beginning of the child's adoption story.

At school adopted children are often asked difficult questions by peers or teachers about their adoption stories. Questions and comments can be generated for a variety of reasons including curiosity, nosiness, or bullying. See Chapter 22 for a discussion of microaggressions often experienced by individuals who have been adopted. When responding to questions and explaining adoption to students, the language and words used should send a message of respect and understanding. If the language of adoption is to be understood, it needs to be included as part of culturally responsive classroom training and teacher preparation curricula. Using adoption-sensitive language will help teach all children that adoption is another way to build a family. See Table 33.2 for adoption-friendly language (adapted from Flanagan, 2015).

The special education process

The federal and state regulations governing the special education process are critical in providing an understanding of the referral process and the rights of the individuals. When considering adopted students for special education, educators must be aware of the circumstances surrounding the adoption, such as the age the child was adopted and the origin of the adoption. For example, students adopted through foster care or internationally adopted students who enter the US school system with no English language skills bring to school their own unique circumstances. These circumstances do not necessarily constitute a referral to special education.

Pre-referral requirements

States are required to use a Multi-Tiered System of Supports/Response to Intervention (MTSS/RtI) approach that provides high-quality structured interventions matched to student needs prior to referral in an effort to improve the identification process. A Multi-Tiered System of Support (MTSS) is an overarching framework that can be an integration of behavioral supports such as PBIS, mental health supports, and academic supports (RtI), all systematically delivered using a range of interventions (Bailey, 2018). MTSS emphasizes a tiered continuum of evidence-based practices within the context of prevention science and implementation research (PBIS Implementation Blueprint, 2015). Using this three-pronged, data-rich approach, all students are seen holistically and referrals to special education are made based on true need and valid diagnoses.

Special education services

Students who enter school with a diagnosed disability are guaranteed services under the Individuals with Disabilities Education Act (IDEA, Individuals with Disabilities Education Act, 2019), which entitles children to a free, appropriate public education and ensures special education and related services to eligible children with disabilities. IDEA governs how states and public agencies provide early intervention, special education, and related services.

Diagnosis is a prerequisite to determining if services are warranted. Subsequent determinants include whether the diagnosis impacts the student's access to curriculum and whether the student needs specially designed instruction (Riccomini, Morano, & Hughes, 2017). Once a diagnosis is determined through academic, behavioral, and/or cognitive assessments, access to services is initiated. When a student is identified by schools as eligible for special education services, they might qualify for one of two types of assistance. One option is the Individualized Education Program (IEP), which provides specially designed instruction, accommodations, modifications, and related services, such as speech-language, counseling, occupational, or physical therapy. A second option is the 504 Plan, which provides accommodations and related services to general education students who are identified with a disability, but do not need special education (National Center for Learning Disabilities, 2017).

English Language Learners/English as a new language

Students adopted internationally have added considerations as they might be learning a new language, while also learning content and skills. Prior to a referral to special education, it is important to decide whether the issues presented are tied to language or a learning disability. One of the most common errors when identifying English Language Learners (ELLs) for special education services is misinterpreting language acquisition as a learning or language disability. This is especially challenging because most internationally adopted children do not continue to use the language of their birth country following adoption, thus cognitive and academic testing in their first language is often not possible. All internationally adopted children should be monitored at school age for aspects of language that are essential to school success, such as verbal memory, sentence comprehension and production, conversational skills, and storytelling (Ellseff, 2013). The possible combined risk factors (i.e., trauma, institutionalization, maltreatment) often have significant impact on the language abilities for older internationally adopted children. Chapter 24 provides an in-depth examination of speech and language development for international adoptees.

School partnerships

Family-school connection

The partnership between the school and the family must be fostered as it is crucial to a student's success. Parental involvement makes a difference in developing student cognitive, social, and behavioral factors that support school outcomes (Beets, Cardinal, & Alderman, 2010). More specifically, among school-aged children, parents' school involvement predicted declines in problem behaviors across elementary grades. Children with more involved parents had enhanced social functioning and fewer adjustment problems (El Nokali, Bachman, & Votruba-Drzal, 2010).

Extensive research exists on the impact of parental involvement in the general population, yet few studies exist on the impact of parent involvement on adopted students at school (e.g., Englund, Luckner, Whaley, & Egeland, 2004; Fan & Chen, 2001). Research does show that adoptive parents tend to have a higher SES, higher education levels, and invest more heavily in their children's cognitive development than nonadoptive parents (Zill & Bramlett, 2014), suggesting that they often have the resources and motivation for high parental involvement. Yet adoptive families are not always well-represented in the school community or considered in the educational curriculum. They might experience marginalization as a result of the lack of inclusion in curricula, multi-racial status, insensitivity, or bias on behalf of school personnel. For example, lesbian and gay adoptive parents might face additional marginalization due to their same-sex relationship (Goldberg, Black, Sweeney, & Moyer, 2017). Given the adversity adoptive families often experience, schools should develop outreach programs that encourage inclusive parental and family engagement.

Individualized education plans

Parental involvement and advocacy are two cornerstones of the special education process. Without the support and advocacy of the parents or family members, IEP meetings lack richness. Unfortunately, IEPs are often written without student input and with fewer goals for independent living skills and postsecondary education. However, in a review of post-adoption IEPs, those written with parental or familial support outlined more specific goals, had a respectful tone, and were overall more comprehensive (Geenen & Powers, 2007).

Every Student Succeeds Act (ESSA)

The Every Student Succeeds Act (ESSA) requires states and districts to develop plans to work collaboratively with families and surrounding communities. The response initiatives that schools and districts design must be implemented through a culturally sensitive lens, while also cultivating a sustainable framework. District support will be key in establishing optimal process and organizational conditions (NYSED, 2013). The goal is to expand efforts to help schools, districts, and states better engage families in education. It is a commitment to supporting parents and families by empowering them and giving them a voice and an opportunity to be engaged. Promoting family–school partnerships at all levels, including representatives from state, district, and local agencies, and national leaders, such as chief state school officers and school board members, can include a variety of methods and activities. Activities can include policy briefings, parent forums, webinars, and informational sessions. The team hopes to reach not only parents and families but district and school personnel as well.

Barriers to engagement

Families often face multiple barriers when it comes to their engagement and involvement in the school, especially when systemic support is lacking or absent. When these barriers are broken down and parents become active members in their child's education, all individuals benefit. For example, when parental engagement becomes a schoolwide goal, opportunities to enhance skills, knowledge, and attitudes of stakeholders increases and engagement is sustained (Mendez, Carpenter, LaForett, & Cohen, 2009).

One barrier to parental engagement is the parents' lack of understanding of the school system necessary to advocate on behalf of their child (Bolivar & Chrispeels, 2010). Unfortunately, educators can create additional barriers that disengage families from school involvement. One example stems from educators' limited understanding of the losses and challenges associated with adoption, given the lack of training on the topic (Smith & Riley, 2006; Wood & Ng, 2001). Also, educators might interpret a lack of parent or family involvement as a lack of caring. They believe adopted children should behave and perform similarly to their nonadopted counterparts because of the underlying assumption that placement in an adoptive family solves the adopted child's difficulties associated with loss, grief, and trauma (Howard, Smith, & Ryan, 2004). Educators might also unwittingly engage in *adoptism*, or the bias that genetically connected families are privileged over those made through adoption.

Overcoming barriers

Educators must take various precautions and practice cultural sensitivity when attempting to engage adoptive families and build trusting relationships. Trust-building practices are necessary to engage adoptive families who might be hesitant to be involved at school. Some impactful methods include using appropriate, adoption-friendly language and asking thoughtful questions. Off-putting and marginalizing questions, such as whether the child is "theirs" or if they are the "real" parents, should be avoided. Adoptive families ultimately decide whether or how much they will reveal to schools about their child's adoption. Families are sometimes reluctant to share, fearing that teachers and staff will make assumptions based on preconceived stereotypes about adopted children (Smith & Riley, 2006). Adoption-sensitive teachers and educators recognize that the world often mistreats adoptive parents and adopted children as "second-best" families. They can use their skills and knowledge to advocate for these families and partner with adoptive families to create a culturally sensitive learning environment (Brabender & Fallon, 2013).

Implications for instruction

Library resources

School libraries are a critical component of school initiatives to develop and maintain a culturally responsive environment. Libraries should have an inviting atmosphere in which all students feel safe to ask questions, see themselves reflected in the literature, and discover more about their own and other cultures (Summers, 2010). School libraries that maintain a diverse collection of how families are built are more likely to establish trust and engagement. Additionally, when students learn academic content while making personal connections through their own cultural frameworks, their learning becomes richer and more meaningful (Gay, 2010).

Family-centered projects

The traditional notion of what constitutes a family is generally no longer representative and has since been replaced with myriad different arrangements. Family-centered history projects and assignments rooted in the notion of the traditional family still exist, despite the awareness of its perils. For children who join families through adoption or foster care, assignments such as bringing in a baby picture or making a family tree can be stressful and anxiety-ridden. These assignments often pressure families to choose between sharing the individual's biological lineage or the adoptive one. Teachers who willingly rearrange lesson plans and redraw assignments long regarded as staples of the classroom are attempting to reflect the growing diversity of their schools. However, there are teachers who refuse to modify assignments, claiming that there is no substitute for traditional genealogical research. The value of genealogical research is not to be disputed, however, allowing students to choose how they will complete the project is key. Every family has a rich history that genetics cannot tell. Alternative suggestions to these popular assignments can be found in the resources section at the end of this chapter.

Pre-service teachers

Teachers need time to engage in explicit reflection on their beliefs and the possible consequences of their beliefs (Fives & Buehl, 2016). As classroom dynamics change, many teacher education programs have added trainings on exploring and challenging beliefs about cultural diversity in education (Trent, Kea, & Oh, 2008). Strong preparation is key in making a dramatic difference in student learning and academic achievement (Darling-Hammond & Youngs, 2002).

Pre-service teachers need to be cognizant of the challenges they will encounter. For internationally adopted students who do not speak English, challenges include communication, socialization, and learning. Many pre-service teachers have concerns about educating ELLs in mainstream classrooms; they are accustomed to working with native English-speaking students (Barron & Menken, 2002) and are not equipped to meet the needs of linguistically diverse students (Pappamihiel, 2007). Other concerns stem from a lack of specific knowledge in the field, a lack of effective teaching strategies, and language differences (Turgut, Sahin, & Huerta, 2016).

Explicit direct instruction

Explicit direct instruction (EDI) was recently identified as one of the 22 "High-Leverage Practices" in special education suggested by the Council for Exceptional Children (McLeskey, 2017). EDI components, such as clear and explicit models and guided practice, reduce cognitive load and its resulting stress on working memory. Students who lack background knowledge and/or automaticity in recalling prerequisite knowledge benefit from EDI (Clark, Kirschner, & Sweller, 2012; Smith, Saez, & Doabler, 2016). For example, internationally adopted children might lack background knowledge of the history of the United States. Therefore, accessing prior knowledge is essential. There are various ways to assess what students know. For example, using predicting guides or using anticipatory sets. These are tools that let the student know what will be discussed and give the students an opportunity to show the teacher what they know, before the lesson begins (see resources for examples).

Resources and assignments

Adoption-friendly language

- Heart to Heart Adoptions, a sponsor of Adoption.org, provides resources across the journey of adoption including sensitive topics such as adoption-friendly language. adoption.org/use-positive-adoption-language
- Adoptive Families is an online subscription including How-To-Adopt and Adoption Parenting Network resources. Adoptive Families addresses issues pre- and post-adoption, including the importance of using and acknowledging adoption-sensitive language. adoptivefamilies.com/talking-about-adoption/positive-adoption-language/
- The United Methodist Church provides an online selection of adoption-related articles in support of using positive adoption language. The United Methodist Church believes that "sometimes we send unintended messages through the language we choose. To help avoid these types of miscommunications, UMC provides a list of positive adoption language." umc.org/what-we-believe/positive-adoption-language-examples-and-resources

Adoption resources for educators and students

- Center for Adoption Support and Education offers mental health services and educational resources for all members of the adoption and foster community. The organization's mission is to "improve the lives of children who have been adopted or in foster care and their families through counseling, lifelong education, and a growing national network of trained professionals." adoptionsupport.org/education-resources/for-parents-families/free-resources-links/

Articles: Schools and adoption

- Pact: An Adoption Alliance is a non-profit organization whose mission is "to serve adopted children of color." Pact has compiled a rich selection of articles and book reviews for educators of adopted children of color. www.pactadopt.org/resources/schools-and-adoption.html

Culturally responsive teaching

- The Education Alliance at Brown University recognizes and supports advancing equitable educational opportunities for all students. The mission of the Education Alliance is "to enhance learning for culturally and linguistically diverse students." By building partnerships with communities and educational organizations, they will apply research to transform instructional practice. www.brown.edu/academics/education-alliance/teaching-diverse-learners/

English Language Learners/adoption resources

- Colorín Colorado is a national website which provides research-based information, activities, and advice to educators and families of ELLs from Pre-K to 12th grade. Colorín Colorado has established itself as "a trusted leader in addressing the urgent challenge of helping ELLs around the country succeed." colorincolorado.org/adoption-and-school-resources-parents-and-educators

Explicit direct instruction

- Dataworks has conducted decades of educational research throughout 45,000 classrooms which has led to a collection of teaching procedures known as Explicit Direct Instruction (EDI). They are designed as interactive teaching strategies to help maximize learning. dataworks-ed.com/research-edu
- The Association for Supervision and Curriculum Development is focused "not just on the academic goals of curriculum, but also on education's broader social dimensions, including the development of students' moral and creative capacities and an understanding of their diverse needs." This collection of resources strives to empower educators to help students achieve excellence and assure they are "healthy, safe, engaged, supported, and challenged." Accessing prior knowledge in Explicit Direct Instruction: www.ascd.org/publications/books/113,005/chapters/Background-Knowledge@-The-Glue-That-Makes-Learning-Stick.aspx

Family engagement

- The US Department of Education has created the Family and Community Engagement Team. The mission and belief of the team is "Raising the next generation is a shared responsibility. When families, communities and schools work together, students are more successful and the entire community benefits. For schools and districts across the US, family engagement is becoming an integral part of education reform efforts." www.ed.gov/family-and-community-engagement?src=rn
- The Global Family Research Project believes that family engagement is a shared responsibility of families and of schools and communities to contribute to a child's learning. The Global Family Research Project works "across boundaries – with early childhood and afterschool organizations, schools, digital media, libraries, museums, and others working on behalf of children and families – to ensure that families are empowered in children's learning, from early childhood to young adulthood." globalfrp.org/Our-Work

Mental health resources

- Bethany Christian Services is a global non-profit organization. In their efforts to bring families together they believe that "strengthening families for the well-being of children is a top priority." Various resources are available for pre- and post-adoption families. https://bethany.org/resources/talking-to-your-kids-about-their-adoption

Family partnerships

- The Southwest Educational Development Laboratory along with the US Department of Education have created a Dual Capacity-Building Framework for School Partnerships, which is designed to act as a platform for the development of family engagement strategies, policies, and programs. www.p12.nysed.gov/turnaround/documents/partners-education.pdf

Special education

- The US Department of Education along with the Office of Special Education Rehabilitative Services (OSERS) is dedicated to improving results for infants, toddlers, children, and youth with disabilities ages birth through 21. The OSERS "understands the many challenges still facing individuals with disabilities and their families and is committed to improving results and outcomes for people with disabilities of all ages." www2.ed.gov/about/offices/list/osers/osep/index.html
- Project IDEAL is part of a teacher preparation program intended to better prepare teachers to work with students with disabilities. Project IDEAL makes available teaching modules including "key concepts, activities, presentations, tests, and media." www.projectidealonline.org/v/special-education-referral-process/

Trauma-informed schools

- The Trauma and Learning Policy Initiative's mission is "to ensure that children traumatized by exposure to family violence and other ACEs succeed in school." traumasensitiveschools.org/
- Documentary: *Paper Tigers*, which tells the story of a school that instituted a trauma-responsive, restorative justice-based culture and saw as a result a significant decrease in dropouts and suspensions. Film: https://kpjrfilms.co/paper-tigers/
- The National Center on Safe Supportive Learning Environments offers information and technical assistance to states, districts, schools, institutions of higher learning, and communities which is focused on improving student supports and academic enrichment. Training Package for Schools: safesupportivelearning.ed.gov/trauma-sensitive-schools-training-package
- The Attachment & Trauma Network's Trauma-Sensitive Schools Initiative is "devoted to creating schoolwide trauma-sensitive reform." The initiative offers professional development programs for educators to help schools understand the effects of early trauma on learning and behavior. creatingtraumasensitiveschools.org/professionaldevelopment/

Assignments

- This resource is a prominent site for adoption books and adoption-related resources which address issues "including, but not limited to, domestic and international adoption, open and closed adoption, transracial adoption, kinship adoption, foster care adoption." adoptionpolicy.org/Adoption_Awareness_Schools.pdf tapestrybooks.com
- Family-Centered Projects: PBS Parents is a trusted resource that is filled with information on child development. PBS Kids' mission is "to use the power of media to open worlds of possibilities for all children, so that every child can reach their full potential in school – and in life." pbs.org/parents/expert-tips-advice/2018/03/navigating-family-heritage-assignments-with-adopted-children/
- Family Tree Alternative: Creating a Family is the national infertility, adoption, & foster care education and support non-profit. Their mission is "to strengthen families through unbiased education and support for infertility patients, adoptive parents, foster parents, and allied professionals." creatingafamily.org/adoption-category/family-tree-assignment-adoption/
- Teaching Genetics: New York Times Blog (May 4, 2010) parenting.blogs.nytimes.com/2010/05/04/teaching-genetics-in-an-adoptive-world/

Library resources/books

- Adoption Network Law Center guides adopting parents and birth parents through every step of their adoption journey. This resource provides ideas and resource to celebrate November as National Adoption Month. https://adoptionnetwork.com/forty-three-ways-everyone-can-celebrate-national-adoption-month
- Books for Children: Adoption Circle has been a leader in "diligently working to preserve the rights of birth parents and children to ensure emotionally healthy and legally sound adoptions." This resource offers age appropriate books about adoption for children. adoptioncircle.org/adoption-resources/book-resources/
- Books for Parents and Children: Heart to Heart Adoptions sponsor of Adoption.com provides resources across the journey of adoption for children and families. adoption.com/11-great-adoption-books-you-should-read
- Chicken Soup for the Soul Entertainment, Inc. builds online video on-demand networks that provide positive and entertaining video content for all screens. aplus.com/national-adoption-month/adoption-books-reading-list?no_monetization=true

References

Adoption Facts. (2013). Adoption research. Retrieved from https://adoptionnetwork.com/adoption-statistics.

An, S. (2013). Schema theory in reading. *Theory and Practice in Language Skills*, *3*(1), 130–134. doi:10.4304/tpls.3.1.130-134

Anderson, S., Medrich, E., & Fowler, D. (2007). Which achievement gap? *Phi Delta Kappan*, *88*, 547–550. doi:10.1177/003172170708800716

Bailey, T. R. (2018) Is MTSS/RTI really that complicated? Let's get back to basics! Retrieved from www.rti4success.org/blog/mtssrti-really-complicated-let's-get-back-basics

Balfanz, R., Byrnes, V., & Fox, J. (2013). Sent home and put off-track: The antecedents, disproportionalities, and consequences of being suspended in the ninth grade. *Journal of Applied Research on Children*, *5*, 1–8.

Barron, V., & Menken, K. (2002). "What are the characteristics of the shortage of qualified teachers to teach english language learners?" Retrieved from www.ncela.fwu.edu/pubs/reports/teacherprep/teacherprep.pdf

Beets, M. W., Cardinal, B. J., & Alderman, B. L. (2010). Parental social support and the physical activity-related behaviors of youth: A review. *Health Education & Behavior, 37*(5), 621–644. doi:10.1177/1090198110363884

Bolivar, J. M., & Chrispeels, J. H. (2010). Enhancing parent leadership through building social and intellectual capital. *American Educational Research Journal, 48*(1), 4–38. doi:10.3102/0002831210366466

Brabender, V., & Fallon, A. (2013). *Working adoptive parents: Research, theory, and therapeutic interventions.* Hoboken, NJ: Wiley.

Bradshaw, C. P., Reinke, W. M., Brown, L. D., Bevans, K. B., & Leaf, P. J. (2008). Implementation of school-wide positive behavioral interventions and supports (PBIS) in elementary schools: Observations from a randomized trial. *Education and Treatment of Children, 31*(1), 1–26. doi:10.1353/etc.0.0025

Brodzinsky, D., & Roberts, M. C. (2011). Children's understanding of adoption: Developmental and clinical implications. *Professional Psychology: Research and Practice, 42*(2), 200–207. doi:10.1037/a0022415

Brodzinsky, D. M. (1990). A stress and coping model of adoption adjustment. In D. Brodzinsky & M. Schechter (Eds.), *The psychology of adoption* (pp. 3–24). New York: Oxford University Press.

Brodzinsky, D. M., & Pinderhughes, E. E. (2002). Parenting and child development in adoptive families. In M. Bornstein (Ed.), *Handbook of parenting: Children and parenting* (pp. 279–311). Mahwah, NJ: Lawrence Erlbaum.

Brown, S. M., Baker, C. N., & Wilcox, P. (2012). Risking connection trauma training: A pathway toward trauma-informed care in child congregate care settings. *Psychological Trauma: Theory, Research, Practice, and Policy, 4*, 507–514. doi:10.1037/a0025269

Centers for Disease Control and Prevention. (2019). Retrieved from www.cdc.gov/violenceprevention/childabuseandneglect/acestudy/about.html.

Chafouleas, S., Johnson, A., Overstreet, S., & Santos, N. (2016). Toward a blueprint for trauma-informed service delivery in schools. *School Mental Health, 8*(1), 144.

Clark, R. E., Kirschner, P. A., & Sweller, J. (2012). Putting students on the path to learning: The case for fully guided instruction. *American Educator, 36*(1), 6–11.

Darling-Hammond, L., & Youngs, P. (2002). Defining "highly qualified teachers": What does "scientifically-based research" actually tell us? *Educational Researcher, 31*(9), 13–25. doi:10.3102/0013189X031009013

Donaldson, E. B. Adoption Institute & CASE. (September 2006). *Adoption in the schools: A lot to learn, promoting equality and fairness for all children and their families.* Retrieved from www.adoptioninstitute.org/publications/adoption-in-the-schools-a-lot-to-learn/

El Nokali, N., Bachman, H., & Votruba-Drzal, E. (2010). Parent involvement and children's academic and social development in elementary school. *Child Development, 81*(3), 988–1005. doi:10.1111/j.1467-8624.2010.01447.x

Ellseff, T. (2013). Changing trends in international adoption: Implications for speech-language pathologists. *Perspectives on Global Issues in Communication Sciences & Related Disorders, 3*(2), 45–49. doi:10.1044/gics3.2.45

Englund, M. M., Luckner, A. E., Whaley, G. J., & Egeland, B. (2004). Children's achievement in early elementary school: Longitudinal effects of parental involvement, expectation, and quality of assistance. *Journal of Educational Psychology, 96*, 723–730. doi:10.1037/0022-0663.96.4.723

Fan, X., & Chen, M. (2001). Parental involvement and students' academic achievement: A meta-analysis. *Educational Psychology Review, 13*(1), 1–22. doi:10.1023/A:1009048817385

Felitti, V. J., Anda, R. F., Nordenberg, D., Williamson, D. F., Spitz, A. M., Edwards, V., … Marks, J. S. (1998). Relationship of childhood abuse and household dysfunction to many of the leading causes of death in adults: The adverse childhood experiences (ACE) study. *American Journal of Preventative Medicine, 14*(4), 245–258. doi:10.1016/S0749-3797(98)00017-8

Fives, H., & Buehl, M. M. (2016). Teachers' beliefs, in the context of policy reform. *Policy Insights from the Behavioral and Brain Sciences, 3*(1), 114–121. doi:10.1177/2372732215623554

Flanagan, A., (2015). Positive adoption language examples and resources. Retrieved from www.umc.org/what-we-believe/positive-adoption-language-examples-and-resources

Gay, G. (2010). *Culturally responsive teaching: Theory, research, and practice* (2nd ed.). New York: Teachers College Press.

Geenen, S., & Powers, L. E. (2007). Tomorrow is another problem: The experiences of youth in foster care during their transition to adulthood. *Children & Youth Services Review, 29*, 1085–1101. doi:10.1016/j.childyouth.2007.04.008

Goldberg, A. E., Black, K., Sweeney, K., & Moyer, A. (2017). Lesbian, gay, and heterosexual adoptive parents' perceptions of inclusivity and receptiveness in early childhood education settings. *Journal of Research in Childhood Education, 31*(1), 141–144.

Gray, D. D. (2012). *Nurturing adoptions: Creating resilience after neglect and trauma.* London: Jessica Kingsley Publishers.

Green, B. L., Saunders, P. A., Power, E., Dass-Brailsford, P., Schelbert, K. B., Giller, E., ... Mete, M. (2015). Trauma-informed medical care: CME communication training for primary care providers. *Family Medicine, 47*(1), 7–11.

Horner, R. H., & Sugai, G. (2015). School-wide PBIS: An example of applied behavior analysis implemented at a scale of social importance. *Behavior Analysis in Practice, 8*(1), 80–85. doi:10.1007/s40617-015-0045-4

Horowitz, G., Domzalski, A. C., & Elizalde-Utnick, G. (2018). Can we teach science in a more culturally responsive way without sacrificing time or content? *Journal of College Science Teaching, 47*(6), 8–10.

Howard, J. A., Smith, S. L., & Ryan, S. D. (2004). A comparative study of child welfare adoptions with other types of adopted children and birth children. *Adoption Quarterly,* 7(3), 1–30. doi:10.1300/J145v07n03_01

Individuals with Disabilities Education Act. (2019). *About IDEA.* Retrieved from https://sites.ed.gov/idea/about-idea/

Leon, I. G. (2002). Adoption losses: Naturally occurring or socially constructed? *Child Development, 73*, 652–663. doi:10.1111/1467-8624.00429

McLeskey, J. (2017). *High leverage practices for special education teachers.* Arlington, VA: Council for Exceptional Children.

Melina, L. R. (2002). *Raising adopted children: Practical reassuring advice for every adoptive parent.* New York: Quill.

Mendez, J. L., Carpenter, J. L., LaForett, D. R., & Cohen, J. S. (2009). Parental engagement and barriers to participation in a community-based preventive intervention. *American Journal of Community Psychology, 44*(1–2), 1–14. doi:10.1007/s10464-009-9252-x

Metzler, M., Merrick, M. T., Klevens, J., Ports, K. A., & Ford, D. C. (2017). Adverse childhood experiences and life opportunities: Shifting the narrative. *Children and Youth Services Review, 72*, 141–149. doi:10.1016/j.childyouth.2016.10.021

National Center for Learning Disabilities. (2017). *The state of LD.* Retrieved from www.ncld.org/identifying-struggling-students

Nickman, S. L. (1985). Losses in adoption: The need for dialogue. *Psychoanalytic Study of the Child, 40*, 365–398. doi:10.1080/00797308.1985.11823039

NYSED. (2013). *Partners in education: A dual capacity-building framework for family-school partnerships.* Retrieved from www.p12.nysed.gov/turnaround/documents/partners-education.pdf

Pappamihiel, E. (2007). Helping preservice content-area teachers relate to English language learners: An investigation of attitudes and beliefs. *TESL Canada Journal, 24*(2), 42–60. doi:10.18806/tesl.v24i2.138

Positive Behavioral Interventions & Supports. (2015). *Implementation blueprint.* Retrieved from www.pbis.org/blueprint/implementation-blueprint.

Riccomini, P. J., Morano, S., & Hughes, C. A. (2017). Big ideas in special education: Specially designed instruction, high-leverage practices, explicit instruction, and intensive instruction. *Teaching Exceptional Children, 50*(1), 20–27. doi:10.1177/0040059917724412

Rogosch, F. A., Oshri, A., & Cicchetti, D. (2010). From child maltreatment to adolescent cannabis abuse and dependence: A developmental cascade model. *Development and Psychopathology, 22*(4), 883–897. doi:10.1017/S0954579410000520

Rosenberg, M. S., Westling, D. L., & McLeskey, J. (2011). *Special education for today's teachers: An introduction.* Upper Saddle River, NJ: Pearson.

SAMHSA, Trauma-Informed Approach: Key Assumptions and Principles, & NCTIC. (2015). Trauma curriculum instructor's guidance. Retrieved from www.nasmhpd.org/sites/default/files/TraumaTIACurriculumTrainersManual_8_18_2015.pdf

Senge, P. M., Cambron-McCabe, N., Lucas, T., Kleiner, A., Smith, B., & Dutton, J. (2012). *Schools that learn: A fifth discipline field book for educators, parents and everyone who cares about education*. New York: Knopf Doubleday Publishing Group.

Smith, J. L. M., Saez, L., & Doabler, C. T. (2016). Using explicit and systematic instruction to support working memory. *Teaching Exceptional Children, 48*(6), 275–281.

Smith, S. L., & Riley, D. (2006). *Adoption in the schools: A lot to learn. Promoting equality and fairness for all children and their families*. Retrieved from Evan B. Donaldson Adoption Institute, www.adoptioninstitute.org/publications/adoption-in-the-schools-a-lot-to-learn/

Sugai, G., & Horner, R. R. (2006). A promising approach for expanding and sustaining school-wide positive behavior support. *School Psychology Review, 35*(2), 245–259.

Summers, L. L. (2010). Culturally responsive leadership in school libraries. *Library Media Connection, 285*(5), 10–13.

Tenner, D. (2017, March 17). Toolkit for foster youth education success: Trauma informed education. Retrieved from http://kids-alliance.org/wp-content/uploads/2018/04/Trauma-Informed-Education-Webinar.pdf

Trent, S. C., Kea, C. D., & Oh, K. (2008). Preparing preservice educators for cultural diversity: How far have we come? *Exceptional Children, 74*, 328–350. doi:10.1177/001440290807400304

Turgut, R., Sahin, E., & Huerta, M. (2016). Changes in preservice teachers' perceptions of preparedness to teach English Language Learners (ELLs) in mainstream classrooms. *Journal of Ethnographic & Qualitative Research, 10*(4), 291–305.

Van, D. D., Juffer, F., IJzendoorn, M. H., Bakermans-Kranenburg, M. J., & Alink, L. R. (2012). Infants' responsiveness, attachment, and indiscriminate friendliness after international adoption from institutions or foster care in China: Application of emotional availability scales to adoptive families. *Development and Psychopathology, 24*(1), 49–64. doi:10.1017/S0954579411000654

van der Kolk, B. A. (2002). Posttraumatic therapy in the age of neuroscience. *Psychoanalytic Dialogues, 12*(3), 381–392. doi:10.1080/10481881209348674

Wood, L., & Ng, N. (Eds.). (2001). *Adoption and the schools: Resources for teachers and parents*. Palo Alto, CA: FAIR.

Zill, N., & Bramlett, M. D. (2014). Health and well-being of children adopted from foster care. *Children and Youth Services Review, 40*, 29–40. doi:10.1016/j.childyouth.2014.02.008

34
POST-ADOPTION SERVICES
Needs and adoption type

Darcey H. Merritt and Rachel D. Ludeke

Post-adoption services are crucial to ensure the relationship between a child and their adoptive family is not adversely hindered due to unattended adjustment challenges, unresolved traumatic issues, or relational deficits (Schweiger & O'Brien, 2005; Zosky, Howard, Smith, Howard, & Shelvin, 2005). Post-adoption services are most effective when based on the specific characteristics, dynamics, and needs of the adoptive family (Schweiger & O'Brien, 2005). This chapter briefly describes post-adoption services, reviews the post-adoption services that have been used for various types of adoptive families, identifies challenges in accessing post-adoptive services, and concludes with recommendations for policy and practice.

Types of post-adoption services

Post-adoption services can be formal and administered through a set structure within post-adoption service agencies (e.g., parent support groups or information and referral services), or informally accessed through family and friends within the adoptive parent's network (Hartinger-Saunders, Trouteaud, & Matos Johnson, 2015). Table 34.1 provides examples of post-adoption services annotated by the type of service and whether the service type is emotional, concrete, or informational. Emotional services include child support groups, family counseling, crisis counseling, or parenting education. These services can be informal; while the formal services are provided within an agency and are often fee-for-service type of operations. Informational services include financial assistance, state information, and referral services through websites, hotlines, workshops, or resource directories. Last, concrete services include access to paid childcare through the use of adoption subsidies, tutoring/academic assistance, respite assistance, or alcohol and drug treatment. While these lists are not all-inclusive, they are a sample of the most often needed and utilized services.

In general, when examining outcomes for these services, research has suggested that they are often beneficial to children and families. Specifically, there is a fair amount of research indicating adoptive families (children and parents) have benefited from the use of adoption support groups wherein the focus is primarily emotional support and information exchange (Bryan, Flaherty, & Saunders, 2010; McDonald, Propp, & Murphy, 2001). Also, post-adoption services can be

Table 34.1 Post-adoption support services

Emotional services	
Service type	Program delivery
Child support groups	Psychoeducational, structured meetings designed to improve the quality of the parent/child post-adoption relationship.
Family counseling	Family counseling can include individual or group counseling in addition to adoption preservation services. These services can be in-home or within the family's community.
Crisis counseling	Crisis counseling (an extension of family or mental health counseling) is usually available for families where a child's mental, physical, or behavioral well-being threatens to dissolve the adoption.
Parenting education	Agency-led in-person training that may be available through workshops, seminars, or lectures or through online services such as blogs, webinars, online trainings, and specialized websites.
Marriage and relationship education	Psychoeducational programs that use a variety of formats to help adoptive parents during the post-adoption process. Formal instruction may take place in the form of lectures, workshops, or retreats
Informational services	
Information and referral services	These services are usually provided through workshops, websites, telephone hotlines, or resource directories, and vary according to state.
Informal help	Informal supports may be available through peer support networks, especially from peers that have already adopted a child or children.
Financial assistance	Adoptive families often need assistance with home, equipment, or vehicle modifications if they have adopted a child with special needs. Financial supports can also take the form of Medicaid, Supplemental Security Income (SSI), Temporary Assistance for Needy Families (TANF), or other county- or state-funded programs.
Concrete services	
Paid childcare	In some states, adoption subsidies can be used to pay for childcare expenses to help defray the out-of-pocket costs for families that qualify.
Tutoring/academic assistance	Some parents seek academic or tutoring for their adopted child(ren) based on their level of academic need (i.e. special needs, behavioral, etc.). These services can be informal or formal and may be provided through agency support or through the school districts directly.
Respite assistance	Respite care is a service that can provide a temporary break for adoptive parents and their new child(ren). It can be formal or informal and in-home or out-of-home depending on the location of the family. Respite care can take the form of summer camps or weekend outings.
Alcohol and drug treatment	Alcohol and drug treatment may be delivered as inpatient or outpatient and is usually for adoptive parents and/or children (depending on the age that they are adopted).

meaningful in ensuring that the relationship between a child and their adoptive family is not hindered due to poor adjustment in familial relationships (Zosky et al., 2005). Parents who participated in or received post-adoption preservation services found these services to be instrumental in their ability to create a stable, safe, and open environment for their adoptive child and also helped to reduce issues related to the child's adjustment in the home. Expressed need and access to these services is based on specific child and family characteristics, situation, and type of adoptive family.

Often, the need for post-adoption services depends on whether the child has prior challenges based on behavioral and emotional difficulties or their developmental stage. An equally important consideration in service provision is whether there are available and accessible post-adoption programs that meet the specific needs of the family in an effort to optimally support the adopted child (Barth & Miller, 2000).

Service needs as a function of adoption type

The US has three primary ways to adopt a child: domestic private adoptions, international/intercountry adoptions, and child welfare system adoptions. Domestic private adoption generally refers to the adoption of children not involved in the child welfare system from the US (Vandivere, Malm, & Radel, 2007). These children, typically infants, are voluntarily placed for adoption by their birth families and are adopted by non-relatives (Raleigh, 2016). Similarly, international/intercountry adoptions involve the adoption of children by non-relatives outside of the US. Finally, children involved in the child welfare system (CWS) were involuntarily removed from their homes due to issues related to child neglect and abuse and can be adopted from the CWS through non-relative foster placement or kinship placement. CWS-involved children are often considered "harder-to-place" due to their older age, race, or special needs (Barth & Berry, 1990; Egbert, 2015). There is large variation in adjustment experiences among the types of adoption. Each of these types of families has specific adoption service needs based on their experiences and child, parental, and situational differences.

Domestic private adoptions

Private adoptions require financial stability from potential adoptive parents and involve many expenses. Unlike CWS-supported adoptions where the government provides subsidized support for families wishing to adopt a child, private domestic adoptions typically require that the adopting family cover out-of-pocket fees, which might include legal fees, medical costs, or adoption agency fees (Raleigh, 2016). Given that these adoptions are expensive, parents adopting through domestic private adoptions are often better able to access support for their children. Typically, children adopted through private means are less likely to experience childhood trauma related to abuse or neglect, parental substance use, or multiple home placements prior to adoption (Howard, Smith, & Ryan, 2008). The current chapter focuses on other adoption types where financial cost is typically a factor in the type of post-adoption services available to the adopting family and their child or children.

International/intercountry adoptions

Families adopting children from other countries often do so without extended periods of visitation and advanced planning for their new child since many US-based adoption agencies have little control over how children and parents are prepared for adoption across countries. Generally, international/intercountry adoptions are much more expensive than domestic CWS adoptions. Parents adopting across countries are not always ideally supported financially by their communities, resulting in financial barriers that impact their ability to provide medically and culturally specific physical and mental health supports for their child (Paulsen & Merighi, 2009). Children adopted from outside of the US are also more vulnerable to attachment difficulties with their adoptive parents and could be affected by grief over the loss of access to their birth parents, disconnection from their homeland, or difficulty acclimating to new culturally specific familial expectations (Masson, 2001; Roberson, 2006). Families formed through international adoption might also be in need of more support to assist with child trauma histories and cultural differences. There is also a dearth of culturally relevant services available for adoptive parents specific to the adopted children (Hegar & Watson, 2013). Despite the challenges of an international adoption, these adoptive families often receive information about post-adoption services more often than the other types of adoptive families and are more likely to access mental health services for their children (Merritt & Festinger, 2013).

Adoptions from child welfare

Children adopted from the CWS may have a pre-adoption history with many out-of-home placements or longer times between placements, and are at risk of poor adjustment with an adoptive family (Moyer & Goldberg, 2017; Wind, Brooks, & Barth, 2007). Children who are older when they enter the CWS, placed with four or more siblings, or identified as African American are also at a higher risk of disruption (Smith, Howard, Garnier, & Ryan, 2006). Additionally, poorer adjustment was noted for those families receiving paid adoption assistance or families with children adopted by non-relatives (Orsi, 2015). Further, older children and those with past trauma histories are more likely to need mental health counseling (Merritt & Festinger, 2013).

Kinship adoptive families often need more concrete and financial supports (e.g., paid child care, respite) to mitigate increased financial burdens on the enlarged family. Kinship care families also tend to rely on informal supports, tutoring, and paid child care, more than other types of adoptions (Merritt & Festinger, 2013). These are just a few examples of nuances regarding newly composed adoptive families who are often quite vulnerable during initial adjustment and intermittently across the life cycle of the adoptive family.

Other accounts of service need, access, and use according to adoption type have been documented highlighting differences between international, CWS non-kin, and CWS kinship adoptions (Merritt & Festinger, 2013). Overall, results of this study indicate CWS non-kinship adoptive families received most of the assessed services at lower rates than international or CWS kinship families; however, non-kin families expressed less need than other types of families with some variation among types of services. While there is variation among services according to types of adoption, all adoption types require post-adoption services and supports which should be selected according to the particular child and family circumstances and histories.

Service use as a function of child and family characteristics

Family dynamics

A variety of characteristics of the child and/or family also determine whether and what types of supports would be needed. In a longitudinal survey of 560 adoptive parents, Wind et al. (2007) provide evidence to suggest that pre-adoption history and preparation can mediate the use of post-adoption services, controlling for child and family characteristics.

Respondents participated in more general post-adoption services than clinical case services. General services included meeting with caseworkers and participation in psychoeducational adoption support groups. The findings suggested that children adopted from CWS might need access to long-term services to ensure their successful transition and adjustment in their new families. Children who are adopted directly from the CWS are often adopted post infancy, suggesting they will engage with an already existing family structure following a significant shift in their living arrangement from state oversight caregivers to private caregivers. As such, children can experience difficulty with adjustment to new family norms and might have difficulty given the decrease in state oversight/support after an adoption has been finalized (Schweiger & O'Brien, 2005). Such challenges could explain accounts of children adopted from the CWS or other institutionalized settings (i.e., orphanages) being referred to mental health services at higher rates than those adopted under other circumstances (Nichols, Martin, & Martin, 2015).

Faulkner and Madden (2012) found that children adopted from the foster care system were more likely to have lived with their birth families at some point during their time under CWS oversight, yet they were less likely to continue to have contact with their birth parents after adoption than children adopted from private adoption agencies. The differences between previously living with birth parents and being adopted by non-relative adoptive parents poses great difficulty adjusting to new home environments coupled with different expectations from new parents, thus requiring specific services aimed at encouraging adjustment (Barth & Miller, 2000; Mullin & Johnson, 1999; Zosky et al., 2005). Moreover, children adopted through the CWS who have experienced a permanent or significantly limited disconnect from their biological families are likely to need support and/or emotional health services as they become accustomed to their adoptive families.

Post-adoption services for youth with special needs

Adopted children with special needs are those who have emotional or physical disabilities, those who have experienced sexual abuse, severe cases of neglect, or traumatic and severe physical abuse, those who are older than one year, and those who are part of a sibling group that needs to be placed with the same adoptive family (Mullin & Johnson, 1999). Parents of children with special needs might be unfamiliar with the most effective methods for responding to issues related to emotional, attentional, or behavioral control (Schweiger & O'Brien, 2005). These adoptions are often much more difficult when compared to adoption of children without special needs, thus, there is an increased need for post-adoption services to develop or maintain perceived trust and support among the newly established family members.

Other pre-adoption risk factors not related to the actual adoption process include environmental, behavioral, or emotional concerns, such as previous child maltreatment and other related traumas, and pre-existing physical or mental health disorders (Wind et al., 2007). Reilly and Platz (2004) surveyed 249 adoptive parents of 373 children to determine the most pressing post-adoption needs of families caring for children with special needs. The study revealed that most families were concerned about medical, dental, and financial supports and subsidies available to meet the needs of their child while citing a lack of in-home supports and counseling as service area gaps. In-home supports were defined as day care, babysitting, and respite care services. These results are supported by previous studies citing a lack of formal and concrete supports as a salient deficiency in available post-adoption services (Barth & Miller, 2000; Berry, Propp, & Martens, 2007; McDonald et al., 2001).

Other considerations for post-adoption access

Other demographic and situational characteristics play a role in optimal adoption adjustment. Age at adoption is considered a risk factor due to the inherent trauma of having been removed from one's birth parent(s) during vulnerable developmental stages. Previous studies have determined that older children and those with previous placement disruptions have been found to be at a greater risk of adoption disruption and poor family adjustment (Barth & Berry, 1990; Barth, Berry, Yoshikimi, Goodfield, & Carson, 1988). Thus, a variety of elements can influence the quality of the caregiver relationship that develops between the adopted child and family, whether optimal adaptability will occur in the child's new environment, and the post-adoption service needs.

Difficulty accessing post-adoption services

The research is mixed regarding associations among types of families, specific needs, availability, and actual receipt of needed supports. Below, we highlight post-adoption services related to post-adoption adjustment in the context of barriers to accessible supports.

There is little consensus regarding the expressed experiences of youth who are adopted or placed into legal guardianship once adoptions are complete. Rolock (2015) suggests this can cause difficulty in tracking the experiences of these youth in an effort to enhance post-adoption services. In addition to overlapping terminology regarding failed adoptions, access and use of post-adoption services by families and children necessary to avoid such outcomes is further complicated by the practice of child welfare agencies in failing to link pre- and post-adoption information specific to children and families. This is especially prominent in cases where information, such as name changes, occur after children are legally adopted. Unclear information makes it increasingly difficult to determine which and how many families are eligible for taking advantage of necessary available post-adoption services. One needs to know which services are accessible according to their specific family member demographics and histories. A clear trajectory is necessary for identifying appropriate post-adoption services specifically related to child and parent circumstances based on pre-adoptive characteristics and current circumstances.

While the majority of research studies focus on the effect of adoption on parents, there is a dearth of research related to how adoption and children's permanency preferences (Merritt, 2011; Merritt & Franke, 2009) impact adopted children's experiential perspectives. Ryan and Nalavany (2003) studied the personal experiences of 17 adoptive children employing a qualitative methodology in an attempt to understand the barriers children face when seeking mental health support, to whom they talk when they need help, and how they cope with the challenges in their relationships with their adoptive parents. The study found that the children grieve the loss of formerly close connections while attempting to build trusting relationships with their new caregivers. They are often afraid to ask for help for fear of harming their new social network of support.

Additional barriers to participation in post-adoption services are the cost of available services, access to services, geographic location, eligibility, suitability of service for family and/or child's needs, awareness of the existence of post-adoption services, and if a child has identified special needs (Dhami, Mendel, & Sothmann, 2007; Egbert, 2015; Festinger &

Maza, 2009; Merritt & Festinger, 2013; Paulsen & Merighi, 2009). Families that tend to access formal services are generally those who have prior experiences with agencies, such as CWS adoptions, those with more financial resources, and those who have received more information about available services, such as domestic private and international adoptive families. As noted by Merritt and Festinger (2013), while families that adopted internationally tended to welcome discussions about the usage of post-adoption services, foster care non-kin families tended to have less desire to discuss post-adoption services and were less likely to utilize such services.

Some adoptive parents report feeling powerless to address their child's behavior and emotional difficulties post-adoption due to inadequate support and services outside of the family, resulting in unmet and unfulfilled expectations regarding the parent–child relationship (Moyer & Goldberg, 2017). In a study of post-adoption experiences of 516 parents in New York City, Festinger (2002) found that parents felt their ability to access post-adoption services was hindered by the cost of services and a lack of information regarding where and which services were available. Furthermore, some parents believed they were cut off from receiving services after the adoption became legal leaving them on their own to ensure the adoptive child's ability to function successfully in their new family home.

Phillips (1990) notes that adoptive parents would be motivated to take advantage of post-adoption services if they were aware that the services existed. Families often do not know that they are eligible to receive such services, or which post-adoption services would be most appropriate for their family and the adopted child. Conversely, not all families require post-adoption services and might not benefit from additional supports. However, for families that do need post-adoption services to help ease the transition of a new child into an existing family structure, the ability to access services can be difficult due to inadequate program resources and/or a lack of understanding regarding available services, particularly those services suited for specific needs (i.e. special needs, adoption of older youth, LGBTQIA services, and so forth).

Practice implications

Research is limited regarding the effectiveness of post-adoption services, evidenced by the dearth of published program evaluations focused on services for adopted children with special needs (Dhami et al., 2007). Practitioners serving adoptive families would greatly benefit from post-adoption service evaluations and best practices, preferably longitudinal accounts focused on the adjustment of adopted children with special needs (e.g., behavioral problems, developmental disabilities).

Schweiger and O'Brien (2005) suggest that utilizing an ecological systems approach to the assessment of adoptive families allows practitioners to thoroughly examine the goodness-of-fit between a child and prospective adoptive family. Employing this approach, goodness-of-fit can be determined based on parental expectations, child characteristics, and existing family functioning. Conducting a comprehensive assessment of children and parents is important to proactively inform both pre- and post-adoption service needs in efforts to bolster the likelihood that there is a sustainable good fit for the child within the new family system. As an example, children with attachment problems might exhibit difficult behavioral patterns, might misunderstand the expectations of their new adoptive parents, and they might struggle with ideal bonding in the context of the parent–child relationship. This is particularly likely if they have previously experienced multiple placement moves or inconsistent caregivers in pre-adoption placement (Hughes, 1999). According to preliminary results, targeted post-adoption services, such as *Right*

Turn in Nebraska, which supports older youth with multiple prior placements and a history of mental health problems, has been beneficial for reducing the number of adoption dissolutions after program completion (Burke, Schlueter, Bader, & Authier, 2018).

Policy implications

As noted above, there is unfortunately a dearth of rigorous evaluations concerning post-adoption services (Dhami et al., 2007), particularly focused on supports and services for children with special needs. Future policy initiatives would be beneficial in encouraging ongoing collaboration between public and private adoption agencies and services to help perform methodologically sound program evaluations. Policies should be regularly updated according to trends in prevalence across adoption types, and with consideration of targeted needs based on child and family characteristics.

Further, the dissemination of information regarding service accessibility according to adoption type and particular child needs is warranted in order to optimally support families based on their specific characteristics. For instance, public awareness campaigns have been found to be quite beneficial in disseminating information about available services and encouraging utilization. The availability of post-adoption support should be a normalized part of the adoption process while emphasizing the need for families, regardless of type of adoption, to access post-adoption supports in a timely manner (Lushey, Holmes, & McDermid, 2018). As adoption type prevalence trends evolve, practitioners and policy makers need to remain aware and prepared to provide the optimal supports according to familial situations and in the context of community and societal changes.

Conclusion

The overarching message from this account of post-adoption service needs, access, and receipt, according to the type of adoptive family, child demographics, and past histories, is that ongoing attention to the adjustment for children and parents across the life cycle of the adoptive family is essential to address the complexity of nuanced, targeted service needs. Moreover, efforts to adhere to our current mandated policy goals should always incorporate a comprehensive pre-adoptive placement assessment in the context of child and family demographics and situational and cultural variations, with consideration of expressed needs and barriers to service access and utilization. In short, post-adoption services are crucial to successful adjustment and the health and well-being of the adopted children and the entire family system.

References

Barth, R. P., & Berry, M. (1990). Preventing adoption disruption. *Prevention in Human Services*, *9*(1), 205–222. doi:org/10.1300/J293v09n01_13

Barth, R. P., Berry, M., Yoshikimi, R., Goodfield, R. K., & Carson, M. L. (1988). Predicting adoption disruption. *Social Work*, *33*(3), 227–233. doi:org/10.1093/sw/33.3.227

Barth, R. P., & Miller, J. M. (2000). Building effective post-adoption services: What is the empirical foundation. *Family Relations*, *49*(4), 447–455. doi:org/10.1111/j.1741-3729.2000.00447.x

Berry, M., Propp, J., & Martens, P. (2007). The use of intensive family preservation services with adoptive families. *Child & Family Social Work*, *12*(1), 43–53. doi:doi.org/10.1111/j.1365-2206.2006.00426.x

Bryan, V., Flaherty, C., & Saunders, C. (2010). Supporting adoptive families: Participant perceptions of a statewide peer mentoring and support program. *Journal of Public Child Welfare*, *4*(1), 91–112. doi:doi.org/10.1080/15548730903563178

Burke, R. V., Schlueter, C., Bader, E., & Authier, K. J. (2018). Post-adoption services for high-risk families and their children: Preliminary results of a state-wide intervention. *American Journal of Family Therapy, 46*(2), 122–138. doi:doi.org/10.1080/01926187.2018.1450687

Dhami, M. K., Mendel, D. R., & Sothmann, K. (2007). An evaluation of post-adoption services. *Children and Youth Services Review, 29*, 162–179. doi:doi.org/10.1016/j.childyouth.2006.06.003

Egbert, S. C. (2015). Supporting and strengthening foster adoptive families: Utah's story of post-adoption service development, delivery, and ongoing evaluation. *Journal of Public Child Welfare, 9*(1), 88–113. doi:doi.org/10.1080/15548732.2014.1001936

Faulkner, M., & Madden, E. E. (2012). Open adoption and post-adoption birth family contact: A comparison of non-relative foster and private adoptions. *Adoption Quarterly, 15*(1), 35–56. doi:doi.org/10.1080/10926755.2012.661333

Festinger, T. (2002). After adoption: Dissolution or permanence. *Child Welfare, 81*(3), 515–533.

Festinger, T., & Maza, P. (2009). Displacement or post-adoption placement? A research note. *Journal of Public Child Welfare, 3*(3), 275–286. doi:doi.org/10.1080/15548730903129889

Hartinger-Saunders, R. M., Trouteaud, A., & Matos Johnson, J. (2015). Post adoption service need and use as predictors of adoption dissolution: Findings from the 2012 National Adoptive Families Study. *Adoption Quarterly, 18*(4), 255–272. doi:doi.org/10.1080/10926755.2014.895469

Hegar, R. L., & Watson, L. D. (2013). Managing special needs and treatment approaches of intercountry adoptees and families. *Adoption Quarterly, 16*(3–4), 238–261. doi:doi.org/10.1080/10926755.2013.790863

Howard, J. A., Smith, S. L., & Ryan, S. D. (2008). A comparative study of child welfare adoptions with other types of adopted children and birth children. *Adoption Quarterly*, 7(3), 1–30. doi:doi.org/10.1300/J145v07n03_01

Hughes, D. A. (1999). Adopting children with attachment problems. *Child Welfare, 78*(5), 541–560. doi:doi.org/10.1.1.474.4940

Lushey, C., Holmes, L., & McDermid, S. (2018). Normalizing post-adoption support for all. *Child and Family Social Work, 23*, 137–145. doi:doi.org/10.1111/cfs.12391

Masson, J. (2001). Intercountry adoption: A global problem or a global solution. *Journal of International Affairs, 55*(1), 141–166. www.jstor.org/stable/24357675

McDonald, T. P., Propp, J. R., & Murphy, K. C. (2001). The postadoption experience: Child, parent, and family predictors of family adjustment to adoption. *Child Welfare, 80*(1), 71–94. Retrieved from: https://search.proquest.com/docview/213804676?accountid=9844

Merritt, D. H. (2011). Should I stay or should I go? Correlates of children's placement preferences. *Journal of Public Child Welfare, 5*(4), 408–425. doi:doi.org/10.1080/15548732.2011.599760

Merritt, D. H., & Festinger, T. (2013). Post-adoption services need and access: Differences between international, kinship, and non-kinship foster care. *Children and Youth Services Review, 35*, 1913–1922. doi:doi.org/10.1016/j.childyouth.2013.09.013

Merritt, D. H., & Franke, T. M. (2009). Should I stay or should I go? Children's placement preferences longitudinally. *Journal of Social Service Research, 36*(1), 46–67. doi:doi.org/10.1080/01488370903333611

Moyer, A. M., & Goldberg, A. E. (2017). "We were not planning on this, but ..." Adoptive parents' reactions and adaptations to unmet expectations. *Child & Family Social Work, 22*, 12–21. doi:doi.org/10.1111/cfs.12219

Mullin, E. S., & Johnson, L. (1999). The role of birth/previously adopted children in families choosing to adopt children with special needs. *Child Welfare, 78*, 579–591. Retrieved from https://search.proquest.com/docview/213804296?accountid=9844

Nichols, T., Martin, M., & Martin, D. (2015). Psychological differences in post-institutionalized internationally adopted children and other groups of children referred for clinical services. *Adoption Quarterly, 18*(4), 311–326. doi:doi.org/10.1080/10926755.2015.1088105

Orsi, R. (2015). Predicting re-involvement for children adopted out of a public child welfare system. *Child Abuse & Neglect, 39*, 175–184. doi:doi.org/10.1016/j.chiabu.2014.10.005

Paulsen, C., & Merighi, J. R. (2009). Adoption preparedness, cultural engagement and parental satisfaction in intercountry adoption. *Adoption Quarterly, 12*(1), 1–18. doi:doi.org/10.1080/10926750902791540

Phillips, R. (1990). Post-adoption services – The views of adopters. *Early Child Development and Care, 59*(1), 21–27. doi:doi.org/10.1080/0300443900590103

Raleigh, E. (2016). An associative marketplace: Foster care, domestic, and transnational adoptions. *Sociology Compass, 10*(6), 506–517. doi:doi.org/10.1111/soc4.12371

Reilly, T., & Platz, L. (2004). Post-adoption service needs of families with special needs children: Use, helpfulness, and unmet needs. *Journal of Social Service Research, 30*(4), 51–67. doi:doi.org/10.1300/J079v30n04_03

Roberson, K. C. (2006). Attachment and caregiving behavioral systems in intercountry adoption: A literature review. *Children and Youth Services Review, 28*, 7. doi:doi.org/10.1016/j.childyouth.2005.07.008

Rolock, N. (2015). Post-permanency continuity. What Happens after Adoption and Guardianship from Foster Care? *Journal of Public Child Welfare, 9*, 153–173. doi:doi.org/10.1080/15548732.2015.1021986

Ryan, S. D., & Nalavany, B. (2003). Adopted children: Who do they turn to for help and why? *Adoption Quarterly*, 7(2), 29–52. doi:doi.org/10.1300/J145v07n02_03

Schweiger, W. K., & O'Brien, M. (2005). Special needs adoption: An ecological system approach. *Family Relations, 54*(4), 512–522. doi:doi.org/10.1111/j.1741-3729.2005.00337.x

Smith, S. L., Howard, J. A., Garnier, P. C., & Ryan, S. D. (2006). Where are we now? A post-ASFA examination of adoption disruption. *Adoption Quarterly, 9*(4), 19–44. doi:doi.org/10.1300/J145v09n04_02

Vandivere, S., Malm, K., & Radel, L. (2007). *Adoption USA: A chartbook based on the 2007 National Survey of Adoptive Parents*. Retrieved from: https://aspe.hhs.gov/system/files/pdf/75911/index.pdf

Wind, L. H., Brooks, D., & Barth, R. P. (2007). Influences of risk history and adoption preparation on post adoption services use in US adoptions. *Family Relations, 56*(4), 378–389. doi:doi.org/10.1111/j.1741-3729.2007.00467.x

Zosky, D. L., Howard, J., Smith, S. L., Howard, A. M., & Shelvin, K. H. (2005). Investing in adoptive families: What adoptive families tell us regarding the benefits of adoption preservation services. *Adoption Quarterly, 8*(3), 1–23. doi:doi.org/10.1300/J145v08n03_01

35

ADOPTION-SPECIFIC CURRICULA IN HIGHER EDUCATION[1]

Bibiana Koh, JaeRan Kim, and Ruth McRoy

An estimated 2 million (2 percent) of all US children and young adults living with their parents are adopted (Kreider & Lofquist, 2014). In the US, children may be adopted from the public foster care system, from private agencies and through attorneys that facilitate domestically born infant or stepparent/second-parent adoptions, or from private agencies that handle intercountry adoptions. The Child Welfare Information Gateway (2016) estimates that 119,514 children were adopted in 2012 and notes that 44 percent were public agency adoptions, 49 percent "other" (i.e., private, stepparent, tribal, etc.), and 7 percent intercountry adoptions. According to the most recent AFCARS Report (2018) from the US Children's Bureau, in FY 2017, 247,631 exited the foster care system and 23 percent or 58,109 of these children were adopted. (For more on adoption statistics, see Chapter 2.)

Current estimates and adoption statistics that report trends over time are only one way to consider the significance of adoption in the US. Another consideration (despite statistical fluctuations) is the systemic impact of adoption in this country. The Dave Thomas Foundation for Adoption (with the Evan B. Donaldson Adoption Institute, 2002) estimated that nearly two-thirds of Americans are impacted by adoption in some way – perhaps by an adoptive family member, a family friend who is adopted, or a family member who has relinquished a child for adoption. The internet has also likely contributed to this impact with the proliferation of information on adoption (e.g., pre- and post-adoption services), including search and reunion processes (Howard, 2012) and the role of DNA genetic testing in these processes (Bahrampour, 2016).

Ecological systems theory (Bronfenbrenner, 1979) can be used to help explain this systemic impact of adoption. At the micro-level, developing adoptees are at the epicenter of the ecological environment. Next, at the meso-level, adoptees and/or their adoptive families intersect with microsystems including a larger kinship/adoptive family network, medical, educational, and social systems. At the exo-level, adoptees (and their families) might be indirectly affected by medical, legal, spiritual, family, and work environment systems. Finally, the macro-level weaves in cultural and societal aspects of adoption – for instance, adoption narratives that might be socially constructed through various media platforms.

The broad range of pre- and post-adoption meso-level services suggest that adoption is a lifelong journey for adoptees and their families (Brodzinsky, 2015; Festinger, 2006; also see Chapter 34 for a comprehensive discussion of services). The need for these services can reflect the numerous developmental issues for children (Grotevant & McDermott, 2014). Adoptees and their families might work with numerous professionals including adoption agency staff, child welfare social workers, medical personnel, and/or mental health counselors when utilizing services (Schweiger & O'Brien, 2005).

One mesosystem within which adoptees and their families are more likely (than the general population) to have contact is the mental health system (Keyes, Sharma, Elkins, Iacono, & McGue, 2008). Researchers have found that adopted children are overrepresented in mental health settings (Brodzinsky, Santa, & Smith, 2016; Tan & Tran, 2013) and often have higher rates of externalizing (Keyes et al., 2008), internalizing, and attention issues (Grotevant & McDermott, 2014) than non-adopted children. Thus, social workers, psychologists, and/or counselors might provide direct practice and clinical services to adoptees, adoptive families, and birth families at some point during the family life cycle (Brodzinsky et al., 2016).

Due to the potential clinical needs adoptees and their families might face (Keyes et al., 2008), adoption professionals providing direct or clinical services to members within the adoption constellation (i.e., birth, foster, and adoptive family members) should be knowledgeable about the intricacies of adoption – including the developmental processes that unfold across the lifespan (Baden & Wiley, 2007; Brodzinsky, 2015; Greco, Rosnati, & Ferrari, 2015; Grotevant & McDermott, 2014). Thus, the education and training of adoption practitioners should reflect the diverse and complex developmental issues (both general and specialized) in adoption that require adoption-specific education and training (Grotevant & McDermott, 2014) – in other words, demonstrating *adoption competency*.

An "adoption competent practitioner" is defined as an educated, licensed mental health professional with the knowledge, skills, and experience to work in adoption (Atkinson, Gonet, Freundlich, & Riley, 2013, p. 166). Adoption competent practitioners should be knowledgeable about developmental and clinical issues in working with adoptees and their adoptive/birth families (Brodzinsky et al., 2016; Stokes & Poulsen, 2014); they should also be knowledgeable of evidence-based approaches that are effective with this specialized population (Atkinson et al., 2013; Barth, Lee, & Hodorowicz, 2017; Brodzinsky, 2013; Casey Family Services, 2003; Morton, 1984; National Child Welfare Resource Center for Adoption, 2007). Both adoptive parents and adoptees have underscored the importance of and the need for adoption competent clinical professionals in various meso-level systems (Atkinson & Gonet, 2007; Atkinson et al., 2013; Brodzinsky, 2015; Grotevant & McDermott, 2014; Ramsey, Brabender, & Fallon, 2013; Riley & Singer, 2016; Siegel, 2013).

From a macro perspective, recent statewide policies underscore the need to bolster the training of adoption competent professionals. For example, The 2014 California Assembly Bill 1790 (AB 1790, 2014) required the California Department of Social Services to convene a work group to identify barriers for children, in need of specialized mental health services, from being served by adoption/permanency trained clinicians. Another example is the five year grant that the Center for Adoption Support and Education (CASE, 2018) received in 2014 from the US Department of Health and Human Services Administration for Children and Families (CASE, 2015). This grant helped CASE establish a National Adoption Competency Mental Health Training Initiative (NTI) to increase adoption competency among child welfare and mental health professionals working with adoptive and guardianship families. Both examples highlight a growing interest in supporting the professional development of adoption competent professionals (see Chapters 31 and 32).

Adoption-specific curricula in degree programs

One might assume that adoption professionals (i.e., adoption agency staff, social workers, mental health providers) might have received some adoption-specific content during their baccalaureate and/or graduate education; however, the research on adoption-specific content in clinical and professional educational programs is limited (Weir, Fife, Whiting, & Blazewick, 2008). For example, in a website review of courses at major public and private universities across disciplines (i.e., psychology, social work, marriage, and family therapy) that included adoption content (e.g., domestic and/or intercountry adoption, permanency planning, adoption research and/or policy, etc.), Ramsey et al. (2013) found only one adoption course that was offered, and this course was offered through the Rudd Adoption Research Program (located in the Department of Psychology and Brain Sciences at the University of Massachusetts, Amherst). A few social work programs offer electives such as "Contemporary Issues in Adoption and Foster Care," which provides an overview of issues, but the content does not have a strictly clinical focus. Often such courses are offered in schools in which a faculty member's research and/or practice is focused on adoption and foster care (Boston College School of Social Work).

Other empirical research has reported similar findings. For instance, a 2008 survey of 224 accredited programs in marriage and family therapy (MFT; Commission on Accreditation for Marriage and Family Therapy Education), social work (Council on Social Work Education), and counseling (Council for Accreditation of Counseling and Related Educational Programs), noted that adoption-specific curricula are scarce (Weir et al., 2008). This study found that existing curricula are more likely to be found in social work programs: 16.3 percent of responding social work programs offered adoption-specific content, compared to 5.2 percent of counseling programs, and 4.8 percent of MFT programs (Weir et al., 2008). Additionally, this study found that social work programs were more likely to offer classroom-based adoption-specific curricula, while MFT programs focused on field-based (i.e., practica) adoption-specific training (Weir et al., 2008). Another study reported that 65 percent of licensed psychologists (N = 210) did not receive adoption-specific coursework in their educational training, and 90 percent reported the need for more adoption-specific training (Sass & Henderson, 2007). This limited research suggests that adoption-specific curricula are needed in professional educational programs (e.g., social work, psychology, MFT, education).

Kolb's learning theory (1981, 1984) would suggest that both didactic and practica formats are needed to account for different learning styles when training adoption professionals. A study by Raschick, Maypole, and Day (1998) adapted Kolb's learning theory (1981, 1984) in the context of field education. For example, *accommodators* (Raschick et al., 1998) might learn best by trying different theories and models (i.e., trial and error, learning by doing) in field practica. For *accommodators*, conceptualization might not come easily. *Divergers* (Raschick et al., 1998) are intuitive learners. Educators who prefer field- to classroom-based learning might lean toward these learning styles. On the other hand, there are two additional learning styles for those with a proclivity for abstract thinking and conceptualization – what Kolb refers to as *assimilators* (Raschick et al., 1998). For these types of innately conceptual learners, classroom-based curricula allow them to conceptualize first, and then later connect this didactic material to their field practicum. Another learning style, *convergers* (Raschick et al., 1998), is strongest with respect to practical ideas/solutions and practice application. These learners are likely to thrive on the integration of classroom- *and* field-based learning; they will also likely complement those with a predilection for abstract thinking (i.e., *assimilators*).

Post-degree adoption training programs

Within the last decade, several post-degree and certificate programs have been developed to address the need for adoption-specific training. Many of these programs emerged at either academic institutions (e.g., Training for Adoption Competency; Certificate Program in Adoption at Rutgers University; Certificate Program in Adoption Therapy at Hunter College; Adoption Competent Practice Program at the University of Denver; Adoption and Foster Care Certificate Program at Rhode Island College; etc.) or adoption agencies (e.g., Kinship Center, Certificate Program in Adoption and Foster Care Therapy from Alexander and Associates in New Mexico; for a more comprehensive list of programs, see Casey Family Services, 2003).

Various barriers such as time, location, enrollment requirements (including type of degree or licensure), and cost may limit the availability and accessibility of these trainings. Additionally, not all adoption professionals seek or have access to additional post-degree training in preparation for their adoption-specific work (Sass & Henderson, 2007). The recent NTI (National Adoption Competency Mental Health Training Initiative) is currently available nationwide via an online site (https://adoptionsupport.org/nti/aboutnti/. It addresses some of these barriers for adoption professionals.

With ecological systems theory (Bronfenbrenner, 1979) as a backdrop, we argue that learning theory and macro-level policy initiatives underscore the need to better prepare adoption competent professionals. Higher education – both undergraduate and graduate curricula – is a crucial element in their training and preparation. Specifically, a comprehensive evaluation of the preparation and training for adoption professionals is needed and should include both degree and post-degree program curricula. Little is known about adoption curricula in higher education degree programs (Ramsey et al., 2013). A 2017 study published in *Adoption Quarterly* (see Koh et al., 2017) addressed this need; the findings of the study are presented below and an expanded discussion of the implications and suggestions for future practice and policy are provided.

Adoption curricula study

Method

This study used purposeful convenience sampling in a two-step data collection process. First, email inquiries for adoption-specific courses were sent to the following professional email lists: (1) Baccalaureate Program Directors for Council of Social Work Education (CSWE) accredited schools; (2) Master of Social Work programs (CSWE accredited); (3) Title IV-E; (4) National Council on Family Relations (NCFR) – adoption focus group; and (5) an adoption research email list managed by a psychology researcher. An announcement was also posted on the Rudd Center for Adoption Research (Department of Psychological and Brain Sciences, University of Massachusetts, Amherst) Facebook page. In addition, 12 adoption researchers from various disciplines (e.g., social work, psychology, family studies) were identified by the authors, emailed individually, and encouraged to submit syllabi. Adoption-specific courses were defined as classes that focused exclusively on adoption or included significant content on domestic and/or intercountry adoption, permanency planning, adoption research and/or policy, and other topics related to adoption.

In phase two, all faculty who emailed syllabi in phase one were invited to participate in an anonymous online Qualtrics survey. Faculty (n = 2) who submitted more than one course syllabus were only invited to participate in the online survey once, resulting in a total of 22 eligible faculty. IRB approval was obtained from the first author's institution.

Results

Phase one: course syllabi

The phase one email lists and adoption researcher inquiries yielded a total of $N = 24$ faculty syllabi from 20 academic institutions ($n = 13$ public; $n = 7$ private) and seven disciplines (see Table 35.1). Data analysis of course syllabi utilized a multi-step process. The first research team member categorized all syllabi according to course focus (based on the course descriptions) resulting in four foci: (1) adoption only, (2) adoption and foster care, (3) child welfare, or (4) other (see Table 35.1). Courses were undergraduate, graduate, or both (see Table 35.1).

Next, to ensure consistent analysis of all course syllabi, the first two research team members independently coded them for themes (defined as categories of course content) and sub-themes (defined as sub-categories within the themes) using thematic content analysis (Braun & Clarke, 2006). Using constant comparison methods (Glaser & Strauss, 2012), the team members compared their identified themes and sub-themes to discuss and reconcile any differences. The resulting themes included the following: clinical, legal/policy, ethics, context, theory, research, and practice/service delivery (see Table 35.2). The rationale for the agreed-upon syllabi themes is consistent with the range of adoption topical areas covered in the literature (e.g., Grotevant & McDermott, 2014). All resulting sub-themes are identified in Table 35.2.

Finally, triangulation of the data helped to check the reliability and trustworthiness of the coding (Creswell & Miller, 2000). Two doctoral students, who had assisted with the teaching of an adoption course and were conducting research on adoption issues, were trained to code by the third research team member. Under the supervision of the third team member, they independently coded a random selection of 20 percent ($n = 5$) of the syllabi for course foci, themes, and sub-themes. Inter-rater reliability was acceptable for the four foci (.80), themes (.71), and sub-themes (.65). The first three team members are the authors of this chapter.

Table 35.1 Overview of phase one adoption curricula course syllabi ($N = 24$)

Discipline	*Syllabi*	*Program*			*Textbook*	*Course focus*			
		UG	*UG/G*	*G*	*Yes*	*AO*	*A/FC*	*CW*	*O*
Social work	11	3*	-	8	8	1	5	4	1
Psychology	4	3	1	-	2	3*	1	-	-
MFT	1	-	-	1	1	-	1	-	-
Family studies	4	4**	-	-	-	3	1	-	-
Human services	2	2	-	-	-	2	-	-	-
Education	1	-	-	1	1	-	-	-	1
Interdisciplinary	1***	-	1	-	1	1	-	-	-

Note: MFT = marriage and family therapy; Program: UG = undergraduate; G = graduate; Course Focus: AO = adoption only; A/FC = adoption/foster care; CW = child welfare; O = other (i.e., grief/loss; identity/adoption).

* One of these social work courses was cross-listed in social work and sociology; it has been included as a social work course.

** One of these family studies courses was cross-listed in both experimental and family studies.

*** This course was cross-listed in counseling, human development, and educational leadership.

Table 35.2 Summary of phase one adoption curricular course syllabi content (*N* = 24)

Theme	Course focus			
	Adoption only n = *10*	*Adoption/foster care* n = *8*	*Child welfare* n = *4*	*Other* n = *2*
Clinical	Referral processes, grief and loss, models/interventions, practice issues (4), psychological affects, counseling the adoption triad, adjustment (2), cultural competence	Role of family therapy, family involvement, psychological effects of adoption/foster care, preparing children for adoption/ guardianship, assessment (2), interventions (4), prevention, grief/loss (4), cultural competence, practice, attachment (3)	Substance abuse (2), abuse and neglect interventions, assessment (3), intervention, problem solving, family violence, practice with social justice framework	Processes related to loss/grief, death/ dying, divorce, interventions
Legal/ policy	Adoption law (4), birthparent rights & responsibilities, policy (5), advocacy (2)	Legal – processes, initiatives, issues (i.e., emancipation, termination of parental rights), guardianship (4), policy (5), comparative policy (state, federal, global)	Legal definitions of abuse & neglect, policy (3), legal issues/processes (2)	
Ethics	Ethics (3), values (1)	Ethics (2)	Ethics (2)	
Context	Types of adoption (domestic, intercountry, kinship) (6), understanding adoption in 21st century, culture (2), race/ethnicity, identity (3), adjustment/ outcomes, heritability, adolescent special issues, language in adoption, history of adoption (4); history of child welfare policies	Types of adoption (i.e., intercountry, kinship, LGBT, special needs, single parent) (5), sociocultural context of adoption/ foster care, impact of early childhood abuse and neglect, role of early adversity, openness, emancipated youth, adaptive functioning, disruptions/ dissolutions (2), cultural competence (2), adaptive functioning, history of adoption/foster care (3), history of child welfare (3)	Effects of poverty (2), diversity, oppression, historical perspective	Cultural/spiritual aspects, identity, sociopolitical, diversity, race, culture, oppression, social justice

(*Continued*)

Table 35.2 (Cont.)

Theme	*Course focus*			
	Adoption only n = *10*	*Adoption/foster care* n = *8*	*Child welfare* n = *4*	*Other* n = *2*
Theory	Developmental considerations/issues (2), neuropsychology, adoption triad perspectives (7), life cycle perspective, theory (2), attitudes/ assumptions about adoption, adoption triad dynamics	Attachment (2), developmental milestones, family life cycle, adoptive identity development	Systems theory, ecological theory, social justice perspective	Attachment, developmental perspective
Research	Adoption research (5), writing literature reviews, data analysis, research team	Research		
Practice/ service delivery	Child welfare, foster care, search and reunion, overview of adoption process, post-adoption support, disruptions (2)	Adoption/foster care (3) Child welfare (3), permanency planning (3), independent living, service needs, aging out, abuse/ neglect, family preservation, current issues in adoption/ foster care, post-adoption services, relinquishment, special issues in adoption (i.e., reunification, disruptions) (4)	Overview of social services (2), child welfare with emphasis on protective services (2), permanency planning, abuse/ neglect, child/ family	Child welfare

Note: Unless otherwise indicated by parenthetical numbers following content area(s), curricular content areas appeared once.

Among the course syllabi received ($N = 24$), 42 percent ($n = 10$) focused solely on adoption. Of these, five disciplines were represented: psychology ($n = 3$), family studies ($n = 3$), human services ($n = 2$), counseling/education ($n = 1$), and social work ($n = 1$). In three cases, the adoption-focused courses were interdisciplinary (counseling/human development/educational leadership, sociology/social work, and experimental/family studies). Each of the aforementioned disciplines included content from these three areas: clinical, theory, and context. Curricular content by discipline varied by content area among the other courses.

Eight courses (offered in different disciplines) had a dual adoption and foster care focus; 50 percent of these courses ($n = 4$) were offered in social work departments/ schools (see Table 35.2). For these courses, the discipline generally framed the course focus. For example, the four social work courses with a dual adoption/foster care focus had a child welfare systems focus, while the course offered in an MFT department had a family therapy focus. All dual-focused courses collectively covered all content areas (see Table 35.2).

Four courses had a child welfare focus (see Table 35.2). These social work courses focused on child welfare practice and services and, as before, the discipline shaped the themes and sub-themes. Each of the child welfare-focused courses had varying levels of adoption and/or foster care content. For instance, while each course focused on child welfare practices and foster care, permanency planning and/or adoption were addressed in one module of the course (e.g., in a module focusing on potential out-of-home placements resulting from child abuse and neglect).

Two of the interdisciplinary courses were categorized as "other." One was a three-credit, ten-unit course on grief and loss that had one unit that addressed grief and loss in the context of foster care and adoption. This course primarily focused on practice/clinical issues using a development, attachment lens. The second course examined education, child welfare, and diversity in a multicultural context. The primary focus of this course was on sociocultural and multicultural contexts; adoption was ancillary (see Table 35.2).

Finally, 58 percent of the courses (n = 14) required textbooks. The remainder of the courses either recommended texts (n = 1) or used empirical journal articles for required readings. For those requiring textbooks, titles varied, but some were used in more than one course (n = 4). Texts that were used in more than one course syllabi included *A Child's Journey Through Placement* (n = 2; Fahlberg, 1991), *Outsiders Within* (n = 2; Trenka, Oparah, & Shin, 2006), *To the End of June* (n = 2; Beam, 2013), and *The Child Welfare Challenge* (n = 3; Pecora, Whittaker, Maluccio, Barth, & DePanfilis, 2009). A complete list of texts listed in all course syllabi is available upon request from the authors.

Phase two: online survey

A total of 22 faculty were invited via email to participate in an online survey. Sixty-eight percent completed the survey (N = 15). Of these, 53 percent (n = 8) of the faculty who responded were from social work programs. Other faculty participants came from a range of other undergraduate and graduate programs including psychology, family studies, and MFT (see Table 35.3).

Table 35.3 Summary of phase two online adoption curricula survey (N = 15)

Discipline	*Courses*	*Program*			*Credit hours*				*Elective*	*Current offering*	
		UG	*M*	*PhD*	*1*	*2*	*3*	*4*	*Yes*	*Yes*	*No*
Social work	8	2	7	1	-	1	7	-	5	7	-
Psychology	3	3	-	-	-	-	2	1	3	-	3
Marriage & family therapy	1	-	1	-	1	-	-	-	1	-	-
Family studies	3	3	-	-	3	-	-	-	2	-	3
Total	15	8	8	1	4	1	9	1	11	7	5

Note: UG = undergraduate; M = Masters; PhD = Doctor of Philosophy

According to survey participants, their course enrollment ranged from two to 25 students. Frequency of these course offerings varied. Nearly three-fourths (73 percent) of the courses were electives and were offered either every quarter or semester (with the exception of one course). As shown in Table 35.2, one-third (n = 6) of the courses are no longer being offered; these courses were in psychology, family studies, and MFT. The social work courses (n = 7) were the only ones currently being offered. Among these, the courses were offered a minimum of once a year (e.g., only once a quarter or semester). One of the seven social work courses was offered based on student interest in the topic of adoption; in another case, the course was being offered for the first time.

Responses varied regarding the reasons why courses were currently offered or had been discontinued. For the courses that are no longer offered (n = 6), the reasons varied and included the following: (a) one-time only course offering (n = 2), (b) course was no longer a Title IV-E requirement (n = 1), and (c) no other faculty member had the adoption background to teach it (n = 3).

Findings on course development and course delivery indicated that instructors had strong ties to adoption. For instance, the courses were developed by faculty (including adjunct) and graduate students (both master's and PhD) who had multiple roles or adoption connections, including instructor, adoption researcher, adoption professional, and adoptee. Additionally, instructors who taught the courses had a connection to adoption such as an adoptive parent (n = 4), birth parent (n = 1), adoptee (n = 4), adoption researcher (n = 4), had an adopted family member (n = 5), and/or the instructor had an adopted friend (n = 9).

Faculty respondents (n =13) indicated that the adoption course feedback was positive and enlightening. For example, one faculty member stated that the course "opened their eyes to the complexities of adoption and families." This respondent continued, "In general [it] heightened their awareness of how stigma (adoption related, race, social class) underlies many dynamics and how, in turn, [it] affects the life trajectory of adoptees, birth parents, and adoptive families." Another instructor wrote, "students said that they had never thought about the negative and social issues surrounding adoption and foster care. Many assumed that it was all 'rainbows' and love after kids are adopted." Yet another instructor commented that the course helped with understanding the unique needs of adoption triad members. Only one instructor (out of n = 13) had received negative feedback and noted that a student felt the course was "too much work" and "too negative regarding adoption."

Phase one: course syllabi updates

Since completion of this study, we contacted the instructors (N = 22) who taught the phase one courses (N = 24; two of the instructors submitted two course syllabi), and we had a 77.2 percent response rate (n = 17). Among respondents, just under one-quarter (22.7 percent; n = 5) reported that they were still teaching the course (in the same and/or a slightly updated version). One instructor reported that a couple of new adoption-specific courses had been started at their institution – although, in both cases, the courses were targeted to a specific population (e.g., first year students or students in an adoption mentoring program). Just over half of the instructors (54.5 percent; n = 12) reported no new updates and/or that they were no longer teaching the course. In some cases, the adoption-specific course was no longer taught due the instructor either changing institutions and/or retiring (n = 5).

Discussion

This adoption curricula study only begins to unveil what is known about adoption-specific curricula in higher education. Three of the major study findings raise important questions about adoption curricula and future training initiatives for adoption professionals. After first outlining these findings, a discussion of educational, practice, and policy implications follows.

This study revealed that adoption curricula come from a wide range of educational disciplines that underscore its interdisciplinary nature: social work, psychology, MFT, family studies, human studies, education, and interdisciplinary studies; this finding is consistent with earlier research findings (Grotevant & McDermott, 2014). The broad scope of other curricular content found in this study – and reflected in this edited volume – supports the interdisciplinary nature of the adoption field. In the case of master's level professional disciplines (i.e., social work, MFT, and counseling), our study findings are similar to Weir et al. (2008). For example, of the disciplines represented in our study, social work dominated: 46 percent of the courses were offered in social work programs. At the exo-level, this suggests that adoptees may be served by adoption professionals educated in a wide range of disciplines.

A second important finding is that while nearly half of the syllabi received were from social work programs, courses that focused solely on adoption came from undergraduate psychology and family studies programs. Notably, neither of these undergraduate degree programs is a stepping stone to the professional licensure (e.g., Licensed Social Worker) that might be required for some adoption professional positions (e.g., child welfare; see Kim, 2011).

This lack of graduate-level courses focused on adoption highlights a missed opportunity. Over 70 graduate-level social work programs offer Title IV-E Child Welfare stipends to students interested in a career in child welfare. In partnership with public child welfare agencies and funded through Federal IV-E grants, students in the IV-E Child Welfare programs are provided tuition stipends for completing a child welfare focused curriculum and field placement in exchange for a commitment to work in public child welfare agencies upon graduation (Barth, Lee, & Hodorowicz, 2017). Some of the curricula submitted for this study integrated adoption content into the required child welfare course for these students. Only one social work course in School of Social Work at the University of Minnesota, required students to take a stand-alone course on permanency and adoption, in addition to another required child welfare course. Other MSW programs, with IV-E Child Welfare programs, could follow this model. Indeed, this finding highlights important links among professional studies curricula (i.e., accredited degree programs that prepare and qualify undergraduate or graduate degree holders to take a professional license exam to practice), professional licensure, and the requisite credentials necessary for adoption professional positions.

As our study findings suggest, adoption curricula are generally interdisciplinary and come from a broad range of academic disciplines; however, it is unknown if any of those working in the adoption field graduated from degree programs that reflect this broad range of disciplines. Anecdotally, adoption professionals have indicated that social workers might be the primary frontline workers in adoption. If so, this might explain, as the study revealed, that nearly half of the course syllabi reviewed came from social work programs. Learning more about the educational programs that the majority of adoption professionals complete is needed to more closely examine the role of adoption curricula in preparing adoption professionals. Thus, additional research is needed to gain a systematic understanding of what adoption professionals, adoptees, adoptive families, and birth families need regarding adoption information. For instance, conducting focus groups at conferences with adoption professionals could be useful in learning more about their adoption training needs.

A third important finding from our study revealed that adoption-only and adoption/foster care course syllabi collectively covered curricular areas important to adoption professionals. For instance, all four types of syllabi (i.e., adoption only, adoption/foster care, child welfare, and other) included a section on developmental theory (i.e., family life cycle) which is consistent with the recognition that adoption is a lifelong journey that, for some, might start with infertility (Freeark et al., 2005).

To better prepare adoption professionals, it is clear that more curricular content should be included in the following areas: (a) adoption contact issues in various types of adoption and processes (e.g., open, mediated, closed, search, and reunion); (b) understanding the multiple perspectives within the adoption constellation (i.e., birth family, adoptive family, adoptees, non-adopted siblings); (c) types of adoption (i.e., same race, transracial, intercountry, LGBT adoptions, single parent, and two parent adoptions; infant and older child adoptions); and (d) communication about adoption and type of adoption contact (i.e., open adoptions, semi-open, closed, use of positive adoption language, etc.). Inclusion of these content areas addresses the complexity of adoption across the lifespan (Baden & Wiley, 2007; Freeark et al., 2005; Zamostny, Wiley, O'Brien, Lee, & Baden, 2003).

Educational implications

As educational institutions are important exo-level systems in the environment of adopted individuals and their families, further examination of the educational implications of our study findings is warranted. While a previous study of clinical training in accredited programs involved an examination of both classroom and field training (Weir et al., 2008), the focus of our study was on didactic, classroom-based learning. While we focused on a content analysis of course syllabi (and found quite a wide range of curricular topics), our study also raises the question about the adoption curricular content delivery (e.g., didactic, field practica) in training adoption professionals.

Kolb's learning styles (1981, 1984; as adapted by Raschick et al., 1998) support the need for both classroom- and field-based learning when educating adoption professionals, regardless of discipline. Thus, any future examination of adoption curricula and training formats (and subsequent implementation) should be in tandem to enhance the education and training of adoption professionals. Existing adoption curricula and post-degree training should be expanded and offered in more academic settings to help in educating and training our next generation of adoption professionals.

Findings from the adoption curricula study (Koh et al., 2017) might have important educational implications in this suggested expansion. Specifically, Koh and colleagues' phase two findings suggested that there could be an institutional, macro-level challenge in recruiting (and retaining) adoption competent faculty to teach these specialized curricula. Without the faculty expertise in adoption, these courses might not be offered and/or might not be an institutional priority. This challenge could be partly addressed by academic institutions that support the need for adoption education and deliberately hire faculty with this expertise. For example, higher education institutions with Title IV-E programs (i.e., in social work departments) might prioritize this curricular focus. Another example of a program that has successfully added this focus is the Rudd Adoption Research Program (located in the Department of Psychology and Brain Sciences) at the University of Massachusetts, Amherst. Clearly, for successful expansion of this content to occur, more higher education programs that are dedicated to adoption-specific curricula are needed to successfully educate the next generation of adoption professionals.

Practice and policy implications

In the context of our study findings, adoption curricula in higher education should include content on the expansive impact of the Internet – and the resulting ethical ramifications on practice – in adoption curricula and training. A report from the Evan B. Donaldson Adoption Institute (Howard, 2012) highlights the significant influence of the Internet on adoption practices. For instance, the Internet has profoundly changed the landscape of search and reunion processes for adoptees, birth families, and adoptive families. Among the recommendations outlined, the report calls for the inclusion of the Internet and social media usage in education and training programs, and a legal evaluation of Internet practices to protect those impacted by adoption. The report also highlights the importance of ethical considerations in regulating adoption practices.

Study limitations

Because our study utilized a convenience sample that drew from professional email lists and adoption researchers (identified by the research team), the findings are not generalizable to the academic disciplines not fully represented in this study. Our phase one small, nonrandom sample included only one "psychology-managed adoption researcher" email list; it did not draw from other general psychology lists. Our small sample might also reflect the fact that there might be a limited number of faculty with the specialized adoption knowledge and qualifications to teach an adoption-specific course. A random phase one sampling frame that drew more comprehensively from multiple disciplines would have strengthened the generalizability of our findings. Phase two results noted that most courses were taught by instructors with personal connections to adoption, but participants were not queried on their preparedness; future research is needed to examine this important topic.

Future directions and recommendations

Based on our study findings, we recommend a sequential series of survey-based research aimed at gaining a broader meso- and exo-level systemic understanding of adoption content. First, surveying a nationally representative sample of adoption professionals currently in the workforce regarding their undergraduate and graduate degree programs would increase understanding of the academic disciplines and professional licensures of current professionals. We suspect that these findings might reveal that some adoption professionals may come from a wide range of disciplines that extend beyond social sciences programs to, for example, medical programs (i.e., nursing, family medicine). Next, a systematic study of academic disciplines should be conducted to obtain a comprehensive, descriptive understanding of the adoption-specific curricular content currently offered in these disciplines. Finally, a survey of adoption professionals' knowledge of other educational venues which might serve to expand their adoption knowledge should be conducted. These venues include pursuing post-degree training programs, utilizing peer-reviewed adoption journals (e.g., *Adoption Quarterly* and *Adoption & Culture: The Interdisciplinary Journal of the*

Alliance for the Study of Adoption and Culture), and attending national adoption conferences (e.g., bi-annual Adoption Initiative Conference; annual Rudd Adoption Conference at the University of Massachusetts, Amherst; annual North American Council on Adoptable Children Conference; the Adoption Exchange Association Annual Conference; and the International Conference on Adoption Research).

We recommend a two-pronged, two-level approach to the education and training of adoption professionals: (a) both classroom- and field-based learning in baccalaureate and/or graduate education, and (b) both degree and post-degree training. Regarding the former, future research should focus on professional disciplines that provide a pathway to professional licensure (e.g., Licensed Independent Clinical Social Worker, Licensed Marriage and Family Therapist, Licensed Professional Counselor). To adequately prepare adoption professionals, field practica should be supported by classroom-based curricular content (effectively delivered to meet various learning styles) in professional studies and higher education. Expanding adoption curricula in academic settings will help educate and train our next generation of adoption professionals who, at the exo-level, work in different medical, legal, and spiritual systems that have an impact on adoptees and their families.

Note

1 This chapter is based on a previously published (2017) article by the same authors in *Adoption Quarterly, 23*(3), 252–265.

References

AB 1790, Chapter 766, California Assembly. (2014). *Foster children: Mental health services Act of 2014.* Retrieved from http://leginfo.legislature.ca.gov/faces/billNavClient.xhtml?bill_id=201320140AB1790

Atkinson, A. J., & Gonet, P. A. (2007). Strengthening adoption practice, listening to adoptive families. *Child Welfare, 86*(2), 87–104.

Atkinson, A. J., Gonet, P. A., Freundlich, M., & Riley, D. B. (2013). Adoption competent clinical practice: Defining its meaning and development. *Adoption Quarterly, 16*(3–4), 156–174. doi:10.1080/10926755.2013.844215

Baden, A. L., & Wiley, M. O. (2007). Counseling adopted persons in adulthood: Integrating practice and research. *The Counseling Psychologist, 35*(6), 868–901. doi:10.1177/0011000006291409

Bahrampour, T. (2016, October 12). DNA's new "miracle": How adoptees are using online DNA registries to find their blood relatives. *Washington Post.* Retrieved from www.washingtonpost.com/local/social-issues/dnas-new-miracle-how-adoptees-are-using-online-registries-to-find-their-blood-relatives/2016/10/12/10433fec-8c48-11e6-bf8a-3d26847eeed4_story.html

Barth, R. P., Lee, B. R., & Hodorowicz, M. T. (2017). Equipping the child welfare workforce to improve the well-being of children. *Journal of Children's Services, 12*(2/3), 211–220. doi:10/1108/JCS-05-2017-0017

Beam, C. (2013). *To the end of june: The intimate life of American foster care.* New York, NY: Houghton Mifflin Harcourt Publishing Company.

Braun, V., & Clarke, V. (2006). Using thematic analysis in psychology. *Qualitative Research in Psychology, 3*(2), 77–105. doi:10.1191/1478088706qp063oa

Brodzinsky, D., Santa, J., & Smith, S. L. (2016). Adopted youth in residential care: Prevalence rate and professional training needs. *Residential Treatment for Children & Youth, 33*, 118–134. doi:10.1080/0886571X.2016.1175993

Brodzinsky, D. M. (2013). *A need to know: Enhancing adoption competence among mental health professionals.* New York, NY: Donaldson Adoption Institute.

Brodzinsky, D. M. (2015). Understanding and treating adoptive families. In S. Browning & K. Pasley (Eds.), *Contemporary families: Translating research into practice* (pp. 35–52). New York, NY: Taylor & Francis Group.

Bronfenbrenner, U. (1979). *The ecology of human development*. Cambridge, MA: Harvard University Press.

Casey Family Services. (2003). Strengthening families and communities: Promising practices in adoption competent mental health services. In *White Paper* (pp. 1–77). New Haven, CT: Author.

Center for Adoption Support and Education (CASE). (2015). *2015 Annual Report*. Retrieved from http://caseannualreport.org/

Center for Adoption Support and Education (CASE). (2018, March 12). *NTI mental health training pilot launch in March 2018*. Retreived from https://adoptionsupport.org/nti/2018/01/04/nti-mh-pilot-2018/

Child Welfare Information Gateway. (2016). *Trends in US adoptions: 2008–2012*. Washington, DC: US Department of Health and Human Services, Children's Bureau.

Creswell, J. W., & Miller, D. L. (2000). Determining validity in qualitative inquiry. *Theory Into Practice*, *39*(3), 124–130. doi:10.1207/s15430421tip3903_2

Fahlberg, V. (1991). *A child's journey through placement*. Indianapolis, IN: Perspectives Press.

Festinger, T. (2006). Adoption and after: Adoptive parents' service needs. In M. M. Dore (Ed.), *The post-adoption experience: Adoptive families' service needs and service outcomes* (pp. 17–44). New York, NY: Child Welfare League of America, Inc.

Freeark, K., Rosenberg, E. B., Bornstein, J., Jozefowicz-Simbeni, D., Linkevich, M., & Lohnes, K. (2005). Gender differences and dynamics shaping the adoption life cycle: Review of the literature and recommendations. *American Journal of Orthopsychiatry*, *75*(1), 86–101. doi:10.1037/0002-9432.75.1.86

Glaser, B., & Strauss, A. (2012). *The discovery of grounded theory: Strategies for qualitative research*. New Brunswick, NJ: Aldine Transaction.

Greco, O., Rosnati, R., & Ferrari, L. (2015). Adult adoptees as partners: The joint task of revisiting the adoption history. *Adoption Quarterly*, *18*(1), 25–44. doi:10.1080/10926755.2014.895468

Grotevant, H., & McDermott, J. (2014). Adoption: Biological and social processes linked to adaptation. *Annual Review of Psychology*, *65*, 235–265. doi:10.1146/psych.annualreviews.org

Howard, J. A. (2012). *Untangling the Web: The Internet's transformative impact on adoption: Policy & practice perspective*. New York: Evan B. Donaldson Adoption Institute.

Keyes, M. A., Sharma, A., Elkins, I. J., Iacono, W. G., & McGue, M. (2008). The mental health of US adolescents adopted in infancy. *Archives of Pediatrics & Adolescent Medicine*, *161*, 419–425. doi:10.1001/archpedi.162.5.419

Kim, H. (2011). Job conditions, unmet expectations, and burnout in public child welfare workers: How different from other social workers? *Children and Youth Services Review*, *33*, 358–367. doi:10.1016/j.childyouth.2010.10.001

Koh, B. D., Kim, J. R., & McRoy, R. (2017). Exploring adoption-specific curricula in undergraduate and graduate degree programs. *Adoption Quarterly*, *20*(3), 252–265. doi:10.1080/10926755.2017.1349698

Kolb, D. A. (1981). Learning styles and disciplinary differences. In A.W. Chickering & Associates. (Ed.), *The modern American college* (pp. 232–255). San Francisco, CA: Jossey-Bass, Inc.

Kolb, D. A. (1984). *Experiential learning: Experience as the source of learning and development*. Englewood Cliffs, NJ: Prentice Hall, Inc.

Kreider, R. M., & Lofquist, D. A. (2014). Adopted children and stepchildren: 2010 (P20-572). *US Census Bureau*. Retrieved from www.census.gov/prod/2014pubs/p20-572.pdf

Morton, T. D. (1984). Training curriculum for workers in adoption of children with special needs. *Adoption & Fostering*, *8*(2), 33–38. doi:10.1177/030857598400800209

National Child Welfare Resource Center for Adoption. (2007). *Adoption competence: A guide to developing an adoption certificate program for mental health practitioners*. Southfield, MI: Spaulding for Children.

Pecora, P. J., Whittaker, J. K., Maluccio, A. N., Barth, R. P., & DePanfilis, D. (2009). *The child welfare challenge* (3rd ed.). Piscataway, NJ: Aldine-Transaction Books.

Ramsey, P., Brabender, V., & Fallon, A. (2013). Meeting the needs of adoptive parents. In V. Brabender & A. Fallon (Eds.), *Working with adoptive parents: Research, theory, and therapeutic interventions* (pp. 213–232). Hoboken, NJ: John Wiley & Sons.

Raschick, M., Maypole, D. E., & Day, P. A. (1998). Improving field education through Kolb learning theory. *Journal of Social Work Education*, *34*(1), 31–42. doi:10.1080/10437797.1998.10778903

Riley, D., & Singer, E. (2016). The need for adoption competent mental health professionals. In R. Fong & R. McRoy (Eds.), *Transracial and intercountry adoptions* (pp. 315–358). New York, NY: Columbia University Press.

Sass, D. A., & Henderson, D. B. (2007). Psychologists' self-reported adoption knowledge and the need for more adoption education. In R. A. Javier, A. L. Baden, F. A. Biafora, & A. Camacho-Gingerich (Eds.), *Handbook of adoption: Implications for researchers, practitioners, and families* (pp. 312–322). Thousand Oaks, CA: Sage Publications.

Schweiger, W. K., & O'Brien, M. (2005). Special needs adoption: An ecological systems approach. *Family Relations*, *54*(4), 512–522. doi:10.1111/j.1741-3729.2005.00337.x

Siegel, D. (2013). Adoption competency in clinical social work. *Social Work Today*, *13*(6), 16. Retrieved from: www.socialworktoday.com/archive/111113p16.shtml

Stokes, L., & Poulsen, S. (2014). Narrative therapy for adoption issues in families, couples, and individuals: Rationale and approach. *Journal of Family Psychotherapy*, *25*, 330–347. doi:10.1080/08975353/2014.977681

Tan, T. X., & Tran, M. (2013). Mental health service utilization in children adopted from foster care, US private agencies and foreign countries: Data from the 2007 National Survey of Adoption Parents (NSAP). *Children and Youth Services Review*, *35*, 1050–1054. doi:10.1016/j.childyouth.2013.04.020

Trenka, J. J., Oparah, J. C., & Shin, S. Y. (2006). *Outsiders within: Writing on transracial adoption*. New York, NY: South End Press.

US Department of Health and Human Services. (2018). *AFCARS Report #25*. Retrieved from www.acf.hhs.gov/cb/resource/afcars-report-25

Weir, K. N., Fife, S. T., Whiting, J. B., & Blazewick, A. (2008). Clinical training of MFTs for adoption, foster care, and child development settings: A comparative survey of CACREP,COAMFTE, and CSWE accredited programs. *Journal of Family Psychotherapy*, *19*(3), 227–290. doi:10.1080/08975350802269517

Zamostny, K. P., Wiley, M. O., O'Brien, K. M., Lee, R. M., & Baden, A. L. (2003). Breaking the silence: Advancing knowledge about adoption for counseling psychologists. *The Counseling Psychologist*, *31*, 647–650. doi:10.1177/0011000003258

INDEX

Locators in **bold** refer to tables though these are not distinguished when concurrent with related text.

For Product Safety Concerns and Information please contact our EU representative GPSR@taylorandfrancis.com
Taylor & Francis Verlag GmbH, Kaufingerstraße 24, 80331 München, Germany

www.ingramcontent.com/pod-product-compliance
Ingram Content Group UK Ltd.
Pitfield, Milton Keynes, MK11 3LW, UK
UKHW051322190926
475701UK00011B/1057

9781032173771